The Migration Conference 2025 Selected Papers

THE MIGRATION
CONFERENCE

UNIVERSITY OF GREENWICH

LATITUDE 51°28'28" NORTH
LONGITUDE 0°00'00"

EAST   WEST

11-17 JUNE   LONDON
2025

The Migration Conference 2025

Selected Papers

Compiled by

Ülkü Sezgi Sözen and İbrahim Sirkeci

UNIVERSITY OF GREENWICH

INTERNATIONAL BUSINESS SCHOOL

TRANSNATIONAL PRESS LONDON

2025

CONFERENCE SERIES: 37

The Migration Conference 2025 Selected Papers

Compiled by Ülkü Sezgi Sözen and İbrahim Sirkeci

Paperback

ISBN: 978-1-80135-168-3

Digital

ISBN: 978-1-80135-169-0

www.tplondon.com

CONTENTS

THE MIGRATION CONFERENCE 2025

Since the first event in 2012, the Migration Conferences have drawn thousands of attendees from around the world. These conferences have been hosted in various cities, including Mexico City (2024), Hamburg (2023), Rabat (2022), London (2012, 2014, 2021, 2025), Prague (2015), Vienna (2016), Athens (2017), Lisbon (2018), Bari (2019), and Tetovo/London (2020). The 14th Migration Conference was hosted by University of Greenwich, London, UK. This event serves as a global forum for academics, policymakers, practitioners, students, and others interested in engaging in meaningful debate and research-driven discussions on the impacts of human mobility worldwide. We are hoping to meet many of you in Bratislava next year.

Supporters of The Migration Conference

Universities

- University of Greenwich, London, UK (TMC 2025 Host)
- Universidad Iberoamericana, Mexico City, Mexico (TMC 2024 Host)
- CENTRUS – Centro Transdisciplinar Universitario para la sustentabilidad
- International Business School (IBS), Manchester, UK (2021-2024)
- University of Notre Dame, USA
- El Colegio de Mexico, Mexico
- Universität Hamburg, Germany (TMC 2023 Host)
- Mohammad V University, Rabat, Morocco (TMC2022 Host)
- South East European University, N. Macedonia (TMC 2020 Host)
- University of Bari Aldo Moro, Italy (TMC 2019 Host)
- University of Lisbon, ISEG and IGOT, Portugal (TMC 2018 Host)
- Harokopio University, Athens (TMC 2017 Host)
- University of Vienna, Austria (TMC 2016 Host)
- Charles University Prague, Czech Republic (TMC 2015 Host)
- Hefei University, Sino-German Economic Development and Innovation Research Centre, P.R. China
- Ruppin Academic Centre, Israel
- Ruhr-Universität Bochum, Centre for Mediterranean Studies, Germany (2019-2023)
- Social Sciences University of Ankara, Global Migration Research Centre, Turkey

- Istanbul Topkapi University, Migration Policies Research Centre, Turkey
- Migration Institute, Finland
- Moscow City University, Russia
- Polissia National University, Ukraine
- Universidade de Lisboa, Research Centre in Economic and Organizational Sociology (SOCIUS), Portugal (2018)
- Symbiosis International University, India
- The Ohio State University, The Global Mobility Project, USA
- Unidad Académica en Estudios del Desarrollo, Mexico
- Universidad de Burgos, Spain
- Universidad Latina de México, Mexico
- Universidad Tecnica Partocular de Loja, Ecuador
- University of Nottingham, Faculty of Humanities and Social Sciences, China (2019-2021)
- West Ukrainian National University, Ternopil, Ukraine
- Yaşar University Jean Monnet Migration Chair, Turkey
- University of Bari, Dipartimento di Scienze Politiche, Italy (TMC 2019 Host)
- Regent's University London Centre for Transnational Business and Management, UK (2018-2021)
- Regent's University London Centre for Transnational Studies, UK (2011-2018)
- University of California Gifford Center for Population Studies
- Danube University Krems, Austria (2011-2017)
- Albrecht Mendelssohn Bartholdy Graduate School of Law, Germany (2019-2023)
- Manisa Celal Bayar University Faculty of Economics and Administrative Sciences, Turkey (2012-2015)
- Celal Bayar University Population and Migration Research Center, Turkey (2012-2015)

migrationconference.net
fb.me/MigrationConference
Email: migrationscholar@gmail.com

Organisations and Companies

- American Chamber in Mexico
- CEEY – Centro de Estudios Espinosa Yglesias
- Consejo Noruego para Refugiados
- Patronato de la Ibero FICSAC
- l'Association Marocaine d'Etudes et de Recherches sur les Migrations (AMERM), Morocco (TMC2022 Host)
- The National Human Rights Council (CNDH), Morocco (2022)
- Austrian Air – Official Carrier for TMC 2016
- Centre for Development Evaluation and Social Science Research (CREDI), Sarajevo, Bosnia and Herzegovina
- Claussen Simon Stiftung, Germany (2023)
- EKKE – The National Center of Social Research, Greece (2017)
- Global Policy and Strategy, Ankara, Turkey (2014)
- Hellenic Sociological Society (2017)
- Institut de Recherche, Formation et Action sur les Migrations, Belgium
- IUSSP International Migration Expert Panel (2011-2015)
- J. Hornig Coffee (2015)
- Ming-Ai (London) Institute, United Kingdom
- Hassan II Foundation for Moroccans Residing Abroad, Morocco (2022)
- Refugee Law Clinic, Hamburg, Germany (2023)
- Ria Money Transfers (2011-2014)
- RGS Population Studies Group, United Kingdom (2011-2014)
- Sustainable Equity and Social Studies Association (SEDER)
- Western Balkans Migration Network (WB-MIGNET), Bosnia and Herzegovina
- ZEIT Stiftung, Ebelin und Gerd Bucerius, Germany (2023)

Cities and Governments

- International Organisation for Migration (2011-2014, 2024)
- National Office of Social and Cultural University Works, Morocco (2022)
- The Ministry of Education, Morocco (2022)
- ISTAT (Italian National Statistics Office) (2019)
- Municipality of Bari, Italy (2019)
- United Nations Population Fund (UNFPA)
- Ordine Assistenti Sociali Regione Puglia, Italy (2019)
- Puglia Regional Administration, Italy (2019)
- Red Cross, Italy (2019)
- Tourism Office of Lisbon (2018)
- Vienna Convention Bureau (2016)

Promoting Journals and Publishers

- Migration and Diversity

- Göç Dergisi
- Border Crossing
- Transnational Education Review
- Yeiya

People

The TMC 2025 Committees:

Executive Team and Conference Chairs:

- Prof Ibrahim Sirkeci, International Business School, Manchester, UK (Chair)
- Prof Özgür H. Çınar, University of Greenwich, UK (Chair)
- Prof Jeffrey H. Cohen, Ohio State University, USA
- Prof Philip L Martin, University of California Davis, USA
- Dr Ülkü Sezgi Sözen, University of Hamburg, Germany
- Dr Karla Angélica Valenzuela-Moreno, Universidad Iberoamericana, Mexico

Transnational Advisory Committee:

- Prof Gudrun Biffl, Krems, Austria
- Prof Özgür H. Çınar, University of Greenwich, UK
- Prof Lucinda Fonseca, University of Lisbon, Portugal
- Prof Elli Heikkila, Migration Institute of Finland, Finland
- Prof Mohamed Khachani, Mohammed V University of Rabat, Morocco
- Prof Beatrice Knerr, Kassell University, Germany and Hefei University, China
- Prof Markus Kotzur, Universität Hamburg, Germany
- Prof Jonathan Liu, International Business School, UK
- Prof Apostolos G Papadopoulos, Harokopio University of Athens, Greece
- Prof Carla Pederzini, Universidad Iberoamericana, Mexico
- Prof João Peixoto, University of Lisbon, Portugal
- Prof Michela C. Pellicani, University of Bari "Aldo Moro", Italy
- Prof Giuseppe Sciortino, University of Trento, Italy
- Dr Karla Angélica Valenzuela-Moreno, Universidad Iberoamericana, Mexico

Transnational Scientific Committee:

Africa

- Agnes Igoye, Ministry of Interior Affairs, Uganda
- Prof Mohamed Khachani, AMERM & Mohammed V University of Rabat, Morocco
- Dr Rania Rafik Khalil, The British University in Egypt, Egypt
- Dr Sadhana Manik, University of KwaZulu-Natal, South Africa
- Prof Claude Sumata, National Pedagogical University, DR Congo

- Dr Ayman Zohry, Egyptian Society for Migration Studies, Egypt

Americas

- Prof Jeffrey H. Cohen, Ohio State University, USA
- Dr José Salvador Cueto-Calderón, Universidad Autónoma de Sinaloa, Mexico
- Dr Ana Vila Freyer, Universidad de Guanajuato, Mexico
- Dr Pascual G. García-Macías, Universidad Técnica Particular de Loja, Ecuador
- Dr Carlos Alberto González Zepeda, Universidad Autónoma Metropolitana-Cuajimalpa, Mexico
- Dr Torunn Haaland, Gonzaga University, USA
- Prof Liliana Jubilut, Universidade Católica de Santos, Brazil
- Prof Philip L Martin, University of California Davis, USA
- Prof Carla Pederzini, Universidad Iberoamericana, Mexico
- Dr Eric M. Trinka, Emory & Henry College, USA
- Karla Angélica Valenzuela-Moreno, Universidad Iberoamericana, Mexico
- Dr Hassan Vatanparast, Saskatchewan University, Canada
- Prof Rodolfo García Zamora, Autonomous University of Zacatecas, Mexico
- Dr Monette Zard, Columbia University, USA

Asia-Pacific

- Prof Ram Bhagat, International Institute for Population Sciences, India
- Dr Jocelyn O. Celero, University of the Philippines Diliman, Philippines
- Dr Sadaf Mahmood, University of Agriculture Faisalabad, Pakistan
- Dr Shweta Sinha Deshpande, Symbiosis School for Liberal Arts, India
- Prof Nicholas Procter, University of South Australia, Australia
- Dr Ruchi Singh, Indian Institute of Management, Bengaluru, India
- Dr AKM Ahsan Ullah, University Brunei Darussalam, Brunei
- Dr Xi Zhao, Hefei University, P.R. China

Central and Eastern Europe

- Dr Merita Zulfiu Alili, South East European University, N. Macedonia
- Dr Olga R. Gulina, Benefit Research GMBH, Germany
- Dr Nermin Oruc, Centre for Development Evaluation and Social Science Research (CREDI), Sarajevo, Bosnia and Herzegovina
- Prof Apostolos G Papadopoulos, Harokopio University of Athens, Greece
- Prof Irina Savchenko, Moscow City University, Russian Federation

Western Europe

- Prof Bahar Baser, Durham University, United Kingdom
- Prof Aron Anselem Cohen, University of Granada, Spain
- Dr Martina Cvajner, University of Trento, Italy
- Dr Carla de Tona, University of Bologna, Italy
- Dr Sureya Sonmez Efe, University of Lincoln, United Kingdom
- Dr Alina Esteves, Universidade de Lisboa, Portugal

- Dr Setenay Dilek Fidler, University of Westminster, United Kingdom
- Prof Monica Ibáñez-Angulo, University of Burgos, Spain
- Dr Gul Ince Beqo, University of Urbino, Italy
- Prof Jonathan Liu, International Business School, United Kingdom
- Dr Lan Lo, University of Nottingham, United Kingdom
- Dr Altay Manço, IRFAM, Belgium
- Dr A. Erdi Öztürk, London Metropolitan University, United Kingdom
- Dr Andrea Romano, Faculty of Law, University of Barcelona, Spain
- Dr Sahizer Samuk-Carignani, University of Pisa, Italy
- Prof Mario Savino, University of Tuscia, Italy
- Prof Giuseppe Sciortino, University of Trento, Italy
- Dr Caner Tekin, Ruhr-Universität Bochum, Germany
- Dr Irene Tuzi, Sapienza University of Rome, Italy
- Dr Ülkü Sezgi Sözen, University of Hamburg, Germany

Near East

- Prof Sebnem Koser Akcapar, Ankara Social Sciences University, Türkiye
- Dr Deniz Yetkin Aker, Istanbul Beykent University, Türkiye
- Dr Tuncay Bilecen, Kocaeli University, Türkiye
- Prof Dilek Cindoglu, Yasar University, Türkiye
- Prof Yaprak Civelek, Anadolu University, Türkiye
- Dr Z. Banu Dalaman, SEDER, Türkiye
- Prof Sevim Atilla Demir, Sakarya University, Türkiye
- Dr İnci Aksu Kargın, Uşak University, Türkiye
- Prof Yakhnich Liat, Beit Berl College, Israel
- Dr Armagan Teke Lloyd, Abdullah Gul University, Türkiye
- Prof Gökay Özerim, Yaşar University, Türkiye
- Dr Md Mizanur Rahman, Qatar University, Qatar
- Dr Betul Dilara Seker, Van Yuzuncu Yil University, Türkiye
- Dr Paulette K. Schuster, Reichman University, Israel
- Dr Onur Unutulmaz, Ankara Social Sciences University, Türkiye
- Dr Deniz Eroglu Utku, Trakya University, Türkiye
- Dr Nevin Karabiyik Yerden, Marmara University, Türkiye
- Dr Pınar Yazgan, Sakarya University, Türkiye

The Migration Conference Technical Organisation Committee

- Dr Aytac Yerden, Gedik University, Turkey (IT)
- Ege Cakir, Henan University, China (Admin)

FROM RULE OF LAW TO RULE OF FORCE: MIGRATION, BORDERS, AND THE RISE OF SECURITISATION

Ülkü Sezgi Sözen and Ibrahim Sirkeci[1]

The 13th edition of The Migration Conference, hosted by the University of Greenwich in London, UK, in June 2025, once again served as a vital global forum for migration studies. As the executive team members of the conference, we are pleased to confirm that nearly 100 parallel sessions took place. In this selection of papers, we present over 60 concise research contributions that collectively offer a vivid, if often sobering, portrait of contemporary global human mobility.

The papers featured herein reaffirm that migration is the defining phenomenon of our era, fundamentally reshaping societies, economies, and legal systems. What emerges most prominently is the growing tension between the legal and policy frameworks designed to regulate mobility and the complex, often spontaneous realities of migrants' lived experiences. Spanning from Chile to China and Japan to Iceland, the scholarship engaged here confronts this tension directly, calling for a multidisciplinary approach that moves beyond single-lens analysis.

From a legal and policy perspective, the proceedings reveal a concerning trend: the escalating externalisation and securitisation of borders. The 'Migration, Law and Policy' section documents how states and supranational bodies increasingly delegate migration control to transit countries – an approach that often prioritises containment over international protection obligations. For instance, one paper analyses Nigeria's role as a crucial hub on West African migration routes, highlighting its entanglement in externalisation regimes and raising critical questions regarding the right to asylum and non-refoulement, particularly in resourced-limited border zones. Similarly, another contribution critiques the administrative accountability of FRONTEX, emphasizing the

---

[1] Dr. Ülkü Sezgi Sözen, LL.M., University of Hamburg, Faculty of Law and the Albrecht Mendelssohn Bartholdy Graduate School of Law, Germany.
Prof. Dr. Ibrahim Sirkeci, International Business School, Manchester, UK.

expanding oversight role of the European Ombudsman as the Agency's reach broadens, a development critics argue may deepen the externalisation of EU borders.

This legal hardening occurs amidst a political landscape increasingly shaped by populist far-right rhetoric, which a paper exploring its impact on migration discourse scrutinises. This environment fosters a "politics of isolation", challenging established human rights standards. For example, the analyses of policies concerning unaccompanied minors in the US and EU demonstrate the substantial legal and ethical challenges involved in protecting vulnerable children in this context. However, hope persists within the law itself: studies from Germany show that human rights-based discourse can still be invoked to address systemic legislative flaws, such as the Asylum Seekers' Benefits Act (AsylbLG), thus opening pathways for social justice and legal reform, even amid political resistance. Crucially, the papers also highlight the urgent need for legal reform to close the protection gap for climate-displaced persons, a gap starkly evident in the Nigerian context, where existing legal frameworks largely overlook drivers such as desertification and coastal flooding.

Research on labour, demographics, and geography demonstrates that migration flows are rarely halted by legal barriers; instead, they are diverted into more hazardous and complex routes. The conference provided detailed, granular data on the socio-economic realities underpinning these movements. Several contributions examine the critical role of remittances, investigating their impact on poverty and inequality across diverse contexts, from Western Balkan countries and Afghanistan to the socio-economic wellbeing of Gulf migrants' families in India.

The papers also map the evolving landscapes of transit and destination, with the 'Migration Geographies' section carefully tracing trans-Saharan pathways and onward migration experiences, such as the resilience of Rwandan refugee women in Cameroon. Mobility is inherently linked to the search for identity and belonging. The 'Identities and Integration' section offers profound insights, including how Chinese immigrants in Hungary negotiate their sense of mother tongue and the challenges faced by unaccompanied children in Turkey as they navigate Berry's acculturation strategies – strategies that, if unsuccessful, risk marginalisation, and thus demand urgent policy intervention.

However, the geographic picture extends beyond movement alone, encompassing the social ecologies within host communities. A paper, for instance, on 'Lived Diversity in Germany's Migration Landscape' contrasts longstanding Turkish-origin residents with post-2015 Muslim immigrants, revealing how intergroup relations are shaped by historical trajectories and shifting power dynamics. Another study on transnational gentrification in Sicily highlights the contradictions associated with lifestyle migrants, who, despite being marketed as catalyst of urban regeneration, may deepen socio-economic inequality and displace vulnerable local populations.

Finally, the 'Skilled Migration and Wellbeing' papers shift focus to the human cost of global mobility. A scoping review synthesises determinants of mental health and wellbeing among young migrants, identifying migration itself as a risk factor for severe mental illness. Alongside studies examining trauma among asylum seekers at the US-Mexico border, these contributions underscore the psychological toll associated with migration, whether voluntary or forced, and emphasize the need for trauma-informed, accessible healthcare policies.

This volume stands as a strong testament to the Migration Conference's founding mission: to foster a global, multidisciplinary dialogue on a frank and friendly platform with academic rigour and encouraging openness. Migration challenges – ranging from border externalisation and integration of unaccompanied minors to the economics of remittances, transit geographies, and trauma – cannot be addressed within a single discipline. Legal frameworks must adapt to demographic realities, and policymakers must ground their decisions in the social and economic insights generated by empirical research albeit academic efforts have been largely overlooked by media and politics.

We extend our sincere gratitude to all leaders, staff and students at the University of Greenwich School of Law and Criminology for their warm hospitality. We encourage readers of this volume not only to engage with these studies but also to participate actively in the ongoing conversation.

Finally, we are delighted to invite you to the 14th Migration Conference, scheduled for September 2026, hosted by the University of Economics and Business in Bratislava, Slovakia. As migration debate continues to reshape the politics around the world, our forum in Bratislava will be a vital space for reflecting on the insights gained thus far and shaping the future directions of migration scholarship, policy, and advocacy.

MIGRATION, LAW AND POLICY

NAVIGATING THE NEXUS OF INTERNATIONAL MIGRATION LAW, CLIMATE CHANGE, AND BORDER MANAGEMENT: A MULTIDISCIPLINARY APPROACH TO ADDRESSING NIGERIA'S MIGRATION CHALLENGES IN THE CONTEXT OF EXTERNALIZATION AND ENVIRONMENTAL DISPLACEMENT

Grace Perpetual Dafiel, Ruqayyah Olaide Abdulaziz, Comfort Onyanta Alli[1]

Introduction

International migration governance is increasingly shaped by deterrence-oriented frameworks that extend beyond state territories, positioning transit states as enforcement proxies. Nigeria, at the heart of West African migration routes, plays a critical role in this evolving architecture. The country participates in externalisation regimes whereby interception, detention, and readmission are delegated to neighbouring states such as Niger, Chad, and Libya through bilateral agreements, technical assistance, and funding mechanisms, including the EU Emergency Trust Fund for Africa. Domestically, Nigeria has strengthened border controls, expanded biometric data-sharing, and facilitated regional readmissions. While these measures enhance capacity to regulate migration, they prioritise containment over protection, constraining access to asylum, challenging non-refoulement obligations, and exposing migrants to elevated risks in fragile, under-resourced contexts.[2]

Climate-induced environmental stressors—desertification, flooding, recurrent droughts, and erratic rainfall—compound socio-economic vulnerabilities, generating both internal and cross-border displacement. Extreme flooding in

---

[1] Dr. Grace Perpetual Dafiel, Veritas University Nigeria, Abuja, Nigeria. E-mails: dafielg@veritas.edu.ng; dafielgrace904@gmail.com: ORCID ID: 0009-0007-5621-3450.
Mrs. Ruqayyah Olaide Abdulaziz, University of Ilorin, Ilorin, Nigeria. E-mail: abdulaziz.ro@unilorin.edu.ng. ORCID ID: 0009-0001-8362-4729
Ms. Comfort Onyanta ALLI, Street Child Care and Welfare Initiative, Lagos, Nigeria. E-mails: comfort@sccwi.org; alli_comfort@yahoo.com
[2] F Gammeltoft-Hansen and M Sorensen, *The Migration–Climate–Externalisation Nexus in Africa* (Routledge 2021) 45–67

2022 affected thirty-four states, increasing internally displaced persons from 3.1 to 5.3 million.[3] Northern Nigeria faces severe desertification, southern coasts endure rising sea levels and floods, while the Middle Belt's erratic rainfall threatens agriculture and food security.[4] Nigeria's migration laws and policies, largely framed around economic and conflict-related displacement, inadequately recognise environmental displacement, leaving climate-displaced persons without legal status, protection, or durable solutions.[5]

This paper examines international migration law and climate displacement in Nigeria, assesses externalisation's impact on sovereignty and rights, evaluates institutional responses, and proposes a multidisciplinary, rights-based governance framework. Evidence-based recommendations aim to recalibrate Nigeria's governance towards legality, resilience, and equitable, rights-consistent burden-sharing.

Conceptual and Theoretical Framework

The intersection of international migration law, climate-induced displacement, and border externalisation requires careful theoretical framing. Core instruments—the 1951 Refugee Convention and 1967 Protocol—protect refugees but exclude climate-displaced persons, creating a legal gap. Complementary frameworks include international human rights law, regional instruments like the ECOWAS Free Movement Protocol (1979), and non-binding instruments such as the 2018 Global Compact for Migration.[6]

Climate displacement encompasses internal or cross-border mobility triggered by climate change impacts, including desertification, flooding, sea-level rise, and ecosystem degradation.[7] Nigeria's vulnerability is evident in NCFRMI data showing post-2022 flood displacement and the Lake Chad Basin crisis, which has left over 11 million people in humanitarian need.[8]

Border externalisation, the translocation of migration control to transit or origin states via partnerships, funding, and operational cooperation, is evident in EU

---

[3] Internal Displacement Monitoring Centre, *Nigeria: 2022 Annual Report on Displacement* (IDMC 2023) 12
[4] O Adepoju, 'Environmental Change and Migration in West Africa' (2020) 18 *Journal of African Migration Studies* 33–55
[5] UNHCR, *Nigeria: Climate-Induced Displacement and Legal Gaps* (UNHCR 2021) 7–9
[6] UN General Assembly, 'Global Compact for Safe, Orderly and Regular Migration' (A/RES/73/195, 2018)
[7] Nigerian Meteorological Agency (NiMet), Climate Variability Reports 2022
[8] National Commission for Refugees, Migrants and Internally Displaced Persons (NCFRMI), Annual Report 2022

initiatives under the Emergency Trust Fund for Africa.[9] These policies, often deploying biometric systems and surveillance, prioritise deterrence and readmission, risking rights erosion and non-refoulement breaches.[10]

Tackling Nigeria's climate-migration challenges requires a multidisciplinary, rights-based strategy combining environmental science, human rights law, and security policy to strengthen resilience and regional cooperation.

Theoretical Framework

The Human Security Paradigm shifts migration governance to people-centred protection, emphasizing dignity, safety, resilience, and alignment with the HRBA and African Charter 1981.[11]

Environmental Justice Theory emphasises the unequal distribution of climate burdens, highlighting the disproportionate impacts on low-emission, climate-vulnerable states like Nigeria.[12]

Securitisation Theory, from the Copenhagen School, explains how migration is framed as a security threat, legitimising extraordinary measures including externalisation.[13]

Environmental Security and Vulnerability Theory conceptualises climate change as a "threat multiplier" exacerbating instability and displacement, framing migration as an adaptive strategy.[14]

Critical Border Studies examines how EU-led externalisation restructures sovereignty, deepens securitisation, and restricts asylum access.[15]

Legal Pluralism highlights the interplay—and tension—between domestic, regional, and international legal regimes, exposing normative gaps in protecting environmentally displaced persons.[16]

---

[9] European Union Emergency Trust Fund for Africa, Migration Partnership Programmes in West Africa (2020)

[10] Gammeltoft-Hansen T and Sørensen N, 'The Migration Industry and Border Externalisation' (2013) 21 Journal of Refugee Studies 3

[11] Adopted 27 June 1981, entered into force 21 October 1986. 1520 UNTS 217

[12] David Schlosberg, *Defining Environmental Justice: Theories, Movements, and Nature* (OUP 2007)

[13] Barry Buzan, Ole Wæver and Jaap de Wilde, *Security: A New Framework for Analysis* (Lynne Rienner 1998) 23

[14] Jon Barnett and W Neil Adger, 'Climate Change, Human Security and Violent Conflict' (2007) 26 *Political Geography* 639

[15] Nick Vaughan-Williams, *Border Politics: The Limits of Sovereign Power* (Edinburgh University Press 2009)

[16] Sally Engle Merry, 'Legal Pluralism' (1988) 22 *Law & Society Review* 869

The international legal framework is fragmented: the 1951 Refugee Convention excludes purely environmental migrants; UNFCCC and Paris Agreement mandate adaptation, while the 2018 Global Compact is non-binding. In *Teitiota v New Zealand*,[17] the UN Human Rights Committee acknowledged climate change as potentially life-threatening but declined to confer refugee status.

Nigeria's 2025 Migration Policy aims for coherence, yet the 2021 Climate Change Act and IDP Policy neglect climate-induced displacement.

Literature Review

Scholarship on the migration–climate–externalisation nexus highlights the insufficiency of current legal frameworks in protecting climate-displaced populations, particularly those outside the 1951 Refugee Convention's scope.[18] Soft-law instruments, including the 2018 Global Compact for Migration, provide guidance but are non-binding; regional frameworks like the Kampala Convention address internal displacement, while EU–Africa externalisation raises sovereignty and rights concerns.[19] In Nigeria, environmental degradation, securitised migration, and governance gaps persist, with climate adaptation largely absent from policy, underscoring the need for a multidisciplinary, rights-based response.

Methodology

This study adopts a qualitative, doctrinal, and interdisciplinary approach to examine international migration law, climate-induced displacement, and border externalisation in Nigeria. It analyses primary legal instruments, including the 1951 Refugee Convention, 1967 Protocol, the Kampala Convention, domestic legislation, and relevant soft-law frameworks. Secondary literature and policy reports contextualise climate impacts, displacement patterns, and governance practices. Using a comparative and normative perspective, Nigeria's externalisation policies are assessed against international protection standards. Triangulated government and agency data inform holistic, evidence-based recommendations integrating climate adaptation, human rights, and humane migration governance.

---

[17] (2020) UN Human Rights Committee Communication No 2728/2016, UN Doc CCPR/C/127/D/2728/2016 (7 January 2020)
[18] Jane McAdam, *Climate Change, Forced Migration, and International Law* (Oxford University Press 2012) 45
[19] Adepoju A, 'Environmental Degradation and Migration Governance in Nigeria' (2020) 12 *Journal of African Migration Studies* 23

Findings

Nigeria's migration governance balances security-focused externalisation with international law obligations; EU-supported agreements with Niger, Chad, and Libya emphasise interception, detention, and return rather than migrant protection.[20] While these measures enhance control over migratory flows, they risk breaching non-refoulement obligations and constraining access to asylum, particularly in under-resourced border zones.[21]

From a human security perspective, Nigerian law largely ignores climate-induced displacement, despite desertification, coastal flooding, and erratic Middle Belt rainfall driving significant internal population movements.[22] This legal invisibility denies climate-displaced persons essential safeguards, entitlements, and pathways to durable solutions. Environmental justice theory further highlights the disproportionate exposure of local communities to climate hazards despite minimal contribution to global emissions.[23]

Externalisation—delegating migration control to transit states—creates legal ambiguities and protection gaps, leaving migrants, including climate-displaced persons, vulnerable to forced returns and abuse.[24] Fragmented capacities of NCFRMI, NEMA, FME, NESREA, and FMHAPA, alongside misaligned domestic and regional policies, hinder integrated climate-migration governance in Nigeria.

Recommendations

As part of its legal and policy reform Nigeria must legally recognise climate-displaced persons, providing protection, status, and durable solutions, aligned with Article 33 of the 1951 Refugee Convention, the Kampala Convention, and ECOWAS protocols.

Secure digital migration platforms and smart border systems, incorporating biometrics and surveillance, enhance efficient, rights-respecting monitoring and support evidence-based policy.

Targeted climate adaptation and disaster risk reduction in hotspots—flood-

---

[20] Thomas Gammeltoft-Hansen and Ninna Nyberg Sørensen, *The Migration Industry and the Commercialization of International Migration* (Routledge 2013) 132

[21] Amnesty International, *Europe's Gatekeeper: EU External Migration Policy and Human Rights* (AI 2020)

[22] NCFRMI, *Annual Report 2022* (Abuja 2023)

[23] David Schlosberg, *Defining Environmental Justice: Theories, Movements, and Nature* (OUP 2007)

[24] Nick Vaughan-Williams, *Border Politics: The Limits of Sovereign Power* (Edinburgh University Press 2009)

prone and drought-affected areas—enhance preparedness and reduce displacement drivers.

Enter into binding rights-based agreements with transit states and advocacy for a global climate-migration legal framework institutionalise protection, responsibility-sharing, and durable solutions.

Conclusion

Climate change increasingly displaces vulnerable Nigerians, intensifying socio-economic instability. Existing legal frameworks inadequately protect climate migrants, exposing them to rights violations. Addressing this requires multidisciplinary, rights-based strategies integrating legal reform, policy development, environmental monitoring, inter-agency coordination, and strengthened institutional capacity. Aligning national laws with international and regional standards, implementing climate adaptation measures, and ensuring accountable externalisation can mitigate displacement drivers, safeguard migrants, and promote resilient, equitable governance that upholds human dignity while balancing societal stability.

References

A Adepoju, 'Environmental Degradation and Migration Governance in Nigeria' (2020) 12 *Journal of African Migration Studies* 23

Amnesty International, *Europe's Gatekeeper: EU External Migration Policy and Human Rights* (AI 2020)

Barry Buzan, Ole Wæver and Jaap de Wilde, *Security: A New Framework for Analysis* (Lynne Rienner 1998) 23

Convention Relating to the Status of Refugees, adopted 28 July 1951, entered into force 22 April 1954, 189 UNTS 137

David Schlosberg, *Defining Environmental Justice: Theories, Movements, and Nature* (OUP 2007)

European Union Emergency Trust Fund for Africa, *Migration Partnership Programmes in West Africa* (2020)

F Gammeltoft-Hansen and M Sørensen, *The Migration–Climate–Externalisation Nexus in Africa* (Routledge 2021) 45–67; 'The Migration Industry and Border Externalisation' (2013) 21 *Journal of Refugee Studies* 3

Internal Displacement Monitoring Centre, *Nigeria: 2022 Annual Report on Displacement* (IDMC 2023) 12

Jane McAdam, *Climate Change, Forced Migration, and International Law* (Oxford University Press 2012) 45

Jon Barnett and W Neil Adger, 'Climate Change, Human Security and Violent Conflict' (2007) 26 *Political Geography* 639

National Commission for Refugees, Migrants and Internally Displaced Persons (NCFRMI), *Annual Report 2022*

Nick Vaughan-Williams, *Border Politics: The Limits of Sovereign Power* (Edinburgh University Press

2009)

Nigerian Meteorological Agency (NiMet), *Climate Variability Reports 2022*

O. Adepoju, 'Environmental Change and Migration in West Africa' (2020) 18 *Journal of African Migration Studies* 33–55

Sally Engle Merry, 'Legal Pluralism' (1988) 22 *Law & Society Review* 869

T Gammeltoft-Hansen and Ninna Nyberg Sørensen, *The Migration Industry and the Commercialization of International Migration* (Routledge 2013) 132

UN General Assembly, 'Global Compact for Safe, Orderly and Regular Migration' (A/RES/73/195, 2018)

UN Human Rights Committee, Communication No 2728/2016, UN Doc CCPR/C/127/D/2728/2016 (7 January 2020)

UNHCR, *Nigeria: Climate-Induced Displacement and Legal Gaps* (UNHCR 2021) 7–9

PARTICIPATION OF POPULISTS IN GOVERNMENT AND ITS IMPACT ON MIGRATION DISCOURSE

Radoslav Štefančík[1]

Introduction

Although anti-immigration rhetoric has long been a staple of populist communication strategies in Western European countries, migration remained a marginal issue in Slovak political discourse until 2015 (Androvičová, 2015). Prior to that year, the topic appeared only sporadically, as it failed to capture the interest of the Slovak public. The situation changed dramatically in 2015, when migration became one of the central themes in political debate. Despite the arrival of thousands of migrants from Africa and the Middle East to Europe, Slovakia was not situated along the main migration routes and thus served neither as a destination nor a transit country. Nevertheless, Slovak populists redirected public attention toward the issue of migration. The rationale behind this shift is straightforward: populist leaders recognized how easily fear of migrants could be used to mobilize their voter base.

Within a few months, terms such as "migrant" and "migration" had acquired negative connotations. It was not only populists who spoke negatively about migrants, but some politicians from the democratic centre also stigmatized migrants. The political discourse in 2015-2016 was characterized by the portrayal of migrants as a multidimensional security risk (Štefančík et al., 2021). The increase in the debate on migration is understandably linked to the migration processes during that period. However, politicians' interest in migration was also influenced by the parliamentary elections held in early March 2016. After the elections, politicians once again pushed migration into the background. More significant discussion of migration did not begin until before the 2023 parliamentary elections. The main populist parties in Slovakia (Smer-SD, SNS, Republika) were in opposition at the time, making it easier for them to criticize the government for poorly guarded state

[1] Prof. Dr. Radoslav Štefančík, Bratislava University of Economics and Business, Bratislava, Slovakia.

borders. Populists once again presented migrants as a threat. Anti-immigration rhetoric was one of the reasons why populists won the parliamentary elections and subsequently formed a government.

Research question, methodology, and theoretical background

This paper aims to examine how Slovak populists addressed the issue of international migration before and after the 2023 elections, when opposition politicians assumed governmental responsibility. It seeks to identify shifts in migration rhetoric among politicians who initially viewed migrants negatively but may have later recognized their potential contribution to the national economy, demographic development, or the social system. The research presented here focuses on the verbal and written statements made by representatives of selected Slovak political parties before and after the 2023 parliamentary elections. Between 2020 and 2023, the Smer-SD party was in opposition.

This study examines how the image of migrants is constructed in political discourse, using discourse analysis as the primary methodological approach. Discourse can be analysed through various frameworks (van Dijk, 1997). Given that this research focuses on how migrants are perceived by political actors, it is appropriate to follow the recommendations of Ruth Wodak (2001), who, in her work on migration discourse, suggests exploring questions such as: How are people named and referred to linguistically? What traits, characteristics, and qualities are attributed to them? What arguments and argumentative strategies are employed by individuals or social groups to justify and legitimize exclusion, discrimination, oppression, or exploitation?

The definition of populism in academic literature is represented mainly by three perspectives. The first refers to populism as a "thin ideology" (Mudde, 2004). In this context, the adjective "thin" is significant because, unlike classical ideologies, populism is based on a simple binary logic: society is divided into two homogeneous and antagonistic groups, "the pure people" versus "the corrupt elite." The second view presents populism as a political strategy (Weyland, 2001). In this view, populism is a form of politics in which a charismatic leader, backed by strong support from their party's membership base and voters, plays a significant role. Finally, the third view presents populism as a communication strategy (Jagers & Walgrave, 2007). Populists employ emotionally charged means of expression to convey their antagonistic attitude towards "the others" or "the foreigners," aiming to achieve the desired effect (Reinemann, 2017). The aim of populist communication strategies is not to inform, but rather to evoke emotions, typically fear and anxiety. Fear is considered an effective way of mobilizing voters (Tannenbaum et al, 2015).

The central category of populist communication is the people, on whose behalf populists speak, defend their interests, and protect them from domestic or foreign enemies. The category of enemy is broad, but in recent years, according to populists, migrants have been among the main enemies of the people. Defining migrants as enemies fits into the binary thinking of us vs. them, the others. Populists perceive migrants as a multidimensional threat. However, the question is how populists perceive migrants when they are in government. Several studies have examined the behavior of populists when they come to power, although this topic was relatively new in political science research until recently. Askim et al (2022) note that populists behave similarly to other political parties in some areas of public administration. The difference, however, lies in the rhetoric they use. Populists differed from non-populist politicians in their communication style and communication priorities. Comparative research (Schwörer, 2022) shows that after entering government, European populists continue their anti-elitist communication, in which the people are the central category. However, populists with government responsibility change the categories of enemies they consider to be enemies of the people. Luo (2024) argues that the change in rhetoric is influenced by a "sense of representation." Populist rhetoric stems from a sense of underrepresentation, which is alleviated after populists come to power.

Migration in Slovak political discourse

Migration has long been a marginal issue in Slovakia's political discourse. Slovakia was not a destination country for migrants. Slovakia was partly a transit country, but in 2015 and 2016, it was not located on the main migration routes. Migration was not at the center of political discourse because the country faced other pressing issues during the transformation process, including the consolidation of democracy, the division of Czechoslovakia, corruption, and cultural and ethical concerns.

In the Summer of 2016, Slovak politicians also began to explore migration as a topic for political discourse. It was only a short period. Following the 2016 elections, old topics resurfaced, and the issue of migration was relegated to the margins of political interest (Dulebová, Štefančík, Cingerová, 2024).

Between 2015 and 2016, several controversial statements were made by Slovak politicians regarding migrants. Slovak politicians presented migrants as a threat, often expressing an interest in protecting the population of Slovakia from non-existent Muslim immigration. Here are a few examples:

> - *Richard Sulík (2015) — "I don't want to live in a society where more Muslim children are born than non-Muslim children. We are against migrants in general" (Folentová, 2016).*

> - *Robert Fico (2016) — "We have to prevent the emergence of a compact Muslim community in Slovakia" (Rohac, 2016).*

The topic of migration also came up before the 2023 parliamentary elections and the 2024 European Parliament elections. Populist politicians visited migrant facilities before the elections and used them for their campaign slogans. Populist election slogans contained various stereotypes: for example, that migrants only come illegally, that they have a specific skin color, or that they are a burden on the social system.

> - Hlas-SD – "*Lower pensions because of migrants — we will not allow that*" (Hlas-SD, 2023).

The statement by the ruling party Hlas-SD is an example of political messaging that links migration to threats to the social system. By saying "*we will not allow that*," politicians are attempting to portray themselves as the "protectors of the nation" against an external enemy, in this case, migration. Politicians thus portray migrants as the cause of the deterioration in the living conditions of the domestic population. This type of rhetoric is based on creating fear and deepening the polarization between "us" and "them," or "the others".

After the parliamentary elections, the situation in the migration discourse changed. Populists formed a government, and the number of Ukrainian migrants grew in Slovakia due to the war in Ukraine. When examining the migration discourse, we can see a change in the rhetoric of Slovak populists. Populists are beginning to distinguish between legal and illegal migrants. Although there are also negative statements about Ukrainian refugees, Prime Minister Fico, who regularly mobilizes anti-immigration rhetoric before elections, has also expressed positive aspects of the migration of Ukrainian refugees:

- Robert Fico – "Ukrainians are a welcome workforce for us" (Pekárková, 2024).

- Robert Fico – "We are preparing laws to help speed up the placement of people from abroad. Note that I mean legal migrants" (Pekárková, 2024).

Fico sees foreign workers as one way to solve the labor shortage in Slovakia. During a visit to Uzbekistan in June 2025, Prime Minister Robert Fico expressed interest in providing 150,000 jobs for foreign workers. It should be noted that the number of migrants living in Slovakia at the end of 2024 was approximately 327,000 (BBF 2025). The statement by the Slovak Prime Minister, quoted below, provides an example of technocratic language that reduces people to mere numbers and economic resources. His language frames migration as a tool for addressing labor shortages, while Fico omits any social, cultural, or ethical aspects of the process. Foreign workers are often presented as objects of preparation and transfer, rather than as subjects with their rights and needs. The quoted statement thus represents a generalizing perspective on labor migration, through which the mobility of people is presented as part of labor market planning.

- Robert Fico – "First and foremost, we are talking about people we need in industry, especially in companies that are part of the automotive industry. However, we are also discussing professions such as nursing. A model has already been developed in Uzbekistan in cooperation with Germany, in which specific professions are being trained directly in Uzbekistan" (Dnes 24 2025).

In the above excerpts, populists also present the positive aspects of migration, unlike in the previous period. However, this discourse is also exclusionary, as people are only welcome if they serve economic interests. The emphasis on "legality" serves to reassure the public that migration will be "under control" by the new government and that there is therefore no reason for the fears.

Conclusion

The cited statements by Slovak populist politicians reveal two levels of migration discourse. Before the parliamentary elections, the emphasis was mainly on the security framework of migration. This framework was based primarily on emotional appeals to fear, uncertainty, and the need to protect the domestic population. Political statements served to mobilize voters through negative framing. Migrants were deliberately portrayed as the cause of social problems faced by the domestic population. This type of discourse is typical of populist rhetoric, which is based on the dichotomy of "us" versus "them," with "us" representing the threatened community and "them" being external actors who disrupt order or, in this case, security. Such discourse is efficient during the pre-election period because it activates collective emotions and reinforces frameworks based on collective identity and the exclusion of others.

After the 2023 parliamentary elections, the statements of Slovak populists who participated in forming the government shifted from an emotional and security framework to a pragmatic language. Negative emotions are absent, fictitious threats are pushed to the margins of political interest, and the economic dimension of migration processes is emphasized. This shift is driven by the need to manage state institutions, address economic challenges, and maintain political legitimacy. This is achieved by emphasizing the differences between "legal" and "illegal" migrants and constantly reiterating the need to protect state borders. The emphasis on legality and increased protection of state borders serves to reassure the public and maintain consistency with previous rhetoric. Politicians thus balance the pragmatic needs of the state with the expectations of their voter base, which was mobilized before the elections through fear and negative portrayals of those involved in migration processes.

In this type of discourse, we can identify the contradictory rhetoric of populist leaders who, while in opposition, use exclusive, nationalist communication strategies, but after coming to power adapt their language to the economic and demographic needs of the state. In discursive analysis, this can be interpreted as a strategic transformation of frameworks (Benford, Snow 2000), which allows politicians to maintain power without losing credibility.

Discourse analysis has succeeded in building on existing theories, according to which populists, after forming a government, create a new image of the enemy and use a different, more politically correct language. However, this does not mean that populists change completely. They present their messages using rhetoric that is more acceptable to broader sections of the population.

Funding acknowledgment:

This text is a result of the project APVV-23-0040, "Migration Discourse in the V4 Countries from the Perspective of Political Linguistics."

Corpus Resources:

Dnes 24 (2025). Potrebujeme 150-tisíc kvalifikovaných pracovných síl, riešením je Uzbekistan. Dnes 24, 9. 6. 2025. https://www.dnes24.sk/fico-potrebujeme-150-tisic-kvalifikovanych-pracovnych-sil-riesenim-je-uzbekistan-463734

Folentová, V. (2016). SaS ide do volieb rozpoltená. Denník N, from<https://dennikn.sk/372555/bilbordoch-reformy-mitingoch-utecenci-sas-ide-do-volieb-rozpoltena/?ref=tit

Hlas-SD (2023). Webový portál strany Hlas-SD. https://strana-hlas.sk/

Pekárková, I. (2024). Ukrajinci sú pre nás vítanou pracovnou silou, vyhlásil Robert Fico v RTVS. Už sa pripravujú zmeny. RTVS, 24.4.2024. https://spravy.rtvs.sk/2024/02/ukrajinci-su-pre-nas-vitanou-pracovnou-silou-vyhlasil-robert-fico-v-rtvs-uz-sa-pripravuju-zmeny.

Rohac, D. (2016). Vote Here for Cronyism, against Liberal Democracy. Politico, February 29, 2016, https://www.politico.eu/article/slovakia-election-robert-fico-visegrad-orban/

References:

Androvičová, J. (2015). Sekuritizácia migrantov na Slovensku – analýza diskurzu. *Sociológia,* 47(4): 319-339.

Askim, J., Karlsen, R., & Kolltveit, K. (2022). Populists in Government: Normal or Exceptional? *Government and Opposition,* 57(4): 728-748.

BBFP (2025). Štatistický prehľad legálnej a nelegálnej migrácie v Slovenskej republike, https://www.minv.sk/?rocenky.

Benford, R. D., & Snow, D. A. (2000). Framing Processes and Social Movements: An Overview and Assessment. Annual. *Annual Review of Sociology,* 26: 611-639.

Dulebová, I., Štefančík, R., & Cingerová, N. (2024). *Language and Security: The Language of Securitization in Contemporary Slovak Public Discourse.* Berlin: Peter Lang.

Jagers, J. & Walgrave, S. (2007). Populism as political communication style: An empirical study of political parties' discourse in Belgium. *European Journal of Political Research,* 46(3): 319-345.

Luo, Y. (2024). We Got Our Guy!: Populist Attitudes after Populists Gain Power. *Socius,* 10.

Mudde, C. (2004. The populist Zeitgeist. *Government and Opposition,* 39(4): 541-563.

Reinemann, C. (2017). Populismus, Kommunikation, Medien. Ein Über-blick über die Forschung zu populistischer politischer Kommunikation. *Zeitschrift für Politikwissenschaft,* 64(2): 167-190

Schwörer, J. (2022). Less Populist in Power? Online Communication of Populist Parties in Coalition Governments. *Government and Opposition,* 57(3): 467-489.

Štefančík, R., Némethová, I. & Seresová, T. (2021). Securitisation of Migration in the Language of Slovak Far-Right Populism. *Migration Letters,* 18(6): 731-744.

Štefančík, R., E. Stradiotová, & Seresová, T. (2022). A Missing Piece: The Absence of Discussion about Integration Policy in the Slovak Migration Discourse. *Migration Letters,* 19(6): 965-981.

Tannenbaum, M., Hepler, J., Zimmerman, R. S., Saul, L., Jacobs, S., Wilson, K., Albarracin,

D. (2015). Appealing to Fear: A Meta-Analysis of Fear Appeal Effectiveness and Theories. *Psychological Bulletin,* 141(6): 1178–1204.

van Dijk, T. A. (1997). What is political discourse analysis. *Belgian Journal of Linguistics,* 11 (1): 11-52.

Weyland, K. (2001). Clarifying a Contested Concept: Populism in the Study of Latin American Politics. *Comparative Politics,* 34(1): 1-22.

Wodak, R. (2001). Discourse-Historical Approach. In: Wodak, R.; Meyer, M. (eds.) *Methods of Critical Discourse Analysis.* London, Thousand Oaks, New Delhi: Sage, pp. 63-94.

THE ADMINISTRATIVE ACCOUNTABILITY OF FRONTEX AND THE PIONEERING ROLE OF THE EUROPEAN OMBUDSMAN

Alessio Laconi

Introduction

Accountability is considered a cornerstone of modern democracies, and as the political relevance of the European Union is constantly increasing, accountability deficits arise and top the agendas of scholars and civil society.

The European Border and Coast Guard Agency (hereinafter Frontex or the Agency) is also part of this debate insofar as since its establishment in 2004 it has witnessed a process of empowerment that rendered it one of the most powerful, both in terms of budget and staff, agencies of the European Union.

Moreover, recent scandals the Agency has been involved in have demonstrated how difficult is controlling its activity and that its *modus operandi* is characterised by an attitude of secretiveness and tendency to cover up violations of obligations aimed at protecting individuals' rights, in particular fundamental rights. This resulted clear after the investigation of the European Anti-Fraud Office (OLAF), whose report led to the resignation of the former Executive Director, Fabrice Leggeri, as complicity in violations of fundamental rights was established. It appeared from the evidence that the Agency, despite being aware of this, did not take appropriate measures to prevent and remedy them.

A similar scenario undermines certain values that form the basis of the European legal system, in particular the rule of law which, intended to ensure that public actions remain within the boundaries set by law, is protected through accountability mechanisms.

The notion of accountability is multifaceted and can assume different meanings depending on the topic the author intends to address. In the present research I embed the notion of accountability provided for by Bovens who defines it as a relationship between an actor, in this case Frontex, and a forum that can pose questions to the former, which has an obligation to respond and justify its conducts.

Moreover, I will refer to administrative accountability that is the form of supervision carried out by *quasi*-legal forums that enforce either administrative or financial control over the conducts and the work of public bodies.

In the European Union, one of the entities designated to perform this form of control is the European Ombudsman (EO) that is regulated by article 228 of the Treaty on the Functioning of the European Union (TFEU) which entitles the former to receive and handle complaints of alleged maladministration by any EU citizen against any of the bodies of the supranational administration.

The *quasi*-legal character of the institution is echoed by article 228 TFEU which provides that the EO cannot investigate on facts that have been the subject of legal proceedings, and thus it cannot constitute a suitable place for the defence of fundamental rights, although, as we shall see, it can provide some form of protection as these rights find a form of manifestation and examination during EO's inquiries.

The European Ombudsman's inquiries into Frontex

The European Ombudsman has decided 62 inquires involving Frontex to date, and to facilitate their analysis they will be divided into four categories: EO's own-inquiries, inquiries regarding access to documents, inquiries regarding fundamental rights[1], and a residual category covering all other subjects not included in the above groups[2];

Furthermore, they will also be grouped according to the period in which the decision was taken, namely after the adoption of Regulation (EU) 1168/2011 that introduced the first safeguards to fundamental rights during operations coordinated by Frontex, and between the adoption of the two main reforms that enhanced the powers of the Agency, Regulation (EU) 2016/1624 and

---

[1] Cases regarding the right of access to documents could be included in fundamental rights category insofar as that is a fundamental right. Yet, considering both the number of inquiries carried out by the EO in the first subject against Frontex as well as the different nature of fundamental rights involved in the second category, I opted to distinguish the two groups.
[2] Most of the cases falling the in category "others" regard either maladministration in public procurements or complaints by former staff for wrong application of Staff Regulations (Regulation 31(EEC), 11 (EAEC).

Regulation /EU) 2019/1896.

The following table show the cases decided by the EO against Frontex:

	EO's own-inq.	F. Rights	Access to doc.	Other
Before Reg. 1168/2011				2
Before Reg. 2016/1624	4		1	5
Before Reg. 2019/1896	1		5	1
After Reg. 2019/1896	3	3	21	13

The table shows how, following the introduction of the first legal obligation upon Frontex to protect fundamental rights with Regulation (EU) 1168/2011, inquiries were launched as more attention was paid to Agency's activities due to increasingly frequent occurrences of deadly accidents and reports of misconducts during the operations, including violation of fundamental rights.

In response to this tendency, European citizens began dedicating growing scrutiny to the activities of the Agency and this explains the growth of the number requests of public access to documents presented to the latter. Individuals sought a mechanism to react to the news of violations perpetrated by Frontex, as well as during its operations, attempting to breach the veil of secrecy that covers its activities.

However, in the aftermath of the adoption of Regulation (EU) 2016/1624 which strengthened Frontex's operational powers, the number of inquiries involving Frontex did not grow; whereas after the adoption of the latest reform, namely Regulation (EU) 2019/1896, which further expanded Frontex's capabilities, the attention on the Agency's activities has reached such levels that it requires adequate oversight in view of the expansion of its powers. In substance, as the powers of the Agency increased so did also the inquiries.

It is in this period that the EO carried out the first three inquiries regarding the possible violation of fundamental rights during the operation although its mandate does not provide proper tools for assessing and eventually addressing the violations which should find scrutiny before the Court of Justice of the European Union instead.

Parallelly, the number of inquiries regarding access to document continued to increase in line with the previous trend, confirming civil society's interest in helping to monitor the legality of Frontex's conduct.

Once upon a time… Frontex

The first relevant inquiries initiated by the EO were own-initiative inquiries which represented the reaction of the institution to the reports of deadly accidents and news of misconducts during the operations, including violation of fundamental rights and lack of transparency.

These have provided the EO with the opportunity to investigate, for the first time, in depth, the internal functioning of the Agency, as observable also by their broad scope of both the object and the conclusions.

In this regard, in case OI/5/BEH-MHZ the Ombudsman evaluated the application of the first fundamental rights safeguards introduced by Regulation (EU) 1168/2011 such as the Code of Conduct and the Fundamental Rights Strategy the Agency was supposed to adopt, as well as the operational measures put in place for the scope. It is noteworthy that in an exchange of opinions through the parts, the Ombudsman completed a series of recommendations that Frontex accepted and slowly incorporated, despite the proposal for a complaint mechanism for receiving denounces of possible violations of fundamental rights by individuals affected during an operation. Therefore, in the annual report that the EO submits to the European Parliament pursuant to Article 228 TFEU, it stressed the importance of this suggestion that the institution eventually introduced including it in Regulation (EU) 2016/1624.

Similarly, and in line with the path undertaken with previous cases, case OI/9/2014/MHZ concerned the real involvement of Frontex during return operations, in particular how, as a coordinator of Joint Return Operations (JROs), it ensures respect for the fundamental rights and human dignity of the individuals being returned. As in previous case, through loyal dialogue with the Agency, the Ombudsman furnished numerous suggestions for improvement in this subject, demonstrating as the protection of fundamental rights begins with efficient administrative practices that aim at that result.

Inquiries on public access to documents

As shown in the table, the majority of the inquiries regarding Frontex fall into the category of public access to documents as the Agency usually denied access to them.

This strand of cases could be divided into two different moments where also two different approaches could be detected: 1) cases regarding the practice of collecting and publishing documents on the website and 2) the management of the request for public access presented by individuals.

In the first cases, the Ombudsman conducted thorough investigations in the Agency's offices, finding relevant mistakes in the management of the documents, for instance it was discovered, by analysing manually some documents, that the officers missed to catalogue some files as Serious Incident Reports, namely those that were object of the request. In another case the Ombudsman provided suggestions for making Agency's website more user-friendly. Further, in another case the EO assessed the typical justification provided by Frontex for denying access to public documents, limiting the abuse to the "overarching interest to public safety" as ground for the denial.

In this first strand of cases, which were decided within a common timeframe prior to the major reform of 2019, it seems that the Ombudsman has taught the Agency good administrative practices for managing internal documents.

In the second series of cases, the scrutiny of the Ombudsman became more intrusive as the Agency did not really cease its practice to deny access due to an "overarching interest to public safety". The Ombudsman thus reacted dismantling the bases grounding such decisions and has succeeded in making Frontex publish the requested documents. In these inquiries, the investigations conducted on Frontex's premises have facilitated the conclusion of an agreement with the Agency as well as a thorough examination of the reasons put forward by the latter.

Fundamental Right before the European Ombudsman

The EO is not the proper forum for addressing these issues, particularly since it can only be invoked by EU citizens, whereas the victims of the violations are mostly third-country nationals. However, its decisions demonstrate it constitutes an important democratic safeguard for fundamental rights.

The inquiries have extensive but well-targeted scope aimed at assessing the application of fundamental rights safeguards, for instance the scarce use of the complaint mechanism, or the lack of transparency regarding the Operational Plans of the operations and the division of competences between the administrations.

The intrusiveness of the scrutiny has achieved important results as following every decision the Agency modified its wrongful practices and thus it made the complaint mechanism more public; it began publishing some Operational Plans, although redacted in almost their entirety; it facilitated access to documents for investigating shipwrecks and accidents.

Conclusions

Following this overview, a general trend in all the inquiries can be detected and shows the cooperative approach of the EO throughout all her investigations. She demonstrated willingness to dialogue with Frontex and aid in improving its administrative practices, which have often proved to be flawed, thus leading to decisions of maladministration.

This is particularly observable in the cases regarding public access to documents as in the cases before 2019 the suggestions were mostly practical, as for instructing Frontex. In other cases, the Ombudsman has shown interest in dismantling practices of secretiveness incompatible with good administration in a democratic order as it is the European Union.

If, on the other hand, cases relating to human rights violations were considered, some important steps must be taken by the side of the Agency that increased its transparency and implemented Ombudsman's recommendations, yet, in the case of the Operational Plans, they are redacted and perhaps with no justification.

Accountability is built progressively insofar as, although it is fundamental in a democratic order, it is made of practices, and these must be developed and then implemented.

The EO is one of the few institutions that thoroughly scrutinised Frontex and the only that succeeded in changing its behaviour. In this regard, its efforts are not isolated as the evidence of the investigations as well as the positions taken by the Agency throughout them, could constitute the basis for enforcing the other mechanisms of accountability, i.e. a position taken by the Agency could be referred to before the Court.

References

Bovens, M. (2007). New Forms of Accountability and EU-Governance. *Comparative European Politics*, 5, 104-120.

Bovens, M. (2010). Two Concepts of Accountability: Accountability as a Virtue and as a Mechanism. *West European Politics*, 33(5), 946-967.

Brandsma, G.J. & Heidbreder, E. & Mastenbroek, E. (2016). Accountability in the post-Lisbon European Union. *International Review of Administrative Sciences*, 82(4), 621-637.

Curtin, D. & Enhert, T. & Morandini, A. & Tas, S. (eds.) (2025). *The European Ombudsman Investigated. From Old Battles to New Challenges.* Oxford: Hart Publishing.

Fink, M. (2018). *Frontex and Human Rights: Responsibility in 'Multi-Actor Situations' under the ECHR and EU Public Liability Law.* Oxford: Oxford University Press.

Gkliati, M. & Rosenfeldt, H. (2019). Accountability of the European Border and Coast Guard Agency: Recent developments, legal standards and existing mechanisms. *Refugee Initiative Law Working Paper 30.*

European Ombudsman. case OI/5/2012/BEH-MHZ.

European Ombudsman. case OI/9/2014/MHZ.

European Ombudsman. case 1616/2016/MDC.

European Ombudsman. case 1767/2017/KM.

European Ombudsman. case 1328/2018/EIS.

European Ombudsman. case 2273/2019/MIG.

European Ombudsman. case OI/5/2020/MHZ.

European Ombudsman. case OI/4/2021/MHZ.

European Ombudsman. case 1885/2023/ACB.

European Ombudsman. case 344/2023/PVV.

European Ombudsman. case OI/3/2023/MHZ.

European Ombudsman. case 219/2024/TM.

Marin, L. (2024). Frontex at the epicentre of a rule of law crisis at the external borders of the EU. *European Law Journal*, 30(1-2), 11-28.

Mulgan, R. (2000). "Accountability": an ever-expanding concept?' *Public Administration*, 78(3), 555–573.

PRESS AND POLITICS: "YELLOW JOURNALISM" AND THE RISE OF THE ZAFER PARTY

Emma Walker-Silverman

Introduction

Since 2014, Turkey has hosted one of the largest populations of refugees in the world (UNHCR, 2024). While the country was initially praised for its generous welcome, as the situation became increasingly protracted local resentment began to mount (McClelland, 2014; Erdoğan, 2022). This trend mirrored rising refugee-host community tensions across much of the region, but its expression in Turkey was unusual.

For the first several years following the outbreak of civil war in Syria and resulting increase in Turkey's refugee population, political parties demonstrated surprising reluctance to politicize the growing public anger toward the situation, in striking contrast to many European countries (Yanasmayan, Üstübici and Kasli, 2019). Traditional media similarly showed unusual reserve in their coverage of the issue. The tendency of news media to sensationalize and exaggerate the threats posed by migrants is well documented (Rasinger, 2010; Wigger, 2019; Harraway and Wong, 2024). Yet for most of the 2010s, media coverage of refugees in Turkey framed them largely as victims rather than threats (Sunata and Yıldız, 2018; Taşdemir and İçten, 2023). As the displacement of Syrians became protracted, both media coverage and political parties became significantly less benevolent. However, while media and politicians are often accused of stoking resentment towards marginalized groups or other scapegoats, in Turkey this shift in tone appears to have followed, rather than precipitated, growing popular backlash against refugees.

Before the social media age, there may have been little to evidence public debate and its interactions with and divergence from political and media elites. Today, deliberations rage across Twitter, Facebook, Instagram, and beyond, leaving a written trail. These discussions capture not only public responses to refugees, but also the conversations that help to shape those responses, from pronouncements by public figures to interpersonal dialogues (McGregor, 2019; Dong and Lian, 2021).

The dataset on which this research was based consists of all tweets posted in Turkish using at least one of a list of designated keywords over the six-month period from November 15th, 2021 to May 15th, 2022. Keywords (listed in the appendix) included the varying terms used for refugees and migrants, the nationalities and ethnic categories most commonly associated with refugees and asylum-seekers, and the terms "racist" and "racism", in order to capture a relevant Twitter debate about whether or not anti-refugee attitudes constituted racism. This resulted in a total of 8,894,968 tweets. I qualitatively analysed a random sample of 500 to map the main themes that appeared to be driving national conversation on the topic.

While there are important differences between refugees, asylum-seekers, and migrants more broadly, I included all of them here both to capture the broadest possible sample of relevant discussions on Twitter, and because these groups are often discussed together and understood as a single topic. Moreover, whether a poster uses the term refugee, asylum-seeker, migrant, or illegal, often indicates more about their stance towards the foreigners in question than it does about their actual legal status.

In recent years there has been a proliferation of research on social media discourse on refugees and immigrants, both globally and in Turkey (Öztürk and Ayvaz, 2018; Bozdağ, 2020; Erdogan-Ozturk and Isik-Guler, 2020; Taşdelen, 2020; Ozduzen, Korkut and Ozduzen, 2021; Özerim and Tolay, 2021; Uluğ *et al.*, 2023; Yılmaz, Elmas and Eröz, 2023; Elmas, Yılmaz and Gürbüz, 2024). However, most of these studies focus on particular events, topics, or hashtags, and tend to focus on shorter time frames. My contribution, which takes a broad construal of the topic followed over the course of six months, allows for the monitoring of changes in focus and intensity over time. It is this dynamic that I explore here.

Results

In this paper I focus on the temporal aspects of the sample's content. The tweets were heavily skewed towards the later months of the study, displaying a dramatic surge in April and May of 2022 relative to preceding months. The scale of the dataset overall, compared with those of previous studies, suggests that this surge may represent an order of magnitude greater engagement with the topic than in previous years – a sentiment shared by press at the time (Karsit, 2022; Sykes, 2022).

Spikes in the popularity of particular subjects on Twitter are typical, usually driven by external events. Some news items were explicitly referenced in the sample, including:

21/11/21: release of video of Greek coast guard pushing back migrant boats (*TRT Haber*, 2021)

21/12/21: revelation of three Syrians burned to death in hate crime in Izmir (*Duvar English*, 2021)

22/2/22: expanded Russian invasion of Ukraine

3/5/22: release of *Sessiz İstila* (Silent Invasion) short film and arrest of director Hande Karacasu (*BBC News Türkçe*, 2022)

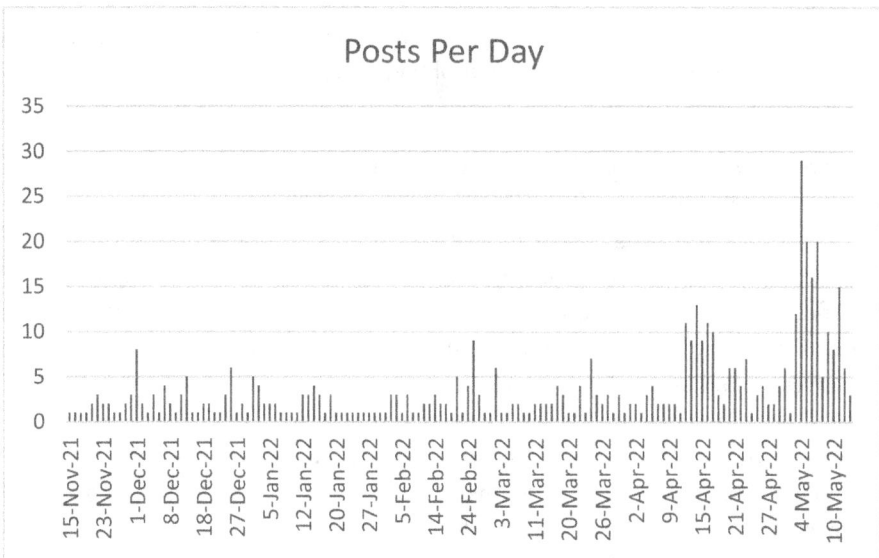

Figure 1 Temporal distribution of randomly sampled Tweets from dataset (n=500)

Yet comparing these dates to the temporal distribution of the 500 randomly sampled tweets demonstrates virtually no correspondence between these events and spikes in Twitter discussion of refugees. Several online events also generated Twitter conversation, including the circulation of several TikTok videos posted by foreign men apparently showing women filmed covertly in public in mid-February, and a series of online jabs exchanged between then

Minister of Interior Süleyman Soylu and Zafer Party leader Ümit Özdağ in late April and early May. Yet these were not referenced in enough tweets to explain the substantial growth in overall volume.

Moreover, there were no obvious changes in the material realities of refugees in Turkey during the period studied. The number of registered foreigners under some form of temporary protection remained fairly constant, and indeed decreased somewhat (though these government figures are widely distrusted) (T.C. İçişleri Bakanlığı Göç İdaresi Başkanlığı, 2025). There were no major policy changes proposed or implemented. Most tweets were not obviously responding to the same event or incident. Yet the change over time is dramatic. What explains this escalation?

Discussion

It is impossible to pinpoint a causal explanation for the intensification of social media discussion of refugees during this time period based on available data. However, the dataset did capture two phenomena, likely interrelated, that may provide some explanation.

The first is what could perhaps be characterized as "yellow journalism". The term, originating from the late 19th century U.S., describes a "sensational style of reporting" featuring dramatic, often lurid headlines and eye-catching illustrations, and marked by an "overreliance on stories of scandal and crime" (Griffin, 2019, p. 4). While media coverage of immigrants frequently mimics some of these tendencies, overrepresenting criminality and negative, threatening narratives (Eberl *et al.*, 2018; Farris and Silber Mohamed, 2018), this has not generally been the case in Turkey. Instead, refugees are most often portrayed in traditional media as victims and aid recipients, particularly in government-controlled outlets (Yaylacı and Karakuş, 2015; Sunata and Yıldız, 2018). Over the past decade, and particularly following the 2016 attempted coup, media ownership in Turkey has consolidated greatly, coming under increasing government influence (Global Media Registry, 2019). While the major outlets are overwhelmingly owned by a handful of holding companies close to the government, the online landscape appears to be facilitating the kind of oppositional media that has become so much more difficult to find elsewhere.

The Twitter sample collected contained a plethora of posts from an array of self-described "independent", "non-partisan", "digital", "new generation" news sites, as their various Twitter bio descriptions assert. These include Aykırı, Whisper Haber, T24, Trajikomik Haber, Conflict, Türk Post, Tele1, BOLD

Medya, BPT Haber, Haber Report , Yeniçağ, and Mülteci Haberler, as well as the since deleted or suspended Sığınmacı Gündemi. While not all of these sites claim all of these descriptors, they seem to be filling a similar niche. All appear to be independent of the four major holding companies that own the majority of the Turkish mediascape, and unlike these news sources, they often focus on storylines explicitly or implicitly critical of government policy. Several feature images of Atatürk on their Twitter profile pages, suggesting a Kemalist political orientation in opposition to the ruling party. Two of the pages, Mülteci Haberler (Refugee News) and Sığınmacı Gündemi (Asylum-Seeker Headlines), as their names suggest, focus explicitly on refugee-related content. That does not mean, however, that they are pro-refugee organizations. Rather, as the bio for Mülteci Haberler declares, they publish "the news which doesn't make it into the national press". In recent years, this appears to consist primarily of valorising and amplifying the rhetoric of anti-refugee politician Ümit Özdağ.

While the journalistic credentials of the "new generation" news sites vary, all appear far more willing to publish content that is uncomfortable to the ruling party than most traditional media is. This includes stories highlighting potential criminal or otherwise antisocial behaviour by people who are or are assumed to be refugees. Over the time period studied, posts of this type increased in both frequency and traction generated.

Comprehensive analysis of crime statistics has found that refugees have had a null or even negative effect on average crime rates in Turkey (Kayaoglu, 2022). Regardless, these provocative stories commanded significant attention on Twitter, eliciting furious comments and calls for the expulsion of all refugees. It was not the first time that these calls were made, or that hashtags declaring refugees unwelcome and demanding they leave the country surged on Turkish Twitter, as documented in previous research. However, in 2021, this rhetoric was for the first time echoed by an institutional actor. With its slogan, "Zafer [Victory] will come, the refugees will go!", the newly formed Zafer Party was answering Twitter's call.

In Turkey's constantly changing political landscape, breakaway parties and shifting alliances are nothing new. Yet even in this context, the Zafer (Victory) Party managed to make a splash. The party was formed by Ümit Özdağ in August of 2021, after his ejection from both the Turkish nationalist MHP (Nationalist Movement Party) and the rival nationalist İYİ (Good) Party. The Zafer Party is described as a far-right, ultra-nationalist, anti-immigrant party and is criticized for having only one issue: opposition to the presence of refugees in Turkey (Türk, 2024).

While its legislative presence has been minimal, the social and cultural impact of the party has been tremendous. In the period studied, Ümit Özdağ and the Zafer Party seemed to burst into the online conversation about refugees and inject it with new life and fresh fury. Özdağ repeated the narratives of refugee criminality reported by the "new generation" news sites, providing a political voice for the fury so many users clearly felt in response (Efe and Ulker, 2024).

Through their mutual amplification, the Zafer Party and "new generation" news sites appeared to contribute greatly to the swell of interest in refugees on Twitter. While the party was formed in August of 2021, it was in early May that it began to garner more significant media attention, aided by a series of attention-grabbing manoeuvres including the release of the *Silent Invasion* short film, which Özdağ funded, and Özdağ's online war of words with Ministry of Interior Süleyman Soylu, which included challenging him to a duel outside his office to prove his honour (Karsit, 2022; Sabah, 2022; Türk, 2024). While Özdağ never got his chance at a duel, he did get the opportunity to speak to dozens of media outlets about the stunt. These antics provided additional fodder for digital news sites and further raised the profile of his chosen issue.

Conclusion

It is difficult to imagine either phenomenon – the spread of "new generation" news site or the rise of Zafer Party – without social media. Over the past decade, the consolidation of traditional media outlets under government influence in Turkey had been largely completed (Bianet, 2021). Social media offered an alternative platform which allowed oppositional narratives to be aired. But in Turkey, as elsewhere, Twitter did more than limit the power of political powerbrokers. It removed all traditional gatekeepers, including those which distinguished empirical reporting from misinformation, rumour-mongering, and outright hate speech (Harari, 2024).

Similarly, the Turkish political system has been increasingly captured by the ruling party. Opposition parties, while representing significant constituencies, have struggled to exert influence over policy (Esen, Gumuscu and Yavuzyılmaz, 2023). The Zafer Party, by contrast, managed to amass demonstrable support entirely independent of electoral processes using social media engagement as a measure of popular support (Sykes, 2022). By the 2023 presidential election, despite Zafer not holding a single seat in Parliament, the party's popularity had convinced both major coalitions to embrace policies and rhetoric imitating its anti-refugee position(Balta, Elçi and Sert, 2023). Moreover, when the election continued to a second round, Zafer was thrust into the position of kingmaker, despite winning only 2.23% of the vote (*Hürriyet*, 2023; Silverman, 2024). On the one hand, this "digital-first" model of political party formation allowed a popular opposition narrative to gain influence in a competitive authoritarian system already largely dominated by the party in power. At some level, this is a victory for democracy. Yet it was achieved through misinformation, xenophobia, the spread of conspiracy theories, and the encouragement of illiberal means and even violence to achieve political aims (Sabah, 2023; Özoflu *et al.*, 2025).

While we may be able to say that it is difficult to imagine either Turkey's "new generation" news sites or the Zafer Party arising without social media, we cannot know whether or to what extent anti-refugee backlash would have arisen in its absence. What is clear is that social media plays a significant but complicated role in relation to both liberal principles and democracy. For those concerned with the rights of those, like refugees, who are dependent on these principles, it is a force that cannot be ignored.

Appendix

Candidate terms were tested for relevance and narrowed down to the following: mülteci (refugee), göçmen (migrant), sığınmacı (asylum-seeker), kaçak (illegal/smuggled), Suriyeli (Syrian), Afgan/Afganlı (Afghan), İranlı (Iranian), İraklı (Iraqi), Pakistanlı (Pakistani), Arap (Arab), ırkçı (racist) and ırkçılık (racism). I used base terms and their plurals, if applicable. Ahmed Gharibeh assisted with data collection, and Dila Falay assisted with data analysis.

References

Balta, E., Elçi, E. and Sert, D. (2023) *The 2023 Elections and Migration Debate in Turkey*. Heinrich Böll Foundation.

BBC News Türkçe (2022) 'Sessiz İstila: Filmin yapımcısı Hande Karacasu serbest bırakıldı', 4 May. Available at: https://www.bbc.com/turkce/haberler-turkiye-61319607 (Accessed: 13 January 2025).

Bianet (2021) *Who owns the media in Turkey*, Media Ownership Monitor. Available at: https://turkey.mom-rsf.org/en/ (Accessed: 31 August 2025).

Bozdağ, Ç. (2020) 'Bottom-up nationalism and discrimination on social media: An analysis of the citizenship debate about refugees in Turkey', *European Journal of Cultural Studies*, 23(5), pp. 712–730. Available at: https://doi.org/10.1177/1367549419869354.

Dong, X. and Lian, Y. (2021) 'A review of social media-based public opinion analyses: Challenges and recommendations', *Technology in Society*, 67, p. 101724. Available at: https://doi.org/10.1016/j.techsoc.2021.101724.

Duvar English (2021) 'Three Syrian workers burned to death in İzmir in racist attack', 22 December. Available at: https://www.duvarenglish.com/three-syrian-workers-burned-to-death-in-turkeys-izmir-in-racist-attack-news-59921 (Accessed: 8 December 2024).

Eberl, J.-M. *et al.* (2018) 'The European media discourse on immigration and its effects: a literature review', *Annals of the International Communication Association*, 42(3), pp. 207–223. Available at: https://doi.org/10.1080/23808985.2018.1497452.

Efe, I. and Ulker, O. (2024) 'Social media, politics, and the rise of the anti-refugee far-right in Turkey', *Journal of Language and Politics* [Preprint]. Available at: https://research.manchester.ac.uk/en/publications/social-media-politics-and-the-rise-of-the-anti-refugee-far-right- (Accessed: 11 December 2024).

Elmas, T., Yılmaz, F. and Gürbüz, N. (2024) '"Refugees from Ukraine are called humans": A corpus-based critical discourse analysis of Turkish tweets about Ukrainian refugees', *Media, Culture & Society*, p. 01634437241271051. Available at: https://doi.org/10.1177/01634437241271051.

Erdoğan, M.M. (2022) *Syrians Barometer 2020: A Framework for Achieving Social Cohesion with Syrians in Turkey*. UNHCR. Available at: https://data.unhcr.org/en/documents/details/91511 (Accessed: 18 November 2024).

Erdogan-Ozturk, Y. and Isik-Guler, H. (2020) 'Discourses of exclusion on Twitter in the Turkish Context: #ülkemdesuriyeliistemiyorum (#idontwantsyriansinmycountry)', *Discourse, Context & Media*, 36, p. 100400. Available at: https://doi.org/10.1016/j.dcm.2020.100400.

Esen, B., Gumuscu, S. and Yavuzyılmaz, H. (2023) 'Competitive yet unfair: May 2023 elections and authoritarian resilience in Turkey', *South European Society and Politics*, 28(3), pp. 359–387. Available at: https://doi.org/10.1080/13608746.2024.2327778.

Farris, E.M. and Silber Mohamed, H. (2018) 'Picturing immigration: how the media criminalizes immigrants', *Politics, Groups, and Identities*, 6(4), pp. 814–824. Available at: https://doi.org/10.1080/21565503.2018.1484375.

Global Media Registry (2019) *Media Ownership Monitor: Turkey, Media Ownership Monitor*. Available at: https://www.mom-gmr.org/en/countries/turkey/ (Accessed: 11 December 2024).

Griffin, B. (2019) *Yellow journalism, sensationalism, and circulation wars*. First edition. New York: Cavendish Square (The Fourth Estate: Journalism in North America).

Harari, Y.N. (2024) *Nexus: A Brief History of Information Networks from the Stone Age to AI*. Great Britain: Fern Press.

Harraway, V. and Wong, J.S. (2024) 'Broad Strokes for "Foreign Folks": A Thematic Content Analysis of Migration within News Articles Containing Migrant Crime', *Journal of Immigrant & Refugee Studies*, 22(1), pp. 37–51. Available at: https://doi.org/10.1080/15562948.2021.1995925.

Hürriyet (2023) 'Zafer Partisi Seçim Sonuçları', 17 May. Available at: https://secim.hurriyet.com.tr/14-mayis-2023-secimleri/zafer-secim-sonuclari/ (Accessed: 31 August 2025).

Karsit, I. (2022) 'Turkey's Far Right Has Already Won', *Foreign Policy*, 12 July. Available at: https://foreignpolicy.com/2022/07/12/turkeys-far-right-has-already-won/ (Accessed: 14 January 2025).

Kayaoglu, A. (2022) 'Do refugees cause crime?', *World Development*, 154, p. 105858. Available at: https://doi.org/10.1016/j.worlddev.2022.105858.

McClelland, M. (2014) 'How to Build a Perfect Refugee Camp', *The New York Times*, 13 February. Available at: https://www.nytimes.com/2014/02/16/magazine/how-to-build-a-perfect-refugee-camp.html (Accessed: 1 December 2024).

McGregor, S.C. (2019) 'Social media as public opinion: How journalists use social media to represent public opinion', *Journalism*, 20(8), pp. 1070–1086. Available at: https://doi.org/10.1177/1464884919845458.

Ozduzen, O., Korkut, U. and Ozduzen, C. (2021) '"Refugees are not welcome": Digital racism, online place-making and the evolving categorization of Syrians in Turkey', *New Media & Society*, 23(11), pp. 3349–3369. Available at: https://doi.org/10.1177/1461444820956341.

Özerim, M.G. and Tolay, J. (2021) 'Discussing the Populist Features of Anti-refugee Discourses on Social Media: An Anti-Syrian Hashtag in Turkish Twitter', *Journal of Refugee Studies*, 34(1), pp. 204–218. Available at: https://doi.org/10.1093/jrs/feaa022.

Özoflu, M.A. *et al.* (2025) 'Populist securitization of migration: The anti-immigrant Zafer Party example in Türkiye', *Mediterranean Politics*, 0(0), pp. 1–28. Available at: https://doi.org/10.1080/13629395.2024.2444763.

Öztürk, N. and Ayvaz, S. (2018) 'Sentiment analysis on Twitter: A text mining approach to the Syrian refugee crisis', *Telematics and Informatics*, 35(1), pp. 136–147. Available at: https://doi.org/10.1016/j.tele.2017.10.006.

Rasinger, S.M. (2010) '"Lithuanian migrants send crime rocketing": representation of "new" migrants in regional print media', *Media, Culture & Society*, 32(6), pp. 1021–1030. Available at: https://doi.org/10.1177/0163443710380311.

Sabah, D. (2022) *Battle of words between Soylu, Özdağ turns into standoff, Daily Sabah*. Available at: https://www.dailysabah.com/politics/battle-of-words-between-soylu-ozdag-turns-into-standoff/news (Accessed: 31 October 2024).

Sabah, D. (2023) *Türkiye debunks disinformation on migrants, refugees, Daily Sabah*. Available at: https://www.dailysabah.com/politics/turkiye-debunks-disinformation-on-migrants-refugees/news (Accessed: 31 August 2025).

Silverman, R. (2024) 'Victory, Even in Defeat: Ümit Özdağ, Sinan Oğan, and The Enduring Influence of The Turkish Far-Right', in *Elections and Earthquakes: Quo Vadis Turkey*. Transnational Press London, pp. 105–116. Available at: https://www.ceeol.com/search/chapter-detail?id=1217537 (Accessed: 12 December 2024).

Sunata, U. and Yıldız, E. (2018) 'Representation of Syrian refugees in the Turkish media', *Journal of Applied Journalism & Media Studies*, 7(1), pp. 129–151. Available at: https://doi.org/10.1386/ajms.7.1.129_1.

Sykes, P. (2022) 'Turkey's Anti-Immigration Challenger Tops Erdogan on Twitter', *Bloomberg*, 20 May. Available at: https://www.bloomberg.com/news/articles/2022-05-20/turkey-s-anti-immigration-challenger-tops-erdogan-on-twitter (Accessed: 31 October 2024).

Taşdelen, B. (2020) 'Twitter'da Suriyeli Mültecilere Karşı Çevrimiçi Nefret Söylemi: #suriyelileriistemiyoruz', *Gümüşhane Üniversitesi Sosyal Bilimler Dergisi*, 11(2), pp. 562–575. Available at: https://doi.org/10.36362/gumus.706944.

Taşdemir, D. and İçten, D. (2023) *Media representation of refugees and migrants in Turkey*. Thessaloniki: Heinrich Böll Stiftung. Available at: https://gr.boell.org/en/2023/06/08/media-representation-refugees-and-migrants-turkey (Accessed: 3 January 2025).

T.C. İçişleri Bakanlığı Göç İdaresi Başkanlığı (2025) *Geçici Koruma*. Available at: https://www.goc.gov.tr/gecici-koruma5638 (Accessed: 1 September 2025).

TRT Haber (2021) 'Yunanistan'dan göçmenlere "insanlık dışı" uygulama', 21 November. Available at: https://www.trthaber.com/haber/gundem/yunanistandan-gocmenlere-insanlik-disi-uygulama-628246.html (Accessed: 8 December 2024).

Türk, H.B. (2024) 'Populist Nationalism and Anti-refugee Sentiment in Turkey: The Case of the Victory Party', *Nationalism and Ethnic Politics*, 30(2), pp. 271–295. Available at:

https://doi.org/10.1080/13537113.2023.2248792.

Uluğ, Ö.M. *et al.* (2023) 'Attitudes towards Afghan refugees and immigrants in Turkey: A Twitter analysis', *Current Research in Ecological and Social Psychology*, 5, p. 100145. Available at: https://doi.org/10.1016/j.cresp.2023.100145.

UNHCR (2024) *Global Focus: Türkiye*, *UNHCR*. Available at: https://reporting.unhcr.org/operational/operations/t%C3%BCrkiye (Accessed: 11 November 2024).

Wigger, I. (2019) 'Anti-Muslim racism and the racialisation of sexual violence: "intersectional stereotyping" in mass media representations of male Muslim migrants in Germany', *Culture and Religion*, 20(3), pp. 248–271. Available at: https://doi.org/10.1080/14755610.2019.1658609.

Yanasmayan, Z., Üstübici, A. and Kasli, Z. (2019) 'Under the shadow of civilizationist populist discourses', *New Diversities*, 21(2), pp. 37–51.

Yaylacı, F.G. and Karakuş, M. (2015) 'Perceptions and newspaper coverage of Syrian refugees in Turkey', *Migration Letters*, 12(3), pp. 238–250.

Yılmaz, F., Elmas, T. and Eröz, B. (2023) 'Twitter-based analysis of anti-refugee discourses in Türkiye', *Discourse & Communication*, 17(3), pp. 298–318. Available at: https://doi.org/10.1177/17504813231169135.

SEEKING TRUTH ACROSS THE MEDITERRANEAN WAVES: UPHOLDING THE RIGHTS OF FAMILIES OF DECEASED MIGRANTS

Charlotte Imhof and Jyothis Mary

Introduction

The 2015 European migrant crisis sparked considerable media attention on the reality of shipwrecks and the bodies they produce to a broad audience increasing awareness about this long-existing reality (Robins S., 2019: 14). 76,593 missing migrants have been reported between 2014 and August 2025, with almost half of the disappearances (32,489) in the sole Mediterranean Sea, which has become a site of escalating numbers of migrant fatalities (IOM, n.d.). More than two-thirds of migrants whose deaths were documented remain unidentified, leaving families and communities grappling with the ambiguous loss of their loved ones (IOM, 2024). People are missing because they are missed. This is the fundamental relational definition of what it means for a migrant to be "missing" and so demands an engagement with the families of the missing (Robins S., 2019: 15). But who can be considered a missing migrant? According to the International Organization for Migration (IOM)'s 'Missing Migrants Project', a missing person is a person who died or who went missing and is presumed to be dead in the process of migration towards an international destination, regardless of the person's legal status to aim the identification of the risks linked to irregular migration journeys (Garcia Borja A. and Black J., 2021). How many of the 32,489 missing migrants in the Mediterranean Sea will have their identity retried and communicated to their families? What are the duties of the European States? Conversely, what are the rights in Europe of loved ones in their quest for the truth?

States' duties as a mirror of the families' rights

The identification of the remains of the people perishing in the Mediterranean Sea represents the decisive starting point, creating both obligations for the State and rights for families.

On the one hand, the State's duties encompass mainly the obligation to take all appropriate measures to search for, locate, and release disappeared persons and, in the event of death, to locate, respect, and return their remains[1]. All the necessary measures to bring those responsible to justice shall be taken[2] and enforced disappearance should constitute an offence under criminal law[3]. Finally, States shall take the appropriate steps with regard to the legal situation of disappeared persons whose fate has not been clarified and that of their relatives in fields such as social welfare, financial matters, family law, and property rights[4].

On the other hand, the rights of families mirror the State obligation. They englobe the right to know the truth regarding the circumstances of the enforced disappearance, the progress and results of the investigation, and the fate of the disappeared person[5]. The right of families mentioned here consists of knowing "the fate of their relatives" by removing this uncertainty[6]. Each victim has the right to know the truth regarding the circumstances of the enforced disappearance, the progress of the investigation, and the fate of the disappeared person[7]. Practically, families have been recognized a 'legitimate expectation' that the dead would be identified by the Pisciatelli Commission's investigation into deaths in the October 2013 Lampedusa shipwrecks (Grant S., 2016: 13). The involvement of the families in the identification process since ante-mortem data from a relative of the dead is likely to be required (Robins S., 2019: 16). Moreover, the victims of enforced disappearance have the right to obtain reparation and prompt, fair, and adequate compensation covering both material and moral damage. Other forms could be envisaged like restitution, rehabilitation, and satisfaction[8]. The gravesites shall be respected, maintained, and marked[9]. Eventually, families should have the opportunity to remember their dead in the place where their remains lie and be given the right to access graves[10]. Where authorities have refused to give families information about the place of burial of a close relative, violations of the right to family life were found (European Court of Human Rights, 2019; Grant S., 2016: 14).

---

[1] Article 4 International Convention for the Protection of All Persons from Enforced Disappearance (ICPPED), 23 December 2010.
[2] Article 3 ICPPED.
[3] Article 4 ICPPED.
[4] Article 24 (6) ICPPED.
[5] Article 24 (3) ICPPED; Article 32 of Additional Protocol (AP) I to the Geneva Conventions from 1977.
[6] Article 32 AP I.
[7] Article 24 (2) ICPPED.
[8] Article 24 (4) and (5) ICPPED.
[9] Article 34 AP I.
[10] Article 32 AP I.

As a result, the rights and obligations exist on paper. However, the reality looks diametrically different: Out of the 16,500 requests recorded by the International Committee of the Red Cross (ICRC) since 2013 for relatives who went missing on their way to Europe, only 285 successful matches have been achieved until December 2023 in around 10 years (Lawrence, F. and al., 2023). How do we bridge this enormous gap between 32,489 missing migrants in the Mediterranean Sea and the 285 matches?

Good practices to uphold the rights of the families

As alluded to before, the identification of the missing bodies remains the central and initial step in the families' way to retrieve their rights. This identification requires accurate documentation in tracing the whereabouts of the missing individuals, timely investigations, codification of data, and a humanitarian approach involving often cooperation among governments. Once a body has been identified, the question arises as to how to enforce the rights of the family. Despite the mentioned challenges, there are some promising practices by European governments such as Italy or Spain, international and non-governmental organizations, and other initiatives that encompass the creation of databases on missing persons and DNA samplings to identify the bodies, as well as practical assistance to the families of the disappeared to identify the whereabouts and the fate of their loved ones.

An important step before the identification of the missing migrants is the recording of the disappearances. For this purpose, the International Commission on Missing Persons (ICPM) works along with the governments of Italy, Greece, Cyprus, and Malta launched the 'Joint Process' to enhance operational cooperation among the countries and a centralized data collection (ICPM, n.d.). Moreover, the 'Missing Migrant Project', by IOM, records the incidents, in alignment with the 'Global Compact on Migration's Objective 8', in which migrants have died in the Mediterranean Sea (IOM, 2024). Additionally, 'Trace the Face' is an online tool launched by the ICRC to help families locate missing relatives by using a virtual photo gallery (ICRC, n.d.). Finally, Boats 4 People, an international coalition made of 11 associations and activists, provides a guide on steps to be taken by the families and supporters to report the missing to the relevant authorities or organizations in the search for their missing ones who perished en route during Mediterranean Sea crossings to Italy (Boats 4 People, 2017).

Regarding the identification of the missing bodies remains, good practices can be outlined particularly in Italy and Spain. In Italy, in 2007, the 'Extraordinary

Commissioner for Missing Persons' was appointed for coordinating the identification of missing migrants and reaching out to the families. The 'National Register of Unidentified Bodies' was set up to record essential information such as physical characteristics as well as where and when the body is located (Italian Government, n.d.). Visual identification and DNA sampling are the two methods adopted by the Italian authorities to identify the deceased person (Robins S., 2019: 19). Therefore, a national DNA database was created under the Ministry of Interior to centralize genetic data information. In Spain, t[he] signed a Memorandum of Understanding with the Spanish Red Cross to address the management of unidentified dead migrants in 2017 (ICRC, 2022: 26). Additionally, the National Center of Missing Persons and the Ministry of Interior manage the 'National Combined DNA Index System', which includes a section for missing persons and unidentified bodies.

When it comes to the enforcement of the rights of the families, the 'Mytilini Declaration for the Dignified Treatment of all Missing and Deceased Persons and their Families as a Consequence of Migrant Journeys' was signed in 2018 for recognizing their rights and duties towards their sufferings due to death or disappearance of their dear ones (The Mytilini Declaration, 2018). Methoria and its Last Rights initiative spearhead its implementation offering continued advocacy, explanatory notes, toolkits, but still calls for broader adoption (United Nations Network on Migration, 2023).

Conclusion

These good practices serve as a beacon of hope for the bereaved families by prioritizing human rights and by treating the dead with dignity over political calculations or migrant control mechanisms, thereby setting examples for the rest of Europe. However, despite these promising initiatives, the questions remain: How can the sufferings of a bereaved be mitigated? Do States uphold the rights of families? Regrettably, in the European context, there is a lack of structured institutional initiatives to ensure justice for the families of the disappeared. The absence of standardized procedures and a single database system for storing data, as well as poor coordination among authorities, create a significant obstacle in effectively conducting searches and investigations for missing migrants. This subsequently denies de facto families the right to truth and justice, leaving them in complete uncertainty. The approach by countries involves prejudices towards families who are denied the right to identify, provide a dignified burial, and travel. Instead, families are revictimized and faced with administrative impediments. Rather than adopting a victim-centric and human rights-based approach, investigating agencies often focus on identifying if a crime has been committed. Moreover, most nations are unprepared and lack the financial resources to address the magnitude of this crisis. Also, while the arrival of living migrants receives attention, the dead or disappeared largely go uncounted. Due to the lack of enforcement of international instruments at the domestic level, often neither a sanction is enforced on the violating States, nor do the families of the deceased receive any compensation. Unfortunately, the journeys of hope turn into an ambiguous loss for their families, making them the indirect victims of this tragedy.

References

Boats 4 People (May 2017). *Dead and Missing at Sea Information Guide for Families and their Supporters, Italy and Central Mediterranean.* https://boats4people.org/wp-content/uploads/2017/05/B4P.Guide_.Families_EN-V2.pdf

European Court of Human Rights (March 14, 2019). Abdullayeva v. Azerbaijan App no 29674/07. https://hudoc.echr.coe.int/eng#{%22itemid%22:[%22001-191545%22

Garcia Borja A. and Black J. (2021). Measuring migrant deaths and disappearances, 66. *Forced Migration Report.* https://www.fmreview.org/issue66/garciaborja-black/

Grant S. (September 2016). Dead and Missing Migrants: The Obligations of European States under International Human Rights Law, IHRL Briefing. *Mediterranean Missing.* https://missingmigrants.iom.int/sites/g/files/tmzbdl601/files/publication/file/Mediterranean-Missing-Legal-Memo-290816.pdf

ICMP (n.d.). *Missing Migrants and Refugees.* Retrieved August 21, 2025, from https://icmp.int/what-we-do/missing-migrants-and-refugees/

ICRC (2022). *Counting the Dead How Registered Deaths of Migrants in the Southern European Sea Border Provide Only a Glimpse of the Issue.* https://missingpersons.icrc.org/library/counting-dead-how-registered-deaths-migrants-southern-european-sea-border-provide-only

ICRC (n.d.). *Trace the Face.* Retrieved August 24, 2025, from Home | Trace the Face

IOM (March 26, 2024). *One in Three Migrant Deaths Occurs En route While Fleeing Conflict.* https://www.iom.int/news/one-three-migrant-deaths-occurs-en-route-while-fleeing-conflict-iom-report

IOM (n.d.). *Missing Migrants Projects.* Retrieved August 21, 2025, from https://missingmigrants.iom.int/project#:~:text=The%20International%20Organization%20for%20 Migration,migrating%20to%20an%20international%20destination; https://missingmigrants.iom.int/

Italian Government (n.d.). *Extraordinary Government Commission for Missing Persons.* Retrieved August 21, 2025 from https://commissari.gov.it/persone-scomparse/https://commissari.gov.it/persone-scomparse/

Lawrence, F. and al. (December 8, 2023). More than 1,000 unmarked graves discovered along EU migration routes. *The Guardian.* https://www.theguardian.com/world/ng-interactive/2023/dec/08/revealed-more-than-1000-unmarked-graves-discovered-along-eu-migration-routes

Robins S. (2019). Analysis of Best Practices on the Identification of Missing Migrants: Implications for the Central Mediterranean (Report No. 2). *Central Mediterranean Route Thematic Report Series.*

The Mytilini Declaration for the Dignified Treatment of all Missing and Deceased Persons and their Families as a Consequence of Migrant Journeys (2018). https://missingpersons.icrc.org/library/mytilini-declaration-dignified-treatment-all-missing-and-deceased-persons-and-their

United Nations Network on Migration (August 15, 2023). *Repository of Practice.* https://migrationnetwork.un.org/practice/declaration-dignified-treatment-all-missing-and-deceased-persons-and-their-families

THE IMPACT OF THE BEST INTERESTS PRINCIPLE ON THE PROTECTION OF MIGRANT CHILDREN: THE VIEWS OF THE COMMITTEE ON THE RIGHTS OF THE CHILD

Jaroslav Větrovský

The Convention on the Rights of the Child is the key legal document governing the status of children in international law. Adopted in 1989 and entering into force in 1990, it now has 196 State parties, making it one of the most widely ratified treaties in the world.

To ensure the effectiveness of the enshrined rights, the Convention provides for the establishment of a supervisory organ, the Committee on the Rights of the Child, which is an independent body of experts overseeing the implementation of the Convention by the State parties. To this end, the Committee has two essential competencies. First, since its inception, the Committee has been empowered to examine periodic reports submitted by all State parties on their progress in children's rights protection.

Second, with the adoption of Optional Protocol No. 3 in 2014, the Committee was granted a new competency to examine individual communications submitted either by children themselves or on their behalf. This competency, however, applies only to those State parties that have also ratified the Optional Protocol. Currently, 53 States are parties to both the Convention and the Protocol.

Many of the rights enshrined in the Convention mirror traditional human rights that we know also from other international treaties. Where necessary, the rights are adapted to the specific circumstances of children. Yet the Convention also contains a small group of rights and obligations that are unique to it and apply exclusively to children. The most prominent of them – and also the most interesting one – is the so-called best interests principle articulated in Article 3(1) of the Convention. According to this provision, children's "best interests" shall be "a primary consideration" in "all actions" concerning them.

In its General Comment No. 14 (2013) the Committee expressed the view that the best interests principle constitutes a threefold concept: an interpretative legal principle, a rule of procedure, and a substantive right. As an interpretative principle, Article 3(1) is often applied as an umbrella provision that integrates all rights guaranteed to children under the Convention. According to the Committee, States are required to apply the provisions of the Convention holistically, given the "interdependence and equal importance" of all the rights set out in the Convention (CRC, *K.S. and M.S. v. Switzerland*, 10 February 2022, CRC/C/89/D/74/2019, § 6.3).

Another way in which the BIP operates as an interpretative tool is by enlarging the usual scope of application of other provisions of the Convention, thereby enhancing the protection normally afforded to children. For example, in a case concerning an arbitrary deportation of an unaccompanied minor to Morocco by Spain, undertaken without any formal procedure, the Committee held that the principle of non-refoulement, when read together with the best interests principle, requires that children must always be guaranteed "the right to access the territory, regardless of the documentation they have or lack, and be referred to the authorities in charge of evaluating their needs in terms of protection of their rights" (CRC, *D.D. v. Spain*, 1 February 2019, CRC/C/80/D/4/2016, § 14.4). The Committee reached this conclusion even though the Convention does not expressly guarantee any right of the child to enter the territory of a potential host State, nor does this right derive from the principle of non-refoulement alone.

The second general function attributed to the BIP by the Committee is that it serves as a foundation for various procedural rights of children and the corresponding obligations imposed on State parties. The first of these obligations is the "legal duty to assess the best interests" of children in all "decisions and actions" affecting them (CRC, *C.C.O.U. et al. v. Denmark*, 19 September 2023, CRC/C/94/D/145/2021, § 8.5). As the Committee has rightly pointed out, such decisions may affect children directly, as in the case of their expulsion, or indirectly, when the child is not the direct target of the measure. For instance, in the case from which the quotation is drawn, the Committee found a violation of the BIP by Danish authorities, although the target of the deportation order was not the child himself but his stepfather.

The second procedural obligation of States stemming from the best interests principle is to ensure that considerations about the child's best interests are included in the reasoning of any decision affecting them. The Committee requires that these considerations be explicitly articulated in the decision and encompass all elements relevant to the assessment. As the Committee pointed out in one of its cases, "[t]he formal and general reference to the best interests of the child by the Finnish Immigration Service, without having considered the author's views, reflects a failure to consider the specific circumstances surrounding the author's case" (CRC, *A.B. v. Finland*, 4 February 2021, CRC/C/86/D/51/2018, § 12.4).

The third procedural obligation of States under Article 3(1) of the Convention is the duty to render an individualized decision, i.e. a decision wherein the best interests are "adjusted and defined on an individual basis, according to the specific situation of the child [...], taking into consideration their personal context, situation and needs" (CRC, *C.E. v. Belgium*, 27 September 2018, CRC/C/79/D/12/2017, § 8.3). In this case, the Committee dismissed the argument of the Belgian government that national authorities were justified in refusing a visa to a Moroccan girl who wished to join her foster parents to Belgium, on the grounds that she could allegedly remain in Morocco with her biological parents. The Committee observed that the reasoning was too general and failed to consider the child's specific situation, in particular the fact that she was born to an unknown father and abandoned at birth by her biological mother (*Ibid.*, § 8.5).

Furthermore, taking the BIP as a procedural rule not only requires that whenever there is a procedure concerning children, their interests must be individually assessed and the decision duly motivated. It also implies the obligation of States to establish a formal process in which all guarantees stemming from the BIP are respected, provided that such a process is lacking.

For example, in several cases concerning the determination of the age of migrant children in Spain, the Committee highlighted the "fundamental importance" of such a determination for the enjoyment of all rights set out in the Convention. It then concluded that there must be a "due process to determine a person's age, as well as the opportunity to challenge the outcome through an appeals process" (CRC, *M.A.B. v. Spain*, 7 February 2020, CRC/C/83/D/24/2017, § 10.3). Of course, the best interests of the child should be a primary consideration in both stages of this process.

The third general function that the Committee ascribes to the BIP is to constitute a substantive right. But the Committee is not very clear in defining the content of this substantive right, nor does it explain how the substantive aspect of the principle is to be distinguished from the procedural one. According to the Committee's general statement, a "substantive right" in this context amounts to "the right of the child to have their best interests assessed and taken as a primary consideration when different interests are […] at stake" (CRC, *General Comment No. 14*, 2013, part I.A). However, the Committee has also made it clear that a State does not violate the Convention merely because its decision does not comply with the best interests of the child concerned.

For instance, in several deportation cases concerning children the Committee held that "a difference in health services" between the State of origin and the State of asylum does not preclude the latter from returning a child to the State of origin (CRC, *G.R. et al. v. Switzerland*, 31 May 2021, CRC/C/87/D/86/2019, § 11.6), even though – we can add – it would clearly be in the child's best interest to remain in a country where health care of a higher standard is available. With respect to the substantive aspect of the Article 3(1), the Committee thus takes the view that the principle does not impose on States an obligation to act in accordance with children's best interests. Rather, States must ensure that when competing interests are weighed in a given procedure, the child's best interests always remain a primary consideration. In all actions concerning children, it must be demonstrated that even when a child's best interests are outweighed, those interests have been assigned primary importance.

UNACCOMPANIED MINOR'S POLICIES. THE CHALLENGE OF THE U.S. AND THE EU SYSTEMS IN ILLIBERAL TIMES

Isabella Miano

Introduction

In the context of growing global instability—marked by inequality, conflict, climate crises, and pandemics—Western democracies have seen a rise in far-right populism and authoritarianism, particularly in the U.S. and EU. This shift has intensified hostility toward immigrants, especially Muslims, and has challenged liberal democratic values. Unaccompanied minors (UAMs), who migrate without guardians, are especially vulnerable due to limited legal migration pathways and their precarious legal status. They often face a paradoxical system where child protection and immigration laws intersect, offering both support and harm. The study explores how UAM policies in the U.S. and EU have evolved over the past decade, swinging like a pendulum between protection and restriction. It examines how recent illiberal trends have influenced these policies and compares the approaches of both regions. The research aims to inform more rights-based, protective policies for UAMs. This work contributes to filling research and policy gaps regarding UAMs in Western democracies.

Unaccompanied Minor's Phenomenon in the U.S. and the EU

In the 21st century, migration has become a central global issue, with unaccompanied minors being a particularly vulnerable group. Historically, children migrating alone were linked to specific crises (e.g., wars, disasters), but their presence in migration flows has grown, prompting international legal attention. While early frameworks like the 1951 Geneva Convention lacked specific provisions for minors, later instruments such as the Convention on the Rights of the Child (1989) and UNHCR Guidelines (1997) began to address their unique needs and rights.

Despite these advances, the phenomenon of UAMs has intensified in recent years due to complex global factors—economic instability, conflict, climate change, and social upheaval—leading to what experts call "mixed migration." In the U.S., since 2013–14, there has been a sharp rise in UAMs from Central America, with broader global origins appearing post-2021. In Fiscal Year (FY) 2022, 149,000 UAMs were encountered at the U.S.-Mexico border. The U.S. faces challenges in processing and protecting these minors, with much of the burden falling on civil society and courts. In the EU, UAMs became a significant concern post-2010, especially after the Arab uprisings and economic crises. The EU issued its first Action Plan for UAMs (2010–2014) and defined UAMs in Directive 2011/95/EU. Unlike the U.S., UAMs in the EU come from a broader range of countries (Africa, Middle East) and typically arrive by sea.

Both regions face ongoing challenges in balancing border control with humanitarian obligations, and the treatment of UAMs is still a critical issue in migration governance. Unaccompanied minors from Africa, the Middle East, and Central America face similar vulnerabilities—poverty, violence, political instability, climate disasters, and lack of opportunities drive their migration. These children often migrate in search of safety, education, or economic opportunity. However, the absence of legal migration pathways forces many into the hands of trafficking networks, leading to irregular and dangerous journeys.

Estimating the global scale of UAM migration is difficult due to inconsistent definitions, data collection methods, and age assessment procedures. Many minors go unrecorded, either because they avoid detection or perish during their journey. This makes UAM migration a pressing and underreported issue for both the U.S. and the EU, gaining political and media attention since 2014–2015.

Research on this group is limited due to their vulnerability and inaccessibility, with most studies focusing on integration rather than cross-national comparisons (e.g., Kulu-Glasgow et al., 2019; Mgebrishvili, 2020; Carvalho Paoletti, 2023; Mejivar & Perreira, 2019; Sanz Caballero, 2021). This study contributes to the underdeveloped field of comparative migration research on UAMs, aiming to bridge gaps in understanding and policy development.

Research Fields and Method

The research is situated within the fields of international relations and humanitarian migration, focusing on unaccompanied minors (UAMs) who may be asylum seekers, refugees, internally displaced persons (IDPs), or victims of trafficking. International humanitarian law and national child protection frameworks govern their status.

The analysis adopts a human security approach (Paris, 2001; Barnett, 2018; Moreno-Lax, 2018; Longo et al., 2023), emphasizing the protection of minors in line with the Best Interests of the Child (BIC) principle from the Convention on the Rights of the Child (CRC, 1989). While humanitarian discourse aims to protect vulnerable migrants, scholars caution that it can also serve as a tool for border control and deterrence (Moreno-Lax, 2018; Panebianco, 2022).

A comparative political science approach is used to examine policy changes in the U.S. and EU over the past decade. The metaphor of a policy pendulum helps illustrate shifts between protective and restrictive stances. The study hypotheses that in recent year there has been a general shift toward more restrictive policies; that illiberal trends have influenced UAM policies due to their dual legal framing, and that The U.S. and EU have adopted a similar approach with regional nuances.

Data are gathered through a Longitudinal desk analysis of legislation, policy papers, academic literature, and media reports. U.S. sources include federal laws, executive orders, and bilateral agreements. EU sources include directives, regulations, and soft law instruments, which require national transposition.

Selected Cases

This study compares the U.S. and the EU as two distinct but influential political systems in managing unaccompanied minors (UAMs) within the broader context of migration governance. The comparison is justified by both humanitarian and political reasons. The U.S. and EU are key destinations along major global migration routes (e.g., Central America, Mediterranean), and both have experienced a surge in UAM arrivals since 2014–2015. These minors face high risks during their journeys and require protection under international and domestic laws.

However, both systems have adopted increasingly securitized approaches to migration since the 1990s, intensified by economic crises, terrorism, and rising xenophobia. Emergency measures have been used to justify exceptional treatment of UAMs. Both regions have experienced an illiberal turn over the past two decades, politicizing immigration and influencing electoral outcomes. While early 21st-century concerns were mostly economic (Akkerman, 2012), recent scholars highlight how cultural threats—not economic ones—drive authoritarian and populist responses to immigration (Norris & Inglehart, 2019).

Policy Evolution for UAM in the U.S. and the EU: A Pendulum Between Protection and Restriction

Both the U.S. and the EU are bound by international conventions such as: Geneva Convention (1951) and its 1967 Protocol; the Convention Against Torture (1984), and the Convention on the Rights of the Child (1989) (ratified by the EU, but not by the U.S.). These frameworks establish the principles like non-refoulement and protection from persecution and torture, the basis for UAM rights. Both systems have their legal building blocks for protecting UAM.

U.S. protective laws for UAM include: the Refugee Act (1980) – formal admission process for unaccompanied refugee minors; the Flores Agreement (1997) – sets standards for detention and care, and the TVPRA (2008) – screens UAMs for trafficking risks but distinguishes between minors from contiguous vs. non-contiguous countries. However, Trump administrations (2017–2020, 2025–) leaned heavily toward restrictive policies, dismantling liberal programs, reinstating Title 42, and limiting legal aid (Gerken, 2024). His rhetoric emphasized fear and exclusion. Biden administration (2021–2024) tried to restore protections (e.g., reopening CAM, ending Title 42), but faced structural and bureaucratic challenges (KIND, 2024). Despite some improvements, UAMs remained in legal limbo.

The EU developed a robust legal framework during the 2010s with the Directive 2013/33/EU, and Regulation 604/2013 which prioritize the best interests of the child. The Action Plan for UAMs (2010–2014) was the only first comprehensive documents. While the Commission promotes a humane approach (e.g., 2021 Strategy on the Rights of the Child), member states have increasingly securitized migration. Recent asylum legislation (New Pact on Migration and Asylum) includes both protective and restrictive provisions (Peers, 2024).

Both regions have seen a rise in authoritarian populism, politicizing migration. Indeed, in the U.S., Trump's policies reflected a cultural backlash (Norris & Inglehart, 2019). In the EU, far-right parties gained more seats in the European Parliament. Despite federal-EU-level restrictions, local actors have implemented protective practices. In Italy, Siracusa's "community of practices" filled policy gaps (Panebianco, 2022) while in the U.S., Operation Apollo under Biden improved UAM processing and reunification (Amuedo-Dorantes et al., 2023). CSOs have used transnational networks to resist far-right narratives (Mat, Chiodi, Schmidtke, 2024). The pendulum metaphor illustrates the tension between humanitarian obligations and securitized migration governance, with both systems oscillating between protection and restriction.

Conclusions

Over the past two decades, global instability—driven by conflict, economic crises, and climate disasters—has led to a significant rise in migration to Western democracies. The arrival of unaccompanied minors (UAMs) in the U.S. (2014) and the EU (2015) was framed as a migration crisis, prompting temporary and securitized policy responses (Menjívar & Perreira, 2019).

The main fundings of this study highlights how both the U.S. and EU prioritized state security over human rights, leading to restrictive policies that often overlooked the specific vulnerabilities of UAMs. However, the U.S. policy pendulum has swung sharply between protection and restriction, heavily influenced by political leadership. Trump's administrations implemented many deterrence-focused policies, while Obama and Biden administrations showed more protective intent, though with limited practical impact. On the contrary, the EU adopted a more structured and protective legal approach but lacks a comprehensive UAM-specific policy. Some restrictive outcomes stem from external agreements with third countries that may not uphold human rights standards.

The main implication for UAMs is that they risk falling into legal limbo, increasing their exposure to exploitation and trafficking. However, the governance complexity of both the U.S. and EU, gives space to local and regional actors who can counterbalance federal-EU-level securitization. For instance: in the U.S., some federal states resist federal enforcement while in the EU, member states vary in implementation based on resources and political will.

References

Menjívar, C. & Perreira, K.M. (2019). Undocumented and unaccompanied: children of migration in the European Union and the United States. Journal of Ethnic and Migration Studies, 45(2), 197–217. https://doi.org/10.1080/1369183X.2017.1404255

Moreno-Lax, V. (2018). The EU Humanitarian Border and the Securitization of Human Rights. Journal of Common Market Studies, 56(1), 119–140.

Panebianco, S. (2022). Migration Governance in the Mediterranean: The Siracusa Experience. Geopolitics, 27(3), 752–772. https://doi.org/10.1080/14650045.2020.1823837

Mat, F., Chiodi, L., Schmidtke, O. (2024). Europeanization as Pragmatic Politics: Italy's Civil Society Actors Operating in the Face of Right-Wing Populism. Social Sciences, 13(205). https://doi.org/10.3390/socsci13040205

Amuedo-Dorantes, C., Bucheli, J., Lopez, M. (2023). Managing Migration Crisis: Evidence from surge facilities and unaccompanied minor children flows. Economic Inquiry, 1–21.

Selected Papers

Gerken, C. (2024). The Power to Exclude: The (Mis)Treatment of Unaccompanied Minors under the Trump and Biden Administration. Human Rights Review, 25(2), 155–177.

KIND (2024). Statement on Office of Refugee Resettlement's Final Unaccompanied Children Program Foundational Rule to Codify Flores Settlement Agreement. Kids in Need of Defense, April 25, 2024.

Peers, S. (2024). The new EU asylum laws: taking rights half-seriously. Yearbook of European Law. https://doi.org/10.1093/yel/yeae003

Norris, P. & Inglehart, R. (2019). Cultural Backlash: Trump, Brexit, and Authoritarian Populism. Cambridge University Press.

EXPLOITATION OF MIGRANT WORKERS IN A PERIPHERAL AREA OF ITALY - METHODOLOGICAL PROPOSALS TO DE-CONSTRUCT ITALIAN MIGRATION POLICIES AND THE ITALIAN CITIZENSHIP REGIME FOR MIGRANTS

Norma Baldino and Margherita Sabrina Perra[1]

Introduction

The exploitation of migrant workers is a persistent structural issue in Italian labour market. Despite extensive academic debate (Ambrosini 2020; Reyneri & Fullin 2011), the phenomenon persists as a structurally embedded dynamics, particularly in contexts marked by employment precariousness and territorial and institutional marginality, informal economy. Migrant workers are disproportionately exposed to irregular, underpaid, and unprotected forms of employment, with heightened effects in peripheral areas, where public policies are fragile and migration is addressed primarily through securitarian rather than inclusive logics.

This paper presents the findings of the CASLIS research project (Countering Labour Exploitation in Sardinia), funded by the Italian Ministry of Labour and coordinated by the Autonomous Region of Sardinia within the framework of the National Programme for Inclusion and the Fight against Poverty 2021–2027, in partnership with the Department of Political and Social Sciences at the University of Cagliari. The project aimed to strengthen institutional capacity to counter migrant labour exploitation through a multilevel and place-based approach, focusing on: (1) analysing the specific features of the Sardinian context; (2) experimenting with participatory methodologies to engage local actors; and (3) proposing shared policy tools, including the establishment of a Regional Observatory on Labour Exploitation.

Sardinia, a large Mediterranean island and an autonomous region of Italy, has a foreign resident population of just 2% (IDOS, 2024), and 97% of its territory is officially classified as inner areas, almost rural (*National Strategic Plan for Internal Areas 2021-2027 (PSNAI)*. It represents a paradigmatic case of intersecting

[1] Norma Baldino and Margherita Sabrina Perra, University of Cagliari, Italy.

marginalities, where labour exploitation is compounded by demographic decline, labour market segmentation, and territorial isolation. Within this framework, the CASLIS project offers a concrete example of institutional innovation, promoting participatory governance models that frame migrant labour not as a threat, but as a strategic lever for social justice and regional development.

Theoretical Framework

This contribution is included in a theoretical framework that connects the analysis of the social construction of otherness with the dynamics of the labour market and forms of territorial marginality. In the Italian regime of migration, policies are often shaped by securitarian logics that construct the migrant as the "Other" — a subject perceived as inherently different and potentially threatening. As widely discussed in Italian sociological literature (Dal Lago 1999; Maneri 2012, 2020; Palidda 2009), this construction translates into institutional practices that associate migrant presence with insecurity and deviance, thereby reinforcing mechanisms of control and marginalisation. Such representations influence how migrants are received or stigmatised, structuring their everyday experience and social positioning.

The figure of the "stranger", as conceptualised in Simmel's classic formulation (1989), remains a critical conceptual tool for analysing mechanisms of exclusion and the construction of belonging. In this perspective, social recognition — as theorised by Honneth (1996) and further elaborated by Sciolla (2002) — is shaped by both cultural and material hierarchies that constrain access to rights and full citizenship.

The construction of otherness must therefore be read alongside the social definition of the migrant as a worker. Migrant identity takes form through social relations that unfold within the labour market, that represents a social space where mechanisms of recognition and exclusion intersect. According to Ambrosini (2020; 2024), migrant workers often develop strategic responses to dominant narratives by constructing alternative forms of belonging and visibility **based on their work experience**.

This perspective is further enriched by a territorial reading of inequality, which shows how marginalisation is spatially embedded yet can also generate place-based practices of resistance, agency, and solidarity (Avola, Cortese & Palidda 2018).

This theoretical lens informed the methodological design of the CASLIS

70

project, guiding its focus on the intersection of migration, labour, and local governance in Sardinia — a context in which labour exploitation is closely intertwined with territorial fragmentation, weak institutional capacity, and the lack of structured public interventions.

Methodology

The research adopted a qualitative approach articulated in three main phases, with the aim of reconstructing the territorial framework of labour exploitation and identifying operational tools to counter it.

The first phase involved a documentary analysis of the regional regulatory and institutional framework, complemented by the examination of project materials, reports, and official documents, in order to identify gaps, discontinuities, and weaknesses in existing governance mechanism.

The second phase consisted in the organisation of four territorial roundtables in areas with a higher incidence of the phenomenon, selected on the basis of socio-occupational indicators and documented cases of labour exploitation. These roundtables served as moments of interinstitutional and cross-sectoral dialogue, involving municipal officials, trade union representatives, social and health service providers, INPS (National Institute of Social Security), INAIL (National Institute for Insurance against Accidents at Work), and non-profit-organisations. They made it possible to gather in-depth knowledge of local specificities, while also highlighting a structural lack of systematic data collection and limited capacity among local authorities to read and interpret the phenomenon of labour exploitation.

The third phase involved semi-structured interviews with key stakeholders, primarily addressed to trade union representatives, from both confederal and grassroots unions, to explore their perspectives, strategies, and the challenges they face in identifying and combating exploitation. Interviews also included public officials, labour inspectors, and civil society actors.

The ultimate objective of the research process was to contribute to the establishment of a Regional Observatory on Labour Exploitation, conceived as a permanent mechanism for monitoring, analysis, and coordination between institutions, local territories, and social actors. The Observatory is intended as a space for participatory observation, aimed at generating applied knowledge and co-producing public policies.

Key Findings: Labour Exploitation and Migrant Conditions in Sardinia

The qualitative fieldwork conducted during the CASLIS project revealed the persistence of structural forms of labour exploitation affecting migrants in Sardinia, particularly in agriculture, hospitality, tourism, and personal services. Migrants are predominantly absorbed into the informal or "grey" economy, which is characterised by high flexibility and seasonality. This configuration disproportionately affects non-EU citizens and asylum seekers, whose labour conditions are shaped by multiple layers of vulnerability.

Among the most critical factors is legal precarity, exacerbated by long delays in residence permits and frequent bureaucratic obstacles, which increase exposure to irregular employment and dependence on employers. Migrants' qualifications and skills are not recognised, leading to widespread deskilling and underemployment. The low quality of available work also leads to frequent cases of overeducation and the dispersion of skills among migrant and native workers.

Added to this is the high adaptability expected of migrant workers, often interpreted as unconditional availability, which results in the acceptance of informal and exploitative working conditions, perceived as inevitable or "normal" in the absence of alternatives.

These dynamics are not isolated incidents but are embedded in the broader socio-economic organisation of the Sardinian territory. The historical figure of the *servo pastore* (servant-shepherd), still visible in small-scale farming, continues to legitimise unpaid or underpaid forms of labour. Gangmastering (*caporalato*) likewise remains a critical structural issue, particularly in the agricultural sector.

Labour exploitation stems not only from economic mechanisms, but also from institutional and structural weaknesses. The reception system (CAS and SPRAR) rarely integrates labour protection into social inclusion pathways, while local institutions suffer from chronic staff shortages, weak coordination, and limited analytical capacity. The lack of disaggregated data and of structured interventions hinders the monitoring and detection of exploitation, especially in sectors like tourism and construction. The isolation of migrant communities, the lack of adequate housing, and the absence of collective mobilisation spaces further exacerbate marginalisation.

In this context, the project underscored the importance of capacity building and awareness-raising actions. It is essential to provide targeted training on labour exploitation mechanisms to local administrations, cultural mediators, and non-profit organisations and NGOs. The involvement of native-speaking mediators can facilitate migrant access to labour rights, inspections, and trade unions. At the same time, institutional roles in labour inclusion and rights protection must be clarified and strengthened.

Conclusions: CASLIS as a Policy Innovation

CASLIS represents a replicable model of intervention that combines academic research, institutional cooperation, and the voice of migrants, within a context marked by demographic decline, labour shortages in rural areas, and growing social fragmentation. Rather than relying on vertical or securitarian approaches, the project developed a methodology rooted in territorial specificities and the active engagement of local stakeholders.

A central innovation lies in the co-design of policies aimed at monitoring and preventing labour exploitation at the local level. This means promoting new principles of multi-level governance and strengthening the role of local administrations—actors that are often under-resourced yet strategically positioned to interpret and respond to complex territorial dynamics.

The project also highlighted the need to include actors traditionally excluded from programming processes, such as Employment Centres, whose involvement is essential to activate meaningful pathways for labour inclusion and social integration.

The most tangible institutional outcome of the CASLIS project is the proposal to establish a Regional Observatory on Labour Exploitation, supported by the University of Cagliari. This Observatory would function as both a space for data collection and knowledge production, and as a strategic platform for participatory policy-making—enhancing the responsiveness of public institutions and fostering shared accountability among governmental bodies, trade unions, and civil society organisations.

By making room for situated knowledge and collective agency, CASLIS shows how academic research can help rethink migration policy from below, producing inclusive, context-sensitive responses to some of the most urgent challenges in contemporary migration governance.

References

Ambrosini, M. (2020). *Sociologia delle migrazioni*. Bologna: Il Mulino.

Ambrosini, M. (2024). *Mobilità umana e costruzione sociale delle frontiere*. Bologna: Il Mulino.

Ambrosetti, E., Paparusso, A., & Strangio, D. (2016). Labour exploitation of migrants in agriculture: Evidence from Southern Italy. *Population and Policy Compact*, 9, 1–8.

Avola, M., Cortese, A., & Palidda, S. (2018). Le forme della marginalità e le resistenze nei territori. In *Processi migratori e nuove disuguaglianze* (pp. 125–147). Milano: FrancoAngeli.

Dal Lago, A. (1999). *Non-persone. L'esclusione dei migranti in una società globale.* Milano: Feltrinelli.

Department for Cohesion Policy and for the South - Presidency of the Council of Ministers, *National Strategic Plan for Internal Areas 2021-2027 (PSNAI) and Annexes, March 2025,* https://politichecoesione.governo.it/it/documenti-ed-esiti-istituzionali/documenti-strategici-di-inquadramento/programmazione-2021-2027/piano-strategico-nazionale-delle-aree-interne-2021-2027-psnai-e-allegati/

Honneth, A. (1996). *The struggle for recognition: The moral grammar of social conflicts.* Cambridge: Polity Press.

International Labour Organization (ILO). (2013). *Italy: Tackling undeclared work – Learning from others.* Geneva: ILO.

Maneri, M. (2012). *Il discorso pubblico sulla sicurezza.* Milano: FrancoAngeli.

Maneri, M. (2020). La costruzione dell'insicurezza e le politiche della paura. In P. Basso (Ed.), *Razza e cittadinanza* (pp. 85–106). Roma: Manifestolibri.

Palidda, S. (2009). *Razzismo democratico. La persecuzione degli stranieri in Europa.* Milano: Agenzia X.

Sciolla, L. (2002). *Processi di riconoscimento e disuguaglianze.* Torino: Utet.

Simmel, G. (1989). *Lo straniero.* In L. Gallino (a cura di), Sociologia. Saggi (pp. 195–202). Torino: Einaudi.

REFUGEE STATUS DETERMINATION: WHY THE 'ZERO-BOATS' AUSTRALIAN MIGRATION POLICY RESULTED IN INCREASED ASYLUM SEEKERS?

Petra Playfair[1] and Amir El-Roubaei[2]

A Fifty-Year History of Australia's Refugee Policy

1975–1983 (Fraser): The Vietnam War created Australia's largest refugee intake: more than 150,000 Indochinese people resettled (Refugee Council of Australia, 2025a). Bipartisanship held, with both major parties endorsing the program. The UN Compact ensured regional cooperation: camps across Southeast Asia were closed, millions resettled or safely repatriated.

It was the foundation moment. Multiculturalism was enshrined as national policy and, for a time, admired abroad (Department of Home Affairs, 2025). Refugee resettlement was not yet a political weapon.

1983–1996 (Prime Ministers Hawke / Keating): Bipartisanship endured, and multiculturalism matured. The Comprehensive Plan of Action managed Southeast Asian flows with UN backing. Refugee resettlement continued successfully, and by the early 1990s the children of that intake were part of Australia's professional and political class. But cracks appeared. Early deterrence policies surfaced (Figure 1): excision of territories from the migration zone, the first use of Temporary Protection Visas (TPVs). The tension between individual rights and social cohesion was named and politicised, foreshadowing the next break (Hafeez-Baig, 2016).

1996–2007 (Prime Minister Howard): Howard transformed asylum into an election weapon. Anti-Asian rhetoric, talk of nationalism and sovereignty, and a deliberate rupture with bipartisanship set the tone. Refugee resettlement continued, but irregular maritime arrivals increased, driven by wars in Afghanistan and Iraq.

---

[1] CEO @ PLAYFAIR® Visa and Migration Services, https://playfair.com.au/team/petra-playfair/
[2] Lawyer @ PLAYFAIR® Visa and Migration Services, https://playfair.com.au/team/amir-el-roubaei/

Policy followed politics: TPVs were introduced, parts of the migration zone were excised, and the legislative foundation for deterrence was laid (McAdam & Purcell, 2008; Knight, 2021).

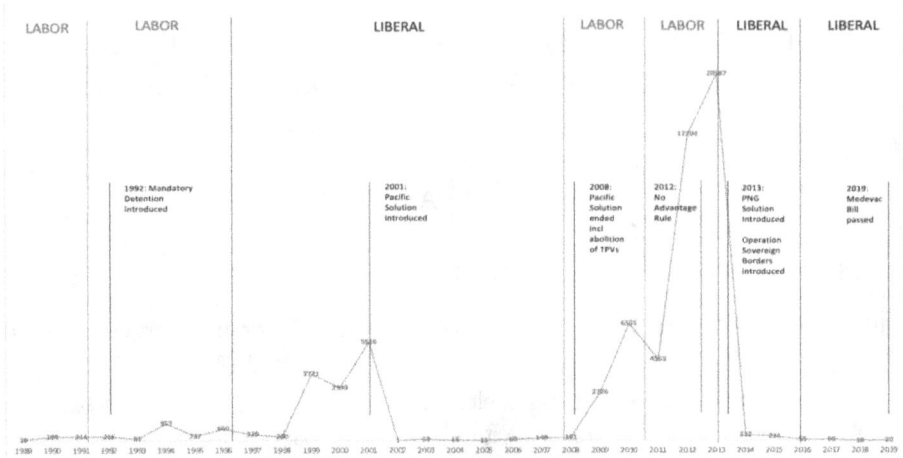

Figure 1. Boat asylum seekers (Playfair et al., 2019).

Data Source: Includes 'assisted takeback' & 'turnback'. Parliamentary Library (Spinks, 2018)

2001–2007

The turning point. Three events anchored asylum in security politics:

The Tampa Affair (Aug 2001): 433 Hazara asylum seekers were rescued at sea; Howard refused the Norwegian cargo ship permission to dock. Within eight days, the "Pacific Solution" was born, resulting in offshore detention on Naùru and Manus (Amnesty International Australia, 2021).

9/11 (Sept 2001): Howard, in Washington on the day of the attacks, aligned Australia with the US "war on terror." Asylum was conflated with terrorism; protecting borders became protecting the nation (McAdam & Purcell, 2008).

Children Overboard (Oct 2001): False claims about the SIEV sinking incident of parents throwing children into the sea dominated headlines. Howard's "We will decide who comes to this country and the circumstances in which they come." speech fused border security with national sovereignty. This rhetoric trumped the voter dissatisfaction with his economic and social policies. His approval surged, delivering an unexpected election victory (Doherty, 2021).

The Pacific Solution introduced in 2001 (Figure 1) reduced maritime arrivals but at a moral cost: indefinite detention, condemned by UNHCR as inhumane. Asylum was no longer an issue of resettlement. It was securitised and electorally profitable.

2007-2013 (Prime Ministers Rudd / Gillard): Rudd sought to dismantle the Pacific Solution. Offshore centres were closed. TPVs were abolished in favour of permanent visas. Policy was aligned with UN obligations. But, as shown in Figure 2, boats returned. Detention centres filled. Riots broke out. Smuggling networks grew more sophisticated, and arrivals surged.

Gillard reintroduced offshore processing. The "no-advantage" rule meant anyone arriving by boat after 13 August 2012 would be detained offshore for Refugee Status Determination (RSD) processing and removing the link for refugee status to a durable solution for resettlement (Playfair et al., 2017). The mainland was excised from processing (Refugee Council of Australia, 2020).

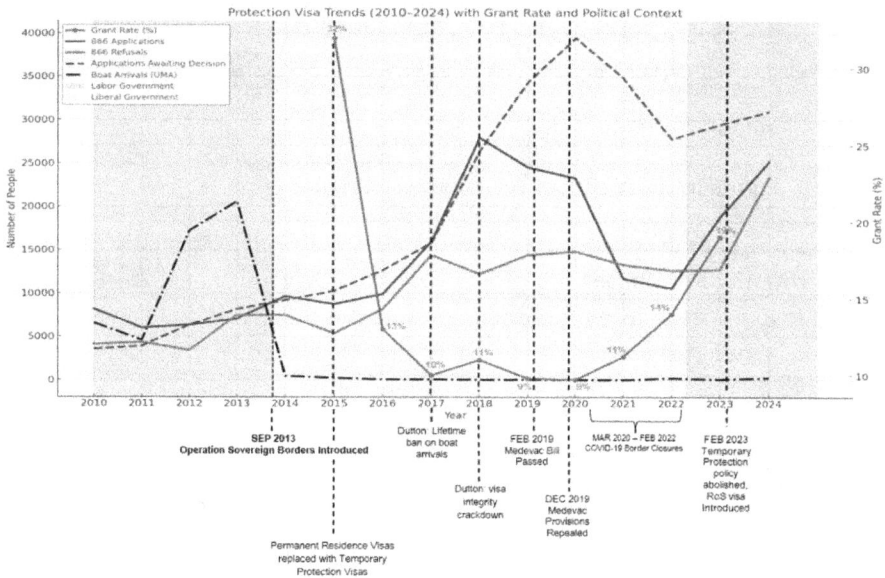

Legend: 866 visa applications (blue), refusals (red), unresolved applications (purple), unauthorised maritime arrivals (navy), primary applications granted annually % (green), political leadership shaded bands (red for Labor, blue for Liberal), policy shifts marked by vertical doted lines for 'Operation Sovereign Borders' (Sep 2013), the Medevac Bill (Feb 2019), COVID-19 onset (Mar 2020), and the abolition of TPVs with the introduction of the RoS visa (Feb 2023).

Figure 2. Australia's Onshore Protection Visa Trends (2010 - 2024). (© 2025 Playfair & El-Roubaei)

2013-2017

By July 2013, Rudd — returned to leadership by his own party — hardened the line further: no one arriving by boat would ever be resettled in Australia. Boat arrivals surged, drownings increased, and "Stop the Boats" became the Coalition's dominant campaign slogan (Refugee Council of Australia, 2020) and leading to a change of government.

On 18 September 2013, under the new Coalition government, 'Operation Sovereign Borders' ('OSB') began. Led by the military, OSB relied on three operational groups: disruption (AFP), detection and interception (Border Force and Maritime Command), and detention and removal (Border Force). Boats were intercepted and returned. The "cone of silence" ensured journalists could not observe turn-backs or offshore centres (Chia et al., 2014). Legislation followed:

- PR visas replaced with TPVs, prohibiting family reunion.

- References to the Refugee Convention were stripped from the Migration Act.

- Rights to independent review were curtailed.

Maritime arrivals dropped to near zero. Offshore deals were struck with the US, and a community sponsorship program was trialled (Chia et al., 2014). But the pressure did not dissipate. It shifted. Despite the collapse in boat arrivals post-2013, demand for protection persisted via other channels, while grant rates remained low and backlogs surged, highlighting institutional strain rather than resolution (Refugee Council of Australia, 2025b; Refugee Council of Australia, 2025c).

From 2014 onward, onshore claims rose. By 2024, more than 25,000 were lodged annually. Refusal rates skyrocketed; grant rates fell below 10%. By 2025, more than 98,000 people were living without resolution, caught in prolonged backlog (Chia et al., 2014).

Discussion

The sharp increase in asylum seekers after the introduction of Operation Sovereign Borders cannot be explained by a single factor. It is the product of intersecting pressures — political, legal, economic, and cultural — that reshaped how protection is sought and how it is denied.

The Politics of Collapse

The decisive break was the end of bipartisanship. For nearly two decades, bipartisan support had underwritten both multiculturalism and refugee resettlement. Once the Political leadership shattered that consensus, asylum became a standing election issue. Each subsequent government doubled down on deterrence not because the numbers demanded it, but because the politics rewarded it. Stopping boats became an electoral currency — a way to demonstrate strength, competence, and control, even as the broader system fell into dysfunction (McAllister, 2003; Knight, 2021).

Media and the Manufacture of Fear

The Tampa crisis, 9/11, and the "children overboard" affair were not just policy events; they were television. Each one staged asylum as danger and borders as the line between order and collapse. By the time Operation Sovereign Borders was introduced, the narrative was set: stopping boats meant safety. What never made the same headlines was the quiet surge in onshore claims by flight arrivals on visitor and student visas and the slow swell of unresolved cases. Fear shaped public perception more effectively than facts ever could.

The Law as Delay

Refugee Status Determination became structurally incapable of resolving claims in a timely manner. Applications took three to five years; tribunal appeals added several more; judicial review added 3-5 years more again. Each layer stretched time. Instead of producing resolution, the legal system produced stasis — a suspended existence that kept people in the community without durable status. In practice, deterrence through delay became an unspoken arm of policy (Ghezelbash et al., 2025; Ghezelbash & Hruschka, 2024).

Bridging Visas and Precarious Inclusion

The Bridging Visa regime allowed refused applicants to live and work while they waited (Department of Home Affairs, 2024). It was pragmatic: large numbers could not be detained, so they were left to sustain themselves (Andrew & Renata Kaldor Centre for International Refugee Law, 2020). But this arrangement created a paradox: people were economically integrated but legally excluded, contributing labour and remittances while denied any pathway to permanence. Precarity was not an accident; it was engineered into the visa system.

Smuggling Networks and Market Adaptation

Deterrence at sea did not kill smuggling; it changed its form. Networks shifted from maritime to aviation, targeting migrants with sufficient resources to obtain student or visitor visas (Australian Federal Police, 2025). These groups were not traditional refugee cohorts but rather educated, urban, and better funded. Smuggling adapted to policy gaps, exploiting the disjuncture between Australia's visa system — designed to encourage tourism and education — and its refugee system, designed to deter (Coyne, 2019).

The Hidden Costs

The cost of offshore detention was heavily scrutinised, but the cost of unresolved onshore claims was not. Years of delay meant people lived in communities with access to Medicare, schools, and limited welfare support. The financial burden was obscured, but the social cost — of leaving tens of thousands in uncertainty, of creating a population neither integrated nor removed — was immense. The system created insecurity on both sides: the public perceived loss of control, and applicants living with perpetual precarity.

The Multicultural Challenge

Australia is already one of the most multicultural nations in the world: half the population are children of migrants; more than a quarter being migrants themselves (Australian Bureau of Statistics, 2022). The issue is not whether diversity can be absorbed. It has been, for decades. The issue is whether the politics of fear will corrode the social contract. Asylum has been cast as the exception to the multicultural story — a category of migration uniquely politicised, uniquely feared. That exception corrodes trust in the system.

Conclusion

Australia's claim to have "stopped the boats" masks a deeper truth: the demand for asylum never ceased, it was merely displaced. What disappeared from the seas re-emerged in airports, in bridging visa applications, in tribunal backlogs. By 2025, nearly one hundred thousand people remain in a protracted state of refusal, technically leading many to deportation but practically unremovable. The policy promise of control has delivered only paralysis.

This is the paradox at the heart of deterrence. Each escalation produces the very conditions it claims to prevent. The Pacific Solution reduced arrivals but manufactured indefinite detention. Operation Sovereign Borders cut off boats but created a vast onshore backlog. Delay, insecurity, and suspicion have become structural features of the system. In effect, deterrence has replaced determination.

The consequences are not only humanitarian but institutional. A refugee system designed to decide claims has become one that suspends them. Law has been stretched into a tool of delay. Politics has converted asylum into a permanent campaign issue. Media has cast irregular migration as existential threat. And in the middle are tens of thousands of people whose lives are held in stasis — permitted to work, denied settlement, tolerated but never accepted.

If the objective is resolution rather than rhetoric, the cycle must be broken. That means restoring bipartisanship so that refugee policy cannot be weaponised in every election cycle. It means building regional cooperation so that responsibility is shared rather than outsourced. Above all, it means re-focusing the Refugee Status Determination process to its original purpose: fast, fair, humane decision-making.

Deterrence can stop boats. It cannot stop asylum. What it creates instead is a politics addicted to its own cruelty, a system that confuses delay for strength, and a society that lives with the corrosive costs of permanent precarity. A different course is possible — but only if political will is rebuilt.

References

Amnesty International Australia. (2021, August 26). *What was the "Tampa affair" and why does it matter?* https://www.amnesty.org.au/what-was-the-tampa-affair-and-why-does-it-matter/

Andrew & Renata Kaldor Centre for International Refugee Law. (2020, November). *Bridging visas* [Fact sheet]. University of New South Wales. https://www.unsw.edu.au/content/dam/pdfs/unsw-adobe-websites/kaldor-centre/2023-09-factsheet/2023-09-Factsheet_Bridging_Visas.pdf

Australian Bureau of Statistics. (2022, June 28). *2021 Census: Nearly half of Australians have a parent born overseas* [Media release]. https://www.abs.gov.au/media-centre/media-releases/2021-census-nearly-half-australians-have-parent-born-overseas

Australian Federal Police. (2025). *People smuggling.* https://www.afp.gov.au/crimes/human-trafficking-and-people-smuggling/people-smuggling

Chia, J., McAdam, J., & Purcell, K. (2014). *Asylum in Australia: 'Operation Sovereign Borders' and international law.* Australian Yearbook of international Law Online, 32(1), 33-64. DOI:10.22145/aybil.32.3

Coyne, J. (2019, February 18). *Air arrivals are Australia's most pressing border security challenge.* The Strategist. https://www.aspistrategist.org.au/air-arrivals-are-australias-most-pressing-border-security-challenge/

Department of Home Affairs. (2024, September 23). *Bridging visa E (BVE).* https://immi.homeaffairs.gov.au/visas/getting-a-visa/visa-listing/bridging-visa-e-050-051

Department of Home Affairs. (2025, March 25). *Our history – Multicultural affairs.* https://www.homeaffairs.gov.au/about-us/our-portfolios/multicultural-affairs/about-multicultural-affairs/our-policy-history

Doherty, B. (2021, August 22). *The Tampa affair, 20 years on: the ship that capsized Australia's refugee policy*. The Guardian. https://www.theguardian.com/australia-news/2021/aug/22/the-tampa-affair-20-years-on-the-ship-that-capsized-australias-refugee-policy

Ghezelbash, D., Dorostkar, K., & Bridle, M. (2025, April 28). *Five ways to tackle Australia's backlog of asylum cases*. University of New South Wales. https://www.unsw.edu.au/newsroom/news/2025/04/five-ways-tackle-australian-backlog-asylum-cases

Ghezelbash, D., & Hruschka C. (2024, September). *A fair and fast asylum process for Australia: Lessons from Switzerland* [Policy brief]. University of New South Wales. https://www.unsw.edu.au/content/dam/pdfs/law/kaldor/2024-10-a-fair-fast-asylum-process-in-australia-lessons-from-switzerland.pdf

Hafeez-Baig, M.J. (2016). *Putting the 'protection' in 'Temporary Protection Visa'*. Bond Law Review, 28(2), 115-147. DOI:10.3316/agispt.20174592

Knight, B. (2021, December 2). *Tampa affair: tracing the fallout on Australia's refugee policy*. University of New South Wales. https://www.unsw.edu.au/newsroom/news/2021/12/tampa-affair--tracing-the-fallout-on-australia-s-refugee-policy

McAdam, J., & Purcell, Kate. (2008). *Refugee protection in the Howard years: obstructing the right to seek asylum*. Australian Yearbook of international Law Online, 27(1), 87-113. DOI:10.1163/26660229-027-01-900000007

McAllister, I. (2003). *Border protection, the 2001 Australian election and the coalition victory*. Australian Journal of Political Science, 38(3), 445-63. DOI:10.1080/1036114032000133985

Playfair, P., Mercado, A. (2017), *Refugee Status Determination Policy and Practice: The Australian Experience*, Chapter 44, The Migration Conference 2017 Proceedings, Transnational Press London.

Playfair, P. (2019), *Refugee Status Determination Policy and Practice: will the current "zero boats" status be sustained by the newly proposed policy of the Australian Labor Party?* Policies of Refuge around the World, TMC 2019 – BARI, ITALY – 18-20 JUNE 2019, (pp 168) from https://www.ceeol.com/search/book-detail?id=851683

Refugee Council of Australia. (2020, May 20). *Australia's offshore processing regime: the facts*. https://www.refugeecouncil.org.au/offshore-processing-facts/

Refugee Council of Australia. (2025a, April 30). *The fall of Saigon: a crisis that changed Australia*. https://www.refugeecouncil.org.au/fall-of-saigon/

Refugee Council of Australia. (2025b, July 27). *Statistics on boat arrivals and boat turnbacks*. https://www.refugeecouncil.org.au/asylum-boats-statistics/

Refugee Council of Australia. (2025c, August 10). *Statistics on people seeking asylum in the community*. https://www.refugeecouncil.org.au/asylum-community/5/

Spinks, H. (2018, July 20). *Boat 'turnbacks' in Australia: a quick guide to the statistics since 2001* (Research Paper Series 2018-19). *Department of Parliamentary Services*. https://parlinfo.aph.gov.au/parlInfo/download/library/prspub/5351070/upload_binary/5351070.pdf

THE LIMITS OF LAW FOR SOCIAL JUSTICE: THE ROLE OF LAW ON RESOURCE EXTRACTION AND GREEN ENERGY DEVELOPMENT ON INDIGENOUS PEOPLES' TERRITORY, IN THE CASE OF THE WAYUU INDIGENOUS PEOPLE IN COLOMBIA

Pilar Balbuena[1]

Introduction

La Guajira in Colombia concentrates the majority of works for the generation of wind energy. Between 2015 and 2022, La Guajira covered 65% of the total wind energy projects in the country, Vargas et al., (2022). As of May 2023, there were 16 wind farms active or under construction across La Guajira, and more than 60 projects are planned or proposed for construction by 2030, González (2023). However so far, the arrival of many of these facilities has generated social tensions, particularly among the Wayuu Indigenous People communities, with accusations of displacement, disagreements, extortion and even violence, González (2023). In Colombia, according to the 2018 DANE (National Population and Housing Census), 4.4% of the population (1,905,617)[2] recognizes itself as a member or belonging to an indigenous culture, with the largest group being the Wayuu, with approximately 380,460 people, representing 20.2% of the country's Indigenous population[3],[4] and 46% of La Guajira.[5]

La Guajira, is a region rich in natural and cultural resources, this territory has

---

[1] Pilar Balbuena, Carleton University. Ottawa, Ontario, Canada.

[2] Cubillos Álzate Julio Cesar, Matamoros Cárdenas Mariana, and Perea Caro Santiago Alberto. 'Boletines poblacionales: Población Indígena Corte a Diciembre de 2019'. Ministerio de Salud, 2020. Boletines Poblacionales : Población Indígena Oficina de Promoción Social.

[3] Hernández Romero, Astrid María Zoraida Hernández, Jhonnathan Chaparro Lizarazo, and Rafael Andrés Urrego Posada. 'Información Sociodemográfica Del Pueblo Wayuu'. Informes de Estadística Sociodemográfica Aplicada. DEPARTAMENTO ADMINISTRATIVO NACIONAL DE ESTADÍSTICA DANE, 2018. Información sociodemográfica del pueblo Wayuu.

[4] Departamento Administrativo Nacional de Estadística, 'Información Sociodemográfica Del Pueblo Wayuu'.

[5] GUERRA LÓPEZ, CARLOS MANUEL. "Proyectos de Energía Renovable En El Territorio Indígena Wayuu. Una Relación Desconectada." *Revista de Derecho Universidad Del Norte* 1, no. 59 (2024): 81–104. https://doi.org/ttps://doi.org/10.14482/dere.59.612.519.

been subject to extensive resource extraction for decades, and there is now a growing interest in developing sustainable energy projects, this paper focuses on wind farm projects. However, the success of these initiatives hinges not only on economic viability but also on social acceptance, which is largely determined by the quality of engagement and consultation processes between corporations and the Wayuu community. On this paper I examine how existing laws impact Indigenous rights, livelihoods, and the environment, and explore how the Wayuu People use legal frameworks to assert their rights.

Theoretical Framework: Colonial Legacies and Law

In this research, I use a theoretical framework that draws on the insights of Arturo Escobar (2011), Walter Mignolo (2005), and Katherine Pistor (2020). Together they argue that the laws governing resource extraction and green energy projects reflect colonial legacies, prioritizing the interests of the nation-state and corporations at the expense of Indigenous rights. Escobar emphasizes that development discourses label Indigenous lands as "underdeveloped," justifying their appropriation under the guise of progress. Mignolo highlights the need for knowledge-based decolonization, asserting that legal frameworks perpetuate colonial legacies that invalidate Indigenous knowledge, beliefs and land claims. Pistor posits that legal structures are designed to favour capitalist interests, creating property rights that align with state goals and marginalizing Indigenous claims. Together, these scholars provide a theoretical framework through which I analyze the limitations of law in addressing social justice Indigenous Peoples.

Legal Context: Colombian Legislation and Indigenous Rights

The Colombian legal framework includes several constitutional articles and laws that ostensibly protect Indigenous rights.

1. Constitutional Articles: [6] Article 332 establishes state ownership of natural resources, stating that the Nation-State owns the subsoil and the natural, non-renewable resources without prejudice to the rights acquired and fulfilled by prior laws. The subsoil and other non-renewable natural resources in accordance with article 332 of the Political Constitution, the territorial sea, the contiguous zone, the continental shelf, the exclusive economic zone, the airspace, the segment of the geostationary orbit, the electromagnetic spectrum

---

[6] SECRETARIO GENERAL, ASAMBLEA NACIONAL CONSTITUYENTE (1991). "Constitución Política 1 de 1991 Asamblea Nacional Constituyente." Gobierno de Colombia, July 6, 1991. https://www.funcionpublica.gov.co/eva/gestornormativo/norma.php?i=4125.

(CP art. 102), as well as the assets that it owns as private property, under the same conditions as individuals (CP Article 58). Article 360 mandates economic compensation for resource extraction. Article 330 governs Indigenous territories in accordance with their customs and traditions.

2. Environmental Protection: Article 80 outlines the state's responsibility to manage natural resources sustainably, and Article 334 empowers the state to intervene in land use and resource exploitation for economic management.

3. Key Legislation: General Environmental Law (Law 99 of 1993) requires that resource exploitation does not harm the cultural identity of Indigenous communities and mandates consultation with them. Law 21 of 1991 protects the rights of Indigenous peoples to resources on their lands, ensuring their participation in management and conservation.

4. International Instruments: The ILO Convention 169, ratified by Colombia, recognizes Indigenous rights and mandates consultation. The UN Declaration on the Rights of Indigenous Peoples (UNDRIP) emphasizes the need for respect and recognition of Indigenous rights globally.

Impact of Resource Extraction on the Wayuu People

In this paper, I discuss the negative effects of resource extraction on the Wayuu community, particularly in the context of large-scale coal extraction (LSCE), as Corral-Montoya et al.,(2022) and Guerra López (2024) research present, and renewable energy projects as discussed by Gonzalez Posso (2023), Guerra López (2024), Rodriguez and Calderón (2024), Pinilla (2024) and González (2023).

These authors research indicates that LSCE has severely disrupted the cultural heritage, social structures, and livelihoods of the Wayuu. The Colombian laws enable corporations to exert considerable influence, framing fossil fuel extraction as a matter of national interest, creating significant wealth for transnational corporations while exacerbating inequalities for Indigenous Peoples, as most economic benefits accrued to the corporations, rather than benefiting the local economy. The introduction of wind farm projects, while framed as sustainable, often disregards the historical claims and rights of the Wayuu. For example, Laws like Law 2099 of 2021 classify these projects as public utilities, allowing for land expropriation without adequate consultation, Gonzalez Posso (2023).

Challenges Faced by the Wayuu People

The Wayuu people face numerous challenges due to the ongoing resource extraction and development projects.

> The corporation's discourse is usually focused on the concept of development, reinforcing their position based on the "importance of taking advantage of the strength of the winds forces," showing their economic activity as an "obligation or imperative" that cannot be avoided." (Guerra López, 2024)

They experienced displacement and violence due to territorial disputes associated with the arrival of corporations. High child mortality rates due to malnutrition and a lack of access to clean water further complicate their living conditions, threatening the Wayuu's cultural identity and traditional practices, Pinilla (2024).

The Role of Free, Prior, and Informed Consent (FPIC)

The concept of Free, Prior, and Informed Consent (FPIC) is central to the discussion of Indigenous rights and resource extraction. As per Rodriguez and Calderón (2024), I highlight the issues related to the implementation of FPIC in the case of the Wayuu People, reporting that they felt excluded from the consultation processes, with corporations often failing to recognize traditional authorities. The legal simplification of Indigenous authority undermines the complex political and social organization of the Wayuu, leading to conflicts over land use and representation. The relationship between the Wayuu and corporations is marked by material inequality, with power dynamics favouring corporate interests over Indigenous rights, Berraondo (2024) and Vázquez & Hodgkins (2021, 22).

Resistance and Advocacy

The Wayuu People have successfully engaged in resistance to protect their rights. They have organized protests, such as blocking access to wind farms, Mejía (2022). Their activism has led to legal challenges against corporations, highlighting the inadequacies of the consultation processes and the need for genuine engagement with Indigenous Peoples, Vega (2023). In this paper, I emphasize the importance of reforms in the legal framework governing resource extraction and energy projects, ensuring that Indigenous rights are respected and prioritized.

Conclusion: The Need for Reforms

With this research, my objective is to highlight the importance of reforms in Colombia's legal framework for better protecting Indigenous rights, with a focus on the case of the Wayuu People and an emphasis on the limitations of existing laws, which appear to serve the nation-state and corporate interests rather than the needs of Indigenous Peoples, as stresses by Rodriguez and Calderón (2024) and Gonzales Posso (2023) that Colombia's existing legal frameworks and land rights policies are exacerbating the inequalities of the Wayuu People by failing to adequately recognize and protect their ancestral land rights with industrial developments like wind energy projects. Implementing inclusive consultation processes that involve including Indigenous people in the entire process is crucial to achieving real, sustainable energy development. Recognizing and valuing Indigenous ontology, knowledge, and governance structures can lead to more effective and just resource management practices. In summary, the intersectionalities between law, natural resources, and Indigenous rights in Colombia highlight opportunities for advocacy and help us understand the broader implications of implementing sustainable energy projects in indigenous peoples' territories.

Future research

Dorn, Felix (2025) research indicates that wind energy projects in La Guajira are seen as a significant investment opportunity. However, these developments have been followed by protests and disruptions from the Wayuu People. The tension centers around the concepts regarding nature and territory, where the Wayuu view the wind as a living entity, the nation-state and corporations see it as a mere resource. To unpack how the Wayúu people see the spiritual and cultural impacts of wind farms built on their ancestral lands, citing arguments about profound disturbance to their way of life and the peace of their sacred sites, for the next phase of this research, I will focus on exploring the question of how can the Wayuu People resistance to wind farms be understood as ontological border resistance.

References

Corral-Montoya, Felipe, Max Telias, and Nicolas Malz. "Unveiling the Political Economy of Fossil Fuel Extractivism in Colombia: Tracing the Processes of Phase-in, Entrenchment, and Lock-In." *Energy Research & Social Science* 88 (2022): 102377. https://doi.org/https://doi.org/10.1016/j.erss.2021.102377.

Cubillos Álzate Julio Cesar, Matamoros Cárdenas Mariana, and Perea Caro Santiago Alberto. *'Boletines Poblacionales: Población Indígena Corte a Diciembre de 2019'. Ministerio de Salud, 2020.*

Boletines Poblacionales : Población Indígena Oficina de Promoción Social., n.d.

Dorn, Felix Malte. "Development in Global Production Networks? Wind Energy and Socio-Ecological Conflicts in La Guajira, Colombia." *Journal of Economic Geography*, 2025.

Escobar, Arturo. *Encountering Development : The Making and Unmaking of the Third World. Princeton,*. NJ: Princeton University Press., 2011. https://doi.org/10.1515/9781400839926.

González, David. "Los Parques Eólicos Dividen a Comunidades Indígenas de Colombia." Dialogue Earth, 2023. https://dialogue.earth/es/energia/368855-los-parques-eolicos-dividen-a-comunidades-indigenas-de-colombia-wayuu/.

Gonzalez Posso, Camilo. "PARQUES SOLARES EN LA GUAJIRA Y EN TERRITORIOS ÉTNICOS WAYÚU – POR CAMILO GONZÁLEZ POSSO." NGO. Indepaz, 2023. https://indepaz.org.co/parques-solares-en-la-guajira-y-en-territorios-etnicos-wayuu-por-camilo-gonzalez-posso/.

GUERRA LÓPEZ, CARLOS MANUEL. "Proyectos de Energía Renovable En El Territorio Indígena Wayuu. Una Relación Desconectada." *Revista de Derecho Fundación Universidad Del Norte* 1, no. 59 (2024): 81–104. https://doi.org/ttps://doi.org/10.14482/dere.59.612.519.

Mejía, Eliana. "Indígenas Wayús Bloquean Vías de Acceso al Parque Eólico En La Guajira." *El Tiempo*, June 1, 2022. https://www.eltiempo.com/colombia/otras-ciudades/indigenas-wayus-bloquean-vias-de-acceso-al-parque-eolico-en-la-guajira-643376.

Mignolo, Walter. *The Idea of Latin America.* Malden, MA: Blackwell Pub, 2005. https://www.are.na/block/3953873.

Pinilla, Bernardo. "Autoridades Indígenas Wayuu y Transición Energética En La Guajira, Colombia." *16* 24 (2024). https://www.uexternado.edu.co/revista-experto/autoridades-indigenas-wayuu-y-transicion-energetica-en-la-guajira-colombia/.

Pistor, Katharina. *The Code of Capital : How the Law Creates Wealth and Inequality.* Princeton, NJ: Princeton University Press, 2020. https://doi.org/10.1515/9780691189437.

Rodriguez, Alexander, and Karen Calderón. "IMPACTOS DE LOS PROYECTOS DE ENERGÍA EÓLICA EN LAS COMUNIDADES INDÍGENAS WAYUU EN LA GUAJIRA, COLOMBIA." *Margens* 18 (2024): 45-62. https://periodicos.ufpa.br/index.php/revistamargens/article/view/17104/11504#.

SECRETARIO GENERAL, ASAMBLEA NACIONAL CONSTITUYENTE (1991). "Constitución Política 1 de 1991 Asamblea Nacional Constituyente." Gobierno de Colombia, July 6, 1991. https://www.funcionpublica.gov.co/eva/gestornormativo/norma.php?i=4125. (n.d.).

Vargas Fernández, Sebastián, and Olimpia Palmar Ipuana. "Energías Renovables En La Guajira: Desafíos y Oportunidades Para Una Transición Energética Incluyente e Intercultural." *Universidad Del Rosario*, 2022.

Vázquez, Karen Hudlet, and Chelsea Hodgkins. "(In)justicia energética en América Latina." *Business & Human Rights Resource Centre*, 2021. https://media.business-humanrights.org/media/documents/reporte_RE_espanol04.08_BgB3kz3.pdf.

VEGA, JOSÉ ANTONIO. "Windpeshi, El Negocio de La Energía Eólica y Las Lecciones Para La Transición Energética." *El Pais*, May 27, 2023. https://elpais.com/america-colombia/2023-05-27/windpeshi-el-negocio-de-la-energia-eolica-y-las-lecciones-para-la-transicion-energetica.html.

INTERSECTIONALITY AND CLIMATE MIGRATION: UNDERSTANDING VULNERABILITIES AND SOCIAL JUSTICE

Betul Dilara Seker

Introduction

Climate change today has global impacts not only in its environmental but also in its social and economic dimensions. Sudden or slowly developing climatic disasters evoke different reactions in individuals and communities. Migratory behavior occupies a prominent place among these reactions. For example, in 2020, 30.7 million people across 149 countries and territories were displaced due to climate-related natural disasters. This number is among the highest since the 38.3 million displacement recorded in 2010 (IDMC, 2021). However, because migration decisions are driven by various contextual factors (de Haas, 2021), determining the exact number of forced migrations due to climate change is difficult (McLeman, 2019). However, it is known that climate change exacerbates the vulnerabilities that force people to leave their homes because it causes serious environmental impacts.

While the definition of climate migration lacks universal consensus, it is generally accepted as the movement of people as a result of sudden or gradual weather and climate changes (McLeman and Gemenne, 2018). This mobility is related to individuals' responses to a climate-related event and is closely linked to personal factors such as local context, socioeconomic status, and health conditions (Lutz and Muttarak, 2017). Forced migration due to climate change is projected to increase in the future, and it is estimated that this number could affect between 150 million and one billion people by 2050. Therefore, climate migration is among the priority issues requiring policy development worldwide (McLeman, 2019). It is also considered important for countries and regions concerned with climate migration to develop policies to manage both internal and external migration.

The impacts of climate change have become more pronounced today, and this has emerged as a significant research topic across many disciplines. Climate migration studies are also attracting attention as an important area of research in this context. Recent studies emphasize the need for a more comprehensive understanding of the social, economic, environmental, and cultural impacts of climate migration on host communities. Similarly, detailed analysis of the livelihoods of climate-induced migrants in their new settlement areas, evidence-based research on internal and international migration processes, the development of long-term migration policies, and the establishment of sustainable livelihood frameworks are necessary (Takahashi, 2024).

Climate migration refers to the temporary or permanent displacement of individuals or communities in response to sudden or gradual changes in the natural environment (McLeman & Gemenne, 2018). Extreme weather events worldwide, particularly rising sea levels, droughts, floods, extreme storms, heat waves, wildfires, and other climate changes, are driving vulnerable populations to seek refuge outside their home countries. In this context, the term "environmental migrants" is used to describe individuals whose living conditions are negatively impacted and who migrate to different regions (Manning & Clayton, 2018).

Climate change negatively impacts not only physical health but also mental health and well-being. As Parker et al. (2016) noted, the likelihood of developing mental health problems increases after natural disasters; this is more pronounced among vulnerable populations such as the elderly, low-income groups, immigrants, and individuals with chronic conditions. Regions that are more vulnerable to climate change due to their geographical location host communities at risk due to factors such as poverty, low education levels, and limited access to healthcare (Manning & Clayton, 2018).

Furthermore, climate migration should be considered as a phenomenon linked to the concept of acculturation, which affects the socioeconomic and environmental balances of not only migrants but also host communities. This situation highlights the need for solution-oriented policies at the national, regional, and international levels (Weissbecker and Czinez, 2011). Climate change should be addressed not only as an environmental problem but also as a significant social justice issue that can deepen social inequalities and lead to intergroup conflict.

Social Identity and Intersectionality

Individuals perceive society by dividing it into categories such as gender, age, ethnicity, and religious affiliation. These categories enable them to understand the social order and their social position. Individuals develop identities with the groups they belong to; these groups provide them with identity and create a sense of belonging. Social identity encompasses the knowledge of belonging to one or more groups, the emotional significance of this affiliation, and the values ascribed to them. The internalization of group identity shapes an individual's social identity and provides a cognitive basis for their social position (Chapman, 2016).

Social identity is a central element in an individual's self-definition and gives meaning to life. For an individual to survive within the social structure, these identity meanings must be shared by group members. Individuals develop self-esteem by prioritizing their ingroup over outgroups in their search for a positive social identity (Weichselbaumer, 2020).

Individuals can belong to multiple groups, and their identities can be inclusive rather than mutually exclusive. Intersectionality provides a detailed framework for understanding the interaction of multiple identities. This concept focuses on what it means for an individual to belong to more than one disadvantaged group (Syed, 2010) and explains how the interaction of different identity categories can lead to discrimination (Manassen & Verkuyten, 2018; Weichselbaumer, 2020).

Intersectionality studies generally focus on the combination of race, ethnicity, religion, and gender (Jordan-Zachery, 2007; Manassen & Verkuyten, 2018). Studies have shown that gender roles, ethnicity, and religion reorganize identity elements.

Vulnerable Groups

While everyone on Earth is affected by climate change, it is striking that its impacts are experienced differently across individuals and communities. These disparities tend to increase levels of social inequality and can also fuel intergroup tensions and conflict. Disadvantaged groups with limited economic and social resources are particularly vulnerable to these impacts. Women, people from poor and minority groups, the elderly, children, people with disabilities, and migrant communities are particularly vulnerable to the impacts of climate change (Dodgen, Donato, & Kelly, 2016; Parker et al., 2016). Women in developing countries, in particular, are directly affected by climate change due to their extensive involvement in agricultural activities (United Nations Population Fund, 2009). Traditional caregiving roles and gender expectations can make women more vulnerable to natural disasters. For example, research shows that older people are at greater risk from the physical impacts of climate change, such as extreme heat, and are more likely to experience mental health problems. Similarly, children are particularly vulnerable to the adverse effects of climate change. Their developing organ systems, small physical structures, and limited independence make children more vulnerable to extreme weather conditions. Early malnutrition and health problems can lead to lasting effects such as developmental delays and reduced economic activity in adulthood. Furthermore, individuals with limited access to healthcare or communities whose livelihoods depend directly on the environment are more vulnerable to the impacts of climate change. Communities that rely directly on environmental livelihoods (agriculture, fishing, tourism) are also at greater risk. Low-income and ethnic minority communities are also more vulnerable to the impacts of climate change. These groups often live in areas with poor infrastructure and are more exposed to extreme weather. A lack of social and economic resources limits their ability to recover from disasters. Furthermore, these communities, which have historically borne a disproportionate burden of environmental injustices, are more severely affected by the impacts of climate change (Manning and Clayton, 2018).

As a result, climate migration has multifaceted impacts on the living conditions of individuals and communities, necessitating the development of solution-oriented policies at the international level. The failure of the international legal system to recognize this group as a refugee remains one of the fundamental problems faced by climate migrants (McLeman, 2019). In this context, the United Nations Sustainable Development Goals and the Sendai Framework for Disaster Risk Reduction recognize this group as highly vulnerable and at risk (Appave et al., 2017). Understanding the vulnerabilities of different segments of society to climate change is critical for developing inclusive and effective adaptation strategies. This necessitates greater consideration of social justice and equity approaches in environmental policies.

Conclusion

Climate change has moved beyond being solely an environmental problem and has become a major global issue affecting social and economic spheres. The impacts of this change are quite diverse and can manifest as slow or sudden disasters, forcing vulnerable groups to migrate. Migration decisions are influenced not only by environmental factors but also by contextual and societal factors. Women, children, ethnic minorities, and economically disadvantaged individuals are among the groups most affected by this situation.

From a social psychological perspective, identity plays a significant role in the migration experience. Climate-induced migration challenges individuals' social identities and requires them to redefine their sense of belonging in new environments. Intersectionality, as a theoretical framework, offers valuable insights into how overlapping identities such as gender, ethnicity, and socioeconomic status shape individuals' experiences and vulnerabilities.

Inclusive and socially conscious public policies are crucial for addressing the multidimensional challenges posed by climate migration. The following recommendations aim to support resilience, social justice, and well-being through approaches that incorporate social psychological perspectives:

1. Culturally Sensitive Adaptation Programs: Initiatives that respect and consider the cultural backgrounds of migrants should be developed. These programs can contribute to easier integration for migrants and the reduction of prejudice in host communities by promoting cultural exchange and mutual understanding.

2. Community Support Networks: The formation of local support groups for climate migrants should be encouraged. These groups can reduce feelings of loneliness and support psychological well-being by providing environments where individuals can share their experiences, access information, and build social connections.

3. Psychosocial Support Services: Accessible mental health services tailored to the needs of climate migrants should be provided. These services should address trauma, identity reconstruction, and adaptation challenges, and focus on promoting resilience.

4. Empowerment through Participation: Climate migrants should be included in decision-making processes such as resettlement and community planning. Enabling individuals to contribute to their new communities can empower them and help them develop a sense of belonging.

5. Intersectionality-Based Policies: Policies should be designed that consider the diverse experiences and needs of climate migrants. Intersectionality-based approaches can contribute to overcoming multidimensional disadvantages by ensuring that support measures are inclusive and effective.

Social justice requires recognizing climate migrants as a vulnerable group that needs to be protected and supported. Advocacy is crucial for the recognition of climate-induced migration within international legal frameworks. Collaboration between social groups, NGOs, and international organizations can contribute to the development of protective measures and the protection of migrants' rights.

The complex interplay of environmental and social factors necessitates a holistic approach to climate migration. By adopting approaches that prioritize intersectionality through social psychological perspectives, policymakers can both address existing challenges and develop compassionate and effective solutions that promote social cohesion, well-being, and resilience among migrants and host communities.

References

Appave, G., Sironi, A., Chazalnoel, M. T., Ionesco, D., & Mokhnacheva, D. (2017). Organizational perspectives: International Organization for Migration's role and perspectives on climate change, migration and the law. In *Research Handbook on Climate Change, Migration and the Law* (pp. 288-315). Edward Elgar Publishing.

Chapman, M. (2016). Veil as stigma: Exploring the role of representations in Muslim women's management of threatened social identity. *Journal of Community & Applied Social Psychology, 26*(4), 354-366.

De Haas, H. (2021). A theory of migration: the aspirations-capabilities framework. *Comparative Migration Studies, 9*(1), 8.

Dodgen, D., Donato, D., Kelly, N., et al. (2016). Ch. 8: Mental health and well-being. In The impacts of climate change on human health in the United States: A scientific assessment (pp. 217-246). Washington, DC: U.S. Global Change Research Program. Available from http://dx.doi.org/10.7930/J0TX3C9H. Accessed January 10, 2025.

Internal Displacement Monitoring Centre (IDMC). (2021). Global Report on Internal Displacement (GRID). Geneva: IDMC. https://www.internal-displacement.org/sites/default/files/publications/documents/grid2021_idmc.pdf. Accessed January 10, 2025.

Jordan-Zachery, J. S. (2007). Am I a black woman or a woman who is black? A few thoughts on the meaning of intersectionality. *Politics & Gender, 3*(2), 254-263.

Lutz, W., & Muttarak, R. (2017). Forecasting societies' adaptive capacities through a demographic metabolism model. *Nature Climate Change, 7*(3), 177-184.

Manassen, A., & Verkuyten, M. (2018). Examining identity intersectionality: Thai marriage migrants in the Netherlands. *International Review of Social Psychology, 31*(1), 1-9.

Manning, C., & Clayton, S. (2018). Threats to mental health and wellbeing associated with climate change. In Psychology and climate change (pp. 217-244). Academic Press.

McLeman, R. (2019). International migration and climate adaptation in an era of hardening borders. *Nature Climate Change, 9*(12), 911-918.

McLeman, R., & Gemenne, F. (2018). Environmental migration research: Evolution and current state of the science. In Routledge handbook of environmental displacement and migration (pp. 3-16). Routledge.

Parker, G., Lie, D., Siskind, D. J., Martin-Khan, M., Raphael, B., Crompton, D., & Kisely, S. (2016). Mental health implications for older adults after natural disasters—A systematic review and meta-analysis. *International Psychogeriatrics, 28*(1), 11-20.

Syed, M. (2010). Disciplinarity and methodology in intersectionality theory and research. *American Psychologist, 65*(1), 61-62.

Takahashi, B. (2024). Latin American immigrants and the environment: acculturation, information sources, and place. *Local Environment, 29*(3), 399-413.

Weichselbaumer, D. (2020). Multiple discrimination against female immigrants wearing headscarves. *ILR Review, 73*(3), 600-627.

Weissbecker, I., & Czinez, J. (2011). Humanitarian crises: The need for cultural competence and local capacity building. In I. Weissbecker (Ed.), Climate change and human wellbeing: Global challenges and opportunities (pp. 79-96). New York: Springer.

EXAMINING THE ROLE OF DUBLIN REGULATIONS IN THE SECURITIZATION OF EU MIGRATION POLICIES AND THE INFLUENCE OF THE FAR-RIGHT

Zeynep Naz Oral

Introduction

In 2015, more than one million migrants entered the European Union (EU). The majority of these individuals were escaping armed conflict and persecution in Syria, Afghanistan, Eritrea, as well as various countries in Africa and the Middle East. (Davis, 2021)

The Dublin III Regulation forms the foundation of the Common European Asylum System (CEAS). It establishes a systematic approach for assigning responsibility to a specific Member State for examining applications for international protection. The regulation seeks to ensure effective access to asylum procedures and to prevent multiple Member States from examining the same application. (EUAA, 2024)

Although the Dublin Regulation was designed to determine which member state should be responsible for examining an asylum claim, it failed to provide substantial assistance to those states receiving a disproportionate share of applications. Dublin III introduced only a limited "early warning, preparedness and crisis management" mechanism, whereby a member state facing particular strain could be invited to prepare a preventive action plan. Under this system, the responsibility remained with the member state itself to adopt the necessary measures to cope with pressure on its asylum system or to remedy existing shortcomings before conditions worsened. (Armstrong, 2020)

This study examines the contribution to the securitization of EU migration policies and how far-right parties influence this process. Instead of promoting solidarity, it has supported stricter border controls and helped create what is often called Fortress Europe, a set of barriers aimed at keeping refugees and migrants out of the EU. Using securitization theory, the essay shows that Dublin reinforced exclusionary policies.

Theoretical Framework

The Copenhagen School's securitization theory offers a useful framework to analyze the transformation of migration from a humanitarian issue into a matter of "security." According to Buzan, Wæver, and de Wilde (1998), securitization occurs when political actors frame an issue as an existential threat, thereby justifying extraordinary measures. At the same time Paris School adds to this view by looking at the everyday practices, routines that help create and maintain insecurity. (Bigo, 2002) From this angle migration becomes a security issue not just through major political statements, but also through the actions of what Bigo calls "professionals of unease management" such as border guards, bureaucrats, policymakers, and security experts. In the context of EU migration policy, institutions such as the Dublin Regulation, Schengen, FRONTEX, EURODAC, and bilateral readmission agreements exemplify how migration has been increasingly governed through a security lens. The European Union has progressively institutionalized a "security continuum" in which migration is framed as a risk to sovereignty, identity, and social order (Guild, Carrera, & Balzacq, 2008). FRONTEX, for instance, has evolved from a border-coordination agency into a militarized actor conducting surveillance, interceptions, and joint operations. The Dublin system reinforces this securitization by requiring border states to act as Europe's "gatekeepers," prioritizing control over protection. (Cross, 2009)

The Dublin Regulation and Fortress Europe

Following the end of the Cold War, internal conflicts began to emerge in Eastern Bloc countries. In addition to tensions in the Balkans, the dissolution of Yugoslavia triggered significant migratory movements by its citizens toward EU member states. Confronted with these flows, EU member states concluded that responses should not remain at the national level but instead be coordinated at the European level. On 15 June 1990, they signed the Dublin Convention, which, after ratification by the national parliaments of the member states, entered into force in 1997. (Moses, 2017)

The Dublin Convention established the conditions necessary for the European Union to develop a common approach to asylum. Within this framework, it was agreed that if an asylum application is rejected in one member state, a new application cannot be submitted in another. This principle was intended to eliminate inequalities arising from the differing legal practices of member states by centralizing asylum applications under a single system. In doing so, the Convention sought to prevent multiple asylum applications and to accelerate decision-making processes. The Dublin Convention thus represented a significant step in the development of common EU migration policies. (ASGI, 2000) However, the constant fluctuation in migration flows toward the EU created tensions within the broader Common European Asylum System, prompting debates over the need to update the Dublin Regulation. (Parliamentary Assembly,2017) Given the failure of European states to establish an effective mechanism to manage asylum and irregular migration, the European Commission announced in 2020 the preparation of a New Pact on Migration and Asylum. (Spehar, 2025) While the Convention marked an important milestone in shaping common EU migration policies, the constant changes in migration flows and the pressures exposed by Dublin revealed that more had to be done to manage asylum fairly and effectively.

Frontline countries like Italy, Greece, and Spain have found themselves carrying the heaviest burden of Europe's asylum system simply because of where they are located. In contrast, wealthier northern and western member states have largely avoided direct responsibility. The Dublin framework, rather than distributing asylum obligations fairly, has created a system that encourages defensive policies and fuels tension between countries. (Santos Vara, 2022)

EURODAC, the EU's biometric database, was established to facilitate the coordination of asylum claims by storing the fingerprints of migrants. This system lets authorities check if someone has already applied for protection in another country. Over time, EURODAC's role has expanded. Now, biometric data is also used for security and law enforcement, which raises concerns about privacy, consent, and surveillance, especially with new reforms under the New Pact on Migration. (Marcu, 2021)

At the same time, FRONTEX, the EU's border and coast guard agency, has expanded dramatically over the past decade. Its budget, personnel, and mandate have expanded, enabling it to coordinate operations both within and outside EU borders, as well as cooperate with third countries on return and readmission policies. Yet FRONTEX has also been implicated in multiple reports of unlawful pushbacks and human rights violations, particularly in the Aegean and Central Mediterranean. These developments show how EU border management has shifted from a primarily humanitarian mission to a security-driven, externalized system of control. (Zhong & Carrapico, 2024)

The way the Dublin system is set up makes countries focus on guarding their borders instead of sharing responsibility. The 2015 migration crisis, when over a million asylum seekers came to Europe, exposed these weaknesses.

(Nascimbene, 2016) Rather than encouraging solidarity, the crisis led to more division. In 2015, Austria built a barrier at Spielfeld and in 2016 added a barrier at the Brenner Pass with Italy. That same year, Hungary erected a fence along its border with Croatia. (Dumbrava, 2022)

This approach, sometimes called Fortress Europe, uses both physical barriers and legal rules to keep people out. Deals with non-EU countries, labelling some places as 'safe' third countries, and using legal loopholes all make it harder for people to get protection. (Armstrong, 2020)

Another way how the Dublin Regulations drive securitization is the political discourse from far right. Government narratives and policies often frame migrants, asylum seekers, and refugees as threats to social stability, fuelling their negative politicization. European migration policy has reinforced this trend by embedding migration within the EU's internal security framework, while restrictive measures, preferential treatment for EU nationals, and indirect support for welfare chauvinism and cultural homogeneity further amplify perceptions of migrants as illegitimate or destabilizing actors. (Huysmans, 2000) From a political standpoint, the inability of European states to share responsibility for asylum seekers has serious consequences for the cohesion of the EU as a whole. The shortcomings of the Dublin system have deepened divisions between member states, particularly at a time when the continent is witnessing a surge in populist nationalism, which only adds to the risk of fragmentation. (Armstrong, 2020)

Parties such as France's Rassemblement National, Italy's Lega, Germany's AfD, and Spain's Vox portray migration as an existential threat to national identity, public safety, and welfare systems. Migrants are depicted as cultural invaders, criminals, or economic burdens. (Halikiopoulou & Vlandas, 2022) In Italy, Matteo Salvini, leader of the Lega, reinforced this narrative by explicitly linking immigration to criminality, declaring: "If I can reduce the number of these crimes, and the presence of illegal immigrants, they can call me racist all they want" (Walt, 2018)

Such rhetoric reinforces a multi-layered securitization: migration becomes a perceived threat to culture, security, and economic stability. Dublin's structural flaws feed this feedback loop, giving far-right actors a platform to justify increasingly repressive measures.

In response to political deadlock over Dublin, the EU introduced the New Pact on Migration and Asylum. The Pact promotes "flexible solidarity," letting member states contribute in various ways through relocation, capacity building, or financial support. Yet this flexibility often allows governments, especially far right or conservative ones, to avoid hosting asylum seekers entirely. Monetary contributions substitute for real responsibility sharing, allowing securitization to continue. (Staykova & Otova, 2025)

This approach carries significant implications for human rights. The securitization of migration compromises fundamental protections, including the right to seek asylum and the principle of non-refoulement, while undermining basic human dignity. Overcrowded detention facilities, protracted asylum procedures, pushbacks at borders, and documented incidents of both legal and physical abuse demonstrate that these challenges are not simply theoretical but have real and harmful effects on the lives of migrants and asylum seekers. (Salgado, Fratzke, Huang, & Dorst, 2024)

Conclusion

Overall, the Dublin system functions less as an impartial mechanism for distributing responsibility and more as a structural driver of migration securitization. Far-right actors have exploited its systemic weaknesses to frame migration as a multidimensional threat, thereby legitimizing restrictive and exclusionary measures. Consequently, the system remains fragmented and inequitable, undermining both the protection of fundamental human rights and the principle of EU solidarity.

Addressing these challenges necessitates more than procedural adjustments; it requires a substantive reorientation in how migration is conceptualized within Europe. Migration should be approached not as a periodic crisis to be managed defensively, but as a persistent transnational phenomenon that necessitates cooperative governance, equitable responsibility sharing, and the consistent protection of human dignity.

References

Armstrong, A. B. (2020). You shall not pass! How the Dublin System fueled Fortress Europe. *Chicago Journal of International Law, 20*(2), Article 13. https://chicagounbound.uchicago.edu/cjil/vol20/iss2/13

Associazione per gli Studi Giuridici sull'Immigrazione. (2000, May). *Dublino: Il meccanismo della Convenzione di Dublino.* https://www.briguglio.asgi.it/immigrazione-e-asilo/2000/maggio/dublino.html

Bigo, D. (2002). *Security and immigration: Toward a critique of the governmentality of unease.* https://migrantsproject.eu/wp-content/uploads/2020/08/Bigo_Security-and-Immigration.pdf

Buzan, B., Wæver, O., & de Wilde, J. (1998). *Security: A new framework for analysis.* Lynne Rienner.

Cross, H. M. (2009). The EU migration regime and West African clandestine migrants. *Journal of Contemporary European Research,* 5(2), 171–187. http://www.jcer.net/ojs/index.php/jcer/article/view/175/148

Davis, K. (2021). The European Union's Dublin Regulation and the migrant crisis. *Washington University Global Studies Law Review, 19,* 259–289.

Dumbrava, C. (2022, October). *Walls and fences at EU borders* (EPRS Briefing No. 733.692). European Parliament Research Service. https://www.europarl.europa.eu/RegData/etudes/BRIE/2022/733692/EPRS_BRI%2820 22%29733692_EN.pdf

European Union Agency for Asylum (EUAA). (2024, June). Section 3.2. The Dublin procedure. In *Asylum report 2024.* https://euaa.europa.eu/

Guild, E., Carrera, S., & Balzacq, T. (2008, October 24). *The changing dynamics of security in an enlarged European Union* (Challenge Paper No. 12).

Halikiopoulou, D., & Vlandas, T. (2022). *Understanding right-wing populism and what to do about it.* Friedrich-Ebert-Stiftung. https://library.fes.de/pdf-files/bueros/wien/19110-20220517.pdf

Huysmans, J. (2000). The European Union and the securitization of migration. *Journal of Common Market Studies, 38*(5), 751–777. https://doi.org/10.1111/1468-5965.00263

Marcu, B.-I. (2021). Eurodac: Biometrics, facial recognition, and the fundamental rights of minors. *European Law Blog.* https://doi.org/10.21428/9885764c.1fc6d748

Moses, L. (2017). The deficiencies of Dublin: An analysis of the Dublin system in the European Union. *Jackson School Journal of International Studies, 7*(2). University of Washington. https://jsis.washington.edu/jsjournal/wp-content/uploads/sites/25/2017/04/Moses_Article.pdf

Nascimbene, B. (2016). Refugees, the European Union and the 'Dublin system': The reasons for a crisis. *European Papers, 1*(1), 101–113. https://doi.org/10.15166/2499-8249/8

Parliamentary Assembly of the Council of Europe. (2017, January 26). *The need to reform European migration policies* (Document No. 14248; Report of the Committee on Migration, Refugees and Displaced Persons, rapporteur: Ian Liddell-Grainger). https://assembly.coe.int/nw/xml/XRef/Xref-XML2HTML-en.asp?fileid=23484&lang=en

Salgado, L., Fratzke, S., Huang, L., & Dorst, E. (2024, July). *Managing international protection needs at borders* (Beyond Territorial Asylum: Making Protection Work in a Bordered World). Migration Policy Institute. https://www.migrationpolicy.org/sites/default/files/publications/mpi-bta_border-processes-2024-final.pdf

Santos Vara, J. (2022). Flexible solidarity in the New Pact on Migration and Asylum: A new form of differentiated integration? In J. Santos Vara & R. A. Wessel (Eds.), *New options for differentiated integration in the European Union* (Vol. 7, No. 3, pp. 1243–1263). *European Papers.* https://doi.org/10.15166/2499-8249/613

Spehar, A. (2025). The EU's New Pact on Migration and Asylum: Towards a long-term sustainable European migration policy? In P. Ekman, B. Lundqvist, A. Michalski, & L. Oxelheim (Eds.), *The depth and size of the European Union in a time of war* (pp. 155–174). Palgrave Macmillan. https://doi.org/10.1007/978-3-031-83441-7_9

Staykova, E., & Otova, I. (2025, August 22). The EU's new migration pact and the limits of flexible solidarity. *The Loop.* https://theloop.ecpr.eu/the-eus-new-migration-pact-and-the-limits-of-flexible-solidarity/

Walt, V. (2018, September 13). 'We Want to Change Things from Within.' *Italy's Matteo Salvini on His Goal to Reshape Europe* [Interview transcript]. *Time.* Retrieved from http://time.com/5394207/matteo-salvini-time-interview-transcript-full/

Zhong, Y., & Carrapico, H. (2024). Frontex goes global: A two-level experimentalist governance analysis of Frontex's international action and its role within the externalisation of EU borders. *Contemporary European Politics, 2,* 1–17. https://doi.org/10.1002/cep4.7

HUMAN RIGHTS DISCOURSE IN REFUGEE AND MIGRANT STRUGGLE AGAINST POLITICS OF ISOLATION

Slađana Branković

This paper engages with the notion of isolation elaborated by the self-organised refugee and migrant movement in Germany. First, as a concept denoting affective and material effects of German and EU migration control policies and infrastructure which define lived experience of people subjected to them. Second, as means of political mobilisation. And finally, as an element of the political reconfiguration of human rights discourse. The paper is based on empirical research conducted within the research project *Human Rights Discourse in Political Protests of Refugees and Undocumented Migrants in Germany and the US[1]*, that is part of the *Human Rights Discourse in Migration Societies* (MeDiMi)[2] research group. The project led by Prof. Dr. Encarnación Gutiérrez Rodríguez focuses on political interventions and articulations of self-organised refugees and migrants from the 1990s until today in Germany and in the USA and the way these address and denounce the tension between human rights as norms and their factual implementation. The analysis for this paper is based on field research and co-labouring (de la Cadena 2015) with organisations *Women in Exile* (WiE) and *The Caravan for the Rights of Refugees and Migrants* (The Caravan) as well as critical discourse analysis of their digital archives (Jäger 2012). In the following pages, I will outline the concept of isolation and sketch out the main points of its political utilisation, and their consequences for the human rights discourse within critical political debates on migration.

Within political work of WiE and The Caravan, isolation is used as an umbrella term that denotes a wide array of infrastructural conditions, institutional practices, and lived experiences these produce. Its invocation makes visible the systemic and institutionalised character of wide array of practices that limit

---

[1] Project is led by Prof. Dr. Encarnación Gutiérrez Rodríguez. The analysis was conducted with support from Basma Al-Moyed, Oscar Herzog Astaburuaga, and Clara Freist. More information at https://www.medimi.de/en/article/69.human-rights-discourse-in-political-protests-of-refugees-and-undocumented-migrants.html

[2] More information on MeDiMi and research agenda at https://www.medimi.de/en/topic/39.research-agenda.html

access to and exercise of basic human rights and needs, including access to health care services, education, freedom of movement, self-determination, building of meaningful inter-personal relations and community, sense of belonging, and participation in societal, cultural, and religious life. These forms of isolation are achieved through a) forms of accommodation, marked by deteriorating conditions, remoteness, and lack of safety and privacy and b) measures of control, such as Bezahlkarte (payment card), Residenzpflicht (residence obligation), and control of movement and of access to services. As The Caravan states, these systematically implemented measures accumulate to a state of dehumanisation (The Caravan 2012a, 7) and serve to exclude migrants from the general society. With it, they diminish the potential to participate in social, cultural, and political life and build prospects for safe, self-determined, and communal future in Germany (The Caravan 2013, 3; WiE 2014, 5; Gutiérrez Rodríguez and Branković 2025).

The notion of isolation as a means of political mobilisation and reconfiguration of human rights discourse functions through a process of translation of lived experience into political expertise (Gutiérrez Rodríguez 2024; Destrooper 2018). We have followed this process discursively beginning with analysis of reports on *Lager*[3] visitations by self-organised migrant and refugee groups, reports on political mobilisation in refugee camps, and finally wider political actions of refugee and migrant networks.

Reports on *Lager* visitations, which describe living conditions and situation in and around accommodation facilities, also contain short interviews or comments made by people living there. These valuable discursive 'snapshots' offer insight into the narratives that unfold through lived experiences of isolation and elaborate affected peoples' epistemological stands on and historical embedding of migration control politics. On this level, the first affective and material effects of isolation are identified as dehumanisation and first historical embedding of perpetuating practices of segregation and isolation are given, as in the following diagnosis of the situation in the Meinersen camp in Lower Saxony, Germany:

> "They threw us into this camp like animals – we're not animals – our children are humans too. You can't treat people like that [...] My grandfather told me

---

[3] *Lager* refers to refugee accommodation in Germany, the Flüchtlingslager or -unterkunft. The term is used by the self-organised movement and people living in refugee camps to emphasise a) colonial continuity of practices of isolation and 'encampment' as well as b) the living conditions resembling 'storage units' which are also termed Lager in German language (Ngari et.al 2024).

what the Nazis were, what their view of humanity was. You find that here too – this is real racism here." (The Caravan 2010, author's translation)

On the second level, these singular experiences and narratives serve as the impulse for political mobilisation in camps and are further negotiated and elaborated through political resistance to dehumanising living conditions and practices of control. Their further theoretical negotiation is disseminated through newsletters and calls for action and mobilisation. In this respect three important processes take place. First, deeper historical analysis of continuity of practices of exclusion, segregation, and isolation is given and solidified as political diagnosis of the politics of migration control in Germany and the EU. Second, three main principles on which political mobilisation and reconfiguration of human rights discourse take place are introduced – solidarity, dignity, and justice. And finally, lived experience under the conditions of isolation and control as well as political work and resistance to it are postulated as (political) expertise on human rights.

The final aspect that stands in focus of this analysis, the expertise on human rights, is, at times, explicitly proclaimed as the following statement illustrates: "The refugees will teach Germany what human rights mean. We will model human rights for you, and then you will say: 'Yes, these are the human rights we dreamed of'" (The Caravan 2012b, 1). This knowledge on human rights is articulated as inherent to the experience of dehumanisation, that materialises through isolation, and is further elaborated through written reports, newsletters, and political actions. One political campaign that took place between 2012 and 2014 centred around a four-day political event, the *International Tribunal of Refugees and Migrants against the Federal Republic of Germany*, makes this particularly visible. The *Tribunal* took place in 2013 in Berlin, mobilising participation of numerous self-organised refugee and migrant groups in Germany and beyond and generating increased discursive production around it – in particular, through calls for participation preceding it and list of accusations that was published in its aftermath.

In the initial call for participation and preparation of the event The Caravan state:

"With this call the tribunal starts today. […] We want to investigate, how far they[4] violate national or international laws. Some act might not be regulated through any law or agreement. In these cases, we claim the right to judge by our human empathies and our

---

[4] "[E]mployees of the state, the state institutions, and the private companies" (ibid.)

dignity. [...] The tribunal is a place of solidarity, where we reach out our hands and claim our right to judge the criminals and the profiteers." (The Caravan 2012c, 4)

This short text already indicates two important notions as characteristics of the political reconfiguration of human rights. First, it indicates that there is a gap between the lived experience of dehumanisation or denial of rights and the (human) rights standards and norms that should be able to address it. And second it positions migrant and refugee activists as experts on the issue at hand while qualities of humanity – empathy and dignity – function as parameters by which violations of human rights are to be judged. Dignity, as well as solidarity, are proposed as central elements of the struggle for justice, and elements missing from legal human rights frameworks. Here, they are only signalled as such, while their further elaboration takes place throughout general discourse of Women in Exile and The Caravan.

Final step of translation of lived experience into human rights discourse is made explicit in the long list of accusations formulated at the *Tribunal*. Here, standardised definitions and notions of human rights are replaced with references that attempt to summarize and capture concrete forms of human rights violations that are reported by people subjected to policies and measures of migration control. These captured experiences are put at the centre of the discourse, marking them as human rights violations only at the end of the text. For example, in the case of addressing inaccessibility of health care services, rather than invoking violation of the right to health, they state "[t]he FRG is accused of enforcing the system of isolation camps, thus [..] endangering refugees' lives by denying them health care" (The Caravan 2014, 3). Similarly, rather than invoking violation of freedom of movement as standardized in (legal) human rights discourse, they state: "The FRG is accused of exerting permanent control and isolation on refugees through restrictions on their residence ('Residenzpflicht', 'residence obligation' law)" (ibid.). Again, human rights are invoked only at the end of the long list of such accusation stating "[t]he FRG is accused of violating our universal human rights and dignity", thus marking all listed forms of violence, isolation, and control as human rights violations.

We see this centring of lived experience as a form of political renegotiation of human rights discourse that indicates a discrepancy between the human rights norms and standards and lived realities of dehumanisation that articulates a need and effort to bridge it. While this contributes to an understanding of *humanrightization* as a dynamic process that is negotiated through legal, political, and everyday discourse (Bast et.al 2025), continuous reproduction and current aggravation of practices, policies, and conditions addressed by the refugee and migrant movement at the *Tribunal* in 2013 until today, once again raises the question of who is centred in this dynamic, whose proposals and theorisations become widely adopted, and why and how political actors subjected to those practices and policies of migration control remain at the edges or outside of this dynamic?

References

Bast, Jürgen, Laura Holderied, and Maximilian Aigner (2025): Humanrightization. Theses on a Theory of Discursive Practice in Migration Societies. Discussion Paper, MeDiMi Working Paper No. 2, https://doi.org/10.22029/jlupub-20079.

Cadena, Marisol de la (2015): Earth Beings. Durham: Duke University Press.

Destrooper, Tine. (2018): On Travel, Translation, and Transformation. In: T. Destrooper & S. Engle Marry (eds.), *Human Rights Transformation in Practice*. Philadelphia: University of Pennsylvania Press. 1-26.

Gutiérrez Rodríguez, Encarnación (2024): Translation as Decolonial Method: On the (Un-)Translatability of Human Rights Demands and the Coloniality of Migration in Refugee Protest in Germany. In: Chambers C. and Demir P. (eds.) Translation and Decolonisation: Interdisciplinary Perspectives. London/New York: Routledge.

Gutiérrez Rodríguez, Encarnación and Slađana Branković (2025): Common Futures for All. Refugee Activism enacting Human Rights between Negation of Rights and *Rexistance* in Germany. Journal für Entwicklungspolitik XXXXI, 2-2025, 75–98, https://jep-journal.com/ausgabe/struggles-for-hope-negotiating-futures-in-times-of-global-crises/#articles

Jäger, Siegfried (2012): Kritische Diskursanalyse: Eine Einführung. Münster: Unrast Verlag.

Ngari, Elisabeth, Encarnación Gutiérrez Rodríguez, and Noémi Adam Onishi (2024): Externalisierung, Menschenwürde und Asyl. In: Krause, Ulrike/Fröhlich, Christiane (eds.): Externalisierung von Asyl. Ein Kompendium wissenschaftlicher Erkenntnisse. https://externalizingasylum.info/de/externalisierungmenschenwuerde und-asyl/, 30.3.2025.

The Caravan (2010): Sie haben uns hier rein geschmissen wie Tiere. https://thecaravan.org/node/2531, 15.08.2025.

(2012a): Damit ein Leben in Würde möglich ist, muss es ein Wandel geben! In: Zeitung der KARAWANE für die Rechte der Flüchtlinge und MigrantInnen, 4/2012, 7.

(2012b): Wir kommen. Zeitung der KARAWANE für die Rechte der Flüchtlinge und MigrantInnen, 4/2012, 1.

(2012c): International Tribunal against Germany. Zeitung der KARAWANE für die Rechte der Flüchtlinge und MigrantInnen, 2/2012, 4.

(2013): Wir waren nicht in der Gesellschaft. Wir waren ausgeschlossen! In: Zeitung der KARAWANE für die Rechte der Flüchtlinge und MigrantInnen, 5/2013, 3.

(2014): We accuse the Federal Republic of Germany! Zeitung der KARAWANE für die Rechte der Flüchtlinge und MigrantInnen, 7/2014, 1-3.

Women in Exile (2014): Challenges of living in the Heim. In: WiE-Newsletter, 2/2014, 5.

HOW HUMAN RIGHTS CAN CHANGE DOMESTIC MIGRATION LAW: THE EXAMPLE OF GERMANY

Frederik von Harbou[1]

This contribution shows how human rights have changed German migration law in the past decades. It examines the extent to which the reception of international human rights law in German legislation has led to transformations of German migration law. It also highlights different forms of references to human rights in the case law on migration law of German courts.

Context, Research Design and Methods

This contribution contains some first results from the research project "Human Rights Transformations of German Migration Law"[2] which is part of the larger interdisciplinary research group Human Rights Discourse in Migrations Society (MeDiMi)[3], funded by the German Research Foundation (DFG) since 2022. MeDiMi follows a practice-theoretical approach and seeks to shed light on the role of human rights in the discursive practices in various fields (e.g. law, politics, culture, professional ethics) of migration societies, among other things on how human rights are used to make claims of migrants' inclusion.[4] As a key concept for MeDiMi, "humanrightization" describes different forms of "doing human rights" in migration societies that need to be understood as dynamic entanglements of law, politics and everyday life, based on human rights law human rights movements and a „human rights consciousness".[5]

"Human Rights Transformations of German Migration Law" is one of ten MeDiMi sub-projects. It explores if and how the reception of international human rights law in legislation and jurisprudence, as well as the practice of legal interventions by NGOs, has led to a human rights transformation of German migration law since 1993, the year in which its constitutional basis was last

---

[1] Professor of Law, Faculty of Social Work, University of Applied Sciences Jena, Carl-Zeiss-Promenade 2, 07745 Jena, Germany, frederik.vonharbou@eah-jena.de.
[2] Cf. www.medimi.de/en/article/65.human-rights-transformations-of-german-migration-law.html.
[3] Cf. www.medimi.de/en.
[4] Bast et al. Human Rights Discourse in Migration Societies. A Research Agenda, MeDiMi Working Paper No. 1, 2023, www.medimi.de/en/article/132.medimi-working-paper-no-1-2023.html, p. 2, 8.
[5] Bast et al., Humanrightization. Theses on a Theory of Discursive Practice in Migration Societies, MeDiMi Working Paper No. 2, www.medimi.de/en/article/237.medimi-working-paper-no-2-2025.html, p. 2-4.

amended,[6] until 2023. It thus examines the intersection of German migration law and international human rights law. German migration law is defined as the branch of the German legal system that deals with the admission to the territory, the determination of the residence status, the right to asylum, social benefits for asylum seekers and persons with toleration status (*Duldung* in German law), and with the integration and naturalization of immigrants.[7] As the term "human rights" is sometimes used ambiguously (e.g. in an ethical sense), a clarification and limitation was necessary. The project therefore examined references to one or more of the 18 most important human rights treaties and declarations from universal and European human rights law.[8]

In the project, the legal doctrinal method is combined with quantitative and qualitative research methods from social sciences (mixed methods approach).[9] In concrete terms, documents relevant to German migration law from federal legislation and the jurisprudence of supreme federal courts are evaluated. These include laws from the 12th to 20th legislative periods of the German Bundestag, expert opinions and expert hearings in the Committee on Internal Affairs of the Bundestag, decisions of the Federal Constitutional Court, the Federal Administrative Court, and the Federal Social Court, as well as briefs that can be assigned to strategic litigation. The corresponding corpuses were first quantitatively indexed with a computer-assisted full text search based on the mention of human rights norms. Quantitatively salient cases were extracted and evaluated in depth by a structuring qualitative content analysis.[10] The following passage will focus on findings from legislation and case law and will not include

---

[6] Namely Art. 16, 16a Grundgesetz (Basic Law), cf. Bundesgesetzblatt (Federal Law Gazette) I 1993, 1002.

[7] The field of law as investigated by the project consists of Art. 16a Grundgesetz (Basic Law), Asylgesetz (Asylum Act, until 2015 „Asylverfahrensgesetz" - Asylum Procedure Act), Aufenthaltsgesetz (Residence Act, until 2004 „Ausländergesetz" – Aliens Act), das Freizügigkeitsgesetz/EU (Freedom of Movement Act/EU), Staatsangehörigkeitsgesetz (Nationality Act), as well as the Asylbewerberleistungsgesetz (Asylum Seekers' Benefits Act).

[8] Namely: Universal Declaration of Human Rights, 1951 Refugee Convention, International Covenant on Economic, Social and Cultural Rights, International Covenant on Civil and Political Rights, International Convention on the Elimination of All Forms of Racial Discrimination, International Convention for the Protection of All Persons from Enforced Disappearance, International Convention on the Protection of the Rights of All Migrant Workers, UN Convention against Torture, UN Convention on the Elimination of All Forms of Discrimination Against Women, UN Convention on the Rights of the Child, UN Convention on the Rights of Persons with Disabilities, European Convention on Human Rights, European Social Charter, Istanbul Convention, European Convention for the Prevention of Torture, Council of Europe Convention on Action against Trafficking in Human Beings, European Framework Convention for the Protection of National Minorities, European Charter of Regional or Minority Languages.

[9] Burzan, Nicole, Methodenplurale Forschung. Chancen und Probleme von Mixed Methods. Weinheim/ Basel: Beltz Juventa 2016; Dobinson, Ian & Johns, Francis, Qualitative Legal Research, In Mike McConville & Wing Hing Chui (Hrsg.), Research methods for law, (S.18-47). Edinburgh: Edinburgh University Press 2007.

[10] Kuckartz, Udo/ Rädiker, Stefan, Qualitative Inhaltsanalyse, Weinheim/ Basel: Beltz Juventa 2024.

those on NGOs and other experts as this was not the focus of the author's work package in the research project.

First Results on German Legislation

The quantitative analysis of German migration legislation between 1993 and 2023 has shown that a total number of 118 explanatory memoranda (*Gesetzentwürfe*) mentioned human rights. In most cases, either the European Convention on Human Rights (ECHR) or the 1951 Refugee Convention were cited. We noticed an increase in references over time with peaks between 2014 and 2020, a time of considerable legislative activity in the field.

To give an example for such a reference, one may take a closer look at the 2015 explanatory memorandum on the reform of German expulsion law.[11] In the words of the legislator of the time: "Expulsion law is being fundamentally reorganised. ... The modifications that the right of expulsion has undergone as a result of supreme court rulings on the requirements of higher-ranking law, in particular the right to respect for private and family life under Article 8 of the European Convention on Human Rights (ECHR), are taken into account in the context of the interest in remaining in the country."[12]

In fact, with the 2015/16 reform of the German Residence Act (§§53–55 Aufenthaltsgesetz), German expulsion law has been redesigned around Article 8 ECHR, abolishing some rigid categories and requiring an integrated balancing that mirrors Strasbourg's criteria of proportionality. To that effect, immigration authorities and administrative courts now conduct an individualised assessment of family life, social ties, duration of residence, conduct and the gravity of offending, explicitly drawing on *Boultif*[13] and *Üner*[14] factors and the heightened protection for settled juveniles in *Maslov*.[15] In practice, authorities must articulate weighty public-interest reasons, calibrate risk, and consider rehabilitation before expelling long-term residents and parents. Overall, German law now operationalises ECHR standards through codified balancing,

---

[11] Gesetz zur Neubestimmung des Bleiberechts und der Aufenthaltsbeendigung, Bundesgesetzblatt (Federal Law Gazette) I 2015, 1386.

[12] Gesetzentwurf der Bundesregierung, Entwurf eines Gesetzes zur Neubestimmung des Bleiberechts und der Aufenthaltsbeendigung, Bundestags-Drucksache 18/4097, 25.2.2015, https://dserver.bundestag.de/btd/18/040/1804097.pdf, p. 1, 23, translation by Frederik von Harbou.

[13] ECtHR, *Boultif v. Switzerland*, Appl. no. 54273/00, Judgment of 2 August 2001.

[14] ECtHR, *Üner v. the Netherlands*, Appl. no. 46410/99, Grand Chamber Judgment of 18 October 2006.

[15] ECtHR, *Maslov v. Austria*, Appl. no. 1638/03, Grand Chamber Judgment of 23 June 2008. Cf. on those decisions: Bast/v. Harbou/Wessels, REMAP, 2nd. ed., Baden-Baden/Oxford: Nomos/Hart 2022, https://www.nomos-shop.de/en/p/human-rights-challenges-to-european-migration-policy-gr-978-3-8487-8244-4, p. 187.

case-sensitive discretion, and structured judicial review, and evidence-based decision-making across federal practice. This is due to the fact that the German legislator incorporated not only the case law of the European Court of Human Rights on Art. 8 ECHR but often even its wording.

First Results on German Case Law

The quantitative analysis of federal German migration case law of decisions by the Federal Constitutional Court, the Federal Administrative Court, and the Federal Social Court between 1993 and 2023 showed a total number of 658 references to human rights. Here again, citations of the European Convention on Human Rights (438 citations) and the 1951 Refugee Convention (188 citations) were by far the most frequent, but also a considerable number of decisions mentioned the UN Convention on the Rights of the Child (20).

To give an example for such a reference, one may take a closer look at a decision on the German Asylum Seekers Benefits Act (*Asylbewerberleistungsgesetz,* AsylbLG). The AsylbLG was introduced in 1993 as part of Germany's "Asylum Compromise." The law established a separate welfare system for asylum seekers, offering reduced benefits compared to regular social assistance. While initially justified by policymakers as appropriate for supposedly temporary stays, the regime has remained controversial, criticised inter alia for discriminatory treatment.[16]

The Federal Constitutional Court, in 2012, has invoked human rights to safeguard minimum subsistence rights and challenge disproportionate benefit reductions for asylum seekers. While it based its main argument on Constitutional rights, it also assessed the AsylbLG against human rights. In the words of the Court: "Migration-policy considerations to keep benefits for asylum seekers and refugees low in order to avoid incentives for migration, which may be set by relatively high benefits compared to international standards, may generally not justify any reduction of benefits below the physical and sociocultural minimum existence (...). Human dignity, guaranteed in Article 1.1 of the Basic Law, may not be modified in light of migration-policy considerations. ... (T)he legislature is also obliged by further requirements emerging from ... international obligations. These include the International Covenant on Economic, Social and Cultural Rights .... Additionally, the United Nations Convention on the Rights of the Child ... contains the obligation that

---

[16] For details see: Frederik v. Harbou, 30 Jahre Sonderrecht. Das Asylbewerberleistungsgesetz im Spiegel der Menschenrechte, Verfassungsblog v. 1.11.2023, https://verfassungsblog.de/30-jahre-sonderrecht/.

the best interests of the child shall be a primary consideration in all legislation".[17] As a consequence, the Court instructed the legislator to revise the AsylbLG in accordance with fundamental and human rights.

A 2023 pilot study by the author of this paper and a colleague on case law on the impact of human rights law on the making and interpretation of the AsylbLG showed that human rights have sometimes brought about systemic changes (like in the cited example), while more often they were invoked (e.g. by lower instance courts) to serve as a corrective to the general legislative assessment in specific constellations characterised by the particular vulnerability of those affected by an administrative measure, e.g. access to (better) medical assistance based on minority and/or disability.[18]

Conclusions

The first results of the study, presented in this short paper, can provide some information on the transformative effects of human rights for domestic migration law. It seems to have a twofold function. It can bring about systemic change or be invoked to handle cases of hardship, e.g. based on multiple vulnerabilities. Parts of German migration law, for example some provisions of the Asylum Seekers Benefits Act, are (still) in conflict with international human rights standards (e.g. the human right to health, Art. 12 Sec. 1 International Covenant on Economic, Social and Cultural Rights).[19] The findings of the sub-project are in line with the findings of the general MeDiMi project which addresses shortcomings in the comprehensive expansion of human rights but also shows the "potential power" of such arguments for the inclusiveness of migration societies.[20]

---

[17] Federal Constiutional Court (*Bundesverfassungsgericht*), Judgment of 18 July 2012 - 1 BvL 10/10; 1 BvL 2/11.
[18] Cf. with further references: Franke/ von Harbou, Das Asylbewerberleistungsgesetz und die Menschenrechte. Zur Argumentationspraxis aus 30 Jahren Gesetzgebung und Rechtsprechung, Zeitschrift für Ausländerrecht 2023, 433.
[19] Cf. with further references: Franke/ von Harbou, Das Asylbewerberleistungsgesetz und die Menschenrechte. Zur Argumentationspraxis aus 30 Jahren Gesetzgebung und Rechtsprechung, Zeitschrift für Ausländerrecht 2023, 433.
[20] Bast et al., Humanrightization. Theses on a Theory of Discursive Practice in Migration Societies, MeDiMi Working Paper No. 2, www.medimi.de/en/article/237.medimi-working-paper-no-2-2025.html, p. 4.

THE INFLUENCE OF SOCIO-DEMOGRAPHIC FACTORS AND MUNICIPAL POLITICAL CONTEXTS ON FOREIGN VOTERS REGISTRATION FOR THE 2024 LOCAL ELECTIONS IN BRUSSELS

Gabriel Timm

Objectives and Justification

The main goal of this study is to explore how political and socio-demographic characteristics at the municipal level influence the registration behavior of foreign voters, encompassing both EU and non-EU nationals, in the 2024 Brussels municipal elections. Brussels represents a particularly relevant context due to its uniquely multicultural demographic profile—foreign nationals account for more than one-third of the population. As these residents are eligible to vote in municipal elections provided they register, their participation (or lack thereof) becomes a significant indicator of democratic inclusion.

Despite eligibility, foreign registration rates remain significantly lower than those of Belgian citizens, prompting a need for comprehensive investigation. While much of the literature focuses on national-level policies or broad comparative studies, this research aims to uncover micro-level patterns, offering valuable insights into local political integration. Addressing this research gap is essential for both academic inquiry and policy formulation, especially in urban settings like Brussels where governance and demographic complexity intersect. Moreover, given growing concerns over political disenfranchisement and civic disengagement in diverse societies, this study contributes to ongoing debates surrounding integration, inclusion, and democratic legitimacy (Bauböck, 2005; Beckman, 2006).

The decision to conduct the research at the municipal level stems from the recognition that political inclusion is often experienced and mediated locally. Unlike national elections, which tend to be shaped by broader ideological narratives, municipal politics frequently deal with more immediate and tangible concerns, which may influence how inclusive or exclusive the context is perceived by foreign residents. Local authorities also play a pivotal role in implementing outreach strategies and administrative processes for registration, making them a crucial institutional layer for understanding variation in participation rates.

Literature Review

Traditional political participation research underscores the impact of socio-economic resources, individual motivations, and institutional arrangements on voter turnout. Seminal contributions such as the Civic Voluntarism Model (Verba, Schlozman & Brady, 1995) and SES theory (Verba & Nie, 1972) highlight education, income, and occupation as core predictors of engagement. These theories were further expanded to incorporate institutional analyses that focus on the design and accessibility of electoral systems (Powell, 1982; Jackman, 1987).

More recently, scholarship has turned to migrant political behavior, which requires contextualizing classical models within frameworks sensitive to issues of mobility, belonging, and integration. The Political Opportunity Structure (POS) theory, introduced by McAdam, Tarrow, and Tilly (1996), focuses on the institutional openness of political systems and the extent to which political elites and policies are responsive to immigrant communities. POS theory has been particularly instrumental in understanding local variations in immigrant participation, suggesting that inclusive political climates foster greater involvement (Koopmans, 2004).

In parallel, Social Capital theory (Putnam, 1993; Fennema & Tillie, 2001) addresses the importance of trust, networks, and civic community. It argues that embeddedness in community organizations and informal social ties enhances political efficacy. Migrants connected to strong civic communities are more likely to be informed, mobilized, and ultimately registered to vote. The concept also draws attention to the interrelationship between social cohesion and political trust, which may be essential for immigrants to feel confident in the usefulness and fairness of their participation.

Human Capital theory, meanwhile, asserts that immigrants' personal resources—particularly education, language proficiency, and length of stay—affect their ability and likelihood to engage with political systems (Morales & Giugni, 2011; Ramakrishnan, 2005). Integration into host societies through naturalization or prolonged residency fosters familiarity with local institutions and increases political literacy. Human Capital is not only a measure of individual capability but also serves as a proxy for readiness to navigate institutional frameworks such as voter registration systems.

Despite these conceptual advances, empirical applications at the municipal level remain underdeveloped. This study seeks to bridge that gap by aligning each hypothesis with these theoretical contributions, offering a comprehensive account of the political engagement of foreign nationals in Brussels. It adds to a growing body of work that emphasizes cities and municipalities as sites of democratic innovation and contestation, particularly in contexts marked by migration and diversity.

Data and Methods

The analysis relies on cross-sectional data from all 19 municipalities of the Brussels-Capital Region. The dependent variables are the registration rates of foreign residents—categorized by EU and non-EU nationality—eligible to vote in the 2024 municipal elections.

Independent variables include:

- Political orientation of the elected mayor (left or right)
- Naturalization rates
- External migration rates (in/out mobility)
- Proportion of foreign residents
- Mean municipal income
- Proportion of residents aged 65 and above

These data were obtained from official sources: STATBEL (the Belgian national statistics office), local electoral bodies, and municipal government websites. The political orientation of each municipal government was determined based on the most recent electoral results and mayoral affiliations.

To gather qualitative insights into municipal strategies, direct email contact was established with each of the 19 municipalities to inquire about specific outreach efforts related to foreign voter registration. While not all municipalities responded, those that did provided valuable contextual information that supported the interpretation of the quantitative data. These responses are archived in the annex.

Given the relatively small sample size and the nature of the variables, Spearman's rank correlation was chosen to detect associations between variables. This method is robust in handling non-normally distributed data. Additionally, to reduce bias from outliers, a refined analysis excluded Saint-Josse-ten-Noode, whose extremely high foreign registration rates were deemed atypical and distortive. The use of both filtered and unfiltered datasets allows for a clearer identification of underlying relationships.

Results and Discussion

Initial results without controlling for outliers indicated several inconclusive or weak correlations. Once Saint-Josse-ten-Noode was excluded, a clearer pattern emerged. Municipalities governed by left-wing mayors tended to have higher registration rates among both EU and non-EU foreign nationals. This aligns with the POS theory's expectation that inclusive political leadership can foster migrant participation. Conversely, municipalities led by right-wing mayors or with a high share of anti-immigrant vote demonstrated lower foreign registration rates, likely due to more exclusionary political messaging and perceived hostility. These findings underscore how political leadership can shape the local climate of inclusion, not just through policy decisions but also through symbolic signals that either encourage or dissuade participation.

Naturalization rates showed a strong positive correlation with registration. This supports the notion from Human Capital theory that formal integration processes enhance civic engagement. In addition, higher proportions of foreign residents also correlated positively with registration, suggesting a "critical mass" effect where social embeddedness and peer influence encourage participation— an idea central to Social Capital theory. In municipalities with dense foreign populations, community networks appear to play a mobilizing role, offering not only information but also social validation for participating in the democratic process.

Socio-economic indicators further supported the theoretical framework. Municipalities with higher average income levels exhibited higher foreign registration rates, in line with SES theory. Similarly, municipalities with a higher proportion of elderly residents tended to have better registration figures, likely reflecting a culture of civic duty and more robust administrative systems that facilitate outreach. Older populations may also demand more transparency and efficiency in municipal governance, indirectly enhancing registration mechanisms available to all residents.

Interestingly, external migration rates were negatively associated with registration. High population turnover appears to weaken the social and institutional embeddedness necessary for political engagement, reinforcing the idea that stability fosters participation. Migrants who frequently move may not build the necessary familiarity or trust in local political institutions, thereby missing opportunities to register.

These patterns suggest that foreign voter registration is a multifaceted phenomenon shaped by structural, institutional, and symbolic elements. Local government actions—ranging from hosting multilingual voter drives to simplifying registration processes—can either mitigate or exacerbate underlying inequalities in civic engagement. Municipalities that invest in inclusion tend to create a virtuous cycle, where increased participation leads to better representation and further incentives for engagement.

Conclusion

This study demonstrates that the electoral engagement of foreign nationals in Brussels is shaped by a combination of political, institutional, and demographic factors. By leveraging a comparative municipal analysis, it reveals significant variation in registration rates that cannot be attributed solely to national laws or eligibility criteria.

Political Opportunity Structures, as manifested through mayoral leadership and policy orientations, emerge as critical determinants of participation. Municipalities that signal openness and actively facilitate inclusion through integration policies, outreach, and institutional accessibility create more favorable conditions for foreign voter registration. Simultaneously, human capital and socio-economic variables—such as naturalization rates, income, and age demographics—serve as important facilitators of civic engagement.

The research faced challenges, particularly regarding access to consistent and detailed data on voter registration by nationality. Additionally, attempts to gather complementary information from municipal administrations and federal electoral bodies were often inconclusive or marked by bureaucratic redirection. These obstacles underscore the importance of transparent, standardized electoral data for future research. Moreover, the lack of centralized information systems hampers scholars and policymakers alike from making informed decisions.

In retrospect, the research also grappled with the difficulty of choosing a methodologically sound yet socially impactful approach. While the statistical analysis provided valuable insights, the study would benefit from qualitative complementarity—such as interviews or content analysis of municipal communications—to better understand the motivations and barriers experienced by foreign residents. A more ethnographic or participatory approach could illuminate how individuals perceive their political inclusion and what practical challenges they encounter when trying to register.

Future research could replicate this study in other Belgian or European metropolitan areas or pursue longitudinal analysis across election cycles to capture trends over time. In addition, more detailed investigation into digital registration tools, language accessibility, and voter education campaigns could illuminate practical levers for improving democratic inclusion. Comparative studies between cities with differing integration policies could also yield valuable insights into best practices.

By centering municipal-level variation, this research contributes to a more granular understanding of political participation in multicultural societies and reaffirms the essential role of local governance in the democratic integration of foreign residents. The study not only advances scholarly discourse but also offers actionable insights for city officials, civil society organizations, and electoral commissions aiming to foster greater civic inclusion among Brussels' diverse and growing population.

References

Bauböck, R. (2005). Expansive citizenship: Voting beyond territory and membership. *PS: Political Science & Politics*, 38(4), 683–687. https://doi.org/10.1017/S1049096505050358

Beckman, L. (2006). *The frontiers of democracy: The right to vote and its limits*. Palgrave Macmillan.

Fennema, M., & Tillie, J. (2001). Civic community, political participation and political trust of ethnic groups. *Connections*, 24(1), 26–41.

Fennema, M., & Tillie, J. (2004). Do immigrant policies matter? Ethnic civic communities and immigrant policies in Amsterdam, Liege and Zurich. In M. Bodemann & G. Yurdakul (Eds.), *Migration, citizenship, ethnos* (pp. 85–105). Palgrave Macmillan.

Goerres, A. (2007). Why are older people more likely to vote? The impact of ageing on electoral turnout in Europe. *The British Journal of Politics and International Relations*, 9(1), 90–121. https://doi.org/10.1111/j.1467-856X.2007.00282.x

Jacobs, D., Martiniello, M., Rea, A., & Teney, C. (2009). Electoral participation of non-national EU citizens in 27 EU Member States. *CEPS Special Report*. https://www.ceps.eu/ceps-publications/electoral-participation-non-national-eu-citizens-27-eu-member-states/

Koopmans, R. (2004). Migrant mobilisation and political opportunities: Variation among German cities and a comparison with the United Kingdom and the Netherlands. *Journal of Ethnic and Migration Studies*, 30(3), 449–469. https://doi.org/10.1080/13691830410001682034

McAdam, D., Tarrow, S., & Tilly, C. (1996). *Comparative perspectives on social movements: Political opportunities, mobilizing structures, and cultural framings*. Cambridge University Press.

Morales, L., & Giugni, M. (Eds.). (2011). *Social capital, political participation and migration in Europe: Making multicultural democracy work?* Palgrave Macmillan.

Norris, P. (2002). *Democratic phoenix: Reinventing political activism*. Cambridge University Press.

Putnam, R. D. (1993). *Making democracy work: Civic traditions in modern Italy*. Princeton University Press.

Ramakrishnan, S. K. (2005). *Democracy in immigrant America: Changing demographics and political participation*. Stanford University Press.

Verba, S., Schlozman, K. L., & Brady, H. E. (1995). *Voice and equality: Civic voluntarism in American politics*. Harvard University Press.

THE CONSTITUTIONAL COURT'S RECENT JURISPRUDENCE AND THE DEPORTATION OF SYRIANS IN THE AFTERMATH OF REGIME CHANGE IN SYRIA

Hande Bingöl[1]

The Legal Framework of the Temporary Protection Regime in Türkiye

Although Turkey's practice of international protection has a long historical background, the first comprehensive legislative framework at the statutory level was introduced with the Law No. 6458 on Foreigners and International Protection. Entering into force in 2013, this legislation established both the international protection regime—comprising refugee, conditional refugee, and subsidiary protection statuses—and, separately, a temporary protection regime (Ergin and Kader, 2024: 89).

The rationale for introducing a temporary protection framework, distinct from international protection, was to provide protection for foreigners arriving in Turkey through mass influxes. As is well known, the statuses of refugee, conditional refugee, and subsidiary protection are granted exclusively on the basis of individualized assessment. However, given that Syrians arrived in Turkey in the form of a mass influx, individualized status determinations could not be conducted, the administrative capacity proved insufficient, and temporary protection status was conferred upon them (Ekşi, 2018: 151).

In essence, the protection needed by individuals fleeing their countries in situations of mass influx is indeed international protection. Yet, due to the state's limited capacity to conduct individual status determination procedures, such persons are collectively placed under temporary protection. As of 29 May 2025, according to the data of the Directorate General of Migration Management, there are over 2,700,000 Syrians under temporary protection status in Turkey.

It should be emphasized that the fact that these individuals are placed under temporary protection does not diminish the obligations of states with respect to

[1] Research Assistant in Private International Law Department, İstanbul University Faculty of Law, Türkiye.

the protection to be afforded to them, nor does it constitute an exception to the principle of non-refoulement (Ergin and Kader, 2024: 96).

The Legal Framework Governing the Deportation of Syrians under Temporary Protection

The principle of non-refoulement has been enshrined in both international instruments and Turkish law as an absolute guarantee applicable to all foreigners. It is codified in the European Convention on Human Rights under the prohibition of torture and inhuman or degrading treatment. Accordingly, individuals may not be returned to territories where they would face persecution, torture, inhuman, or degrading treatment or punishment (Ergin, 2024: 69).

In Turkish law, the principle of non-refoulement is explicitly articulated in Article 4 of the Law No. 6458 as applicable to all foreigners. Furthermore, the Temporary Protection Regulation stipulates that every individual within its scope benefits from this guarantee. Even in the event that temporary protection comes to an end, those concerned remain within the ambit of the non-refoulement principle.

This raises the question: Can holders of temporary protection status be deported? The legislation does not provide a clear provision on this point. Law No. 6458 allows for the deportation of international protection status holders only in three narrowly defined circumstances. The unsettled issue is whether these same grounds may also be applied to deport individuals under temporary protection (Çelikel and Gelgel, 2024: 127).

A seminal decision on this matter is the Constitutional Court's judgment of 11 November 2015 in *"K.A."*. In that case, the applicant, a Syrian national, was subject to a deportation order on the ground that he posed a threat to public order and public security. The applicant lodged an individual application before the Constitutional Court, claiming that deportation to Syria would expose him to the risk of being killed, tortured, or otherwise ill-treated, thereby violating his right to life. Of particular importance for our purposes, the Court asserted in its reasoning that holders of temporary protection status could not be deported. However, an examination of the legislation reveals no such explicit rule (Aydoğmuş, 2017: 243).

In more recent judgments, the Constitutional Court appears to have adopted a more accurate and nuanced approach to the deportation of Syrians. For instance, in its 2023 decision in *"Hüsam İbrahim"*, the Court assessed whether the deportation of the Syrian applicant, against whom a deportation order had been issued, would violate his right to life. The Court grounded its analysis squarely on the principle of non-refoulement, holding that the applicant's claims regarding the risk of ill-treatment upon return had to be duly examined by the administration. The Court found that the administration had disregarded the real risk posed by deportation to Syria, and in reaching this conclusion, it referred to the prevailing security conditions in the country of origin, as well as to judgments of the European Court of Human Rights and reports of international organizations.

Does the Current Situation in Syria Permit Conditions for Safe Return?

Since the fall of the Assad regime on 8 December 2024, hopes of return have been rekindled among Syrians. After fourteen years of civil war, many Syrians have once again begun to contemplate the possibility of returning to their homes. Yet, the overthrow of the regime does not in itself render Syria a safe country of return. Indeed, in its statement released immediately thereafter, the United Nations acknowledged that although the risks emanating from the Assad regime had ceased, other dangers persisted and the overall situation in Syria remained unstable. The UN further called upon all states to continue to afford protection to Syrians within their territories and to abide scrupulously by the principle of non-refoulement.

Turning to developments in Turkey since 8 December 2024, the Directorate General of Migration Management granted, between 1 January and 1 July 2025, "go and see visits" to temporary protection beneficiaries in order to support voluntary returns and facilitate planning thereof. Under this arrangement, beneficiaries were permitted to travel to Syria and back up to three times within a six-month period.

According to the May 2025 report of the United Nations High Commissioner for Refugees (UNHCR), interviews conducted in Gaziantep and Konya with individuals who had made use of these visits revealed that they found the arrangement beneficial, yet they also reported acute psychological distress upon witnessing the scale of destruction in Syria. Moreover, many expressed a profound sense of estrangement arising from the vast social and cultural transformations in their homeland. Only a small minority indicated any willingness to return permanently, and only on the condition that living conditions improved substantially. Similarly, interviews conducted in Hatay revealed a desire among Syrians to return, yet also underscored major obstacles such as insecurity, inadequate infrastructure, and uncertainty surrounding the provision of basic necessities such as water, food, and sanitation. Particularly noteworthy were the views expressed by Syrian women: they stated that in Turkey they were better able to resist early marriage and domestic violence, which made them feel more empowered. They stressed that safeguarding women's rights and security in Syria would be indispensable for enabling a safe return.

As of 15 May 2025, UNHCR reported that more than 200,000 Syrians had voluntarily returned. The question nonetheless remains: is Syria truly suitable for return? Reports of international organizations indicate that the country still lacks sufficient resources to sustain large-scale returns.

First, Syria remains unable to meet basic needs such as food, shelter, healthcare, electricity, and water. Thirteen years of war have left most urban centers in ruins, with hospitals, schools, and power grids devastated. Moreover, despite the fall of the Assad regime, sanctions initially imposed during its rule have continued to impede reconstruction efforts. A positive development in this respect was the announcement on 13 May by former U.S. President Donald Trump that all sanctions on Syria had been lifted.

Another grave concern lies in ongoing, indiscriminate acts of violence. Although Syria's transitional leadership pledged to end hostilities, violence—particularly against specific groups such as Alawites in coastal cities—has persisted. Clashes also continue between the new administration's security forces and remnants of the deposed regime's armed elements.

The issue of property and cadastral records constitutes yet another major barrier to safe return. The destruction of land and property registries during the civil war has gravely undermined ownership rights. Restoring and protecting such rights in the post-war period poses a formidable challenge, particularly for displaced persons who may be unable to assert their claims in the absence of official documentation.

A further threat is posed by landmines and unexploded ordnance left behind after fourteen years of conflict, which continue to endanger lives across residential areas and agricultural lands. According to the International NGO Safety Organization, since 8 December 2024 such remnants have claimed more than 250 lives and injured many more.

Humanitarian aid delivery also remains fraught with obstacles. Under the Assad regime, aid was tightly controlled, subject to government approval, and often obstructed. Although the regime has fallen, independent international humanitarian organizations still face significant bureaucratic impediments and difficulties in cooperating with local authorities.

It is thus evident that the conditions prevailing in Syria since 8 December 2024 do not yet provide a safe environment for the return and sustainable reintegration of Syrians. This conclusion has also been reflected in the most recent jurisprudence of the Constitutional Court concerning the deportation of temporary protection beneficiaries. In its judgment of 15 January 2025, concerning a Syrian national who was deported on the grounds of having worked without a permit, the administrative authorities had issued a deportation order without specifying the destination country or identifying a safe third country. The Court held that any deportation order must specify the country of return and must be preceded by a detailed assessment of the risks involved. Furthermore, the Court underlined that there was no basis for departing from its earlier jurisprudence on the inadmissibility of deportation to Syria. Accordingly, the Constitutional Court confirmed that the deportation of Syrians to their country of origin is not a viable legal possibility under present conditions.

References

Aydoğmuş, A. Y. (2017). Türk Hukukunda Geçici Korumadan Yararlananların Sınır Dışı Edilmesi, MHB, Y. 37, S.2, 223- 255.

Çelikel, A& Gelgel, G. (2024). Yabancılar Hukuku, İstanbul: Beta.

Ekşi, N. (2018). Yabancılar ve Uluslararası Koruma Hukuku, İstanbul: Beta.

Ergin, A.D. (2024). İlticaya Erişim Hakkı: 6458 Sayılı Yabancılar ve Uluslararası Koruma Kanunu Bakımından Bir Değerlendirme. In: Ergin, A.D.& Kader, Y. (eds.) *6458 Sayılı Yabancılar ve Uluslararası Koruma Kanunu'nun 10. Yılında Türkiye'de Uluslararası Koruma ve Göç*, İstanbul: Oniki Levha, 57- 95.

Ergin, A.D& Kader, Y. (2024). Uluslararas Koruma ve Geçici Koruma Rejiminde Geçicilik Unsuru: "Geçici" Olan Nedir?, İnsan Hakları Yıllığı, C.42, S.2, 79-122.

ECONOMICS, WORK AND MIGRATION

EXPLORING THE TREND AND PROCESS OF INDIAN LABOUR MIGRATION TO GULF COUNTRIES: A CASE STUDY OF MURSHIDABAD DISTRICT

Abbasuddin Sk[1] and Subrata Purkayastha[2]

Introduction

Labour migration is defined by the International Organization of Migration (IOM, 2008) as the movement of individuals from one state to another for work-related reasons. At present about 167 million labour work in a country other than their country of birth. (ILO, 2024). India is one of the leading countries in the world that produces labour migrants. (Parida& Raman, 2018; Mallick, 2022) The GCC nations emerge as an important destination for the unskilled and semi-skilled migrants from India (Chanda, 2012; Oommen, 2016). The discovery of Oil reserve in the GCC countries and its commercial exploitation have fueled economic expansion and fast urbanisation (Ramadan, 2015; Elessawy, 2021), this has increased demand for cheap adaptable labour from India leading to migration of semi-skilled and unskilled labourers from economically disadvantaged backgrounds to GCC countries (Varghees, 2023; Naz, 2024). Recent studies suggest the exploitation of migrant labour in GCC countries on issues of labour rights, working conditions, and the lack of social security protections (Afsar, 2009; Naithan&Jha, 2009; Ahmad & Khan, 2011; Oommen, 2016). Apart from this, labourers often face cultural and language barriers, making it difficult to integrate into Gulf society. Gulf economies' recent shift, economic crises, and job competition have sparked significant return migration to India, with mixed results for individuals, where some have gained, others have failed to earn and are often labelled as "Gulf victims" in their respective villages (Sahoo&Goud, 2013; Rahman & Yong, 2015). In this context, this paper analyses the trend and process of labour migration from Murshidabad to GCC countries.

---

[1] Abbasuddin Sk, Research scholar, Dept of Geography, North-Eastern Hill University, Shillong, Meghalaya,793022, India. E-mail: abbasgeography@gmail.com
[2] Dr. Subrata Purkayastha, Associate Professor, Dept of Geography, North-Eastern Hill University, Shillong, Meghalaya,793022, India. E-mail Id:spurkayastha@nehu.in

Database and Methodology

Government data from the Ministry of External Affairs has been assessed from 2008 onwards to suggest the volume and trend of migration from Murshidabad district to GCC countries. A non-probability purposive sampling technique was used to generate primary data through interviews with key informants. Focus Group Discussion (FGD) were conducted with village elders and migrants currently living in the three selected villages, viz Salua, Tentulia, and Rahigram, sending maximum migrants to GCC. Six migrants were selected as Key Informants to relate their experience on the migration process and hurdles faced. Three village elders representing their respective villages were also selected as key informants. The paper is based on interviews with ten case studies. Information on the motivating factors leading to such migration, the role of money lenders, obstacles faced in the host countries, and the socio-economic status of the migrants upon returning home has been gathered. An agent provided information on the recruitment process, procurement of passports, visas, tickets, and jobs in the host country, for a stipulated fee.

Each transcript has been carefully examined to find commonalities and differences in the migration process. Simple statistical techniques have been used to present the volume of migration. For the trend in the volume of labour emigration to GCC countries, the *Least Squares Method of Karl Pearson* has been used. The formula for the Trend line is Yc=a+bx. (Young, 2007)

Results and Discussion

1. Trend in Labour Migration

Murshidabad district is experiencing a significant number of migrant workers moving to Gulf countries. The trend of migration since the year 2008 indicates a gradual positive growth in the initial period, followed by a sharp decline during the COVID-19 pandemic, and then a surge from 2022 to 2024. (figure1) The least square method indicates an upward trend in recent years, with Saudi Arabia emerging as the preferred destination and Bahrain as the least preferred destination (Table 1)

Table 1: The year-wise volume of emigration from Murshidabad district to GCC countries (2008 to 2024)

Year	GCC Countries (Number of migrants, with percentage in parentheses)						Total	Growth Rate in %
	Saudi Arabia	Kuwait	United Arab Emirates	Bahrain	Oman	Qatar		
2008	1055	21	301	2	258	150	1787	-
	(59.04)	(1.17)	(16.84)	(0.11)	(14.43)	(8.39)	(100)	
2009	1591	50	77	2	160	90	1970	10.24
	(80.76)	(2.54)	(3.90)	(0.10)	(8.12)	(4.57)	(100)	
2010	2045	48	67	2	100	41	2303	16.90
	(88.80)	(2.40)	(2.90)	(0.09)	(4.34)	(1.78)	(100)	
2011	3082	52	97	3	108	43	3385	46.98
	(91.04)	(1.54)	(2.87)	(0.08)	(3,19)	(1.27)	(100)	
2012	3510	77	68	9	71	87	3822	12.90
	(91.84)	(1.99)	(1.78)	(0.23)	(1.86)	(2.28)	(100)	
2013	1216	116	47	2	3	59	1443	-62.24
	(84.27)	(8.04)	(3.26)	(0.14)	(0.21)	(4.09)	(100)	
2014	2983	328	155	2	31	81	3580	148.10
	(83.32)	(9.16)	(4.33)	(0.06)	(0.87)	(2.26)	(100)	
2015	17900	728	573	18	191	227	19637	488.51
	(91.39)	(3.71)	(2.92)	(0.09)	(0.97)	(1.16)	(100)	
2016	17304	833	459	27	134	177	18934	-3.57
	(91.39)	(4.40)	(2.42)	(0.14)	(0.710)	(0.93)	(100)	
2017	6202	717	426	38	240	106	7729	-59.18
	(80.24)	(9.28)	(5.51)	(0.49)	(3.10)	(1.370)	(100)	
2018	3914	953	377	63	176	236	5719	-26.00
	(68.43)	(16.66)	(6.59)	(1.01)	(3.08)	(4.13)	(100)	
2019	1606	265	102	17	43	33	2066	--63.87
	(77.73)	(12.83)	(4.94)	(0.82)	(2.08)	(1.60)	(100)	
2020	1889	149	101	47	22	34	2242	07.85
	(84.26)	(6.65)	(4.50)	(2.10)	(0.98)	(1.52)	(100)	
2021	1658	207	46	59	150	263	2383	06.29
	(69.58)	(8.69)	(1.93)	(2.47)	(6.29)	(11.03)	(100)	
2022	8241	1058	99	73	324	165	9960	317.96
	(82.74)	(10.62)	(0.99)	(0.73)	(3.25)	(1.66)	(100)	
2023	6242	825	482	83	276	411	8319	-16.47
	(75.03)	(9.92)	(5.79)	(0.10)	(3.32)	(4.94)	(100)	
2024	4070	566	885	83	234	258	6096	-26.72
	(66.76)	(9.28)	(14.52)	(1.36)	(3.84)	(4.23)	(100)	
Total	84508	6993	4362	530	2521	2461	101375	---
	(83.36)	(6.90)	(4.30)	(0.52)	(2.49)	(2.42)	(100)	

Source: *Ministry of External Affairs, Govt. of India*

Figure 2 Emigration rate from Murshidabad District to GCC Countries:2008-2024

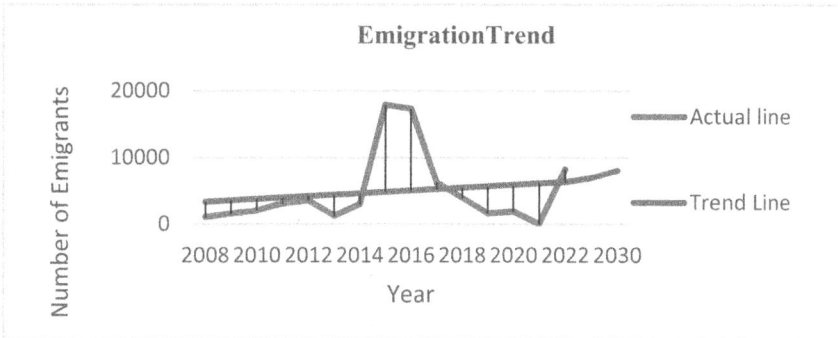

The Process of Labour Migration

From the case studies, the process of migration has been discussed in distinct phases.

Phase I: Decision making and Motivation:

The process are influenced by push factors such as low wages, lack of employment opportunities in Murshidabad as it is one of the poorest district, located in the flood plains of Ganga, prone to floods creating havoc leading to life, property and land loss hence the marginalized rural population here often migrate to the larger urban centers of India as well as the GCC countries in search of better wages and employment opportunities. It is interesting to note that the family members, relatives, and friends usually act as the catalyst who encourage migration to the GCC countries as wages are higher there. From FGD it is observed that the family members sometimes pressurize the would-be migrants to move to GCC countries by citing examples of gulf returnees who have improved their life condition in their respective villages on returning back, having gained in financial and social assets.

Phase-II: Migration process

There are two processes for migrating - the first process involves family members or friends living in the host country, helping in the immigration process and also finding employment in the host country. The second process is through Brokers and Local agents. The agencies from GCC take in contractual labour force for which they send their requirement to the brokers stationed in Mumbai. The Mumbai office then contacts the local agents stationed at Murshidabad, the agents recruit the labour force for a substantial fee collected from the migrants usually on an installment-basis, but the migrant has to pay the entire amount of the fee before he leaves for the host country. One of the key informants disclosed the process. The agent arranges the entire travel, including passport, visa, medical clearance, the job in the host country, the contract on the nature, and duration of the job, including daily wages, accommodation in the host country. The migrants often borrow money to pay these agents from the local Money lenders, friends and family members usually at exorbitant interest rate for which they often mortgage their land and other valuables. Once the migrants reach the GCC countries, they sometimes face challenges due to a lack of proper written contract and rules, lack of knowledge on the actual amount of wages to be provided by the private recruiting agency stationed in the host countries. Field observation suggests that the agents often dupe the migrants as the migrants lack in education and exposure to the complex nature of migration and the prevailing *Kafala system* operating in GCC countries. The migrants face various challenges and find adverse conditions in the host country, which becomes difficult for some to adapt. They prefer to return back but are unable to do so as their passports are taken away by the respective *Kafeel* (sponsor).

Phase III: Migration and stay in the host country

The *Kafeel* takes the passport and visa of the migrant to create a proper identification document, known as the *Iqama*. The *Iqama* is generated after 15 to 20 days. Most migrants highlight the positive aspects of living in the GCC. However, in some cases, migrants have experienced unsatisfactory living conditions and problems in regard to food and accommodation. In some cases, the *Kafeel* does not return the passport in time. One such key informant related his experience of migrating to Saudi Arabia due to the devastating flood in the year 2000 as his land and home were washed away by the fury of flood waters and he decided to migrate in order to support his family back home, The migrant contacted an agent and took loan from the local money lender at a high rate of interest in order to meet the financial requirement in the migration process. On arrival in Saudi Arabia, his condition became worse. He was denied adequate food and accommodation, and for four years, the *kafeel* prevented him from communicating with his family members, neither paid him the promised wage as per the contract. It is interesting to note that our field findings can be substantiated by a National English newspaper, Sabrang India (16th February 2018), reporting the torture, denial of proper food and threats to nine Bengali-speaking Indian migrants in Saudi Arabia. Similarly, a Local Bengali newspaper, Aajkaal (18th November 2023), reported that a migrant from Murshidabad went missing in Saudi Arabia. News18 Bengali (Media- 28th July 2023) reported that a migrant has been jailed in Saudi Arabia. 4th Feb 2024, News18 Bangla reported the death of a migrant from Murshidabad in Saudi Arabia. Field data suggest that only one key informant reported adverse conditions in the host country.

Phase IV – Return migration

As migration to GCC is contractual in nature without any family members, return migration is a must for all migrants. The determinants for return migration also include visa issues, low wages, harsh working conditions, health issues, job loss, and scams by both Indian agencies and the Kafeel. Field data suggests that return migration is usually without much challenges but a few of the migrants reports that the process of returning migration is also challenging as sometimes the Kafeel falsely implicates the migrants and reports to police resulting to deportation called *Kuruch*(Exit) In some other cases, migrants wishing to return home escape from their Kafeel by bribing the informal channels who ultimately report to police. The other determinants for return migration are- expiry of the contract, visa, unsatisfactory job conditions, including low wages.

Conclusion

The volume of migration from Murshidabad has been increasing over the years. It must be mentioned here that Murshidabad, located in the fertile lower Ganga plains of India, is teeming with millions of people whose main stay in life is traditional agriculture. With climate change, this region gets impacted by frequent hazardous floods, leading to land and property loss; hence, a large army of unskilled and semiskilled labour force moves out in search of better livelihood opportunities. Field investigation suggest that some of these migrants often fall prey to the *Kafala System* which marginalizes them further as migration to GCC involves huge expenditure which is often borrowed from the local money lenders and if these migrants cannot adapt to the conditions in their host countries or are duped by the agents they come back without much earning, falling prey to the vicious cycle of poverty, while some migrants report a success story as they can remit cash and kind back home or bring back enough cash thereby improving their socio-economic condition and status in this rural setup.

References

Afsar, R. (2009). Unraveling the vicious cycle of recruitment: Labour migration from Bangladesh to the Gulf States (Working Paper). Geneva: International Labour Organisation

Ahmad, I., & Khan, B. A. (2011). Indian migrants in Gulf states: Issues and problems. *The Indian Journal of Political Science*, 1143-1164.

Anjum, F. (2017). Indian diaspora in GCC countries. *International Journal of Research Culture Society*, *1*(10), 82-88.

Chanda, R. (2012). Migration between South and Southeast Asia: Overview of trends and issues.

Elessawy, F. M. (2021). The abnormal population growth and urban sprawl of an Arabian Gulf City: the case of Abu Dhabi City. *Open Journal of Social Sciences*, *9*(02), 245.

IOM(2008). Retrieved on 27th February, 2025, from https://www.iom.int/resources/info-sheet-labour-migration

Kohli, N. (2014). Indian migrants in the gulf countries. *Developments in the Gulf Region*, 115-147.

Mallick, F. (2022). Recent Trends of International Migration from India. *International journal of humanities, engineering, science and management*, *3*(01).

Naithani, D. P., & Jha, A. (2009). Challenges faced by expatriate workers in the Gulf Cooperation Council countries. *Naithani, P. and Jha, AN (2010). Challenges faced by expatriate workers in the GCC countries. International Journal of Business and Management*, *5*(1), 98-104.

Naz, S. (2024). Navigating Lives: The Impact of Men's Gulf Migration on "Left-Behind" Women in India's Changing Landscape,*UJ Press University of Johannesburg,85-107*

Oommen, G. Z. (2016). South Asia-Gulf migratory corridor: Emerging patterns, prospects and challenges. *Migration and Development, 5*(3), 394-412.

Oommen, G. Z. (2016). South Asia-Gulf migratory corridor: Emerging patterns, prospects and challenges. *Migration and Development, 5*(3), 394-412.

Parida, J. K., & Raman, K. R. (2018). India: Rising trends of international and internal migration. In *Handbook of migration and globalisation* (pp. 226-246). Edward Elgar Publishing.

Rahman, M. M., & Yong, T. T. (2015). International migration and development in South Asia: An introduction. In *International migration and development in South Asia* (pp. 1-21). Routledge.

Rajan, S.I. (2018). Demography of the Gulf Region. In: Chowdhury, M., IrudayaRajan, S. (eds) South Asian Migration in the Gulf. Palgrave Macmillan, Cham. https://doi.org/10.1007/978-3-319-71821-7_3

Ramadan, E. (2015). Sustainable urbanization in the Arabian Gulf region: Problems and challenges. *Arts and Social Sciences Journal, 6*(2), 1-4.

Sahoo, A. K., & Goud, T. C. (2013). Migration, Return and Coping Patterns: A Study of Gulf Returnees in Andhra Pradesh, India. *IMDS Working Paper Series*, 17.

Varghese, V. J. (2023). Labour migration to the Gulf and India's emigration governance: Expanding bounds of protection. *Millennial Asia*, 09763996231177584.

World Migration Report. (2024). IOM, Geneva. Retrieved on 23th July 2025.

Young, P. V. (2007). *Scientific social surveys and research* (Fourth). Prentice Hall of India, New Delhi, 341-345

THE IMPACT OF INTERNATIONAL MIGRATION ON THE DEMOGRAPHY AND ECONOMY OF MOROCCO

Zaynab Benabdallah[1] and Djamila Chekrouni[2]

Introduction

International migration has emerged as one of the defining phenomena of the 21st century, both in terms of its scale and its multidimensional repercussions. It is reshaping demographic, economic, and social balances in both countries of origin and destination. In 2019, approximately 281 million people were living outside their country of origin, representing 3.6% of the global population (United Nations, 2020). These flows are driven by economic disparities, conflicts, climate change, and the pursuit of better living conditions.

In this rapidly evolving context, Morocco presents a particularly relevant case study. Located at the crossroads of migration routes between sub-Saharan Africa and Europe, the country displays a hybrid profile: it is both a country of significant emigration especially of young graduates and a transit zone, or even a destination, for migrants coming from sub-Saharan Africa. This dual role produces contrasting effects on Moroccan society, profoundly altering its demographic structure and economic balances, while also creating new political and social challenges.

This leads to a central question: How has international migration influenced Morocco's demographic and economic dynamics in recent years, and what are the implications for national public policy?

Theoretical and Empirical Literature Review

International migration is a complex phenomenon with diverse impacts, simultaneously affecting both origin and destination countries in demographic, economic, and social dimensions. In host countries such as France, Germany,

[1] Doctor of Economics, FSJES-AGDAL, UM5-RABAT benabdallah.zaynab@hotmail.com, https://orcid.org/0000-0002-4907-2131

[2] Professor of Economics, FSJES-AGDAL, UM5-RABAT d.chekrouni@gmail.com, https://orcid.org/0000-0001-8158-2986

or the United Kingdom, migrants—generally young and of working age help offset demographic aging by renewing the labor force and supporting social systems, including pensions and public health (Willekens et al., 2017; Espenshade, 2001). This demographic dynamism is essential for maintaining the balance of aging societies.

Conversely, origin countries, particularly in Sub-Saharan Africa and Eastern Europe, experience the negative effects of migration, notably the exodus of young workers and graduates, which accelerates the aging of the active population and weakens social and economic structures (OECD, 2019). This "brain drain" constitutes a significant barrier to sustainable development, especially impacting vital sectors such as health and education (Docquier and Rapoport, 2009).

Economically, the arrival of low-skilled migrants in host countries can create labor market tensions, with risks of wage suppression and increased competition for low-skilled jobs (Borjas, 2003). However, highly skilled migrants play a key role in innovation and economic growth, particularly in strategic sectors like technology, health, and sciences (Dustmann and Frattini, 2014).

Moreover, remittances sent by migrants to their countries of origin represent an important source of income for households and can contribute to financing essential public services. However, this dependence exposes these countries to economic vulnerabilities in the face of external shocks (Ratha, 2003). Additionally, migration accelerates urbanization processes, posing challenges in infrastructure and urban planning, especially in developing countries where lack of appropriate policies can degrade living conditions (UN-Habitat, 2020; Henderson and Kriticos, 2018).

Empirical studies highlight a progressive convergence of migrants' demographic and social behaviors with those of local populations, notably regarding fertility and cultural integration, reflecting a process of adaptation to the host country's norms (Adserà and Ferrer, 2014). For example, in Europe, although migrants initially exhibit higher fertility rates, these tend to align with those of native populations over successive generations (Adserà and Ferrer, 2023).

Economically, immigration generally contributes to overall employment growth and strengthens the competitiveness of host economies (Dustmann et al., 2024). In the United States, migrants' impact on innovation is particularly significant, with about a quarter of patents filed between 2010 and 2020 involving at least one foreign-born inventor (Kerr and Kerr, 2023).

Finally, in origin countries, despite the loss of young active workers representing a depletion of human capital, diaspora remittances play a crucial role in supporting public budgets, as illustrated by the Philippines, where these transfers finance nearly 12% of national health and education expenditures (Hugo et al., 2022). Migration also promotes political reforms aimed at mobilizing the diaspora and mitigating the negative effects of brain drain.

Migration management thus requires significant institutional adjustments, notably in housing, health, education, and language integration, to foster migrants' social inclusion and optimize their demographic and economic contributions (OECD, 2024). These multidimensional dynamics call for integrated public policies that address the specific challenges faced by both origin and host countries.

Stylized facts

Migration is a historical and structural marker of Morocco's socio-economic development. Initially a country of emigration to Europe, the Kingdom has, over the past two decades, also become a transit country and increasingly a destination for thousands of sub-Saharan African migrants, particularly following the tightening of European border controls.

In the early 2000s, sub-Saharan migrants in Morocco were seen as "temporary." Today, however, a growing number are settling permanently, contributing to urban diversity but also increasing pressure on social services, the informal job market, and housing especially in northern regions and around Casablanca.

At the same time, Moroccan emigration continues at a steady pace, particularly among young graduates. This trend is fueling a concerning brain drain, weakening key sectors such as healthcare, engineering, and education. More than 5 million Moroccans currently live abroad mainly in Europe and send home nearly $8.5 billion annually, representing around 7 to 8% of the country's GDP. These remittances provide crucial support for households especially the elderly but their potential to finance productive initiatives (entrepreneurship, training, local projects) remains underexploited.

In 2024, Morocco also faces several structural challenges: an aging population (with the fertility rate falling to 2.3 children per woman), persistent unemployment (especially among youth and women), and rapid urbanization (64% of the population now lives in urban areas). These transformations demand more regionally balanced policies, labor market reforms, and better utilization of human capital including talent from the diaspora.

Data and Methodology

The primary objective of this study is to examine the impact of net migration on Morocco's demographic and economic dynamics. To do so, we utilize key demographic indicators such as fertility rate, birth rate, death rate, age group distribution, and total population to analyze the effect of migration on the demographic structure.

On the economic side, the study focuses on key variables including GDP per capita, unemployment rate, and urbanization rate, thus allowing for an assessment of the economic consequences of migration.

The models are estimated using the Ordinary Least Squares (OLS) method, with rigorous statistical tests, notably Student's t-tests, to verify the significance of the estimated coefficients. The analysis covers the period from 2010 to 2022, relying primarily on reliable data from the World Bank of Morocco.

Results

Demographic Impact

The analysis reveals a statistically significant negative relationship between net migration and the youth population (15–24 years), suggesting a persistent outflow of young and often highly educated individuals. This dynamic contributes to:

A reduction in the share of the active and innovative segment of the population

Accelerated demographic aging

Weakened endogenous human capital formation

In contrast, the working-age population (25–59 years) exhibits a positive and significant influence on population growth, reinforcing labor force stability and demographic momentum. The elderly population (60+), while generally considered a demographic burden, shows a moderate positive association with household welfare outcomes, primarily due to remittances received from emigrant family members, which help support elderly dependents.

Trends in fertility and birth rates show a gradual decline, in line with regional demographic transitions. However, delayed childbearing and decreasing family sizes point toward structural shifts in reproductive behavior, leading to slower natural population growth despite relatively stable birth rates.

Economic Impact

Net migration is found to have a negative and statistically significant impact on GDP per capita, reflecting the loss of productive human capital and a potential erosion of innovation and labor productivity. This effect is particularly pronounced in the context of high-skilled emigration and the limited reinvestment of remittances into productive sectors.

On the other hand, urbanization rate displays a positive and robust correlation with GDP per capita, suggesting that urban agglomeration economies—including improved access to services, infrastructure, and labor markets—play a central role in driving growth. These findings align with urban economic theories that emphasize the benefits of capital concentration and labor specialization.

Unexpectedly, unemployment rate shows a positive correlation with GDP per capita, a counterintuitive result. This may be explained by:

Structural transformation of the labor market, where lower-productivity or informal jobs are phased out

Technological substitution and increased capital intensity, leading to higher average productivity but also greater joblessness

Possible temporal lags between output growth and employment creation

Comparative Insights

Cross-country comparisons underscore heterogeneity in migration effects:

In Tunisia and Spain, migration mitigates demographic decline and supports pension systems by compensating for low fertility.

In Egypt and Italy, the demographic and economic effects of migration are limited, possibly due to restrictive policies or structural economic rigidities.

Algeria and Senegal benefit from large youth cohorts, sustaining demographic dynamism, whereas their economic gains from migration remain mixed.

Urbanization consistently emerges as a strong predictor of growth across countries such as Spain, Tunisia, Algeria, and Jordan, reinforcing the importance of strategic urban policy.

Conclusion

International migration profoundly shapes Morocco's demographic and economic dynamics. While the loss of young workers weakens the country's productive potential and accelerates demographic aging, remittances play a compensatory role by supporting families, reducing poverty, and creating opportunities for local investment.

The study also highlights that urbanization, when effectively managed, can be a powerful driver of economic growth. However, rapid urbanization requires more equitable spatial planning to prevent the deepening of regional inequalities.

In light of these challenges, integrated public policies are essential: tackling brain drain, improving the integration of migrants residing in Morocco, ensuring fair management of South-South migration flows, and mobilizing the diaspora in a more strategic way. It is crucial for Morocco to develop a migration approach based not only on border security, but also on human capital, economic diplomacy, and social inclusion.

References

Ager, A. (2019). *Le partenariat euro-africain sur la migration : coopération marocaine. Politique internationale.*

Borjas, G. J. (2003). *The Labor Demand Curve is Downward Sloping. Quarterly Journal of Economics.*

Docquier, F., & Rapoport, H. (2009). *Migration and Development: The Role of Remittances. World Bank.*

Dustmann, C., & Frattini, T. (2014). *The Fiscal Effects of Immigration to the UK. The Economic Journal.*

Greene, W. H. (2018). *Econometric Analysis (8th ed.).* Pearson.

Haut Commissariat au Plan (HCP, 2024). *Population du Maroc – Rapport démographique.*

Khachani, M. (2009). *The Impact of Migration on the Moroccan Economy.*

OECD (2024). *Economic Survey of Morocco.*

OIM (2020). *Rapport sur la migration au Maroc.*

UN-Habitat (2020). *World Cities Report: The Value of Sustainable Urbanization.*

Willekens, F., et al. (2017). *The Impact of Migration on the Demographic and Economic Structure of Host Countries. Population and Development Review.*

Wooldridge, J. M. (2019). *Introductory Econometrics: A Modern Approach.* Cengage Learning.

World Bank (2024). *Perspectives économiques du Maroc.*

World Bank (2024). *Rapport sur les transferts de fonds et l'économie du Maroc.*

LABOUR OUT-MIGRATION IN ODISHA: PROCESSES, DETERMINANTS, AND OUTCOMES

Budhadev Mahanta[1]

Introduction

Migration has become a major global and national issue over the past few decades. It has become a key livelihood strategy in developing regions, driven by economic inequality, environmental pressures, and socio-political factors (De Haas, 2010). In countries like India, internal migration is a vital yet overlooked issue, especially in states like Odisha, where rural migration is increasing due to agricultural distress, job scarcity, poverty, and seasonal unemployment. Additionally, the state has experienced both inter-state and intra-state labour outflows, influenced by a complex interplay of push and pull factors (Parida, 2016; Mishra, 2016 & 2020). Meanwhile, pull factors such as better wages, regular work, and education in urban destinations further incentivise migration (Kundu and Saraswati, 2012). However, migrants are a heterogeneous category in India and elsewhere (Srivastava & Sasikumar, 2003; Srivastava, 2020). Regionally focused studies are more likely to capture localised migration processes, determinants, and outcomes, particularly at the household and village levels.

Literature Review

Migration theory highlights that people move due to a combination of push and pull factors. Economic determinants such as wage differentials and employment opportunities are central (Harris & Todaro, 1970), while poverty, demographic pressure, education, and marriage also influence decisions. Environmental stressors like droughts or climate change (Black et al., 2011). The process of migration is explained by both individual and household perspectives: neoclassical theory views migration as a cost–benefit calculation (Todaro, 1969), whereas the New Economics of Labour Migration (Stark & Bloom, 1985) emphasizes household strategies for income diversification. Migration networks

[1] Doctoral Research Scholar at the Centre for the Study of Regional Development, Jawaharlal Nehru University, New Delhi, India. E-mail Id: bmahantajnu@gmail.com and budhad34_ssf@jnu.ac.in

(Massey et al., 1993) reduce risks and costs, while Piore's (1979) dual labour market theory highlights the structural demand for cheap migrant labour in host economies. The outcomes of migration are complex: sending areas gain remittances, skills, and investment but may face labour shortages and dependency (de Haas, 2010). At the household level, migration enhances income and mobility but may also lead to precarity, exploitation, and identity struggles (King, 2013). Thus, migration is a multidimensional process with mixed consequences for origin, destination, and migrants themselves.

Studies show that temporary migration is often shaped by economic hardship and social vulnerability. Limited farmland, low agricultural income, and weak livestock holdings are key drivers (Haberfeld et al., 1999; Deshingkar & Start, 2003). Seasonal migration is particularly common among Scheduled Tribes and Scheduled Castes, reflecting its distress-driven nature (Deshingkar & Start, 2003; Keshri & Bhagat, 2012). At the same time, employment opportunities, higher wages, and the costs of separation strongly influence short-term migration (Parida & Madheswaran, 2012). Social networks also play a critical role in facilitating and sustaining these movements (De Haan et al., 2002).

Methodology

Sampling Design:

We utilised multiple sampling methods for our research. In the first stage, we chose Odisha through purposive sampling, focusing on its history of out-migration and rural poverty. In the second stage, we selected migrant households from each of the villages using stratified random sampling, with agricultural landholding categories (landless, marginal, small, and medium) serving as the basis for stratification. Similarly, control households (non-migrant households) were also selected proportionately from the same landholding groups. Households were randomly chosen from each category, with the number of households selected from each group being proportional. Finally, we collected data through in-depth interviews and focus group discussions (FGDs).

Sample size:

We used Yamane's (1967) method for sample size. A total of 400 households, including 100 non-migrant households, has been collected.

Empirical Model:

We used a logit model to determine the factors influencing workers' decisions to migration. The model can be written as:

$$L_i = ln(P_i/1 - P_i) = X_i'\beta + u_i$$

Where, L_i is the logit, u_i is the stochastic error term,

Pi is the probability of decision to migration, and P = 1 if there is at least one household member who has migrated for over 30 days within the past year, and 0 otherwise.

Xi is the vector of independent variables such as per capita land, average monthly agricultural income, wage different between origin and destination places, castes, hh size, age squared and education squared.

In addition, we also used average treatment effect (ATT), which estimates the expected difference in outcomes between households that migrated and comparable households that did not, based on their propensity scores.

Result:

Whose migration and Why?

The characteristics of migrants vary significantly between long-term and short-term migrants (Keshri and Bhagat, 2012, 2013). Analysing the background characteristics of short-term migrants and their households provides valuable insights into the social and economic factors driving migration (Mishra, 2016, 2020; Sucharita, 2020; Nienkerke et al., 2023). Insights from our field survey indicate that households with marginal and small landholdings are more likely to migrate temporarily due to the low income in agriculture, they are migrating for their livelihoods. While social group wise migration, similar to Deshingkar & Stark (2003) and Keshri & Bhagat (2012), we found that socially deprived groups, such as Scheduled Tribes (ST) and Scheduled Castes (SC), migrate more than other social groups. In the case of education backgrounds, most of them have experienced with secondary education.

When asked why they are migrating, half of the respondents stated that they are migrating due to insufficient employment opportunities in their localities, followed by landless and low earnings in agriculture. Similar results have also been found by several researchers, such as Parida (2016), and Mishra (2016 & 2020). The logit regression result shows that average monthly agricultural income has a negative association with migration. In contrast, the wage gap between the home and destination areas shows a positive relationship. Additionally, age squared has a negative relation, indicating migration decreases with increasing age due to health issues. Similarly, education squared also shows negative effects, suggesting migration decreases at higher education levels.

During the FGDs, some differences also came out very sharply. Most of the migrants are not focused on agriculture due to wild animals (e.g., elephants). They invest in agriculture, but during the harvesting time, wild animals destroyed the crops. This happens every year. Some of them also would like to do agriculture, but there are no irrigation facilities. Thus, they would not like to do agriculture or invest in agriculture. That's why they are forced to migrate for their livelihoods to fulfil the household needs.

Migration Processes

The migration process may have inherent characteristics that impact the outcome (Mishra, 2020). However, social networks significantly influence most individual and family migration decisions. We found that neighbours are significant factors in the migration process, followed by kinship and friends. These migration networks monitor and control labour from origin to destination, along with their choice of destination and occupations. As a results, they were faced discrimination, including differences in behaviours and wages at the workplace.

Outcome:

Effects of Migration on Households' Expenditure Patterns:

Based on the ATT results from the propensity score matching analysis, migration appears to have a mixed impact on household expenditure patterns when comparing treated (migrant) and matched control (non-migrant) groups. We found that migrant households spend significantly less on monthly per capita food and non-food consumption. Similarly, there is a marginally significant reduction in the share of expenditure on food, which may reflect changes in dietary patterns. However, migrants allocate a significantly higher share of their budget to non-food (e.g. clothing, utilities and other household services), durable goods and housing construction. Additionally, migrants spend a greater share on social and cultural events, highlighting their continued engagement in community activities despite migration. At the same time, no significant differences were observed in overall monthly consumption, loan repayment, education, health, or agricultural-related expenditures.

These results consistently indicate that rural families in Odisha tend to prioritise spending on assets that offer immediate improvements to their living standards, rather than on assets that could boost their future earning capacity, such as investments in human capital or other productive assets.

Agrarian Change Through the Voices from the Field

As working-age males migrate away, there is a shortage of agricultural labor, especially during peak seasons like sowing and harvesting. As a result, agricultural wage rates have increased, and there has been a rise in female participation in agricultural work, particularly among Scheduled Tribe (Adivasi) and Scheduled Caste (Dalit) households.

Additionally, we have observed changes in land use and crop patterns. Due to migration and the lack of local labour, many households are leasing out their land or leaving it fallow. Some are shifting towards horticulture crops where market access and irrigation are available. Furthermore, migration serves as a source of agrarian investment; migrant households are using their remittances to purchase seeds and fertilizers, as well as to rent agricultural machinery like tractors and power tillers.

"Now the boys go outside for work, and only women are left in farming. Work doesn't get done fully, so we do only one crop now."- FGDs

Conclusion

Labour out-migration in Odisha is driven by limited non-farm employment opportunities, low agricultural income, and various socio-economic factors, leading to significant impacts on local communities. To address these challenges, it is crucial to strengthen rural employment opportunities by enhancing the implementation of the Mahatma Gandhi National Rural Employment Guarantee Scheme (MGNREGS), ensuring consistent job availability throughout the year, and promoting skill development programs tailored to local needs. Additionally, improving access to irrigation, agricultural inputs, and affordable credit options for migrant families and women farmers can significantly boost agricultural productivity. Implementing effective measures to protect crops from wild animals will also encourage farmers to invest in their fields. Furthermore, fostering gender inclusion in agriculture by empowering women through training and resources will enhance their participation and contributions. Creating platforms for knowledge exchange among migrant and non-migrant households can strengthen community ties and promote sustainable agricultural practices. By addressing these areas, Odisha can reduce out-migration factors and cultivate a more resilient rural economy.

Acknowledgement:

I express my sincere gratitude to all those who have supported me in completing this research work. I am deeply indebted to my supervisor, Prof. Deepak Kumar Mishra, whose guidance, constructive criticism, and encouragement have been invaluable throughout my Ph.D. journey. This research forms an integral part of my Ph.D. thesis.

References

Black, R., Adger, W. N., Arnell, N. W., Dercon, S., Geddes, A., & Thomas, D. (2011). The effect of environmental change on human migration. Global environmental change, 21, S3-S11.

De Haan, A., Brock, K., & Coulibaly, N. (2002). Migration, livelihoods and institutions: contrasting patterns of migration in Mali. Journal of Development Studies, 38(5), 37-58.

De Haas, H. (2010). Migration and development: A theoretical perspective. International migration review, 44(1), 227-264.

Deshingkar, P., & Start, D. (2003). Seasonal migration for livelihoods in India: Coping, accumulation and exclusion (Vol. 111). London: Overseas Development Institute.

Dodd, W., Humphries, S., Patel, K., Majowicz, S., & Dewey, C. (2016). Determinants of temporary labour migration in southern India. Asian Population Studies, 12(3), 294-311.

Haberfeld, Y., Menaria, R. K., Sahoo, B. B., & Vyas, R. N. (1999). Seasonal migration of rural labor in India. Population Research and Policy Review, 18(5), 471-487.

Harris, J. R., & Todaro, M. P. (1970). Migration, unemployment and development: a two-sector analysis. The American economic review, 60(1), 126-142.

Keshri, K., and R.B. Bhagat. (2012). Temporary and Seasonal Migration: Regional Pattern, Characteristics and Associated Factors. Economic and Political Weekly 47 (4): 81–88.

Keshri, K., and R.B. Bhagat. (2013). Socioeconomic Determinants of Temporary Labour Migration in India: A Regional Analysis. Asian Population Studies 9 (2): 175–195.

King, R. (2013). Theories and typologies of migration: An overview and a primer.

Massey, D. S., Arango, J., Hugo, G., Kouaouci, A., Pellegrino, A., & Taylor, J. E. (1993). Theories of international migration: A review and appraisal. Population and development review, 431-466.

Massey, D. S., Alarcón, R., Durand, J., & González, H. (1990). *Return to Aztlan: The social process of international migration from western Mexico* (Vol. 1). University of California Press.

Mishra, D.K. (2016). Seasonal Migration from Odisha: A Field View. In Internal Migration in Contemporary India, ed. D.K. Mishra, 263–290. New Delhi: Sage.

Mishra, D. K. (2020). Seasonal migration and unfree labour in globalising India: Insights from Field surveys in Odisha. *The Indian Journal of Labour Economics, 63*(4), 1087-1106.

Munshi, K. & Rosenzweig, M. (2006). Traditional institutions meet the modern world: Caste, gender, and schooling choice in a globalising economy. The American Economic Review, 96(4), 1225–1252.

Nienkerke, I. M., Thorat, A., & Patt, A. (2023). From distress migration to selective migration: Transformative effects of agricultural development on seasonal migration. *World Development Perspectives, 29*, 100483.

Parida, J. K., & Madheswaran, S. (2012). Higher wages, cost of separation, and seasonal migration in India. Bangalore, India: Institute for Social and Economic Change.

Piore, M. J. (1979). Birds of passage: Migrant labour and industrial societies. Cambridge University Press.

Stark, O., & Bloom, D. E. (1985). The new economics of labor migration. The american Economic review, 75(2), 173-178.

Srivastava, R. (2012). Internal migration in India: An overview of its features, trends and policy challenges. Workshop Compendium, Vol. II: Workshop Papers, National Workshop on Internal Migration and Human Development in India. New Delhi, India: UNESCO/ UNICEF.

Sucharita, S. (2020). Socio-economic determinants of temporary labour migration in Western Jharkhand, India. *Millennial Asia*, *11*(2), 226-251.

Todaro, M. P. (1969). A model of labor migration and urban unemployment in less developed countries. The American economic review, 59(1), 138-148.

Yamane, T. "Statistics: an introductory analysis, 1st edn, Harper and Row, New York." (1967).

FEMINTEGRA - EXPLORING THE LABOR TRAJECTORIES OF ROMANIAN IMMIGRANT WOMEN IN THE PROVINCES OF BARCELONA, LLEIDA, VALENCIA, AND CASTELLÓN

Ioana-Felicia Marin[1]

Introduction

Spain has transformed from a country of emigration to a major destination for international migrants. During the 20th century, millions of Spaniards emigrated to countries like France and Germany for work. Their remittances supported Spain's economy, aiding modernization. After joining the European Economic Community in 1986, Spain's economic growth and stability attracted migrants, shifting its demographic and labor dynamics.

Romanian migration to Spain followed several phases. Initially limited and politically driven before 1989, it intensified post-communism due to economic hardship. Romania's 2007 EU accession enabled free movement, prompting one of the largest migration flows to Spain. By 2022, Romanians accounted for 12.6% of Spain's foreign population, though numbers declined due to economic crises, EU mobility, the pandemic, and return migration.

This study uses mixed methods—survey, participant observation, interviews, and labor data analysis—to explore Romanian women's labor integration. Key factors include EU mobility, visa liberalization, and social networks. Most women work in low-status sectors like hospitality, retail, cleaning, caregiving, and agriculture. Interviews reveal occupational shifts and aspirations for upward mobility, though barriers like overqualification and discrimination persist. The study also distinguishes pioneer migrants from newer generations, informing culturally sensitive labor policies.

It addresses three questions:

How have Romanian women become a key labor force in Spain?

[1] Ioana-Felicia Marin, University of Valencia, Spain.

How are they integrated across employment sectors?

What factors determine their labor integration?

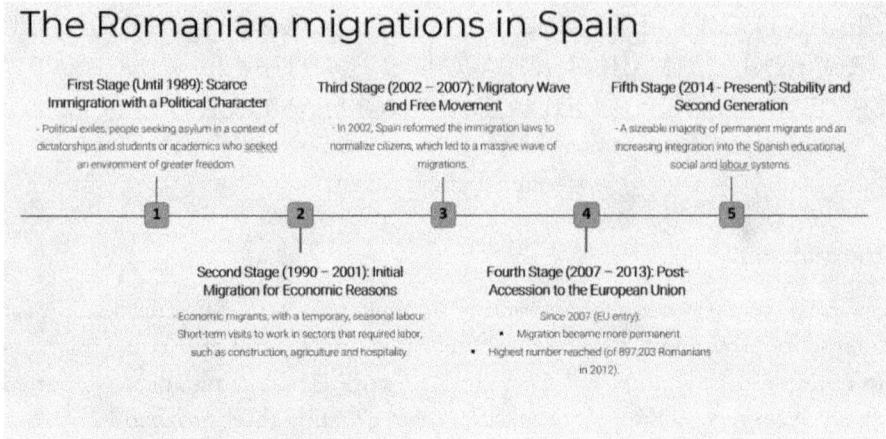

Figure 1: The Romanian Migrations in Spain

Source: Prepared by the author

Romanian Migration in Spain: origin and characteristics

Romanian migration has diversified since the 1980s, with EU accession in 2007 easing movement and Spain emerging as a major destination due to labor demand and cultural proximity. Concentrated in Madrid, Catalonia, Valencia, and Andalusia, migrants are mainly young people working in construction, agriculture, domestic work, and hospitality. This migration causes brain drain in Romania (Ferro, 2004; Nedelcu, 2000). While highly qualified Romanians benefit from institutional support, irregular migration relies on personal networks. The community has stabilized through family reunification, second-generation growth, and entrepreneurship, playing a vital role in Spain's economy and society.

2.1 First Stage (until 1989): Political Migration under Dictatorship

Under Ceauşescu's regime, emigration was tightly controlled. Harsh austerity, surveillance, and repression limited mobility. Migration was rare and mostly political—exiles, asylum seekers, and academics faced high personal risks. Romanian presence in Spain was marginal (Marcu, 2009). After the 1989 revolution, political drivers gave way to economic motives amid deep socio-economic crisis.

2.2 Second Stage (1990–2001): Early Economic and Diversified Migration
Post-communist Romania's economic collapse triggered legal, circular migration to Western Europe, especially Spain, Italy, and Germany (Anghel et al., 2016; Viruela, 2004). Migrants included seasonal workers and professionals. Short-term visas, cultural ties, and church networks supported integration, with regional patterns shaping destinations—e.g., Transylvanians to Spain, Moldavians to Italy.

2.3 Third Stage (2002–2007): Migration Surge and EU Pre-Accession Romania's 2002

Visa liberalization and Romania's 2002 EU accession agreement spurred mass migration to Spain. Economic growth and labor demand—especially in agriculture and construction—fueled this surge. Migrants relied on social networks and informal transport. Migration became circular and informal (Sandu, 2006; Diminescu, 2002a, 2000b), often seen as a post-socialist rite of passage (Horváth, 2008). By 2006, over 400,000 Romanians lived in Spain.

2.4 Fourth Stage (2007–2013): EU Membership and Migration Reconfiguration
EU membership in 2007 expanded mobility, though Spain imposed labor restrictions (2007–2009, 2011–2013). Migration stabilized, with more families reuniting. Spain's recession, however, triggered returns or onward migration. Programs like DIASPORA-START-UP encouraged return, but most were short-term. EU citizenship supported continued circularity, especially among youth (Marcu, 2013). The Romanian population peaked at 800,000 in 2012.

2.5 Fifth Stage (2014–Present): Stability, Settlement, and Second Generation
Post-2014, migration shifted toward long-term settlement and civic engagement (Stan y Erne, 2014). The second generation increasingly integrates into education and the labor market. Yet, challenges like overqualification and discrimination persist. As of 2024, over 600,000 Romanians reside in Spain.

Decline and Transformations of Romanian Migration in Spain

As of 2022, Romanians were the second-largest foreign group in Spain, with 627,478 residents—a sharp decline from nearly 900,000 in 2012. Factors include the 2008–2013 economic crisis, EU mobility, COVID-19, improved conditions in Romania, and an aging migrant population. Spain's lack of talent retention and rising costs also pushed many to leave. By 2024, the population dropped to just over 620,000, impacting sectors like hospitality and care work. Return migration has economic and social implications, yet policies have largely overlooked long-term settlement or qualified return, missing an opportunity to harness the migrants' skills for mutual benefit.

Principales grupos de extranjeros en España

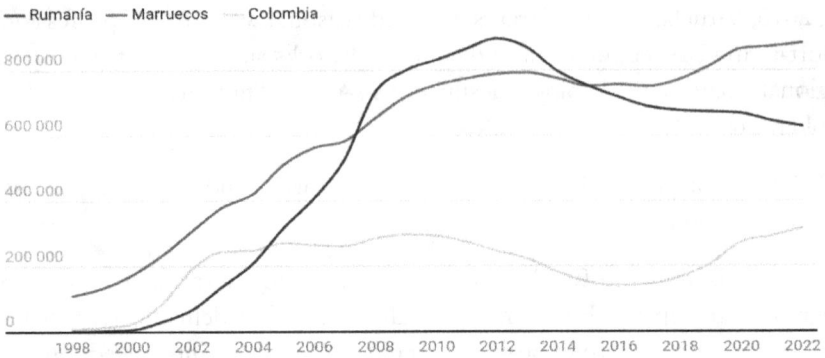

Figure 2: Main groups of foreigners in Spain (1998-2022).

Source: INE, El Debate, Created with Datawrapper

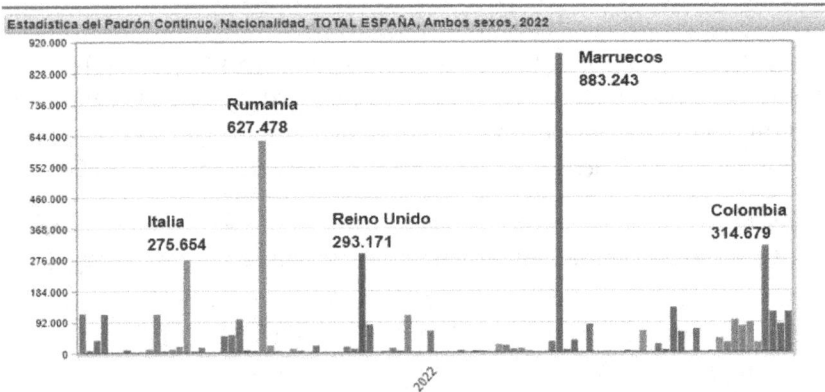

Figure 3: Continuous Register Statistics, Foreign Population by Nationality and Year (2022).

Source: INE data as of January 1, 2022, and author's processing.

Puesto ⬦	País ⬦	2024[35] ⬦	2022[36] ⬦	2020[37] ⬦	2012[38] ⬦	2001[39] ⬦	2000[40] ⬦	Núcleos ⬦
1	Marruecos	920 693	714 243	709 945	788 563	233 415	173 158	Marroquíes en España
2	Rumania	620 463	627 478	667 378	897 137	31 641	6 410	Rumanos en España
3	Colombia	578 477	314 679	273 050	273 176	87 209		Colombianos en España
4	Italia	325 358	275 654	252 008	191 713	34 689	27 874	Italianos en España
5	Venezuela	325 254	212 064	189 110	58 916	16 549	12 119	Venezolanos en España
6	Reino Unido	272 404	293 171	262 885	397 892	107 326	99 017	Británicos en España

Figure 4: Continuous Population Registry Statistics, Foreign Population by Nationality and Year.

Source: INE data

Romanian Women: Gender Roles, Identity, Migration Drivers, and Integration Challenges

During Romania's communist era, women were extensively incorporated into education and the workforce. However, traditional patriarchal norms persisted and were reinforced by Ceaușescu's pro-natalist policies, such as the coercive "menstrual police" (Navaz and Bordonaba, 2007). This legacy continues to shape Romanian migrant women's identities, where caregiving and domestic responsibilities are moral obligations and expressions of love. The ideal of the "good housewife" remains deeply ingrained, often clashing with Spain's more egalitarian gender norms.

Why Do Romanian Women Choose Spain?

Cultural and linguistic proximity—both countries speak Romance languages—facilitates integration. Shared values like religiosity, family, and tradition ease cultural adaptation. Romanian women are drawn to high-demand sectors like agriculture and domestic work, valued for their reliability despite low pay and poor working conditions. Spain's climate and lifestyle also enhance well-being. Moreover, strong community networks in cities like Castellón and Barcelona offer emotional support, job access, and bureaucratic help, often through family, churches, or associations.

Main Challenges Faced by Romanian Women

Migration often leads to "identity grief," as described by Berry (1997). Women oscillate between cultures, facing stress and emotional strain influenced by language skills, age at migration, and available support (Sandu, 2005). Labor market segmentation compounds their vulnerability. Many face "occupational downgrading" despite qualifications (Kofman and Raghuram, 2015) and remain stuck in informal, underpaid roles lacking protections (Lutz, 2011; Oso and Parella, 2012). Bureaucratic obstacles further hinder access to residency, healthcare, and social services (García Castaño et al., 2014), especially for those in irregular employment. Limited Spanish proficiency exacerbates dependence and limits autonomy (Calavita, 2005), though community associations help bridge this gap (Sandu, 2005).

Cultural Identity and Community Networks

Despite challenges, Romanian migrants actively preserve cultural identity. The Romanian Orthodox Church, with over 120 parishes in Spain, serves as a vital hub for spiritual and social support. Associations provide vocational training, legal aid, and gender violence support. Romanian-language media, like *Occidentul Românesc*, reinforce cohesion and collective memory. Regular travel to Romania sustains dual belonging.

Digital Networks

In areas with fewer formal supports, online platforms like Facebook host Romanian groups that share job offers, legal advice, childcare tips, and migration experiences. A 2024–2025 participant observation in Catalonia and Valencia revealed recurring themes: employment, paperwork, logistics, and identity reflection. These digital spaces support resilience, introspection, and evolving notions of belonging.

Labor Integration of Romanian Immigrant Women in Catalonia and the Valencian Community: Profiles, Challenges, and Evolving Dynamics

The labor integration of Romanian immigrant women in Spain—particularly in Catalonia and the Valencian Community—offers critical insights into the intersections of gender, migration, and labor in the post-pandemic era and amidst recent labor reforms. Drawing from official sources such as the SEPE and the Spanish Social Security database (TGSS), this study analyzes employment patterns, contract types, and sectoral participation, highlighting structural challenges and changes.

Procedencia País de nacionalidad	País	Pers. Extranjeras *	% variac. 2023/2022
TABLA 2 AFILIADOS PERSONAS EXTRANJERAS POR PROCEDENCIA Y PAÍS DE NACIONALIDAD			
Países UE	Rumanía	328.545	0,79
	Italia	174.664	10,76
	Portugal	63.927	5,33
	Francia	56.961	4,87
	Bulgaria	55.714	-1,10
	Alemania	47.453	5,63
	Polonia	31.683	5,03
	Países Bajos	19.901	8,75
	Bélgica	12.607	6,53
	Suecia	9.120	6,49
	Resto países UE	52.613	7,29
	Total Países UE	853.188	4,32
Países No UE	Marruecos	319.433	5,68
	Colombia	174.583	37,81
	Venezuela	148.324	19,28
	China	115.952	3,66
	Perú	70.708	30,93
	Ecuador	69.815	-0,08
	Ucrania	65.694	9,2
	Reino Unido	63.880	-0,69
	Honduras	60.656	17,87
	Argentina	56.728	16,04
	Resto países No UE	646.794	6,85
	Total Países No UE	1.792.567	10,71

Figure 5: Foreign Affiliates by Origin and Country of Nationality

Source: Prepared by the SEPE Employment Observatory based on data from the MISSM. Social Security, December 30, 2023

Demographic Profile and Employment Characteristics

As of 2023, foreign nationals accounted for 12.76% of all workers registered with Social Security in Spain, with Romanians representing the largest EU labor group (328,545 affiliates), of whom nearly half are women. Most Romanian women are aged between 35 and 54, reflecting a stable, working-age profile. They are primarily employed under the General Social Security Regime, with many also working in hospitality, retail, domestic and agricultural sectors. These jobs are typically low-skilled, unstable, and poorly paid, although Spain's 2022 labor reform has brought some improvements in contract stability.

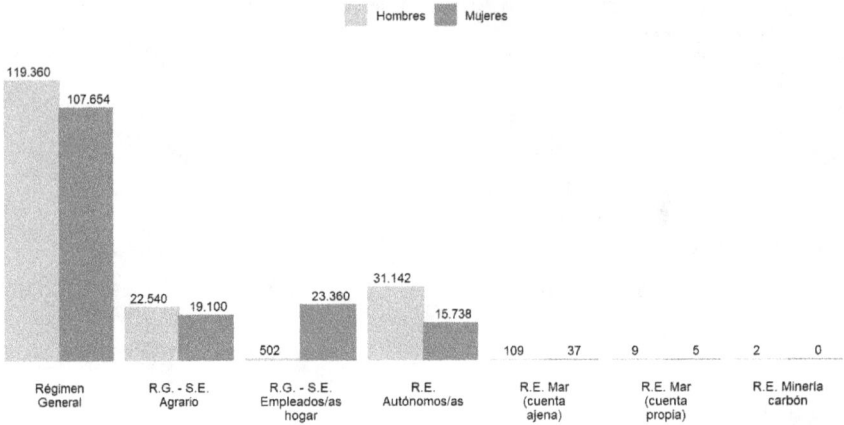

Figure 6: Romanian nationals registered in the labor force by system and sex. 09/29/2023

Source: Social Security - MISSM

Labor Reform and Contractual Trends

The 2021 labor reform promoted permanent contracts and aimed to reduce temporary employment. By 2023, 57% of contracts given to foreign workers were indefinite, although Romanian women still experienced high contract turnover (averaging 2.28 contracts per person). While female employment has increased post-pandemic, migrant women continue to face lower rates of permanent contracts and are overrepresented in part-time and temporary roles.

Modalidad contractual	Contratos				% colectivo	% variación 2023/22
	Jornada Completa	J. Tiempo parcial	Fijos discont.	Total		
Indefinido ordinario (bonificado/no bonificado)	736.157	375.386	831.807	1.943.350	31,79	18,86
Indefinido personas con discapacidad ordinarios	541	292	99	932	5,43	-0,85
Conversión ordinaria	57.069	25.284	13.533	95.886	19,54	-64,28
Total indefinidos	793.767	400.962	845.439	2.040.168	30,81	7,13
Obra o servicio	0	0	-	0	0,00	-100,00
Circunstancias de la producción	926.996	356.096	-	1.283.094	19,79	-9,47
Sustitución	112.160	71.342	-	183.502	13,43	4,70
Temporal personas con discapacidad	942	440	-	1.382	6,47	-9,85
Sustitución jubilación anticipada	0	-	-	0	0,00	-100,00
Jubilación parcial	-	77	-	77	0,32	-2,53
Relevo	151	149	-	300	3,58	1,01
Obtención práctica profesional	3.283	953	-	4.236	8,66	-29,82
Formación en alternancia	5.082	-	-	5.082	10,15	23,23
Investigador predoctoral en formación	1.400	-	-	1.400	23,80	19,15
Vinculado programas políticas activas empleo	11.277	1.861	-	13.138	4,85	45,24
Financiado con fondos europeos	1.262	170	-	1.432	8,06	37,30
Artistas y personal técnico o auxiliar	25.455	807	-	26.262	8,29	-
Duración determinada Contrato de acceso de personal investigador doctor	199	-	-	199	43,64	-
Otros	12.694	6.934	-	19.628	9,46	-27,87
Total temporales	1.100.903	438.829	-	1.539.732	17,45	-22,89
Total contratos	1.894.670	839.791	845.439	3.579.900	23,18	-8,24

TABLA 7. CONTRATACIÓN DE PERSONAS EXTRANJERAS POR TIPO DE CONTRATO Y JORNADA LABORAL

Figure 7: Hiring of foreign workers by type of contract and working hours

Source: Prepared by the SEPE Employment Observatory based on SISPE data. 2023

Sectoral and Regional Distribution

Romanian women are concentrated in hospitality, retail, cleaning, and caregiving. In Catalonia, most are registered in Barcelona and Tarragona, especially under the General Regime and as domestic workers or self-employed.

AfUdExtranjeros por Período, Provincia y Régimen. Mujer, UNION EUROPEA.

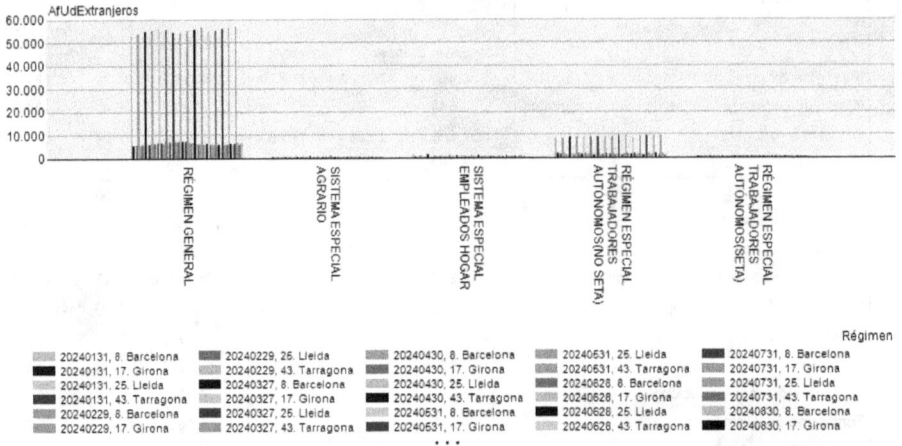

Figure 8: Foreign affiliates last day of the month, by period, regime, province, European Union, sex

Source: Social Security - MISSM

In the Valencian Community, their labor force is centered in cleaning, hospitality, retail, caregiving, and seasonal agriculture. Notably, many women are also self-employed, developing businesses in areas like aesthetics, food services, or selling Romanian products.

AfUdExtranjeros por Período, Provincia y Régimen. Mujer, UNION EUROPEA.

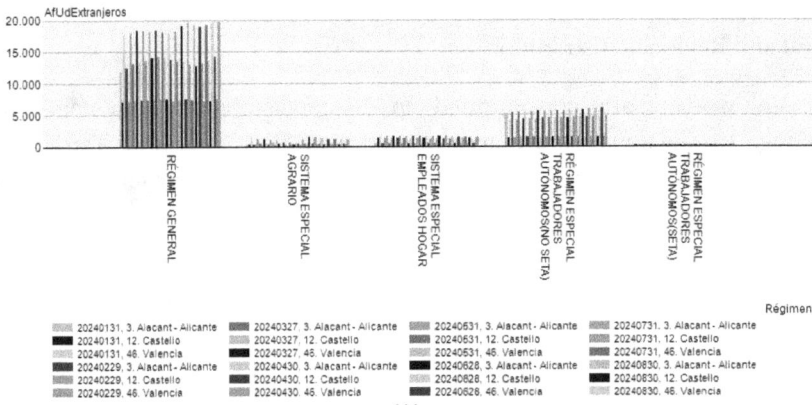

Figure 9: Foreign affiliates last day of the month, by period, regime, province, European Union, sex

Source: Social Security - MISSM

Domestic and Care Work: Informality and Vulnerability

The domestic and care sector remains one of the most precarious for Romanian women. An estimated 36% work without formal contracts or social security. Over 80,000 women in Catalonia and around 54,000 in the Valencian Community work in this sector—over 60% of them migrants. Despite legislative advancements (e.g., Spain's ratification of ILO Convention 189), implementation remains weak, and inspections in private homes are rare (El País, 2024).

Qualitative and Intergenerational Perspectives

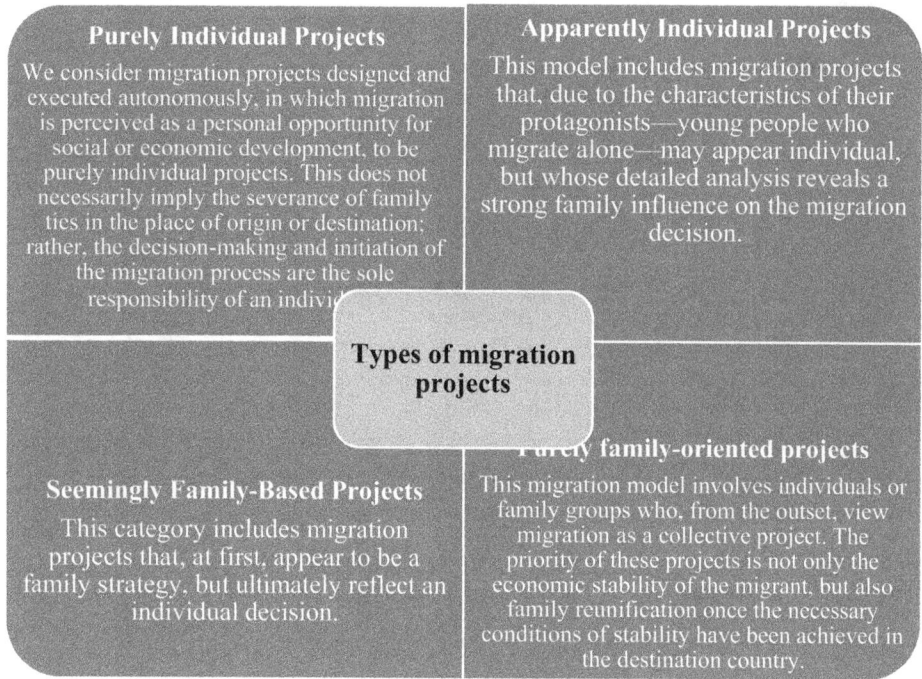

Purely Individual Projects

We consider migration projects designed and executed autonomously, in which migration is perceived as a personal opportunity for social or economic development, to be purely individual projects. This does not necessarily imply the severance of family ties in the place of origin or destination; rather, the decision-making and initiation of the migration process are the sole responsibility of an indivi

Apparently Individual Projects

This model includes migration projects that, due to the characteristics of their protagonists—young people who migrate alone—may appear individual, but whose detailed analysis reveals a strong family influence on the migration decision.

Types of migration projects

Seemingly Family-Based Projects

This category includes migration projects that, at first, appear to be a family strategy, but ultimately reflect an individual decision.

Purely family-oriented projects

This migration model involves individuals or family groups who, from the outset, view migration as a collective project. The priority of these projects is not only the economic stability of the migrant, but also family reunification once the necessary conditions of stability have been achieved in the destination country.

Figure 10: Types of migration projects

Source: Prepared by the author

The study's qualitative phase (2024–2025) involves interviews and surveys in Barcelona, Valencia, Castellón, and Lleida. It explores labor trajectories, strategies for adaptation, and the gap between migrants' aspirations and labor market realities. The research distinguishes between "pioneer" migrants (arriving in the early 2000s) and newer generations (including their daughters), revealing generational differences in qualifications, expectations, and barriers.

While pioneers often entered low-skilled sectors with minimal institutional support, younger women tend to have higher education, sometimes earned in Spain, but still face challenges such as overqualification, lack of professional networks, and structural racism. Migratory projects fall into four categories—individual, family-driven, or mixed—and motivations range from cultural admiration for Spain to escaping difficult conditions in Romania (e.g., corruption, limited opportunities).

These findings highlight the need for intersectional policies that recognize diverse trajectories and support upward mobility.

References

Achotegui, Joseba (2002). "Migración y salud mental: el síndrome del inmigrante con estrés crónico y múltiple (síndrome de Ulises)". *Revista Norte de Salud Mental.*

Anghel, Remus Gabriel, Ioana Manafi, Anatolie Coşciug and Monica Roman (2016). "International Migration, Return Migration, and Their Effects: A Comprehensive Review on the Romanian Case". SSRN Electronic Journal. DOI: 10.2139/ssrn.2895293

Aparicio, Rosa (2007). "Las "segundas generaciones" en España". Cuadernos europeos de Deusto, vol. 36, pp. 19-56.

Aparicio, Rosa and Liliana Suárez (2007). "Migración rumana en España. Retos de estudios de la migración europea". Migraciones, vol. 21, pp. 7-23. https://revistas.comillas.edu/index.php/revistamigraciones/article/view/2871.

Arango, Joaquín and Ramón Mahía (2017). Migraciones y mercados laborales en España. Salamanca: Ediciones Universidad de Salamanca

Berry, John W. (1997). Immigration, acculturation, and adaptation. Applied Psychology.

Bleahu, Ana (2004). Romanian migration to Spain: Motivations, networks and strategies. En New patterns of labour migration in CEE. Cluj: AMM

Calavita, Kitty (2005). Immigrants at the Margins: Law, Race, and Exclusion in Southern Europe. Cambridge: Cambridge University Press

Ciobanu, Ruxandra Oana and Tim Elrick (2008). "Migration network and policy impacts: insights from Romania-Spain migrations". Global Networks, vol. 9(1), pp. 100-116. DOI: 10.1111/j.1471-0374.2009.00244.x

Diminescu, Dana (2002a): "Stratégies roumaines". Plein Droit, vol. 55, pp.6. http://www.gisti.org/doc/plein-droit/55/strategies.html

Diminescu, Dana (2002b): "La désinstitutionalisation de l'hospitalité et l'intégration par le bas". Ville, Ecole, Integration, vol. 131, décembre. Dossier: "Nouvelles migrations, nouvelles formes de migrations", vol. 5.

Ferro, Anna (2004). Romanians email from abroad. A picture of the highly skilled labour migrations from Romania. International Roundtable on Brain Drain and the Academic and the Intellectual Labour Market in South East Europe, Bucharest, 18-19 June 2004.

García Castaño, Francisco Javier, et al. (2014). La inmigración en España: Evolución y perspectivas. Madrid: CIS

Horváth, István (2007). "Focus migration". Country Profile, vol. 9, pp- 1-10.

Horváth, István (2008). "The culture of migration of the rural Romanian youth". Journal of

Ethnic and Migration Studies, vol. 34(5), pp. 771-86.

Kofman, Eleonore and Parvati Raghuram (2015). Gendered Migrations and Global Social Reproduction. London: Palgrave Macmillan

Lazaridis, Gabriella and Maria Koumandraki (2007). "Albanian Migration to Greece: Patterns and Processes of Inclusion and Exclusion in the Labour Market". European Societies, vol. 9(1). DOI: 10.3986/dd.2018.1.10

Lutz, Helma (2011). The New Maids: Transnational Women and the Care Economy. London: Zed Books

Marcu, Silvia (2009). "Del este al oeste. La migración de rumanos en la Unión Europea: Evolución y características". Migraciones internacionales, vol. 5(1). https://doi.org/10.17428/rmi.v5i16.1107

Marcu, Silvia (2013). "La movilidad transfronteriza de los rumanos en España en tiempos de crisis". Revista Internacional de Sociología, vol. 71(1), pp. 115-141. https://doi.org/10.3989/ris.2012.01.18

Navaz, Liliana Suárez and Paloma Crespo Bordonaba (2007). "Familias en movimiento. El caso de las mujeres rumanas en España". Migraciones. Publicación del Instituto Universitario de Estudios sobre Migraciones, vol. 21, pp. 235-257. https://revistas.comillas.edu/index.php/revistamigraciones/article/view/2898

Nedelcu, Mihaela F. (2000). "Instrumentalizarea spaţiilor virtuale. Noi strategii de reproducere şi conversie a capitalurilor în situaţie migratorie". Sociologie Românească, vol. 2, pp. 80-96.

Oliver Alonso, Josep (2012). "Migraciones, género y trabajo en España: Retos y políticas de integración". Papeles de Economía Española.

Oso, Laura and Sònia Parella (2012). "Inmigración género y Mercado de trabajo: una panorámica de la investigación sobre la inserción Laboral de las mujeres inmigrantes en España". Cuadernos de relaciones laborales, vol. 30(1), pp. 11. https://revistas.ucm.es/index.php/CRLA/article/view/39111/37724.

Parella, Sònia (2019). "Mujeres migrantes en el mercado laboral español: Vulnerabilidad y estrategias de supervivencia". Revista Internacional de Sociología.

Potot, Swanie (2002): "Quand les migrants balkaniques rencontrent ceux venus du Sud". Rencontres. http://www.afebalk.org/rencontres2002/textes/S.Potot.pdf

Radu, Cosmin (2001). "De la Crângeni – Teleorman spre Spania: antreprenoriat, adventism şi migraţie circulatorie". Sociologie Românească, vol. 1-4, pp. 215-31.

Sandu, Dumitru (2005). "Dynamics of Romanian Migration in Spain and Italy: Comparative Perspectives". Journal of Ethnic and Migration Studies.

Sandu, Dumitru (2006). "Migration Waves from Romania, 1990-2006". International Migration Review.

Stan, Sabina and Roland Erne (2014). "Explaining Romanian labor migration: from development gaps to development trajectories". Labor History, vol. 55(1), pp. 21-46. DOI: 10.1080/0023656X.2013.843841

Stănculescu, Manuela Sofia and Victoria Stoiciu (2012). Impactul crizei economice asupra migratiei fortei de munca din Romania. Bucureşti: Paideia. DOI: 10.13140/2.1.1446.1128

Viruela Martínez, Rafael (2004). "El recurso de la emigración. balance durante la transición en Rumania". Papeles del Este, vol. 9.

World Bank. (2018). Moving for Prosperity: Global Migration and Labor Markets. Washington, DC: Banco Mundial

BBDD Estadísticas TGSS. https://w6.seg-social.es/PXWeb/pxweb/es/

European Commission. (2020). Integration of migrants in the European Union: 2020 report.

Publications Office of the European Union.
https://migrant-integration.ec.europa.eu/library-document/eu-migrant-integration-statistics-2020_en

Los riesgos del trabajo doméstico: "Los jefes piensan que somos como Superman". https://elpais.com/economia/2024-09-21/los-riesgos-del-trabajo-domestico-los-jefes-piensan-que-somos-como-superman.html

Observatorio Permanente de la Inmigración (OPI). Estadísticas. https://www.inclusion.gob.es/web/opi/estadisticas

Principales series de población desde 1998. Población extranjera por Nacionalidad, provincias, Sexo y Año. https://www.ine.es/jaxi/Tabla.htm?path=/t20/e245/p08/&file=03005.px&L=0

2023 Tendencias del Mercado de Trabajo en España, Observatorio de las Ocupaciones, Servicio Público de Empleo Estatal, Madrid. https://www.sepe.es/SiteSepe/contenidos/observatorio/Que-es-el-Observatorio/2023_Tendencias_Mercado_Trabajo.pdf

2024 Informe del Mercado de Trabajo de los Extranjeros Estatal, Datos 2023. Servicio Público de Empleo Estatal, Madrid. Consulta realizada en la página web del Servicio Público de Empleo Estatal (SEPE): https://www.sepe.es/SiteSepe/contenidos/que_es_el_sepe/publicaciones/pdf/pdf_mercado_trabajo/2024/Informe-del-Mercado-de-Trabajo-de-las-Personas-Extranjeras.-Estatal-2024--Datos-2023-.pdf

2024 Informe del Mercado de Trabajo de las Mujeres Estatal Datos 2023. Servicio Público de Empleo Estatal, Madrid. https://www.igualdadenlaempresa.es/recursos/CentroDocumentacion/docs/Informe_del_Mercado_de_Trabajo_de_las_Mujeres_2024.pdf

2024 Informe del Mercado de Trabajo de Valencia. Datos 2023. Servicio Público de Empleo Estatal, Madrid. https://www.sepe.es/SiteSepe/contenidos/que_es_el_sepe/publicaciones/pdf/pdf_mercado_trabajo/2024/Mercado-de-Trabajo-2024-VALENCIA--Datos-2023-.pdf

2024 Informe del Mercado de Trabajo de Barcelona. Datos 2023. Servicio Público de Empleo Estatal, Madrid. https://www.sepe.es/SiteSepe/contenidos/que_es_el_sepe/publicaciones/pdf/pdf_mercado_trabajo/2024/Mercado-de-Trabajo-2024-Barcelona--Datos-2023-.pdf

EFFECT OF REMITTANCES ON POVERTY IN THE WESTERN BALKAN COUNTRIES

Nevila Mehmetaj[1]

Introduction

The Western Balkans is a region with a complex economic and demographic history, characterized by large migration flows, economic transition, and post-conflict reconstruction efforts. Countries such as Albania, Kosovo, and Bosnia and Herzegovina have some of the highest emigration rates globally, leading to a substantial inflow of remittances from their diasporas. According to the World Bank (2023), remittances to low- and middle-income countries reached over $669 billion in 2022, demonstrating their critical role in global development financing. Unlike foreign direct investment (FDI) and foreign aid, remittance flows are often countercyclical and less volatile, providing a reliable safety net during crises such as the 2008 financial crisis or the COVID-19 pandemic. In the Western Balkans, remittances account for a significant share of GDP, ranging from 6–15% in most countries. Kosovo, for example, relies on remittances for over 18% of GDP, reflecting the size and influence of its diaspora. Remittances have been used primarily for household consumption, education, and housing investments, but their potential to alleviate poverty and promote inclusive development remains a subject of debate. Some scholars argue that remittances create dependency, reduce labor market participation, and widen income inequality (Chami et al., 2008). Others emphasize their stabilizing role, particularly in fragile economies, where they provide access to basic needs and capital for small-scale investments (Adams & Page, 2005).

This paper seeks to contribute to this ongoing debate by focusing on the empirical link between remittances and poverty in the Western Balkans. The central hypothesis is that remittances have a poverty-reducing effect in west Balkan countries. The analysis also examines other macroeconomic determinants, such as trade openness, external debt, inflation, and human capital, to understand their role in shaping poverty dynamics in the region.

---

[1] Nevila Mehmetaj, University of Shkodra, Albania.

Literature Review

The literature on remittances and poverty presents a mixed picture, reflecting differences in methodology, data quality, and regional context. Globally, studies by Adams and Page (2005) and Ratha et al. (2022) provide strong evidence that remittances have a poverty-reducing effect. Their analysis of cross-country data found that a 10% increase in per capita remittances led to a 3.5% decline in poverty rates. However, the developmental impact of remittances is not uniform and depends on factors such as financial infrastructure, migration networks, and government policies.

In the Western Balkans, migration has been a defining feature of economic life since the 1990s. Research by Gëdeshi and Jorgoni (2012) shows that remittances have been essential for supporting household consumption in Albania, especially in rural areas where job opportunities are scarce. Similarly, IMF (2020) studies highlight that remittances acted as a stabilizing force during the global financial crisis, helping the region maintain macroeconomic stability. However, Kapur and McHale (2019) caution that remittances can create moral hazard, discouraging governments from investing in social protection programs and labor reforms.

Other studies use panel econometric methods to explore these dynamics at a regional level. Most research is country-specific, with qualitative approaches dominating literature. This study contributes to filling this gap by applying FMOLS to a 22-year panel dataset, providing robust evidence on the long-term relationship between remittances and poverty in the region.

Data and Methodology

This study uses annual panel data from 2000 to 2022 for six Western Balkan countries: Albania, Bosnia and Herzegovina, Kosovo, Montenegro, North Macedonia, and Serbia. The data is sourced from the World Bank's World Development Indicators, IMF's World Economic Outlook, and UNDP's Human Development Reports. Kosovo's data are supplemented from regional statistical agencies due to limited availability. The dependent variable is the poverty headcount ratio, measured as the percentage of the population living below the national poverty line. Independent variables include remittance inflows (% of GDP), GDP per capita, trade openness (exports + imports % of GDP), external debt (% of GDP), inflation (annual %), and human capital (measured through mean years of schooling). The empirical model is specified as follows:

$$Poverty_{it} = \alpha + \beta 1 Remittances_{it} + \beta 2 Income_{it} + \beta 3 Trade_{it} + \beta 4 Debt_{it} + \beta 5 HumanCapital_{it} + \beta 6 Inflation_{it} + \mu_i + \varepsilon_{it}$$

where i denote countries and t denotes years. This study employs the Panel Fully Modified Ordinary Least Squares (FMOLS) method to analyze the effect of remittances on economic performance across the Southeast Balkan (SEE6) countries. FMOLS was selected over traditional panel OLS to address non-stationarity, enabling robust long-run relationships to be estimated. FMOLS, introduced by Phillips and Hansen (1990), is widely used for panel data with cointegrated variables. It corrects for both endogeneity and serial correlation by modifying the least squares estimator, producing unbiased and efficient parameter estimates. This makes it suitable for small-sample panels with strong cross-sectional dependence, as is typical in studies of small regions like the Western Balkans. And this is particularly important when examining remittance impacts in countries where macroeconomic indicators are highly persistent over time.

Table 1: Descriptive Statistics

Variable	Mean	Std. Dev.	Min	Max
Poverty (%)	18.4	5.7	9.1	30.2
Remittances (% GDP)	10.5	3.8	3.4	18.6
Income per capita (USD)	6,900	1,450	3,200	9,800
Trade Openness (% GDP)	85.3	15.4	55.2	120.3
Debt (% GDP)	58.2	12.3	40.1	80.7
Human Capital Index	0.72	0.08	0.55	0.85
Inflation (%)	3.8	2.1	0.5	8.5

Empirical Results and Discussion

The FMOLS estimates indicate that remittances exert a statistically significant negative effect on poverty, supporting the hypothesis that remittances reduce poverty rates in the region. Income growth is strongly associated with declining poverty, while debt and inflation exacerbate vulnerability. Human capital also plays a crucial role, with education positively influencing long-term poverty reduction. Country-specific analysis reveals variations: Albania and Kosovo, with higher remittance-to-GDP ratios, show the most pronounced poverty-reducing effects, whereas Serbia demonstrates weaker effects due to more diversified income sources.

Table 2. FMOLS Estimation Results

Variable	Coefficient	t-Statistic	Significance
Remittances	-0.145	2.18	$p < 0.05$
Income per capita	-0.272	4.91	$p < 0.01$
Trade Openness	-0.053	1.74	$p < 0.1$
Debt	0.089	2.10	$p < 0.05$
Human Capital	-0.191	3.23	$p < 0.01$
Inflation	0.067	2.45	$p < 0.05$

The FMOLS estimation results provide critical insights into the determinants of poverty in the Western Balkans. Remittances have a statistically significant negative coefficient, confirming their role in poverty alleviation. A 1% increase in remittance inflows as a share of GDP is associated with an approximate 0.15% reduction in poverty. Income growth exerts the strongest influence, underscoring the importance of economic expansion in lifting households out of poverty. Human capital development, measured through education, also has a strong poverty-reducing effect. In contrast, higher external debt and inflation exacerbate poverty, signalling macroeconomic vulnerabilities. Trade openness shows unsignificant effect, suggesting that while globalization can support growth, its direct impact on poverty requires complementary social and institutional reforms.

Conclusion

This study investigates the effect of remittances on poverty in six Western Balkan countries (Albania, Bosnia and Herzegovina, Kosovo, Montenegro, North Macedonia, and Serbia) using panel data from 2000 to 2022. By applying the Fully Modified Ordinary Least Squares (FMOLS) methodology, the analysis captures the long-term relationship between poverty and several macroeconomic determinants, including remittances, income, trade openness, external debt, human capital, and inflation.

Key findings indicate that remittances have a statistically significant poverty-reducing effect, particularly in countries with large diaspora communities and robust remittance inflows such as West Balkan countries. Income growth is the strongest determinant of poverty reduction, highlighting the importance of sustained economic growth. Human capital, proxied through education, plays a critical role in lowering poverty levels over time. Conversely, high debt and inflation increase vulnerability, underscoring the need for macroeconomic stability.

This study contributes to regional policy discussions by providing empirical evidence on how migration and remittances can be strategically integrated into economic planning to reduce poverty and accelerate development. The study recommends that governments and policymakers strengthen financial inclusion, promote the use of formal remittance channels, and create diaspora engagement strategies to channel remittances toward productive investment. Complementary reforms in education, trade policy, and debt management will be essential to maximizing remittances' developmental potential.

References

Adams, R. H., & Page, J. (2005). Do international migration and remittances reduce poverty in developing countries? World Development, 33(10), 1645–1669.

Chami, R., Fullenkamp, C., & Jahjah, S. (2008). Macroeconomic consequences of remittances. IMF Staff Papers, 51(1), 55-75.

European Commission. (2022). Western Balkans economic report. Brussels: European Union.

Gëdeshi, I., & Jorgoni, E. (2012). Albanian migration and remittances: Trends and impacts. South-East European Journal of Economics and Business, 7(1), 69–83.

IMF. (2020). Regional economic outlook: Europe. Washington, DC: International Monetary Fund.

Kapur, D., & McHale, J. (2019). The global migration of talent: Implications for development. Oxford University Press.

Phillips, P. C. B., & Hansen, B. E. (1990). Statistical inference in instrumental variables regression with I(1) processes. Review of Economic Studies, 57(1), 99–125.

Ratha, D., De, S., & Plaza, S. (2022). Migration and development brief 36: Remittances resilience. World Bank.

UNDP. (2021). Human development report: Western Balkans. United Nations Development Programme.

World Bank. (2023). World development indicators. Retrieved from https://data.worldbank.org

Appendix

Figure 1.

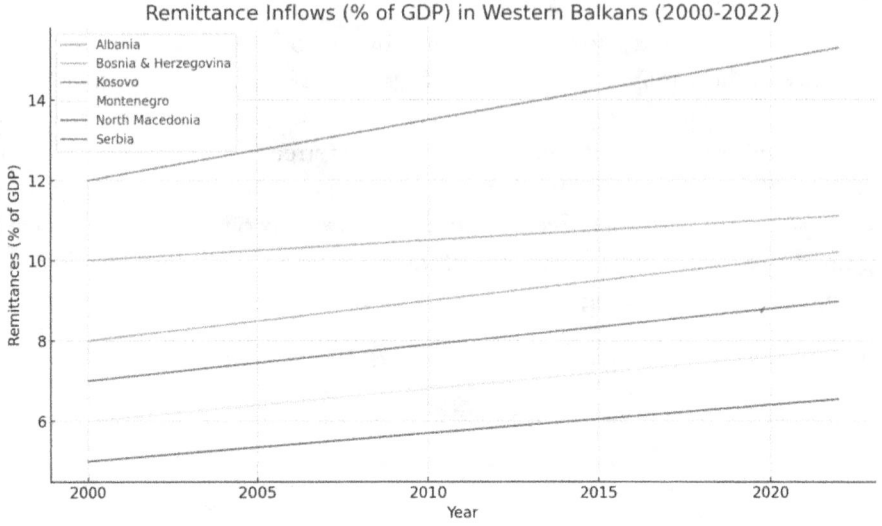

Remittance Inflows (% of GDP) in Western Balkans (2000-2022)

Source: Author's calculations

Figure 2.

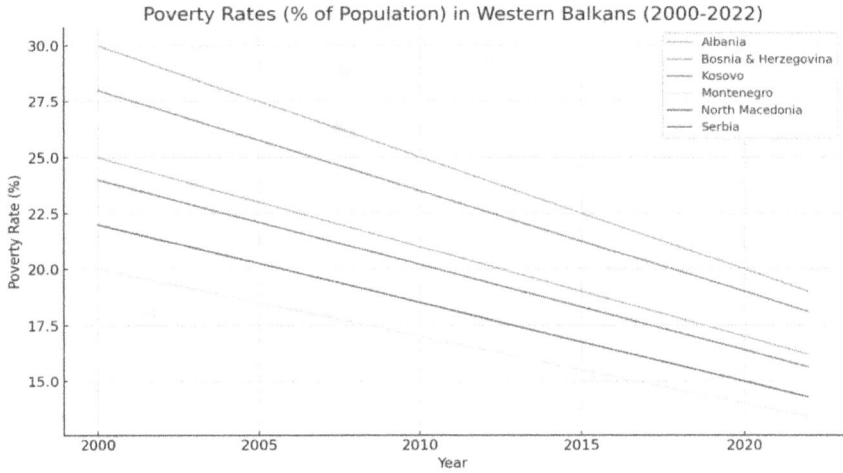

Poverty Rates (% of Population) in Western Balkans (2000-2022)

Source: Author's calculations

Figure 3.

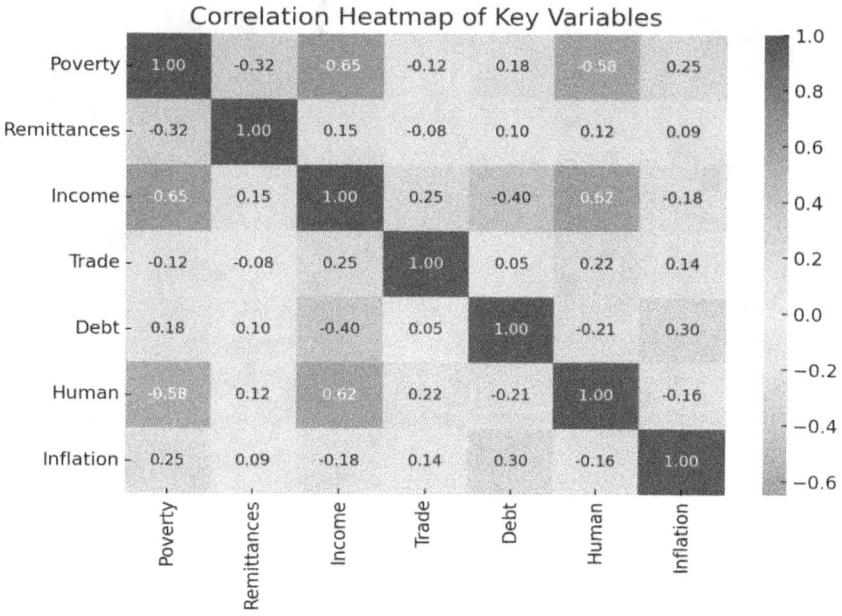

Correlation Heatmap of Key Variables

Source: Author's calculations

IMPACT OF REMITTANCES ON SOCIO-ECONOMIC WELLBEING OF GULF MIGRANTS FAMILY: A STUDY ON DALIT WOMEN DOMESTIC WORKERS FROM ANDHRA PRADESH TO GULF COUNTRIES

Sreenivasulu and Mekala Sagar [1]

Introduction

Women domestic workers migrating from Andhra Pradesh to the Gulf countries occupy a critical yet underexplored space in international labour migration. Their journeys are shaped by a complex web of challenges at both ends of migration—ranging from exploitation and stigma in the destination countries to systemic hurdles in recruitment, financial arrangements, and social perceptions in the home country. While existing studies have highlighted the vulnerability of migrant women workers, there is limited attention to the caste-based differences in migration pathways and the utilisation of remittances. In particular, Scheduled Caste women face distinct barriers during the recruitment and migration process, though evidence on differential experiences at the destination remains limited.

This study examines the socio-economic implications of women's migration, focusing on how remittances transform household livelihoods and rural social structures. Beyond immediate income gains, remittances play a pivotal role in enabling migrant households to purchase land, acquire productive assets, build houses, invest in children's education, and reduce poverty. At the same time, the inflow of earnings from Gulf migration alters social hierarchies and reshapes perceptions of women's mobility, particularly within historically disadvantaged communities.

The paper is structured into five sections. Section II gives an overview of impact of remittances on women migrant's families. Section III analyses the economic impact of remittances on migrant households, focusing on income, assets, and investments. Section IV explores the evolving social status of Gulf women

[1] Sreenivasulu, Associate Professor, Centre for Economics and Social Studies Hyderabad.
Mekala Sagar, Research scholar, Dept. of Economics, Centre for Economics and Social Studies Hyderabad.

domestic workers across different caste groups within rural society. Finally, Section V presents the conclusions of the paper.

Overview of Impact of remittances on women Gulf migrants' families

Remittances, the financial transfers made by migrant workers to their families, are central to both internal and international migration. Classical theories such as those of Ravenstein (1885), Lewis (1954), Harris & Todaro (1970), and Lee (1966) highlight wage differentials, labour supply-demand imbalances, and expected income as drivers of migration. Later contributions by Stark & Bloom (1985) and Lucas & Stark (1985) advanced the New Economics of Labour Migration (NELM), which positioned remittances not only as household support but also as instruments of community-level development and poverty reduction. At the micro level, remittances meet immediate consumption needs, reduce poverty, and allow investments in education, health, housing, and productive assets (Adams & Page, 2005; Oberai & Singh, 1980; Kapur, 2004). They also generate spillover benefits within rural communities. At the macro level, remittances strengthen foreign exchange reserves, contribute to balance of payments, and stimulate economic growth, though they may also exacerbate inequalities (Lucas, 2003). Their multiplier effects vary significantly across countries, ranging from modest in Greece (1.7) to high in Mexico (3.2) (Adelman & Taylor, 1990).

The literature highlights distinct gendered patterns in remittance behaviour. Studies (INSTRAW, 2000; IOM) show that migrant women often remit a larger share of their earnings compared to men, despite receiving lower wages. Women tend to allocate remittances toward food, healthcare, and education, while men direct more towards consumer goods or investments in land and livestock. This shift in women's financial contributions has reshaped household decision-making and gender relations. Migrant women, particularly when they become heads of households, gain autonomy, reduce dependence on extended families, and employ others to reduce their domestic and agricultural workload (Van Rooij, 2000; De Haas, 2007). In India, remittance patterns are complex due to internal migration flows and socio-economic diversity. Families remain the key unit for remittance utilization, mirroring global trends. However, women domestic workers migrating from disadvantaged Scheduled Caste and Backward Class households face distinct vulnerabilities, including unfree labour, unpaid wages, and discrimination. Yet, their remittances are transformative: they enable children's education, asset creation, and house construction, while also challenging entrenched agrarian hierarchies and caste-based domination in rural labour markets.

Economic Status of Migrant Households

Remittances have played an important role in improving the economic status of poor households particularly SC households whose main occupation is agricultural labour in the village. After migration their economic situation has changed. Their human development indices show rise in education levels, health and employment and reduced poverty. Thus, the impact of Gulf migration on household economic situation is better in terms of income levels and living conditions.

Table 1.0: Average Remittances and Utilisation in Last 6-12 Months (Rs.)

District/ Social Category		Remittances sent in last 6 months/1 year	Remittances Used for Household Consumption	Remittances Used for Children's Education	Remittances Used for Health	Remittances Used for Repaying Debt	Remittances Used for Acquiring Assets	Money Saved for Self at Destination
East Godavari	S C	3340000 (100)	376000 (11.26)	288000 (8.62)	50000 (1.5)	2156000 (64.55)	0	470000 (14.07)
	B C	3560000 (100)	472000 (13.26)	40000 (1.12)	0	2430000 (68.26)	18000 (0.51)	600000 (16.85)
	O C	3254000 (100)	551000 (16.93)	40000 (1.23)	40000 (1.23)	1946000 (59.8)	377000 (11.59)	300000 (9.22)
	Total	10154000 (100)	1399000 (13.78)	368000 (3.62)	90000 (0.89)	6532000 (64.33)	395000 (3.89)	1370000 (13.49)
YSR Kadapa	S C	4006000 (100)	630000 (15.73)	720000 (17.97)	60000 (1.5)	1310000 (32.7)	786000 (19.62)	500000 (12.48)
	B C	3494000 (100)	414000 (11.85)	140000 (4.01)	70000 (2)	1530000 (43.79)	460000 (13.17)	880000 (25.19)
	O C	4300000 (100)	631000 (14.67)	428000 (9.95)	86000 (2)	1960000 (45.58)	849000 (19.74)	346000 (8.05)
	Total	11800000 (100)	1675000 (14.19)	1288000 (10.92)	216000 (1.83)	4800000 (40.68)	2095000 (17.75)	1726000 (14.63)

Source: Field study.

Note: Percentages are given within parentheses.

Table 1.0 indicates that the primary aim of women migrating as housemaids is to increase family income, repay debts, and build assets for a better life. In the last six months to one year, total remittances amounted to ₹1.15 crore in East Godavari and ₹1.18 crore in YSR Kadapa, with the latter contributing more across social groups. In YSR Kadapa, OCs (₹43 lakh) and SCs (₹40.06 lakh) remitted the most, while in East Godavari, BCs (₹35.6 lakh) led slightly ahead of SCs and OCs. Expenditure patterns show distinct priorities. Debt repayment dominated, accounting for 64.33% in East Godavari and 40.68% in YSR Kadapa—highest among BCs and SCs in East Godavari, and among OCs and BCs in YSR Kadapa. Household consumption formed a modest share (≈14%

in both districts), but SCs and OCs in YSR Kadapa spent the most on this category. Education emerged as a key priority for SCs, with 8.62% of remittances in East Godavari and 17.97% in YSR Kadapa directed to children's schooling, reflecting aspirations for long-term social mobility. Asset acquisition was far higher in YSR Kadapa (17.75%) than East Godavari (3.89%), driven by OCs and SCs in the former, while SCs in East Godavari reported no investment in assets. Overall, the findings underscore that while debt repayment remains the foremost use of remittances, SC households in particular are leveraging earnings for education, and YSR Kadapa migrants show greater inclination toward asset creation, signalling differentiated pathways of socio-economic progress across caste groups.

Table 1.1: Purpose of Utilisation of Remittances in Last 6-12 Months

(Percentage)

District	Caste	Business	Children's Education	Clearing Debts	Purchasing Permanent Assets	Saving in Banks	Grand Total
East Godavari	SC	18.18 (4)	22.73 (5)	13.64 (3)	45.45 (10)	0.00 (0)	100 (22)
	BC	18.18 (4)	22.73 (5)	13.64 (3)	45.45 (10)	0.00 (0)	100 (22)
	OC	13.64 (3)	22.73 (5)	13.64 (3)	45.45 (10)	9.09 (2)	100 (22)
	Total	16.67 (11)	22.73 (15)	13.64 (9)	45.45 (30)	3.03 (2)	100 (66)
YSR Kadapa	SC	9.09 (2)	31.82) (7)	4.55 (1)	36.36 (8)	13.64 (3)	100 (22)
	BC	15 (3)	35 (7)	10 (2)	30 (6)	10 (2)	100 (20)
	OC	9.09 (2)	13.64 (3)	4.55 (1)	54.55 (12)	18.18 (4)	100 (22)
	Total	10.94 (7)	26.56 (17)	6.25 (4)	40.63 (26)	14.06 (9)	100 (64)

Source: Field study.

Note: Figures in parentheses indicate number of migrants.

Table 1.1 presents the utilisation of remittances by migrant women in the two study districts over a period of six months to one year. The findings indicate that the largest share of remittances was invested in permanent assets—45.45 percent in East Godavari and 40.63 percent in YSR Kadapa. In East Godavari, this pattern was consistent across all social groups, whereas in YSR Kadapa, OCs (54.55 percent) invested the most in asset creation. The second major use of remittances was education. In East Godavari, 22.73 percent of funds were directed to children's education, a trend consistent across social groups. In YSR Kadapa, spending on education was slightly higher (26.56 percent), with BCs

(35 percent) and SCs (31.82 percent) allocating a significant portion of their remittances to schooling. This suggests a growing recognition of education as a pathway for upward mobility, especially among disadvantaged groups. Repayment of debts accounted for 13.64 percent of remittance use in East Godavari and 6.25 percent in YSR Kadapa, reflecting the temporary reliance on loans during migration. Savings for future needs were modest in East Godavari (3.03 percent) but notably higher in YSR Kadapa (14.06 percent). Caste variations were evident: in East Godavari, SCs and BCs reported no formal savings, while in YSR Kadapa, OCs and SCs set aside funds in banks.

Social Status of Migrant Workers

Scheduled Castes (SCs), traditionally positioned at the lowest rung of the social hierarchy, have historically suffered from poor education, limited assets, and dependence on agricultural labour. Gulf migration has brought transformative change to their lives. Through remittances, SC women migrants have been able to construct houses, invest in their children's education, and acquire productive assets such as land. Many have shifted from farm labour to non-farm activities, with some entering self-employment, thereby reducing dependence on caste-based agrarian relations. This shift explains the decline in farm labour households in the villages, as remittances are increasingly channelled into non-agricultural investments. Despite the stigma historically attached to single women's migration for domestic work, attitudes are gradually changing as women across caste groups migrate to the Gulf. In East Godavari, 90.91 percent of migrant women reported that migration improved their lives, and only a small fraction felt their families faced disrespect. In YSR Kadapa, while 56.13 percent reported no impact, 21.88 percent felt their families gained respect, with SC households particularly noting improved social standing. Across both districts, the majority of families acknowledged progress after migration, though a few reported no change. Women's work itself has not fundamentally changed— shifting from agricultural labour at home to domestic service abroad—but the economic outcomes have redefined their perceptions of job satisfaction. Most women migrate out of economic necessity rather than preference for the nature of work. Yet, their responses reveal significant satisfaction with Gulf employment: 90.63 percent of YSR Kadapa women expressed happiness with their jobs, especially among OCs and BCs, followed by SCs. In East Godavari, satisfaction was lower at 50 percent, though still notable, particularly among BC and SC women. These findings underscore that, despite persistent stigma and challenging working conditions, Gulf migration has enabled women, especially from marginalized communities, to achieve higher incomes, greater household security, and improved social recognition.

Conclusions

The study concludes that Gulf migration has significantly transformed both the economic well-being and social relations of women domestic workers and their households. While all communities benefit from higher incomes compared to local work, the impact is particularly striking among Scheduled Caste (SC) migrants, who have channelled remittances into children's education, asset creation, and housing, thereby securing greater social mobility and reducing caste-based wage discrimination. The weakening of traditional patron-client ties with upper-caste women and the visible construction of new houses reflect these shifts in rural power structures. Nevertheless, societal stigma surrounding women's migration remains pervasive, especially towards SC women in YSR Kadapa. Overall, Gulf remittances emerge not only as a means of economic sustenance but also as a catalyst for reconfigured social hierarchies, enhanced aspirations, and more equitable labour market relations in rural Andhra Pradesh.

References

Adams, R. H., Jr., & Page, J. (2005). Do international migration and remittances reduce poverty in developing countries? *World Development, 33*(10), 1645–1669. https://doi.org/10.1016/j.worlddev.2005.05.004

Adelman, I., & Taylor, J. E. (1990). Is structural adjustment with a human face possible? The case of Mexico. *The Journal of Development Studies, 26*(3), 387–407. https://doi.org/10.1080/00220389008422158

De Haas, H. (2007). *Remittances, migration and social development: A conceptual review of the literature* (No. 34). United Nations Research Institute for Social Development. https://www.unrisd.org/unrisd/website/document.nsf/(httpPublications)/D531921B6A07D5A6C12573240036D5A0

Harris, J. R., & Todaro, M. P. (1970). Migration, unemployment and development: A two-sector analysis. *The American Economic Review, 60*(1), 126–142.

Kapur, D. (2005). Remittances: The new development mantra? In S. M. Maimbo & D. Ratha (Eds.), *Remittances: Development impact and future prospects* (pp. 331–360). World Bank. https://doi.org/10.1596/0-8213-5794-8

Lee, E. S. (1966). A theory of migration. *Demography, 3*(1), 47–57. https://doi.org/10.2307/2060063

Lewis, W. A. (1954). Economic development with unlimited supplies of labour. *The Manchester School, 22*(2), 139–191. https://doi.org/10.1111/j.1467-9957.1954.tb00021.x

Lucas, R. E., & Stark, O. (1985). Motivations to remit: Evidence from Botswana. *Journal of Political Economy, 93*(5), 901–918. https://doi.org/10.1086/261341

Lucas, R. E., Jr. (2003). Macroeconomic priorities. *The American Economic Review, 93*(1), 1–14. https://doi.org/10.1257/000282803321455133

Oberai, A. S., & Singh, H. K. (1980). Migration, remittances and rural development: Findings of a case study in the Indian Punjab. *International Labour Review, 119*(2), 229–241.

Ravenstein, E. G. (1885). The laws of migration. *Journal of the Statistical Society of London, 48*(2), 167–235. https://doi.org/10.2307/2979181

Stark, O., & Bloom, D. E. (1985). The new economics of labor migration. *The American Economic Review, 75*(2), 173–178.

Van Rooij, A. (2000). *Women of Taghzoute: The effects of migration on women left behind in Morocco* (Master's thesis). University of Amsterdam.

IMPACT OF MIGRANTS' REMITTANCES AND COVID-19 ON HOUSEHOLD POVERTY AND INEQUALITY: A CASE STUDY OF MAZAR-I-SHARIF, BALKH PROVINCE, AFGHANISTAN

Baqir Khawari[1]

Introduction

Afghanistan remains one of the poorest and most fragile countries globally, with poverty and income inequality deeply entrenched despite decades of development interventions. National poverty rates have risen alarmingly from 34% in 2007/08 to 54.5% in 2017, and further to an estimated 85% in 2022, driven by conflict, economic instability, and the COVID-19 pandemic ((NSIA, 2021; UNDP, 2021). In urban centers such as Mazar-i-Sharif, these challenges are acute, with prior studies reporting poverty rates exceeding 80% and significant income disparities among households (Hall, 2014). Against this backdrop, migration has emerged as a critical survival strategy, with millions of Afghan migrants sending remittances that support household consumption, education, and health needs ((Wickramasekara et al., 2006; Murrugarra et al., 2011). While the poverty-reducing effects of remittances are well-documented globally, their role in mitigating poverty and inequality under conditions of compounded crisis, such as pandemics in fragile contexts, remains underexplored. This study examines whether and how international and domestic remittances have alleviated household poverty and reduced income inequality in Mazar-i-Sharif before and during the COVID-19 pandemic. By providing empirical evidence from an urban fragile setting, this research contributes to understanding the stabilizing yet limited role of remittances in addressing structural poverty and inequality in Afghanistan.

Methodology

This study employs a quantitative cross-sectional design to analyze the impacts of remittances and the COVID-19 pandemic on household poverty and income inequality in Mazar-i-Sharif, Afghanistan. A multi-stage random sampling

[1] Baqir Khawari, Department of Economics, Samangan Higher Education Institute, Aybak, Afghanistan. E-mail: b.khawari@osce-academy.net

technique was used to select households from four urban districts (Nahiyahs) within the city. The target sample size was 1,100 households; however, after accounting for non-responses, the final dataset comprised 1,060 households.

Primary data were collected through structured surveys administered between May and July 2021, covering two reference periods: pre-COVID-19 (March 2019–March 2020) and during COVID-19 (March 2020–March 2021). Poverty was measured using Foster-Greer-Thorbecke (FGT) indices to assess headcount, gap, and severity, while income inequality was analyzed through Gini coefficients and Lorenz curves. Statistical analyses included descriptive statistics, independent t-tests to compare poverty and inequality across periods and remittance statuses, and binary logistic regression to estimate the association between remittances and household poverty risk, controlling for household demographic and socio-economic characteristics. Data were analyzed using STATA 17 and Microsoft Excel.

Results

The Foster-Greer-Thorbecke (FGT) poverty indices demonstrate substantial reductions in poverty when remittances are included in household income. Using the income-based approach, the poverty headcount ratio (HCR) in 2019/20 was 88.7% before remittance inclusion, declining significantly to 69.6% after inclusion. Similarly, during the pandemic year (2020/21), the HCR increased to 93.3% without remittances but decreased to 77.3% after accounting for them. The poverty gap (PG) also declined markedly, from 41.1% to 24.2% in 2019/20 and from 50% to 28.7% in 2020/21. The poverty severity index (PGS) followed the same trend, falling from 23.1% to 11.2% in 2019/20 and from 31.7% to 13.4% in 2020/21. Independent t-tests confirmed that all reductions were statistically significant at the 1% level, underscoring the critical role of remittances in poverty alleviation (see Table 1).

Furthermore, the Gini coefficient results indicate that remittances modestly reduced income inequality. In 2019/20, the Gini coefficient was 0.257 without remittances and decreased to 0.240 with their inclusion. In 2020/21, the Gini rose to 0.289 in the absence of remittances but dropped substantially to 0.217 when remittances were included (see Table 2). Lorenz curve analyses corroborate these findings, showing that remittances shifted income distribution marginally towards lower-income households (see Figure 1 & 2). Notably, the redistributive effect of remittances was more pronounced during the pandemic, although overall inequality remained substantial.

Table 1: Comparison of Poverty Indices Before and After Remittance Inclusion in Mazar-i-Sharif, 2019/20 and 2020/21

Poverty Indices	Stages	Income-based approach				
	First Stage	2019/20 (Pre-C)	Sig	2020/21 (D-C)	Sig	Pre-C vs D-C
HCR	Before including remittances (B)	88.68	A < B***	93.3	A < B***	Pre-C < D-C***
	After including remittances (A)	69.62		77.26		Pre-C < D-C***
PG	Before including remittances (B)	41.09	A < B***	50.02	A < B***	Pre-C < D-C***
	After including remittances (A)	24.23		28.65		Pre-C < D-C***
PGS	Before including remittances (B)	23.14	A < B***	31.65	A < B***	Pre-C < D-C***
	After including remittances (A)	11.24		13.44		Pre-C < D-C***

Table 2: Gini Coefficient Reductions Due to Remittances (Pre- and During COVID-19)

Gini Coefficient (G)	Gini coefficient (2019/20) (Pre-C)			Gini coefficient (2020/21) (D-C)		
	Before Including Remittances (B)	After Including Remittances (A)	Percentage point of reduction	Before Including Remittances (B)	After Including Remittances (A)	Percentage point of reduction
	0.257	0.24	0.017	0.289	0.217	0.072

Figure 1: Lorenz Curve with (b) and without (a) Including Remittances during 2019/20

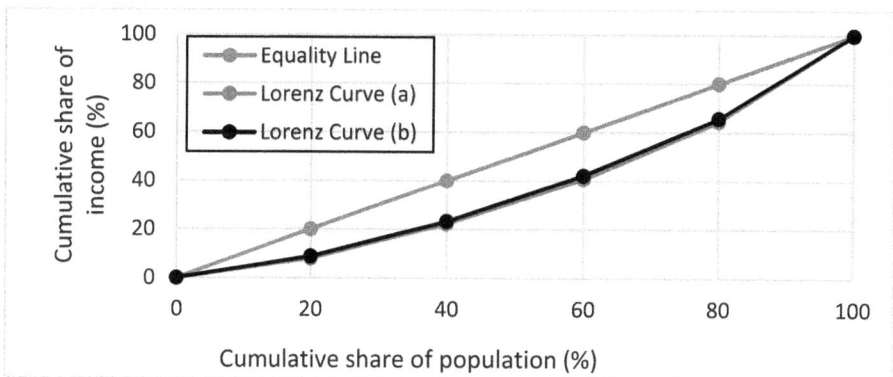

Source: The Authors' Own Work

Figure 2: Lorenz Curve with (b) and without (a) Including Remittances during 2020/21

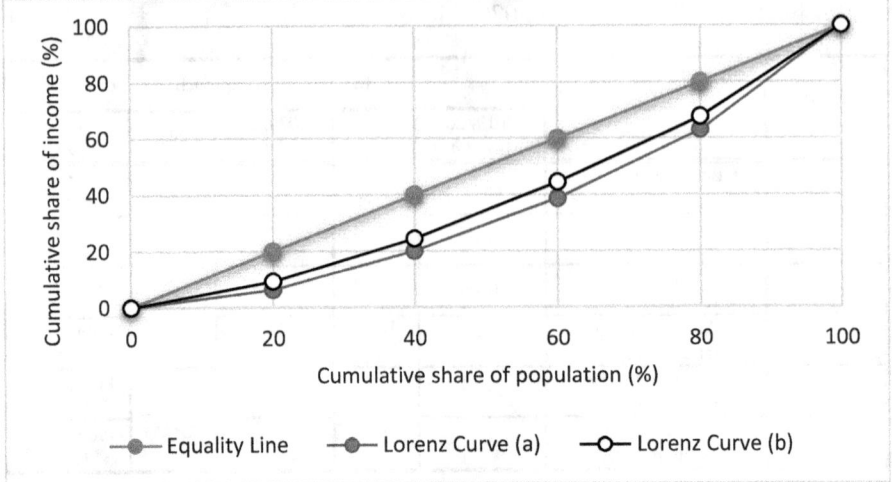

Source: The Authors' Own Work

Specifically, Logistic regression analysis revealed that both international and domestic remittances were significantly associated with reduced household poverty risk. Specifically, a 1% increase in per capita international remittances reduced the probability of a household being poor by 4.5% in 2019/20 and by 3.7% in 2020/21. Domestic remittances reduced poverty likelihood by 3% and 2.5% in the respective periods. These effects were statistically significant at the 1% level. Among control variables, household size was positively associated with poverty risk, while the education level of the household head, the presence of university-educated household members, and a higher male-to-female ratio were significantly and negatively associated with poverty (see Table 3).

Overall, the results underscore that while remittances provided a critical financial buffer against poverty and modestly improved income distribution, their capacity to fully offset the adverse economic impacts of the COVID-19 pandemic remained limited, highlighting the persistence of structural poverty and inequality in Afghanistan's urban context.

Table 3: Logistic Regression Results: Determinants of Household Poverty, 2019/20 and 2020/21

Periods	2019/20				2020/21			
variables	Coefficient	Standard Error	Odds ratio	Marginal Effect	Coefficient	Standard Error	Odds ratio	Marginal Effect
international-remit	-0.3527722	0.0205672***	0.7027373	-0.0451002	-0.3451861	0.0232637***	0.7080886	-0.0371119
Domestic-remit	-0.2316575	0.0223658***	0.7932178	-0.0296163	-0.2303476	0.0264533***	0.7942575	-0.0247653
HH-size	0.5108436	0.0840147***	1.67E+00	0.0653089	0.601269	0.1093578***	1.82E+00	0.064644
HHh-educ	-0.0975592	0.0184391***	9.07E-01	-0.0124725	0.1528932	0.0197948***	8.58E-01	-0.016438
Gen-HHh	-0.5314088	0.1721335*	0.5877763	-0.0679381	0.7803557	0.1462431	0.458243	-0.0838981
Age of HHh	0.132278	0.0445034***	1.141426	0.0169111	0.0162156	0.0421112	1.016348	0.0017434
Age squared of HHh	-0.0015086	0.0003886***	0.9984926	-0.0001929	-0.0004533	0.0004172	0.9995468	-0.0000487
HH member with university education	-0.4253602	0.0689921***	0.6535343	-0.0543803	-0.3344465	0.0847181***	0.7157342	-0.0359572
Percentage of Male	-0.0229827	0.0060499***	0.9772794	-0.0029382	-0.0192072	0.0063784***	0.9809761	-0.002065
Number of observation	1060				1,060			
Peseudo R2	0.3486				0.3626			
LR chi2(15)	453.81				412.09			
Prob > chi2	0.00000				0.0000			
Log likelihood	-423.96605				-362.18226			

Note: The standard error, ***p<0.01, **p<0.05, *p<0,1.

Discussion

This study examined the impact of migrants' remittances and the COVID-19 pandemic on household poverty and income inequality in Mazar-i-Sharif, Afghanistan. The results reveal that remittances significantly reduced poverty incidence, depth, and severity across both the pre-pandemic and pandemic periods, with international remittances exerting a stronger poverty-reducing effect than domestic remittances. This finding aligns with global evidence demonstrating the vital role of remittances in supplementing household incomes, especially in fragile settings where formal social protection systems are limited or absent.

However, the study also finds that the poverty-reducing effect of remittances weakened during the pandemic, as overall poverty rates increased substantially despite continued inflows. This suggests that while remittances serve as a critical coping mechanism, their effectiveness is constrained under systemic shocks that simultaneously reduce migrant earnings and increase household dependence on transfers. The persistence of high poverty rates, even among remittance-receiving households, underscores the limitations of remittances in addressing the structural drivers of poverty such as unemployment, inflation, and restricted economic opportunities in Afghanistan.

In terms of income inequality, the inclusion of remittances modestly improved income distribution, as indicated by reductions in the Gini coefficient and upward shifts in Lorenz curves, particularly during the pandemic. This suggests that remittances had a redistributive effect by increasing the income shares of lower quintiles. However, the overall magnitude of this effect remained limited, with inequality remaining substantial in both periods. This reflects the structural nature of income concentration in urban Afghanistan and highlights that while remittances can mitigate inequality to some extent, they cannot overcome institutional and market barriers that perpetuate disparities.

The regression results further underscore the significance of education and household demographics in shaping poverty outcomes. Households with higher educational attainment were less likely to be poor, highlighting the protective role of human capital investment. Conversely, larger household sizes were associated with higher poverty risks, reflecting demographic pressures on limited income resources.

These findings contribute to the growing literature emphasizing the conditional effectiveness of remittances. In Afghanistan's context, remittances provide an essential financial buffer but are insufficient to achieve sustainable poverty reduction and equitable economic development in the absence of broader structural reforms. Thus, while remittances remain a lifeline for many households, policies aiming to enhance their development impact should be integrated with strategies that address systemic economic vulnerabilities, improve access to education and employment, and strengthen social protection mechanisms. This comprehensive approach is necessary to ensure that remittances can support not only short-term household survival but also long-term poverty alleviation and inclusive growth in fragile states.

Conclusion

This study examined the role of migrants' remittances in alleviating household poverty and reducing income inequality in Mazar-i-Sharif, Afghanistan, before and during the COVID-19 pandemic. The findings demonstrate that remittances significantly reduced poverty incidence, depth, and severity, with international remittances having a stronger effect than domestic transfers. Remittances also modestly reduced income inequality by improving the income shares of lower-income households, particularly during the pandemic. However, despite their positive impacts, remittances were insufficient to fully offset the economic shocks of COVID-19, and poverty and inequality remained structurally high. These results underscore that while remittances are a critical short-term safety net, they cannot replace comprehensive development policies and structural reforms needed to achieve sustainable poverty reduction and equitable growth in Afghanistan.

Policy Implications

The findings highlight the need for policies that enhance the effectiveness of remittances as a development tool. First, improving access to affordable, secure, and efficient remittance transfer channels, particularly digital systems, can maximize their reach and impact. Second, financial literacy programs targeting remittance-receiving households should be implemented to promote effective utilization for productive investments, savings, and long-term resilience. Third, targeted social protection measures are essential for non-recipient households, who remain highly vulnerable. Finally, integrating remittance data into national poverty monitoring frameworks can improve policy design and ensure that remittance flows complement broader economic and social development strategies in fragile contexts like Afghanistan.

References

Hall, S. (2014). Urban Poverty Report: A Study of Poverty, Food Insecurity and Resilience in Afghan Cities. Danish Refuge Council and People In Need, Kabul, Afghanistan. https://www.clovekvtisni.cz/media/publications/729/file/1433502328-pin-drc-afghanistan-2014-a-study-of-poverty-food-security-and-resilience.pdf

Murrugarra, E., Larrison, J., & Sasin, M. (2011). Migration and Poverty Toward Better Opportunities for the Poor. https://openknowledge.worldbank.org/handle/10986/2535#:~:text=Through%20remitta nces%2C%20migration%20provides%20a,strategy%20in%20times%20of%20distress

NSIA. (2021). Income and Expenditure & Labor Force Surveys Report 2020. National Statistic and Information Authority, Kabul, Afghanistan. Accessed on September 6, 2022. https://fscluster.org/sites/default/files/documents/income-and-lobar-force-survey-2020-

15.pdf

UNDP. (2021, September 9). Afghanistan on the brink of universal poverty: UN. Al Jazeera and News Agencies. https://www.aljazeera.com/news/2021/9/9/nearly-all-afghans-to-plunge-into-poverty-by-mid-2022-warns-un

Wickramasekara, P., Sehgal, J., Mehran, F., Noroozi, L., & Eisazadeh, S. (2006). Afghan households in Iran: Profile and impact. *International Migration Programme International Labour Office.* https://www.researchgate.net/profile/piyasiri-wickramasekara/publication/238707241 afghan households and workers in iran profile and impact/links/02e7e528328a011079000000/afghan-households-and-workers-in-iran-profile-and-impact.pdf

IDENTITIES AND INTEGRATION

LAS PATRONAS. WOMEN'S AGENCY, EXPERIENCES, AND RESILIENCES AROUND TRANSIT MIGRATION

Fanny Margot Tudela Poblete and Jesús Antonio Madera Pacheco

Introduction

Understanding the agency of *Las Patronas* requires situating their practices within the border transformations of migration in Mexico and Central America, marked by structural tensions, multiple vulnerabilities, and institutional challenges (resulting from Trump's migration policies) that shape both risks and opportunities for collective action.

In 2025, human mobility across Mexico is still driven by the persistent economic inequality, political and criminal violence. Still, it has increased due to the environmental crises, political persecution, and multiple deportations. The restrictive and reinforced barriers to regular transit, policies of migrant "dispersion" across Mexican territory, and the militarization of internal and external borders are increasing the vulnerabilities of the people who cannot travel in a "documented" way. This creates a highly contradictory space: the nation-states' reinforcement of the narrative of globalization is the worst aspect of this complexity.

It is essential to note a significant shift in the actual migratory context under Donald Trump's administration, as the United States' migration policy has become increasingly restrictive. A national emergency was declared at the southern border, which justified the deployment of military personnel to support Customs and Border Protection (CBP) operations. These measures were accompanied by the resumption of mass deportations and the establishment of new quotas for Immigration and Customs Enforcement (ICE) arrests.

Mexico has a particularity for the geographic localization, the people migrate to the U. S. and pass through, but also, especially after the 2018 exodus, Mexico is also seen as a country of residence, and until now, the different types of migrants are "cohabiting" in the same space: the same migrants can try to pass, stay or even sometimes get back to their countries. In addition to this, the people who migrate and pass through Mexico are changing too; now there are individuals

193

from Asia, Africa, and Europe trying to pass through or stay in Mexico, applying for a visa, seeking refuge, or remaining undocumented.

According to the OECD (2024), the number of people applying for a migratory process is increasing, but at the same time, the policies and requirements are being tightened. For example, the National Migration Institute (INM) is having changes and working with the government to "manage" and help the non-documented migratory flow with measures as the installation of humanitarian points on major railway routes or the assisted return.

Still, this institutional support is not enough the passage of the people[1] carries with the basic needs of every human being: to eat, to clean, to sleep, etc., and they cannot have access easily, so most of the migrants can have it thanks to the chained actions of international organizations, governmental institutions, but mainly of the society, people who wanted to help and the existing collectives that support and protect Central Americans as they pass through Mexican territory.

The reactions and actions to support migrants are typically initiated by ordinary people who rush to help in this situation; their actions can be individual, but those that occur collectively or have a significant impact are more notable. Within this scenario, *Las Patronas* stands out as a crucial collective actor. The way Central American migrants view Mexico has also changed, as it was initially seen as just a country of transit. However, after 2018 and the "exodus", Mexico is seen as a destination land (asylum, refuge, work, etc.).

The collectives, such as Las Patronas, are comprised of ordinary people, and most of them do not have a profession in caring for others. However, as they carry out their actions and recognize their context and resources through experience, they specialize in what they do, from advocating for people to raise awareness about the migratory phenomenon to providing assistance and defence for Central Americans in situations of danger. The analysis of these elements is articulated in conjunction with Norman Long's agency and actor-oriented analysis. This paradigm enables us to observe everyday elements and prioritize our experiences.

This study follows that logic, focusing on the agency of migrant-support collectives, their contexts, and the collective actions they undertake, all of which

---

[1] According to the OIM (Why Is It So Difficult to Collect Data on Irregular Migration? 2025), it is difficult to have the exact data of undocumented migrants due to the very nature of the problem and the lack of reliable data. Estimates suggest that they represent a significant portion.

are dynamic and constantly evolving. To capture this complexity, it is essential to establish the analytical standpoint from which reality is observed. We chose the actor-oriented approach of Norman Long, which considers how local traditions, global systems, and external interventions intersect through the interaction of actors and structures.

Agency and the Multi-sited Ethnography

Agency is fundamental to understanding the role of groups surrounding the migrant phenomenon, as it brings visibility to actors often overlooked in traditional sociological theories. From this perspective, ordinary individuals, drawing on their everyday experiences and resources, process their realities, make collective decisions, and form networks aimed at protecting and supporting Central American migrants in transit through Mexico.

In an actor-oriented analysis, individuals become social actors when they participate in local spaces, assume leading roles, and use identity and cultural diversity as tools to create networks and collective action. This approach emphasizes that social processes are shaped not only by the agency of these actors but also by their interaction with external interventions, such as global systems, local structures, and cultural traditions. For Long (2007), the agency:

It refers to the ability to know and act, and to the way in which actions and reflections constitute social practices that impact or influence actions and interpretations of oneself and others (...). The agency is therefore composed of a complex mix of social, cultural, and material elements (Long, 2007: 442).

Agency can be understood as the set of capacities that enable actors to process their lived experiences and the social context in which they are situated. The focus is on the dynamic relationship between their reality, experiences, knowledge, and the small details of everyday life—les petites choses— and the spaces where their actions are made.

In this sense, the methodology must be dynamic also, and put the attention on these details, so the ethnography is prioritized as the methodological approach in this research, given the contemporary context in which migration policies are shaped by globalization and hegemonic political discourses, and where virtual platforms provide access to information that would otherwise be unavailable.

Multi-sited ethnography (Marcus, 2014) enables the researcher to trace the mobility of subjects, objects, and symbolisms across diverse cultural, social, symbolic, and economic contexts, linking physical sites—such as shelters and community dining halls—with virtual spaces like Facebook or YouTube. This perspective enables the recognition of multiple lifeworlds, which, although distinct, complement each other and share common threads.

For this reason, multi-sited ethnography was employed, enabling the analysis of collectives' practices across both physical spaces—such as shelters—a space in movement, like La Bestia, and virtual or symbolic arenas, like social networks. This methodology enables the interweaving of diverse territories of action while accounting for their similarities, differences, and connections. Within this framework, the study examines Las Patronas as a case, integrating theoretical debates on agency and actor-oriented analysis with empirical findings that highlight the significance of grassroots humanitarian action.

Las Patronas and their actions

The number of transit migrants in Mexico has increased since 2018. With the new political panorama, the flow and the objectives are changing but not stopping, just to put an example, between October 2018 and March 2019, more than 300,000 Central Americans crossed Mexico aiming to reach the United States or settle in Mexican territory (Nájar, 2019), a figure that doubled the annual flows estimated in previous years. Between 2021 and 2024, the number of administrative records of people entering the U.S. without proper documentation rose from 309,692 to 1,234,698 cases (Burgos, 2025).

As the migrants use alternate ways (which are not always safe) to cross the border, consequently and by the "irregularity" of their transit, they suffer violent acts by subjects, organizations, or institutions; that is to say, they are the subject of multiple violence, including the symbolic charge.

In this context, people and collectives that emerge to support Central American migrants are often comprised of individuals without formal training in social work, such as religious leaders, students, and homemakers. So, why do they help? "Women are no longer passive recipients of welfare aid but seen by men and themselves as agents of change: dynamic promoters of social transformations that can alter the lives of both women and men" (Sen, 2000: 233).

According to Sen, women are changing their reality with the experience and the "routine" actions as cooks or caregivers. This is the situation of Las Patronas, a group of women based in La Patrona, a small community in Veracruz, Mexico. They have been working since 1995 to provide humanitarian aid to migrants traveling to the United States, especially whom is traveling on La Bestia.2 They start with a "spontaneous" action of sharing food with passing migrants; their beginning was with their own resources, and over time, they begin to form networks, collaborate with other collectives, or seek additional help.

Their actions now include preparing and distributing meals, offering shelter, and advocating for the rights of migrants. Their work has become emblematic of solidarity and humanitarian resistance in the face of increasingly restrictive migration policies. They have not stopped working for more than 30 years. The women are constantly adapting their actions to different scenarios, such as the exodus of migrants or the COVID-19 pandemic.

This collective has two fundamental characteristics, apart from being led by women; the first is that it is mainly composed of family members (mother, sisters, and granddaughter), and the second is that its dining room has a designated space. However, the most critical actions are performed in a moving space, that is, La Bestia, where they provide food during the train's passage.

The rationality in actor-oriented analyses refers to the other resources the individual possesses, such as their own experience, personal skills, or prior knowledge, like caring for a child or cooking. In this case, Las Patronas, driven by feelings of empathy or love, have triggers that prompt their actions. Emotions, for Long (2007), shape the sense of actions because they are associated with motivations and values that will influence their logic of action that led to taking specific strategies with what they have at their disposal, like it might be, to take off part of your pantry to give to someone else or to get up 5 am to cook 20 kilos of rice to strangers.

Las Patronas emerged from personal experiences and motivations, such as the desire to help, the recognition of migrants' hunger, and the empathy felt toward the families traveling north. When these individual actions and feelings were shared and legitimized collectively, particularly among the women and their families who make up the group, the initiative gained strength as a community project. Rooted in a specific territorial context—the proximity to the route of La Bestia—and shaped by their own economic and cultural conditions, Las Patronas organized themselves as a response to the humanitarian needs of migrants.

This collective has developed strategies to know how to react to situations that

---

2 Freight trains transiting through Mexico, the migrants use them to cross the country.

might seem obvious, such as having extra staff to help care for migrants, an exodus, or when the migrants are injured. The direct organization of Las Patronas is related to the family context of the dynamic agents, specifically whether any of the women have small children or are responsible for their husbands or the household, leaving them with little time to do anything else. Although the organization and roles outlined in Las Patronas are seen more horizontally, since each woman chooses the day that suits her best, there is also an order for decision-making, such as the establishment of collective coordination.

It is important to highlight that these women had to "fight" for their freedom to act, since most of them could not help outside their home or do anything that their parents, brothers, or husbands would not allow. The "public" recognition of certain rights of action of Las Patronas reaffirms the importance of the agency of women. In 2013, their efforts were recognized with Mexico's National Human Rights Award, highlighting the contrast between state-level securitization measures and community-driven responses centered on empathy, dignity, and human rights. This could be a "simple" award, but public recognition had an impact on their actions and the reach of it.

Las Patronas and their actions start with the desire to solve a basic need, such as eating. The trigger was to provide food because, for them, every human being must have access to it. "I am nobody, I just feed these people, give them a bag of food and give them water, and how they receive me with so much love?" (Patrona 2, 2017).

The dynamism in women's actions, in this case, Las Patronas, is connected to fundamental needs such as transit through Mexican territory, clothing, or medical care, but also to various situations that require flexibility and improvisation. They have been influenced by improvisation and routine since their formation, being "ordinary" women who do not have training in humanitarian care or cooking. The actions they have taken are based on what they have learned in their lives.

Conclusion

In this Research, actor-oriented analysis supports the presentation of a new subject, the women in *Las Patronas* who observe the experience and, through rational and reflective processes, build their agency. Considering that there is a multiplicity of actors and consequently desires, capacities, and practices, a definition of agency is constructed in the fourth chapter. This perspective enabled us to highlight the everyday aspects of what the collectives experienced. The emphasis on everyday things is what distinguishes collectives, as well as their impact and the way they act.

References

Burgos, J. (2025, septiembre 9). Se incrementa la migración en tránsito por México. *Criterio.hn.* https://criterio.hn/migracion-en-transito-por-mexico-paso-de-300-mil-personas-a-mas-de-1-millon-cepal/

Long, N., & Long, A. (1992). Battlefields of knowledge: the interlocking of theory and practice in social research and development. Routledge.(1976). *Essays in Self-Criticism.* London: New Left Books.

Long, N. (2007). Sociología del desarrollo: una perspectiva centrada en el actor. San Luis Potosi: CIESAS

Marcus, G. E. (2014). Etnografía en/del sistema mundo. El surgimiento de la etnografía multilocal. Alteridades, (22), 111–127.

Nájar, A. (2019, abril 24). La «histórica» oleada de cientos de miles de migrantes de todo el mundo que está llegando a México. BBC News Mundo. https://www.bbc.com/mundo/noticias-america-latina-48033101Badiou, A., Bourdieu, P., Butler, J., Didi-Huberman, G., Khiari, S., Rancière, J. (2016). *What is A People?* New York: Columbia University Press.

ONU Migración Americas. (2025, septiembre 11) Why is it so difficult to collect data on irregular migration? | . https://lac.iom.int/en/blogs/why-it-so-difficult-collect-data-irregular-migration

Organisation for Economic Co-operation and Development. OECD.(2024, noviembre 14). .Mexico: International Migration. https://www.oecd.org/en/publications/international-migration-outlook-2024_50b0353e-en/full-report/mexico_d1b0bd46.htmlAlthusser, L.

Sen, A. (2000). Libertad y desarrollo. Bogotá: Editorial Planeta. Distrito Federal

REFUGEES IN NEUTRAL PORTUGAL DURING THE SECOND WORLD WAR: HOSPITALITY AND INTRANSIGENCE

Carolina Henriques Pereira[1]

Introduction

During the summer of 1940, following the German occupation of the major countries of Western Europe, thousands of Jews fled the territories occupied by the Nazis in search of salvation. However, only a part of them reached Portugal and, consequently, travelled to overseas destinations. From the end of June, and especially throughout the first half of July 1940, Portugal became crowded with desperate refugees seeking entry into what was the last "free port" of Europe. The refugees who sought temporary refuge in Portugal (rather than exile, as this was not permitted by the regime) mostly went to North America, South America, and England. However, some remained in Portugal after the war ended under special circumstances, either because they had rebuilt their lives there or because they were afraid to live outside Europe. Some also didn't want to return to their countries of origin.

At the time, Portugal was largely unknown and therefore not a particularly attractive place to transit through or to seek exile. From the limited information they had about this small southwestern European country, gleaned from brief propaganda and tourist articles in French magazines such as *Marie Claire*, *Jour de France*, and *Match*, the refugees knew that Portugal was a predominantly poor country governed by a dictatorial regime that was very wary of foreigners, especially communists, entering its territory. Cascais and Estoril were the best-known places on the coast near the capital. Known as the "Costa do Sol", these places were often compared to the French Riviera. Along with Lisbon, these were the only places in Portugal that refugees had heard of. Therefore, they were the places where everyone wanted to live temporarily. However, Estoril and Cascais were mainly where the royalty, diplomats, renowned artists, and, in short, the *crème de la crème* of European society stayed at the time. The bulk of

---

[1] PhD. University of Coimbra – Faculty of Arts and Humanities and the Center for the History of Society and Culture (CHSC-FLUC), Portugal. Email address: chpereira@fl.uc.pt

the refugees, unknown to the public, ordinary men, women, and children, settled temporarily in the capital, Lisbon, or in thermal and bathing resorts in the central and coastal areas of the country. Although both Jewish and non-Jewish refugees entered Portugal at different stages between 1933 and the end of the war in 1945, the majority arrived during the spring and summer of 1940.

Given its position of neutrality, Portugal ended up playing (although against its will) a fundamental role in hosting refugees during the Second World War. The "Estado Novo" was a regime deeply nationalist, conservative, and anti-communist, ruled with firm hand by António de Oliveira Salazar, and like other European fascisms, such as Italy and Germany, Salazar's ideological discourse was based on traditions, heritage, heroic deeds, and the greatness of the nation, as opposed to the clear decadence of those days, from his perspective. However, the regime was eventually confronted with the actions of one of its diplomats in France, which the state considered clear disobedience. The consul in Bordeaux, Aristides de Sousa Mendes (1885-1954), granted transit visas free of charge and indiscriminately to all who requested them, going against the circulars in force (which foresaw the loss of autonomy of their consuls in issuing transit visas for the country) and, above all, Salazar's orders. During the disciplinary proceedings he faced at the hands of the Portuguese government in the summer of 1940, shortly after the events in question, Sousa Mendes stated the following in his defence:

> "I tried to honour the mission entrusted to me and defend our good name and prestige. As Portugal's representative, I was addressed by some of the most eminent people from countries with which we have always enjoyed the best relations. In general, they expressed appreciation and consideration for Portugal, a hospitable and welcoming country where they could find peace and rest from suffering and fatigue. In my opinion, their words are the greatest reward for what I did for them."[2].

Salazar disregarded Sousa Mendes' extensive explanations and failed to recognise the importance of his humanitarian act, which he ultimately exploited to his advantage. He used Sousa Mendes' case as an example to discourage others from ignoring or disobeying his orders. He therefore removed the consul from his diplomatic career, sentencing him to forfeit half his salary, after which

---

[2] Diplomatic Historical Archive of the Ministry of Foreign Affairs (Lisbon, Portugal), Disciplinary Proceedings of Aristides de Sousa Mendes, S2.1. E6. P7/ 14962, letter from Sousa Mendes dated August 10, 1940, p. 9. Author's translation.

he was to retire[3]. Although the consul was forcibly removed by the regime, the refugees publicly and privately recognised the importance of his role in rescuing them. Ultimately, it is impossible to discuss the presence of refugees in Portugal during the Second World War without acknowledging his actions. One example is the French writer Gisèle Quittner Allatini (1883-1965), who did not shy away from telling what she thought about him, referring to Sousa Mendes as a man of great qualities and a source of "honor for your country"[4]. The main escape route used by refugees with transit visas issued by the consulate in Bordeaux passed through cities such as Bayonne, Burgos, and Salamanca, with the refugees entering the country through the border town of Vilar Formoso. Thus, despite being opposed, the Portuguese authorities had to allow the refugees to enter at the Vilar Formoso border crossing, "since Spain would not allow them to return to France through its territory, because they had 'a good visa for Portugal from a Portuguese consul' [5], according to the director of the PVDE [political police], Agostinho Lourenço". While the majority of those who made it to Portugal had some possessions, many were ordinary people with few resources and no connections. Those who had exhausted all their financial and material resources by selling their possessions, such as cars and jewellery, to sustain their stay, as well as those who arrived impoverished, were helped by various national and international Jewish and non-Jewish organisations.

A testimony by a Czech refugee who entered the country in June 1940 shows us the widespread perception of Portuguese hospitality: "(…) when the train reached the border station at Vilar Formoso, the passengers were asked to disembark. Nobody was allowed to continue to Lisbon. Smiling villagers emerged from all sides, bearing baskets of food and offering us bread, cheese, and fruit. This unexpected display of human kindness visibly improved everyone's mood"[6]. Despite the numerous reports of hospitality, the Portuguese government was determined to keep the refugees out of the country. Although it did not manage to stop them, it tried to cause them bureaucratic inconvenience and difficulties to force them to leave for other destinations as soon as possible. It is therefore important to dispel the widespread notion of national hospitality and recognise that the treatment of refugees by most Portuguese authorities was very different from the positive reactions of local

---

[3] Diplomatic Historical Archive of the Ministry of Foreign Affairs (Lisbon, Portugal), Disciplinary Proceedings of Aristides de Sousa Mendes, S2.1. E6. P7/ 14962, letter dated October 30, 1940.
[4] DHAMFA (Lisbon, Portugal), S2.1. E6. P7/ 14962, letter dated August 12, 1940.
[5] Cláudia Ninhos, *O essencial sobre Aristides de Sousa Mendes*, Lisbon, Imprensa Nacional Casa da Moeda, 2021, p. 76.
[6] Maria Bauer, *Beyond the Chestnut Trees*, New York, The Overlook Press, 1984, p. 105.

populations who lived with them during their brief stay in Portugal. Upon entering the Portuguese border, the refugees were dispersed by the authorities to different locations around the country.

This was done on purpose to prevent the spread of modern, democratic, and *avant-garde* ideals in the Portuguese capital. Only those who already had all the necessary paperwork (visas and sea tickets) to leave Portugal quickly were sent there. They were then concentrated in thermal and bathing resorts on the coast and in the centre of the country that had the logistical capacity to accommodate greater numbers (places designated as "fixed residences"), such as Caldas da Rainha, Curia, Ericeira, and Figueira da Foz. Although the creation of "fixed residences" was compulsory, it gave refugees more freedom and better living conditions. However, they were forbidden to move more than 5 km without permission from the local political police, and they had to revalidate and/or apply for a new residence permit from the PVDE every 30 days. In these microcosms, where the government had concentrated the refugees, the local population was acutely aware of the foreigners' presence.

To combat the idleness resulting from waiting incessantly for visas and sea passages to overseas countries, the refugees made the most of their temporary stay in the country by going to the beach, going for walks, playing sports, going to the cinema, and visiting social and gambling establishments such as casinos. They also took part in dances and shows organised for local charities whenever possible. One of the events was a piano recital, held at the Figueira da Foz Casino on 17 July 1940, featuring two renowned pianists: Witold Malcuzynski (1914-1977) and Colette Gaveau (1914-?). This charity recital, in aid of relief work in Figueira da Foz, was a huge success, so another session was scheduled for 29 July 1940. The Portuguese writer Luís Cajão (1920-2008) referred to the show as a tremendous success, stating that "In a provincial town, the concert made a reasonable profit for the time"[7].

However, despite their urgent need to leave Europe for permanent residences elsewhere, the refugees made a point of thanking the Portuguese people and authorities for their hospitality when they left and shortly after they arrived. This is because the refugees still believe that the way they were welcomed by Portugal was substantially more positive than the welcome they received in other transit countries, such as France and Spain, where refugees were held in internment

---

[7] Luís Cajão, *As torrentes da memória. Histórias e inconfidências do arco-da-velha*, Lisbon, Palas Editores, 1979, p. 14 and *O Figueirense*, July 24 1940, p. 1.

camps rather than in open spaces (towns and villages) without walls or barbed wire as in Portugal. It should be noted, though, that the Portugal hospitality was not politically or economically disinterested, and historically it is necessary to distinguish between the rigid and indifferent actions of national authorities and the helpful, understanding, and emotional attitude of local populations.

In summary, it is important to recognise that, despite its small size, Portugal played a central role in the history of refugees during the Second World War. However, due to Salazar's restrictive policies, Portugal was primarily a country of transit rather than a definitive place of exile during this period. Salazar only tolerated refugees in his country for a short time, creating bureaucratic hassles and trying to speed up their departure. Salazar also took credit for the humanitarian act of the consul whom he had severely punished to save the regime and the Portuguese colonies, thereby gaining favourable international public opinion in the process. The Portuguese population generally favoured the presence of refugees, showing solidarity with these foreigners and living closely alongside them despite occasional conflicts relating to their stay in Portugal.

In essence, our communication sought to demonstrate how the presence of refugees in Portugal during this period was characterised by the population's natural hospitality and the regime's firm intransigence. However, it also emphasised the significant role played by a neutral country like Portugal in the temporary reception of refugees fleeing war, racial and religious persecution, and the Nazi Holocaust.

ACCULTURATION OF UNACCOMPANIED CHILDREN IN TURKEY: CHALLENGES AND POLICY IMPLICATIONS

Betul Dilara Seker

Introduction

Every year, unaccompanied minors are forcibly displaced worldwide due to various reasons. Children may migrate for reasons such as war, conflict, famine, education, etc. However, children can also be actors in their families' migration projects. In other words, methods such as first sending the child to a foreign country and then having family members follow them are also being tried (İçduygu, 2024:11). Therefore, migration has a wide international, national, and local impact. It can be said that children are the most negatively affected by migration movements. Therefore, the problem of unaccompanied minors across various age groups is experiencing a gradual increase in the number of unaccompanied minors (Dost & Gökez, 2024). Due to its geographical location, Turkey is observed to be both a transit and destination country in the migration process. Migration is classified as regular or irregular depending on the mode of entry into the destination country. The number of irregular migrants in Turkey has been rapidly increasing over the last fifteen years. Those who enter the country regularly, that is, registered, are called migrants or asylum seekers or refugees, depending on their mode of migration and their legal status in their destination. While these groups have their own unique characteristics, it is known that children, especially unaccompanied minors, are at greater risk and vulnerability in different migration statuses. A healthy parent-child relationship has a protective effect on young individuals who have not yet completed their physical and psychosocial development in coping with traumatic experiences (Betancourt & Khan, 2008). However, children's deprivation of this relationship negatively impacts them. Therefore, it can be said that unaccompanied children are in a riskier position than their peers in many respects. Studies show that unaccompanied children witness more traumatic events than children who migrate with their families (Kaya et al., 2020). Similarly, it is known that unaccompanied children in the destination country experience social exclusion, victimization of hate crimes, and difficulty holding on to life due to the inability to establish healthy peer relationships and the marginalizing rhetoric of peer bullying and media (KOREV, 2017). Furthermore, unaccompanied children are known to be the most at-risk group in child trafficking, where children are exploited for illegal adoption, organ transplantation, sexual or labor purposes, or similar malicious purposes (Atasü-Topçuoğlu, 2019).

Unaccompanied Minors in Turkey

Any person under the age of eighteen is considered a child. This group, referred to as "unaccompanied children" in the literature, is defined in the UNHCR Guidelines on Determining the Best Interests of the Child as "unaccompanied children or unaccompanied minors" (Dost and Gökez, 2024).

General procedures for asylum seekers and refugees are regulated by international conventions and national laws. However, situations involving children are addressed within the framework of the UN Convention on the Rights of the Child and domestic legal regulations, based on non-discrimination, the child's best interests, and the right to survival, development, and participation. Turkey, with a policy that respects the right to survival and development of every child, including refugee and refugee children, aims to: It is known that available resources are distributed indiscriminately (Kaya et al., 2020). It is known that unaccompanied children experience social exclusion, victimization of hate crimes, and difficulty in maintaining their lives because of their inability to establish healthy peer relationships, peer bullying, and marginalizing media discourse (KOREV, 2017). When these children are placed in institutional care, they face the obligation to leave the institution after the age of 18 if they are not continuing their education. One in every two refugees in Turkey is a child. Meeting the material and spiritual needs of unaccompanied children and protecting them from all forms of abuse is the responsibility of states parties to the UN Convention on the Rights of the Child. Because detention and similar practices applied to unregistered adult foreigners may not be appropriate for children, unaccompanied children receive special treatment by states during border control procedures. It is known that, in Turkey, existing resources are distributed without discrimination, with a policy that respects the right to life and development of every child, particularly for asylum-seeking and refugee children (UNICEF, 2017). Practices based on the child's rights of participation and best interests are generally implemented together (Kaya et al., 2020).

According to Article 3 (1) (m) of the Law on Foreigners and International Protection, an unaccompanied child is a child who enters Turkey without the accompaniment of a parent or an adult, either by law or custom, or who remains unaccompanied after entry. According to Article 66 of this law, unaccompanied children have special needs; they are covered by Child Protection Law No. 5395 and are under the responsibility of the Ministry of Family and Social Services. As a rule, there is no legal distinction between unaccompanied foreign children under the age of 18 and Turkish citizen children in Turkey (Ekşi, 2024:19). Child support centers have been established in the provinces of Konya, Ağrı, Yozgat, Gaziantep, Bilecik, Erzincan, Istanbul, and Van for unaccompanied minors arriving in Turkey from countries such as Afghanistan, Somalia, Sudan, Iraq, and Syria.

Children face numerous risks before, during, and after migration (Kayma, 2024). However, reaching their destination and ultimately seeking asylum and humanitarian protection does not offer a solution for unaccompanied refugee minors. Unaccompanied refugee minors often face a variety of challenges, ranging from racist and discriminatory harassment to complex immigration and legal bureaucracies that systematically disrupt or prevent their access to education (Aleghfeli & Hunt, 2022). Unaccompanied refugee minors (UNMs) are at high risk for mental health problems (Jore et al., 2020).

Acculturation and Challenges in Unaccompanied Minors

Existing literature has focused primarily on acculturation among young people who migrate with family members (e.g., research on parent-child acculturation differences; see Birman, 2006; Schwartz et al., 2016), but much remains unknown about acculturation among unaccompanied youth who migrate without families maintaining their culture of origin (Garcia & Birman 2022). Acculturation should be understood as a lifelong negotiation process between the culture of origin/heritage and the host culture (Berry et al., 2006). In fact, this acculturation process cannot be generalized to all unaccompanied minors. Furthermore, given that many unaccompanied minors are male, transferring acculturation data to female groups may be problematic.

Acculturation can be understood as a multidimensional, dynamic process that involves simultaneously adopting aspects of the receiving country and maintaining aspects of the homeland. Berry's most frequently cited acculturation model distinguishes between four main acculturation strategies: assimilation, marginalization, integration, and separation (Berry, 2006). Assimilation describes a strategy in which members of a minority group do not maintain their cultural identity and become strongly oriented toward the host country. In contrast, a separation strategy describes individuals' desire to maintain their cultural identity, while there is no orientation toward the host country. An integration strategy occurs when individuals orient toward both their home country and their host country. Finally, marginalization describes the strategy adopted by individuals who are neither orientated toward their home country nor their host country (El-Awad et al., 2021). Regarding the distribution of preferred acculturation styles among refugees, Copoc (2019) showed that the majority of adult Syrian refugees in Germany demonstrated either an integration (48.4%) or assimilation (42.4%) strategy. Since the acculturation process is always influenced by the attitudes of the receiving society, a similar distribution of acculturation strategies exhibited for unaccompanied minors in Germany can be expected. However, since unaccompanied minors have to deal with both acculturation and developmental tasks simultaneously (Berry et al., 2006), these results may not be generalizable. However, understanding these factors can help facilitate the acculturation process of unaccompanied minors and, consequently, improve their mental health and social inclusion.

Conclusion

This study examines the acculturation processes of unaccompanied minors in Türkiye, aims to shed light on gaps in the literature, and offers guiding recommendations for policymakers. The findings reveal that unaccompanied minors face numerous challenges during the pre-migration, migration, and post-migration periods. These challenges have profound impacts not only at the individual but also at the societal level.

The inadequate statistical data on unaccompanied migrant children worldwide and in Türkiye makes it difficult to understand the true extent of the problem. Identifying, registering, and quickly determining the legal status of these particularly vulnerable children is vital to protecting them from various risks (Düzel & Alış, 2018). Struggling to meet basic needs such as shelter and nutrition, these children later face serious problems in areas such as human trafficking, criminal gangs, and access to education, healthcare, and social services.

The migration experience of unaccompanied children is quite complex due to traumatic experiences and lack of psychosocial support. Problems experienced in basic areas such as institutional care, education, and social integration negatively impact these children's long-term adaptation processes. They also frequently face social problems such as peer bullying, social exclusion, and exposure to the marginalizing language of the media.

Within the framework of Berry's acculturation models, it is crucial to understand which strategies unaccompanied children adopt among integration, assimilation, separation, and marginalization. The prevalence of marginalization and segregation strategies, particularly among these children, highlights the need for more comprehensive policies to support social cohesion. Integrating unaccompanied children by preserving their own culture while also embracing the culture of the host society plays a critical role in both individual and social well-being.

This study offers important recommendations for public policies. First and foremost, the basic living conditions of unaccompanied children must be improved. It is recommended that the physical and service infrastructure of shelters be strengthened, qualified care personnel be employed, and care plans tailored to the children's individual needs be developed. Furthermore, expanding psychosocial support services, language education, and social activities that promote social cohesion will contribute to more effective management of this process.

Refugee and asylum-seeking children, regardless of their ethnicity, religious beliefs, or country of origin, are important actors who will shape the future of the entire world. Therefore, contributing to their healthy development means building a more just, safe, and peaceful future. Public policies should facilitate these children's access to education, health, and social services, and improve the quality of these services. In education, programs aimed at overcoming language barriers and curricula that enhance cultural sensitivity should be developed.

International migration policies and scientific studies focusing on unaccompanied minors are crucial for better understanding their psychological needs and supporting their social inclusion. Migration should not be associated solely with problems and shortcomings; it should also focus on the resilience and skills necessary for successful psychological adaptation. Programs promoting acculturation should provide knowledge of the host society's culture, increase social participation, and strengthen cultural sensitivity. Furthermore, public policies should support initiatives that reduce prejudices against refugees and immigrants and build bridges between the native population and those who arrive (Usama et al., 2021). Ensuring a safe and supportive transition for unaccompanied refugee children, in particular, is vital for a sustainable society.

Consequently, the acculturation process of unaccompanied minors requires a multifaceted approach. Policies supporting social cohesion should be designed to ensure both individual well-being and social integration. Collaboration among public institutions, local governments, and civil society organizations is crucial in this process. Furthermore, conducting more academic research in this area and taking this research into account by policymakers will contribute to a more robust integration process for unaccompanied minors.

References

Aleghfeli, Y. K., & Hunt, L. (2022). Education of unaccompanied refugee minors in high-income countries: Risk and resilience factors. *Educational Research Review, 35,* 100433. https://doi.org/10.1016/j.edurev.2022.100433

Atasü-Topçuoğlu, R. (2019). Türkiye'de göçmen çocukların katılım hakkı. *Itobiad: Journal of the Human & Social Science Researches, 8*(1), 408-430.

Berry, J. W. (2006). Acculturation: A conceptual overview. *Acculturation and parent-child relationships,* 13-32.

Berry, J. W., Phinney, J. S., Sam, D. L., & Vedder, P. (2006). Immigrant youth: Acculturation, identity, and adaptation. *Applied Psychology, 55*(3), 303-332. https://doi.org/10.1111/j.1464-0597.2006.00256.x

Betancourt, T. S., & Khan, K. T. (2008). The mental health of children affected by armed conflict: Protective processes and pathways to resilience. *International Review of Psychiatry, 20*(3), 317-328. https://doi.org/10.1080/09540260802090363

Birman, D. (2006). Measurement of the" acculturation gap" in immigrant families and implications for parent–child relationships. *Acculturation and parent-child relationships,* 113-134.

Copoc, P. (2019). Acculturation of Syrian refugees in Germany: Using a variation of the multidimensional individual difference acculturation (MIDA) model in a new context. *Studies in Undergraduate Research at Guelph, 11*(1), 1-12.

Dost, S., & Gökez, S. (2024). Sığınmacı refakatsiz çocukların korunması ve hukuki temsili. *Süleyman Demirel Üniversitesi Hukuk Fakültesi Dergisi, 14*(1), 421-463.

Düzel, B., & Alış, S. (2018). Düzensiz göçle gelen Suriyeli mülteci çocuklar bağlamında Türkiye'de refakatsiz göçmen çocukların durumu ve başlıca risklerin değerlendirilmesi. *Asia Minor Studies, 6*(1), 1-20.

Ekşi, N. (2024). AHİM kararlarında refakatsiz çocukların geri gönderme merkezlerinde tutulması. *Göç Yolunda Kadın ve Çocuk* (s. 19). Polis Akademisi Yayınları.

El-Awad, U., Fathi, A., Vasileva, M., Petermann, F., & Reinelt, T. (2021). Acculturation orientations and mental health when facing post-migration stress: Differences between unaccompanied and accompanied male Middle Eastern refugee adolescents, first- and second-generation immigrant and native peers in Germany. *International Journal of Intercultural Relations, 82,* 232-246. https://doi.org/10.1016/j.ijintrel.2021.03.005

Garbade, M., Eglinsky, J., Kindler, H., Rosner, R., Sachser, C., & Pfeiffer, E. (2023). Factors affecting the acculturation strategies of unaccompanied refugee minors in Germany. *Frontiers in Psychology, 14,* 1149437. https://doi.org/10.3389/fpsyg.2023.1149437

Garcia, M. F., & Birman, D. (2022). Understanding the migration experience of unaccompanied youth: A review of the literature. *American Journal of Orthopsychiatry, 92*(1), 79-95. https://doi.org/10.1037/ort0000591

İçduygu, A. (2024). Kırılgan göçmen kategorileri. In S. Yıldız, M. R. Baygeldi, Z. M. Özdemir, S. Emik, & Ş. Demirel (Eds.), *Göç Yolunda Kadın ve Çocuk* (Rapor No: 87, s. 195). Polis Akademisi Yayınları.

Jore, T., Oppedal, B., & Biele, G. (2020). Social anxiety among unaccompanied minor refugees in Norway: The association with pre-migration trauma and post-migration acculturation related factors. *Journal   of   Psychosomatic   Research,   136,* 110175. https://doi.org/10.1016/j.jpsychores.2020.110175

Kaya, H., Gündüz, G. B., & Erden, H. G. (2020). Mülteci ve sığınmacı çocuklarda yüksek yararın değerlendirilmesi. *Toplum ve Sosyal Hizmet, 31*(2), 764-790.

Kayma, D. (2024). Geçici Koruma Altındaki Suriyeli Çocuklar. *Afyon Kocatepe Üniversitesi Sosyal Bilimler Dergisi, 26*(1), 308-328.

KOREV.   (2017). *Refakatsiz   sığınmacı   çocuklar   çalıştayı   sonuç raporu.* https://www.korev.org.tr/files/document/refakatsiz-siginmaci-calistayi.pdf

Schwartz, S. J., Unger, J. B., Baezconde-Garbanati, L., Zamboanga, B. L., Córdova, D., Lorenzo-Blanco, E. I., ... & Szapocznik, J. (2016). Testing the parent–adolescent acculturation discrepancy hypothesis: A five-wave longitudinal study. *Journal of Research on Adolescence, 26*(3), 567-586.

Unicef. (2017). *Çocuk çocuktur: Yollardaki çocukların şiddet, istismar ve sömürüden korunması.*

Usama, E. A., Fathi, A., Vasileva, M., Petermann, F., & Reinelt, T. (2021). Acculturation orientations and mental health when facing post-migration stress: Differences between unaccompanied and accompanied male Middle Eastern refugee adolescents, first- and second-generation immigrant and native peers in Germany. *International Journal of Intercultural Relations, 82,* 232-246. https://doi.org/10.1016/j.ijintrel.2021.03.005

EXPECTED IDENTITIES: TIBETANS IN-EXILE AND THE PRESSURES OF TIBETANNESS

Jack McMahon

Introduction

As it has become further accepted that identities are fluid, non-fixed and multifaceted, the need to engage with identity at the level of the refugee or those who are stateless has become increasingly more significant. This has resulted in discussions and analysis of identity becoming far more complicated, moving away from binary understandings and instead adopting the unknown, such as those concepts of hybridity within the *third space* of identity introduced by Bhabha (2004). The condition then of being a refugee or stateless provides a tangible third space, both being experienced and lived. Those within this space must forge an identity that exists somewhere within the expectations of their host nation as well as their own community that surrounds them. For Tibetans living in the condition of exile, refugee and statelessness since 1959, this much is true.

It is evident that whilst the ideal of being Tibetan, or the notion of what a Tibetan should be was discussed throughout literature as well as the community, the actual conception of Tibetanness, or what it was to be Tibetan presented as a sort of *grey area*, with many different interpretations existing. The aim of this article then is not to identify the singular state of being a Tibetan, but instead to unpack where this idea of a cohesive Tibetan identity emerged from and how it manifests today.

Understanding *Tibetanness:*

This aforementioned *grey area* is important and reflects the third space that was alluded to by the important works of Bhaba (2004). For the Tibetan identity, there is an importance in seeking to understand where this notion of a Tibetanness, or a homogenising of identity has come from, given that the three states of Tibet have always carried with them their own distinctive identifying factors.

During the Qing Dynasty (1644 – 1912), Tibet[1] as it is now contextually understood was a congregation of different states, kingdoms or tribal groups whose influence and power fluctuated in relation to the patterns of Qing rule. The reality was that the idea of a homogenised, unified nation of Tibet had not yet gained prominence during the period of Qing rule (Samuels, 1993).

The period of independence which was first declared by the Thirteenth Dalai Lama Thubten Gyatso in 1913 has been purported by some to be the event that consolidated the idea of Tibet as a nation. This may have been true in the areas where the Tibetan government had most influence, primarily being U-Tsang, yet it did not result in a great deal of impact or move towards a unified understanding of Tibet on those far away from Lhasa in the Tibetan states of Kham and Amdo (Shakya, 1993).

Notions of this lateness to national unity have been challenged by Tibetans such as Rinchen Lhamo, who wrote as early as 1926 about the idea of a Tibetan nation, writing that 'the Tibetans are a homogenous nation, bound together by the ties of race, of historical tradition and of a distinctive social, political and material civilisation held in common' (Lhamo, 1926, p. 60). Lhamo wrote their testaments regarding Tibet after settling in the United Kingdom, primarily as a response to criticism of Tibet's lack of development. In an effort to counter this critique, it made sense for Lhamo to respond to the European critics that the place they were critical of actually had the precursors that the Europeans had themselves set out as essential for the success of a people, one such parameter being a strong sense of the nation.

Amongst all of these interpretations, it is Norbu (1992) who provides the more contemporary position in that unity only came once the Tibetan identity became politicised. Their timeframe for the politicising of Tibetan identity coincides with the events of March 1959, being the Tibetan uprising and subsequent flight of the Dalai Lama and his followers to India. In the moments before the national uprising in March of 1959, refugees from Kham and Amdo entered Lhasa as they fled Chinese occupation, creating an important opportunity for these "Tibetans" who had scarcely come into contact with each other to finally do so. It was these interactions, in the eyes of Norbu (1992), that created the

---

[1] When I speak of Tibet, I am referring to its historical territories of U-Tsang, Kham and Amdo, as it is referenced within the Tibetan exile community. The Chinese state of the Tibetan Autonomous Region does not encompass the entirety of these regions, with the traditional territories of Amdo and Kham being subsumed by the states of Qinghai, Gansu, Sichuan and Yunnan. For Tibetans in-exile, this is important, and reflects one of the key historical injustices experienced since the CCP victory in the Chinese Civil War in 1949.

need to unite.

To be Tibetan:

Consider once more Bhabha's (2004) third space, a place where hybrdities of identity emerge that create complex, multifaceted identities across any one singular identity paradigm. It is in this space that identities are empowered through new forms of expression or agency that may differ from the traditional avenues of identity formation, allowing for a more diverse representation across the entire group that may owe to the identity. This diversification is reflected in the complex *Tibetan* identity that blurs U-Tsang, Kham and Amdo together, reflecting the scope of Tibetanness. Within these hybridities, Tibetans are being forced to negotiate between the past, present and future in an effort to adapt to the modern changes occurring around them whilst also doing their best to keep the past with them as well. There is a genuine feeling amongst the Tibetans in-exile that they owe a great deal to their past, and without the past playing some sort of role in their lives, it makes the condition of exile much more difficult to make sense of or to commit to. This sort of duty or obligation shone through in some of the participants that I spoke with. Consider the following which were responses to the question of: What does it mean to be Tibetan?

> "To be Tibetan is to be a fighter for our country. Because we lost our country and nowadays, we are going to lose our culture…so here we have to work hard, and when we have a good opportunity, we try to explain our situation to others." (Tenzin*[2])

> "My forefathers, being a Tibetan, the responsibility passed to me, and I have to take it. Whether I wish for it or not. I have to take it. And this responsibility I have to pass to future generations. That's what I'm feeling at an individual level. And then, as a people, or with the status of being a Tibetan. We have to take the responsibility of our past history, and we have to take responsibility of the present situation, we have to take it and think about the future of Tibetans." (Passang*)

Within perceptions of Tibetanness there is a clear role that memory plays, in that it is this ongoing negotiation between what people feel that they should be as a Tibetan (operating on the level of the individual), as opposed to what they feel they should be doing as a Tibetan (operating on the level of the group). This condition was best summarised by Said (2021) in their lecture titled: "Intellectual

---

[2] * This name and all names going forward are pseudonyms, implemented in order to protect the participants and those around them.

Exile: Expatriates and Marginals",[3] who said:

> 'there is a popular but wholly mistaken assumption that being exiled is to be totally cut off, isolated, hopelessly separated from your place of origin. Would that surgically clean separation were true, because then at least you could have the consolation of knowing that what you have left behind is, in a sense, unthinkable and completely irrecoverable. The fact is that for most exiles the difficulty consists not simply in being forced to live away from home, but rather, given today's world, in living with the many reminders that you are in exile, that your home is not in fact so far away, and that the normal traffic of everyday contemporary life keeps you in constant but tantalising and unfulfilled touch with the old place. The exile therefore exists in a median state, neither completely at one with the new setting nor fully disencumbered of the old, beset with half-involvements and half-detachments' (p. 370-371).

In Said's nuanced words, this in betweenness and lack of stability not only presents the mental state of exile, but it also has direct connections with identities in exile as well, being those hybridities that have emerged in this apparent third space.

Tibetan refugee identities

Given the agreed upon perspective that it was the politicisation and flight of Tibetans into exile that gave way to the idea of Tibetanness, the act of identifying as a refugee has important connections with interpretations and expressions of identity for those Tibetans living in exile.

The label of *refugee* signifies legally what is meant to be a temporary condition, yet considering that many refugees around the world, including Tibetans in exile, have lived their entire lives as refugees, this presents itself as a sometimes-redundant conceptualisation of how being a refugee is. To address this misconception, Nguyen's (2019) conceptualising of *refugeetude* becomes useful. They say that 'refugeetude describes a coming into consciousness of the forces that produce and structure "refuge" and "refugee"' (p. 110). Refugeetude then looks at the status of being a refugee as a structural component of one's identity, a far cry from just being a word with legal implications relating to temporariness. It seeks to understand being a refugee as a way of life, a subjective experience that can be as purpose filled as one who is not a refugee. This serves to further challenge widespread discourses that surround the state of being a refugee as one of helplessness, despair or victimisation. Furthermore, given that India

---

[3] This particular lecture was given as a part of the BBC Reith Lecture Series and was broadcast on July 7, 1993. The transcript is taken from a collection of Said's collected works.

possesses no refugee law, the Tibetan case represents a time where subjectivity is able to rise above that which is legally defined. This was demonstrated by some participants that I discussed the sense of being a refugee with:

> "(I am) a refugee of course. Although the term doesn't really apply, at least in legal terms…Tibetan refugees, as we call ourselves, are not exactly considered as refugees as such. (Pause) You know, of course, anybody who is kicked out of their land is a refugee." (Tashi*)

> "It's very conflicting because…legally, we are not refugees here (India), but given our (pause), my, mental state and our social position right now, we claim ourselves as a refugee." (Dadon*)

Of course, not all Tibetans are refugees. This raises the circumstances of those Tibetans living inside of Tibet, who are not refugees, yet have obvious components of Tibetanness. This difference does not make one group more or less "Tibetan", just reflecting one of the many aspects of an identity, with the condition of being a refugee serving as a factor of hybridity. It would thus be safe to assume that those Tibetans inside of Tibet would reflect a Tibetanness that looks different to that which has emerged in exile.

Conclusion

An investigation of Tibetanness provides a way to understand the ramifications of the politicisation of an identity, and how this manifest into everyday life. As members of the exile population continue to balance what they perceive is expected of them, stemming from their community, history and status as a refugee within their own personal lives, it is most likely that the scope of Tibetanness will continue to expand. Some challenges for Tibetanness are on the horizon, primarily being the increased outward migration from India to other nations as well as the angst that surrounds the Dalai Lama's reincarnation process. These are challenges that the community exile population is aware of, and concerns surrounding what it will do to Tibetan identities are growing.

Therefore, future engagements regarding Tibetanness should consider the complexity of the identity and use it as a scope for reflection as to how it has continued to evolve. If the opportunity were ever to arise for a detailing of perceptions of identity for those Tibetans inside of Tibet, it would be of high importance and would provide an important point of connection between those inside and outside of Tibet.

References:

Bhabha, H.K., 2004. *The Location of Culture*. London: Routledge.

Lhamo, R., 1926. *We Tibetans*. London: Seeley, Service & Co.

Nguyen, V., 2019. Refugeetude: When does a refugee stop being a refugee. *Social Text*, *37*(2), pp.109-131.

Norbu, D., 1992. *Culture and the politics of Third World nationalism*. London ; New York: Routledge.

Said, E., 2021. *The Selected Works of Edward Said: 1966–2006*. Bloomsbury Publishing.

Samuel, G., 1993. *Civilized Shamans: Buddhism in Tibetan Societies*. Washington, D.C.: Smithsonian Institution Press.

Shakya, T., 1993. Whither Tibet? *Himal*, 6(6), pp.8–10.

THE CONCEPT OF FILIAL PIETY AMONG CHINESE MIGRANTS IN IRELAND

Liwei Zhu

Introduction

Filial piety, in Chinese, is translated as 孝 (Xiào) or 孝顺 (Xiàoshùn). The character for 孝 is composed of two parts: the upper component represents senior people, while the lower part signifies a son. Vertically, this character reflects the responsibility of caring for one's parents and the hierarchical structure of a traditional family (McCormack & Blair, 2015).

The concept of filial piety is deeply rooted in Chinese society, largely shaped by the teaching of Confucian and his successors. Traditionally, it may refer to support, respect parents and continuing the family lineage by having children (Legge, n.d.; Tang, 1995).

This paper is a part of findings from the research titled as "Values migration: The influence of Christianity and traditional Chinese values on the cross-cultural adaptation of Chinese migrants in Irish society", which was completed in 2013. It may limit the direct applicability of the findings to the current context. To address this, the paper has been supplemented with a review of recent literature, as shown in the next section. This situates the findings within recent academic discourse — specifically, empirical research exploring the concept of filial piety among contemporary Chinese populations, including overseas Chinese. Additionally, changes in relevant factors over time (e.g. immigration policies) have been considered when interpreting the results.

Literature Review

Bedford & Yeh critique the traditional view of filial piety as a fixed set of rules (Bedford & Yeh, 2021; Yeh & Bedford, 2003). This doesn't really work well across different cultures. They propose a model, called Dual Filial Piety, or DFPM. This model breaks filial piety down into two types: Reciprocal Filial Piety, which is based on genuine gratitude and a more equal, horizontal relationship between parents and children; and Authoritarian Filial Piety, which is more about obedience and a strict, hierarchical relationship.

Some researchers tested DFPM, and support its universality, also highlight personality and moral cognition (Qiao et al., 2021), and psychological motivations (Lim et al., 2022) for filial piety beyond traditional Confucian norms.

Some research doesn't examine DFPM but reveals the importance of filial piety among Chinese diasporas. In Canada, senior people have lower expectations of filial responsibility but still value and hope for emotional care from their children (Zhang, 2022). In addition, the perceived filial piety among the older Chinese immigrants in the Netherlands generally exceeded expectations, called "filial piety sufficient" which can enhance emotional well-being in older adults adapting to new environments (Cheung et al., 2022).

Furthermore, studies on filial piety among Chinese Christians in New Zealand (Wang, 2022) and Taiwanese Christians in the U.S. (Chen, 2006) show that while people reinterpret traditional duties to their parents through a Christian lens—giving priority to biblical teachings when there's a conflict—they still hold onto the core value of honouring their parents. Additionally, Christianity encourages families to move away from strict authority and instead focus on open dialogue and mutual respect. Rather than parents having total control, children are supported to be more independent and to express themselves, which helps create a more balanced and personal family relationship (Chen, 2006).

All of the above studies focus exclusively on filial piety, either connected to religious influence or not. In contrast, this research looks at a bigger picture—how values and religious practices are changing among the participants, and the interaction with their cross-cultural adaptation. This research examined the following values: filial piety, ancestor worship, Feng Shui, the selection of auspicious dates, the belief that good behaviour brings good fortune and vice versa, and views about social issues mentioned in passing during the interviews. The findings show that, of the values examined, filial piety is the most maintained among the participants. Furthermore, as this is qualitative research, it provides insight into the concept of filial piety among a small group of Chinese migrants in Ireland.

Data and Methods

Following the approval of ethical clearance, the author conducted 22 in-depth interviews with Chinese migrants recruited via snowball sampling (Holstein & Gubrium, 1995). It started with semi-structured interviews and then moved to unstructured interviews as I became more experienced. The participants include both long-term and short-term residents, with a mix of genders and different beliefs. Their Chinese origins range from mainland China, Hong Kong, and Malaysia.

I used Classic Grounded Theory (Glaser, 1978) to guide the entire process of data collection and analysis. Grounded theory primarily focuses on understanding the basic social processes involved in human interaction. I conducted open, line-by-line coding to shape the empirical data. Data analysis followed systematic coding, categorization, and memoing processes, ensuring that findings are deeply rooted in participants' lived experiences. Out of this process, five key categories related to filial piety emerged: pragmatic support, psychological well-being, a special form of reciprocity, obedience and reinterpretation through a Biblical lens.

Results and Discussion

Pragmatic support

Mr Li explained how he practices filial piety with great responsibility toward his family. For him, filial piety means treating parents well and meeting their needs: If elderly parents lack money, children should help them. If they are sick, care for them. We eat well and dress well, and they should too. Mrs. Hua and Mrs. Lin said, as children often felt sad, they could not be with their parents or help with daily chores.

Psychological well-being

Although Mr Li emphasised the importance of financial support for parents, he believed that the most important thing for parents was psychological satisfaction. Make sure to support them not just financially but emotionally too. In fact, most participants' parents don't need financial support but want frequent contact, with their children through phone or internet. Seven participants said that they kept in touch by phone with their parents and visited home regularly. Mr. Qi also called and visited his parents but found it hard to have common topics to talk about with them.

A special form of reciprocity

Filial piety is regarded by the participants as a form of reciprocity, whereby one is expected to return the favour of their parents' nurturing and upbringing, as indicated in a Chinese idiom 养儿防老 (yǎng ér fáng lǎo), meaning "raising children to ensure care in old age". Many participants expressed a strong sense of duty to return home to care for their parents when they get aging, especially as the only child of them. For example, Mrs. Zhao and Mrs. Fang planned to leave Ireland permanently to look after their elderly parents in China, even though they had long-term residence permits. This is partly because challenges in extended family reunions primarily due to restrictive immigration and family reunification policies in Ireland.

Obedience

Both Mrs. Cheng and Mr. Ma come from very traditional Chinese families where filial piety means obeying parents completely. Mrs. Cheng, for example, had to obey her parents' wishes, including not marrying an Irish man, to show her filial piety. Ms. Shang, an only child of her family, also showed filial piety by following her mother's wishes. She has lived in Ireland for 10 years but returned to China due to unemployment. She got a good position in China, however, she had to move to Australia, for by doing this her mother could join her there according to the Australian immigration policy. Her mother believed 外国的月亮圆 (wàiguó de yuèliàng yuán）, literally meaning is the western moon is rounder. This reflects a common Chinese view of the West as better. Although Ms. Shang struggled with depression at first, she gradually adapted to her life in Australia. All this is to honour her mother through obedience. This dimension reflects the remnants of hierarchy in Chinese traditional parental relationships embedded in traditional concept of filial piety.

Reinterpretation through a Biblical lens

Mr. Wu believes filial piety is the foundation of his Buddhist belief. He sees no conflict between the two and acknowledging filial responsibilities in both material and emotional needs. Mr. Li identifies as Protestant but has some uncertainties about his faith. However, he clearly states the duties of filial piety in physical and psychological aspects. Whereas some participants adjust their understanding and practice of filial piety as they engage with Christian teachings. For instance, after becoming a Christian, Mrs. Cheng gave up ancestor worship, which is against biblical teaching though she was skilled at. Therefore, she cannot obey her parents' wishes in this matter because doing so would contradict her faith. Likewise, In the case of Mrs. Zhao, who loves her parents and stays close to them emotionally, but she believes filial piety must align with Bible teachings. If her parents asked her to stop worshiping God, she wouldn't obey, as faith comes first. She cited Ephesians 6:1-3, saying children should obey parents "in the Lord". She is one of the participants who expressed the possibility of having to return home to care for her elderly parents.

Conclusions, limitations and recommendations

The research findings both resonate with existing literature and offer unique insights into the cross-cultural adaptation processes of Chinese migrants in Ireland. All the participants uphold the value of filial piety. This concept among the participants retains its traditional core value of honouring parents, involving both practical supports, care, and emotional supports, and obedience to parents. It is considered a special form of reciprocating the care and upbringing provided by parents. The only aspect missing from traditional understanding is an emphasis on continuing the family lineage by having children. Additionally, Christian Chinese reinterpret filial piety in light of Scripture. Furthermore, practice of filial piety for the participants can result in a loss of human capital to the receiving country, as some migrants who have already settled down may have to return to China permanently to care for their ageing parents due to challenges to reunite extended families.

As a qualitative study, the findings cannot be generalized to all Chinese in Ireland. For future research, I recommend a mixed-methods approach with a longitudinal design, focusing on practical societal applications and aiming to inform relevant policymaking.

References

Bedford, O., & Yeh, K.-H. (2021). Evolution of the Conceptualization of Filial Piety in the Global Context: From Skin to Skeleton. *Frontiers in Psychology, 12.* https://doi.org/10.3389/fpsyg.2021.570547

Chen, C. (2006). From Filial Piety to Religious Piety: Evangelical Christianity Reconstructing Taiwanese Immigrant Families in the United States1. *International Migration Review, 40*(3), 573–602. https://doi.org/10.1111/j.1747-7379.2006.00032.x

Cheung, S.-L., Krijnen, W. P., Fu, Y., van der Schans, C. P., & Hobbelen, H. (2022). Filial Piety and Mental Health Among Older Chinese Immigrants in the Netherlands. *Gerontology and Geriatric Medicine, 8*, 23337214221083470. https://doi.org/10.1177/23337214221083470

Holstein, J. A., & Gubrium, J. F. (1995). *The Active Interview.* SAGE Publications.

Legge, J. (n.d.). *The Analects of Confucius (from the Chinese Classics).* Https://Www.Gutenberg.Org/Files/3330/3330.Txt. Retrieved 22 July 2025, from https://www.gutenberg.org/cache/epub/3330/pg3330.html

Lim, A. J., Lau, C. Y. H., & Cheng, C.-Y. (2022). Applying the Dual Filial Piety Model in the United States: A Comparison of Filial Piety Between Asian Americans and Caucasian Americans. *Frontiers in Psychology, 12.* https://doi.org/10.3389/fpsyg.2021.786609

McCormack, J., & Blair, J. G. (2015). *Thinking through China.* Rowman & Littlefield Publishers.

Qiao, X., Lv, Y., Aldbyani, A., Guo, Q., Zhang, T., & Cai, M. (2021). Chaos May Prevail Without

Filial Piety: A Cross-Cultural Study on Filial Piety, the Dark Triad, and Moral Disengagement. *Frontiers in Psychology, 12*. https://doi.org/10.3389/fpsyg.2021.738128

Tang, Z. (1995). Confucianism, Chinese culture, and reproductive behavior. *Population and Environment, 16*(3), 269–284. https://doi.org/10.1007/BF02331921

Wang, Y. (2022). "Cross Is Fix": Christianity and Christian Community as Vehicles for Overcoming Settlement Crises of Chinese Immigrant Families. *Religions, 13*(2), Article 2. https://doi.org/10.3390/rel13020119

Yeh, K.-H., & Bedford, O. (2003). A test of the Dual Filial Piety model. *Asian Journal of Social Psychology, 6*(3), 215–228. https://doi.org/10.1046/j.1467-839X.2003.00122.x

Zhang, W. (2022). Perceptions and expectations of filial piety among older Chinese immigrants in Canada. *Ageing & Society, 42*(3), 497–520. https://doi.org/10.1017/S0144686X20000902

RELIGIOUS REFUGEES IN THE 21ST CENTURY - THE CASES OF AFGHANISTAN AND SYRIA

Alexia Kapsambeli

Introduction

The 21st century has witnessed a significant rise in global refugee crises, with conflict, violence, and persecution driving millions of people away from their homes. According to data from the United Nations, by the end of June 2024, 122.6 million people worldwide were forcibly displaced from their homes due to persecution, conflict, violence, human rights violations, and events seriously disturbing public order. Among those were 43.7 million refugees. There were also 72.1 million internally displaced people and 8 million asylum seekers. While some refugees settle in neighboring countries, others face difficulties.

Refugee Legal Protection

The centerpiece of international refugee protection is the 1951 Refugee Convention and 1967 Protocol relating to the Status of Refugees. They are based on Article 14 of the Universal Declaration of Human Rights 1948, which recognizes the right of persons to seek asylum from persecution in other countries. The 1951 Refugee Convention and its 1967 Protocol provide the internationally recognized definition of a refugee and outline the legal rights to which they are entitled.

A refugee, according to the Convention, is someone unable or unwilling to return to their country of origin owing to a well-founded fear of being persecuted for reasons of race, religion, nationality, membership of a particular social group, or political opinion.

The Geneva Convention provides five reasons for persecution based on which refugee status is recognized. These are race, religion, nationality, membership of a particular social group, and political opinion.

Religious persecution has been one of the most common causes of forced displacement. It is not surprising that religion is recognized as one of the main reasons for persecution by the Geneva Convention relating to the Status of

Refugees. (Susanna Trotta and Elena Fiddian-Qasmiyeh, 2022)

As for religious freedom, the Universal Declaration of Human Rights affirms the right broadly as freedom of thought, conscience, and religion in article 18. (H. Knox Thames, 2024)

Religious Refugees in the Past

Religious intolerance is not new. Firstly, Christianity faced significant persecution in ancient Rome, as it was said to be a threat to the polytheistic beliefs of the period.

At the end of the fifteenth century, religious minorities, in particular Jews and Muslims, in Spain faced significant persecution and were often targeted by the Spanish Inquisition. The goal of the Inquisition was to ensure religious uniformity.

According to Dr Israel Charny who was the president of the International Association of Genocide Scholars, in Turkey between 1913 and 1922 more than 3.5 million Armenian, Assyrian, and Greek Christians were massacred in a state-organized and state-sponsored campaign of destruction and genocide. This Christian Holocaust is viewed as the precursor to the Jewish Holocaust in WWII.

Religious Refugees Today

Nowadays religious freedom is a basic human right, but it is under threat in many parts of the world.

From China and Iraq to Nigeria and North Korea, religious persecution is not uncommon.

Religious persecution can be defined as systematically hostile or ill-treatment towards an individual or a group because of their religious beliefs.

The Case of Afghanistan

The most characteristic cases are those of Syria and Afghanistan.

More than four decades of violent conflict, political instability, natural disasters, the coronavirus pandemic, and economic challenges have caused Afghans to make up one of the largest refugee populations worldwide.

Shortly after the takeover in August 2021, the Taliban stated, that human rights in general would be respected in Afghanistan 'within the framework of Islamic law'. However, the conditions of religious freedom have deteriorated, under the Taliban government.

The Taliban enforces a strict interpretation of Sharia law, which is not found in other Islamic countries. Their policies severely restrict fundamental human rights, including the right to thought, conscience, belief, and religion. This situation has led to a significant decline in religious freedom for minorities, women, and individuals who hold different interpretations of Islam. Therefore, they have created an environment of fear for religious minorities.

 As the Human Rights Watch organization claimed, religious minorities often operate in secret, living in constant fear of being outed and subjected to brutal punishments. They are denied the freedom to gather, worship, or express their beliefs openly.

As the International Christian Concern (ICC) stated, "The Taliban are working to completely erase Christianity or any religious minority from the country."

The Taliban are also failing to protect Afghanistan's religious minorities from violence. The Islamic State of Khorasan Province (ISKP), the armed extremist group that is the Islamic State's (ISIS) affiliate in Afghanistan, has continually attacked Shia, Sufi, and non-Muslims, and in particular Hazaras. Hazara is a Shia Muslim ethnic group that has faced discrimination and abuse by successive Afghan governments for over a century. Under the previous Taliban rule in 1996-2001, several massacres of Hazaras took place. With the Taliban back in power, the Hazara have been increasingly concerned for their safety. (United States Department of State, 2023)

According to the annual report of the UN High Commissioner for Human Rights, "Despite some progress over the last two decades, minorities in Afghanistan have never enjoyed full protection of their human rights, and this is the case with religious minorities in particular."

Religious persecution, particularly by the Taliban, has resulted in a significant number of people fleeing their homes, both internally and as refugees seeking safety in other countries. There is no doubt that the situation in Afghanistan contributes to a global refugee crisis.

The Case of Syria

The second characteristic case of our days is Syria. In the past, Syria was a country with a rich history and culture. Religion was an essential part of Syrian society, and it played a significant role in shaping the culture and values.

Syria had a vast religious diversity with Sunni Muslims being the largest religious group, approximately 70 percent of the population. There were also Alawites, Twelver, and Ismaili Shias. Christians (both Orthodox and Catholics), Druze, and Yazidis made up the rest of the population. Christians were divided into several branches, including Greek Orthodox, Syriac Orthodox, Armenian Orthodox, Melkite Catholics, and Syrian Catholics. The Druze were a small religious minority in Syria, making up only about 3 percent of the population. The Yazidis were a Kurdish-speaking religious minority in Syria that made up less than 1 percent of the population. (Gilad James, 2023)

The government had recognized and tolerated religions, and it had ensured that all religions had equal rights and opportunities to practice their faiths. The constitution declared the state shall respect all religions and shall ensure the freedom to perform religious rituals as long as these "do not disturb the public order."

Although Syria was a Sunni-majority nation, it was ruled by the Alawite Assad family since 1974 Bashar al-Assad was said to be a protector against the rise of extremist jihadist groups. Many Syrian Christians in major areas like Damascus, Homs, and Aleppo preferred Assad's government to rebel administrations because rebel groups were dominated by extremists such as Al-Qaida's affiliate Hay' at Tahrir al-Sham (HTS), the Islamic State group (ISIS), and the Syrian National Army (SNA), all of which committed atrocities against Christians and other religious minorities in areas under their control. (Joseph Daniel, 2025)

Members of the European Parliament asked the Commission about the situation of Greek Orthodox Christians in Syria. They mentioned that residents were forced to flee their family homes, religious leaders were abducted, churches were destroyed and archaeological sites dating back to the Hellenistic period have been damaged. Islamic organizations have even poisoned the traditional beverages of the Greek Orthodox Christian community, in a bid to engineer their extinction. They added that Greek Orthodox Christians in Syria have become the victims of a coordinated genocide. (George Epitideios, 2015)

In October 2019, Turkey invaded northern Syria and created a so-called "safe zone" along the Syrian Turkish border, where it used Arab Islamic fighters to control Kurdish and Christian areas. Radical Islamic groups seized Christian properties, restricted religious practices, and imposed demographic changes by settling families linked to these armed groups.

When the Islamic militant group Hayat Tahrir al-Sham (HTS) conquered Assad's forces and took control of major Syrian cities in December 2024, Christians and other minorities were fearful of the potential changes under the new regime. They promised they would not enact radical religious policies, but as time passed, persecution against Christians and other minorities intensified. Militants attacked churches, desecrated cemeteries, forced Christian women to adhere to Islamic dress codes, and confiscated Christians' homes. Christmas trees were burnt, and large demonstrations took place demanding protection for Christians. Furthermore, the leader of the Druze minority denounced a campaign of genocide and criticized the power of Islamists in Syria.

Syria, at one time boasting as one of the most religiously tolerant countries in the Middle East, now finds itself to be one of the worst persecutors in the world. In 2011, Syria was placed on the "World Watch List," a ranking of the top 50 countries with the worst persecution of Christians, at number 38 meaning the country had moderate persecution. Today it ranks number 5 in the world as it is now considered to have severe persecution of Christians. (United States Commission on International Religious Freedom, 2022)

Syria remains one of the largest displacement crises globally, with over 14 million people forcibly displaced since the conflict began in 2011.

Conclusion

There is no doubt that religion plays a vital role in society. The Refugee Convention provides five reasons for persecution based on which refugee status is recognized. One of these reasons is religion. Totalitarian regimes often suppress religious minorities to maintain absolute control and enforce uniformity. This happens in the cases of Afghanistan and Syria. This situation, war, and persecutions, leads millions of people fleeing away from their homes. It is recommended the international community press the governments of these two countries to uphold their obligations under international human rights law.

References

Susanna Trotta and Elena Fiddian-Qasmiyeh, June 2022, "Chapter 7: Religions and Forced Migration" "The State of the Evidence in Religions and Development" Joint Learning Initiative on Faith and Local Communities, https://jliflc.com/wp-content/uploads/2023/02/SoE-chapter-7.pdf

H. Knox Thames 2024, "Ending Persecution Charting the Path to Global Religious Freedom" University of Notre Dame Press, https://www.google.gr/books/edition/Ending_Persecution/alz5EAAAQBAJ?hl=el&gbpv=1&dq=persecution+because+of+religion&pg=PT10&printsec=frontcover

Arthur   Gonzaga   "Christian   Persecution   in   Ancient   Rome"
https://www.scribd.com/document/824688889/Christian-Persecution-in-Ancient-Rome

"Notes on the Genocide of Christians of the Ottoman Empire" https://www.greek-genocide.net/index.php/overview/internal/notes-on-the-genocide-of-christians-of-the-ottoman-empire

United States Department of State-Office of International Religious Freedom, 2023 "International Religious Freedom Report for 2023" https://www.state.gov/wp-content/uploads/2024/04/547499_AFGHANISTAN-2023-INTERNATIONAL-RELIGIOUS-FREEDOM-REPORT.pdf

Gilad Jame, 2023, "Introduction to Syrian Arab Republic" Mystery School, https://www.google.gr/books/edition/Introduction_to_Syrian_Arab_Republic/91DAEA AAQBAJ?hl=el&gbpv=1&dq=religion+syria&pg=PT24&printsec=frontcover

Joseph Daniel, 2025, "A Summary of What's Unfolding in Syria" https://www.persecution.org/2025/01/07/a-summary-of-whats-unfolding-in-syria/

George Epitideios, 2015 "Genocide of Greek Orthodox Christians in Syria" European Parliament https://www.europarl.europa.eu/doceo/document/E-8-2015-004733_BG.html

"El lider de la minoria drusa de Siria denuncio una 'campana genocida' y critic al poder islamista" 2025, Infobae, https://www.infobae.com/america/mundo/2025/05/01/el-lider-de-la-minoria-drusa-de-siria-denuncio-una-campana-genocida-y-critico-al-poder-islamista/

United States Commission on International Religious Freedom, 2022, "Overview of refugees fleeing-religious persecution globally" https://www.uscirf.gov/sites/default/files/2022-05/2022%20Factsheet%20-%20Refugees%20Fleeing%20Religious%20Persecution%20Globally.pdf

"Persecuted religious minorities in Syria devastated by attacks", 2025, https://globalchristianrelief.org/christian-persecution/stories/religious-minorities-persecuted-christians-in-syria-under-attack/

LIQUID SPATIOTEMPORALITY: FROM NOMADIC TO SEDENTARY TO NOMADIC

Bilal Salaam

Introduction

Ibn Khaldun & Zygmunt Bauman

Ibn Khaldun's Muqaddimah is a cornerstone of sociology and historiography. A central aspect of the theory of humanity developed within Muqaddimah was social group movement to and from a bedouin to sedentary society as natural.[1]

Zygmunt Bauman was a major figure in social theory whose work spanned modernity, postmodernity, and ethics. His concept of liquid modernity highlighted the instability of contemporary life, where identities and institutions are fluid, and his writings traced how consumerism, bureaucracy, and fragmentation reshape moral and social experience.[2][3][4]

Thesis

This essay examines the fluidity of human settlement patterns over time and space, challenging the dichotomy of nomadism and sedentary life. Employing Hegelian and Bourdieusian frameworks, it synthesizes Ibn Khaldun's and Zygmunt Bauman's concepts to illustrate the persistence of the nomadic lifestyle as a recurring pattern in human history. emphasizing the fluidity of spatiotemporality, this essay highlights the continuous shifts in human settlements in response to social factors,

Analysis

Khaldun On Nature & Habit

Ibn Khaldun emphasizes the importance of time in the development of a people towards intelligence and simultaneously away from nature and towards evil.

---

[1] Baali, "Society, State and Urbanism" 28
[2] Smith, "Zygmunt Bauman", 192
[3] Smith, "Zygmunt Bauman", 192
[4] Smith, "Zygmunt Bauman", 192

The existence of Bedouins is prior to, and the basis of the existence of towns and cities. Likewise, the existence of towns and cities results from luxury customs pertaining to luxury and ease, which are posterior to the customs that go with the bare necessities of life. Bedouins are closer to being good than sedentary people.[5]

Integral to the concept of the sedentary-nomad dichotomy is that it is not simply a dichotomy. It is a circle that ends where it began, and if as Khaldun says, nomads precede, then there will be a return to that nomadism.

All habits are corporeal. Habits are qualities and colors of the soul. When the soul has been colored by a habit, it is no longer in its natural state.[6]

A major distinction between Khaldun's argument regarding the differences between supposed sedentaries and nomads is that over time, technical habits have been developed by sedentaries, in contrast to nomads. Unknown to Bedouins, these habits can be perceived as intelligence.

sedentary people have refined technical habits and manners as far as customary activities and sedentary conditions are concerned, all of them things that are unknown to the Bedouins.[7]

Simultaneously, Khaldun posits that the naivete or naturalness of the so-called nomad(as bedouin) inclines him towards an inherent goodness relative to the intel-heavy complexified sedentary.

Anything natural has precedence over luxury[8]

...the soul in its first natural state of creation is ready to accept whatever good or evil may arrive and leave an imprint upon it. Muhammad said: "Every infant is born in the natural state. When customs proper to goodness have been first to enter the soul of a good person and his (soul) has thus acquired the habit of (goodness, that person) moves away from evil and finds it difficult to do anything evil. The same applies to the evil person when customs (proper to evil) have been first to affect him.[9]

Habitus-Agency is Not Habit's Agency

---

[5] Khaldun, "Muqaddimah", 164
[6] Khaldun, "Muqaddimah", 556
[7] Khaldun, "Muqaddimah", 559
[8] Khaldun, "Muqaddimah", 11
[9] Khaldun, "Muqaddimah", 165

One of the reasons for the use of the term habitus is the wish to set aside the common conception of habit as a mechanical assembly or preformed program, as Hegel does when in the Phenomenology of Mind he speaks of habits as dexterity.[10]

Erez Naaman of American University in his 2017 article Nurture over Nature: Habitus from al-Fārābī through Ibn Khaldūn to ʿAbduh makes a concerted effort to equivocate Ibn Khaldun's use of the concept of habit with habitus. Naaman makes the distinction between the Aristotelian use of the term habitus and the Bourdieusian use. If Khaldun had used the term habitus to refer to what Naaman translates from malaka, or habit, which is a particular disposition, then Aristotle's habitus and Khaldun's habit (translated as habitus by Naaman) would be in alignment with one another. This is not the case, though. While habit is a trait or disposition acquired through practice, for Bourdieu, habitus is…

> "a learned set of preferences or dispositions by which a person orients to the social world. It is a system of durable, transposable, cognitive schemata or structures of perception, conception and action."[11]

So, not only is Bourdieu's habitus different from habit in that it is a set of habits, it also is in relation to the social world, some amorphous, set or subset of social entities whose existence Bauman "liquefiers" might argue against. Yet, for an anthropologist, whose goal it is to create the illusion of differences among groups of people, rather than either acknowledging a collective actor-network theory, humanity, or better yet, the ability of the critical consciousness of individuals to create meaning for themselves based on their own conscious agency, this way of thinking dialecticizes *an other* (another) in a positivist sense.

> Through the habitus, the structure which has produced it governs practice, not by the processes of a mechanical determinism, but through the mediation of the orientations and limits it assigns to the habitus's operations of invention.[12]

Here, for Bourdieu, habitus is a product of structure. There is no accounting for the ways that habitus can be influenced by the agent. Society is not simply made of structures. It is not simply made of habituses. The social have not completely relinquished their determinacy of the static state. A Hegelian *Phenomenology of the Mind*, ontic and existential in nature, would disagree with Bourdieu's singular perspective.

---

[10] Bourdieu, "Outline of A Theory", 218
[11] Bourdieu, "An Invitation to Reflexive", 27
[12] Bourdieu, "Outline of A Theory", 92

Circumstances, situations, customs, and so on, which show themselves on one side as something given, and on the other as within this specific individuality, reveal merely indeterminate nature of individuality.[13]

Hegel argues that individuality can maintain an indifferent stance, remaining neither influenced by nor opposing external influences, which suggests a situation where the individual remains unaffected by society's habitus or systemic customs. He posits that the effect of outside influences on an individual, and the specific nature of their effect, depend completely on the individual's intrinsic characteristics. Asserting that an individual has been shaped by specific situations only reaffirms the predisposition(habit) of the individual to be molded by that situation. The habits, customs, and societal states perceived as outside the individual also exist within that individual, affirming the indeterminate nature of that individuality. This implies that specific situations alone are not the sole determinant of individuality.

This is non-materialist and pro-agency at its core. It is clear from these Neo-Hegelian, existential phenomenological conceptualizations juxtaposed with Bourdieu and Khaldun's concepts that habit is not habitus, rather the former is dictated by the individual, albeit it influenced by systems, while the latter is a theorization of a degree of separation from the system at most, and at the least it is a relabelling or reproduction of the system itself.

Liquid Spatiotemporality's Space and Time

Tony Blackshaw, creator of the concept of liquid leisure, in his Routledge handbook of Leisure Studies encapsulates Bauman's writing approach as that which "enable(s) the reader to read dispositionally"[14]. One might think of these dispositions as congruent with Bourdieu's disposition that he uses to refer to the individual behaviors that make up the sets which create a habitus. Dispositionality, which might also be referred to as character, nature, inclination or attitude permeates Bauman's work on many levels. His concept of liquidity, rooted in the phenomenological individual nature of Hegelian approaches of how societies become, are concerned with experience, however repetitious, as a major influence on habit, nature and identity.

Habitual conduct is thus the sedimentation of past experience or learning. Thanks to regular repetition, it relieves us from the need to think, calculate, and

---

[13] Hegel, "Phenomenology of The Mind", 304.
[14] Blackshaw, "Routledge Handbook of Leisure Studies", 170.

make decisions in many of our actions just as long as the circumstances we encounter appear in a regular pattern.[15]

It can be said that habit and nature are synonymous, or at the least, that patterns (and it is important to consider the racination of the driving force behind these patterns) shape, not only habits, but what is presumed to be natural. To be faced with the decision to comply, to resist, in a passive sense, or to radically be critically conscious is to decide the level of one's individuality. If one, by chance, would like to be relieved from being critical and making decisions, s/he may acquiesce.

> However appalling and horrifying (similar, repeated events) might have been at their first appearance within sight, they become, through the monotony of their repetition, 'normalized', made 'ordinary' – things just as things are by their nature; in other words, they are trivialized, and the function of trivia is to amuse and entertain, rather than shock.[16]

> If pressed, we might allude to tradition: "this is the way things have always been done;' or "this is how it is:' What we are doing here is to suggest that the length of time in which these habits have persisted lends them an authority that is not normally the object of questioning.[17]

The shock of the alteration of a space can be lessened over time, wherein an eventual authority can be given to habits or natural actions which at one point may have been questioned or changed. Liquid spatiotemporality can lead us to the conclusion that an alteration of time can be lessened over space as well. That is to say, as we broaden our purview of community the impact of changing habits (or even habitus) will, in turn, not be so drastic.

> The result of these transformations may be the need to defend, or return to, "the old ways:' Targets become the newcomers who represent new ways of being, or those that do not believe in the old ways and so cannot belong to a journey that seeks the unity embodied in nostalgic calls. Pierre Bourdieu wrote of this process within what he called "fields" of social relations in terms of people pursuing strategies of "orthodoxy" or "heresy" depending on the fit between their dispositions and social context."[18]

And so, orthodoxy here, as Bauman explains Bourdieu, necessitates tradition and is in juxtaposition with new ways of being. This is a factor of spatial crowding(repetition) over time in order to change what is not new to what is

---

[15] Bauman, "Thinking Sociologically", 58.
[16] Bauman, "Born Liquid", 30.
[17] Bauman, "Thinking Sociologically", 62.
[18] Bauman, "Thinking Sociologically", 31.

new. This liquid spatiotemporality is a desensitization by way of repetition. Badawis preceded the Hadaris in time, so Khaldun claims and so, traditions, habits and nature as illusions of time and space eventually become acceptable. Rather than accepting the temporal influence of tradition, the radical-minded might ask why, not simply as an unfounded rebellious transgressor, but as a seeker of reason and truth, and a simultaneous maker of one's own meaning.

> We inhabit spaces and places that inform and are informed by the meaning we attach to them. The significance of such meaning is variable and can be characterized as a series of concentric circles exhibiting varying degrees of comprehension, each one being larger than the next. The smaller spheres in which we interact are more familiar because they exhibit rules and behavior we understand, and we know how to respond to the routines of interaction.[19]

Liquid Habit(us)

The "us" of Habitus is parenthetical in this title, because the liquidity of modernity has made it so. Nostalgia as fleeting memory will not erase these parentheses. The influence of "us" on the habitus has given way to the influence of the habit of the individual.

> Living a liquid modern life… alerts us to the fact that not only are we conscious of our being as individuals and that there is no external categorization powerful enough to compete with that crucial awareness, but also that in searching for some overarching narrative of meaning on which to base our lives, we are more likely to prioritize our own needs at the expense of the needs of
>
> *others.*[20]

> The era of unconditional superiority of sedentarism over nomadism and the domination of the settled over the mobile is on the whole grinding fast to a halt. We are witnessing the revenge of nomadism over the principle of territoriality and settlement. In the fluid stage of modernity, the settled majority is ruled by the nomadic and exterritorial elite.[21]

Whether it is right or wrong, evil or good, luxurious or simple, there should be consideration regarding the shift of the perception that sedentarism is less aspirational than it once historically was.

---

[19] Bauman, "Thinking Sociologically", 92
[20] Blackshaw, "Routledge Handbook of Leisure Studies", 171
[21] Bauman, "Liquid Modernity", 28.

Conclusion

This essay has examined the fluidity of human settlement patterns over time and space, challenging the traditional dichotomy of nomadism and sedentary life. It synthesized the concepts of Ibn Khaldun and Zygmunt Bauman to illustrate the persistence of nomadic lifestyles throughout history, highlighting the continuous shifts in human settlements in response to social factors.

Broader Implications

The essay's findings have broader implications for understanding human societies. They suggest that human settlement patterns are not fixed but rather dynamic, evolving in response to various social, economic, and environmental factors. By recognizing the fluidity of spatiotemporality, we can gain a deeper understanding of how societies adapt and change over time. This perspective challenges us to rethink traditional narratives of progress and development, acknowledging the complexities of experience and the confluence of cultural practice.

References

Baali, F. (1988). Society, state, and urbanism: Ibn Khaldun's sociological thought. State University of New York Press.

Bauman, Z., & Leoncini, T. (2018). Born Liquid. Polity Press.

Bauman, Z. (2013). Liquid Modernity. Polity Press.

Bauman, Z. (1990). Thinking sociologically. B. Blackwell.

Blackshaw, T. (2020). Routledge Handbook of Leisure Studies. Taylor & Francis Group.

Bourdieu, P. (2006). Outline of a theory of practice. Cambridge University Press.

Hegel, G. (2017). Phenomenology of Spirit (the Phenomenology of Mind). Rehak, David.

Khaldun, I., & Rosenthal, F. (2020). Muqaddimah - Volume 1: An Introduction to History. Independently Published.

Smith, D. (2013). Zygmunt Bauman: Prophet of Postmodernity. Polity Press.

FORCED MIGRATION AND GETTING COHESION OF SYRIAN CHILDREN

Vildan Mahmutoğlu[1]

Introduction

Syrian refugees who migrated to Türkiye were allowed to become "urban refugees" after 2013. The number of refugees living in camps that year decreased from 270,000 to 60,000. They have started to live side by side with the local people in the cities. Besides being a target country, Türkiye is also a transit country. For these two reasons, it has received a large number of immigrants (Erdoğan, pp. 72-73). According to current data (14.08.2025), the number of Syrians under temporary protection in Türkiye is 2,539,073 (Temporary Protection (goc.gov.tr)).

After briefly summarising the situation with numbers, it is clear that the most important issue that emerges is social cohesion. Because a very large portion of Syrian refugees in Türkiye do not live in camps, but in cities. It is also quite difficult for such a large society to live in tune with another society. This study was conducted with children who watched the "Walk of Amal" performance in Izmir. The puppet named Amal, which gives the performance its name, represents a 9-year-old Syrian girl and has crossed borders on foot. In a study conducted with children who watched this performance, the social adaptation of immigrant children to the community they live in was investigated through their school and education. They live side-by-side with the host community in the school they continue attending due to their age, where they arrived through forced migration. Thanks to the education they receive at school, which they attend due to compulsory education, they are experiencing a social adaptation process different from that of their families.

The main question of the study also emerges here: What is the impact of the education children who have migrated due to forced displacement receive in school on their social adaptation?

[1] This work has been supported by the Scientific Research Projects Commission of Galatasaray University under grant number SBA- 2022-1110.

241

The path to social cohesion

One of the most important topics discussed today regarding migration is social cohesion. Before the issue of social cohesion, assimilation was at the heart of migration debates. The academic study of assimilation began at the Chicago School. Since the beginning of the 20th century, the Chicago School has produced influential works in urban research. In 1830, Chicago was a place with a total population of 100 people, but by 1930, its population becomes with a population 3,373.753. The reason Chicago grew so large is due to its breakthroughs in trade, finance, and transportation. In addition to the population impact of Chicago's economic breakthroughs, the immigration it received along with the American Civil War also increased the population. As Southern blacks arrived with great hope, the number of immigrants in the city increased significantly. This wave of migration becomes a problem that needs to be controlled (Serter, 2013: 68-69). Between 1916 and 1970, 7 million African Americans migrated to Chicago in a constant wave of migration from the South to the North. Before this wave of migration, Chicago had a 2% Black population, which increased to 33% during the Great Migration (chicagohistory.org).

In this increasing migration environment, as questions arise about how to live with immigrants, one of the earliest theories in the field begins to be discussed. This theory, called the "melting pot," began to be discussed as a view that supports assimilation and states that all races should adapt to the place, The Chicago School argues that incoming minorities will adapt to their new environment and will eventually fully integrate into society. The melting pot theory, which is the adaptation of minority groups to culturally, politically, and economically dominant groups, has received much criticism. There is a metaphorical transition from the melting pot, considered the most accurate path, to the idea of a "salad bowl." A new idea of pluralism emerged in the 1960s, conceptually similar to the idea of a salad bowl. This theory suggests that individuals need to protect their cultures, which are at risk of being lost, and that it is necessary to live in a multicultural society. The idea of a salad bowl is more integrative than a melting pot and more protective of the identities and cultures it encompasses. But those who criticise this idea also say that, of course, one can be selective about the ingredients to be put in the salad (Berray, 2019:143). After the salad bowl metaphor, the idea of multiculturalism is emphasised as a new perspective. Perspectives on multiculturalism also differ. For example, Kymlicka looks at the issue from an individual perspective. Kymlicka says that regardless of which group an individual belongs to, they have rights as an individual. Because all citizens are free and equal (Hazır, 2012:4-8).

The discussion of the idea of multiculturalism has brought to light the necessity of preserving all cultures in society as they are. However, there are also criticisms against this view. Because dialogue does not develop between cultures that are protected in the same way. The new concept that will replace multiculturalism is interculturalism, and interculturalism emphasises mutually developing dialogue (Chow, Multiculturalism. - EBSCO)

The relationship between social cohesion and education

Children and adolescents form different relationships at different stages of their lives; for example, building relationships with parents, managing relationships with school, and establishing a study routine for academic success. In addition to these, immigrant children also have to establish new relationships related to life in their new location. In addition to the usual difficulties encountered in a new settlement, the process of adapting to the new location adds further problems, such as learning a new language and understanding the cultural codes of the new place (Doğan, 2020: 27-28).

J. Berry, who proposed four models of cultural adaptation, defines members of minority communities with this model. In the acculturation adaptation model, attitudes are referred to as "acculturation attitudes." Acculturation attitudes develop in the following four forms: integration, assimilation, separation, and marginalisation (Berry, 1997). Being included in formal education is one of the most important factors that facilitates the integration of immigrants into their new location. As language proficiency increases with education, the adaptation process becomes much easier (Saygın, Hasta, 2018:325).

Since 2012, basic policies have been put on the agenda in Türkiye to address this mass migration. Although they were initially considered "guests" upon their arrival, work on child-focused education was initiated because there were children among the visitors. To prevent Syrian children from becoming a "lost generation," ministry and provincial commissions were established for education starting in 2013, and decisions were made for their inclusion in formal education. Support courses have also started for them to learn Turkish outside of formal education. (Documentation of the educational intervention for Syrian children under temporary protection in Turkey – final report. Pdf (unicef.org))

Sample and Method

The population of this study consists of Syrian children who are mandatory migrants and who watched Amal's walk performance and attend Seniha Mayda Primary School. Amal's walking route started in Türkiye and ended in

Manchester, England. In-depth interviews with children who observed Amal's walking performance and participated in events with her focused on the contribution of the training they received during the adaptation process. Some of the children who left Syria with the outbreak of the civil war either came to Türkiye as babies or started school there, but their education was interrupted. It is clear that some consequences of the traumas experienced in both forms will emerge. Therefore, education and school life are an important stage for children's social adaptation.

Ethical approval was obtained before starting the research. In-depth interviews were conducted with 12 students. Throughout the interviews, only audio recordings were made, and the children's names were not mentioned in any part of the study. The children participating in the study are Syrian children who are in school.

Findings

The children interviewed are only identified by the letter G. No name is mentioned in this study. When asked if they like school, all the children answered positively. G1, who said he also has friends at school, said, "My favourite thing about this place is the friendship. I didn't have any friends in Syria. I have friends here."

When asked if he had any friends, G4 replied, "I have both Syrian and Turkish friends." As Berry stated, education plays an important role in personal variables. Syrian children said they also make friends outside with the children they know from school.

To the question of whether children generally liked the education in Türkiye, they responded, "I like it very much. The teachers are very good. They are understanding. They love us very much." It is clear that, as in Berry's classification, there is a positive trend towards integration as a result of education and the positive behaviour of teachers.

Again, to understand social cohesion, the question was asked, "Do you participate in activities here?" To the question, "I also agree with those in school, I used to be shy and wouldn't participate in events. When I went to 5th grade, I participated in April 23rd. I said I could do it. I did it. He answered, "as." With children participating in formal education, a path has opened for them to communicate with the host community. Additionally, the supplementary Turkish classes opened in schools have accelerated children's language learning. Most of the children also stated that they spoke Turkish with their siblings at home.

Conclusion

There are difficulties experienced by children who have come through forced migration from Syria in the integration process. The study showed that the school they attended had a positive impact on their ability to cope with these challenges and social adjustment. They said they were able to play games with the children they met at school, even outside of school. The teachers' good and non-discriminatory behaviour in helping children adapt to school also had a positive impact on integration. With Turkish language courses also offered in schools, children are able to integrate into society more easily.

References

Berry, J (1997), Immigration, Acculturation, and Adaptation, **Applied Psychology: an International Review,** 1997.46 (1). 5-68,

Berray, M. (2019).A Critical literary review of the melting pot and salad bowl asimilation and integration theories, **Journal of Ethnic and Cultural Studies,** (Vol 6) no 1 . 2019

Doğan, A. (2020), "Göçmen çocuk ve ergenlerin uyum sürecini etkileyen risk ve koruyucu faktörler "ed: Doğan, A. Kağnıcı, D.Y. **Göçmen Çocuk ve Ergen Kültürleşme, Uyum ve Eğitim,** Nobel Yayıncılık.

Erdoğan, M.M. (2018) **Suriyeliler Barometresi,** İstanbul Bilgi Üniversitesi Yayınları, İstanbul.

Erder, S., (2020) "Göçmenlik, mültecilik ve değişen uyum anlayışı" (27-50), (der: Gül, Dedeoğlu, Nizam), **Türkiye'de Mültecilik, zorunlu göç ve toplumsal uyum** içinde, Bağlam Yayıncılık, İstanbul

Hazır, M. (2012)"Çokkültürlülük Teorisine Çağdaş Katkılar ve Bireysel Haklar-Grup Hakları Ekseninde Çokkültürlülüğü Tartışmak", (1-28), **Akademik İncelemeler Dergisi,** Cilt 7, Sayı1.

Saygın,S., Hasta,H,(2018), "Göç, Kültürleşme ve Uyum", **Psikiyatride Güncel Yaklaşımlar,** 10(3):312-333 doi:10.18863/pgy.364115

Serter,G.(2013). **Şikago Okulu Kent Kuramı: Kentsel Ekolojik Kuram Planlama,**23(2):67-76 doi: 10.5505/planlama.2013.98608

Web Sites

Geçici koruma yabanci kimlik no (goc.gov.tr).

Great Migration (chicagohistory.org).

Mülteci (goc.gov.tr)

Multiculturalism. - EBSCO

T.C. İçişleri Bakanlığı Göç İdaresi Başkanlığı - geçici koruma

geçici koruma (goc.gov.tr) 01. 08. 2025

Türkiye'de geçici koruma altında olan Suriyeli çocuklara yönelik eğitim

SKILLED MIGRATION AND WELLBEING

DETERMINANTS OF MENTAL HEALTH AND WELLBEING OF YOUNG MIGRANT POPULATIONS: A SCOPING REVIEW

Melanie Rees-Roberts[1], Palmira Ramos[1], Jade Fawkes[1], Dunishiya De Silva[1], Oluwatomi Shobande[2], Francesca Gan[2], Sally Kendall[1]

Introduction

Current international evidence suggests increased prevalence of poor wellbeing and mental health in migrant populations compared to native born populations, with migration a precipitating factor for mental illness (Bhugra, 2014; Virpaksha et al, 2014). Risk factors for poor mental health and wellbeing can include pre-existing vulnerabilities, individual characteristics, migration and post-migration experiences, adverse new environments, complexities in new local systems, language difficulties and cultural disparities (Bhugra, 2014; Bowe, 2017; Virpaksha et al, 2014). Despite good physical health at migration, the impact of wider determinants of health such as these contribute to the development of unhealthy lifestyles, poor wellbeing and as a result poor mental health over time (Maggi et al, 2010).

Data from the Migration Data Portal estimates 24% of migrant populations worldwide are children and young people with 13% being children under the age of 18 and 11% being young people aged 18-24 (Migration Data Portal, 2025). In these younger populations, migration has been shown to be linked to severe mental illness, such as psychosis, particularly for those under the age of 18 (Kirkbride et al, 2017). Given the impact of early adverse experiences in forming successful adult lives, it is critically important to understand what underlies these disparities (Short et al, 2020). Furthermore, vulnerable groups exist based on individual characteristic risk factors such as sex or ethnicity but also due to experiences such as forced migration (Marley and Mauki, 2019).

To support the health of young migrant populations, it is important to identify individual risk factors for poor mental health and wellbeing, but also to

[1] Centre for Health Services Studies, University of Kent, Canterbury, UK
[2] Public Advisors for the project were young migrant women from Kent, UK.
Corresponding Author: Dr M Rees-Roberts, Centre for Health Services Studies, University of Kent, Canterbury, CT2 7NZ. Email: m.rees-roberts@kent.ac.uk

understand the social, environmental and wider determinants entrenching these issues. Gaining a better and more consistent understanding of the impact that migration has on mental health and wellbeing may lead to improvement in support, care, methods for early detection and mechanisms for prevention for this rising global population.

This article presents a scoping review of existing literature with the aim of understanding the current evidence of risk factors, experiences and determinants of poor mental health and wellbeing in young migrant populations. This evidence is synthesised with the potential to inform public health policy and support the testing of relevant interventions to meet the needs of this population.

Methods

This scoping review was conducted as one work package of a project examining the mental health and wellbeing of young migrant women. The protocol is published on the funder website (Rees-Roberts, 2022). The scoping review protocol was guided by established scoping review methodology (Arksey and O'Malley, 2005; Pham et al, 2014).

The search was developed and conducted by an experienced research librarian and conducted across the following literature databases: Medline (Ovid), Embase (Ovid), Cinahl, ERIC, Social Policy & Practice, Web of Science, PsycInfo and Scopus. An initial search strategy was designed in Medline (Ovid) with text words contained in the titles and abstracts of relevant articles, and MeSH or relevant index terms then used to develop a full search strategy. A wide range of search terms to identify articles detailing risk factors or determinants of health with data was used and included: emigrants, immigrants, transients, migrants, adolescent/young adult/teenager, mental health, mental health need, mental Disorders/Stress, psychological, mental, or emotional adjectives including need, stress, distress, disorder, problem, well-being, adaptation, psychological, resilience, psychological/psychology. Terms for young women and refugees were included as potential vulnerable groups already identified from the literature and particularly important for public health. The same search strategy was then used in additional databases listed above and articles exported for analysis in April 2022. Reference lists of all included sources of evidence were screened for additional relevant studies. Relevant sources of unpublished studies/grey literature were identified through known third sector organisations websites, relevant repositories and by searching Google and Google Scholar.

Articles included were original peer-reviewed or grey literature articles in English, published from January 2000 to April 2022. Publications needed to consider young migrant adolescents or young people aged 4-24. Articles needed to present at least one outcome measure for mental, emotional or psychological health or wellbeing and/or related wider determinants of health for the population group of interest. Studies needed to be concerned with migrants settling within a country in Europe or North America.

All article titles and abstracts were screened independently by two members of the project team (PR, MRR) with any conflicting selections discussed until consensus was achieved. The following data was extracted in an Excel (Microsoft Office 365) spreadsheet: author(s), journal, year of publication, study design, characteristics of migrant participants, country, age of participants, type of data collection and comparators if applicable, study analysis, outcomes measured, and key findings including factors identified to be associated with mental health and/or wellbeing (key findings were collated in Word, Microsoft Office 365).

The scoping review findings were synthesised and organised using a narrative approach, comparing and contrasting findings and evaluating their relative worth (validity, reliability, and generalisability). The organised narrative and key findings were presented to the projects two lived experience public advisors (OS and FG) who made comments which were reflected on and included in the final narrative of the scoping review.

Results

The search identified 1648 potentially eligible articles relevant to the mental health and wellbeing of young migrant populations (Figure 1). After screening titles and abstracts, forty-four articles were identified as potentially meeting the full eligibility criteria. Twenty-four articles were excluded on assessing the full paper contents leaving twenty articles selected for data extraction (Table 1).

The majority (n=13) of these involved cross-sectional study designs with medium to large sample sizes from n=500 (Sirin et al, 2019) to n=276,165 (Chiu et al, 2012) carried out within a single country or from data collected across several countries. Four comprised longitudinal studies comparing first and second generation adolescent migrants (Bowe, 2017; Motti-Stefanidi et al, 2020; Dura-Vila et al, 2013) or immigrant families over time (Sirin et al, 2019). A single scoping review and two systematic reviews (Guruge and Butt, 2015; Marley and Mauki, 2019; Nakeyar et al, 2018) were also included. All articles consider adolescents ranging from age 11 to 29.

Within a United Kingdom (UK) context, five of the selected peer-reviewed articles were either conducted solely with UK data (n=3) (Bowe, 2017; Dura-Vila et al, 2013; Samara et al, 2020) or with cross-sectional international data which included information from the UK (n=2) (Chiu et al, 2012; Delaruelle et al, 2021). Of those conducted solely with UK data, two were longitudinal (Bowe, 2017; Chiu et al, 2012) and one cross-sectional (Samara et al, 2020). The two systematic reviews included studies in the UK (Marley and Mauki, 2019; Nakeyar et al, 2018).

Figure 1: Selection of articles for scoping review

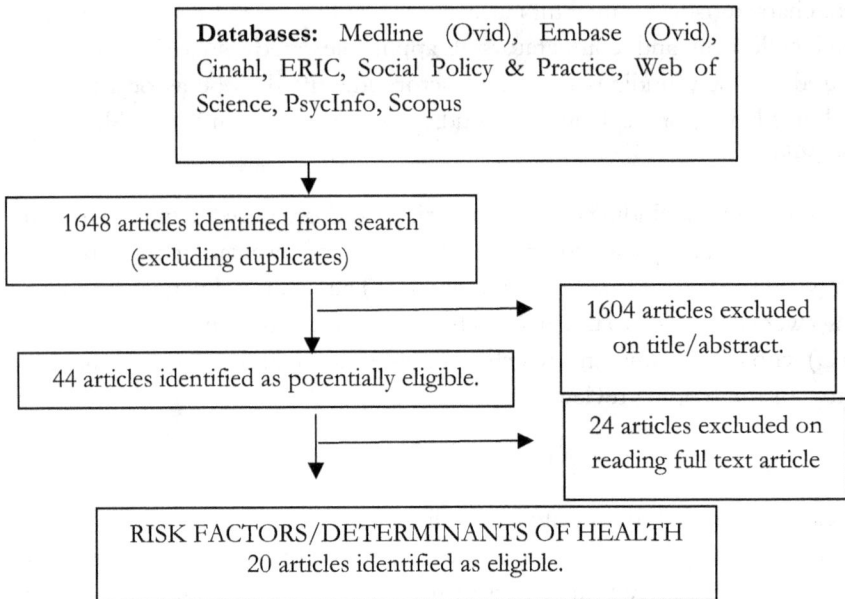

Databases: Medline (Ovid), Embase (Ovid), Cinahl, ERIC, Social Policy & Practice, Web of Science, PsycInfo, Scopus

1648 articles identified from search (excluding duplicates)

1604 articles excluded on title/abstract.

44 articles identified as potentially eligible.

24 articles excluded on reading full text article

RISK FACTORS/DETERMINANTS OF HEALTH
20 articles identified as eligible.

Most studies highlighted the disparities between native born and migrant adolescent mental health and wellbeing (Guruge and Butt, 2015; Marley and Mauki, 2019; Nakeyar et al, 2018; Delaruelle et al, 2021) whilst others support a migrant paradox, whereby migrant populations (including in adolescent studies) appear to have no difference or notably better mental health and wellbeing than native born adolescents (Duinhof et al, 2020; Georgiades et al, 2013). There is some evidence that good mental health and wellbeing may be associated with shorter time since migration but also with age where poor mental health is exacerbated during teenage and early adult years (Sirin et al, 2019). This reflects our finding of some inconsistency or potential genuine differences in the overall literature about migratory effects on mental health and wellbeing potential due to contextual factors.

Most young migrants cope well during migration (Neto, 2009) and undergo a process of adaptation that does not impact on their mental health and wellbeing. Interestingly, evidence suggests that migratory impact on mental health and wellbeing is independent of socio-economic status (Duinhof et al, 2020; Beiser et al, 2015). However, acculturative stress can increase the risk of mental health problems (Sirin et al, 2019). We do not address the complexity and process of acculturation in this synthesis, focussing only on particular factors or determinants considered important for good/poor mental health in adolescent migrant populations. However, it is acknowledged that the dynamic process, complexities and particular experiences of acculturalisation (be it bidirectional or unidirectional) can impact on adolescent migrant mental health outcomes (Sirin et al, 2019).

It was clear from the literature that forced migration, refugee status and being an unaccompanied minor were particularly strong risk factors for poorer mental health and wellbeing linked to significant trauma and discrimination during and post-migration (Spaas et al, 2022; Derluyn et al, 2009). Gender differences were also apparent with one article reporting no gender risks (Duinhof et al, 2020), whilst other studies illustrated differential burden of mental health illness in young women (Chiu et al, 2012; Guruge and Butt, 2015; Neto, 2009; Chau et al, 2012; Alivernini et al, 2019). Evidence supported higher rates of psychopathology, assault and lower self-esteem in females, particularly as a result of gender inequality, discrimination and a less positive attitude and feeling of belonging at school (Guruge and Butt, 2015; Alivernini et al, 2019; Chiu et al, 2012; Lebenbaum et al, 2021).

The articles provided a wide range of evidence into the determinants affecting migrant adolescent mental health and wellbeing which are summarised in Figure 2 showing the identified risk or protective factors for mental health and wellbeing in young migrants and for particular vulnerable groups.

Table 1: Final selected articles for wider determinants of health and risk factors for young migrant populations including young women

Reference	Title	Journal	Study design	Population Age	Sample size	Study country
Guruge and Butt, 2015	A scoping review of mental health issues and concerns among immigrant and refugee youth in Canada: Looking back, moving forward	Canadian Journal of Public Health	Scoping review	13-29	17 articles	Canada
Hjern et al, 2013	Migrant density and well-being - a national school survey of 15-year-olds in Sweden.	European Journal of public health	Cross-sectional	15	76229	Sweden
Duinhof et al, 2020	Immigration background and adolescent mental health problems: the role of family affluence, adolescent educational level and gender.	Social Psychiatry and psychiatric epidemiology	Cross-sectional	11-16	1054	Denmark
Delaruelle et al, 2021	Mental Health in Adolescents with a Migration Background in 29 European Countries: The Buffering Role of Social Capital.	Journal of youth and adolescence	Cross-sectional	11, 13, 15	121751	International: 29 countries, including Scotland
Bowe, 2017	The immigrant paradox on internalizing symptoms among immigrant adolescents.	Journal of adolescence	Longitudinal study	14-15	15770	UK
Chau et al, 2012	School difficulties in immigrant adolescent students and roles of socioeconomic factors, unhealthy behaviours, and physical and mental health.	BMC public health	Cross-sectional	11-16	1559	France
Chiu et al, 2012	Immigrant students' emotional and cognitive engagement at school: a multilevel analysis of students in 41 countries.	Journal of youth adolescence	Cross-sectional	15	276165	International: 41 countries, including UK
Beiser et al, 2015	Cultural distance and emotional problems among immigrant and refugee youth in Canada: Findings from the New Canadian Child and Youth Study (NCCYS).	International journal of intercultural relations	Cross-sectional	11-13	2074	Canada
Lebenbaum et al, 2021	Association of source country gender inequality with experiencing assault and poor mental health among young female immigrants to Ontario, Canada.	BMC Public Health	Cross-sectional	6-29	299228	Canada
Neto, 2009	Predictors of mental health among adolescents from immigrant families in Portugal.	Journal of Comparative family studies	Cross-sectional	15.54	755	Portugal

Reference	Title	Journal	Study design	Population Age	Sample size	Study country
Sirin et al, 2019	Acculturative Stress and Mental Health: Implications for Immigrant-Origin Youth.	Paediatric clinics of North America	Longitudinal study	15	500	United States of America
Alivernini et al, 2019	Support for Autonomy at School Predicts Immigrant Adolescents' Psychological Well-being.	Journal of Immigrant and minority health	Cross-sectional	15/16	3130	Italy
Georgiades et al, 2013	Emotional and behavioural problems among adolescent students: the role of immigrant, racial/ethnic congruence and belongingness in schools.	Journal of youth adolescence	Cross-sectional	12-18	77150	United States of America
Motti-Stefanidi et al, 2020	Longitudinal interplay between peer likeability and youth's adaptation and psychological well-being: A study of immigrant and non-immigrant adolescents in the school context.	International journal of behavioural development	Longitudinal study	13	1118	Greece
Spaas et al, 2021	Mental Health of Refugee and Non-refugee Migrant Young People in European Secondary Education: The Role of Family Separation, Daily Material Stress and Perceived Discrimination in Resettlement.	Journal of Youth and Adolescence	Cross-sectional	11-24	1366	International: 5 European countries, not UK
Derluyn et al, 2009	Mental health problems in separated refugee adolescents.	Journal of adolescent health	Cross-sectional	11-18	1294	Belgium
Dura-Vila et al, 2013	Mental health problems of young refugees: duration of settlement, risk factors and community-based interventions.	Clinical Child Psychology	Longitudinal intervention	3-17	102	UK
Samara et al, 2020	Examining the psychological well-being of refugee children and the role of friendship and bullying.	British Journal of Educational Psychology	Cross-sectional	6-10	269	UK
Marley and Mauki, 2019	Resilience and protective factors among refugee children post-migration to high-income countries: a systematic review.	European Journal of public health	Systematic review	6-23	11 articles	International – studies in single countries only
Nakeyar et al, 2018	The psychological needs of refugee children and youth and best practices for filling these needs: A systematic review	Clinical Child Psychology and Psychiatry	Systematic review	5-18	18 articles	International studies in single and multiple countries

Figure 2: Identified determinants of mental health and wellbeing in young migrant populations.

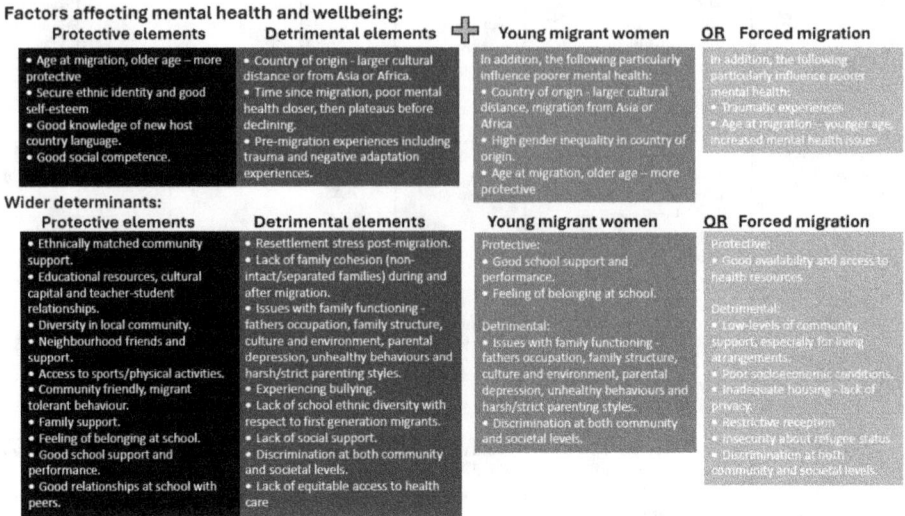

Factors affecting mental health and wellbeing:

Protective elements	Detrimental elements ➕	Young migrant women	OR Forced migration
• Age at migration, older age – more protective • Secure ethnic identity and good self-esteem • Good knowledge of new host country language. • Good social competence.	• Country of origin - larger cultural distance or from Asia or Africa. • Time since migration, poor mental health closer, then plateaus before declining. • Pre-migration experiences including trauma and negative adaptation experiences.	In addition, the following particularly influence poorer mental health: • Country of origin - larger cultural distance, migration from Asia or Africa • High gender inequality in country of origin. • Age at migration, older age – more protective	In addition, the following particularly influence poorer mental health: • Traumatic experiences. • Age at migration – younger age, increased mental health issues

Wider determinants:

Protective elements	Detrimental elements	Young migrant women	OR Forced migration
• Ethnically matched community support. • Educational resources, cultural capital and teacher-student relationships. • Diversity in local community. • Neighbourhood friends and support. • Access to sports/physical activities. • Community friendly, migrant tolerant behaviour. • Family support. • Feeling of belonging at school. • Good school support and performance. • Good relationships at school with peers.	• Resettlement stress post-migration. • Lack of family cohesion (non-intact/separated families) during and after migration. • Issues with family functioning - fathers occupation, family structure, culture and environment, parental depression, unhealthy behaviours and harsh/strict parenting styles. • Experiencing bullying. • Lack of school ethnic diversity with respect to first generation migrants. • Lack of social support. • Discrimination at both community and societal levels. • Lack of equitable access to health care	Protective: • Good school support and performance. • Feeling of belonging at school. Detrimental: • Issues with family functioning - fathers occupation, family structure, culture and environment, parental depression, unhealthy behaviours and harsh/strict parenting styles. • Discrimination at both community and societal levels.	Protective: • Good availability and access to health resources. Detrimental: • Low-levels of community support, especially for living arrangements. • Poor socioeconomic conditions. • Inadequate housing - lack of privacy. • Restrictive reception. • Insecurity about refugee status. • Discrimination at both community and societal levels.

Discussion

This project aimed to understand the existing evidence on determinants of mental health and wellbeing in young migrant populations. We identified a number of useful studies to understand risk and protective factors for mental health and wellbeing in this population; however, contradictory findings were observed indicating that context such as country of origin and reception experiences may play a key role as determinants of health. Factors of particular importance were having good school support, a feeling of school belonging and good academic performance (Sirin et al, 2019; Chau et al, 2012). Discrimination was a significant player in influencing poor mental health and wellbeing across all young migrant populations at school, community, and societal levels (Sirin et al, 2019; Guruge and Butt, 2015; Georgiades et al, 2013). From a UK context, despite inclusion in one cross-sectional study identifying mental health and wellbeing risk for young migrants across several European countries, there is little research on risk factors for poor mental health and wellbeing (Bowe, 2017; Dura-Vila et al, 2013; Samara et al, 2020). The literature identified a number of factors that may identify at risk groups, including females, dysfunctional or fragmented families, forced migration, being an unaccompanied young person or having experienced significant trauma early in life or as a result of migration.

Due to the risk of increased mental health problems over time for young migrants (Virupaksha et al, 2014; Bhugra et al, 2014; Sirin et al, 2019), fostering resilience in this population is a public health concern, especially with existing disparities in and limited access to children's mental health services. Overall, there needs to be better awareness of risks and protective factors in this population guiding interventions for support including understanding changing needs over time which was less well evidenced due to the cross-sectional nature of many existing studies. This would enable targeted approaches to support and identify those most at risk whilst enabling services to take a whole person approach, flexible enough to adapt to differing needs for support and covering practical aspects of adaption and functioning (e.g. language acquisition, signposting and support using services), social competence, establishing connections/relationships and psychological wellbeing (Alivernini et al, 2019).

Conclusion

There are a number of large-scale studies, mostly cross-sectional in nature that evidence determinants of mental health and wellbeing in young migrant populations. Migratory experiences and contexts are particularly important to consider which result in more severe vulnerabilities in mental health and wellbeing, for example forced migration. Further research would benefit from in depth longitudinal studies of migratory effects on young people including in depth analysis of contexts important for supporting mental health and wellbeing.

References

Alivernini F, Cavicchiolo E, Manganelli S, et al. (2019). Support for Autonomy at School Predicts Immigrant Adolescents' Psychological Well-being. Journal of Immigrant & Minority Health, 21(4):761-6.

Arksey H and O'Malley L. (2002). Scoping studies: Towards a methodological framework. International Journal of Social Research Methods, 8(1):19-32.

Beiser M, Puente-Duran S, Hou F (2015). Cultural distance and emotional problems among immigrant and refugee youth in Canada: Findings from the New Canadian Child and Youth Study (NCCYS). International Journal of Intercultural Relations, 49:33-45.

Bhugra D, Gupta S, Schouler-Ocak M, et al. (2014). EPA guidance mental health care of migrants. Eur Psychiatry, 29(2):107-15.

Bowe AG (2017). The immigrant paradox on internalizing symptoms among immigrant adolescents. Journal of Adolescence, 55:72-6.

Chau K, Baumann M, Kabuth B, et al. (2012). School difficulties in immigrant adolescent students and roles of socioeconomic factors, unhealthy behaviours, and physical and mental health. BMC Public Health, 12(1):453.

Chiu MM, Pong SL, Mori I, et al. (2012). Immigrant students' emotional and cognitive engagement at school: a multilevel analysis of students in 41 countries. Journal of Youth & Adolescence, 41(11):1409-25.

Delaruelle K, Walsh SD, Dierckens M, et al. (2021). Mental Health in Adolescents with a Migration Background in 29 European Countries: The Buffering Role of Social Capital. Journal of Youth & Adolescence, 50(5):855-71.

Derluyn I, Mels C, Broekaert E (2009). Mental health problems in separated refugee adolescents. 2009. Journal of adolescent health, 44:291-297. doi:10.1016/j/jadohealth.2008.07.016.

Duinhof EL, Smid SC, Vollebergh WAM, et al. (2020). Immigration background and adolescent mental health problems: the role of family affluence, adolescent educational level and gender. Social Psychiatry & Psychiatric Epidemiology, 55(4):435-45.

Dura-Vila G, Klasen H, Makatini Z, et al. (2013). Mental health problems of young refugees: duration of settlement, risk factors and community-based interventions. Clinical Child Psychology & Psychiatry, 18(4):604-23.

Georgiades K, Boyle MH, Fife KA (2013). Emotional and behavioural problems among adolescent students: the role of immigrant, racial/ethnic congruence and belongingness in schools. Journal of Youth & Adolescence, 42(9):1473-92.

Guruge S and Butt H (2015). A scoping review of mental health issues and concerns among immigrant and refugee youth in Canada: Looking back, moving forward. Canadian Journal of Public Health Revue Canadienne de Sante Publique, 106(2):e72-8.

Hjern A, Rajmil L, Bergstrom M, et al. (2015). Migrant Density and well-being - a national school survey of 15-year-olds in Sweden. Canadian Journal of Public Health, 23(5):823-828. doi:10.1093/eurpub/ckt106.

Kirkbride JB, Hameed Y, Ioannidis K, et al. (2017). Ethnic Minority Status, Age-at-Immigration and Psychosis Risk in Rural Environments: Evidence from the SEPEA Study. Schizophr Bull, 43(6):1251-61.

Lebenbaum M, Stukel TA, Saunders NR, et al. (2021). Association of source country gender inequality with experiencing assault and poor mental health among young female immigrants to Ontario, Canada. BMC Public Health, 21(1):1-12.

Maggi S, Ostry A, Callaghan K, et al. (2010). Rural-urban migration patterns and mental health diagnoses of adolescents and young adults in British Columbia, Canada: a case-control study. Child Adolesc Psychiatry Ment Health, 4:13.

Marley C and Mauki B (2019). Resilience and protective factors among refugee children post-migration to high-income countries: a systematic review. European Journal of Public Health, 29(4):706-13.

Migration Data Portal (GMDAC) IsGMDAC.: The bigger picture (Accessed 2025). Available from: https://www.migrationdataportal.org/themes/child-and-young-migrants#:~:text=Child%20Migrant%20Stocks&text=In%202020%2C%20UN%20DESA%20estimated,per%20cent%20among%20children%20globally.

Motti-Stefanidi F, Pavlopoulos V, Mastrotheodoros S, et al. (2020). Longitudinal interplay between peer likeability and youth's adaptation and psychological well-being: A study of immigrant and non-immigrant adolescents in the school context. International Journal of Behavioural Development, 44(5):393-403.

Nakeyar C, Esses V, Reid GJ (2018). The psychosocial needs of refugee children and youth and best practices for filling these needs: A systematic review. Clin Child Psychol Psychiatry, 23(2):186-208.

Neto F (2009). Predictors of mental health among adolescents from immigrant families in Portugal. Journal of Family Psychology, 23(3):375-85.

Pham MT, Rajić A, Greig JD, et al. (2014). A scoping review of scoping reviews: advancing the approach and enhancing the consistency. Res Synth Methods, 5(4):371-85.

Samara M, El Asam A, Khadaroo A, et al. (2020). Examining the psychological well-being of refugee children and the role of friendship and bullying. British Journal of Educational Psychology, 90(2):301-29.

Short A, Bolton J and Baram, T (2020). Mechanisms by which early-life experiences promote enduring stress resilience or vulnerability. Stress Resilience: Molecular and Behavioral Aspects Book Chapter. DOI: 10.1016/B978-0-12-813983-7.00012-4

Sirin SR, Sin E, Clingain C, et al. (2019). Acculturative Stress and Mental Health: Implications for Immigrant-Origin Youth. Pediatric Clinics of North America, 66(3):641-53.

Spaas C, Verelst A, Devlieger I et al. (2022). Mental health of refugee and non-refugee migrant young people in European secondary education: A study of immigrant and non-immigrant adolescents in the school context. Journal of Youth Adolescence, 51:848-870. doi:10.1007/s10964-021-01515-y

Virupaksha HG, Kumar A and Nirmala BP (2014). Migration and mental health: An interface. J Nat Sci Biol Med, 5(2):233-9.

Data Availability Statement

The data used in this article comes from already published research articles and papers. Articles are fully referenced within this article and are freely available to access online through academic journal online libraries and journal websites or on the wider internet.

Declaration Of Interests

The authors have no conflicts of interest.

Authorship Statement

The study was co-led by PR and MRR. The scoping review search was conducted by a trained librarian. PR and MRR conducted the article selection and analysis with support from SK for dis-agreements in article selection and analysis advice. O and FG as public advisors reviewed the synthesised themes and provide input and comments which were incorporated into the results.

Funding Statement

This work was supported by the National Institute for Health and Care Research (NIHR) Public Health Research programme (Award number NIHR 135216). The authors (MRR, SK, JF, DdS) are also supported by funding from the NIHR Applied Research Collaboration Kent, Surrey, Sussex (ARC KSS, NIHR 200179). The views expressed are those of the author(s) and not necessarily those of the NHS, the NIHR or the Department of Health and Social Care.

Ethical Approval Statement

This work does not require ethical approval as it is a review of existing published literature.

Acknowledgements

We would like to thank the experienced librarian who supported the search for relevant articles. We would like to thank the study advisory group for help and advice on the project. Finally, we thank our public co-authors who have been committed and supported through this work.

THE DUAL IMPACTS OF INTERNATIONAL MEDICAL MIGRATION: NIGERIAN DOCTORS IN THE UK AND THE CONSEQUENCES FOR NIGERIA'S HEALTHCARE SYSTEM

Mohammed Abdullahi

Introduction

The international migration of medical professionals is increasingly recognised as both a benefit and a challenge for global health systems. This paper explores these dual impacts, specifically through the lens of Nigerian medical doctors migrating to the United Kingdom (UK). Drawing extensively on original research conducted as part of a doctoral thesis, this study employs a rigorous mixed-methods approach integrating surveys, qualitative interviews, and policy document analysis to provide a nuanced examination of medical migration. It aims to contribute significantly to ongoing discussions around migration policy, healthcare workforce management, and the global distribution of medical resources.

Nigerian doctors migrate primarily due to the structural deficiencies within Nigeria's healthcare system. These deficiencies include inadequate salaries, poor working conditions, political instability, limited career progression opportunities, and insufficient medical infrastructure (Misau et al., 2010; Abdullahi, 2020; Ossai et al., 2020). These factors act as powerful incentives pushing doctors out of Nigeria towards more favourable employment contexts abroad. Specifically, the UK's healthcare system offers structured career paths, advanced training opportunities, access to state-of-the-art medical technology, and globally respected qualifications that Nigerian doctors find particularly attractive (Sveinsson, 2015; Adebayo, 2019; Abdullahi, 2022).

Survey findings from the study underscore these push and pull factors. Nigerian doctors consistently identify career advancement and professional development opportunities available in the UK as critical drivers of migration. Additionally, economic stability, competitive salaries, and structured professional pathways strongly influence their decisions (Abdullahi, 2022). Qualitative interviews reveal that professional aspirations are frequently intertwined with personal goals such as improved quality of life and enhanced family stability, thus further reinforcing migration decisions (Abdullahi, 2022).

This movement offers substantial benefits for individual Nigerian doctors, particularly regarding professional growth, economic stability, and improved living standards. Doctors working in the UK report significant advancements in their clinical skills, specialisation opportunities, and professional credibility on a global scale (Abdullahi, 2022). The financial advantages provided by the NHS system facilitate improved economic conditions for these professionals and their families, leading to significant remittances back to Nigeria. These remittances play a crucial role in community development and local economic stability within Nigeria (Taslakian, Garber, and Shekherdimian, 2022).

Nevertheless, the impact of this migration is deeply problematic for Nigeria's healthcare system. The continuous loss of trained doctors exacerbates workforce shortages and intensifies existing inadequacies within the national healthcare infrastructure (Ossai et al., 2020; Onah et al., 2022). Rural areas and underserved communities suffer disproportionately due to fewer available healthcare professionals, thereby increasing health disparities and reducing the quality of care (Ossai et al., 2020; Abdullahi, 2022).

The economic impact of this brain drain is also considerable. Nigeria invests heavily in the education and training of its medical professionals, with an average investment of approximately $66,000 per doctor (Obamiro et al., 2020). However, when these doctors migrate, Nigeria experiences significant financial losses, including forfeited returns on investment and increased costs associated with continually training new healthcare workers to replace those lost to migration (Abdullahi, 2022). This ongoing loss compounds economic strain and undermines sustainable health development.

Despite these challenges, the Nigerian diaspora contributes positively through remittances, philanthropic activities, and medical missions. These contributions provide short-term relief and essential support to Nigeria's healthcare sector, particularly in areas severely impacted by workforce shortages (Taslakian, Garber, and Shekherdimian, 2022; Wariri et al., 2024). However, these efforts alone cannot sufficiently address the structural deficiencies driving medical migration.

To mitigate the negative impacts of medical migration, effective policy interventions are critically needed. The Nigerian government has introduced several policy initiatives, such as the National Diaspora Policy (2021), aimed at engaging the diaspora community more systematically. However, implementation gaps, lack of coordination, and insufficient resource allocation have limited the effectiveness of these initiatives (Yakubu, Musa, and Nnochiri, 2022). Addressing these shortcomings requires comprehensive strategies that target root causes, including improving healthcare infrastructure, enhancing remuneration and working conditions, and creating more attractive career opportunities domestically (Abdullahi, 2022; Yakubu, Musa, and Nnochiri, 2022).

Moreover, strategic international collaboration and ethical recruitment practices are essential in addressing medical migration sustainably. The World Health Organization's Global Code of Practice on the International Recruitment of Health Personnel emphasises destination countries' responsibility to manage recruitment ethically and minimise negative impacts on healthcare systems in source countries. The UK, as a major beneficiary of Nigerian medical professionals, has an ethical obligation to implement recruitment practices that protect Nigeria's healthcare system from further deterioration. This includes providing structured support for Nigerian doctors practising in the UK, facilitating skill transfer, and fostering opportunities for professional exchange and collaboration (Abdullahi, 2022).

Additionally, fostering return migration represents a vital but underutilised approach to mitigating the negative consequences of medical migration. Doctors returning to Nigeria after periods of employment in the UK often bring back valuable expertise, innovative clinical practices, and strengthened professional networks. These returnees can significantly contribute to local healthcare improvement, training and mentorship of junior medical staff, and the overall strengthening of Nigeria's healthcare system (Sveinsson, 2015; Abdullahi, 2022). Nevertheless, return migration remains low due to persistent systemic barriers within Nigeria, including political instability, inadequate healthcare infrastructure, and limited career advancement opportunities (Abdullahi, 2022).

Findings from in-depth interviews indicate that Nigerian doctors abroad frequently express a desire to contribute positively to their home country's healthcare sector. However, many remain deterred by the ongoing socio-economic challenges and uncertainties regarding professional reintegration (Abdullahi, 2022). Policies designed to incentivise return migration must therefore comprehensively address these systemic challenges. Practical incentives could include improved healthcare infrastructure, guaranteed professional opportunities, competitive remuneration packages, and robust institutional support for returnees (Yakubu, Musa, and Nnochiri, 2022).

Strengthening diaspora engagement platforms could further optimise contributions from Nigerian medical professionals abroad, even in the absence of physical return. Digital technologies, telemedicine initiatives, and virtual knowledge-transfer platforms could enable diaspora professionals to actively contribute to training, clinical consultations, and healthcare policy development remotely (Abdullahi, 2022). Implementing such strategies could enhance the sustainability of Nigeria's healthcare workforce management by leveraging international medical expertise effectively.

In conclusion, the migration of Nigerian medical doctors to the UK presents clear individual benefits but poses significant systemic challenges for Nigeria's healthcare system. Addressing these dual impacts requires targeted, evidence-based policy responses. Nigeria must tackle structural barriers driving emigration through sustainable reforms, increased healthcare investment, and targeted incentives for professional retention. Simultaneously, the UK and other destination countries must adopt ethical recruitment practices, support diaspora engagement, and facilitate knowledge transfer.

This research underscores the need for strategic international collaboration in managing global healthcare workforce mobility. By integrating robust policy interventions with effective diaspora engagement and return migration incentives, it is possible to mitigate negative impacts and harness medical migration as a strategic asset for Nigeria's healthcare development.

References

Abdullahi, M. (2020). What Are The Return Propensities of Nigerian Medical Doctors In The UK? In *The Migration Conference 2020 Proceedings: Migration and Integration*, 59-63. Transnational Press London.

Abdullahi, M. (2022). Return Migration: Decision-making among Nigerian Physicians working in the NHS. In *The Migration Conference Proceedings*.

Adebayo, E. (2019). Migration of health professionals from Nigeria: A critical review. *International Journal of Public Health*, 7(2), 12-17.

Misau, Y. A., Al-Sadat, N., & Gerei, A. B. (2010). Brain-drain and health care delivery in developing countries. *Journal of Public Health in Africa*, 1(1), e6.

Obamiro, K., et al. (2020). Economic implications of health professionals' migration. *Human Resources for Health*, 18, Article 66.

Onah, M. et al. (2022). Impacts of doctor migration on healthcare delivery in rural Nigeria. *Rural and Remote Health*, 22(2), 6538.

Ossai, E., et al. (2020). Medical brain drain and its implications for Nigeria's health sector. *Pan African Medical Journal*, 36(32).

Sveinsson, K. (2015). Making a contribution: New migrants and belonging in multi-ethnic Britain. *Runnymede Trust*.

Taslakian, B., Garber, K., & Shekherdimian, S. (2022). Diaspora engagement in global health: The role of medical professionals from LMICs. *Global Health Action*, 15(1), 201-210.

Wariri, O., et al. (2024). Mitigating healthcare workforce shortages through diaspora engagement: Insights from Nigeria. *Journal of Global Health Reports*, 8, e2024059.

Yakubu, A., Musa, N., & Nnochiri, U. (2022). Policy responses to medical brain drain in Nigeria: A critical analysis. *African Health Sciences*, 22(3), 1-10.

THE ACCESSIBILITY OF MIGRANTS TO EQUINE-ASSISTED THERAPY FOR TRAUMA TREATMENT ASSOCIATED WITH PTSD

Caroline Erviksæter[1]

Introduction

When discussing mental health care for migrants, particularly those who have fled conflict zones and experienced trauma, it is crucial to understand the unique barriers they face. These barriers include language, cultural differences, and religious factors, which significantly impact their ability to access traditional therapeutic modalities (Kirmayer et al., 2011). Among various treatment options for trauma-related disorders such as Post-Traumatic Stress Disorder (PTSD), equine-assisted therapy (EAT) has emerged as a compelling alternative that could address some of these accessibility issues.

Understanding PTSD in Migrants

PTSD is a complex psychological condition that can develop after a person experiences a traumatic event. Symptoms may include intrusive memories, heightened anxiety, emotional numbing, and difficulties in interpersonal relationships (American Psychiatric Association, 2013). For migrants, the challenges associated with PTSD are often amplified due to their inability to articulate experiences that led to their trauma. They may encounter additional stressors, including loss of social networks, cultural dislocation, and economic instability, which exacerbate their psychological distress (Reed et al., 2012). As traditional therapeutic approaches often rely heavily on verbal communication, individuals who face language barriers or cultural differences may find it challenging to engage fully in such therapy (Hinton et al., 2014). Furthermore, migration itself can be a traumatic experience, encompassing dangers such as violence, exploitation, and separation from loved ones. The stigma surrounding mental health in some cultures can also discourage individuals from seeking help, leading to untreated symptoms that severely hinder their ability to adapt

[1] Caroline Erviksæter, Western Norway University of Applied Sciences, Department of Health and Care Sciences, Svanehaugvegen 1, 6812 Førde, Norway. E-mail: 240045@stud.hvl.no

to new environments. It is essential to develop culturally sensitive interventions that recognize the unique experiences of migrants, allowing for alternative forms of expression, such as art or community support, which can foster healing and resilience. Building trust within therapeutic relationships is crucial, as it encourages individuals to share their struggles and embark on a path toward recovery.

Equine-Assisted Therapy as an Intervention

Equine-assisted therapy presents a unique therapeutic model that may mitigate some of the challenges faced by migrants. EAT involves the use of horses as part of the therapeutic process, where patients engage in various activities with the horse, facilitated by a trained therapist. This interaction enables participants to develop non-verbal communication skills, emotional awareness, and a sense of control, which can be particularly beneficial for those struggling with PTSD (White-Lewis, 2019).

One of the key components of EAT is the horse's capacity to respond to human emotions without judgment, providing an environment of safety and acceptance. This non-judgmental quality can alleviate the pressure individuals may feel in traditional therapeutic settings, enabling them to express emotions more freely (Badin et al., 2022). The horse serves not only as a companion but also as a mirror, reflecting participants' emotional states and promoting self-awareness through the process of interaction (Schmidt et al., 2022).

Moreover, the physical presence of a horse can ground individuals, helping them reconnect with their bodies and emotions, which is particularly important for those experiencing dissociation or emotional numbness—common symptoms of PTSD. The structured activities involved in EAT also promote routine and purpose, which can foster a sense of normalcy in the often chaotic lives of migrants. Additionally, the bond that forms between the participant and the horse can cultivate trust and empathy, skills that are often compromised in individuals with PTSD. By bridging the gap between verbal and non-verbal communication, EAT provides an alternative avenue for expression and healing, making it a powerful intervention for migrants navigating the complex terrain of trauma recovery. The holistic nature of this therapy supports not just emotional healing but also helps in rebuilding social connections and enhancing overall well-being.

Overcoming Accessibility Barriers

1. Language and Communication

Language barriers significantly hinder migrants' access to mental health services. Many therapists may not be fluent in the migrant's primary language, limiting effective communication and understanding of the nuances of their experiences. EAT addresses this issue by emphasizing non-verbal communication, allowing participants to engage with their emotions without the constraints of language (Antonovsky, 1996). The therapeutic bond with the horse can transcend linguistic differences, creating a safe space for emotional expression.

2. Cultural Sensitivity

Cultural differences can also pose challenges in the therapeutic relationship, where conventional methods might not align with individual beliefs or values. EAT is adaptable and can be tailored to suit the cultural backgrounds of participants.

For instance, horses can be seen as symbols of freedom and healing across various cultures, which can resonate positively with migrants experiencing trauma (Baun et al., 2006). Thus, the cultural adaptability of EAT makes it a viable option for diverse populations, fostering a sense of empowerment and agency.

3. Emotional Safety and Trust Building

For many migrants, building trust with mental health providers can be a significant challenge, especially when discussing traumatic experiences. Traditional therapy often involves delving into painful memories, which can induce anxiety and reluctance to engage (Mäkelä et al., 2019). EAT encourages a gradual buildup of trust through interactions with horses, which can help to establish rapport before moving onto more challenging topics. This process allows participants to develop emotional safety and fosters a healthier therapeutic alliance (Field, 2018).

Methodology: Qualitative Research Design

To explore the accessibility and effectiveness of equine-assisted therapy for migrants suffering from PTSD, a qualitative research design will be employed. This design focuses on the lived experiences of participants and allows for an in-depth understanding of the nuances surrounding their therapeutic journeys (Kvale & Brinkmann, 2015)

1.Participants

The study will involve various stakeholders, including migrants who have accessed EAT, practitioners in the field, and employees at therapy centers. This diverse participant pool will provide rich insights into the effectiveness and perceptions of EAT for trauma treatment across different contexts.

2. Data Collection

Semi-structured interviews will be conducted, guided by a carefully constructed interview template. This approach allows for flexibility in responses, enabling participants to share their experiences in their own words while ensuring that key areas of interest are covered (Patton, 2015). The interview guide will be developed to avoid language barriers, employing simple language and visual aids where necessary, to facilitate understanding and comfort (Hinton et al., 2014).

3. Analysis

Thematic analysis will be employed to analyze the interview data, identifying key themes and patterns that emerge from the participants' narratives. This approach allows for the exploration of shared experiences and the unique challenges faced by migrants undergoing equine-assisted therapy for PTSD (Braun & Clarke, 2006). A focus will be placed on understanding their perceptions of accessibility, emotional benefits, and cultural adaptations of EAT.

The Significance of the Study

Understanding the effectiveness and accessibility of equine-assisted therapy for migrants is vital for several reasons. First, the findings could contribute significantly to the field of trauma-informed care by illustrating how EAT can serve as a potential alternative for those unable to access traditional therapeutic modalities. With increasing numbers of migrants facing psychological distress due to war, displacement, and resettlement challenges, innovative treatment options are paramount in improving overall mental health outcomes (Malterud, 2021).

Second, this research could promote greater awareness of the unique needs of migrant populations in mental health settings, encouraging practitioners to adopt culturally competent care practices. By examining how EAT can be integrated into existing therapeutic frameworks, the study aims to enhance the cultural sensitivity and effectiveness of interventions for diverse groups (Mæland, 2021).

Lastly, the study seeks to highlight the potential of horses as effective facilitators of healing, showcasing how non-traditional therapeutic methods can make a meaningful difference in the lives of individuals grappling with the lasting effects of trauma. By infusing the therapeutic process with creativity and adaptive techniques, there is potential for groundbreaking advancements in trauma treatment.

Conclusion

In conclusion, the accessibility of equine-assisted therapy for migrants suffering from PTSD presents a promising area for further research and intervention development. As traditional therapeutic avenues may often be limited by language barriers, cultural sensitivities, and emotional safety concerns, EAT offers a unique alternative that may more effectively address the complex needs of this population. The qualitative research proposed aims to deepen the understanding of EAT's accessibility and efficacy, ultimately contributing to the advancement of trauma-informed care among migrants.

The implications of this study extend to practitioners, policymakers, and mental health advocates engaged in addressing the mental health care needs of diverse populations. The exploration of equine-assisted therapy as a viable treatment option has the potential to inspire innovation, foster cross-cultural understanding, and facilitate healing for those affected by trauma.

References

- American Psychiatric Association. (2013). Diagnostic and statistical manual of mental disorders (5th ed.). Arlington, VA: American Psychiatric Publishing.
- Antonovsky, A. (1996). The salutogenic model as a theory to guide health promotion. *Health Promotion International*, 11(1), 11–18.
- Badin, L., Alibran, É., Pothier, K., & Bailly, N. (2022). Effects of equine-assisted interventions on older adults' health: A systematic review. *International Journal of Nursing Sciences*, 9(4), 542–552.
- Baun, M. M., Johnson, R. A., & McCabe, B. W. (2006). Human-animal interaction and successful aging. In A. H. Fine (Ed.), *Handbook on animal-assisted therapy: Theoretical foundations and guidelines for practice* (2nd ed., pp. 287–302). Academic Press.
- Braun, V., & Clarke, V. (2006). Using thematic analysis in psychology. *Qualitative Research in Psychology*, 3(2), 77–101.
- Field, A. (2018). *Discovering statistics using IBM SPSS Statistics* (5th ed.). SAGE Publications.
- Hinton, D. E., Pich, V., & Chhean, P. (2014). Cultural concepts of distress in Cambodian refugees: PTSD, depression, anxiety, and the cultural insult syndrome. *Cultural Medicine & Psychiatry*, 38(2), 152–173.
- Kirmayer, L. J., Guzder, J., & Rousseau, C. (2011). Cultural consultation: A model of mental health service for the 21st century. *Canadian Journal of Psychiatry*, 56(5), 110–115.
- Kvale, S., & Brinkmann, S. (2015). *Interview: Det kvalitative forskningsinterview som håndværk* (3rd ed.). Hans Reitzel.

Selected Papers

- Malterud, K. (2021). Kvalita*tive forskningsmetoder for medisin og helsefag* (4th ed.). Universitetsforlaget.
- Mæland, J. G. (2021). *Forebyggende helsearbeid: Folkehelsearbeid i teori og praksis* (5th ed.). Universitetsforlaget.
- Mäkelä, M., Luoma, I., & Kivimäki, M. (2019). *Psychological trauma and mental health in refugees: A systematic review.* European Journal of Psychotraumatology, 10(1), 1622071.
- Patton, M. Q. (2015). *Qualitative interviewing: A method of qualitative research.* Sage Publications.
- Reed, R. J., et al. (2012). *The impact of migration on mental health.* International Journal of Social Psychiatry, 58(4), 345–357.
- Schmidt, L. L., Johnson, S. N., Genoe, R., Jeffery, B., & Crawford, J. (2022). *Social interaction and physical activity among rural older adults: A scoping review.* Journal of Aging and Physical Activity, 30(3), 495–509.
- Stergiou, A., Tzoufi, M., Ntzani, E., & Varvarousis, D. (2017). *Therapeutic effects of horseback riding interventions: A systematic review and meta-analysis.* American Journal of Physical Medicine & Rehabilitation, 10, 1.
- White-Lewis, S. (2019). *Equine-assisted therapies using horses as healers: A concept analysis.* Nursing Open, 7(1), 58–67.
- White, R. L., Babic, M. J., Parker, P. D., Lubans, D. R., Astell-Burt, T., & Lonsdale, C. (2017). *Domain-specific physical activity and mental health: A meta-analysis. American Journal of Preventive Medicine,* 52(5), 653–666.

PRESERVING YOUTH MENTAL WELLBEING IN WARTIME MIGRATION CRISIS: EDUCATORS' REFLECTION

Gražina Čiuladienė, Nomeda Gudelienė, Janina Ovčinikova[1]

Introduction

Children fleeing war experience continuing traumatic occurrences and stressors due to living through transformed social situations, deteriorated life conditions, and general uncertainty (Schwartz et al., 2022). The opportunity to access education in a host country is considered a way to overcome war trauma through establishing a secure environment of care and support for refugee pupils. The European Parliamentary Assembly emphasizes the importance of ensuring migrant children access to quality education that contributes to their capacity development and helping them reach their full potential (Onses-Segarra, 2024). Schools play a crucial role in refugee integration process (Nazuruk et al., 2024; Vandekerckhove and Aarssen, 2020; Shoshani, 2021). In particular, the responsibility for implementing educational and integration solutions in this area rests primarily with teachers. Therefore, exploring the experiences of teachers is necessary to facilitate integration, observe obstacles, and suggest improvements.

The research aims to examine the perceptions, practices and challenges Lithuanian teachers face when educating migrant children, especially Ukrainian war refugee adolescence who arrived after the Russia's full-scale invasion in Ukraine in February 2022. The tasks include identifying the experiences of educators working in multilingual environment; examining the challenges of teaching pupils suffering from war caused traumas; provide recommendations for strengthening migrant integration in Lithuanian schools.

Education institutions not only provide academic knowledge but also facilitate integration into the cultural, linguistic, and social life of the host society (Goździak, E. M., & Popyk, A., 2024; Popyk, 2023). Although multicultural from the middle ages, during the last decades Lithuania was a rather

[1] Gražina Čiuladienė, Nomeda Gudelienė, Janina Ovčinikova, Mykolas Romeris University, Lithuania. E-mails:
grazina.ciuladiene@mruni.eu; ngudel@mruni.eu; janinaovcinikova@gmail.com

homogenous culture. The war in Ukraine caused an influx of Ukrainian and Russian speaking children and teenagers, most with traumatic experiences, into Lithuanian society and schools. Teachers following Lithuanian curriculum were not prepared to sudden multilingual and intercultural communication, missing knowledge on trauma-informed pedagogy and inclusion based social fabric.

Cultural intelligence and respecting individual needs are important in general education, especially in the context of migration. Research suggests that teachers lacking intercultural awareness and not being able to communicate in pupil's mother tongue unintentionally marginalize migrant children (Banks, 2015; Gay, 2018; Portes & Rumbaut, 2014; Suárez-Orozco et al., 2018). Majority of Ukrainian refugees arrive into host countries with trauma caused by war, family separation and home loss. It affects socio-psychological well-being but also academic life resulting in lack of concentration, learning delays and higher school drop-out rates (Fazel et al., 2012). As the migrant flows have been increasing in Lithuania during the last decade, teachers often encounter these challenges without adequate psychological and linguistic training.

For the last decades migration in Lithuania was understood in terms of Lithuanians leaving the country and returning. Before 2022, about 82% of migrants were returnees. However, the situation has changed during the last years and especially after the start of Russia's caused war in Ukraine. In Lithuania, 97 963 Ukrainian refugees including 22 524 children and adolescence were registered (State Data Agency, 2025). This influx of war affected people has changed the country demographics and caused challenges for Lithuanian teachers, educators and child welfare workers.

Majority of Ukrainian children and teenagers immediately after arriving in Lithuania continued their education in public and private schools taught in Lithuanian, Russian or Polish. Some schools with the Ukrainian language of instruction were started, employing Ukrainian refugees as teachers, school psychologists and social pedagogues. For example, the school "Gravitas Schola" enrolling approximately 500 pupils of all ages was formed in March 2022 by a group of Lithuanians and accommodated at Mykolas Romeris University (MRU). In the following school years nearly 180 pupils (grades 8-11) have been studying in MRU premises, smaller children in other parts of Vilnius, and different education and recreational events were hosted by the university.

The research methodology included a qualitative research aimed to record teachers' subjective perceptions and experiences with the focus on intercultural interactions, professional preparedness, and classroom dynamics. Nine teachers participated in the study. Semi-structured interviews were carried out in April-May 2023. The teachers were asked about the experiences in teaching classes that include Ukrainian war refugees, challenges they face, their practice in teaching bi-lingual classrooms and addressing war-traumatized pupils. The interviews were transcribed, coded, grouped into similar topics and interpreted.

Results

The research results have revealed three major groups of answers: 1) limited capacity to satisfy pupil individual linguistic needs; 2) lack of knowledge how to teach pupils who have war-caused traumatic experiences; 3) need for constant profession development with regard to multiculturalism.

First, communication with the war migrants has appeared as a critical challenge. Children and adolescence from Ukraine spoke Ukrainian and Russian while Lithuanian pupils and young teachers spoke Lithuanian and English while older teachers spoke Russian. A language barrier prevents communication with both the teachers and the peers. the migrant children do not speak Lithuanian, hardly any English, and the teachers do not speak Ukrainian. Russian became not only a tool to communicate with the teacher (if the teacher knows Russian), but also to communicate with peers, so the circle of peers narrowed down to only those children who knew Russian. Migrant children learned Lithuanian during the language lessons, as well as during extra lessons, which is far from enough to be able to understand and engage in regular classes and relationships. Lithuanian fluency was understood as a prerequisite for learning engagement. Teachers attributed the responsibility for developing language skills to pupils, positively evaluating those who made progress. The ability to understand others and express oneself verbally is a crucial prerequisite for academic, psychological, and sociocultural adaptation. Inability to understand teaching content was the major obstacle in the classroom, respondents reported. This, in turn, unintentionally put teachers and pupils in the risk of violation of equal opportunities and discrimination resulting in school drop-out among the Ukrainian war refugees. In line with other research (e.g., Vrdoljak et al., 2024), the language barrier is be viewed as the major source of reported challenges, influencing all aspects of the integration process.

Second, educating children and adolescence who have encountered war-related traumas such as loss or injury of family members or acquaintances, displacement, fear and uncertainty about the future was mentioned by several respondents. Knowledge gap of trauma-informed education placed emotional tensions for teachers and other pupils indicating the need of psychological support. Without receiving adequate socio-psychological support Ukrainian pupils started to avoid school which finally led to drop-outs.

Third, teachers reported that they were left by themselves and felt not prepared to work in multicultural and multilingual classrooms. As prior to the war in Ukraine there was no need to receive training on intercultural teaching, the war in Ukraine revealed the gap of preparedness. The need to understand the basic issues of different cultures and language teaching was emphasized suggesting to include it in teacher education and professional development.

The research results have revealed that in times of wars and social challenges teachers need systemic support and training, especially about trauma-informed pedagogical practice. The teachers also emphasized the importance of language assistance, supporting migrants in language acquisition, and knowledge of multilingualism and multiculturalism. The findings highlight that meeting pupil individual linguistic and sociopsychological needs is a prerequisite for teaching and learning academic discipline content. As language barriers pose major obstacles to teaching, refugee well-being and integration, it is suggested to initially place refugees in their familiar linguistic environment with intensive host country language courses.

To conclude, the research presents how Russia's caused war in Ukraine challenged Lithuanian general education system and provided opportunities to build more culturally, linguistically, and psychologically sensitive and supportive schools. The study underscored to need embed multiculturalism and multilingualism as well as trauma-informed courses into teacher training and professional development. The research reveals broader challenges schools in many European countries accepting migrants faced, with particular focus on Lithuania, historically homogenous country that suddenly faced big scale of war affected Ukrainian children and adolescence. It pointed to the need to include intercultural intelligence, inclusive curriculum development and trauma-informed teaching into national teacher preparation system to build a resilient and socially coherent society.

References

Banks, J. A. (2015). Cultural diversity and education: Foundations, curriculum, and teaching. Routledge.

Goździak, E. M., & Popyk, A. (2024). Navigating and negotiating borders in primary and secondary education: Ukrainian children in Polish schools. *Human Organization, 83*(3), 289–302. https://doi.org/10.1080/00187259.2024.2389522

Fazel, M., Reed, R. V., Panter-Brick, C., & Stein, A. (2012). Mental health of displaced and refugee children resettled in high-income countries: Risk and protective factors. The Lancet, 379(9812), 266–282.

Gay, G. (2018). Culturally responsive teaching: Theory, research, and practice. Teachers College Press.

Portes, A., & Rumbaut, R. G. (2014). Immigrant America: A portrait. University of California Press.

Popyk, A. (2023). Migrant children and schools: Educational and social integration in host societies. International Journal of Sociology of Education, 12(1), 45–63.

Nazuruk, S., Ruszkowska, M., Budyk, O., Dąbrowska, I. , and Sokolowska, B. (2024). Experiencec of the Polish teachers of primary schools in working with war refugee students from Ukraine – selected problems, limitations and implications for pedagogical practice. *Education*, 3 (13), 1-14.

Onsès-Segarra J. and Domingo-Coscollola, M. (2024) Integration of migrant children in educational systems in Spain: stakeholders' views. *Intercultural Education*, 35(2), 156-170, DOI: 10.1080/14675986.2024.2314394

Schwartz, L., Nakoecha, M., Campbell, G., Brunner, D., Stadler, Ch., Schid, M., Fegert, J.M., and Burgin, D. (2022). Addressing the mental health needs and burdens of children fleeing war: a field update from ongoing mental health and psychosocial support efforts at the Ukrainian border. *European Journal of Psychotraumatology*. 13, 2101759

Shoshani, A. (2021). Transcending the reality of war and conflict: effects of a positive psychology school-based program on adolescents' mental health, compassion and hopes for peace. *The Journal of Positive Psychology*, 16 (4), 465-480.

State Data Agency. 2025. *Švieslentė. Karo pabėgėliai iš Ukrainos*. Vilnius: Official Statistics Portal. Available at: https://osp.stat.gov.lt/ukraine-dashboards [Accessed 19 Aug. 2025].

Suárez-Orozco, C., Motti-Stefanidi, F., Marks, A., & Katsiaficas, D. (2018). An integrative risk and resilience model for understanding the adaptation of immigrant-origin children and youth. American Psychologist, 73(6), 781–796.

Vandekerckhove, A., and Aarssen, J. (2020). High time to put the invisible children on the agenda: supporting refugee families and children through quality ECEC. *European Early Childhood Education Research Journal*, 28 (1), 104-114.

Vrdoljak, A., Stanković, N., Čorkalo Biruški, D., Jelić, M., Fasel, R., and Butera, F. (2024). "We would love to, but…"—needs in school integration from the perspective of refugee children, their parents, peers, and school staff. *International Journal of Qualitative Studies in Education*, 37 (2), 512-529.

A GROUNDED THEORY EXPLORATION OF WELLBEING FOR WOMEN WHO HAVE BEEN FORCIBLY DISPLACED AS A RESULT OF TRAUMA CAUSED BY CONFLICT, BASED ON THE EXPERIENCE OF PARTICIPANTS LIVING IN UGANDA

Helen Harrison

Introduction

This research aimed to explore the experiences of two groups of women living in Uganda who have been displaced by war and are rebuilding their lives in refugee and displacement communities. While the initial focus was on their experiences and understanding of wellbeing in the context of war-related displacement, the data collected broadened the scope beyond wellbeing alone. Both groups had received trauma counselling services from a Ugandan non-profit with which the author has a professional (non-financial) connection.

The study focused on two groups of displaced women living in Uganda:

South Sudanese Refugees (SSR):

These women fled the ongoing civil war in South Sudan, which began with the country's independence in 2016 (Pinaud, 2021). By 2023, there were 2,292,482 South Sudanese refugees under the UNHCR mandate, with nearly 1 million hosted in Uganda (UNHCR, 2024). The participants in this study lived in a UNHCR-recognised refugee settlement in northern Uganda.

Acholi Internally Displaced Persons (IDPs):

These women were displaced due to the two-decade war between the Lord's Resistance Army (LRA) and the Ugandan government, which ended in 2006. The conflict displaced nearly 1.6 million people (Amone-P'Olak et al., 2014) many of whom moved to urban areas, including the 'Acholi Quarters' in Kampala, where the study's Acholi participants now reside.

Since the end of UNHCR humanitarian aid in 2012, Uganda no longer recognizes IDP status and residents of Acholi Quarters consequently face ongoing challenges including poor access to basic services and insecure land and housing tenure (Mallett, 2010).

Justifying the research

Forcibly displaced women as the participant group

As of mid-2024, 122.6 million people were forcibly displaced worldwide, including 68.3 million internally displaced persons and 37 million refugees. Uganda hosts about 1.7 million refugees, primarily from South Sudan, the DRC, and Burundi (UNHCR, 2024). Refugee studies often present a homogenised view of refugee experiences, neglecting gender-specific analysis. The UNHCR's definition of a refugee lacks a gendered lens, despite evidence that displacement impacts people differently based on gender (Ghorashi, 2021). This has led to the marginalisation of women's voices and the problematic grouping of women and children, which obscures adult women's unique needs (Freedman & Freedman, 2007). The study aims to address these gaps by centring the experiences of displaced women.

Wellbeing as the initial focus

Wellbeing is central to the UN Sustainable Development Goals (SDGs, 2024) and widely studied, yet data from the Global South is limited (Disabato et al., 2016). The Capability Approach (Sen, 1993; Nussbaum, 2011) challenges traditional Western, middle-class male perspectives by valuing diverse lived experiences and highlighting human diversity and multiple wellbeing dimensions. Despite this, there is little research on wellbeing among women refugees in the Global South, especially displaced women in Uganda. This study aims to address that gap by exploring their unique experiences and views of wellbeing.

Study design

This study is based on constructivist grounded theory and feminist standpoint paradigms, which support the examination of gendered experiences and power dynamics while centring participants' voices (Tyagi, 2014; Charmaz, 2014). Data collection involved open, unstructured interviews, with interpreters assisting participants in speaking their native languages. Ethical approval was granted by both the University of Gloucestershire and Gulu University research ethics committees, and research permission was obtained from the Ugandan National Council of Science and Technology (UNCST).

Research in practice

This study employed a Grounded Theory approach, enabling simultaneous data collection and analysis, supported by ongoing memo writing (Birks & Mills,

2023). Initial individual interviews generated early codes, which were refined into focused codes through additional interviews, culminating in a theoretical code that informed the final grounded theory. The research included interviews with six South Sudanese and sixteen Acholi women. Early interviews used open-ended questions to explore personal understandings of wellbeing post-displacement, centring participant voices. Subsequent group interviews focused on emerging themes while allowing individual input. Communication was facilitated by female Acholi-speaking interpreters, and data was gathered through recordings, field notes, and visual aids. Ethical standards, including informed consent, were upheld, and researcher reflections were used to deepen the analysis.

Analysis and findings

In line with grounded theory approach, analysis utilised a constant comparative approach, with the initial analysis, and resultant initial codes informing subsequent data collection. In this study the initial codes and categories were encapsulated in conceptual model figure 1.

Figure 1 illustrates a conceptual journey from a pre-conflict life with acceptable wellbeing (1), through the trauma of external violence (2) that renders life unliveable (3), followed by forced displacement (4) leading to a new, more liveable situation (5). The time (6) taken for these stages varied across individuals, as did the nature of their transitions. The perception of a "liveable" life also differed and evolved over time (8), with changing criteria for wellbeing and liveableness (7).

The study focused on the conceptual model's category of *reimagining liveable space*, which included the interconnected properties of *liveableness*, *wellbeing*, and *community*, and the research concentrated on this theme for further data collection and analysis. Theoretical coding centred on this category, and subsequent interviews explored its components until theoretical saturation was achieved. During this process, a new category, *temporariness*, also emerged and was examined similarly. Constant comparative analysis was used throughout to compare data across interviews and ensure category saturation.

Figure 1: Conceptual model of the initial categories identified, (property of

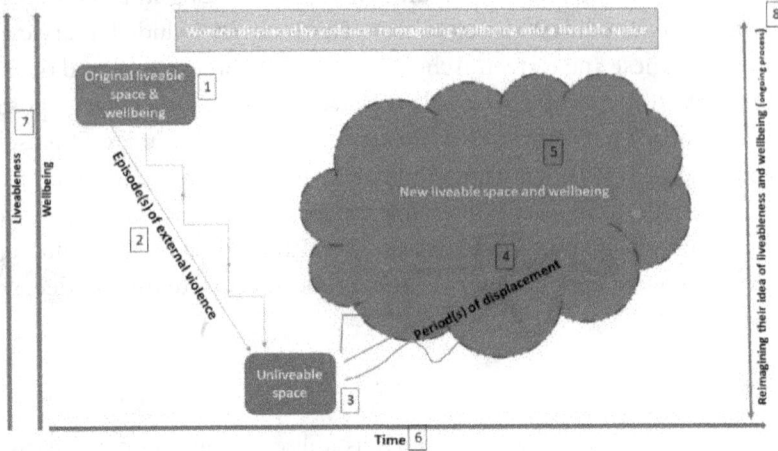

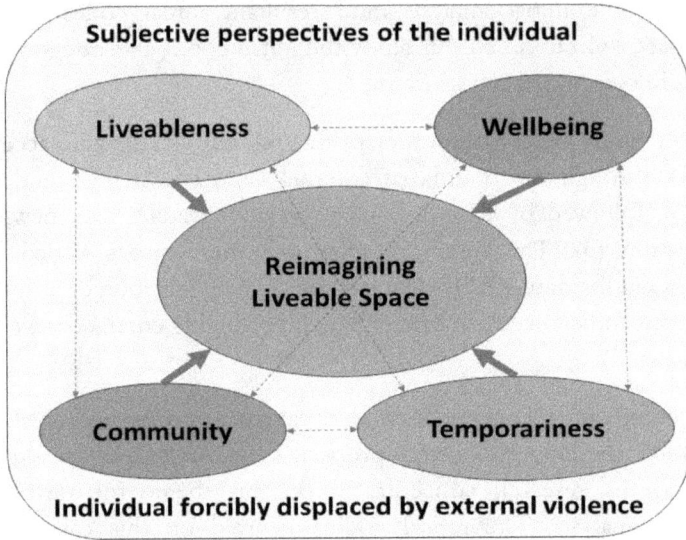

Fig 2: Updated conceptual model, *(property of author)*

author)

By the end of the analysis stage an updated conceptual model (figure 2) had been developed.

This illustrates how the theoretical concept of *reimagining liveable space* connects with its four categories—wellbeing, liveableness, community, and temporariness—while emphasizing the subjective nature of individual perspectives.

Findings

Although the study initially focused on wellbeing among women forcibly displaced by war, the main findings centred on the theoretical code of *reimagining liveable space*, encompassing four key categories: *wellbeing, liveableness, temporariness,* and *community*.

Reimagining liveable space

The concept of *liveable space* refers to a temporary refuge where displaced individuals feel safe enough to stop fleeing—such as refugee camps, safe houses, or private homes. Though not permanent, these spaces provide a secure environment for individuals and their dependents.

Reimagining liveable space is a dynamic process influenced by shifting priorities. Initially centered on safety and basic needs, displaced individuals' perceptions evolve to include goals like education, employment, independence, and a sense of home—signifying broader definitions of wellbeing and community as stability increases.

Most displaced women received psychosocial support, which they credited with enhancing wellbeing and empowering long-term decision-making. This support often contributed to a reimagining of liveable space, with some women developing a stronger sense of belonging, while others retained a longing for home and a feeling of impermanence.

Initially, many sought familiar communities, but over time, preferences shifted toward those offering better services and opportunities, reflecting evolving definitions of liveableness. The pace of reimagining varies, shaped by trauma, recovery time, personal circumstances, and host community conditions. Greater opportunities may slow the process, while limited resources can accelerate aspirations for change.

The emergent grounded theory

The final version of the grounded theory that emerged from this study was:

Women who have undergone forced displacement due to profound, personal experience of gender-based violation and abuse through violent external episodes will demonstrate a reimagining of what constitutes a liveable space with the passing of time and as influenced by the interconnectedness of their individual, subjective perceptions of wellbeing, liveableness, community, and temporariness.

To test the robustness of the theory as part of the solidification process, it was assessed against the grounded theory pre-requisite that an emergent theory should fulfil the requirements of fit, work and relevance, and modifiability (Lomborg and Kirkevold, 2003). Each of these conditions was satisfactorily met, and the theory was also shown to address deviant cases which provided further evidence of the robustness of theory (Haning, 2021).

Importance of the findings for future use / Contribution and value-add

The findings from this study, and the emergent grounded theory, provide a platform from which to draw a number of learning points pertinent to the practices of service providers working with forcibly displaced people.

One learning point is that Wellbeing, liveableness, temporariness, and community are deeply interconnected and non-hierarchical concepts for women who have experienced trauma. They influence one another in complex, subjective ways that vary by individual and context. This interdependence highlights the importance of considering these concepts together when designing support services and evaluating outcomes.

Service providers should recognize that *reimagining liveable space* is an ongoing process, affecting a client's goals during trauma counselling. As perceptions shift over time, support strategies may need to adapt. However, current programs often offer only short-term interventions. A key recommendation is for counselling agencies to move beyond one-time support and develop longer-term approaches that build resilience and accommodate evolving needs.

Each of the four grounded theory categories—liveableness, wellbeing, temporariness, and community—has multiple properties influencing a displaced person's healing. These include factors like safety, gender, mental health, mutuality, and choice. Given this complexity, organizations should review their practices to ensure clients have the space and support to explore all relevant areas during the healing process.

Given the subjective nature of trauma, it is essential to treat each woman as an individual and listen to her unique perspective. While group therapy can offer valuable benefits like shared information and social support (Nakimuli-Mpungu, *et al*, 2015), organizations must avoid assuming that all participants have similar experiences or needs.

A key learning is the importance of considering the needs of host communities alongside those of displaced people. Educating and supporting host communities can foster acceptance and peaceful coexistence. Without this, displaced individuals may face rejection and added trauma, hindering their recovery.

This research uniquely integrates the four interconnected components of liveable space rather than focusing on them individually. This innovative approach, grounded in participants' experiences, offers valuable insights and practical applications for supporting displaced and traumatized people. The study's findings have significant potential to influence policy and future global research.

References

Amone-P'Olak, K. et al. (2014) 'Postwar Environment and Long-Term Mental Health Problems in Former Child Soldiers in Northern Uganda: The Ways Study,' *Journal of Epidemiology and Community Health*, 68(5), pp. 425–425

Birks, M. and Mills, J. (2023) *Grounded Theory: A Practical Guide*. 3rd edition. Sage. London.

Charmaz, K. (2014) *Constructing Grounded Theory*. 2nd edition. Sage, London.

Disabato, D. J. *et al.* (2016) 'Different types of well-being? A cross-cultural examination of hedonic and eudaimonic well-being', *Psychological Assessment*, 28(5), pp. 471–482.

Freedman, J. and Freedman, J., (2007).' Who are the "Refugee Women"?' *Gendering the International Asylum and Refugee Debate*, pp.21-4

Ghorashi, H., (2021). 'Normalising power and engaged narrative methodology: Refugee women, the forgotten category in the public discourse.' *Feminist Review*, *129*(1), pp.48-63.

Haning, M. (2021) 'The Role and Influence of Performance in School Music Programs: A Grounded Theory'. *Journal of Research in Music Education*, 69(1), 85-104.

Lomborg, K. and Kirkevold, M., (2003). 'Truth and validity in grounded theory–a reconsidered realist interpretation of the criteria: fit, work, relevance and modifiability.' *Nursing Philosophy*, *4*(3), pp.189-200.

Mallett, R. (2010) 'Transition, Connection and Uncertainty: IDPs in Kampala,' *Forced Migration Review*, (34), pp. 34–35.

Nakimuli-Mpungu, E., *et al*, (2015). 'Group support psychotherapy for depression treatment in people with HIV/AIDS in northern Uganda: a single-centre randomised controlled trial.' *The Lancet HIV*, *2*(5), pp.e190-e199.

Nussbaum, M.C., (2011) *Creating capabilities: The human development approach*. Harvard University Press. London.

Pinaud C, (2021) '*War and genocide in South Sudan.*' Cornell University Press, Ithaca, NY:. Available at: https://library.oapen.org/handle/20.500.12657/62027

SDGS. (2024). '*Sustainable Development Goals*', United Nations. Department of Economic and Social Affairs Sustainable Development. https://sdgs.un.org/goals (accessed 03/02/2025)

Sen, A. (1993) 'Capability and well-being', Edited by M.C. Nussbaum and A. Sen. *The quality of life*. Oxford University Press, Oxford, pp30-53

Tyagi, R. (2014) 'Understanding Postcolonial Feminism in Relation with Postcolonial and Feminist Theories', *International Journal of Language and Linguistics*, 1(2), pp. 45-50.

UNHCR (2024), *Refugee statistics*, https://www.unhcr.org/refugee-statistics/ (accessed

UNCERTAINTIES UPON UNCERTAINTIES: AN ETHNOGRAPHIC RESEARCH ON THE MIGRATION EXPERIENCES OF BRITISH NATIONAL (OVERSEAS) MIGRANTS IN THE UK

Lok Yee Liona Li

Introduction

On 30 June 2020, Hong Kong entered a new era with the sudden enactment of the National Security Law (NSL). The law criminalised acts of sedition, secession, terrorism, and collusion with foreign powers, and immediately altered the lives of many. For young people especially, the city's future appeared increasingly uncertain.

Against this backdrop, the UK government introduced the British National (Overseas) [BN(O)] visa scheme, presented as a demonstration of its "historic and moral commitment" to Hong Kongers (Home Office, 2020, p. 3). The scheme provided a settlement route for those holding BN(O) status, granting the right to reside, work, and study in the UK, with a path to citizenship after six years. By March 2024, 144,400 people had relocated under this pathway (Home Office, 2024).

This paper examines the migration experiences of young BN(O) migrants in the UK. It argues that their journeys, stretching from pre-departure decisions to settlement challenges, exemplify "uncertainties upon uncertainties". By situating these experiences within debates on forced and voluntary migration, uncertainty, and youth, the paper shows how the BN(O) case complicates conventional categories and offers insights into migration shaped by layered political, temporal, and generational dynamics.

Literature Review

Migration is often classified along a spectrum of voluntariness, with forced migration implying coercion and voluntary migration implying choice. Yet, as Bakewell (2021) and others argue, these boundaries are blurred. The BN(O) visa scheme bears hallmarks of voluntary migration: financial proof, visa fees, health requirements, and was framed by policymakers as a matter of individual choice. However, decisions to leave were made under the shadow of political repression and the extraterritorial reach of the NSL, making safe return uncertain. Some migrants, therefore, describe their move as "forced exile", revealing a disjuncture between official categorisation and lived realities.

The concept of uncertainty further illuminates these experiences. Distinct from risk, which refers to calculable probabilities, uncertainty highlights open-ended, indeterminate conditions (Horst & Grabska, 2015). Migration generates and is shaped by uncertainty, from opaque bureaucratic processes to unpredictable futures in both origin and host societies. BN(O) migrants face temporal uncertainties – waiting for decisions, deferring life plans; and spatial uncertainties – from where they will settle to whether return is possible. Such uncertainties are also socially produced, requiring analysis of how they are lived and negotiated.

Finally, the paper takes a relational approach to youth. Rather than a chronological category, youth is understood through social expectations, intergenerational relations, and disrupted life transitions (Hopkins & Pain, 2007; Robertson, 2018). Migration reroutes and delays milestones such as education, employment, and family formation, producing anxieties about "falling behind". For young BN(O) migrants, these disruptions are intertwined with political rupture, deepening the sense of uncertainty across the life course.

Methodology

This research adopts an ethnographic approach, drawing on in-depth interviews and participant observation with 17 young BN(O) migrants in the UK between 2021 and 2023. Participants were selected using convenience sampling methods and included individuals spanning recent graduates to mid-career professionals, representing a variety of migration backgrounds.

Fieldwork included attending community gatherings, shadowing everyday routines, and informal conversations. This has enabled the exploration of lived experiences beyond policy framings, foregrounding the meanings young migrants attach to uncertainty and belonging.

Ethical considerations were central, given participants' potential vulnerabilities under the NSL's extraterritorial provisions. Pseudonyms are used throughout and identifying details have been removed.

Findings and Analysis

1. The Decision to Leave: Choice or Exile?

For many participants, the decision to migrate was both urgent and reluctant, often described in terms such as "forced exile" or "fleeing" their home. Parents of young protest participants framed the BN(O) visa as a "lifeboat" – a crucial means of securing safety for their children amid fears of surveillance and arrest. Similarly, journalists, activists, and professionals affiliated with disbanded organisations highlighted their heightened personal precarity, which left them with little real choice but to leave.

Yet, alongside these urgent pressures, some participants also recognised the "privileges" embedded in the BN(O) scheme. Unlike asylum seekers, BN(O) migrants were required to demonstrate financial means, pay visa fees, and organise their own travel arrangements. However, upon arrival, they were granted the ability to work, study, and live with relative freedom.

This dual reality reveals migration under the scheme as a complex process shaped by both constraint and opportunity. It was propelled by fear and repression, and also heavily influenced by migrants' available resources and family circumstances. Such complexity challenges the adequacy of simple binary labels like "forced" versus "voluntary" migration, underscoring the need for a more nuanced understanding.

2. Living with Uncertainty

During the application process, many participants faced prolonged waits for visa approval and unexpected bureaucratic hurdles, such as scheduling and completing the required tuberculosis (TB) test at designated clinics in Hong Kong.

Once in the UK, young BN(O) migrants encountered new uncertainties. Some under threat back home often arrived without clear plans for settlement. They could only rely on contingency accommodation, such as Airbnb, moving frequently from one temporary place to another. This precariousness in housing often spilled over, affecting their ability to secure steady employment, pursue education, and build social networks.

Temporal uncertainty was pervasive. Participants described their lives were "on hold". They had been delaying their decisions about further study, careers, or even relationships until their immigration status felt secure. As one noted, "I am always waiting…for the visa, for a job, for a future I can't see.". Despite the

BN(O) scheme's legal clarity, this prolonged precariousness echoed experiences common in forced migration.

Spatial uncertainty also emerged subtly. While many appreciated cultural familiarity – in language, institutions, and colonial legacies – they were unsettled by everyday differences in social norms and work culture. Feelings of dislocation deepened with the realisation that return to Hong Kong might no longer be possible out of safety concerns. As one participant put it, "Home is 12 hours away, but unreachable.".

3. Youth, Transitions, and Interrupted Timelines

Youth highlighted the complex ways migration disrupted life trajectories. Most participants had to restart their paths in the UK by pursuing additional studies, taking entry-level jobs, or internships. These created a palpable sense of delay compared to peers who remained in Hong Kong. Others faced accelerated responsibilities, such as supporting parents with limited English, navigating bureaucracy for family members, or becoming primary breadwinners. Migration thus reshaped not only individual timelines but also generational roles. The pressure to "catch up" or "not fall behind" was intense, compounding anxieties already rooted in Hong Kong's highly competitive social environment.

Yet, alongside these challenges, participants emphasised resilience and adaptability. Some welcomed the chance to "start fresh", describing how they "had nothing to lose" and appreciated living in an environment freer from political constraints and relentless peer competition. In this way, youth became a space not only of vulnerability but also of agency, where migrants actively redefined their identities and aspirations in the face of uncertainty.

4. Negotiating Belonging

Belonging proved to be a complex and ongoing process for BN(O) migrants. Although they were officially welcomed under the rhetoric of "historic responsibility" and recognised as BN(O) "citizens" (Home Office, 2020, p. 3), many experienced various forms of exclusion. Institutionally, they remain excluded from certain social benefits and public funds. Beyond these formal barriers, several participants reported experiences of racialisation in workplaces and public spaces. Furthermore, many felt homogenised under the label "BN(O) migrants", a category that fails to capture the diverse motivations behind their migration and the complexities of their identities.

Community networks such as mutual aid groups and churches have played a crucial role in helping migrants navigate settlement by offering practical assistance and emotional support. However, reliance on these networks sometimes reinforced a sense of parallel existence, which potentially delayed fuller integration into wider society.

Belonging was further complicated by identity struggles within the Hong Kong diaspora itself. Migrants grappled with questions about what it means to be a "Hongkonger" in exile: Must they "suffer" to claim this identity? Are they considered genuinely Hongkonger if they visit a Chinese restaurant in Chinatown or no longer following news about political prosecutions in Hong Kong? Such debates continue to circulate within the UK's Hong Kong community.

At the same time, many migrants felt estranged from their home city, which increasingly no longer felt familiar due to political autocratisation and the closure of well-known shops and restaurants. The growing presence of China-owned chain stores deepened their sense of dislocation, complicating their connection to "home".

Conclusion

The BN(O) migration scheme is often presented as a voluntary and orderly pathway for Hongkongers seeking new lives in the UK. However, the lived experiences of young migrants reveal a far more complex reality. Their journeys show how migration is shaped by overlapping uncertainties, including political repression at home, bureaucratic delays and precarious conditions abroad, and interrupted life-course transitions that blur the distinction between choice and exile.

Analysing these experiences through the lenses of forced versus voluntary migration, uncertainty, and youth highlights the inadequacy of rigid policy categories. The case of BN(O) migrants demonstrates that migration is rarely a matter of pure choice or coercion. Instead, it is an ongoing negotiation of constraints and possibilities across time and space.

For young migrants especially, uncertainty is not a temporary obstacle but a defining condition. It influences how they imagine their futures, take on responsibilities, and construct a sense of belonging. These realities leave many in a state of "permanent temporariness". Understanding their experiences demands moving beyond policy framings towards the everyday realities of navigating "uncertainties upon uncertainties".

Acknowledgement

I would like to thank my supervisors, Mahardhika Sjamsoe'oed Sadjad and Roy Huijsmans, for their invaluable support, and all participants who generously shared their experiences for this research.

References

Bakewell, O. (2021). Unsettling the boundaries between forced and voluntary migration. *Handbook on the Governance and Politics of Migration*, pp.124–136. doi:https://doi.org/10.4337/9781788117234.00017.

Home Office (2020a). *Hong Kong British National (Overseas) Visa Policy Statement.* CP. 280, London: HMSO.

Home Office. (2024). Safe and Legal (Humanitarian) routes to the UK. GOV.UK. https://www.gov.uk/government/statistics/immigration-system-statistics-year-endingmarch-2024/safe-and-legal-humanitarian-routes-to-the-uk#british-national-overseas-bnoroute

Hopkins, P. and Pain, R. (2007). Geographies of age: thinking relationally. *Area*, 39(3), pp.287–294. doi:https://doi.org/10.1111/j.1475-4762.2007.00750.x.

Horst, C. and Grabska, K. (2015). Flight and Exile—Uncertainty in the Context of Conflict-Induced Displacement. *Social Analysis*, 59(1), pp.1–18. doi:https://doi.org/10.3167/sa.2015.590101.

Robertson, S. (2018). Migrant, interrupted: The temporalities of 'staggered' migration from Asia to Australia. *Current Sociology*, 67(2), pp.169–185. doi:https://doi.org/10.1177/0011392118792920.

GESTATIONAL DIABETES MELLITUS IN SOUTH ASIAN IMMIGRANT WOMEN IN CANADA: CAUSES, CONSEQUENCES, AND MANAGEMENT

Loshana Sivanarul

Introduction

Gestational diabetes mellitus (GDM) is an emerging global health problem, with a recent meta-analysis reporting a worldwide prevalence of 14.7% (Saeedi et al., 2021). Regional variations exist, ranging from 5.4% in Europe to 13.9% in Africa (Nguyen et al., 2018). In Canada, GDM diagnoses have quadrupled over the past two decades, showing both rising prevalence and improvements in diagnostic measures (Dłuski et al., 2022). Risk factors for GDM include modifiable aspects such as obesity, maternal age, changes in screening thresholds, and ethnic diversity, as well as non-modifiable factors such as genetic predisposition and family history of diabetes (Metzger et al., 2007; Lamri et al., 2022). These factors overlap with those observed in type 2 diabetes (T2DM), highlighting that women with a parent diagnosed with T2DM are more susceptible to GDM and have an increased likelihood of developing T2DM later in life (Jang et al., 1998; Vounzoulaki et al., 2020).

Canada's growing cultural diversity, driven by immigration, has significant implications for public health. Immigrants accounted for 23% of the population in 2021 and are projected to reach 30% by 2036 (Government of Canada, 2023a; Brosseau and Dewing, 2018). Population-based studies across high-income countries consistently show that immigrant women, particularly from South Asia (SA), face a higher risk of GDM than native-born women (Kragelund Nielsen et al., 2022). SA women experience 2.3 times higher GDM risk, with rates of 7.7% compared to 3.3% in non-Asian populations (Kandasamy et al., 2020). With GDM contributing to the rising prevalence of diabetes worldwide, projected to increase by 59.7% between 2021 and 2050, urgent preventive measures are required (Ong et al., 2023).

This dissertation explores GDM in SA immigrant women in Canada, examining how cultural, linguistic, and socio-economic factors influence access to care and pregnancy outcomes. Using the Social-Ecological Model (SEM) to categorise barriers and the COM-B framework to guide behavioural interventions, this study identifies challenges and proposes strategies to improve maternal and neonatal health in this vulnerable population.

Background

Gestational diabetes mellitus (GDM) is a metabolic disorder characterised by chronic hyperglycemia during pregnancy in women without prior diabetes (Plows et al., 2018). The Hyperglycemia and Adverse Pregnancy Outcomes (HAPO) study demonstrated that GDM is associated with increased maternal and neonatal complications, including preeclampsia, caesarean sections, and macrosomia (Metzger et al., 2008). Early identification is essential, as interventions such as lifestyle and dietary modifications, metformin, or insulin therapy can mitigate many adverse outcomes (Crowther et al., 2005).

International migration refers to individuals relocating across national borders from their place of birth (United Nations, 2023). This review focuses on South Asian (SA) immigrants in Canada, including both recent arrivals and long-term residents, while excluding refugees due to their unique circumstances (Yu et al., 2007). Figure 1 illustrates Canada's immigrant population trends, highlighting a significant proportion from Asia, accounting for 62% of recent arrivals between 2016 and 2021 (Norris, 2022). Migrants often face language barriers, limited access to services, and socioeconomic marginalisation, which can impede healthcare access (Suphanchaimat et al., 2019).

South Asians constitute 7.1% of Canada's population and encompass diverse ethnicities, languages, religions, and cultural practices (Government of Canada, 2023b; Waxler-Morrison et al., 2011). Recognising this diversity is crucial, as individual risk factors and cultural practices influence pregnancy outcomes. Despite Canada's publicly funded Medicare system, immigrants—particularly those without permanent residency or undocumented status—may face obstacles accessing care (Garasia et al., 2023; Martin et al., 2018). Private insurance or out-of-pocket payments can be costly, particularly for low-income families (Caulford and D'Andrade, 2012).

Studies indicate that SA immigrant women experience higher rates of adverse pregnancy outcomes than Caucasian counterparts, including GDM, preterm birth, and stillbirth (Davies-Tuck, Davey, & Wallace, 2017; De Graaff et al., 2022). Addressing these disparities requires culturally tailored healthcare strategies that consider genetic, environmental, and social determinants. Understanding these intersecting factors forms the foundation for effective interventions to improve maternal and neonatal outcomes among SA immigrant women.

Methodology

A systematic literature review was conducted to explore the causes, consequences, and management of GDM in SA immigrant women. Databases including PubMed, Scopus, and Web of Science were searched using keywords such as "gestational diabetes," "South Asian," "immigrant," "Canada," and "maternal health." Inclusion criteria were peer-reviewed articles published in English over the last 15 years focusing on SA populations. Studies addressing refugees, asylum seekers, or populations outside Canada were excluded. Relevant studies were filtered, analysed, and synthesised to identify key themes including genetic predisposition, cultural and dietary influences, preconception care, healthcare access, psychosocial factors, and interventions using behavioural frameworks such as COM-B.

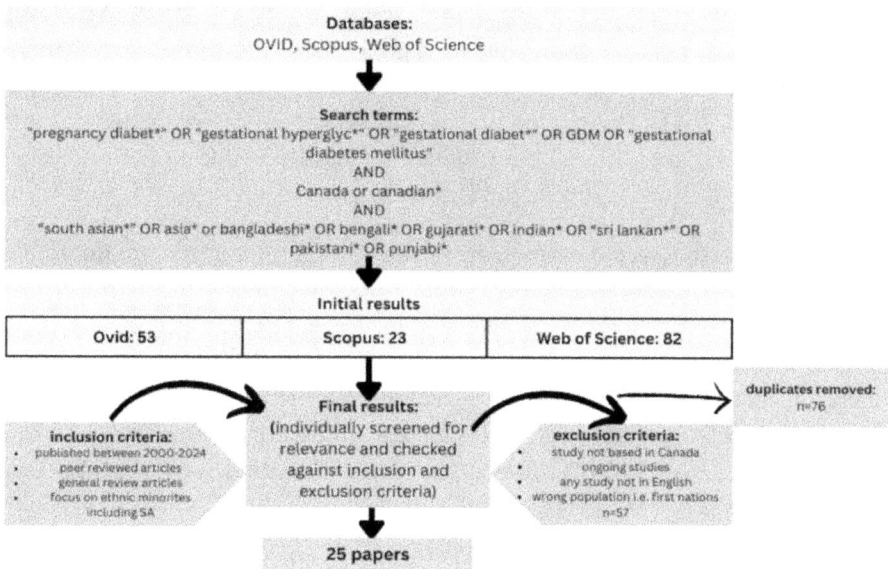

Figure 1: Literature review search

Discussion

Causes and Risk Factors

The literature reveals multiple factors influencing GDM risk in SA immigrant women, including genetic predisposition, dietary patterns, cultural beliefs, and socioeconomic circumstances. Despite lower BMI compared to Caucasians, SA women tend to exhibit greater abdominal obesity, contributing to increased insulin resistance and elevated GDM risk (Anand et al., 2017; Retnakaran et al., 2006; Huang et al., 2015). Conventional BMI thresholds underestimate obesity prevalence in this population; for example, using a BMI ≥ 30 kg/m² identified only 19% as obese, whereas a revised threshold of ≥ 25 kg/m² identified 58% of SA women in the Fraser Health population (Fraser Health Authority, 2015; Razak et al., 2007).

Hormonal differences also play a role. Lower adiponectin levels in SA women, even at lower BMI, are associated with reduced insulin sensitivity (Retnakaran et al., 2004). Elevated levels of the protein RBP-4 may serve as a potential biomarker for GDM, though further research is required (Huang et al., 2015).

Preconception care is essential in mitigating GDM risk. Promoting optimal pre-pregnancy weight, balanced diets, and physical activity improves metabolic outcomes (Anand et al., 2013, 2017; De Souza et al., 2019). However, implementation is challenging due to high rates of unplanned pregnancies among immigrant women, estimated at over 50% in Canada (Black et al., 2015; Oulman et al., 2015). Integrating preconception care into family planning and sexual health services offers opportunities for targeted education and lifestyle interventions (O'Brien, Grivell, and Dodd, 2016).

Immigration status, acculturation, and exposure to obesogenic environments further influence GDM risk. Recent immigrants often display higher prevalence rates than long-term residents, potentially due to genetic factors combined with environmental exposures in host countries (Read et al., 2021). Acculturation involves adopting the host culture's values while modifying original cultural practices, affecting diet, activity, and healthcare utilisation (Ahmed and Lemkau, 2000). Stress and social isolation may also exacerbate metabolic risk (Ho et al., 2023; R.O. Yeung et al., 2017).

The Healthy Migrant Effect

The Healthy Migrant Effect suggests that immigrants often arrive in a host country with better overall health compared to the native population, typically due to self-selection and generally higher baseline health (Ali, 2002; McKay, Macintyre, and Ellaway, 2003; Pérez, 2002). Among SA immigrant women in Canada, this effect is initially evident through lower rates of smoking and alcohol consumption, and higher consumption of vegetables, reflecting cultural norms and upbringing (Anand et al., 2016; Fraser Health Authority, 2015).

However, over time, this health advantage diminishes as immigrants adapt to the host country's lifestyle, which may include increased consumption of processed foods, reduced physical activity, and exposure to obesogenic environments (Newbold, 2006; Zaidi, Couture-Carron, and Maticka-Tyndale, 2013). Acculturation, social isolation, and stress associated with resettlement can further exacerbate these risks, particularly for recent immigrants, increasing susceptibility to gestational diabetes mellitus (GDM) and future type 2 diabetes (R.O. Yeung et al., 2017; Ho et al., 2023).

From a COM-B perspective, the decline in health behaviours illustrates changes in **opportunity** (environmental influences) and **motivation** (beliefs and habits) over time. Culturally tailored interventions, including diet and physical activity support, preconception counselling, and education about GDM risks, are crucial for maintaining beneficial behaviours and mitigating the rise of GDM among SA immigrant women. Early engagement with healthcare providers can help sustain the initial health advantage, reduce complications, and support long-term metabolic health.

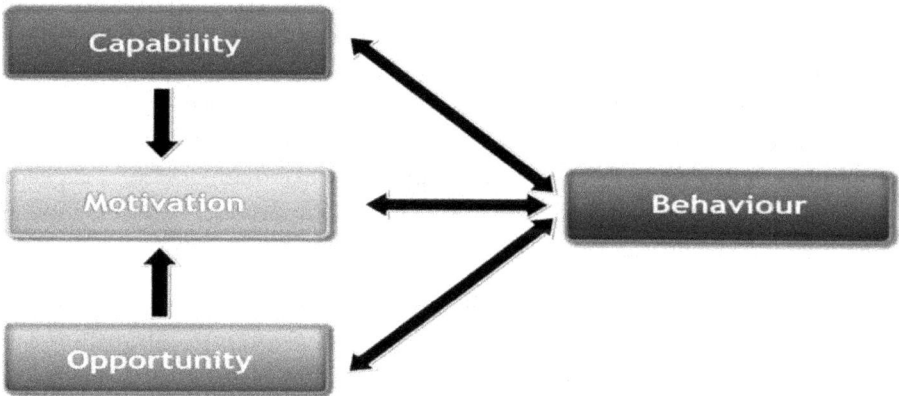

Figure 2: COM-B model

Cultural Influences on Diet and Exercise

Cultural norms significantly shape dietary habits, exercise behaviours, and adherence to medical recommendations. SA diets are traditionally carbohydrate-rich, including rice, chapati, and deep-fried vegetarian dishes, complicating dietary modification in GDM (Bandyopadhyay, 2021; Tzotzis et al., 2023). Vegetarian women, in particular, may consume excessive carbohydrates, highlighting the need for culturally sensitive dietary guidance (Bandyopadhyay, 2021; De Sequeira et al., 2019).

The COM-B framework—capability, opportunity, and motivation—offers a structured approach to behaviour change. Capability relates to knowledge and skills, emphasizing culturally adapted education. Opportunity encompasses environmental and social factors, such as access to dietitians, transportation, and social support. Motivation includes beliefs and habits, often driven by concern for the unborn child, although sustaining behaviour postpartum remains challenging (Michie et al., 2011; Banerjee et al., 2016).

Exercise-related beliefs also affect adherence. Cultural norms sometimes promote sedentary behaviour during pregnancy due to perceived safety, potentially conflicting with clinical advice (Vyas et al., 2012; De Sequeira et al., 2019). Tailored interventions can help women make informed choices while respecting cultural practices.

Family Support and Healthcare Access

Family involvement is critical in GDM management. Multigenerational households often assist with meal preparation, medication adherence, and monitoring lifestyle behaviours, although conflicting advice may arise (De Sequeira et al., 2019; Tzotzis et al., 2023). Engaging family members in education enhances adherence and supports collaborative care. Language barriers can impede comprehension, necessitating interpreter services, though inconsistencies may lead to miscommunication.

Healthcare access challenges include long wait times for dietitian services, transportation difficulties, and inconvenient clinic locations (Vogel, 2017; Haigh et al., 2023). Improving accessibility and integrating services at local clinics can reduce barriers and enhance engagement in GDM management.

Psychological Impact

The diagnosis of GDM can induce anxiety, stress, and feelings of loss of control, particularly due to frequent blood glucose monitoring and dietary restrictions (Bandyopadhyay, 2021; Haigh et al., 2023). Recent immigrants may experience heightened psychological stress, compounded by acculturation pressures and limited social support (De Sequeira et al., 2019). Providing counselling and mental health support is crucial for promoting wellbeing and adherence.

Consequences for Mothers and Newborns

GDM has substantial long-term implications. Mothers are at increased risk of type 2 diabetes and cardiovascular disease postpartum (Bainey et al., 2019; Anand et al., 2016; Ho et al., 2023). Newborns often display the "thin-fat" phenotype—low birth weight with high abdominal adiposity—predisposing them to insulin resistance and cardiometabolic risk (Anand et al., 2013; Desai et al., 2021). These outcomes align with the thrifty phenotype hypothesis, suggesting fetal adaptations to maternal metabolic stress confer survival advantages but increase long-term health risks. Early recognition and intervention are essential to mitigate adverse outcomes in both mothers and infants.

Conclusion

Managing GDM in SA immigrant women requires a culturally sensitive, multifactorial approach that addresses genetic predisposition, dietary and lifestyle practices, preconception care, psychological support, and social determinants. Interventions using the COM-B framework, ethnicity-specific BMI criteria, and family-inclusive education can improve adherence, maternal health, and neonatal outcomes, reducing the intergenerational burden of metabolic disease. Tailored strategies are essential to enhance healthcare accessibility and support long-term behavioural changes, ultimately promoting better health outcomes for both mothers and their children.

A CONCEPTUALIZATION OF SCHOOL CITIZENSHIP FOR THE NEW CITIZENS OF SCHOOLS IN TÜRKIYE: THE RIGHTS AND RESPONSIBILITIES OF IMMIGRANT/REFUGEE STUDENTS AND PARENTS

Ali Faruk Yaylacı[1]

Introduction

Türkiye, with its long migration history and the more recent large-scale influx of refugees, has emerged as a central country of migration. Since the outbreak of the Syrian civil war in 2011, the country has experienced unprecedented migration flows, hosting over five million foreigners, many of whom are children and young people of school age. This demographic reality places education at the heart of debates on migration and integration. Following Türkiye's open-door policy in 2011, refugee children's access to education expanded significantly, with enrolment rates reaching nearly 70 per cent. Yet, despite this progress, important challenges remain. The perception of refugees as *temporary guests* has hindered the establishment of comprehensive and permanent educational policies. The absence of strong, holistic strategies continues to limit the role of education in fostering mutual adaptation between the host society and newcomers. At the same time, education remains critical for building social cohesion and promoting harmony between different communities.

From this perspective, examining the situation of migrant and refugee students and their families through the lens of *school citizenship* provides valuable insights. Organisational citizenship theory, when adapted to the school context, conceptualises schools as communities where students, teachers, administrators, parents, and staff act as *citizens* bound by mutual rights and responsibilities. This framework highlights how school membership reflects not only educational but also social and political dimensions of belonging. Historically, however,

[1] Prof. Dr., Kütahya Dumlupınar Üniversitesi, ali.yaylaci@dpu.edu.tr, ORCID:0000-0003-4459-3410
The full text of the presentation is based on the project work titled "New Citizens of Schools: The Position of Immigrant/Refugee Students and Their Parents in the Turkish Education System" (Anadolu University Scientific Research Project, SBA-2024-2479).

citizenship has operated as an exclusionary category, granting broader rights to citizens than to non-citizens (Özkan, 2019). Tracing back to ancient Greek society, only the children of noble citizens were entitled to education, considered *small citizens* (Yolsal Murteza, 2023). Similarly, Turner (2001) emphasises how citizenship continues to marginalise immigrants, undocumented migrants, and ethnic minorities. Within schools, this exclusionary logic often extends to migrant, refugee, or foreign students, limiting their rights and recognition.

Analysing the educational experiences of these students and their parents within the framework of school citizenship therefore deepens understanding of their rights and responsibilities. Such an approach not only contributes to the integration of newcomers but also supports the development of inclusive, sustainable education policies in line with Türkiye's contemporary migration reality. The organisational citizenship approach seeks to counter the negative effects of neoliberalism in education, which often positions school members as service providers and recipients. Organisational citizenship behaviours, defined as voluntary and unrewarded actions beyond formal role descriptions, nonetheless enhance organisational effectiveness (Organ, 1988; Podsakoff, MacKenzie, Paine & Bachrach, 2000; Graham & Van Dyne, 2006). Graham (1995) expanded this concept through political philosophy, introducing *civic virtue*, which emphasises responsible participation in organisational life. His perspective, grounded in philosophy and political science, is considered foundational to the organisational citizenship framework (Yaylacı, 2016). Educational institutions, in this sense, may be viewed as *political communities* or *quasi-states* (Yaylacı, 2015).

Within the organisational citizenship framework (Yaylacı, 2004, 2011, 2015, 2016), citizenship represents the legal, social, and educational interactions between schools and their members. This relationship, which shapes rights and responsibilities, extends to teachers, students, administrators, support staff, and parents. The notion of *school citizenship* (Yaylacı, 2024) adapts this concept to education, recognising school members as *citizens* with varying rights and responsibilities depending on their roles (Yaylacı, 2011, 2016, 2024).

In this context, the aim of this study is to examine the rights and responsibilities of migrant and asylum-seeking students and parents—new *citizens* of Turkish schools—within the framework of school citizenship. Based on research in schools in Eskişehir, this study discusses how school–citizen relations, conceptualised through organisational and school citizenship, illuminate the educational challenges of asylum seekers and contribute to developing mutual cohesion. Ultimately, this perspective provides a holistic framework for the school citizenship approach rooted in organisational citizenship theory.

Method

In order to conceptualise the rights and responsibilities of migrant and asylum-seeking students and parents, who are the new citizens of schools in Türkiye, this study was designed as qualitative research. Data were collected through surveys and interviews. The study group was reached using purposive and snowball sampling techniques. A total of 41 participants were included: 21 refugee students and 20 refugee parents from schools attended by refugee students in Eskişehir, Türkiye.

Findings and Discussion

The processes through which refugee families are recognised within the education system, and through which perceptions of their rights are constructed, are often limited, fragmented, or shaped by structural constraints (Dryden-Peterson, 2015). The findings of this study likewise reveal that parents' and students' views regarding their rights and responsibilities in schools are significantly shaped by their experiences as refugees. A detailed examination of participants' statements indicates that rights are mostly articulated in fragmented, ambiguous, or individualised ways, whereas responsibilities are expressed more clearly, collectively, and in action-oriented terms. This supports the broader conclusion of the study that responsibilities are emphasised more than rights.

The statements of parents in this study reveal uncertainty and lack of knowledge concerning rights. Some parents explicitly stated that they were unaware of their entitlements. For example, one participant noted: "I have no idea. I don't know what my responsibilities are or what I am entitled to" (Parent-8), underlining the absence of any form of orientation or guidance. This statement is a striking example of how limited rights awareness can be among parents. The literature similarly emphasises that ambiguities regarding rights are often linked to lack of information, language barriers, and complex bureaucratic processes (Due, 2021; OECD, 2022).

Structural constraints associated with refugee status also play a significant role in shaping perceptions of rights. For instance, one participant remarked: "I have been here for six or seven years. We came here under the supervision of the United Nations. They gave us an identity card. We live here but we have no rights. For example, we cannot leave the city. We need to get an appointment and permission to travel" (Parent-2). Such words demonstrate that rights are perceived not only within the school context but also as part of the broader restrictions permeating everyday life. This finding resonates with the literature, which highlights that refugees' perceptions of rights are not confined to the education system but are directly shaped by the opportunities and constraints of wider migration regimes (Boukhari, 2025).

Nevertheless, some parents with greater awareness conceptualised education not solely as an academic activity but also in terms of human and children's rights. As one participant explained: "Human rights, children's rights are very important. Because what we call education is actually a very broad phenomenon. It is not just mathematics or Turkish. But in many countries, only these subjects are taught" (Parent-3). This perspective draws attention to the holistic dimension of education, beyond academic achievement alone. The literature supports this approach, noting that education serves not only academic purposes but also as a vehicle for social and cultural integration (Gandarilla Ocampo, vd., 2021). Other parents, however, emphasised the importance of religious education, drawing on cultural traditions from their countries of origin.

Another recurring theme among parents was the demand for equal treatment in schools. As one parent stated: "In classes, in schools, children should be treated well" (Parent-9), highlighting the right of children to be respected in educational settings. Some parents also recounted discriminatory experiences involving their children and teachers.

Students' perceptions of rights, in contrast, were more individualised and rooted in daily experiences compared to those of parents. One student expressed the desire for social acceptance, stating: "I just want us to be friends… that they don't shout" (Student, 15). Another adopted a more universal perspective: "Education must be equal for all students; this is a right" (Student, K, Iraq). These findings show that students' perceptions of rights are closely linked to being treated equally, avoiding exclusion in peer relations, and having their voices heard. As Due (2021) stated that students' understanding of rights is strongly connected to social acceptance and peer relationships.

Overall, the findings indicate that statements concerning rights were limited, fragmented, and often grounded in personal experiences. While parents tended to frame rights in relation to structural constraints and systemic exclusion, students focused on equality and acceptance in everyday school life. In contrast to the ambiguity and fragmentation of rights-related statements, both parents and students articulated responsibilities in clear, specific, collective, and action-oriented ways. This demonstrates that refugee families' interactions with the school system are defined more through obligations, while rights remain largely invisible (OECD, 2022; Boukhari, 2025).

Parents generally defined their responsibilities in terms of supporting their children's educational progress and adapting to school rules. For example, one parent stated: "Of course, we are responsible for ensuring that they behave according to the rules. Taking our children to school and picking them up on time. If something happens, we should immediately go if called. Of course, we will fulfil this responsibility" (Parent, E, Afghanistan). Other statements likewise highlight parents' strong sense of responsibility in actively participating in the educational process and ensuring their children are treated appropriately. However, some parents also emphasised the difficulties they faced in fulfilling responsibilities due to economic and social constraints.

Students' understanding of responsibilities was also clear and concrete. For instance, one student stated: "Students must obey school rules and respect teachers" (Student, K, Azerbaijan), emphasising that responsibilities were centred around discipline and respect. Other students defined their responsibilities through practical examples such as listening to lessons, avoiding fights, and maintaining classroom order. Parents' expectations were also seen to align with these views.

The findings reveal a striking imbalance between rights and responsibilities. For both parents and students, rights were defined ambiguously, in limited terms, and often through personal experiences, whereas responsibilities were articulated much more clearly, concretely, collectively, and in action-oriented ways. While parents perceived rights mainly through structural restrictions, students focused on the pursuit of equality in daily school life. Responsibilities, however, were marked by strong consensus and clarity. These findings are consistent with the research, which highlights the tendency for rights to become invisible while responsibilities are centralised in the educational experiences of migrants and refugees, indicating that educational participation is often defined primarily through obligations (Gandarilla Ocampo, vd., 2021; Boukhari, 2025).

Conclusion

The findings of this study reveal a clear imbalance between how rights and responsibilities are perceived by migrant and refugee families. While responsibilities were expressed in concrete, collective, and action-oriented terms, rights were often described in fragmented, ambiguous, and individualised ways. Parents tended to frame rights within broader structural constraints, whereas students focused on equality, friendship, and social acceptance in daily school life. This contrast demonstrates that participation in education for migrant families is shaped primarily through obligations rather than entitlements. The emphasis on responsibility reflects families' strong commitment to supporting their children's education and adapting to school rules. At the same time, the lack of clarity regarding rights highlights limited awareness, insufficient guidance, and systemic barriers.

These findings underline the importance of developing inclusive and holistic educational policies that strengthen the visibility of rights while maintaining shared responsibilities. Schools, as key spaces of socialisation, have the potential to balance this relationship by fostering both belonging and equality. Addressing these gaps would not only support the educational success of migrant and refugee students but also contribute to social cohesion and mutual adaptation within the wider society.

References

Boukhari, A. (2025). The relational refugee child: Towards trauma-informed, culturally and linguistically inclusive approaches. *UNHCR Education Research Digest*, July 2025. UNHCR

Due, C. (2021). Inclusive education for students from refugee or migrant backgrounds. International Journal of Inclusive Education, 25(11), 1276-1290.

Dryden-Peterson, S. (2015). Refugee education: The crossroads of globalization. Educational Researcher, 44(9), 473-482

Gandarilla Ocampo, M., Bennouna, C., Seff, I., Wessells, M., Robinson, M. V., Allaf, C., & Stark, L. (2021). We are here for the future of our kids: Parental involvement in refugee adolescents' educational endeavours in the United States. *Journal of Refugee Studies*, 34(4), 4300–4321

Graham, 1986, 1991, 1995

Graham, J. W. (1995). Leadership, moral development, and citizenship behavior. Business Ethics Quarterly, 5(1), 43-54.

Graham, J. W. & Van Dyne, L. (2006). Gathering information and exercising influence: Two forms of civic virtue organizational citizenship behavior. Employee Responsibilities and Rights Journal, 18(2), 89–109

OECD. (2022). The resilience of students with an immigrant background: Factors that shape well-being. OECD Education Working Papers, No. 270. OECD Publishing

Organ, D. (1988). Organizational citizenship behavior: The good soldier syndrome. Lexington Books

Özkan, I. (2019). Yeni vatandaşlık türleri: Çağdaş bir tipoloji mi? [New Citizenship Types: Is It A Contemporary Typology]. D.E.Ü. Hukuk Fakültesi Dergisi, 21(Özel Sayı), 2205-2251.

Podsakoff, P. M., MacKenzie, S. B., Paine, J. B., & Bachrach, D. G. (2000). Organizational citizenship behaviors: A critical review of the theroetical and empirical literature and suggestions for future research. Journal of Management, 26(3), 513–563.

Turner, B. S. (2021). Contemporary citizenship: Four types. Journal of Citizenship and

Globalisation Studies 1(1):10-23.

Yaylacı, A.F. (2004). İlköğretim okulu yönetici ve öğretmenlerinin örgütsel yurttaşlık davranışları. [Organizational citizenship behaviors of primary school administrators and teachers].[Doctoral Dissertation]. Ankara Üniversitesi Eğitim Bilimleri Enstitüsü, Ankara

Yaylacı, A. F. (2011). Örgütsel yurttaşlık sistemi [Organizational citizenship system]. Uşak Üniversitesi Sosyal Bilimler Dergisi, 4(1), 73-92.

Yaylacı, A. F. (2015). Eğitim örgütleri için yeni yapı önerisi: Örgütsel yurttaşlık sistemine ilişkin bir kavramsallaştırma girişimi [New structure proposal for educational organizations: A conceptualization attempt for organizational citizenship system] İçinde: Prof. Dr. İbrahim Ethem Başaran'a Armağan, Ankara: PEGEM Akademi

Yaylacı, A. F. (2016). Rights and responsibilities of teachers and parents as school citizens: A qualitative study based on organizational citizenship. Education, 137(2), 233-247.

Yaylacı, A. F. (2021). Türkiye'de Örgütsel Yurttaşlık (Vatandaşlık) Çalışmaları Bağlamında Eğitim Örgütleri İçin Makbul Yurttaş Arayışı [The search for acceptable citizens for educational organizations in the context of organizational citizenship studies in Türkiye] İçinde: Prof. Dr. İnayet Aydın'a Armağan, (Eds. Oğuz, E., Yılmaz, K.) PEGEM Akademi pp. 435-452.

Yolsal Murteza, E. (2023). Çocuk Haklarının Kısa Felsefi Tarihinde 'Çocuklar için Felsefe' ['Philosophy for children' in a brief philosophical history of children's rights]. *Bursa Uludağ Üniversitesi Fen-Edebiyat Fakültesi Felsefe Dergisi Kaygı*, 22 (3), 681-702.

TRANSNATIONAL GENTRIFICATION IN SICILY: LIFESTYLE MIGRANTS AND INEQUALITY

Valeria Holguin Arcia

Introduction

In recent years diverse trends of global mobility, such as North to South, have been making an impact in peripheral and semi-peripheral countries. Lifestyle migration is one of these trends: a form of temporary or permanent relocation where individuals from wealthier countries move to less affluent regions (O'Reilly, 2000). Unlike other forms of migration, lifestyle migration is motivated by climate, culture, cost of living, desire for slower paces of life, and accompanied by relative privilege in terms of citizenship which facilitates the move (McGarrigle, 2022). In some southern European countries these flows are being state-led and expected to have a trickle-down effect. Palermo, Sicily demonstrates how lifestyle migration and tourism intersect to produce transnational gentrification; reshaping urban spaces, housing (Cocola-Gant & Lopez-Gay, 2020) and culture which instead might be exacerbating inequalities and displacing local population.

This paper draws on preliminary findings and utilizes qualitative and quantitative data, as well as ethnographic analysis through focus groups with locals, in-depth interviews with lifestyle migrants from the Global North[1] and Palermitan residents/service workers. Due to the limited availability of official government statistics on the number of Global Northerners residing within Italy/Sicily, a common issue when studying this phenomenon (Diana & Maddaloni, 2018) this study relies on approximate figures derived from expatriate community groups in Palermo and tourism data.

---

[1]For this study the term "Global North" follows the classification of the UN Trade and Development organization, as well as Wallerstein's World Theory System classification of 1997 which includes Southern European countries as semi-peripheries, making a visible economic divide within the North-South of Europe. For this case the Global North is understood as: Canada, United States, Denmark, Estonia, Finland, Iceland, Ireland, Latvia, Lithuania, Norway, Sweden, United Kingdom, Belgium, Netherlands, Luxembourg, Germany, Australia and New Zealand.

Theoretical Framework

Migration studies highlight push and pull factors as central to understanding mobility (Lee, 1969). While economic necessity and political turmoil may be the main drive for many Global South migrants, lifestyle migrants are largely pulled by cultural imaginaries (Hayes & Zaban, 2020). This intersects with the concept of gentrification, originally defined as the transformation of working-class neighborhoods by middle-class influx (Glass, 1964). In its transnational variant, gentrification is driven by mobile elites from the Global North seeking affordable real estate, cultural authenticity, and leisure (Sigler & Wachsmuth, 2016; Hayes, 2018).

Richard Florida's (2002) "creative class" can be used to situate many of these lifestyle migrants (digital nomads, start-ups and retirees) as cultural consumers who accelerate urban transformations, by prioritizing lifestyle. Disparity of income, spike of temporary rentals and the substitution of local business for multinationals are results of both mobilities.

Sicily and Southern Europe

The South of Europe continues to experience a high influx of tourism and lifestyle migration partly as result to the 2008 financial crisis and the neoliberal policies to stimulate the economy (Mendes, 2018). Post Covid-19, these large mobilities have resulted in furthering already existing inequalities between Northern and Southern Europe, leaving the North as an economic hub and the South to depend on tourism and foreign influx.

Sicily occupies a peripheral position within Europe and a unique history of diverse colonial rule, it has since experienced economic disparity within itself and later with the industrialized North. On the other hand, during the second part of the 20th century Palermo, the island's capital, endured decades of depopulation and urban neglect due to organized crime and weak governance (Picone & Schicelli, 2013).

Demographic shifts have continued within the 2000's. Sicily has experienced one of Italy's highest rates of population decline. Aging population, low fertility rates and brain drain being main causes. In 2022, 1 out of 4 students left Sicily to pursue upper education in other regions, this primarily due to labor market scarcity and informality. Meanwhile foreign arrivals are incentivized and expected to rescue the economy, with many politicians claiming that the South can live off tourism, forgetting the impact Covid-19 had on this industry. By 2024, Palermo hosted nearly 9 million visitors, contrasting with a relatively small but affluent expatriate community of 2,000 active members to 9,000 temporaries [2], this community was stated as crucial when choosing Palermo as their destination. These numbers still leave Palermo to be the most densely populated city in Sicily with around 600,000 people.

Transnational Gentrification in Palermo

The influx of lifestyle migrants has altered Palermo's urban fabric. In 2024, Palermo was named Italy's capital for digital nomads, making it the number one city chosen by remote workers in Italy, primarily due to its great weather and cheap housing. This has led the government to invest €34 million euros in digitalizing the region, another €73 million in Palermo's historic center restauration, and €135 million allocated towards tourism infrastructure. Locals on the other hand see another picture with housing costs surging within the last 5 years, with reported average rents varying in increase depending on the area from €150–250 per room to €500–800 per apartment, leaving the city center. Platforms such as Airbnb have commodified residential stock, with 7,000 listings reported in the city center in 2025, majority owned by property management groups, making 30% of apartments in Palermo dedicated to short term rentals (InsideAirbnb, 2025) (Observatorio Tecnocasa, 2024) (PalermoToday, 2024) (La Repubblica, 2025). As a result, long-term residents face displacement, echoing patterns of urban exclusion elsewhere in Southern Europe (Cocola-Gant & Lopez-Gay, 2020).

The addition of Palermo to the UNESCO list in 2015, was a key moment where the market prioritized tourism. Between 2000-2016, around 20,000 small and medium economic activities ceased operations in part due to lack of demand, however in the following years it was filled by tourism-related services (Prestileo, 2020). Another wave of urban changes has sparked in the historic center in the last years, where autoethnographic observation determined 11 local shops shut down to be replaced by franchises such as KFC.

Culturally, lifestyle migrants value Sicilian traditions, food, and landscapes, but rarely integrate linguistically or socially. Only three of 20 interviewed migrants spoke Italian, and only two held local employment, many of which have been

---

[2] The group "Palermo Expats, Foreigner, Digital Nomads and International People" on Facebook holds 9,000 participants who according to its founder are permanent or temporary residents in the city. This group also holds a WhatsApp community of more than 2,000 participants who engage in 20 subgroups according to different activities and interests, such as sports, women's group, parents and families, over 35+, investment, language exchanges, buying and renting property, social dinners and Q&A. Besides activities proposed by the participants the local founders post a weekly schedule with everyday activities hosted by them.

living in Palermo or Italy for long periods. When asked if identified as a migrant of expat, almost all responded expat, even if many claimed not to know the difference, a common reason was because they arrived legally, or they had a job. This reinforces a dichotomy between "expats" and "migrants," where Northerners are viewed as economic and social enrichers while Global South migrants are framed as having integration problems.

Socio-Economic Impacts

The city seems to be changing but not in response to the needs of residents. Out of Palermo's population, 48% is not part of the labor force, and of the remaining, 14% are unemployed; this leaves Palermo with one the least economically active population, while medium household income remains around €16,000 annually (INPS, 2023). Among interviewed service workers, the highest reported monthly income was €1,000, with many workers engaged seasonally and without contracts, with only some wages being declared.

By contrast income requirements for digital nomad visas and elective residence permits begin at €26,000 and €32,000 respectively, producing a structural gulf between incoming migrants and locals.

Part of the packages to attract foreign residents include tax incentives, for foreign retirees (ERV) this would mean a 7% flat rate for retirees in southern Italy, compared to 25–40% for locals. Digital nomads, and other EU freelancers moving their tax residence to a Southern Italian city, hold a 70% exemption on their taxable income.

Public services have suffered some strains. Since 2020, 115 schools have closed, and most recently in 2025, 600 teaching positions have been closed. While healthcare investment had €140 million cut (Palermo Today, 2024). Infrastructure prioritizes tourists as well, with main sources of transportations like buses leaving peripheral workers underserved to prioritize city center and touristic routes, a problem that was mentioned in groups and through observation between 2022-2025.

Residents' and Lifestyle migrants: two sides of a city.

The perspectives of Palermo's temporary and permanent inhabitants reflect one city lived through different experiences. Service workers describe low wages, precarious employment, and linguistic demands imposed by foreign consumers. Lifestyle migrants emphasize affordability and cultural admiration, while expressing frustration at limited English proficiency among locals, and not much desire to learn the local language. Local business owners appreciate urban regeneration and improvements in safety but acknowledge dependency on tourist spending, as well the transformation of their offer to please these customers. Meanwhile, residents highlight unaffordable rents, displacement pressures, and the dominance of foreign-owned Airbnb properties in their buildings, making community living difficult and lonely. Commentary from social media expat groups further reveals how lifestyle migrants construct Palermo as an "affordable paradise," often disregarding the systemic challenges faced by locals. Local grassroot groups protesting over Touristification and gentrification in the city center have used logos as "treat the migrant as you treat the tourist", "tourist everywhere, basic services nowhere" and the unfortunate phrase many tourists repeat, "I am your economy, you are welcome", in protests as a way of bringing awareness to the unregulated flow that spikes inequality. On the other hand, the city center has been also plagued with many forms of street art, which call out the foreign influx in the last years, having no one to claim them but with strong mentions of gentrification equalizing colonialism.

Conclusion

The case of Palermo exemplifies the contradictions of lifestyle migration and transnational gentrification. While marketed as engines of regeneration and growth, these processes deepen socio-economic inequality, displace vulnerable residents, and commodify culture for external consumption. Integration discourses remain uneven, demanding assimilation from Global South migrants while overlooking the privileges of Northern expatriates. Without regulatory frameworks to redistribute benefits and protect local livelihoods, Sicily risks perpetuating cycles of dependency and exclusion. Further research should interrogate how peripheral regions can balance cultural preservation with economic openness in the face of global mobility.

References

Cocola-Gant, A. & Lopez-Gay, A. (2020). Transnational gentrification, tourism and the formation of 'foreign only' enclaves in Barcelona. *Urban Studies, 57*(15), 3025–3043.

Florida, R. (2002). *The Rise of the Creative Class.* New York: Basic Books.

Glass, R. (1964). *London: Aspects of Change.* London: MacGibbon & Kee.

Hayes, M. (2018). *Gringolandia: Lifestyle Migration under Late Capitalism.* Minneapolis: University of Minnesota Press.

Hayes, M. & Zaban, H. (2020). Lifestyle migration and gentrification in the Global South. *Urban Studies, 57*(15), 2999–3014.

InsideAirbnb. (2025). Palermo Listings. Available at: [online database]

La Repubblica. (2025). "Tourism in Sicily: Palermo at 8.9 million visitors." *La Repubblica,* 10

January.

Lee, E. (1969). A theory of migration. *Demography, 3*(1), 47–57.

Mendes, L. (2018) 'Tourism gentrification in Lisbon: The panacea of touristification as a scenario of a post-capitalist crisis', in David, I. (ed.) *Crisis, Austerity and Transformation: How Disciplinary Neoliberalism is Changing Portugal.* London: Lexington Books, pp. 25–46.

O'Reilly, K. (2000). *The British on the Costa del Sol: Transnational identities and local communities.* London: Routledge.

PalermoToday. (2024). "Via Roma businesses close amid tourism boom." *PalermoToday*, 15 November.

Picone, M. & Schicelli, M. (2013). Urban regeneration in Palermo: from neglect to revitalisation. *Journal ofMediterraneanUrban Studies, 8*(2), 115–132.

Prestileo, F. (2020) 'Geografie del turismo a Palermo. Un monopolio territoriale', *Etnografie del Contemporaneo*, 3(3), pp. 49–61

Sigler, T. & Wachsmuth, D. (2016). Transnational gentrification: Globalisation and urban change. *Urban Studies, 53*(4), 705–720.

Zuk, M., Bierbaum, A., Chapple, K., Gorska, K. & Loukaitou-Sideris, A. (2018).

Gentrification, displacement, and the role of public investment. *Journal of Planning Literature, 33*(1), 31–44.

THE PSYCHOLOGICAL TOLL OF MIGRATION: FACTORS INFLUENCING TRAUMA IN ASYLUM SEEKERS AT THE U.S.-MEXICO BORDER

Renee M. Frederick, Ashley Bautista, Dan O'Connell, Alfonso Mercado, Luz Garcini, and Amanda Venta

Introduction

The journey to arrive at the southern border of the United States (U.S.) and Mexico is perilous for many Latinx migrants. Approximately 25% originate from the Northern Triangle of Central America (El Salvador, Guatemala, and Honduras; Banda et al., 2025), and they face numerous dangers along the way including violence, kidnapping, extortion, rape, serious illness or injury, and even death (Shetty, 2014). Despite these risks, thousands of migrants continued to arrive at the border each month throughout 2024 (Gramlich, 2024). Furthermore, Latinx migrants arrive at the border with high rates of mental and physical problems, including posttraumatic stress symptoms (PTS; Venta, 2019).

The prevalence of PTS among Latinx immigrants may be explained, in part, by the risk of experiencing a potentially traumatic event along the way to the U.S. Recent literature has begun documenting the trauma exposure that Latinxs often experience during their journey (DeBrabander & Venta, 2022; Mercado et al., 2024; Perreira & Ornelas, 2013). However, few studies focus exclusively on the role of migratory experiences on post-migration PTS in Latinx individuals. During the migration journey, individuals have reported traumas related to family separation, exposure to violence (physical and sexual), extortion, and kidnapping (Grafft et al., 2022; Gudiño et al., 2011; Shetty, 2014). Further, a recent study on migrants at a respite center in Texas found that 6 in 10 women experienced violence during their migration journey to the U.S., and that both the number of traumatic experiences and experiences of physical and sexual violence were associated with increased levels of PTS (Banda et al., 2025). While prior research has investigated the types of traumas experienced and their associations with PTS, less is known about what other demographic or migration factors might be associated with PTS among migrants (e.g., age, traveling alone compared to traveling with family). By identifying key risk factors that contribute to post-migration PTS, this research can guide policy to make visa and asylum processing more compassionate and effective. Furthermore, the current study can equip healthcare systems and community organizations with information needed to better serve recent immigrants and address their unique mental and physical health needs.

Therefore, the current study sought to investigate various potential statistical predictors of posttraumatic distress for recently arrived migrants at the border of the U.S. and Mexico. Particularly, it was hypothesized that sex and age would be associated with PTS, with women and older migrants reporting higher symptom levels. Furthermore, it was hypothesized that experiencing trauma during the migration journey and traveling with family would be positively associated with PTS.

Method

Procedures

The current study was approved by the University of Houston Institutional Review Board. The study consisted of in-person interviews and biometric data collection conducted at two sites: at a respite center in McAllen, Texas, United States and an encampment site in Reynosa, Tamaulipas, Mexico. After providing informed consent, all participants were interviewed by trained research assistants. Data for this current study were gathered at the border of the U.S. and Mexico in May 2023, and all interviews were conducted in Spanish.

Measures

Migration Factors. The *Migration Experiences Interview* (MEI; DeBrabander & Venta, 2022) is a semi-structured interview that was used to assess experiences before, during, and after migration. The MEI includes open-ended questions about an individual's motivation for migration, elements about the migration itself (e.g., who they travelled with, how they travelled to the U.S., and who paid for the journey), as well as questions about how their experience in the U.S. relates to their expectations.

Posttraumatic Stress Symptoms. The *Impact of Events Scale - Revised* (IES-R; Weiss & Marmar, 1997) was used to measure distress caused by traumatic events. The IES-R measures the severity and type of posttraumatic stress symptoms experienced by an individual. Items correspond to symptoms of PTSD according to the DSM-IV criteria. Respondents are asked to identify a specific stressful life event and then indicate how much they were distressed or bothered during the past seven days by each of the listed symptoms.

Participants

Participants included 290 recently arrived migrants at the U.S.-Mexico border seeking asylum. All participants identified as Latinx or Hispanic, with 61.7% of participants identifying as female. Participants' ages ranged from 18-71, though the median age was 28.5. The breakdown of participants' country of birth can be found in Table 1.

Table 1 Participant Country of Birth

	n	%
Colombia	28	9.7
Cuba	3	1
Dominican Republic	1	0.3
Ecuador	5	1.7
El Salvador	13	4.5
Guatemala	26	9
Honduras	138	47.6
Mexico	13	4.5
Nicaragua	2	0.7
Peru	6	2.1
Venezuela	55	19
Total	290	100

Results

A multiple regression analysis was conducted to examine how migration related factors were associated with posttraumatic stress symptoms. The full regression model, which included sex, age, trauma exposure during migration, and family travel arrangements, was significant and explained 15.5% of the variability in posttraumatic distress as measured by the IES-R [$F(4, 285)=14.219$, $p<.001$, $R^2_{adj}=.155$]. Results are presented in Tables 2 and 3. The multiple regression analysis revealed that sex ($p<.01$), experiencing/witnessing a trauma during migration ($p<.001$), and family travel arrangements ($p<.05$) were linked to increased posttraumatic stress symptoms. Results indicated that age was not a significant factor linked to PTS in this context. Sex, dummy coded such that male = 0 and female = 1, showed a significant effect, indicating that being a female was associated with higher levels of PTS. Moreover, results indicated that traumatic experiences during migration and traveling with children were both associated with increased symptoms of posttraumatic distress for migrants arriving at the southern border.

Table 2 ANOVA[a]

Model		Sum of Squares	df	Mean Square	F	Sig.
1	Regression	30605.037	4	7651.259	14.219	<.001[b]
	Residual	153359.460	285	538.103		
	Total	183964.497	289			

a. Dependent Variable: Total Impact of Events Score
b. Predictors: (Constant), Family Travel, Migration Journey Trauma, Age, Sex

Table 3 Coefficients[a]

Model	Unstandardized Coefficients		Standardized Coefficients			95.0% Confidence Interval for B	
	B	Std. Error	Beta	t	Sig.	Lower Bound	Upper Bound
1 (Constant)	21.590	5.784		3.733	<.001	10.205	32.975
Sex	8.409	2.859	.162	2.941	.004	2.781	14.037
Age	-.071	.151	-.025	-.469	.640	-.368	.226
Migration Journey Trauma	18.992	3.091	.333	6.144	<.001	12.908	25.077
Family Travel Arrangements	6.634	2.811	.131	2.360	.019	1.101	12.168

a. Dependent Variable: Total Impact of Events Score

Discussion

This study aimed to investigate correlates of posttraumatic distress in migrants seeking asylum at the U.S.-Mexico border. Findings support the notion that specific migration conditions (i.e., migration trauma and traveling with family) and demographic factors (i.e., being female) are indeed associated with higher levels of posttraumatic stress symptoms after migration. These results align with prior work demonstrating that migrants arriving at the U.S.-Mexico border are likely to have experienced significant trauma and subsequently have an elevated risk of experiencing posttraumatic stress symptoms (Banda et al., 2025; Mercado et al., 2024; Venta, 2019). Although not examined in this study, previous research has found that 6 in 10 women experience sexual assault during migration and this factor was associated with elevated PTS (Banda et al., 2025). Moreover, families are often separated along the route, leading to a disruption of important attachment bonds and increased symptoms of PTS (Cohodes et al., 2021; Grafft et al., 2022; Miller et al., 2018; Venta et al., 2024).

Overall, this study underscores the importance of understanding the challenges migrants face along their journey to the U.S. and how these challenges influence their health and wellbeing, along with specific risk factors that may lead to increased PTS. It is important that healthcare professionals improve and implement trauma screening for this population to address the unique needs of migrants and asylum seekers. Specifically, these screeners should ask about factors related to the migration journey itself, as research–including the current study– has shown that these factors may impact mental health. Screeners should be embedded in the immigration process and should also be disseminated to medical, psychological and community service providers to help direct individuals to appropriate mental health services.

Additionally, this work calls for developing more humane immigration policies, as Latinx migrants are exposed to trauma prior to and during migration, and emerging research has found that specific immigration policies were associated with additional psychological harm for migrants. For example, the Remain in Mexico policy has been associated with additional exposure to traumatic events and hazardous living conditions (Mercado et al., 2024). Under this policy, migrants are forced to wait in Mexico while living in tents or makeshift encampments (Mercado et al., 2024). Individuals have reported experiencing physical and sexual violence, harassment, and kidnapping while waiting for asylum appointments from the Mexican side of the border (Mercado et al., 2024). Other policies lead to family separation during processing, screening, detention, and deportation (Venta, 2019), and one study by Miller et al. (2018) found that family separation can exacerbate symptoms of posttraumatic stress disorder, depression, and anxiety.

Finally, more research is needed on protective factors that may buffer detrimental psychological and health outcomes in this group. In a global context, this study provides valuable insights into the challenges faced by asylum seekers and highlights the critical role of supportive policies and tailored healthcare services in protecting the well-being of migrants.

References

Banda, F., Torres, A., Morales, F., Palomin, A., Venta, A., Garcini, L., & Mercado, A. (2025).

Types of traumatic experiences and cultural values associated with posttraumatic stress in recently immigrated asylum-seekers from Central America. *American Journal of Community Psychology*, *n/a*(n/a). https://doi.org/10.1002/ajcp.12806

Cohodes, E. M., Kribakaran, S., Odriozola, P., Bakirci, S., McCauley, S., Hodges, H. R., Sisk, L. M., Zacharek, S. J., & Gee, D. G. (2021). Migration-related trauma and mental health among migrant children emigrating from Mexico and Central America to the United States: Effects on developmental neurobiology and implications for policy. *Developmental Psychobiology*, *63*(6), e22158. https://doi.org/10.1002/dev.22158

DeBrabander, M., & Venta, A. (2022). Migration experiences of Central American youth: Developing a new measure. *Psychiatry Research*, *314*, 114652. https://doi.org/10.1016/j.psychres.2022.114652

Grafft, N., Rodrigues, K., Costas-Rodriguez, B., & Pineros-Leano, M. (2022). Latinx immigrants and complex layers of trauma: Providers' perspectives. *Journal of Latinx Psychology*, *10*(4), 291–303. https://doi.org/10.1037/lat0000210

Gramlich, J. (2024, October 1). Migrant encounters at U.S.-Mexico border have fallen sharply in 2024. *Pew Research Center*. https://www.pewresearch.org/short-reads/2024/10/01/migrant-encounters-at-u-s-mexico-border-have-fallen-sharply-in-2024/

Gudiño, O. G., Nadeem, E., Kataoka, S. H., & Lau, A. S. (2011). Relative impact of violence exposure and immigrant stressors on Latino youth psychopathology. *Journal of Community Psychology*, *39*(3), 316–335. https://doi.org/10.1002/jcop.20435

Mercado, A., Venta, A., Morales, F., Palomin, A., Garcini, L., Silva, M., & Domenech Rodríguez, M. M. (2024). Trauma in the American asylum process: Experiences of immigrant families under the migrant protection protocols. *Psychological Trauma: Theory, Research, Practice, and Policy*, *16*(Suppl 2), S379–S388. https://doi.org/10.1037/tra0001368

Miller, A., Hess, J. M., Bybee, D., & Goodkind, J. R. (2018). Understanding the mental health consequences of family separation for refugees: Implications for policy and practice. *American Journal of Orthopsychiatry*, *88*(1), 26–37. https://doi.org/10.1037/ort0000272

Perreira, K. M., & Ornelas, I. (2013). Painful Passages: Traumatic Experiences and Post-Traumatic Stress among U.S. Immigrant Latino Adolescents and their Primary Caregivers. *International Migration Review*, *47*(4), 976–1005. https://doi.org/10.1111/imre.12050

Shetty, S. (2014, February 20). *Most Dangerous Journey: What Central American Migrants Face When They Try to Cross the Border*. Amnesty International USA. https://www.amnestyusa.org/updates/most-dangerous-journey-what-central-american-migrants-face-when-they-try-to-cross-the-border/

Venta, A. (2019). The Real Emergency at Our Southern Border Is Mental Health. *Journal of the American Academy of Child & Adolescent Psychiatry*, *58*(12), 1217–1218. https://doi.org/10.1016/j.jaac.2019.05.029

Venta, A., Bautista, A., Cuervo, M., Mercado, A., Garcini, L. M., Colunga-Rodríguez, C., Ángel-González, M., Preciado-Rodríguez, T. M., Cardenas, F. P., Sotelo, K. V., & Payan, T. (2024). Family Separation at the US and Mexico Border Continues. *Journal of the American Academy of Child & Adolescent Psychiatry*, *63*(7), 670–672. https://doi.org/10.1016/j.jaac.2023.09.546

Weiss, D. S., & Marmar, C. R. (1997). The Impact of Event Scale—Revised. In *Assessing psychological trauma and PTSD*. (pp. 399–411). The Guilford Press.

FATHERING IN INTERNATIONAL MARRIAGE FAMILIES: INTERGENERATIONAL COMPARISON OF FATHERING PRACTICES AND NEGOTIATIONS OF MIXEDNESS AMONG JAPANESE MIGRANT MEN IN THE PHILIPPINES

Jocelyn O. Celero[1]

Introduction

Mixedness is a social identity people obtain through forming constellations or inheritance of two or more cultures (Singla 2015, 110). While it characterizes societies in Asia, mixed racial and ethnic identities have gained scholarly attention only in the recent times (Fozdar and Rocha 2017; Rocha et al. 2018; Rocha and Aspinall 2020, 681). Inter-Asian ethnic boundary crossing and newer forms of mixedness are regarded as resultant of increased migration, intercultural contact, and diversity.

The emergence of international marriages and families is an enduring outcome of cross-border migration. Mixed children of Filipino and Japanese parentage, for instance, are born outside of the Japanese territory. In 2012 alone, there were around 16,000 children born to one or two parents with Japanese nationality outside of Japan (Takeda 2018). It is unknown, however, whether these 16,000 identify as mixed, and how many mixed children are born to only one or two Japanese parents (Torngren and Okamura 2020, 920). Even more underexplored are the lived experiences of parents raising mixed children.

The current study deals with the experiences of Japanese men raising Japanese-Filipino children. It considers how mixed parenting entails transmitting life worlds, transferring experiences as a foundation of children's mixed identity, building their awareness of the diverse societies and cultures, and influencing them through prevailing images and meanings attached to cultures and societies (Murad 2005). Extant literature has depicted how fathers (e.g., Japanese) in migrant families either are *absent (*except Hoang and Yeoh 2011, Lee and Koo 2006, Satake 2004) or occupy persistent roles as breadwinners and child carers

---

[1] Jocelyn O. Celero, Asian Center, University of the Philippines-Diliman

(Ishii-Kuntz 1994, Ishi-Kuntz et. al. 2004). In raising Japanese-Filipino children, a study on Filipino migrant mothers in Tokyo finds that these women adopted a combination of assimilating, maintaining and switching childrearing strategies depending on their ethno-cultural, legal and social resources (Celero 2012). This study, however, failed to analyze the involvement of Japanese fathers. Therefore, the present research aims to make visible their role as active fathers, contributing to the childrearing, socialization, and acculturation of their children. Considering a generational lens suggests exercising reflexivity (Woodman and Wyn 2015) through highlighting "heterogeneity in and between generations". Operationalizing this lens in the context of this study, it is established that Japanese men's fathering approaches are fundamentally shaped by their age, educational background, and social realities.

In analyzing the fathering practices of Japanese men belonging to different generational backgrounds, this research is guided by the following questions:

1)   What is stable over time and space?

2)   What socio-cultural changes and new risks affect Japanese fathers in raising Japanese-Filipino children?

3)   How are the pervasive inequalities in terms of class, ethnicity and gender affecting them and their families?

This qualitative research aims to make a generational comparison of Japanese men's strategies of fathering mixed children, comparing those who became parents in the 1990s and those in the 2010s. These two generations of intermarried Japanese were impacted by intertwining trends of migration and education system in and between Japan and the Philippines.

Research Methods

This study builds upon semi-structured interviews with five Japanese fathers conducted between 2012 and 2015 face-to-face while doing my PhD fieldwork in Tokyo, and another five Japanese men, based in Manila, Bulacan, and Cebu, Philippines, were interviewed online between 2022-2024 with the assistance of a male research colleague. The online interviews lasted between two and four hours using zoom. The participants were interviewed using a mix of Filipino, Japanese, and English languages, depending on the proficiency and comfortability of respondents in expressing themselves. Having done ethnographic research on Japanese-Filipino families for the last 13 years, I encountered numerous methodological issues and attempted to develop approaches for overcoming them. I documented my research experiences in a vlog found in this link: <u>Researching the Intimate: Methodological Issues and</u>

<u>Insights into studying Japanese-Filipino Intermarriages</u> – 国際結婚移民: アジアにおける家族とライフストーリー . Extracted and collated from the interviews are the following themes: personal background,

educational and work experiences of both parents, childrearing arrangements, language education, school choice, spouse views, and future plans/aspirations that may entail transnational migration of families.

Findings

Demographic Profile

The data obtained for this research suggest that the two generations of Japanese fathers differ in terms of demographic characteristics. As Table 1 shows, the older generation, or those who married prior to the 2000s, depict the broader trends in intermarriages and mixed family life in Japanese society. First, older Japanese men sought their spouse at an *omise* (bar) in Japan where Filipinas were employed as entertainers. Notice that their age gap can be as huge as more than 20 years old.

Second, this group's marriage to a Filipina was in Japan which was instrumental to the latter's re/marriage to secure legal status and permanent residency, which provides stability for these families to live and settle in Japan. The lack of marriage is also evident, as in the case of Okada, who lived for more than a decade in Manila before relocating the family to Tokyo to be with his Filipina partner, and for the sake of their children's Japanese language education.

Thirdly, nucleating, which denotes co-residence between parents and children only, is a common family strategy among the families of older-generation Japanese fathers. Through remarriage, they may form a new family, while Filipino women become disconnected from their children from the previous family of one's Japanese spouse. Children from previous marriage may become estranged from Japanese fathers, as well as his newly formed family. In terms of family arrangement, the older group ventures in split-to-reunited in Japan (i.e. children are left-behind in the Philippines while Japanese and Filipino parents work in Japan) and circular patterns, in which family settles in Japan but

323

occasionally travels to the Philippines for vacation or education of children (Celero 2015, 2016).

Table 1. Older group

	Name of Couple	Age* (at the time of interview)	Education	Occupation	Children	Status (prior to marriage with Filipina)	Years of Marriage* (at the time of interview)
1	Higashi	62	HS graduate	Business owner turned taxi driver	20 y/o, 18 y/o	Divorced	21 (2013)
2	Nakano	55	university graduate	Company employee	2 children (19 y/o, 17 y/o)	Single	20 (2015)
3	Okada	70	High school graduate	Transnational business (construction services, apartments)	3 children (20, 18, 14 y/o)	Married to a Japanese	19 years of partnership (since 2013)
4	Tanaka	80	High school graduate	Retired businessman	1 child (21 y/o)	Divorced	16 years (2017)
5	Ota	61	High School graduate	Retired businessman	2 older children (age undisclosed) from previous (Japanese) relationship	Divorced	17 years

In comparison, Japanese men who married Filipinas, belonging to the younger generation, are those whose marriage was after the 2000s. They possess characteristics that reflect wider migration and societal trends between the Philippines and Japan. Their site of intercultural contact is online, as in the case of the Uminos who dated online for years, while others found their Filipina spouse while living in the Philippines. Located in the two metropolises are multinational and Japanese companies that either deploy Japanese workers, or recruit Japanese who are already based in the Philippines and have acquired relevant work experiences such as teaching English to Japanese, has knowledge of doing business in the country.

Second, the couples in this group have an age gap of more than 10 years, making them relatively younger at the time of union compared to the previous group. Unlike the previous group, these men practice years of cohabitation. Marriage only becomes instrumental to Japan-bound family migration, which enables these couples to lead a relatively more flexible family setup, and nurture intimacy and trust before agreeing to register their union at the civil registry office. Getting married is oftentimes influenced by social integration needs in the Philippines (e.g. 'prerequisite' to one's child's admission to Japanese school. The younger generation Japanese fathers build a rather blended transnational family setup. Some of them adopt children of Filipinas from previous marriage/partnership, and they facilitate establishing connection between their Filipino spouse, Japanese-Filipino children, and Japanese grandparents.

Table 2. Younger group

	Name of Couple	Age	Education	Occupation/work	Children	Status (prior to marriage with Japanese)	Years of Marriage
1	Miki	50	University graduate	teaching Japanese, business owner	19 y/o, 10 y/o, 5 y/o with Clarita	Single	20 (2022)
2	Honda	53	university graduate (Bachelor of Laws)	English school manager, company employee (return to Japan)	divorced with a kid from previous marriage; 8 y/o daughter with Gina	Divorced	12 (2022)
3	Umino	58	University graduate	Savings and FOREX (money changer services)	5 y/o daughter with Amelia	divorced with a daughter	8 (2022)
4	Kimura	33	University graduate	Company employee	8 y/o, 5 y/o	Single	11 (2014)
5	Onda	62	University graduate	Company employee	14 y/o, 12 y/o	single	17 (2008)

Third, according to family-migration arrangements, the younger Japanese parents engage in circular migration towards Japan for education and employment, while the family settles either temporarily or permanently in the Philippines, dependent hugely on the Japanese husband's economic activities, such as when he sets up a business in the Philippines.

Fathering Mixed Japanese-Filipino Children: A Generational Comparison

This section draws a comparison between two groups of Japanese fathers. The older group recollects their fathering experiences in the 1990s, while the second group consists of younger ones whose parenting experiences began in the 2010s. In fathering mixed children, Japanese men contribute in the aspect of school selection, language acquisition, and transnationalizing their children's schooling experiences.

School selection

Integral to Japanese men's fathering is selecting schools for their children. The older group of Japanese fathers shared that they would search for 'suitable' schools in the Philippines that offer Japanese language class, and affordable school fees. They greatly influence their children to go to Japan due to its perceived "better" economic prospects. Their school-related decision-making is tied to the rigid gendered division of labor in family life, in which the fathers adhere to the breadwinning roles, while mothers take on more of caregiving and providing emotional support to their children. By contrast, the younger group, regards searching for desirable schools a dual/shared parental task. When choosing a school, Japanese father consider the distance between their residential location/domicile and the school their child is supposed to attend. The second consideration pertains to the available economic opportunities for them as Japanese in the Philippines. Some respondents disclosed how their decision to set up a business in the Philippines coincided with their aspiration to retire there during old age. Japanese men across generations actively are involved in selecting schools for their children but they differ in terms of their considerations and approaches to selecting schools.

Language acquisition

Ensuring that mixed children attain a certain level of competence in dual or multiple languages is an aspiration shared by most Japanese fathers. Yet, they do not perceive that languages that Japanese-Filipino children should learn— Japanese, English, Filipino among other local languages in the Philippines—to be of equal value in honing their linguistic competence.

The older generation-Japanese fathers in this research tend to put premium on teaching Japanese language and social manners to their children at a young age. Even highly educated fathers would send their kids to a Japanese (language) school in Japan to fulfill this learning goal. Others would support sending kids to the Philippines to learn English and connect with Filipino family in the process. The older Japanese fathers in my study do not commonly support learning Filipino and local languages. In my previous study (Celero 2012), Filipina single parents who assert their cultural influence on their children often easily circumvent such.

The younger group of Japanese fathers, meanwhile, also teach Japanese language and social manners themselves. But compared to the previous group, they tend to rely on multimedia resources and the Internet for teaching. They tend to utilize the Youtube channel and smart phones to teach the language. They purchase a variety of learning materials such as CDs, flashcards, charts of hiragana and katakana, as well as devices (e.g., laptop, iPad). These Japanese fathers also use online spaces to interact with other Japanese men living in the Philippines. They create blogs to document everyday life as a mixed family particularly in the Philippines to inspire others to overcome difficulties in raising children. They also use social media platforms in seeking advice on better teaching methods, disciplining techniques, and work-life balance.

In aiming for language proficiency for their mixed children, the generational convergence between Japanese fathers lies in giving primacy over learning Japanese language, as well immersing them to Japanese social manners during formative years. The difference between young and old Japanese fathers lies in their strategies for harnessing the linguistic ability and socialization experiences of their children.

Transnational Education

Transnational education is another dimension of Japanese men's fathering practices, which entails moving between Japan and the Philippines, through physical or virtual mobility, in order to access educational opportunities available in both contexts. The older-generation Japanese fathers incorporate vacation trips as part of family lifestyle and providing learning opportunities for the children. The younger-generation Japanese fathers venture in transnational education of their children in distinctive way: a combination of online learning, onsite schooling (international school for children of expats), and student exchange programs outside of the Philippines.

In transnationalizing the educational experiences of their mixed children, it could be observed that the generational divergence between the two groups of Japanese fathers lies in the ways they rationalize the importance of diversifying the learning opportunities and technologies apart from reconfiguring the role of Japan and the Philippines in the accumulation of language and cultural competencies. A significant divide is also found in the ways their economic status shapes the affordance of co-presence and co-parenting with their Filipino spouses. The younger fathers, who are mostly entrepreneurs based in the

Philippines, have more freedom and resources for parenting. Therefore, they combine several methods for transnationalizing the educational experience of their children, compared to the older group.

Conclusion

This research on generational comparison of Japanese fathering strategies suggests several stable trends over the last three decades since the growing number of Japanese-Filipino families in both Japan and the Philippines. First, across generations, there is pervasiveness of breadwinning and education roles (e.g., teaching Japanese language) expected of Japanese fathers. But this is not necessarily gendered/masculine obligation. Second, these families also face financial instabilities that often influence migration and transnational family life decisions as well arrangements that Japanese fathers and their Filipina spouses pursue. When faced with hardships, during the pandemic in particular, Japanese fathers would consider crossing borders in consideration of the educational needs of their children, and their capabilities to support them. Third, Japanese fathers perceive the uneven place utilities that the Philippines and Japan have on the life trajectories of their children. As discussion, the unequal value of Japanese, English and Filipino languages along with the disparity in the geopolitical ad economic relevance of Japan (i.e. a first world country) and the Philippines (i.e. a third world) in global hierarchy of nations inform the repertoire of educational and acculturation strategies that Japanese fathers deployed.

Over time, meanwhile, there have been shifts that have significantly affected the parenting experiences of Japanese men. First, there is an ongoing ideological shift is evident in the loosening of gender dichotomy as parenting endeavors become more collaborative between parents. Second, caregiving role has been less idealized (i.e. *ikumen*) especially in the context of Japan, and has been more realized in the Philippines where fathers have more autonomy over their time and resources for fathering. Third, there is a perceived hierarchy of languages (English, Japanese, Filipino) that shape the life aspirations Japanese fathers may have for their children. Differing generations of Japanese men view and live migration to Japan as partly driven by a confluence of economic and educational goals for their children.

To conclude, this paper has shown that the dynamics of parenting among Japanese men in mixed, Japanese-Filipino families include decisions around school selection, language acquisition, and transnational education for and with their children and to some extent, Filipina mothers. In raising mixed children outside of Japan, Japanese fathers constitute a diversity of parents negotiating their socio-economic parental background, cultural capital, and cosmopolitan sensibilities.

References

Celero, J.O. (2012) Managing ethnic identities: Filipino mothers' patterns of rearing Japanese-Filipino children (JFC) in Japan. MA Thesis, Sophia University, Japan.

Celero, J.O. 2015. "Towards a Shared Future?": Transnational Identity and Belonging of Japanese-Filipino Families in Japan. In The Age of Asian Migration: Continuity, Diversity and Susceptibility Vol. II, edited by Yuk Wah Chan, Heidi Fung, and Grazyna Szymanska Matusiewicz, 67–94. UK: Cambridge Scholars Publishing.

Celero, J.O. (2016). Japanese-Filipinos' Transnational Pathways To Social Mobility: Education, Occupation And Life Aspirations. PhD thesis, Waseda University, Japan.

Hoang, L. A., & Yeoh, B. S. (2011). Breadwinning wives and "left-behind" husbands: Men and masculinities in the Vietnamese transnational family. *Gender & Society*, 25(6), 717-739.

Ishii-Kuntz, M. (1994). Paternal involvement and perception toward fathers' roles: A comparison between Japan and the United States. *Journal of Family Issues*, 15(1), 30-48.

Ishii-Kuntz, M., Makino, K., Kato, K., & Tsuchiya, M. (2004). Japanese fathers of preschoolers and their involvement in child care. *Journal of Marriage and Family*, 66(3), 779-791.

Koo, H., & Lee, Y. J. (2006). Wild geese fathers' and a globalised family strategy for education in Korea. *International Development Planning Review*, 28(4), 533-553.

Kukutai, T. H., & Broman, P. (2016). From colonial categories to local culture: Evolving state practices of ethnic enumeration in Oceania, 1965–2014. *Ethnicities*, 16(5), 689-711.

Rocha, Z. L., & Aspinall, P. J. (2020). Introduction: Measuring mixedness around the world. *The Palgrave international handbook of mixed racial and ethnic classification*, 1-25.

Rocha, Z. L., & Fozdar, F. (Eds.). (2017). *Mixed race in Asia: Past, present and future*. Taylor & Francis.

Satake, M. 2004. "Filipina-Japanese Intermarriages: A Pathway to New Gender and Cross-Cultural Relations." *Asian and Pacific Migration Journal*, 13 (4): 445-473.

Singla, R. (2015). Intermarriage and mixed parenting, promoting mental health and wellbeing: Crossover love. Springer.

Takeda, S. (2018). Global ka jidai no kokueki to fukusuu kokuseki no zehi wo megutte [On "National Interest" in the Era of Globalization and the Pros and Cons of Multiple Nationality]. *Kokusaichiikigakukenkyu,21*, 35–50.

Torngren and Okamura 2020. Recognition of Multiracial and Multiethnic Japanese: Historical Trends, Classification, and Ways Forward. In The Palgrave Handbook of Mixed Racial and Ethnic Classification, edited by Zarine L. Rocha and Peter J. Aspinall, 911–933. Cham, Switzerland: Palgrave Macmillan

Woodman, D., & Wyn, J. (2015). Class, gender and generation matter: using the concept of social generation to study inequality and social change. *Journal of Youth Studies*, 18(10), 1402-1410.

THE ENIGMA OF RETURN IN BRITISH MIDDLE EASTERN NARRATIVES

Elena Violaris

Introduction

This paper explores how two novels about second-generation British-Arabs, and an essay about a British-Iranian academic, propose nuanced ways of considering the transformative possibilities of 'return' to an ancestral country in which one has never lived. To describe these possibilities, I coin two terms: catalytic return, when a visit to the country of descent initiates personal transformation, and episodic return, where recurring childhood visits create a personal archive of memories and sensations that are drawn upon or reinterpreted in adulthood.

My focus on return arose from the initial observation that both Robin Yassin-Kassab's *The Road from Damascus* (2008) and Isabella Hammad's *Enter Ghost* (2023) – two second-generation British-Arab novels, written fifteen years apart – open with a return visit to the region of descent: Syria in *Damascus*, and Haifa and the West Bank for the Palestinian protagonist of *Enter Ghost*. In both cases, the visit is driven by an existential alienation that contrasts with the material needs that underpinned the previous generation's migrations. The interior transformation emphasised in the novels has prompted comparisons with the bildungsroman genre. A New York Times review of *Enter Ghost* has commented on how '*Enter Ghost* ... centers on a woman undergoing [an] existential growth spurt', a belated 'coming of age', even though the protagonist is thirty-eight.[1] Moreover, C. E. Rashid analyses *The Road from Damascus* in terms of Mark Stein's 'novels of transformation'.[2] Stein suggests this a genre in black British fiction that adapts the bildungsroman – with its Germanic origins in the formation of the white male – to the experiences of British ethnic minorities. Stein argues:

---

[1] 'Hamlet, and a Political Awakening, Stir in the West Bank', Lily Meyer, *New York Times*, March 31 2023, https://www.nytimes.com/2023/03/31/books/review/isabella-hammad-enter-ghost.html [Accessed 4 September 2025].

[2] C. E. Rashid, 'British Islam and the Novel of Transformation' in *Journal of Postcolonial Writing*, Vol. 48, No. 1, February 2012, 92–103 (p. 95).

The process of formation brings about the construction of … an identity, [where] the efficacy of the novel of transformation, then, is directed inward, at the protagonists of the texts.[3]

I argue that return contributes to this formation of identity by revealing hidden family histories which are charged with political and philosophical implications. In this, I hope to challenge the wholesale dismissal of return as an illusory romanticisation. This kind of approach is evident in Rashid's analysis of Yassin-Kassab's novel:

> If our protagonist seems to have visited Damascus with the purpose of concretizing his identity and his place in the world, he has returned disillusioned with his Syrian heritage, family and wife.[4]

Yet 'disillusionment' is not the only effect, nor the sole purpose, of the opening scene If return fails to complete the intended restoration of identity, it acts as a catalyst for a different kind of transformation. I will now illustrate this catalytic effect through a close reading of the novels, starting with *Damascus*.

At the opening of the novel, 31-year-old Sami's reasons for visiting Syria are reiterated as lists. His reasons for going are to 'reconnect with his roots, remember who he was, find an idea, in that causal order'.[5] By 'find an idea', Sami is referring to his struggle to complete a PhD, so this comment illustrates his belief that cementing his personal identity will help his professional ambitions. Yet the constant listing, of both motivations and surroundings, indicates Sami's failure to map himself both cognitively and geographically; he possesses piles of information that he cannot shape into a narrative, collection without cohesion. 'Feeling foreign' (1) in Syria, he realises that he cannot 'remember' who he is in a place he has never lived; the memory he seeks lies beyond the individual, in a collective or imagined past, recalling a comment made by British-Arab academic Ramy Aly, who describes his move to Dubai: 'I had left the UK in an attempt to "return" to an Arab world that I had never left to begin with'.[6]

Aly's comment appears in his ethnographic study *Becoming Arab in London*, which he positions as straddling 'formal ethnography of the "other" and auto-ethnography'.[7] Such interweaving of personal and scholarly modes reflects the education-inflected character of British Middle Eastern postmigrants, many of

---

[3] Mark Stein, *Black British Literature: Novels of Transformation*, Ohio State University Press, 2004, p. 30.
[4] Rashid, p. 95.
[5] Robin Yassin-Kassab, *The Road From Damascus,* Penguin, 2009, p. 38. Further references are taken from this edition and cited inside the text.
[6] Ramy Aly, *Becoming Arab in London*, Pluto Press, 2015, p. 3.
[7] Aly, p. 1.

whose families migrated to Britain to study and remained because of conflict in their countries of descent. This academic context also Sami's journey in *Damascus*: 'As a proper academic, like his father before him, he'd be able to get it all back on course – his place in the world, his marriage, his mother. So he believed' (2). The authorial aside ('so he believed') adds an irony, corresponding with Franco Moretti's comment on the need for readers of a bildungsroman to access insight beyond the partial vision of the protagonist.[8] In addition, this passage shows how Sami's causal logic is unstable. In the previous section, we saw how 'remember[ing] who he was' was supposed to help him to 'find an idea', but now academic success appears to be the solution to his personal issues. The reversibility reveals that neither issues is causing the other, but both are symptomatic of a deeper root: Sami's unresolved relationship with his deceased father and estrangement from his mother, both of which underpin his animosity towards religion, his academic struggles and his alienation. This is not to say that there is a totally linear cause-and-effect, but unpacking the enigma of this history provides a key to the process of resolving the other issues in the protagonist's life.

To address this enigma, we can turn to the ways in which return catalyse *formation*: the reconstruction of a more robust form of identity. When Sami visits his aunt in Syria, he discovers a traumatised relative, who was tortured for years after his involvement in an Islamic group was betrayed by an informant Sami intuits that his father was the informant but this is initially encrypted in symbols; after the visit, he has a nightmare of a horse bearing his dead father's face. This is the 'enigma' of return, where the root of the word 'enigma' – 'to speak allusively or obscurely', with etymological origins in 'fable' (OED) – suggests both secrecy and instruction, aligning with the pedagogical logic of the bildungsroman. At the end of the chapter, then, Sami intuits that 'things were complex, that nothing was simple… There were paths… other than the one his father had trodden' (10–11). And yet, 'It would take a summertime for the realization to sink into his core' (11). By depicting the realisation of 'another path', the title of the opening chapter, the opening scene of return is a microcosm of Sami's conversion, which is not quite as straightforward as from atheism to Islam, but from fixity to flexibility, rigidity to tolerance. The signs of the opening cohere in the novel's final chapters, with Sami's reconciliation with his mother Ironically, this occurs just after Sami is profiled post-9/11 for growing a beard, only to be offered a role as an informant by the British police (336). Sami's refusal to be an informant symbolically rejects his father's betrayal,

---

[8] Franco Morretti, *The Way of the World: the Bildungsroman in European Culture*, Verso, 1987, p. 56.

and the narrative resolves through a formal symmetry: the betrayal discovered at the beginning is negated at the end. Sami's return *to* Damascus, then, is catalytic precisely because it is enigmatic: the power of the return lies in what is disclosed slowly, symbolically, through acts of interpretation, which are undertaken on the road *from* Damascus. Return is revelation rather than reversal.

The highly politicised nature of personal relationships is also a feature of *Enter Ghost*, where the protagonist Sonia's summer visits to Haifa are set against the backdrop of the Palestinian intifadas. This phase of episodic return ends in Sonia's mid-twenties, due to the death of grandparents, the demands of her acting career, and the sense that any political obligation to visit was fulfilled by her sister. Testimonies from interviews I have conducted with British postmigrants reflect a similar pattern: the death of grandparents is often a turning point, signalling the end of the obligatory family visits and the beginning of a different phase, in which the relationship to the ancestral country either grows distant or is maintained through individual agency. For Sonia's sister Haneen, the post-childhood phase of return takes the form of a permanent move to Tel Aviv, where she works as a university lecturer. For Sonia, however, return is deferred until she reaches an impasse in her personal life, following a miscarriage, divorce and failed affair with a married theatre director.

The significance of episodic return in the novel hinges on Sonia's recurring memory of visiting the West Bank in her youth, and encountering a young man called Rashid who was on a hunger strike. The memory returns at several critical points, prompting both its reconceptualisation and practical action. First, Sonia had assumed that Rashid had survived, but Mariam, a theatre director and old family friend, inadvertently reveals that he had died. Sonia also discovers that her sister Haneen had known he had died – Mariam says 'it's part of her narrative of why she became an academic' – and feels betrayed that her sister hadn't told her.[9] This revelation indirectly pushes her a step further in creating a *new* relationship with her heritage by agreeing to participate in Mariam's performance of Hamlet in the West Bank. Participation in this play enables an alignment of Sonia's personal and professional roles, allowing her new opportunities for a Palestinian identity that she had previously hesitated to claim. The second resurfacing of this memory is when Sonia confronts Haneen for not telling her about Rashid's death towards the end of the novel. Haneen admits that this was partly because she wanted to 'protect' her sister, but also

---

[9] Isabella Hammad, *Enter Ghost*, Vintage, 2024, p. 137. Further references are taken from this edition and cited inside the text.

'want[ing] to keep him for myself' (266). The confrontation provides a kind of closure, and Sonia reconciles with her sister by suggesting they attend a demonstration in Jerusalem together. The episode thus initiates political action. If *Enter Ghost*, with its intertextual references to *Hamlet*, engages with the tropes of tragedy, the confrontation of these memories of Rashid embodies one of Hammad's moments of recognition. In her recent essay, 'Recognising the Stranger', Hammad articulates that '[a]ll writers have tics, a particular repertoire of moves that recur', identifying her own as 'recognition scenes, or moments of what Aristotle in his *Poetics* called *anagnorisis*': a kind of realisation of something one knew all along.[10] Here, episodic return lays the baseline for a recognition – as re-cognition, rethinking – of politically-charged memories, leading to action in the present.

Moving from fiction to the form of the essay, an alternative conception of episodic return is presented in an article by British-Iranian academic Arianne Shahvisi, who describes her childhood visits to Iran through the vocabulary of Harry Potter. Shahvisi emphasises the shifts in value enacted through the movement from England to Iran and vice versa: how racism in England correlated with celebrity treatment in Iran, or the transformation from being 'dark, weird, hairy, short kids with bad clothes in England to being fair, tall, cool and worldly in Iran'.[11] Taking the form of an essay rather than a novel, Shahvisi's article does not hinge on a particular *moment* of revelation, but on a *reversibility* which is formative in a more cumulative way. It is not crystallised into a particular enigma or discovery – like Sami and the betrayal, or Sonia's memory of Rashid – which throws into relief the particular demands of literary *plot* in shaping and extrapolating postmigrant experiences.

Of course, episodic return is not possible for all postmigrants Those who have no family in the country of descent, or who are struggling economically, or whose countries are at war, are often unable to undertake periodic visits. Several of my interviewees described conflicts in Syria or Iraq as reasons why they could not visit as children. In her essay, Shahvisi also describes how her own phase of episodic return came to an end, while a new phase was not able or available to begin: 'the complexities – personal and political – of navigating both identities as an adult have produced a state of fear, guilt, heartache and nostalgia that amounts to a kind of exile.' In 'Reflections on Exile', Edward Said critiques the

---

[10] Isabella Hammad, *Recognising the Stranger*, Pern Press, 2024, p.8.
[11] Arianne Shahvisi, *"Iran was Our Hogwarts": My Childhood between Tehran and Essex*, The Guardian, 2021, https://www.theguardian.com/lifeandstyle/2021/sep/23/a-mudblood-in-tehran-my-childhood-between-iran-and-england [Accessed 4 September 2025].

romanticisation of exile, but acknowledges some 'positives' in its making possible an 'originality of vision':

> Most people are principally aware of one culture, one setting, one home; exiles are aware of at least two, and this plurality of vision gives rise to an awareness of simultaneous dimensions, an awareness that – to borrow a phrase from music is contrapuntal. … For an exile, habits of life, expression or activity in the new environment inevitably occur against the memory of these things in another environment. Thus both the new and the old environments are vivid, actual, occurring together contrapuntally. There is a unique pleasure in this sort of apprehension.[12]

The postmigrant who has experience of this 'episodic return' does not necessarily have *habits of life* recalled, but moments of transition, as in Shahvisi's article, which emphasises juxtapositions, movements back-and-forth, rather than a linear experience of one place followed by another. In light of this, we might reframe Said's *contrapuntal* metaphor into an *ostinato*: a repetitive motif. This articulates a particular postmigrant ontology, where the significance of the episodic visits does not always lie in a linear teleology but in the perpetual possibility of transformation, its reversibility and relativity

To summarise, I hope to have shown how British Middle Eastern postmigrant narratives can challenge the illusory idealisation of a mythical homeland. Through the bildungsroman structure, return offers the potential for a teleological transformation. In *Damascus*, return initiates the resolution of enigmas, contributing to familial reconciliation, while in *Enter Ghost*, the reinterpretation of past experiences stimulates new perspectives, prompting Sonia to participate in collectives which strengthen her Palestinian identity. Contrasting these novels with Arianne Shahvisi's essay reveals a non-fictional variant of episodic return that privileges reversibility over teleology. Return may not offer resolution, but it can disorient in order to reorient, constituting another tool in diasporic identity formation.

---

[12] Edward Said, 'Reflections on Exile' in *Reflections on Exile: & Other Literary & Cultural Essays*, Granta, 2000, pp. 173-186 (186).

ARTIST AS CITIZENSHIP: (IM)MOBILITY & (NON)BELONGING AMONG CHINESE ARTISTS IN THE NETHERLANDS

Ziyue Lu[1]

Introduction

In much of the migration literature, citizenship has been conventionally understood in relation to the category based on civil, social and political rights (Marshall 1992). My use of the term here departs from this normative framework. Rather, I borrow from its conception of "gradation" (Walsh 2011) and "quasi-membership" from "temporary rights to work and residence to denizenship in the form of permanent residency" (Robertson 2013, 79). In other words, citizenship is conceptualized neither as a fixed legal status nor an endpoint of national belonging, but as a gradational, precarious relationship to the state, experienced by migrants in degrees, in a spectrum of rights, (visa) practices and subjective attachments.

The participants in this study – Chinese artists and art students in the Netherlands – belong to what has been theorized as 'middling migrants' (Yeoh et al. 2003), that is, individuals who neither fall into the elite circuits of global capital (Ong 1999) nor the legally invisible sphere of undocumented laborers. Their migration is both enabled and constrained by their (family's) class status, artistic and educational capital, and also the Dutch funding and visa infrastructures.

Drawing on semi-structured interviews and year-long participant observation, this paper explores how these artists experience mobility as/and immobility and how they navigate belonging in transnational liminality. I argue that these migrant artists embody "partial citizenship": their migration status determines that they do not hold a membership bestowed once and for all, but conditioned by bureaucratic uncertainty, economic precarity and visa-dependent temporality. I conclude by proposing to understand them as a group inhabiting a particular configuration of "diasporic citizenship," where identity, belonging,

---

[1] PhD candidate, anthropology department, University of Amsterdam

and mobility are persistently shaped through the structures and subjectivities of migration.

Methodology and Fieldwork Context

This paper is based on a year of ethnographic fieldwork conducted in different cities in the Netherlands with Chinese artists, complemented by semi-structured interviews. The participants were mostly in their twenties and thirties, some of them recent graduates and art students of Dutch art academies. Their lives were deeply entangled in visa regimes, family relationships back in China, and the Dutch funding system for artists. The data presented here is drawn from everyday conversations and formal interviews with artists in their studios and other social gatherings.

Mobility as Immobility

Transnational mobility is often celebrated as a privilege of the cosmopolitan class. Yet for many migrants, mobility is lived at the expense of immobility. On one level, immobility is reflected in physical, social and legal restrictions faced by migrants themselves. On another, it is also the immobility of others, in this case, certainly the family, the "left-behind" parents, who partially countered the flipside of migration by way of material and/or emotional support. For example, a participant recalled the eight-month wait before he could collect his residence card. This was even before the Covid-19, when the bureaucratic process already appeared unpredictable. He described the period of waiting as "absolutely tiring, even crippling," for there was nothing he could do other than wait, with no job, no income, only bodily reactions that alarmed him of the limp of reality. This eight-month was "like a waste" given the fact that the visa was only valid for a period of two years, and he felt, then, he had only one year left.

Many art students and graduates spoke about the struggles of sustaining themselves as an artist after graduation, as they had to both balance creative work and seek financial possibilities to sponsor their visa application. While their educational mobility was initially enabled and continuously supported by their parents and the remittance from China, there was always a fear of not being able to make a living and to obtain a residence permit after their student visa ran out. This everyday precarity and temporality resulted in a heavy sense of anxiety among participants, some of whom told me that they could hardly sleep or do anything else while working/waiting for the visa. There seemed to be what I call a "time-visa-deadline" triangle that hung itself like a ghost in the long tunnel of migration, a process during which migrants' "bodies, capabilities, relationships and bank accounts laid bare to the scrutiny of the immigration regime" (Robertson 2013, 8). More often than not, participants ended up in a process of, in their own words, "applying for visa just for the sake of visa" (为了签证而签证 weile qianzheng er qianzheng).

Mobility as Privilege

Meanwhile, mobility was also experienced as a form of privilege. As mentioned, family support is a large part of what sustains the student migration. Most participants shared a class-based capacity to pursue education and art abroad, made possible by their families' socioeconomic capital. The parental support was not only a financial matter of covering tuition and living costs, but it also provided a space for their children abroad to experiment with uncertain artistic careers, in a place they knew very little about. Certainly, privilege is not a constant. In this case, it is used as a migration strategy which brings access to visa and citizenship, and it is also a condition and discourse mutually constitutive to precarity and marginalization as participants move through time and space and become migrants in another country, embodying localized relations of power (Mapril 2014; Robertson & Roberts 2022; Hussain 2019; Baas 2017; Cederberg 2017; Rye 2019). Privilege, in this way, is inseparable from the vulnerability of migrants' positions in a foreign environment, where their middle-class aspirations and imaginations of a mobile future remained tethered to the strict and shifting demands of the Dutch immigration regime.

(Non)belonging in the Liminal Space

How, then, do migrants account for their embodied experience and enact belonging even when excluded from full citizenship? In my study, many artists articulated a sense of (non)belonging in ways that resisted the all-too-familiar discourse of "in-betweenness," which is often reduced to a broad immigrant talking point. Participants' narratives of belonging can be both pragmatic and affective. For example, when asked about her sense of belonging in the Netherlands after having lived in many places in the world, one artist answered with a Chinese idiom, 既来之, 则安之 (jilaizhi zeanzhi), meaning, "Take things as they come," or, "Since we have come, we may as well stay and make the best of it." A similar remark from another artist reads: "As a migrant, I will be a migrant wherever I go, but I still want to do things here, with other migrants and make local connections." Some also noted that, simply, "Home follows the person, home is where I am."

These words reflect a mode of belonging rooted not in a fixed national membership or legal inclusion from the state. Rather, they help to imagine and deliver a space of belonging by looking at transnational liminality with acceptance and compliance; or for the better, as a coping method to treat the complex, if contradictory positionality of the migrant in relation to privilege and precarity. By embracing mobility as a condition of life, participants claim their own home(making) in the place of residence, and create alternatives of attachment which neither romanticize cosmopolitan freedom, nor simply reduce their experience to marginalization.

Rethinking Migrant Subjectivities Through "Diasporic Citizenship"

The experiences of the Chinese artists suggest the need for a new framing of migrant subjectivity. Rather than treating "artist" as merely a profession, I propose to think of the practice of the artist-migrant as a socio-cultural form of citizenship, not least because the creative nature of the artist's work already assumes a socio-cultural contribution to the host society. Whether artistic, bureaucratic or affective, these migrants demonstrate different ways of negotiating and claiming their place in a shared transnational liminality.

I draw on the term "diasporic citizenship" for two reasons. First, "diaspora" is a word often used by Chinese artists themselves, and generally among cultural migrants in describing their living condition, especially in recent years amidst intensified political climates. This gives the concept an emic as well as etic potential to both "speak about" and "speak to" the subjects in question.[2] Second, diasporic citizenship foregrounds both the precarity of migrants' political and economic position in the country of residence, and their cultural mobility across transnational networks. It highlights relational dynamics of privilege, belonging, and identity without assuming a stable citizenship status in a single nation-state.

Thinking through the framework of diasporic citizenship allows us to see how migrant artists function as creative agents between the state and its immigration regimes. Their very struggle for visa-dependent mobility not only reproduces citizenship as an ongoing process of negotiation with multiple actors, but also challenges us to rethink citizenship beyond the endpoint of national belonging. Moreover, the term can be used as a method by migrants themselves to

---

[2] My idea here is inspired by anthropologist Xiang Biao's (2021) introduction of the word "suspension" (悬浮 xuanfu), which is developed as an emic-etic term to both theorize social facts from within, and lend itself to subjects who can describe and *problematize* their own living conditions.

understand and narrate their mobility plan and space of belonging, especially when excluded from full citizenship of the host country.

Conclusion

By emphasizing artists' own narratives and experiences, this paper discusses how migrants live out a structural inequality that renders them "partial citizens" whose membership is contingent on bureaucratic conditions, economic capacities and affective resilience. I bring forward the idea of "diasporic citizenship" to not only speak about the precarious nature of migration itself, but also to speak to these very migrant artists in their experience of mobility as both immobility and privilege, and (non)belonging beyond national circumstances. Further, the concept can provide a useful lens for capturing the ambivalence of transnationality shaped by visa regimes and class-based capacity and precarity. Citizenship, then, is far from being a static legal status but a dynamic practice lived and articulated by migrants themselves.

References

Baas, Michiel. 2012. Imagined Mobility: Migration and Transnationalism Among Indian Students in Australia. Anthem Press.

Cederberg, Maja. 2017. "Social Class and International Migration: Female Migrants' Narratives of Social Mobility and Social Status." Migration Studies, January, mnw026.

Hussain, Yasmin. 2019a. "'I Was Professor in India and Here I Am a Taxi Driver': Middle Class Indian Migrants to New Zealand." Migration Studies 7 (4): 496–512.

Mapril, José. 2014. "The Dreams of Middle Class: Consumption, Life-Course and Migration Between Bangladesh and Portugal." Modern Asian Studies 48 (3): 693–719.

Marshall, Thomas Humphrey, Thomas B. Bottomore, and Tom Bottomore. 1992. Citizenship and Social Class. Pluto Perspectives. London: Pluto Press.

Ong, Aihwa. 1999. Flexible Citizenship: The Cultural Logics of Transnationality. Duke University Press.

Robertson, Shanthi. 2013. Transnational Student-Migrants and the State: The Education-Migration Nexus. Springer.

Robertson, Shanthi, and Rosie Roberts. 2022. "Migrants 'in-between': Rethinking Privilege and Social Mobility in Middle-Class Migration." In Rethinking Privilege and Social Mobility in Middle-Class Migration. Routledge.

Rye, Johan Fredrik. 2019. "Transnational Spaces of Class: International Migrants' Multilocal, Inconsistent and Instable Class Positions." Current Sociology 67 (1): 27–46.

Walsh, James P. 2011. "Quantifying Citizens: Neoliberal Restructuring and Immigrant Selection in Canada and Australia." Citizenship Studies 15 (6–7): 861–79.

Xiang, Biao. "Suspension: Seeking Agency for Change in the Hypermobile World." Pacific Affairs 94, no. 2 (2021): 233–50.

Yeoh, Brenda S.A., Katie D. Willis, and S. M. Abdul Khader Fakhri. 2003. "Introduction: Transnationalism and Its Edges." Ethnic and Racial Studies 26 (2): 207–17.

MIGRATION GEOGRAPHIES

TRANS-SAHARAN PATHWAYS AND TRANSIT EXPERIENCES AMONG SUB-SAHARAN MIGRANTS: A QUALITATIVE SYSTEMATIC REVIEW

Mawutor Fleku and Sarah Kwakye[1]

Introduction

International migration has surged, with 281 million migrants globally in 2020, up from 153 million in 1990 and 84 million in 1970, comprising 3.6% of the global population (UN Migration, 2021). In Africa, internal migration reached 21 million in 2020, up from 18 million in 2015, while African-born migrants outside the continent doubled since 1990, with 11 million in Europe, 5 million in Asia, and 3 million in North America (UN Migration, 2021).

This review examines trans-Saharan migration, where sub-Saharan migrants from West and East Africa cross the Sahara to reach Europe via transit countries like Libya and Morocco. Driven by economic and political factors, this route is cost-effective and requires less documentation (Flahaux & De Haas, 2016; Kaiyoorawongs, 2016; Ntenhene, 2021). West African migrants are often economic migrants, while East Africans are frequently refugees, facing perilous Sahara crossings and Mediterranean voyages (IEEE, 2018). Transit countries are temporary stops en route to final destinations (Berriane & de Haas, 2012; Vives, 2011).

The trans-Saharan journey involves human trafficking, smuggling, exploitation, and severe shortages of food and water, with risks of suffocation or dehydration deaths (UNODC, 2010; IEEE, 2018). Authorities often exploit migrants, and mistreatment is common (Andersson, 2014; IEEE, 2018). In Libya and Morocco, migrants face racism, discrimination, and arrests despite valid documentation (Achtnich, 2021b; Bendra, 2019; Davison & Davison, 2017). Strict border controls and readmission agreements prolong stays, exacerbated by high onward travel costs (Araújo, 2011; Perrin, 2008; Thorsen, 2018; Snel et al., 2021).

---

[1] Mawutor Fleku, Sarah Kwakye, University of Ghana, Ghana.

Coping strategies include returning home, prayer (used by 50–75% of Somali and Ethiopian refugees), and seeking organizational support (DeFreece, 2016; Weldemariam et al., 2023). Post-2011 Arab Spring reforms aimed to improve human rights, but knowledge gaps persist regarding transit experiences (Liolos, 2013). This review analyzes qualitative studies from 2012–2023, addressing:

1. What challenges do sub-Saharan migrants face during their journey, and how do they cope?

2. What challenges do they encounter in Libya and Morocco, and how do they navigate these?

Theoretical Considerations

Trans-Saharan migration involves movement from sub-Saharan Africa through the Sahara to Europe, driven by economic, political, and conflict-related factors (IEEE, 2018). A Giddens-inspired structurationist approach frames this study, focusing on structure (social rules, norms, institutions) and agency (individuals' ability to act within constraints) (Wolfel, 2005). Migrants are active agents navigating challenges to improve their conditions (Marcelino & Farahi, 2011; Snel et al., 2021; Üstübici, 2016a). Qualitative methods are recommended to explore these dynamics (Achermann, 2021; Fidler et al., 2023).

Methods

Design

This qualitative systematic review adheres to PRISMA guidelines (Page et al., 2021).

Search Strategy

Scopus and Google Scholar were searched for qualitative studies from 2012–2023, post-Arab Spring. The Population Context Outcome (PCO) framework guided searches, targeting sub-Saharan migrants, pathways, transit experiences in Libya/Morocco, and coping strategies (Davoudi-Kiakalayeh et al., 2017). Keywords included "Sub-Sahara*," "migra*," "path* SAME Morocco," "lived-experience*," and "cop*."

For the first question (pathways and coping), a Scopus search (November 6, 2023) yielded 378 documents, reduced to 167 (2012–2023), and 113 after keyword refinement, with two selected. A Google Scholar search produced 286 articles, none suitable. For the second question (transit challenges), a Scopus search (November 9, 2023) yielded 94 documents, reduced to 54, with three selected. A Google Scholar search identified 282 articles, none included.

Identification, Screening, and Eligibility

From 420 records (248 Scopus, 172 Google Scholar), 16 duplicates were removed, leaving 404 for screening. Eligibility criteria included qualitative studies in English, 2012–2023, focusing on sub-Saharan migrants' experiences in Libya/Morocco. Sixteen studies were included.

Assessment of Methodological Quality

Studies were appraised using the JBI Critical Appraisal Checklist, evaluating methodology, methods, and findings alignment. All studies represented participants' perspectives adequately, and none were excluded.

Analytical Strategy

Thematic analysis was used for its flexibility (Braun & Clarke, 2021). Themes were extracted from studies on pathways, challenges, and coping strategies, then synthesized to address research questions.

Results

Sixteen studies produced 89 findings, grouped into 12 categories and 19 key findings. Journey challenges include:

- Human trafficking and exploitation: Smuggling and abuse by traffickers (UNODC, 2010).

- Resource scarcity: Food and water shortages, with risks of suffocation or dehydration (IEEE, 2018).

- Abuse by authorities: Systematic exploitation (Andersson, 2014).

In Libya and Morocco, challenges are:

- Racism and discrimination: Hostile media and public spaces (Davison & Davison, 2017).

- Unlawful arrests: Detentions despite documentation (Achtnich, 2021b; Bendra, 2019).

- Financial barriers: High costs for onward travel (Thorsen, 2018).

- Border controls: Strict regulations and readmission agreements (Araújo, 2011; Perrin, 2008).

Coping strategies include:

- Language acquisition: Learning Arabic to reduce discrimination.

- Community building: Forming migrant groups for support.

- External support: Seeking human rights organizations' assistance.

- Spiritual coping: Prayer, used by 50–75% of Somali/Ethiopian refugees (DeFreece, 2016).

- Return migration: Returning home when challenges are overwhelming (Weldemariam et al., 2023).

Discussion

Findings reflect Giddens' structuration theory, where structures (e.g., border policies, racism) constrain migrants, yet agency enables coping through language learning, community formation, and spirituality. Post-Arab Spring reforms have had limited impact (Liolos, 2013). Arabic learning centers in sub-Saharan countries could reduce discrimination, while partnerships with human rights organizations could enhance safety.

Conclusion

Sub-Saharan migrants face severe challenges during trans-Saharan migration and in transit countries, navigating these through resilient coping strategies. Establishing Arabic learning centers could mitigate discrimination, while policy interventions should strengthen support systems for migrant well-being.

References

Achermann, C. (2021). Understanding migration through a structurationist lens. *Migration Studies*, 9(2), 123–145.

Achtnich, M. (2021b). Mobility and immobility in transit: Sub-Saharan migrants in Libya. *Journal of Ethnic and Migration Studies*, 47(4), 789–806.

Andersson, R. (2014). *Illegality, Inc.: Clandestine migration and the business of bordering Europe*. University of California Press.

Araújo, S. (2011). Readmission agreements and their impact on African migrants. *African Migration Review*, 5(2), 45–67.

Bendra, N. (2019). Discrimination and detention: Sub-Saharan migrants in Morocco. *Migration Policy Review*, 12(3), 101–120.

Berriane, M., & de Haas, H. (2012). African migrations: Continuities and transformations. *African Studies Review*, 55(1), 1–19.

Braun, V., & Clarke, V. (2021). Thematic analysis: A practical guide. *SAGE Publications*

Davoudi-Kiakalayeh, A., et al. (2017). PCO framework for systematic reviews. *Systematic Reviews Journal*, 6(1), 89–95.

Davison, J., & Davison, L. (2017). The black danger: Media portrayals of African migrants in Morocco. *Journal of African Media Studies*, 9(2), 201–215.

DeFreece, A. (2016). Spiritual coping among African migrants. *Journal of Refugee Studies*, 29(3), 321–340.

Fidler, R., et al. (2023). Structuration theory in migration research. *International Migration Review*, 57(1), 45–68.

Flahaux, M. L., & De Haas, H. (2016). African migration: Trends, patterns, drivers. *Comparative Migration Studies*, 4(1), 1–25.

IEEE. (2018). Trans-Saharan migration: Challenges and risks. *IEEE Migration Report*, 2018.

Kaiyoorawongs, W. (2016). Economic drivers of trans-Saharan migration. *African Economic Review*, 8(2), 56–78.

Liolos, J. (2013). Post-Arab Spring migration dynamics. *Middle East Studies Journal*, 15(4), 123–140.

Marcelino, P. F., & Farahi, S. (2011). Agency in migration: A structurationist perspective. *Migration Studies*, 3(2), 89–110.

Ntenhene, F. (2021). Political instability and migration in Africa. *Journal of African Politics*, 10(1), 34–50.

Page, M. J., et al. (2021). PRISMA 2020 statement: Updated guidelines for systematic reviews. *Systematic Reviews*, 10(1), 89.

Perrin, D. (2008). Border controls and African migration. *Journal of Border Studies*, 4(3), 67–85.

Snel, E., Bilgili, Ö., & Staring, R. (2021). Prolonged transit: Sub-Saharan migrants in North Africa. *Journal of Migration Research*, 7(2), 101–119.

Thorsen, D. (2018). Financial constraints in transit migration. *Migration and Development*, 7(3), 321–339.

UN Migration. (2021). *World Migration Report 2020*. International Organization for Migration.

UNODC. (2010). *Human trafficking in the Sahel: A UNODC report*. United Nations Office on Drugs and Crime.

Üstübici, A. (2016a). Transit migration in North Africa. *Journal of Ethnic and Migration Studies*, 42(5), 701–718.

Vives, L. (2011). Transit migration in the Maghreb. *Migration Policy Brief*, 6(2), 23–40.

Weldemariam, K., et al. (2023). Return migration as a coping strategy. *African Migration Journal*, 10(1), 78–95.

Wolfel, R. (2005). Structuration theory and migration. *Sociological Review*, 53(3), 456–478.

THE TRANSFORMATIVE ODYSSEY: AGENCY AND RESILIENCE IN THE ONWARD MIGRATION OF RWANDAN REFUGEE WOMEN IN CAMEROON

Signe Made Carelle Michèle[1]

Introduction: The Context of Migration in Africa and Fundamental Concepts

Crises and Conflicts as Drivers of Population Mobility

In Africa, crises and conflicts are major factors in population mobility, prompting individuals to move, often across national borders, in search of security. This dynamic is a well-documented phenomenon in migration literature, where social conflicts are identified as a fundamental cause of intra-regional migration on the continent (Adepoju 2002; Manning, 2022).

The Rwandan genocide in the mid-1990s is an emblematic illustration of this reality, having led to the displacement of over one million individuals to neighboring nations such as the Democratic Republic of Congo, Uganda, and Tanzania (UNHCR, 2000). This massive displacement marked the beginning of a long pilgrimage for many refugees, who were seeking refuge from insecurity.

The Feminization of Migration: The Emergence of Female Autonomy

Historically, migration studies linked female migration primarily to conjugal reasons or dependence on male figures. However, this approach has been challenged by the emergence of an increasingly documented phenomenon: the "feminization of migration" (Gouws, 2007). This concept describes a paradigm shift where women migrate not because of family constraints, but for personal aspirations or, more pragmatically, in search of refuge in times of war.

The emergence of women as autonomous migratory actors is not a simple, deliberate choice, but rather a direct response to the disintegration of traditional family structures and the collapse of security that conflict generates. The crisis and the loss of male protectors (husbands, fathers) forced these women to

---

[1] Signe Made Carelle Michèle, University of Yaoundé 1, Cameroon.

assume roles that were once unthinkable, transforming a survival constraint into a new form of autonomy and migratory decision-making.

Onward Migration: A Survival Trajectory

"Onward migration" is defined as a spatial trajectory involving prolonged stays in two or more destination countries (Ahrens and King, 2023, p 5). Turcatti (2022) describes this settling and departure of the migrant as a succession of movements motivated by undesirable situations. In the case of post-genocide Rwandan refugees, this migratory approach is perceived as a survival strategy in times of crisis (Puppa, 2018), shaped by previous experience.

However, there is a conceptual tension between the notion of strategy and the reality of an involuntary journey. While the term strategy implies some planning, the itinerary of Rwandan refugee women was the result of a series of forced reactions to persistent insecurity, as evidenced by the persecution and massacres they endured in host countries (particularly the Democratic Republic of Congo). The search for better living conditions, acceptance, and integration (Koser & Kuschminder, 2016) transformed what was initially a chaotic flight into a progressive quest for stability. This was not a choice between several ideal options, but rather the only possible survival option, which makes the journey both strategic (because it leads to survival) and fundamentally involuntary.

The Journey of Rwandan Women: A Post-Genocide Case Study

Methodology and Qualitative Approach

This study is based on a qualitative approach grounded in the analysis of life stories collected from 10 women who fled Rwanda during the conflict period. The methodology deliberately targeted women from different social classes and marital statuses to gather more diverse opinions and allow for a more in-depth study of the challenges they faced. This methodological approach emphasizes the importance of recognizing that the experience of female migration is not monolithic, but is modulated by socioeconomic and family status, which makes it possible to grasp the complexity and nuances of individual journeys in a crisis situation.

The Context of the Flight and the Trajectory of Wandering

The wave of cross-border migration that followed the official end of the Rwandan conflict in July 1994 was mainly motivated by fear of reprisals and the lack of guarantees of a peaceful life once the Rwandan Patriotic Front came to power (Umutesi, 2000; FIDH and Human Rights Watch, 1999). Once outside Rwandan territory, refugees were confronted with new challenges, including the terror sown by former Hutu military personnel who discouraged them from returning to Rwanda. Literature and the stories collected from women mention that refugees were also pursued and massacred by the Alliance of Democratic Forces for the Liberation of Congo-Zaire and by the new Rwandan government (Binet, 2014; Bradol & Le Pape, 2016). The collected narratives confirm this climate of tension and uncertainty, where refugee camps, like the one in Congo-Zaire (now the DRC), became sources of insecurity.

A testimony from Signé's (2024) article reports a journey marked by an unplanned but vital onward migration:

> It is war, the war in Rwanda in 1994 made us leave the country to come here. Now, the path was not like Kigali-Cameroon. It was Congo Kinshasa (DRC), road to the Central African Republic (CAR), moreover we crossed all these paths. Cameroon because there was more stability. Arrived in Congo (Kinshasa), there were problems between the different regimes, Mobutu-Kabyla. The camp of refugees was attacked, going to the Central African Republic was not easy. It was in Cameroon that we found stability and that we had to integrate.

The author highlights the motivations for this onward migration of Rwandans all the way to Cameroon. This itinerary, in which flight became a constant search for security, reveals a process of adaptation and progressive learning in the face of hostility and insecurity. What began as an unorganized migration became, through the force of circumstances, a targeted search for integration and peace.

Vulnerability and Agency: The Refugee Woman, an Actor in Her Own Survival

The Development of Resilience in the Face of Violence

The migration of women is often analyzed from the perspective of vulnerability, particularly in the face of sexual violence. During their migratory journey, women are called upon to overcome challenges related to power relations or male domination (Tyszler, 2018). Vulnerability is a reality that highlights a fundamental psychological and social mechanism: the development of resilience. Parson's (2021) argument is that immigrant women demonstrate resilience as a result of the sexual violence they suffer at borders. This conception of the woman as a simple victim is transformed into an actor who shapes her own migratory project (Stock, 2012).

Women's Decision-Making Power in Their Migratory Journey

Although distinguished by its character of vulnerability and constraint, the migration of refugee women is also marked by their ability to make decisions. Women have the capacity to decide on their mobility by choosing their different destinations (Shaffer & Stewart, 2021). These women are not simple victims who suffer, but actors who, in situations of extreme atrocities, develop agency and decide on their future situations. This decision-making power is not unlimited freedom, but a strategic power exercised in survival conditions. In contexts where choices are severely restricted, the simple act of choosing to continue a journey to avoid a new wave of violence, or to marry for protection, becomes a significant act of agency that redefines autonomy. Agency does not eliminate vulnerability, but develops in parallel and in reaction to it.

Transformations of Roles and Family Challenges

The Rwandan Woman: From Homemaker to Family Pillar

Traditionally, Rwandan women were "under the male cover," their life being limited to the "household" and raising children, without being "allowed to do anything" beyond this domestic sphere, as one interviewee stated:

> For several years, the needs of the Rwandan woman were focused on her husband. So, she, she is the mother of the house, she has children, she raises the children, but she has no other life in fact. Her life is limited to the household. She is not allowed to do anything (...) Today, things have evolved a lot. It has improved a lot.

However, the new realities of migration forced these women to change roles. In the context of war, their status and vulnerability, often perceived as a weakness, became an asset (Freedman, 2017). They were, for example, more favored than men by employers, finding jobs in fieldwork or domestic work. Women with a higher level of education had the possibility of serving as intermediaries with refugee aid organizations. This resilience gave the Rwandan woman a new role as provider and family support, and she became the central pillar of her family, assuming responsibility for the survival of her family.

The Dilemmas of Motherhood in Times of Crisis: An Extreme Burden

One of the aspects of this migratory experience is motherhood in times of war. A testimony reveals the impossible decisions that mothers had to make. One interviewee stated: "We didn't want the children behind... We had to hide, and walk silently, because the rebels were always chasing us". To escape ambushes, women were forced "to abandon their children in the forests or along the way". This decision illustrates the ultimate dilemma of survival. This act of abandonment, although it seems to contradict motherhood, is an extreme form of maternal agency in a context of impossibility. It is the ultimate act of protection, where the sacrifice of a part (the child) is the only way to save the whole (the survival of the fleeing group).

Male Absence and the Woman's Dual Role

The transformation of family roles was accentuated by the absence of men, who were often forcibly conscripted into military conflicts. The conflict between the Sassou Nguesso and Lissouba regimes in 1997 required the reinforcement of troops with Rwandan refugees who had military training (Le Pape, 2001). An interviewee reported on this: "They engaged our soldiers in the war in Congo Brazzaville (...) Sassou had to use our soldiers to reinforce his army and come to power". Stripped of a male and paternal figure, the Rwandan woman had to assume a dual role: that of father and mother of the family. This external constraint further forced these women to double their efforts to provide for the family's needs and the children's education, which has permanently reshaped the family unit and responsibilities within the household. The crisis is not only an agent of displacement but also a catalyst for social transformation and the redefinition of gender identities.

The Specific Challenges of Single Young Women and Their Survival Strategies

Increased Vulnerability to Sexual Violence

The situation of single young refugee girls represents a case of particular vulnerability. The absence of a spouse or a close parent leads to permanent exposure to multiple sexual violences (Callamard, 2002). Single young Rwandan refugee women were perceived as a " bargaining chip " for the survival of other community members with smugglers (at the DRC-Republic of Congo border), forced to offer their bodies to allow other community members to access canoes. Their status as an unprotected woman worked against them, placing them in a position of exploitation. Migrant women in this vulnerable situation develop strategies that increase their power of action and decision-making (Tyszler, 2023).

Default Marriage as a Protection Strategy

In the face of the challenges of famine and sexual violence, default marriage appeared as a way out. For these young women, uniting with a man was a protection strategy, the man being considered "a protector" and a "shield" against sexual predators. Unlike marriages imposed by force or physical violence in times of war (Bélair, 2006), this decision is presented as an act of decision-making power over how their migratory journey would unfold. The young Rwandan woman chooses one type of relationship (marriage) to escape another, more violent and more arbitrary one (rape and exploitation). This act of decision, although made in desperate circumstances, is an affirmation of autonomy and the will to survive with a certain degree of control over one's own destiny.

Conclusion

The journey of Rwandan refugee women is an illustration of a complex dynamic. Although the refugee woman is mostly perceived from the perspective of her vulnerability, whose fate depends on the individuals around her, this analysis reveals a more nuanced reality. Migration in times of crisis, with its atrocities and constraints, has forced a reinvention of roles and the emergence of a powerful capacity for adaptation.

References

Ahrens, J., & King, R. (2023). Onward migration and multi-sited transnationalism: Complex trajectories, practices and ties. Springer.

Bélair, K. (2006). Unearthing the Customary Law Foundations of "Forced Marriages" During Sierra Leone's Civil War: The Possible Impact of International Criminal Law on Customary Marriage and Women's Rights in Post-Conflict Sierra Leone. *Columbia Journal of Gender and Law, 15*(3).

Binet, L. (2014). Traque et massacres des réfugiés rwandais au Zaïre et au Congo (1996-1997). MSF.

Bradol, J.-H., & Le Pape, M. (2016). Génocide et crimes de masse. L'expérience rwandaise de MSF (1982-1997). CNRS Éditions.

Callamard, A. (2002). Refugee women: A gendered and political analysis of the refugee experience. In Global changes in asylum regimes (pp. 137-153). Palgrave Macmillan UK.

Della Puppa, F. (2018). Ambivalent mobilities and survival strategies of Moroccan and Bangladeshi families in Italy in times of crisis. *Sociology, 52*(3), 464-479.

Freedman, J. (2017). Women's experience of forced migration: Gender-based forms of insecurity and the uses of "vulnerability." In J. Freedman, Z. Kıvılcım & N. Özgür Baklacıoğlu (Eds.), A Gendered Approach to the Syrian Refugee Crisis (pp. 125-141). Routledge.

Gerard, A. (2014). Violent and circuitous pathways: Women's experiences in exiting Somalia. In A. Gerard, The Securitization of Migration and Refugee Women (pp. 95-120). Routledge.

Human Rights Watch & FIDH (1999). Aucun témoin ne doit survivre. Le génocide au Rwanda. Karthala.

Le Pape, M. (2001). Une guerre contre les civils. Crash (MSF).

Manning, A. (2022). Counting and Categorizing African Migrants, 1980-2020: Global, Continental and National Perspectives. In M. De Haas & E. Frankema (Eds.), Migration in Africa: Shifting Patterns of Mobility from the 19th to the 21st Century (355-375). Taylor & Francis.

Pason, N. C. (2021). Violence and resilience across borders in Handbook of Culture and Migration. Edited by Jeffrey H. Cohen and Ibrahim Sirkeci. 263–273.

Shaffer, M., & Stewart, E. (2021). Refugees on the move: resettlement and onward migration in final destination countries. In J. H. Cohen and I. Sirkeci (Eds.), *Handbook of Culture and Migration* (341-350).

Signé, M. (2024). Socio-economic Integration Strategies of "Former Rwandan Refugees" in Yaoundé, Cameroon. *Journal of Critical Global Issues, 1*(1), 3.

Stock, I. (2012). Gender and the dynamics of mobility: reflections on African migrant mothers and 'transit migration' in Morocco. *Ethnic and Racial Studies, 35*(9), 1577-1595.

Umutesi, M.-B. (2000). Fuir ou mourir au Zaïre : le vécu d'une réfugiée rwandaise. L'Harmattan.

UNHCR (2009). "Le génocide rwandais et ses répercussions" dans Les Réfugiés dans le monde. (This report offers a detailed analysis of the mass exodus and the militarization of refugee camps).

LIVED DIVERSITY IN GERMANY'S MIGRATION LANDSCAPE: INTERACTIONS BETWEEN TURKEY-ORIGIN RESIDENTS AND POST-2015 "MUSLIM" IMMIGRANTS

Melisa Çelik[1]

Introduction

The past decade has been marked by intense debates and political mobilizations surrounding international migration "crises." Although the global share of migrants has not increased dramatically (de Haas, 2023), significant changes have occurred in the global order and the characteristics of migrant populations. Migration research has explored diverse issues, yet in many European countries, studies have remained largely focused on the binary distinction between natives and migrants. In Germany, post-war reconstruction facilitated the recruitment of migrant labourers from the late 1950s. By 2024, 25.6% of the population has a migration background (Destatis, 2025). Despite this, intergroup relations among different ethnic communities remain underexplored. This paper focuses on relations between long-established Turkish-origin migrants and post-2015 arrivals from Muslim-majority countries, using Elias' established–outsider figuration as a theoretical lens.

Turkish migrants constitute the largest foreign-origin group, with Syrians now the third-largest, alongside growing Afghan and Iraqi populations (Destatis, 2021). The outbreak of war in Ukraine added approximately 1.3 million refugees. The new refugee arrivals have intensified references to "Muslims in Germany," though this label does not necessarily reflect shared belonging. Early representative surveys showed that migrants of Turkish origin, alongside Russian-Germans, were among the most concerned groups during the initial refugee influx (SVR-Migration, 2016). Similarly, established migrants from Iran expressed attitudes toward newly arrived "Muslim" immigrants that closely resembled those of the majority population (Sadeghi, 2019).[2] Russian-Germans

[1] Melisa Çelik, University of Munster, Germany. E-mail: melisa.celik@uni-muenster.de https://orcid.org/0000-0001-6175-1201
[2] In this paper, the terms *"migrant"* and *"inter-migrant"* are used to refer to both migrants and individuals with migration backgrounds. Although many established individuals do not have a personal migration history and

also engaged in boundary-making, distancing themselves from "Muslim" refugees and asylum seekers (Goerres et al., 2018), while some Turkish-origin and German entrepreneurs blamed new "Muslim" migrants for undermining the local market (Steigemann, 2020). Evidence also suggests that first-generation migrants' positive views of newcomers decline over time (Šedovič & Dražanová, 2025). While sect, ethnicity, and language can mark group differences (Türkmen, 2024), they represent only part of the complex processes shaping social positioning and intergroup perceptions.

Theoretical Framework

Elias defines figurations as shifting power dynamics over time, shaped by interdependencies between individuals or groups (Elias, 1978). From this perspective, the established–outsider figuration is conceptualized as a form of intergroup relation rooted in unequal power balances, length of residence, group cohesion, and patterns of perception. This framework enables us to move beyond static structure–agency dichotomies. It allows us to understand figurations as dynamic, processual networks of relationships that evolve over time, shaped by power balances, historical contexts, and shared experiences (Elias, 1978). I argue that this conceptual framework also provides an analytical lens for examining shifting hierarchies within inter-migrant relationships; minority groups can reproduce power asymmetries internally. Figurations evolve as successive migration waves unfold, nation-state policies concerning migrants change, and as public discourses and societal responses shift. Intergroup boundaries and unequal power balances emerge, consolidate, and persist, accompanied by the formation of "we" and "they" images. Such developments arise from the interconnected dynamics that groups create, shape, and sustain through their interactions (Elias, 2006). Elias connects group charisma or group disgrace to "we–they" images, which are shaped by access to power resources and interactions over time. These theories resonate strongly with my research, as I also trace shifting power hierarchies. In the early stages of labour migration from Turkey to Germany, hierarchies were explicitly structured as native versus guest workers. Today, however, I argue that we observe racialized communities with citizenship alongside newer migration waves, which represent emerging figurations aligned with Elias' core principles:

---

were born and raised in Germany, the term is retained to describe relationships between non-majority groups. I use 'Turkish-origin' referring to Turkish nationality, considering participants had other ethnic backgrounds such as Kurdish or Arabic. Similarly, the term *"Muslim"* appears in quotation marks, as in the studies referenced it often functions as a proxy for country of origin rather than an indication of the individuals' actual religious beliefs.

interdependent power structures that continuously change.

The established group has nearly seventy years of history, which tragically includes many forms of racist violence, from neo-Nazi murders to arson attacks, harsh labour conditions, lower wages compared to German counterparts, residence in overcrowded worker dormitories, and segregation into separate Turkish classes at schools (Castles & Kosack, 1973). Despite the emergence of a fourth generation and symbolic events such as dual citizenship rights, Turkish-origin populations in Germany remain a racialized group. At the same time, their positioning is characterized by internal diversification in terms of class position, political representation, and comparatively higher levels of integration. By contrast, the recent phase of asylum admissions following the infamous *"Wir schaffen das"* discourse created new pathways for migration. This period brought new migrant generations into a country that had finally begun to recognize itself as a country of immigration. Compared to the guest worker generation, these groups encountered broader social welfare provisions and more institutional support upon arrival. Many being war refugees, reached Germany through perilous journeys, underwent complex asylum processes (excluding Ukrainians), and are now expected to meet demanding bureaucratic and societal requirements (Etzel, 2022). Their legal precarity, comparatively limited linguistic capital, and heightened cultural visibility situate them in more vulnerable structural locations. The motives, migratory trajectories, societal responses, and state policies clearly differentiate older and newer migration patterns for the groups examined in this research. At the same time, many visible and more covert commonalities continue to shape intergroup relations in significant ways.

Methodology

This research employs multi-sited ethnography across German cities including Bremen, Mülheim a. d. Ruhr, Bielefeld, Essen, Bochum, Gütersloh, Aachen, and Minden. The empirical analysis comprises 35 in-depth semi-structured interviews and 5 expert interviews, with fieldwork ongoing since 2021. Sampling was purposive to capture diversity in age, gender, class, hometown, religious background, and ethnicity. The approach is informed in part by feminist methodology, prioritising participants' own frameworks for understanding integration, belonging, group identity, and conflict, and incorporates self-reflexivity based on my migration history and prior work with refugees, family networks with established Turkish-origin communities, participation in language courses with recently arrived migrants. Data collection combined interviews with participant observation, conducted mainly in workplaces or homes to engage with living conditions, economic practices, and social relations.

Fieldwork also included mosque gatherings, migrant associations, weddings, and women's meetings.

Emerging Figurations and Intergroup Relations

Findings show that established Turkish-origin migrants and newcomers both perceive themselves as distinct groups, while each group is itself highly heterogeneous, complicating any notion of a unified category of "Muslims in Germany." Despite recognition of many shared experiences (such as Muslim othering, the impact of the Israel-Gaza war on German politics, rising anti-Muslim crimes and rhetoric, racialisation, and institutional racism) the subjects of this research consistently emphasized a distinction between old and new migrants. Turkish-origin participants often referred to earlier guestworker generations, e.g. Italians, Greeks, and Portuguese, as their counterparts who *"earned their place in Germany"*. By contrast, newcomers frequently highlighted disparities in institutional and societal responses, particularly when comparing their experiences with those of Ukrainians. At the same time, established Turkish-origin migrants recognized that Germans often perceive them together with "Muslim" newcomers as a single category, while newcomers acknowledged that earlier Turkish migration paved the way for new arrivals in positive ways. An established Turkish man remarked that newcomers *"gather in parks with entire families,"* which he believed *"frightens Germans"* because it is unfamiliar to them. A newcomer Syrian man also acknowledged these dynamics, observing that *"Turks and Kurds were here long before; it helps us, but some of our people should adapt."* These accounts highlight how outsiders' self-image is strongly shaped by established groups' perceptions, consistent with Elias and Scotson's analysis of group relations (1994[1965]).

These emerging figurations are marked by patterns of discontent and avoidance, often expressed through moving out of certain neighbourhoods, upward class mobility, and boundary-making practices (Brubaker, 2004). Drawing on Elias and Scotson's concept of social closure (1994[1965]), it becomes evident that shared Islam does not function as a unifying force; nor do sectarian or ethnic differences fully explain the dynamics. Instead, criticisms of newcomers often revolve around refugee stereotypes, such as being *"welfare state abusers"* or lacking proper manners and everyday behaviour, referring to lack of integration. As one established Turkish woman explained, she avoids certain streets because *"people speak too loudly, sit outside their doors, and behave carelessly in traffic."* Another interview partner criticized Syrians, Bulgarians, and Ukrainians for *"living off welfare,"* adding that Germans accept Ukrainians more readily because *"they look like them."* Importantly, many of these established migrants are themselves religious, underscoring that this is not solely secular–religious or sectarian conflict. Rather, a discourse of deservedness, rooted in earlier migration histories, strongly shapes processes of identification and boundary-making, instead of culturalisation of conflict (Hüttermann, 2015). The "right to Germany" is framed as something earned through hardship, with narratives of labour and sacrifice replacing nationalist bloodline claims with a legacy of work. Within this moral economy of reciprocity (Wimmer, 2013), there is a marked reluctance to share progress with newcomers. As one established religious woman explained, earlier generations *"did every kind of work, lived in the cheapest houses, and didn't give up,"* while newcomers are seen as unwilling to take difficult jobs, demanding better conditions, and remaining within their own groups.

The analysis also highlights complex interdependencies that stretch across national borders and institutional frameworks. Along with historical and cultural relations, many refugees in Germany passed through Turkey as a transit country or lived there temporarily, sometimes maintaining family ties there. A Syrian woman recalled her family's two-year stay in Turkey, but felt excluded: *"Since we had a fancy car, locals didn't like us. We had so many unpleasant looks."* Such accounts point to ambivalent positions between host, transit, and destination societies. Interdependencies are equally evident in the political and institutional realm, as rising far-right politics in Germany shapes hierarchies of belonging. An established Turkish man noted that while newcomers are often targeted by debates on remigration, he felt that such measures *"would not apply to us."* At the same time, institutional structures of the German labour market further shape migrants' possibilities for participation. An Afghan man explained how lengthy bureaucratic procedures around asylum applications can leave people *"spending eight years doing nothing,"* creating conditions of marginalization that hinder both employment and language acquisition. In precise terms, newly emerging established-outsider figurations in Germany show that Turkish-origin migrants tend to distance themselves not only from "Muslims" broadly, but from all newcomers, whereas post-2015 arrivals from Muslim-majority countries generally hold more positive attitudes toward earlier migrant generations and concerned primarily with bureaucratic challenges. Both groups remain aware of their "Ausländer" identity and highlight the disparities between legal and societal treatment of Ukrainian refugees.

Conclusion

"Wir schaffen das, oder?" (We can manage it, right?) reflects a widespread perception among participants that Germany has struggled to manage refugee policies effectively. The findings show that a lack of sustained contact between

groups fuels the reproduction of stereotypes (Schönwälder et al., 2016) and reinforces we–they *images*. Belonging emerges as situational, conditional, and strategically negotiated, shaped by unequal power balances between established groups and newcomers. Policies that classify refugees as good or bad complicate these processes of identification and belonging, not only for new arrivals but also for long-established migrants. Religion, ethnicity, or culture alone cannot account for intergroup tensions. Viewed through Elias' concept of the established–outsider figuration, these dynamics demonstrate how figurations evolve in relation to interdependencies, historical trajectories, and changing political regimes. My analysis underscores that migration-related diversity is not static but a dynamic sociological phenomenon of lived diversities. Emerging figurations and evolving intergroup relations therefore require greater scholarly attention, particularly in light of their implications for unequal power balances.

References

Brubaker, R. (2004). *Ethnicity without groups*. Harvard University Press.

Castles, S., & Kosack, G. (1973). *Immigrant workers and class structure in Western Europe*. Oxford University Press.

De Haas, H. (2023). *How migration really works: A factful guide to the most divisive issue in politics*. Random House.

Destatis. (2021). *Bevölkerung und Erwerbstätigkeit: Ausländische Bevölkerung – Ergebnisse des Ausländerzentralregisters. Fachserie 1, Reihe 2*. Retrieved March 24, 2025, from https://www.destatis.de

Destatis. (2025, May 22). *Gut jede vierte Person in Deutschland hat eine Einwanderungsgeschichte* (Pressemitteilung Nr. 181). Retrieved August 8, 2025, from https://www.destatis.de/DE/Presse/Pressemitteilungen/2025/05/PD25_181_125.html

Elias, N. (1978). *What is sociology?* Columbia University Press.

Elias, N. (2006). *The collected works of Norbert Elias*.

Elias, N., & Scotson, J. (1994). *The established and the outsiders: A sociological enquiry into community problems* (2nd ed.). Sage. (Original work published 1965)

Etzel, M. (2022). New models of the "good refugee": Bureaucratic expectations of Syrian refugees in Germany. In *Permitted outsiders* (pp. 127–146). Routledge.

Goerres, A., Spies, D. C., & Kumlin, S. (2018). The electoral supporter base of the Alternative for Germany. *Swiss Political Science Review, 24*(3), 246–269. https://doi.org/10.1111/spsr.12300

Hüttermann, J. (2015). Figurational change and primordialism in a multicultural society: A model explained on the basis of the German case. In *After integration* (pp. 17–42). Springer VS.

Sadeghi, S. (2019). Racial boundaries, stigma, and the re-emergence of "always being foreigners": Iranians and the refugee crisis in Germany. *Ethnic and Racial Studies, 42*(10), 1613–1631. https://doi.org/10.1080/01419870.2018.1451220

Sachverständigenrat deutscher Stiftungen für Integration und Migration (SVR). (2016). *Viele Götter, ein Staat: Religiöse Vielfalt und Teilhabe im Einwanderungsland. Jahresgutachten 2016 mit Integrationsbarometer*. Retrieved March 7, 2024 from https://www.svr-migration.de/wp-content/uploads/2016/04/SVR_JG_2016-mit-Integrationsbarometer_WEB.pdf

Schönwälder, K., Petermann, S., Hüttermann, J., Vertovec, S., Hewstone, M., Stolle, D., & Schmitt, T. (2016). *Diversity and contact: Immigration and social interaction in German cities.* Springer.

Steigemann, A. (2020). 'Multi-culti' vs. 'another cell phone store': Changing ethnic, social, and commercial diversities in Berlin-Neukölln. *Cosmopolitan Civil Societies: An Interdisciplinary Journal, 12*(1), 83–105. https://doi.org/10.5130/ccs.v12i1.6777

Šedovič, M., & Dražanová, L. (2025). Migrant and non-migrant views on immigration in Europe. *European Journal of Population, 41*(1), 1–38. https://doi.org/10.1007/s10680-024-09672-1

Türkmen, G. (2024). The politics of believing and belonging: Increasing diversity among Muslim immigrants in Germany. *International Migration Review.* Advance online publication. https://doi.org/10.1177/01979183241234567

Wimmer, A. (2013). *Ethnic boundary making: Institutions, power, networks.* Oxford University Press.

DRAWING STRENGTHS: TRAUMA-INFORMED EXPRESSIVE ARTS FOR ASYLUM-SEEKING CHILDREN IN A HUMANITARIAN RESPITE CENTER AT THE US-MEXICO BORDER

Alfonso Mercado, Kim Nguyen-Finn, Cecilia Garza, Andy Torres, Francisco Banda, Erin Tovar, Ricardo Robles[1]

Introduction

Title IV of the Homeland Security Act of 2002 establishes three criteria as the legal definition for unaccompanied minors (UMs) (Homeland Security Act of 2002, 6 U.S.C. §§ 201-311). These are: 1) the individual has no lawful immigration status, 2) is below the age of 18, and 3) has no parent or legal guardian in the US or no such caregiver is available to assume custody. According to statistics from United States Customs and Border Protection (2025), arrivals of UMs saw a recent peak of 6,827 in December of Fiscal Year 2025, down from a peak of 13,462 in December of Fiscal Year 2024 and has since maintained steady at or below 1,000 encounters per month. After their encounter with Border Patrol agents, UMs are entered into the Unaccompanied Refugee Minors Program where they receive indirect financial support, healthcare, and other services (Mercado & Venta, 2022).

Peaks of arrivals and the possibility of future escalations warrant an expansion of the provider care toolset such that they can accommodate UMs' need for culturally tailored, trauma-informed care. This is important as UMs have been recognized as a vulnerable group due to high rates of traumatic experiences such as witnessing violence against others and being subject to abuse themselves (Venta & Mercado, 2019). Culturally tailored expressive arts interventions pose one such possible addition. Ample research supports the effectiveness of expressive arts interventions. Most notably, de Freitas and colleagues (2019) found that asylum-seeking youth and their parents attributed improved emotional safety and sense of normalcy to a creative expressive workshop.

---

[1] The University of Texas Rio Grande Valley, United States.

Morison and colleagues (2022), meanwhile, conducted a meta-analysis that confirmed art-based interventions were associated with reduced posttraumatic stress disorder symptom levels among samples of general youth with trauma(s). These expressive arts interventions are also conducive to cultural tailoring via relatively simple modifications to activities such that participant language preferences, values, and traditions are incorporated into the program.

This study is a qualitative exploration of a novel design for an expressive arts intervention program piloted with a sample of UMs at a respite center in deep South Texas. The structure and design of the program are reported followed by a brief review of participant engagement and facilitator reflections. Implications for similar programs are discussed as well as strengths and limitations.

Method

Participants

Participants in this project were recently arrived UMs and asylum-seeking immigrants who had been processed by U.S. Customs and Border Patrol and temporarily placed at a humanitarian respite center along the U.S.–Mexico border. Demographic characteristics were not formally collected in order to protect the confidentiality of all participants. The approximate group size varied by session with a range of two to twelve.

In addition to the child participants, a team of facilitators contributed to the planning and delivery of the program. This team included four doctoral students in clinical psychology who were responsible for session facilitation and documentation, one licensed psychologist who supervised the intervention and ensured adherence to trauma-informed principles, and one licensed professional counselor–supervisor (LPC-S) with extensive experience in expressive arts interventions who guided the development of activity agendas. A local artist also collaborated by assisting with creative design particularly through supporting canvas-based projects and providing materials. This interdisciplinary team ensured that the intervention incorporated clinical expertise, expressive arts practices, and culturally responsive approaches.

Setting

All activities took place at a Catholic Charities Humanitarian Respite Center at the US-Mexico border in South Texas. The shelter provides human respite services including food, water, shelter, and opportunities to contact family members or arrange further travel. Within this context, the expressive arts sessions were embedded as trauma-informed, culturally sensitive, and responsive programming designed to support children during a period of heightened stress and transition. All activities were performed in the context of the center's mission statement, *"restoring human dignity"* to ensure legal and cultural alignment with their scope of service (*see* https://catholiccharitiesrgv.org/get-help/humanitarian-respite-center/)

Procedures

Children engaged in three semi-structured sessions that incorporated expressive arts and movement-based expressive practices. Each session was facilitated by the doctoral student team with oversight from the licensed psychologist and activity guidance from the LPC-S expressive arts specialist. The local artist assisted during the creative activities and supported the children with art materials. Sessions lasted approximately 45 minutes and were conducted in small groups to foster a safe and supportive environment.

Session 1

In the first session, children completed the activity *Las emociones de mi corazón*, in which they drew inside and outside of a heart. Items or memories placed inside the heart represented positive experiences or sources of happiness, whereas objects drawn outside the heart represented memories or experiences they wished to forget. This activity allowed the children to express themselves regarding their journey via drawings/coloring with minimal written expression tasks. Doctoral students and LPC-S guided all children in a group-like structure that included 1) mindfulness breathing, 2) introduction to the group facilitators, 3) group instructions, 4) distribution of expressive arts materials, 5) sharing completed task / expressive arts with fellow children, and 6) closing belly-breathing exercises.

Session 2

The second session, *Lo que me ayuda a ser fuerte* ("What helps me be strong"), featured age-stratified tasks: older children were asked to write or draw about themselves, family, and life experiences that bring them joy; middle-aged children focused on drawing objects or experiences that make them happy; and younger children were given the opportunity for free drawing. This logistical update to session #1 facilitated group cohesion, allowed each doctoral student to co-facilitate with greater group management skills, and permitted the children participants to engage in developmentally relevant activities. The tasks 1-5 listed in Session 1 above were also included in this activity.

Session 3

The third session was a "kiddie yoga" activity that incorporated animal-inspired poses such as the lion, giraffe, crocodile, and tree, paired with affirmations, mindfulness meditation, paced breathing, and playful self-regulation strategies. The session was conducted in a "yoga circle" style where the lead facilitator, author KF, demonstrated the movements and breathing instructions. This session agenda consisted of 1) mindfulness breathing, 2) introduction to the group facilitators, 3) group instructions, 4) following and copying movements of the kiddie yoga facilitator while doctoral students followed along and helped new participants integrate into the "yoga circle" and 5) exiting deep breathing as a closing activity.

Data Collection and Reflections

Rather than collecting quantitative or identifying data, facilitators documented qualitative reflections following each session, as well as behavioral observation of the group dynamics. This was documented in a journal style. Each facilitator was tasked to write a brief journal entry at the end of each group to record their own experience as facilitator, working with migrants, UMs, and with asylum-seekers. Children's artwork was considered part of the expressive process rather than systematically analyzed. The emphasis remained on creating a supportive space and generating insights into the applicability of trauma-informed expressive arts in humanitarian settings following the center's mission of "restoring human dignity."

Results

Across the three sessions, children demonstrated high levels of engagement with the expressive arts and mindfulness activities. Thematic patterns emerged from facilitator reflections and observations of the children's participation. First, children consistently expressed both positive and negative experiences through artwork. In the *Las emociones de mi corazón* activity, many children filled the interior of the heart with colorful drawings of family, friends, pets, and favorite activities, while the outer portions often depicted darker or absent figures, symbolizing experiences they wished to forget. This pattern reflected the duality of resilience and trauma frequently described in research on unaccompanied minors (American Psychological Association, 2024; Morrison et al., 2022).

Second, the *Lo que me ayuda a ser fuerte* activity highlighted children's ability to identify sources of strength and joy. Older children tended to articulate themes of family, cultural identity, and education, while younger participants often emphasized play and familiar comforting objects. These age-related distinctions emphasize the importance of developmentally appropriate activities in expressive arts activities.

Third, the yoga and mindfulness session fostered noticeable enthusiasm and group cohesion. Children engaged playfully in poses such as lions, giraffes, and crocodiles, often laughing and encouraging peers. Facilitators noted that even children who were initially hesitant became more participatory as the session progressed. The integration of positive affirmations and paced breathing was observed to promote calmness and self-regulation, with some children spontaneously repeating the affirmations after the activity concluded.

Additionally, facilitators identified three overarching themes: (a) children demonstrated resilience by naming or drawing protective factors, (b) group activities promoted a sense of safety and belonging within a temporary and uncertain environment, and (c) the inclusion of an interdisciplinary facilitation team enriched the quality and adaptability of sessions. The presence of a local artist was particularly impactful as children were enthusiastic about the opportunity to use professional art materials and work on canvas creations which many had not previously experienced.

Discussion

This expressive art project with UMs and migrant families demonstrates the feasibility and cultural sensitivity of implementing trauma-informed expressive arts. The three-session program provided children with opportunities to express both positive and negative experiences through art, to reflect on sources of resilience, and to engage in playful yoga and mindfulness activities. Facilitator reflections highlighted that children readily engaged with the activities, often using artwork to externalize difficult experiences while simultaneously identifying protective factors such as family, culture, and play. The yoga session offered children strategies for embodied self-regulation during a time of instability as seen in other studies (Freitas Girardi et al., 2019; Morrison et al., 2022).

This expressive arts model reflects prior research emphasizing culturally responsive and interdisciplinary approaches via drawing, canvas painting, and movement-based therapy (e.g., yoga) to alleviate the participants from written expression tasks that can be burdensome and alienate those with developmental delays or severe cognitive problems amid traumatic response (Freitas Girardi et al., 2019; Morrison et al., 2022). Nonetheless, the absence of systematic data collection and the transient setting limit the ability to draw causal conclusions about intervention outcomes. Future research should incorporate psychological measures, follow-ups, and mixed-methods evaluation to better capture the effects of expressive arts in humanitarian contexts.

Conclusion

The findings suggest that expressive arts can serve as culturally responsive strategies for supporting unaccompanied minors during humanitarian transitions. Even brief sessions provided meaningful opportunities for resilience-building and emotional expression. Interdisciplinary teams remain critical to deploy trauma-informed programming in migrant and underserved care settings.

References

American Psychological Association. *Psychological Science and Immigration Today.* (2024)

APA. Presidential Task Force on Immigration and Health. Retrieved from https://www.apa.org/pubs/reports/psychological-science-and-immigration-today.pdf.

de Freitas Girardi, J., Miconi, D., Lyke, C., & Rousseau, C. (2020). Creative expression workshops as Psychological First Aid (PFA) for asylum-seeking children: An exploratory study in temporary shelters in Montreal. *Clinical Child Psychology and Psychiatry, 25*(2), 483–493. https://doi.org/10.1177/1359104519891760

Homeland Security Act of 2002, Pub. L. No. 107-296, 116 Stat. 2135 (2002) (codified as amended in 6 U.S.C. §§ 201-311)

Mercado, A., & Venta, A. (2022*). Cultural competency in psychological assessment: Working effectively with latinx populations.* Oxford University Press, Incorporated.

Morison, L., Simonds, L., & Stewart, S.-J. F. (2022). Effectiveness of creative arts-based interventions for treating children and adolescents exposed to traumatic events: A systematic review of the quantitative evidence and meta-analysis. *Arts & Health, 14*(3), 237–262. https://doi.org/10.1080/17533015.2021.2009529

United States Customs and Border Protection. (2024, August 6). Southwest Land Border Encounters | U.S. Customs and Border Protection. U.S. Customs and Border Protection. Retrieved from https://www.cbp.gov/newsroom/stats/southwest-land-border-encounters

Venta, A. C., & Mercado, A. (2019). Trauma Screening in Recently Immigrated Youth: Data from Two Spanish-Speaking Samples. *Journal of Child and Family Studies, 28*(1), 84–90. https://doi.org/10.1007/s10826-018-1252-8

STORIES OF ESOL IN SUFFOLK, ENGLAND

Amna Smith

Introduction

Presented in this article are excerpts of the stories and experiences of ESOL learners. ESOL (English for Speakers of Other Languages) refers to English language instruction for individuals living in English-speaking countries who are learning English as an additional language (Hann et al., 2021). ESOL provision often serves refugee, asylum-seeking, and immigrant populations. The terms "refugee" and "asylum seeker" are frequently conflated in UK discourse, despite important legal distinctions. A refugee is someone forced to flee their country due to conflict or a credible fear of persecution, seeking protection in another state. An asylum seeker is someone whose application for refugee status is still under review (UNHCR, 2023). This conflation can negatively impact public perception and policy, with asylum seekers and refugees often viewed unfavourably in the UK (Tong and Zuo, 2019), leading to serious consequences for their safety and wellbeing (Rosen and Young, 2016). As of May 2024, an estimated 120 million people were displaced globally (European Civil Protection and Humanitarian Aid Operations, 2024). Refugees and asylum seekers face numerous barriers to accessing ESOL provision. In this study, "barriers" are defined as any factor that obscures or limits learning opportunities (Choudhry, 2022).

Theoretical Framework

This section introduces the theoretical frameworks guiding the study. The first is Brown's adapted (2021) *Emancipation Continuum*, which examines ESOL provision as a pathway to societal inclusion. It highlights systemic barriers that limit learners' agency, which is their ability to reflect on and act within their circumstances (Schwandt, 2001). Brown outlines three models of integration: assimilation, integration, and inclusion, showing how each shapes social structures that either empower or constrain immigrants. The second framework is Choudhry's (2022) intersectional approach, used to explore barriers at the individual level. It considers how personal histories, circumstances, and migration pathways influence learners' access to and experience of ESOL provision.

Research questions

This study aims to answer the following research questions.

1. How do ESOL learners from a refugee or asylum-seeking background, living in Suffolk, encounter barriers to learning at an individual level? What are the stories surrounding these barriers?

2. How do ESOL teachers and refugee support staff narrate the barriers that their learners encounter? What cannot be mitigated at a societal level?

3. What are the goals and aspirations of the learners, and which factors at the societal and individual level facilitate the learners' goals and aspirations?

For this article, research question 1 will be addressed in detail.

Methodology

This study adopts a constructivist approach, recognising multiple realities shaped by lived experience. It uses narrative inquiry, specifically, narrative interviews, as the primary method of data collection. As Clandinin and Connelly (2000) note, the interviewer's actions and responses influence how participants share their stories. Narrative inquiry is inherently autobiographical; as both ESOL practitioner and researcher, my own experiences shaped the inquiry's direction.

Participants were selected through purposive and convenience sampling. Staff were chosen based on their job role, and learners based on English proficiency and willingness to participate. While the study aimed to include learners with very low English and literacy levels, an underrepresented group, sadly, this was beyond its scope. An exclusion criterion of E1 (CEFR A1 equivalent) was applied. All participants were recruited through the researcher's professional network, with additional learners recruited via snowball sampling, for example, through tutors who shared the study with their students.

The study included seven ESOL learners, four female and three males, ranging in age from 18 to 54. Participants originated from Ukraine, Kosovo, Iran, and Afghanistan, with national identities including Ukrainian, British, Albanian,

Iranian, Kurdish, and Afghan. They spoke a range of languages, including Kurdish, Albanian, Dari, Pashto, Polish, Russian, and English. Most were married with children, and their education levels varied from college diplomas to university degrees. This diverse group reflects a wide spectrum of linguistic, cultural, and educational backgrounds, offering rich insight into the lived experiences of ESOL learners in Suffolk.

This study used reflexive thematic analysis, following Braun and Clarke (2006, 2012, 2021), to identify and interpret patterns within interview data. This approach involves ongoing reflection and revision of codes as understanding evolves (Braun and Clarke, 2021). Widely used across disciplines and not tied to a specific theoretical framework, thematic analysis has faced critique but is valued for its flexibility and rigour when applied systematically (Howitt, 2016). An experiential, reflexive thematic analysis was used to interpret participant meaning, following Braun and Clarke's (2021) guidelines. Coding was conducted manually in Excel, with interview excerpts used to generate codes and themes. Themes were grouped under broader barriers to ESOL learning, such as "individual life circumstances."

A research assistant reviewed selected transcripts to 'sense-check' the coding logic (as in Byrne, 2022), revealing close alignment with minor semantic differences. This collaborative approach supported the rigour and reflexivity of the analysis. The researcher used NVivo's autocode function to analyse transcripts, but it missed many participant nuances. To address this, manual coding was conducted within NVivo, allowing for more accurate theme identification. Final themes from tutors, support staff, and learners were grouped into static sets, each representing a key barrier to ESOL learning based on participant perceptions and researcher interpretation.

Findings

To address Research Question 1, this section presents novel findings from learner data. Below is a thematic map detailing the themes produced by participants during interviews.

For the purposes of this article, excerpts of learner interview will be presented. A key barrier identified was "location and living in Suffolk" highlighted in ESOL Learner 1's account as limiting opportunities to speak and practise English. Following Braun and Clarke's (2022) guidance, findings and analysis are integrated to contextualise the data.

Figure 1. Thematic map

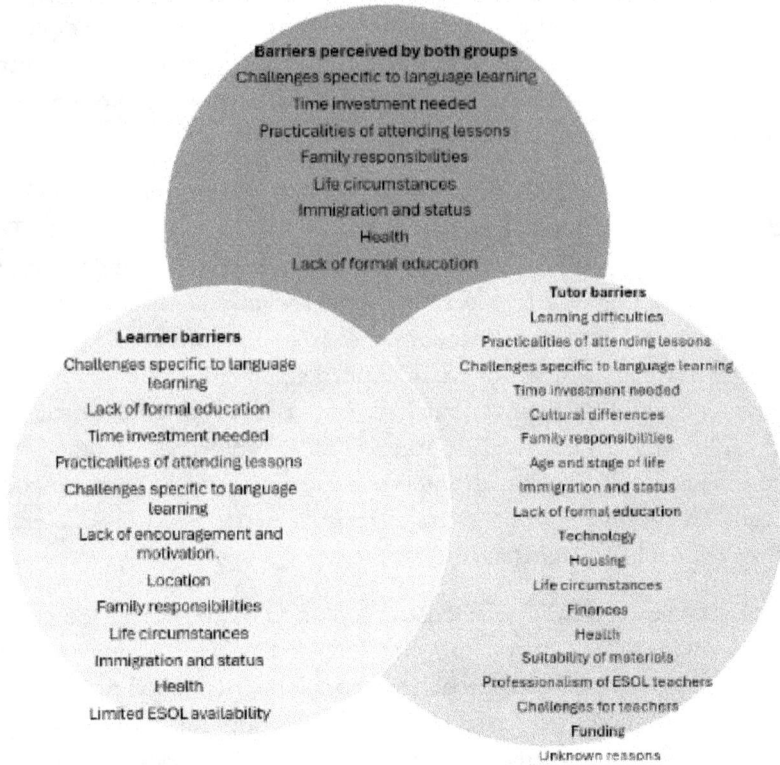

Barriers perceived by both groups
Challenges specific to language learning
Time investment needed
Practicalities of attending lessons
Family responsibilities
Life circumstances
Immigration and status
Health
Lack of formal education

Tutor barriers
Learning difficulties
Practicalities of attending lessons
Challenges specific to language learning
Time investment needed
Cultural differences
Family responsibilities
Age and stage of life
Immigration and status
Lack of formal education
Technology
Housing
Life circumstances
Finances
Health
Suitability of materials
Professionalism of ESOL teachers
Challenges for teachers
Funding
Unknown reasons

Learner barriers
Challenges specific to language learning
Lack of formal education
Time investment needed
Practicalities of attending lessons
Challenges specific to language learning
Lack of encouragement and motivation.
Location
Family responsibilities
Life circumstances
Immigration and status
Health
Limited ESOL availability

> ESOL Learner 1: You know what I notice when I used to live in Essex? There are only English people, and my English was better then, and...here we have in [name redacted] for example, we have more different people from other countries, and they speak their languages and English. I use only maybe in school, but it's not often... and I'm I'm not happy with this so I need to be with the English people. I need to absorb all this.

Living in Suffolk was identified as a barrier to ESOL learning by ESOL Learner 1 and Support Staff participants, who cited ruralisation schemes and lack of local service information as contributing factors. ESOL Learner 1, a degree-educated Ukrainian refugee who arrived via the resettlement scheme with family, accessed strong ESOL provision and arrived with the right to work. While arriving with family may offer emotional support and resilience (Corbin and Hall, 2019), this assumption requires further investigation. The participant's education level also supports the researcher's hypothesis that educational background influences the barriers ESOL learners face.

ESOL Learner 1 accessed a free 12-week online English course, available exclusively to Ukrainian refugees before October 2024. Flexible scheduling made the course accessible for those with family or work commitments. While rural location was identified as a key barrier, this may lessen as the learner settles. Having children also created opportunities to use English in daily interactions. While Learner 1 benefited from strong ESOL provision and family support, Learners 4 and 5 faced very different challenges as unaccompanied minors. Learners 4 and 5, who arrived as unaccompanied asylum-seeking children from Kurdistan and Iran, lacked family support, and were housed in hostels with limited resources. Learner 5 and Learner 4 were notably reluctant to discuss family.

> Researcher: Tell me about your family.

> ESOL learner 5: *Not really* [participant didn't want to talk about family].

> Researcher: *Tell me about your family.*

> ESOL learner 4: *Like, how many brothers do I have? How is my family?*

> Researcher: *Yeah.*

> ESOL learner 4: *I have like, uh, two brother and two sisters, and they (are) younger than me.*

> ESOL learner 4: *Yeah, I haven't seen them for like three years.*

> Researcher: *Ok. Are they in Iran?*

> ESOL learner 4: *They are in back home, yeah.*

Learners 4 and 5 arrived in the UK alone, without family support or formal education, and had limited access to public funds after age 19. They relied on ESOL and college education for stability, though escaping poverty may take years. Even with refugee status, they must achieve sufficient English proficiency and gain recognised qualifications, an extended process, especially given their current ESOL provision of just 5–6 hours per week during term time. Learner 1's proactive approach and access to online courses contrast sharply with Learner 5's limited resources and vulnerability. This disparity underscores how prior education and family support shape ESOL outcomes.

> Researcher: Why are you learning English?

> ESOL learner 5: Because, if you don't, this country, all speak English, if you don't speak English, it's like you're deaf, you don't know nothing.

Learner investment in English is shaped by future aspirations (Newman et al., 2013). ESOL Learner 5 recognised the value of English for improving life chances and employment. However, stark disparities exist between Learners 1, 4, and 5 in terms of support and opportunity. Unaccompanied minors like Learners 4 and 5 remain vulnerable to poor educational outcomes (Aleghfeli & Hunt, 2022), reflecting broader policy and societal inequities. While this research cannot resolve these issues, it aims to raise awareness among policymakers and educators. Learners 4 and 5 had minimal prior education, which influenced their English proficiency and the depth of their responses—contrasting sharply with Learner 1's experience.

A notable contrast between Learners 1 and 5 was their willingness to be recorded; Learner 1 was comfortable with video recording, while Learner 4 declined voice recording but allowed note-taking. This may relate to national identity and public perception. Ukrainian refugees, often women (Grabowska et al., 2023), with higher education, have received a positive reception in the UK, unlike male asylum seekers from Afghanistan, Iraq, and Kurdistan, who face prejudice and media-driven mistrust (Tong & Zuo, 2019). Such experiences may lead to reluctance in engaging with authority or formal processes. These learners often have disrupted education and require patient, informed support (Aleghfeli & Hunt, 2022). Gender dynamics may also influence participation, given the researcher's identity. These accounts illustrate how individual life circumstances, such as family separation and prior education, act as barriers to ESOL learning, directly addressing Research Question 1. These assumptions will be explored during the follow-up data collection phase of this study. In response to Research Question 1, ESOL Learner 1 identified living in Suffolk as a barrier to learning, contrasting it with her more supportive experience in Essex, where she had greater opportunities to speak English. This perception may evolve as she settles and builds connections in Suffolk and will be revisited in follow-up data collection. As narrative inquiry captures evolving experiences, further data is needed to deepen and refine these findings.

Significance of study

This study is timely post-Brexit and post-Ukraine, aligning with the Home Office's Step Ahead program to support refugee ESOL learning. Effective ESOL provision offers strong returns, often repaying public costs within five months (Hann et al., 2021). It also highlights a unique, feminised Ukrainian refugee group and aims to amplify underrepresented voices, informing integration, ESOL planning, and support services. Enhanced ESOL provision reduces isolation and risk for refugees, improves access to education and work, and supports autonomy (Sidaway, 2022). With many ESOL learners being women (Choudhry, 2022), it also advances SDGs 4 and 5 ahead of the 2030 deadline.

Next steps and implications

Living in Suffolk emerged as a barrier to ESOL learning, with current provision and materials falling short of refugee learners' needs. A local guide listing services and entitlements could help address knowledge gaps. Some findings are based on researcher assumptions and will be explored further in follow-up data.

References

Aleghfeli, Y.K. & Hunt, L. (2022) Education of unaccompanied refugee minors in high-income countries: Risk and resilience factors, *Educational Research Review*, Volume 35, 2022, 100433, ISSN 1747-938X, https://doi.org/10.1016/j.edurev.2022.100433.

Braun, V., & Clarke, V. (2006). *Using thematic analysis in psychology. Qualitative Research in Psychology*, 3(2), 77–101.

Braun, V., & Clarke, V. (2012). *Thematic analysis*. In H. Cooper (Ed.), *APA handbook of research methods in psychology* (Vol. 2, pp. 57–71). APA

Braun, V., & Clarke, V. (2021). *Thematic analysis: A practical guide*. Sage.

Brown, S. (2021) 'The emancipation continuum: analysing the role of ESOL in the settlement of immigrants' *British Journal of Sociology of Education*, Issue 42(5) pp.864-880

Byrne, D. 'A worked example of Braun and Clarke's approach to reflexive thematic analysis.' *Qual Quant* 56, 1391–1412 (2022). https://doi.org/10.1007/s11135-021-01182-y

Choudhry F. (2022) *An Investigation of the barriers experienced by female Muslim ESOL learners whilst being in education*. Choudry, F. Theses submitted for doctorate in education, Staffordshire University (2022) p.1-193.

Clandinin, D. and Connelly, F. (2000). *Narrative Inquiry: Experience and Story in Qualitative Research*. Jossey-Bass

Corbin, J. and Hall, J. (2019). 'Resettlement post conflict: Risk and protective factors and resilience among women in northern Uganda' *International Social Work*, 62(2), pp.918-932. https://doi.org/10.1177/0020872818755863

European Commission for European Civil Protection and Humanitarian Aid Operations (2023) https://civil-protection-humanitarian-aid.ec.europa.eu/what/humanitarian-aid/forced-displacement_en#:~:text=At%20the%20end%20of%202022,Syria%2C%20Ukraine%2C%20and%20Afghanistan. (accessed on 14/11/2023).

Grabowska, I., Jastrzebowska, A., and Kyliushyk, I. (2023). 'Resilience Embedded in Psychological Capital of Ukrainian Refugees in Poland.' *In Migration Letters*, 20(3), pp.421–430. https://doi.org/10.47059/ml.v20i3.2887

Hann, N. Willott, J. Graham-Brown, N. Roden, J. & Tremayne, D. (2021). *What is Suitable and Effective ESOL for Refugees?* Compiled for Migration Yorkshire January 2021

Howitt,D. (2016) *Introduction to Qualitative Research Methods in Psychology*. Pearson Education, Australia, 2019.

Newman, M. & Patiño-Santos, A. & Trenchs-Parera, M. (2013). Linguistic Reception of Latin American Students in Catalonia and Their Responses to Educational Language Policies.

International Journal of Bilingual Education and Bilingualism. 16. 195-209. 10.1080/13670050.2012.720669.

Rosen, M and Young, A. (2016) *Who are Refugees and Migrants? What makes People leave their homes?* Wayland Publishing, 2016.

Schwandt, T. (2001) Dictionary of qualitative inquiry, 2nd Edition. Sage Publishing.

Sidaway, K. (2022). 'Exploring the motivation of women studying in a multilevel ESOL class in England.' *TESOL J. 2022;13:e61518.* https://doi.org/10.1002/tesj.615

Suffolk Refugee Support (2023) Proceedings from the AGM October, 2023, Suffolk, England.

Tong, J. and Zuo, L. (2019) 'Othering the European Union through constructing moral panics over "immigrants" in the coverage of migration in three British newspapers, 2011-2016'. In The *International Communication Gazette* 2019 Vol. 81 (5) pp.445-469

United Nations High Commissioner for Refugees (2023) *Refugee Definition.* Available at: https://emergency.unhcr.org/protection/legal-framework/refugee-definition [accessed on 23/11/2023].

TALES OF A YIDDISH LAND - EXPLORING YIDDISH DIASPORIC TERRITORIALITY IN NEW YORK THROUGH AUTOBIOGRAPHICAL NARRATIVES

Ariel Roemer[1]

Introduction

The following article presents the results of an exploratory research regarding a set of 8 autobiographies held by the Institute of Jewish research (YIVO) in New York. The texts analysed are in the collection "American Jewish Autobiographies, 1942-1970" (RG 102). The writings from Yiddish speaking Jews revolve around the mass migration period in the United States from the 1880s to 1924, when approximately 23 million immigrants mainly from Eastern and Southern Europe docked in the country. In the Jewish case, the region that they came can be called the Yiddishland located between Eastern Poland, Ukraine, Western Russia, Belarus, Lithuania and Romania. Specifically, New York, is the city envisaged in this research by the high concentration of Jews arriving while it was the main port of entry for the newcomers (Diner & Bontempo, 2022)

To approach the accounts, two analyses were made. One was a thematic analysis searching for elements in the texts that could show three aspects of migrations identified by a previous reading: Belonging to the homeland; Being a migrant; Integration in the country. The second analysis was made through a discourse analysis by grasping how the writers depicted the places that they made present by remembrance in the text. This also meant an approach on how different meanings were imprinted in places that these migrants experienced throughout their lives.

The Jewish Migration from Eastern Europe to the United States (1880-1924)

To understand the context of what the immigrants wrote about, it is

---

[1] Ariel Roemer, Université de Libre de Bruxelles, Erasmus Mundus Master's MITRA, Belgium.

fundamental to apprehend the time span of the mass migration period in the United States. Although it is the period when most of immigrants arrived, this is also the moment when new mechanism of control and surveillance are being implemented.

What mostly marks this period is the 1882 Ban on Chinese Migration, the first law being implemented to restrict completely the arrival of one specific ethnic group in the country. Until this point, policies regarding migration were not made in a federal level. Nevertheless, the winds of politics were blowing towards anti-immigration movements, based on racial theories, to block undesired groups that would not contribute to an U.S. American *ethos* and economy (Diner & Bontempo, 2022). This made not only the infrastructure to receive and control these immigrants more robust, but detailed statistics were being produced.

Considering the Jewish case, Anti-semitism is usually counted as the only factor for emigrating, nevertheless, other strong aspects of the changing times they were living influenced their decisions. Mostly, the process of industrialisation in Eastern Europe caused a fast-paced urbanisation, breaking down traditional economic networks that connected small towns and villages, which made Jews and non-Jews to migrate to bigger towns and cities and towards the United States. Added by this, the improvement of communications with *landslayt*[2] established networks of solidarity to facilitate the arrival of others. Finally, the means of transportations created more ship lines that could transport more people faster (Diner, 2004).

Despite these conditionings, migrating depended on several structures that embraced specific elements, and family organisation determined also who would migrate first, who would come afterwards, who would be the breadwinner and so on as exemplified by Wagner (1942-1970, p. 96): "But when I told it to my mother, she began to cry and said she would die if I go to such a far country, that she would never see me again."

1924 marks the end this period with the National Origins Act, that established a quota system for each of the nationalities from Europe. This made eastern and southern Europeans to decrease their arrival and for Jews, to change their community organisations and their gaze towards their homelands.

---

[2] Term in Yiddish to talk about a countryman.

The autonomization of the U.S. American-Jewish community after 1924

After 1924, two movements are influential to change the configuration of the U.S. American Jewish community. The first is caused by the effective implementation of the quota system caused by the National Origins Act, massively decreasing the arrival of landslayt in the harbours. The second, although not new, grows significantly in politics, which is the anti-immigration movement merged with Anti-semitism (Diner, 2004).

In this configuration, the Jewish community generally sought ways to showcase their adoption of U.S. American mainstream values. Simultaneously, organisations that would mimic white protestant models started to rise such as social clubs, Jewish schools and summer camps, while other organisations would gather Jews so they could keep their values, mostly inside the conservative movement (Diner, 2004). What changed significantly was the conception of belonging. Once, Yiddish speaking would mainly find their roots in Eastern Europe with language, the Jewish socialist party (Bund), the Yiddish theatre and literature. In the 1920s to find settlement, there was a period of transition and identification with the values of the host country. Furthermore, the local differences from the hometowns start to fade in the mixture among themselves (Diner, 2004).

Not only because of the changes in the United States that the community looked towards another direction, but because of the destruction that they witnessed in their hometowns after World War I. In this aspect, in retrospective, the mutual-aid association connected to the hometowns (landsmanshaftn) promoted literature contests and publications that emphasized grasping the pieces of memory alive in the immigrants who tried to build an image of comfort for a shattered world that they could not return anymore. The Yiddishland was fading while served as a guidance for the first generation of migrants (Czendze, 2021; Wolff, 2013).

YIVO, founded in 1925, in Vilnius carried this weight of, being an academic and cultural institution, assembling a world that since the end of the 19th century was being transformed. When it arrived in New York in 1940, escaping from the World War II, it had to serve itself from the needs that the U.S. American Jewry was facing to build identification amongst themselves and to integrate to the host society without losing its roots (Cohen, 2000).

The American-Jewish autobiography contest in 1942

In 1942, bearing the ideas of building self-identification and assembling a comprehensive archive of personal accounts regarding migration, YIVO launched The American-Jewish autobiography contest. In their announcements they asked for daily life descriptions with accuracy and no flourishing, even though the subject proposed was *"Why I Left Europe and What I Have Accomplished in America*. This firstly confused the participants who still being from a lower middle class or within the labour movement did not see themselves accomplishing what could be expected from the American Dream, nevertheless, with further motivations, especially from the scientific director Max Weinreich, a total of 223 autobiographies were sent from different parts of the United States, Canada, Mexico and Cuba.

For the writers their objectives differed from the organisation. For them it was relevant that someone was interested in reading their stories, especially a respected academic institution in their views. But mainly, it was a moment that they could stop and make a life balance of their trajectory.

What did they write?

From the corpus of 223 autobiographies, 8 were chosen as they were typed in English (considering the fluency of the researcher and the duration of the research). Nevertheless, the writers in this group shared the period of migration, the region and all were young men. Considering the social markers related to their profiles and what could be grasped by their accounts, it was possible to identify, and analyse excerpts related to situations that related to belonging to the homeland; being a migrant; and integrating in the new country.

Harry Mann (1942-1970) illustrates his belonging with the Jewish condition while expresses some kind of assimilation or appreciation for the Russian culture: "I began to feel a kinship with Russian culture and things Russian in general. Yet it could not be called a process of assimilation. Our family was an average lower middle class Jewish family where pure Yiddish was spoken, and where the Jewish life of the town was reflected." (p. 5) at the same time he identifies himself as part of a persecuted group in a tender age, bringing the understanding that still he was felt as a stranger in this society.

The perception of being a migrant could be faced through struggle for material existence and discrimination or through specific places of sociability that migrants built for themselves. The different accounts such as from Mann (1942-1970) "Things were not made easier because I was a Jew from Russia and still spoke with a trace of a foreign accent. (...) I was beginning to lose respect for myself and regard for America as the golden land of opportunity." (p. 17-18) and Podell (1942-1970) "I ate gefilte fish on Fridays, worked on Saturdays, went to the Jewish theatre on Sundays, and attended socialist meetings at Rutgers's Square during the rest of the days. (p. 90) show us these different perceptions.

Finally, integration could be presented through different shades that might have not followed the white protestant ideals. Mann (1942-1970) shows discontent with the secular Jewish culture, which made him prefer regular U.S. entertainment as a way towards assimilation; Podell (1942-1970) brings that for him was much easier to pal with other Russian Jews who worked with him and were in the same social level; and Wagner (1942-1970) did integrate through one of the unions in the garment sector, which had a major Jewish participation.

Landscapes of memory

When writing about their experiences, it is possible to see how these migrants had an active process of memory building through the recreation of places and landscapes that were not linear, neither completely coherent. In some cases, shaped by their age and the feelings transmitted by the texts, Eastern Europe is described as place of comfort and later a place of disgrace, mostly when they talk about their decision to leave it all behind with hopes of finding a better life in the United States. What does not happen so often are thorough description of New York. It is possible to understand that during the 1940s with news about the war, following the trend of the earlier landsmanshaft literature, there was a need to preserve and solidify a image of a place that somehow was remembered with care. Mostly because the first generation of Jewish migrants was still dislocated in the United States (Soyer, 1986).

The excerpts from Wagner (1942-1970) illustrate the ambiguity in his standpoint reflecting years after his childhood and subsequent migration. When describing about the town of Dembno he says, "Its soil is fertile; and its inhabitants are prosperous." (p. 117), but when docking at the Battery Park in New York he cites himself "Sholem Aleichem – Hello, America', (…) How beautiful! I looked up to the sky; it seemed much bluer and the sun much brighter than in the old country." (p. 150)

Final thoughts

After submerging in the accounts of the 8 selected autobiographies some considerations might be drawn, without forgetting that the research was focused on a specific group of Jewish immigrants even considering the whole range of autobiographies in the YIVO's collection.

Firstly, the appropriation of the New York urban space is seen through adopting the U.S. American values and its way of life while building a new identity, not from a detailed description of the places they inhabited. Secondly, the themes related to belonging, migration and integration were mostly associated with social markers that would highlight a difference in their subjectivation. This means that they would identify their belonging, for instance when this was related to their social class in the country of origin or the traditions associated with this territory. Last, though not talking directly about diaspora their reterritorialization process in New York brings elements, mainly through community organisation that kept links between the two sides of the Atlantic. In this sense even the community organisations they integrated had roots on the old land while existing in the United States as a way to settle in the new country.

Finally, the main reflection that might be extrapolated to other diasporic communities is the challenge of conveying the duality of the subjectivity based on a severance that makes *hereness* and *elsewhereness* inhabit a person or a group of people.

References

Primary resources

Carasnik, S (Nekhemie) (1942-1970), Autobiography. American-Jewish Autobiographies (RG 102 Box 14, Folder 173), YIVO Institute for Jewish Research, New York, NY, United States.

Greene, J. (1942-1970). Autobiography. American-Jewish Autobiographies (RG 102 Box 11, Folder 118), YIVO Institute for Jewish Research, New York, NY, United States.

Kligsberg, M. (1946). Socio-psychological problems reflected in the Yivo autobiography contest / YIVO Archives, Moses Kligsberg, RG 719

Mann, H. (1942-1970) Autobiography. American-Jewish Autobiographies (RG 102 Box 14, Folder 170), YIVO Institute for Jewish Research, New York, NY, United States.

Moshe, S. B. (1942-1970) Autobiography. American-Jewish Autobiographies (RG 102 Box 16, Folder 198), YIVO Institute for Jewish Research, New York, NY, United States.

Podell, M. (1942-1970) Autobiography. American-Jewish Autobiographies (RG 102 Box 15, Folder 178), YIVO Institute for Jewish Research, New York, NY, United States.

Rudnick, L. J. (1942-1970) Autobiography. American-Jewish Autobiographies (RG 102 Box 51, Folder 400), YIVO Institute for Jewish Research, New York, NY, United States.

Shapiro, M. (Em. S.) (1942-1970) Autobiography. American-Jewish Autobiographies (RG 102 Box 5, Folder 34), YIVO Institute for Jewish Research, New York, NY, United States.

Wagner, E. (1942-1970). Autobiography. American-Jewish Autobiographies (RG 102 Box 6, Folder 45), YIVO Institute for Jewish Research, New York, NY, United States.

YIVO Institute for Jewish Research. (1942-1970) Unarranged Material, American-Jewish Autobiographies (RG 102, Box 53), YIVO Institute for Jewish Research, New York, NY, United States.

YIVO Institute for Jewish Research. (1942) Autobiography Contest - Announcements, 1942. (RG

719 Box 32, Folder 667), Moses Kligsberg Papers.

YIVO Institute for Jewish Research, New York, NY, United States. YIVO Institute for Jewish Research (1942-1970) American Jewish Autobiographies 1942-1970's. YIVO Institute for Jewish Research (RG 102), New York, NY, United States

Secondary resources

Cohen, J. (2000). *Discourses of Acculturation: Gender and Class in East European Jewish Immigrant Autobiography, 1942.* PhD Thesis, University of Massachussets, (Order No. 9991400). Available from ProQuest Dissertations & Theses Global. (304614996). https://www.proquest.com/dissertations-theses/discourses-acculturation-gender-class-east/docview/304614996/se-2

Clifford, J. (1994). *Diasporas.* Cultural Anthropology, 9 (3), 302–338. http://www.jstor.org/stable/656365

Czendze, O. (2021). *In Search of Belonging: Galician Jewish Immigrants Between New York and Eastern Europe,* 1890–1938. PaRDeS : Journal of the Association for Jewish Studies in Germany, 27, 69-83. https://doi.org/10.25932/publishup-53285

Diner, H. R. (2004). *The Jews of the United States, 1654 to 2000* (1st ed.) Berkeley: University of California Press.

Diner, H. R. & Bon Tempo, C. J. (2022) *Immigration. An American History.* New Haven: Yale University Press

Haesbaert, R. (2010). *Território e multiterritorialidade: um debate.* GEOgraphia, 9(17). https://doi.org/10.22409/GEOgraphia2007.v9i17.a13531

Hall, S. (2018). Essential Essays (Two-Volume Set): Foundations of Cultural Studies and Identity and Diaspora. Durham: Duke University Press.

Kriwaczek, P. (2005). Yiddish Civilisation: the rise and fall of a forgotten nation. New York: Vintage Books

Kobrin, R. (2006). *The Shtetl by the Highway: The East European City in New York's Landsmanshaft Press, 1921-39.* Prooftexts, 26(1–2), 107–137. https://doi.org/10.2979/pft.2006.26.1-2.107

Wolff, F. (2013). *The Home that Never Was: Rethinking Space and Memory in Late Nineteenth and Twentieth-Century Jewish History.* Historical Social Research / Historische Sozialforschung, 38(3 (145)), 197–215. http://www.jstor.org/stable/23644532

Soyer, D. (1999). *Documenting Immigrant Lives at an Immigrant Institution: Yivo's Autobiography Contest of 1942.* Jewish Social Studies, 5(3), 218–243. http://www.jstor.org/stable/4467560

Soyer, D. (1986). *Between Two Worlds: The Jewish Landsmanshaftn and Questions of Immigrant Identity.* American Jewish History, 76(1), 5–24. http://www.jstor.org/stable/23883236

Moore, D. D., Gurock, J. S., Polland, A., Rock, H. B., Soyer, D., & Linden, D. L. (2017). *Jewish New York: The Remarkable Story of a City and a People.* New York: NYU Press. https://doi.org/10.2307/j.ctt1pwt9bw

Santos, M. (2020) A Natureza do Espaço; Técnica e Tempo, Razão e Emoção. (4th ed.) São Paulo: EDUSP.

Silvain, G. & Minczeles, H. (1999) *Yiddishland.* Corte Madera: Gingko Press.

ROOTEDNESS AND STAYING AMIDST OUT MIGRATION IN RURAL GUATEMALA

Helen Hobson

Introduction

The research study took place in Santa Eulalia, a rural municipality of Huehuetenango, Guatemala. The ongoing violence from capitalist exploitation and military counterinsurgency in the 20th century has pushed many in this region toward international migration. A 2022 study of the region indicates that 80% of families have at least one immediate family member in the United States. Yet even with this strong culture of migration, there are young adults who demonstrate strong aspirations and agency to stay put.

Theoretical Framework

With the focus of my study on those who stay in an area with high levels of outmigration, the aspirations-capabilities theoretical framework is helpful in the way that it allows for complex dynamic interactions of the many factors that affect (im)mobility decisions. The framework goes beyond the individualistic, rational actor model of migration. Because migration and staying occur in diverse contexts, the structures affecting capabilities to migrate can be very distinct. Furthermore, the often-nonlinear nature of the human experience can mean that aspirations and agency to migrate or stay can shift as a result of changes in structures and the surrounding discourse.

Outstanding theoretical questions from literature:

To what extent are migration and staying co-constituted?

What are the retain and repel factors that matter for decisions to stay?

What role do non-economic factors play in decisions to stay?

Conceptualization of Rootedness

Scholars have struggled to conceptualize the attachment that humans have to a place and a community. I argue for a conceptualization of rootedness that comes out of Indigenous and decolonial feminist paradigms which allows for

389

the complex dynamic nature of and meaning attributed to the human experience; these are paradigms that go beyond the dualistic, linear assumptions of Western thinking and scholarship. My work draws on critical new materialism, experiential phenomenology, and Maya ontology that foreground daily lives and experiences, emotions, and bodies as sites for theorizing. For this study, rootedness is: Embodied and emotional connections that humans develop and sustain as part of a becoming self, entangled in relationships with the human and more-than-human worlds.

Research Site and Data Collection

Santa Eulalia is a municipality of 54,000 people and 99% are Maya. The quality-of-life indicators are well below the region and the nation. Participants range in age from 20-40, live in the town center, and do not currently aspire to migrate internationally. Only 3 of the 35 participants did not finish high school, and 50% have some university study. About half have an immediate family member in the United States. Data consists of 35 semi-structured interviews, field notes, analytical memos, and auto-ethnographic journal entries.

Results

Theme 1: Comfort

The interview asks several questions that explore people's ties to the human and more-than-human worlds of Santa Eulalia. The responses demonstrate their deeply embodied and emotional relationships to people, places, practices, objects, and the natural world. I have coded these responses as "Comfort" because it captures how the senses and the emotions together generate rootedness.

Many expressed the safety and security they feel in the community in comparison to other communities and the sense of freedom that gives them in their daily lives. Some also attribute the feeling of freedom to the natural world of their rural municipality. Care and solidarity in their relationships came up very frequently. They describe the daily care they exchange with others in the town. One person shared about the deep family unity that surrounded one of their nine siblings who felt like he needed to migrate to the United States. One woman offered the priest as an example of deep caring and even the patron saint Eulalia as showing caring through miracles.

Comfort is also generated by Maya traditions and practices that are deeply sensory. The melodies and sons of the marimba are present at any life event and are part of the hum of daily life. The visual and tactile features of women's beautiful traditional clothes were praised by both women and men alike as they described the many sensory experiences of religious celebrations. Many shared their love of the corn, beans, squash, and greens that they grow themselves and have prepared for generations.

Talking about the comforts of the natural world and family relationships elicited emotional expressions of beauty, love, and gratitude. Many people shared that the cold, rainy climate feels comfortable and describe their body's adaptation to it. They showed me their photos of the of sunrises and sunsets, rain, clouds, mountains, spider webs, and dew drops on plants. Expressions of gratitude came as they reflected on the role of their loved ones in their feelings of comfort. Many are grateful to the Herculean efforts of their parents and siblings both in Santa Eulalia and in the US for helping to fund their education and also how these loved ones contribute to the economy of Santa Eulalia, allowing them to stay and fight here. Several expressed gratitude and love for their grandparents and ancestors in general for fighting for survival and for preservation of their Maya traditions.

Theme 2: Loss

All that we love will also be lost, so looking at loss can help us understand rootedness. The people I interviewed shared deep losses in a context of high levels of structural violence, dangerous border crossings, and undesired changes in family relationships, as well as perceived loss of Maya culture. During the months I was in Santa Eulalia, death from many causes was very present in people's lives, and the embodied sense of loss it generates was palpable in the mourning and celebration in the cemetery for the Day of the Dead and All Saints' Day.

When asked about the effects of long-term migration on Santa Eulalia, everyone spoke about absence, abandonment, and betrayal as painful sources of loss that they or someone they know has experienced. With a man in the United States, there is the absence of a father figure for children, or an abandonment of the family in Santa Eulalia to feed money to alcohol or other vices, or betrayal by the man who finds another woman and creates a new family.

Another loss centers on the vulnerability of the Maya identity and traditions in the face of transnational influences. Some lament the decreased use of the Maya Q'anjob'al language by the youngest generation, while others criticize the increasingly commercialized and folklorized expressions of Q'anjob'al identity they find inauthentic and superficial. They worry about the survival of Maya cosmology. These losses then contribute to aspirations to stay and to the agency of their ongoing process of becoming and creating a fulfilling life.

Theme 3: Becoming and Agency

All the people I interviewed have the aspiration to stay, so what they shared with me were the motivation, mindset, and passion that underlie their desire for a fulfilling life. Their primary motivations are around their family. Several spoke of how being attentive to their mother or honoring parents who sacrificed for them are guiding their decisions. Those who have children state that they do everything so that their children do not have to struggle in the same way they have. Others shared about family in the United States that they have not seen in person for 20 years who motivate them in part by sharing how hard life is in the there.

A common mindset they shared is related to entrepreneurship and the necessity for risk, investment, sacrifice, hard work, and struggle to achieve success. Curiosity is another mindset that pushes them toward education and exploring opportunities. The passions they shared seem to come from places of loss or rootedness. Several shared what led them to pursue particular careers- the death of someone or the injustice of their own experiences made them want to be a voice for change. Several shared their passion for promoting long term development and prosperity of their community.

Having land and building a house is a fundamental aspiration that is challenging economically without remittances. These individuals demonstrate incredibly high levels of agency in their efforts and struggles to have an economically viable life within structures that constrain their capabilities. Low wages, inflated prices, and government neglect mean that incredible effort is needed in a family to cover basic expenses, especially when there is not help from remittances. Because education options are limited in Santa Eulalia, many left at age 15 to go to the regional capital or to Guatemala City to work and pay for their studies. Others work several jobs in Santa Eulalia to pay for tuition for vocational training in the regional capital on the weekend. Because of poor roads, professionals such as teachers or nurses at times have lived in the communities where they work during the week and go home only on the weekends. Opening small businesses as additional income is very common among most of the people I talked to.

In addition to financial obstacles, many cited the nepotism and need for bribes they face when trying to get a formal job as a professional. Because of an under-resourced health system, illness becomes a huge obstacle and at times generates a shift in aspirations. Living in an area with limited and unreliable infrastructure means that the time necessary for day-to-day activities in a cold, rainy, muddy place becomes an obstacle.

Discussion/Implications

To summarize, what is rootedness for the young adults in this context? I argue that it is embodied relationships with both the human and more-than-human worlds that offer comfort in the continual presence of loss and that guide their aspirations and agency in a non-linear process of becoming. In applying the theoretical framework in the context of my study, talking about staying necessitates talking about migration, so this supports the idea that they co-constitute one another. It is also clear that separating economic from non-economic factors for staying would not be useful because often the non-economic retain factors fuel the efforts needed to sustain an economically viable path without migration.

The March 2025 issue of *Migration and Human Security* is devoted specifically to advocating for the dignity and agency that are implied in the human rights to migrate, return, stay, and to not have to migrate. Citing failures of the "addressing root causes" attempts by Western countries, which try to force staying, approaches foregrounding rootedness are held up as ones that consider a community's own needs and aspirations to stay. My study offers an even more comprehensive approach to rootedness that is important for practitioners and policy makers genuinely interested in listening to communities.

References

Blanco, Juan. 2019. Sobre el pensar intercultural-decolonial: El proyecto intercultural-decolonial del pensamiento maya contemporáneo en Guatemala. Guatemala City: Editorial Maya 'Wuj.

Coole, Diana, and Samantha Frost, eds. 2010. "Introduction." New Materialisms: Ontology, Agency, and Politics. Durham, NC: Duke University Press,

De Haas, Hein. 2014. "Migration Theory: Quo Vadis?" International Migration Institute's Working Paper Series No. 100,

Johnson, Mark. 2007. The Meaning of the Body, Aesthetics of Human Understanding. Chicago: University of Chicago Press.

Kerwin, Donald, Tom Hare, and Maria Estela Rivero Fuentes. 2025. "The Right to Stay, Migrate and Return: Conceptualizing Freedom, Examining Diverse National Contexts and Exploring Policy Implications. Journal of Migration and Security 13(1): 3-29.

Merleau-Ponty, Maurice. 1962 [1945]. Phenomenology of Perception. Routledge.

Saavedra, Cinthya M., and Ellen D. Nymark. 2008. "Borderland-Mestizaje Feminism: The New Tribalism." Handbook of Critical and Indigenous Methodologies 255 .

Schewel, Kerilyn. 2019. "Understanding Immobility: Moving Beyond the Mobility Bias in

Migration Studies." Interna tional Migration Review: 328-355.

Stockdale, Aileen, and Tialda Haartsen. 2018. "Editorial Introduction: Putting Rural Stayers in the Spotlight." Population, Space, Place 24: 1-8.

Wilson, Shawn. Research Is Ceremony: Indigenous Research Methods. Fernwood Publishing, 2020.

MOTHER TONGUE: A SURVEY AMONG CHINESE IMMIGRANTS LIVING IN HUNGARY

Szandra Ésik[1]

Introduction

This study investigates the complex relationship between language use, identity, and integration among Chinese immigrants residing in Hungary, with a particular focus on the concept of mother tongue. The research is motivated by the increasing demographic significance of the Chinese community in Hungary, where preliminary data from the Hungarian Central Statistical Office (2024) reports a population of 21,150 Chinese citizens as of January 1, 2024, surpassing other immigrant groups such as Ukrainians and Germans. The study aims to elucidate how Chinese immigrants relate to their mother tongue within the context of migration, social integration, and identity formation, contributing to broader discussions on multilingualism, language retention, and policy implications in immigrant communities.

The theoretical framework draws upon linguistic and sociocultural theories of language identity, emphasizing the multifaceted and fluid nature of the mother tongue. Traditional definitions, such as Bloomfield's (1933) conception of the mother tongue as the first language learned and the native speaker's competence, are critically examined alongside more nuanced perspectives by Skutnabb-Kangas (1984, 2000) and Rampton (1990). These scholars highlight the emotional, social, and contextual factors influencing language identification, proposing flexible, individual-centered models that accommodate multilingual realities and the dynamic nature of language allegiance and inheritance. The study underscores that the relationship between language and identity is not deterministic but shaped by personal, familial, and societal variables.

Employing a mixed-methods research design, the study integrates quantitative questionnaire data with qualitative interviews to capture a comprehensive picture of language attitudes and practices. Participants include school-age

[1] Dr Szandra Ésik, Assistant Professor, Chinese Department, Eötvös Loránd University, Budapest, Hungary. E-mail: esik.szandra@btk.elte.hu. ORCiD: https://orcid.org/0000-0002-1818-4915

children (grades 5–12) and adults over 18, with profiles reflecting diverse migration backgrounds, including first-generation immigrants, second-generation descendants, and individuals with varying degrees of integration. Data collection commenced in October 2023, with questionnaires comprising closed questions on language use, proficiency, and attitudes, complemented by in-depth telephone interviews totaling 578 minutes of recorded material. The questionnaires were completed by 28 students and 87 adults, with responses in Chinese, Hungarian, or both, revealing patterns of language interchangeability and preference. The interviews provided contextual insights into individual language histories, identity perceptions, and community practices, illustrating the complex interplay between external circumstances and internal identity processes.

Quantitative findings reveal that most school-age respondents (16 out of 28) and a significant proportion of adults identify Chinese as their mother tongue, although many report stronger proficiency or more frequent use of Hungarian. Notably, some children born in Hungary or who have never lived in China still consider Chinese their mother tongue, often linked to family heritage and cultural identity. Conversely, a subset of respondents, despite long residence or birth in Hungary, identify Hungarian or bilingual identities, emphasizing the emotional and social dimensions of language affiliation. The self-assessment of language skills indicates variability, with some children rating their Chinese proficiency as low due to difficulties in writing Chinese characters or limited exposure, yet still maintaining a strong cultural connection. The intrinsic motivation to learn Chinese persists across age groups, driven by familial ties and cultural identity, despite external challenges such as community insularity and language attrition.

Qualitative data deepen understanding of these patterns, illustrating how community practices, social networks, and institutional support influence language maintenance. Participants describe a predominantly closed Chinese community in Budapest, where social interactions, religious activities, media consumption, and education reinforce Chinese language use. Private schools and community organizations employ native teachers and Chinese curricula, fostering language retention but also contributing to a degree of linguistic insularity. Interviewees express a sense of cultural pride and identity rooted in family and heritage, with some perceiving physical traits and appearance as markers of Chinese identity, which can influence language attitudes and integration experiences. The narratives reveal that language use is often context-dependent, with code-switching and language mixing common in informal settings, reflecting the fluidity of bilingual identities.

The study also explores the variability in the concept of mother tongue among participants, referencing Skutnabb-Kangas' (2000) and Rampton's (1990) models. Many respondents emphasize emotional and social factors over purely linguistic competence, supporting a flexible, individual-centered understanding of mother tongue. For instance, some respondents who have acquired Hungarian proficiency at a high level still consider Chinese their mother tongue due to familial and cultural ties. Conversely, others with limited Chinese skills maintain a strong cultural identity linked to Chinese heritage. The findings suggest that the traditional, static definitions of mother tongue are inadequate for capturing the lived realities of immigrant communities, where language and identity are intertwined in complex, evolving ways.

The implications of these findings are multifaceted. For language maintenance, the data underscore the importance of community institutions, family practices, and media in sustaining heritage languages. Educational policies should recognize the diversity of language backgrounds and support bilingual education and cultural programs that foster both linguistic proficiency and cultural identity. From an integration perspective, the research highlights that language is a key marker of identity but not a sole determinant of social inclusion; community insularity and physical traits also play significant roles. Policymakers should consider promoting intercultural dialogue and language learning initiatives that bridge community boundaries and facilitate integration.

Limitations of the study include its relatively small sample size and geographic concentration in Budapest, which may limit generalizability. The reliance on self-reported data introduces potential biases, and the cross-sectional design precludes tracking changes over time. Future research should adopt longitudinal approaches to monitor shifts in language attitudes and identity, especially among second-generation immigrants and children of mixed marriages. Further studies could also explore the impact of language policies, media influence, and educational practices on heritage language maintenance and identity construction.

In conclusion, this research affirms that the concept of mother tongue among Chinese immigrants in Hungary is highly individualized, shaped by emotional, social, and contextual factors. While traditional linguistic definitions provide a foundation, they must be complemented by flexible, socioculturally informed models that acknowledge the fluidity of language and identity. The findings contribute valuable insights into the dynamics of language maintenance, cultural identity, and integration in immigrant communities, offering implications for policy, education, and community development aimed at fostering multilingualism and social cohesion in diverse societies.

References

Bloomfield, L. (1933): *Language*. London: Allen & Unwin: 43.

Rampton, B. (1990). „Displacing the 'native speaker': expertise, affiliation and inheritance," IN: *ELTE Journal Volume 44/2*: 97–101.

Skutnabb-Kangas, T. (1984). *Bilingualism or Not. The Education of Minorities*. Clevedon: Multilingual Matters Ltd.

Skutnabb-Kangas, T. & Dunbar, R. (2000). *Indigenous Children's Education as Linguistic Genocide and a Crime Against Humanity?* A Global View. Gáldu: Resource Centre for the Rights of Indigenous Peoples

SMALL STATE RESPONSE TO MIGRATION TRANSFORMATION: BALTIC REGIONAL EXPERIENCE

Santa Barone-Upeniece[1]

Introduction

Migration policy formation is a complex process influenced by both internal structural factors and external institutional pressures (Castles, 2004). The Baltic states, which are recognized in academic literature as small states according to population size, territory and economic influence (Lamoreaux & Galbreath, 2008), represent a unique case study in small state migration governance, where post-socialist transformation, EU integration and geographical position create specific challenges. This study analyses the period from 2016 to 2023, when structural changes in migration patterns occurred in the Baltic states. While Lithuania experienced a dramatic transition from negative to positive migration balance, Estonia maintained a consistent positive balance, and Latvia demonstrated fluctuating trends with persistent challenges, which overall indicates the evolving role of these countries in European migration dynamics.

The significance of this research extends beyond regional analysis. As the European Union faces demographic challenges and labour shortages, understanding how small states transform from emigration to immigration destinations provides valuable insights for policy development. The Baltics case is particularly relevant as these countries share similar historical experiences of Soviet occupation, EU accession in 2004, and significant emigration following the 2008 financial crisis, yet have developed varying migration trajectories in recent years.

Theoretical Framework

In theoretical literature, small state migration governance is conceptualized as seeking balance between national sovereignty and international obligations (Lindberg & Borrelli, 2019). This balance becomes particularly complex in the context of EU membership, where freedom of movement principles intersects

[1] Santa Barone-Upeniece, University of Latvia, Latvia

with national migration policies and security concerns.

Castles (2004) points out that migration policy formation is often influenced by two false assumptions: the economic belief that people migrate only for income maximization purposes, and the bureaucratic belief that regulations can effectively regulate migration flows. Together, these assumptions create the illusion that migration can be "turned on and off like a tap" (Castles, 2004). This framework is particularly relevant for understanding Baltic states' policy responses, as they have attempted to manage both emigration of their citizens and immigration of third-country nationals through various regulatory mechanisms.

Lee's (1966) push-pull theory provides an analytical framework for understanding migration factors, identifying four migration-determining factors: push factors at the place of origin, pull factors at the destination, intermediate obstacles, and personal factors. In the Baltic context, this framework allows analysis of the structural transformation from emigration (dominated by push factors) to immigration (dominated by pull factors) models. Recent scholarship by Hazans (2016) examining Baltic migration in the context of economic crisis and Vorotnikov & Habarta (2021) analysing post-Soviet migration patterns to the Baltic States provides empirical evidence for applying these theoretical frameworks to the region.

Methodology

This study employs a mixed-methods approach combining quantitative data analysis with policy document review. The quantitative analysis is based on migration statistics from 2016-2023, using data from:

- Eurostat population and migration databases;

- National statistical offices (Central Statistical Bureau of Latvia, Statistics Lithuania, Statistics Estonia);

- OECD International Migration Outlook reports (2023, 2024);

- National migration departments' annual reports.

The comparative analysis framework examines all three Baltic states as similar cases with variations, allowing for identification of both common patterns and country-specific factors. Key indicators analysed include:

- Net migration rates per 1,000 inhabitants;

- Migration origin structures and diversification indices;

- Return migration proportions;

- Integration policy measures and their outcomes.

Data limitations include methodological changes in Latvia's population counting system in 2023 and varying definitions of return migration across countries. Where such limitations exist, they are explicitly noted in the analysis.

Migration Transformation: Empirical Analysis

Overall Migration Balance Dynamics

Empirical data reveals structural changes in migration patterns across all three Baltic states during the period from 2016 to 2023. The transformation demonstrates varying speeds and trajectories of change, reflecting different policy approaches and structural conditions.

Table 1. Net international migration indicators of the Baltic states (per 1000 inhabitants), 2016-2023

Year/ Country	Latvia	Lithuania	Estonia
2016	-6,2	-8,7	0,8
2017	-4,0	-7,3	4,0
2018	-2,5	-0,4	5,3
2019	-1,8	3,9	4,1
2020	-1,7	7,4	2,8
2021	-0,2	7,0	5,3
2022	11,7	25,5	29,5
2023	-1,7	15,7	10,1

Source: Eurostat, 2025. Population change - crude rates of total change, natural change and net migration plus adjustment

Latvia demonstrates the most volatile migration dynamics among the three states. The country experienced prolonged negative migration balance from 2016-2020, with gradual improvement from -6.2 to -1.7 per 1000 inhabitants. The near-zero balance in 2021 (-0.2) suggested potential transformation, but this proved temporary. The spike in 2022 (11.7), was primarily driven by Ukrainian refugee arrivals rather than structural change, as evidenced by the return to negative balance in 2023 (-1.7).

The 2023 figures require particular attention: initial calculations showed positive migration (1.3), but were revised to negative (-1.7) following the implementation of a new population estimation methodology by the Central Statistical Bureau. This methodological change created a break in the time series, with 2022 data remaining uncalculated under the new method, making direct year-to-year comparisons problematic.[2] Despite this methodological limitation, the revision from positive to negative suggests that Latvia's actual migration situation may be less favourable than initially assessed.

Lithuania achieved the most remarkable transformation, shifting from the worst position among Baltic states in 2016 (-8.7) to regional leadership in attracting immigration. The turning point occurred in 2019 when migration balance became positive (3.9), followed by sustained growth reaching 25.5 in 2022 and maintaining strong positive levels (15.7) in 2023. While this transformation suggests comprehensive policy reforms in migration management and integration support, specific measures and their implementation details would require further investigation. The documented evidence includes Lithuania's flexible approach to Ukrainian refugee employment, where mandatory language requirements were removed for several occupations (OECD, 2023, p.101), and the achievement of a 66% employment rate among Ukrainian refugees (OECD, 2024, p.58), the highest in the Baltic region.

Estonia maintained the most stable positive trajectory throughout the period, never recording negative migration balance. Starting from modest positive levels (0.8 in 2016), Estonia showed consistent growth pattern (4.0-5.3 range during 2017-2021), with exceptional increase in 2022 (29.5) due to Ukrainian refugees, before stabilizing at sustainable levels (10.1) in 2023. This stability reflects Estonia's early adoption of digital governance systems facilitating immigration procedures and consistent economic growth providing employment opportunities.

Structural Factors Behind Varying Trajectories

The varying migration trajectories may reflect underlying structural differences, though comprehensive comparative data on economic indicators requires additional research. Available evidence suggests varying policy approaches and

---

[2] CSB of the Republic of Latvia (CSB). IBE010. Long-term international migration by country group 1990 - 2024. Note: The population count for early 2023 and 2024 was recalculated using a new population estimation methodology. This affects the volume of migration flows and results in a methodological break in the time series. The 2022 migration data have not been recalculated, therefore they are not fully comparable with the population count at the beginning of 2023

implementation capacities across the three states.

What is documented is the differential integration success of Ukrainian refugees, which may serve as an indicator of broader integration capacity: Lithuania achieved a 66% employment rate, Estonia 54%, and Latvia 30% (OECD, 2024, p.58). These differences suggest varying institutional capacities and policy approaches, with Lithuania removing language requirements for certain occupations (OECD, 2023, p.101), though systematic comparison of broader economic and labour market indicators would strengthen this analysis.

Migration Flow Diversification and Origin Structure

The transformation from emigration to immigration destinations has been accompanied by fundamental changes in migration composition.

Latvia: From Regional to Global

Latvia's immigration increased from 8,345 (2016) to 18,710 (2023) (CSB, 2025), a 124% increase. The most dramatic change is the surge in Asian migration, particularly from India (1,241 immigrants in 2023, compared to 114 in 2016) and Central Asian countries (951 from Uzbekistan, Tajikistan, and Kyrgyzstan combined). This represents a notable shift from post-Soviet to more diversified migration patterns. Return migration remains significant at 38% (7,190 persons), while ethnic diversity increased from 30 to 59 registered ethnicities (CSB, 2025).

Lithuania: Structural Reorientation

Lithuania's transformation is most pronounced: total immigration increased from 31,395 (2016) to 66,920 (2023). The composition significantly changed from 80% return migration in 2016 to 75% foreign immigration in 2023. Central Asian countries became the dominant source with 10,874 immigrants, followed by Belarus (15,675) and Ukraine (10,539) (2023 Migration Yearbook, p.17). This shift reflects deliberate policy reorientation from diaspora return to international labour recruitment.

Estonia: European Integration Model

Estonia maintains consistent positive migration balance throughout the analysed period. Total immigration grew from 14,822 (2016) to 26,414 (2023). The 2023 structure showed Ukraine (13,082), returned Estonians (5,758), and EU citizens (2,983) as main components (Statistics Estonia, 2025). The relatively high proportion of EU citizens in the migration flow (approximately 11%) distinguishes Estonia's pattern, though further research would be needed to determine whether this reflects deliberate policy choices or other factors.

Estonia achieved a 54% employment rate among Ukrainian refugees in 2023, with concentration in processing industry, administrative and support services, and wholesale and retail trade (OECD, 2024, p.58).

Policy Responses and Governance Challenges

The Baltic states have undertaken various reforms in migration management, though comprehensive documentation of specific measures requires further research.

Documented reforms include:

Latvia began modernizing its Unified Migration Information System in 2023, introducing e-services for residence permits (OECD, 2024, p.93).

Lithuania demonstrated flexibility in integration approaches, exempting Ukrainian refugees from mandatory language requirements for certain occupations (OECD, 2023, p.93).

Following Russia's invasion of Ukraine in 2022, all three Baltic states implemented coordinated restrictive measures. Estonia, Latvia, and Lithuania jointly banned entry for Russian citizens holding Schengen short-stay visas for non-essential purposes, with exceptions for humanitarian cases. Additionally, Estonia and Latvia enacted legislation allowing citizenship revocation from naturalized citizens who threaten national security (OECD, 2023, p.98, 226, 245).

While these examples suggest broader reform efforts across all three countries, systematic documentation of legislative and administrative changes, their implementation timelines, and effectiveness would strengthen the analysis. The varying employment rates of Ukrainian refugees (30% in Latvia, 54% in Estonia, 66% in Lithuania) suggest possible differences in administrative capacity and policy implementation, though establishing direct causal links would require further investigation.

Conclusions

This analysis of Baltic migration patterns (2016-2023) reveals varying speeds of transformation toward positive migration balance, with all three states showing transformation trends, though at different paces and with varying sustainability. Lithuania transformed from the highest emigration rate (-8.7 per 1000 in 2016) to sustained positive migration (15.7 in 2023), while Estonia maintained consistent positive balance throughout the period. Latvia's fluctuating pattern, including methodological revision of 2023 data from positive to negative, suggests persistent structural challenges.[3]

The differential integration of Ukrainian refugees - employment rates of 66% in Lithuania, 54% in Estonia, and 30% in Latvia (OECD, 2024 p.58) - suggests possible differences in institutional approaches, though establishing causal relationships would require comprehensive policy analysis and consideration of labour market structures. Lithuania's removal of language requirements for certain occupations (OECD, 2023, p.101) exemplifies policy flexibility that may contribute to integration success.

Migration composition shows notable changes. Lithuania's shift from 80% return migration (2016) to 75% foreign immigration (2023), with increased Central Asian immigration (2023 Migration Yearbook, p.16-17), suggests an evolving migration pattern, though longer-term data would be needed to confirm whether this represents permanent structural change. Latvia shows increasing diversification with immigrants from 59 ethnicities by 2023 (CSB, 2025), while Estonia maintains significant EU citizen presence (Statistics Estonia, 2025).

These preliminary findings suggest that small states may transform at different speeds, as indicated by Lithuania's trajectory. Latvia's experience particularly demonstrates that transformation is not inevitable even under similar external pressures, **raising questions about whether** these represent genuinely different models or temporary variations in similar transformation processes

The study identifies several areas requiring further research: most urgently, systematic documentation of specific migration policies and their implementation across all three states, the relationship between specific policies and outcomes, long-term integration trajectories, and the impact of geopolitical factors evidenced by coordinated restrictions on Russian and Belarusian nationals (OECD, 2023, p.98, 226, 245). Methodological challenges in migration measurement, highlighted by Latvia's data revision, suggest caution in cross-country comparisons.

---

[3] CSB of the Republic of Latvia. IBE010. Long-term international migration by country group 1990 - 2024. Note: The population count for early 2023 and 2024 was recalculated using a new population estimation methodology. This affects the volume of migration flows and results in a methodological break in the time series. The 2022 migration data have not been recalculated, therefore they are not fully comparable with the population count at the beginning of 2023

The Baltic experience 2016-2023 provides initial evidence of evolving migration patterns, though available data limitations - particularly regarding specific policy measures and their implementation - mean this study should be considered a preliminary mapping rather than definitive causal analysis. While variations in outcomes suggest possible differences in policy approaches and implementation capacity, systematic comparative policy research would be necessary to establish whether these represent fundamentally different transformation models or temporary differences in timing and pace of similar processes.

References

Castles, S. (2004). The Factors that Make and Unmake Migration Policies1. *International Migration Review*, *38*(3), 852-884. https://doi.org/10.1111/j.1747-7379.2004.tb00222.x

Hazans, M. (2016). Migration experience of the Baltic countries in the context of economic crisis. In Labor Migration, EU Enlargement, and the Great Recession. DOI: 10.1007/978-3-662-45320-9_13

Lamoreaux, J. W., Galbreath, D. J. (2008). The Baltic States As 'Small States': Negotiating The 'East' By Engaging The 'West.' *Journal of Baltic Studies*, *39*(1), 1–14. https://doi.org/10.1080/01629770801908697

Lee, E. S. (1966). A Theory of Migration.

Lindberg, A., Borrelli, L. M. (2019). All quiet on the 'Eastern front'? Controlling transit migration in Latvia and Lithuania. *Journal of Ethnic and Migration Studies*, *47*(1), 307–323. https://doi.org/10.1080/1369183X.2019.1575719

Vorotnkov, V., Habarta, A. (2021). Migration from post-Soviet countries to Poland and the Baltic States: Trends and features. Baltic Region, 13(4), 79-94. https://doi.org/10.5922/2079-8555-2021-4-5

OECD (2023), *International Migration Outlook 2023*, OECD Publishing, Paris. https://doi.org/10.1787/b0f40584-en.

OECD (2024), *International Migration Outlook 2024*, OECD Publishing, Paris. https://doi.org/10.1787/50b0353e-en

CSB of the Republic of Latvia, 2025; International long-term migrants by citizenship, IBE060.

CSB of the Republic of Latvia, 2025; Long-term international migration by ethnicity 2011 – 2024, IBE040.

Migration Department under the Ministry of the Interior of the Republic of Lithuania. (2024). 2023 Migration Yearbook.

Statistics Estonia: Official Statistics Portal, 2025; RVR08: External migration by age group, sex and citizenship.

POLITICAL DISSENT AND MIGRATION: THE MONTENEGRIN EXPERIENCE IN COMMUNIST YUGOSLAVIA

Jelisaveta Blagojević

Introduction

Aims and Context

The study of political emigration from the Socialist Republic of Montenegro (SR Montenegro)[1], one of the six constituent republics of the Socialist Federal Republic of Yugoslavia (SFRY), offers a revealing insight into the complex intersections of ideology, state repression, and Cold War geopolitics. In the aftermath of the Second World War, Yugoslavia emerged under the one-party rule of the League of Communists of Yugoslavia (LCY), led by Josip Broz Tito. Within Montenegro, the League of Communists of Montenegro (LCM) assumed a decisive role in political, economic, and social life.

This paper seeks to examine the causes, dynamics, and consequences of political emigration from Montenegro during the communist period, with particular attention to the years following the Tito–Stalin split of 1948 and the subsequent Inform-Bureau crisis[2]. Montenegro's experience was shaped by its unique socio-economic conditions, its historical relationship with Russia, and the disproportionate presence of pro- Inform-Bureau sentiment in its population. This combination created both an unusually high incidence of political persecution and a notable pattern of exile.

Historical Background and the Inform-Bureau Crisis

In 1945, Yugoslavia stood among the victorious states of the anti-fascist coalition. Its leadership had relied heavily on Soviet military and political

---

[1] At the Fourth Session of the Montenegrin Anti-Fascist Assembly of National Liberation (CASNO) in Cetinje, held from 15 to 17 April 1945, the Federal State of Montenegro was established as part of the Democratic Federal Yugoslavia (DFY). With the adoption of its first constitution on 31 December 1946, it was renamed the People's Republic of Montenegro, and in April 1963—along with all other Yugoslav republics—it was re-designated as a "socialist republic."

[2] Inform-Bureau - Informational Bureau of Communist and Workers' Parties.

support during the war, and the Soviet model loomed large as a blueprint for postwar reconstruction. Montenegro, heavily devastated by wartime destruction, was one of Yugoslavia's poorest regions — with a shattered economy, widespread illiteracy, and a small population.[3]

These conditions fostered an almost complete political reliance on the Communist Party, seen as the only vehicle for national recovery. Montenegro became the Yugoslav republic with the highest party membership, with Montenegrins believing they were building "a new society free from exploitation".[4] The Soviet Union, as the "Slavic motherland" and historic protector against Ottoman rule, occupied a revered place in Montenegrin political imagination. Stalin himself was regarded as an ideological and moral authority, and the 1945 Treaty of Friendship, Cooperation, and Mutual Assistance between the USSR and Yugoslavia seemed to confirm a permanent strategic alliance.[5]

The shock of 1948, when relations between Belgrade and Moscow collapsed over questions of foreign policy, economic planning, and interpretations of socialist orthodoxy, was therefore especially profound in Montenegro. The Cominform Resolution of 28 June 1948 accused the leaders of the Communist Party of Yugoslavia of "embarking on a path of secession from the unified socialist front against imperialism, betraying the cause of the international solidarity of the working people, and shifting to positions of nationalism."[6]

Montenegrin communists, more than those in most other republics, openly sympathized with the Soviet position. This reflected not only deep-seated Russophilia but also skepticism toward Yugoslavia's economic capacity without Soviet aid.[7] Many viewed the Soviet Union as infallible in matters of socialist construction. Consequently, when the LCY rejected the Cominform's demands at its Fifth Congress (July 1948) ističući da je kritika CK SKP „netačna, nepravilna i nepravedna"[8], a significant portion of Montenegro's party membership and broader public opposed the official line.

---

[3] Kovačević, 1998a, p. 127.
[4] Ibid, p. 128.
[5] Ibid, pp. 127-130.
[6] Rezolucija Informacionog biroa komunističkih partija o stanju u Komunističkoj partiji Jugoslavije (Bukurešst, 28 jun 1948) u >1948< *Jugoslavija i Kominform – pedeset godina kasnije*, Beograd: Fakultet političkih nauka, Pravni fakultet, Arhiv Jugoslavije, Službeni list SRJ, Međunarodna politika, Podgorica: Istorijski institut Crne Gore, p. 294.
[7] Kovačević, pp. 131-132.
[8] Kovačević, 1998b, p. 58

The regime responded forcefully. Four of the nine members of the Provincial Committee of the LCY for Montenegro — Božo Ljumović, Vuko Tmušić, Niko Pavić, and Radivoje Vukićević — were removed for "undermining party unity".[9] Surveillance intensified to unprecedented levels: UDB-a (the State Security Service) operated an all-encompassing system of political policing, interrogating every party member and treating all social contacts as potentially subversive.

Traditional Montenegrin kinship and moral codes — based on clan solidarity, hospitality, and personal honor — eroded under the weight of suspicion. By the end of 1948, 93 party members had been expelled in Montenegro for pro-Inform-Bureau positions; 53 of them were arrested, alongside 20 non-party citizens. Even minor gestures or private remarks could be construed as anti-state activity.[10]

Example of the Party's Records on Expelled Members, Provincial Committee of the Communist Party of Yugoslavia for Montenegro, box no. 15, 1948.

Escalation of Repression and Emigration

In 1949, repression in Montenegro deepened significantly. Nearly half of the arrests (47%) carried out by the UDB that year were later judged unjustified by

---

[9] Kovačević, 1998a, p. 133.
[10] Ibid, 135.

federal prosecutors. Blažo Jovanović, Montenegro's foremost political figure—himself under constant security surveillance—publicly condemned the harassment of prisoners' families.[11] Despite his warnings, such appeals had little practical effect. Torture became a routine investigative method, with detainees forced to confess to both genuine and fabricated crimes. The death toll in Montenegrin prisons and camps reached 63 during this period.[12] Notably, Montenegro had the highest per capita proportion of Inform-Bureau supporters in Yugoslavia, accounting for 1.06% of its population.[13]

Yugoslavia, including Montenegro was under a police state marked by pervasive surveillance and mutual distrust.[14] Faced with systematic harassment, arrests, and social ostracism, many dissenters sought to escape Yugoslavia/Montenegro. The primary immediate refuge was Albania, then ruled by Enver Hoxha, a staunch Stalinist whose regime maintained close ties with Moscow. For Montenegrin Inform-Bureau loyalists, Albania was a vital transit point in the hope of eventually relocating to the Soviet Union. Propaganda from across the Albanian border—including smuggled editions of the newspaper *Nova borba*—helped sustain anti-Titoist morale.[15] Armed groups infiltrated Montenegro from Albania, prompting increased border security and further arrests. Many escape attempts failed tragically; for example, in January 1949, the entire District Committee Bureau of Bijelo Polje, led by Ilija Bulatović, was killed within two weeks of attempting to cross into Albania.[16] By 1957, a total of 403 individuals had defected from Montenegro: 321 to Albania, 63 to the Soviet Union, and 19 to other Eastern Bloc countries.[17]

At the broader Yugoslav level, a total of 16,288 people were arrested and punished, over 308,000 were expelled from the Party between 1948 and 1955, and 4,928 found themselves in emigration in socialist countries during and after the conflict.[18]

Many were already abroad—serving as diplomats, students, or workers in socialist countries—and simply refused to return. A substantial share of the

[11] Ibid, 143.
[12] Ibid, 141.
[13] Ibid, 140.
[14] Kovačević, 1998b, p. 63.
[15] Kovačević, 1998a, p. 138.
[16] Ibid, 136.
[17] Report of the Central Committee on Emigrants, State Archive of Montenegro, fonds *Central Committee of the League of Communists of Montenegro*, box no. 118, 1957.
[18] Crtice iz historije. (2019, December 14). *Politička emigracija nakon Rezolucije Informbiroa*. historija.info. https://historija.info/politicka-emigracija-nakon-rezolucije-informbiroa/

émigrés belonged to national minorities such as Russians, Czechs, Hungarians, and Bulgarians, who often felt particularly vulnerable to political persecution.[19] Most sought refuge in neighboring socialist states, with Bulgaria and Albania absorbing the largest numbers, due to pre-1948 political ties and hopes for a swift political reversal in Belgrade. Hungary, Romania, and the USSR also hosted significant Yugoslav émigré communities. In the Soviet Union alone, 718 Yugoslav citizens—mostly students or military trainees—chose to remain after 1948.[20]

This Yugoslav political emigration, largely composed of individuals who had been abroad at the time of the Tito-Stalin split, expressed vigorous resistance and opposition to Tito's regime. They formed the *League of Yugoslav Patriots for the Liberation of the Peoples of Yugoslavia from the Yoke of the Tito-Ranković Clique and Imperialist Slavery*, which published periodicals such as *For a Socialist Yugoslavia* and *Our Struggle*.[21] The Union was led by notable Montenegrins including General Pero Popivoda and Radonja Golubović, a former Yugoslav ambassador to Romania. Meanwhile, Inform-Bureau émigrés in Prague were represented by figures like Pero Ivanović, former President of the Supreme Court of Montenegro.[22]

Return under Watch: The Post-Stalin Era of Yugoslav Emigration

Stalin's death in 1953 and Khrushchev's subsequent policy shifts led to a thaw in Yugoslav–Soviet relations. The 1955 Belgrade Declaration signalled normalization, encouraging some émigrés to return.[23] By 1957, 1,026 individuals had returned.[24] In Montenegro, of the 403 defectors, 101 returned (mainly from Albania), 14 died in emigration, and 288 remained abroad as of 1957.[25]

However, the détente was fragile. The 1956 Hungarian uprising, Belgrade's refusal to sign the 1957 Declaration of Twelve Communist Parties, and the adoption of a new LCY program in 1958 reignited ideological tensions.[26] Dogmatic socialist states — notably Albania and China — resumed anti-Yugoslav campaigns, prompting a partial re-mobilization of Inform-Bureau

---

[19] Previšić, 2012, p. 173.

[20] Ibid, p. 176.

[21] Luburić, 1997, pp.6-8.

[22] CANU: Crnogorska akademija nauka i umjetnosti, Crnogorska politička emigracija (1918–1991), In *Leksikon diplomatije Crne Gore*. Retrieved August 12, 2025, from https://leks.canu.ac.me/web/ldcg.php?OID=2506

[23] Kovačević, 1998a, p. 144.

[24] Crtice iz historije. (2019, December 14)

[25] Report of the Central Committee on Emigrants, State Archive of Montenegro, fonds *Central Committee of the League of Communists of Montenegro*, box no. 118, 1957.

[26] Previšić, 2012, p. 180.

émigrés.

With the adoption of the Amnesty Law in 1962, tensions eased; travel restrictions were loosened, some emigrants were issued permanent passports, and family visits within the socialist bloc were permitted. The number of émigrés under criminal prosecution fell from 1,157 in 1958 to 151 by 1964, with prosecutions focusing primarily on those involved in violent or espionage activities.[27]

Nevertheless, repatriates were never fully trusted. Security services monitored them closely, recording political opinions and associations. While many adapted to civilian life and achieved material stability, none regained political influence. Inform-Bureau loyalty remained the single most disqualifying political stigma in socialist Yugoslavia.

Conclusion

Montenegro's unusually high rate of Inform-Bureau support and emigration reflected a convergence of historical sentiment, economic vulnerability, and political culture. The deep-rooted affection for Russia, shaped by wartime alliance and postwar dependence, made the Soviet ideological model especially persuasive. Consequently, the abrupt rupture with Moscow was perceived not merely as a foreign policy shift but as a betrayal of foundational revolutionary principles.

Repression in Montenegro was intensified by the republic's small size and close-knit communities, where surveillance and denunciation permeated all social layers. The erosion of clan solidarity under political loyalty pressures left lasting scars on local society. Thus, for Montenegrin society, the Inform-Bureau episode marked a fracture in both political culture and collective identity. The interplay of state coercion, community divisions, and exile fostered a legacy of mistrust toward political authority and complicated Montenegro's relationship with the broader Yugoslav project.

Understanding this history enriches comparative studies of political migration, authoritarian governance, and post-conflict reconciliation. It also underscores the necessity of acknowledging and integrating the experiences of political exiles into the national historical narrative—not as marginal episodes, but as central to the story of twentieth-century Montenegro.

---

[27] Ibid, p. 181.

References

CANU: Crnogorska akademija nauka i umjetnosti. *Crnogorska politička emigracija (1918–1991)*. In *Leksikon diplomatije Crne Gore*. Retrieved August 12, 2025, from https://leks.canu.ac.me/web/ldcg.php?OID=2506

Crtice iz historije. (2019, December 14). Politička emigracija nakon Rezolucije Informbiroa. *historija.info*. https://historija.info/politicka-emigracija-nakon-rezolucije-informbiroa/

Kovačević, B. (1998). "O Informbirou u Crnoj Gori" u *1948 Jugoslavija i Kominform – pedeset godina kasnije*, Beograd: Fakultet političkih nauka, Pravni fakultet, Arhiv Jugoslavije, Službeni list SRJ, Međunarodna politika, Podgorica: Istorijski institut Crne Gore.

Kovačević, B. (1998b). "Informbiro i Crna Gora" u Lakić, Z. (Ed.). *Goli otok, 1949–1956: radovi sa okruglog stola, Podgorica, 27. juna 1995*. Podgorica: Crnogorska akademija nauka i umjetnosti.

Luburić, R. (1997). Jugoslovenska informbiroovska emigracija: između iluzija i stvarnosti (1948–1953). *Istorijski zapisi*, 1, 1–26. Retrieved from https://istorijskizapisi.me/wp-content/uploads/2021/05/LUBURIC-Jugoslovenska-informirovska-emigracija.pdf

Party's Records on Expelled Members, Provincial Committee of the Communist Party of Yugoslavia for Montenegro, box no. 15, 1948.

Previšić, M. (2012). Informbiroovska emigracija. *Historijski zbornik*, 65(1), 171–186. https://hrcak.srce.hr/117735

Report of the Central Committee on Emigrants, State Archive of Montenegro, fonds Central Committee of the League of Communists of Montenegro, box no. 118, 1957.

THIS IS WHY WE STAY

Andres Hijar[1]

This study will focus on the reasons two long-standing ethnic communities in Mexico do not migrate to the United States. The Zoques in Tuxtla, Gutierrez, Chiapas, and Raramuri, also known as Tarahumaras in Ciudad Juárez, Chihuahua. As Augustin Hernandez, a Zoque drummer answered when confronted by the question of why he stayed in poverty-stricken Chiapas, "no, for what. We have everything here. *La fiesta, la musica, la comida.*" [2] Likewise, Teresa Villalobos, a Raramuri in charge of the Center for Gender Violence by the state government as well as an official interpreter related. "Yes, it is true. I only knew of one, but he came back, no families migrate, they stay in Mexico. I travel all over the Sierra conducting workshops, I have for 25 years, and no we do not go to the United States." [3]

I will show that the reasons why individuals from these groups do not migrate to the United States as communities, as their fellow ethnic counterparts in Mexico have for decades, stems from these groups ability to enact local political and economic control. For decades, the struggle for local space has provided them with a sense of community, which has permitted them to exercise political and religious power. In their minds, they will never possess that type of power in the United States. As Serafina, a Raramuri living in Juárez said to me, "my husband told me to come to Juárez, there is land for us there and we can continue to speak Raramuri and continue la fiesta as well."[4]

The Zoques urban presence in Tuxtla performing their celebrations, combining Christianity with long time pagan rituals goes back to colonial times, despite the animosity and occasional hostility from ecclesiastical authorities.[5]

---

[1] Dr. Andres Hijar, assistant professor of history at Georgia Gwinnett College, United States.
[2] Interview with Agustin Hernandez, Zoque drummer, June 2019.
[3] Interview with Teresa Villalobos, March 2021
[4] Interviews with Serafina Gloria Gonzales, March 2021 and Interview with Maria Dolores Gonzalez, April 2021
[5] Dolores Aramoni, *Los refugios de los sagrado: religiosidad, conflict y Resistencia entre los zoques de Chiapas* (Mexico: CONACULTA, 1992).

For example, an incident in 2004 illustrates an often-adversarial relationship between the Zoque and the Catholic Church in Tuxtla. "In Tuxtla, they stole our Virgin del Rosario in 2006. We celebrated in the 16th century. They argue we are doing terrible things, but what they really wanted was the money from the celebrations, so they wanted to control it. This caused pain for the mayordomia" 6 according to an interview with Sergio de la Cruz. Clearly, Zoques and church officials had power struggles over money and space. Moreover, the Zoque consider the images they venerate as actual living beings, resting in those physical places. Again, space surfaces as a crucial factor in the Zoque's sense of power, as Vázquez said when asked whether Zoques in Tuxtla asked the church for permission to take over the church. "No, we do not. We just go to church; there are too many of us."7

In Juárez, Raramuri have a space reserved only for those identified as Raramuri located in the *colonia* Plutarco Elias Calles in the periphery of the city. "It was founded in 1987 by a Raramuri from Chihuahua. He led to the demand that the land was only Raramuri, but I do not remember his name. Later there was Chencho de Rocheache; He led, and we had the land so that it would stay Raramuri." 8 As in Chiapas, power struggles over political and economic issues drove Raramuris into conflicts with the church. At first, the Catholic Church had a space within the *colonia,* "particularly two Franciscans, nuns too, but this was brief. It did not go well."9

Raramuri in the *colonia* elect their authorities as, "there is a president and two governors. The governor is the one that talks with the authorities. We have a meeting every fifteen days. The president gives land to the people, but there is none left. Our meetings are independent of government representatives. Now, we have *chabochis* there, the dance is not the same though. If a Raramuri falls in love with a *chabochi*, they must pay rent."10

Raramuri vote by raising their hand and usually elect the one that is "studied." 11 Young people do not participate. There is a fifty peso fine for missing any meetings and three hundred pesos for not participating in communal work. The allocated money "goes to many places including the kitchen."12 Thus, the

---

6 Interview with Sergio de la Cruz Vazquez
7 Ibid
8 Interview with Don Indalecio Castillo
9 Ibid
10 Ibid
11 Ibid
12 Ibid

Raramuri in Juárez have acquired independent urban physical spaces in which the continuation of their cultures as they understand it takes place independent from authorities and the church.

The Zoque have also taken over various parts of Tuxtla going back to colonial times.[13] The Zoque in Tuxtla go back to the pre-classic era (2500 BCE to 200 BCE) as supported by linguistic and archaeological evidence that shows communities belonging to the Mixe-Zoque-Popoluca made their way from the Pacific to the gulf. Thus, the Zoque inhabited a valley located between the hills and mountains surrounding El Canon del Sumidero. They called this valley Coyatocmo or "place where bunnies abound."

The introduction of Catholicism developed one of the most important rituals in Zoque culture today, the *Meque*, or *fiesta*. As Cecilio Hernandez said "we are Zoques for *la fiesta* and the music, without music, there is no fiesta, and there would not be Zoque." [14] These rituals centered on the venerations of certain images, such as Virgen del Rosario, or la Virgen del Carmen or de Dolores. Modern-day Zoque in Tuxtla organize to celebrate their local saint day as they did five hundred years ago. However, modern Zoques still connect these celebrations to pre-Hispanic pagan rituals of land and fertility, revolving around music, food, and dance as they did pre-contact openly in the church grounds.

Archeologists and Zoque drummer Sergio de la Cruz affirmed these concepts when talking about the *Meque*, "many of these celebrations have to do with the agricultural cycle. In February, starts with cleaning the fields, or the Corpus Christi during harvest, and in June we dance for the rain, while outsiders think it is religious, it is more than that."[15]

For the Zoque, the connection between sacred and space does not end there. The term *cowina* refers to a "religious place dedicated to the gods in which all family members participate as *cowinas*." This is a Mesoamerican spatial arrangement, in which the entire family participates in the continuation of traditions and rituals. Thus, going back three centuries, the Zoque in Tuxtla have celebrated and paid homage to the Virgin of Copoya both in the private and public realm. The public celebrations last for two months and directly relate to the cargo system, the latter, which goes back to pre-colonial times, makes sure that there is s system in place that elects *mayordomo*s, who oversee the

---

[13] Ibid. fiesta means celebration,
[14] Interview with Cecilio Hernandez
[15] Interview with Sergio de la Cruz Vazquez

celebrations, assisted by other members of the community with different titles.[16] There is also music, dance, food and other massive celebrations, which allows all members of the community to participate. This allows the Zoque to continue their connections with other Zoques, sharing their traditions, image venerations and knowledge in a society that preserves the past by bringing these traditions to the present. These rituals revolve around music and dance, in which performers wear traditional clothing. As Agustin Hernandez said to me when asked about the connection between the fiesta and music, "Without it, there would be no *meque,* no fiesta because the fiesta is the music, the music makes the fiesta, without music, then there is no *meque.*"[17] Music also serves as a vehicle for continuity as there also elements of egalitarianism, which according to spatial contestations theory leads to a certain degree of agency when it comes to change and continuity.[18] Zoque musicians have passed down their musical dating back to colonial time; this is the case with Don Ramon Chacón, who is responsible for mentoring most of the *tamborerors* (drummers) and *piteros* (flautist) that play in Tuxtla today. His grandfather trained him. Chacon's commitment to the community has permitted the young men in Tuxtla have a degree of agency within their spaces. This fact keeps surfacing in the interview for most, "Yes, here we are something, I am a drummer, over there, what?"[19] Expertise and knowledge forms the glue that keeps this identity going. As a result, Zoques do not see immigration to the United States as a step above compared to their current conditions. In fact, they see Mexico as a place, in which they can have a degree of agency. These sentiments exist despite the long-time hostile relationships between Mexican political and economic elites vis-s-vis native group. Most interviewees consider Mexico "their *patria*" and Juárez, or Tuxtla as the place they love despite significant racism and violence, but only because they occupy it, or as Cecilio Hernandez said, *"we live here. It is Mexico that is why we love it."*[20]

The perception among themselves that the Raramuri can utilize their language in their respective spaces within Mexico is another crucial factor that compels them to stay. Few Raramuri speak Spanish amongst themselves and when they do, they only speak it when is an absolute necessity. "Yes, we try to preserve our language, we teach our daughters to continue," said Marta.[21] Conversely,

---

[16] Ibid
[17] Interview with Agustin Hernandez
[18] Ibid
[19] Ibid
[20] Interview with Cecilio Hernandez, March 2019
[21] Interview with Marta Cruz, June 2015.

most Zoques in Tuxtla have gradually lost the ability to speak Zoque and consequently few know the language today. The loss of language is one of the sacrifices/consequences of urbanization, as Leopoldo said: "we have to speak Spanish, school, stores, all its in Spanish."[22]

This paper has shown that the Zoque and Raramuri venerate and consider their physical spaces sacred because of their ancestors, in this case the *Anayahuare* and the *Cowina,* respectively. These perceptions allow them to invest in the space that their ancestors have occupied for centuries. Their ability to claim space in an urban setting has made this continuation possible. These factors put together have created a mindset dictating that these activities can only take place in Mexico. As a result, they do not migrate to the United States as a community, they have not established roots in the United States as their counterparts do, and few individuals have known to migrate. This study argues that this is the result of the ability of these two groups to engage in religious, political, and economic decisions within their community that makes them feel valued and respected. Moreover, these two groups have found certain niches that have earned them an extra degree of respect and notoriety that adds to their sense of space, identity, expertise, and nationalism, such as skilled musicians or marathon runners, as it is with the Zoque and Raramuri respectively. These ideas altogether inevitably connect them to their space, land and eventually nation.

References

Primary Sources
Interview with Agustin Hernandez, Zoque drummer, June 2019
Interview with Teresa Villalobos, March 2021
Interviews with Serafina Gloria Gonzales, March 2021
Interview with Maria Dolores Gonzalez, April 2021
Interview with Sergio de la Cruz Vazquez
Interview with Elva Reyes Tapia, January 2021
Interview with Cecilio Hernandez, March 2019
Interview with Marta Cruz, conducted by author, March 22, 2006
Interview with Don Indalecio Castillo

Secondary Sources
Charles Gibson, The Aztecs Under Spanish Rule, Stanford University Press, 1964
Dolores Aramoni, *Los refugios de los sagrado: religiosidad, conflict y Resistencia entre los zoques de Chiapas* (Mexico: CONACULTA, 1992)
Jose Neumann, Luis Gonzalez (ed.) *Historia de las Rebeliones en la Sierra Tarahumara.* Editorial

---

[22] Interview with Leopoldo Gallegos, February 2020.

Camino, Chihuahua, 1991

Paul Vanderwood, *The Power of God and the Guns of Government*, Stanford University Press, 1998

Andres Hijar, *The Myth of Madera*, Thesis dissertation, University of Texas at El Paso, 2002

Alan Weisman's essay on the Tarahumara. Gilbert Joseph and Timothy Henderson, *The Mexico Reader*, Duke University

LATIN AMERICAN MIGRATION TO TÜRKIYE: MOTIVATIONS, EXPERIENCES, AND PROSPECTS

Elif Sena Garrido Forner

Introduction

Migration has always been central to human history, yet its patterns and drivers constantly evolve. Today, Latin America is among the world's most dynamic regions of out-migration, with millions leaving in response to insecurity, political turmoil, and economic decline. Most scholarship and policy discussions emphasize migration toward the United States, Spain, or other European states. In contrast, Türkiye rarely appears in analyses of Latin American migration, despite growing evidence that the country has become a non-traditional yet increasingly visible destination.

Türkiye's global migration profile is often associated with refugees and displaced persons from neighboring regions, particularly Syria, Iraq, and Afghanistan. However, in recent years the country has also attracted migrants from more distant geographies, including Latin America. Although numerically small, these flows are striking because they cross cultural, linguistic, and geographic boundaries. They raise important questions about how and why Türkiye attracts migrants from the other side of the world.

This paper investigates the motivations and experiences of Latin American migrants in Türkiye, with a focus on two dimensions. First, it analyzes the push and pull factors shaping these movements, ranging from economic crises and political instability in origin countries to the accessibility, affordability, and opportunities offered by Türkiye. Second, it explores the role of soft power; scholarships, cultural diplomacy, and media through which Türkiye presents itself as an appealing destination.

Conceptual And Theocratical Background

Migration theory has long relied on the push–pull framework, which explains mobility as the outcome of adverse conditions in the origin country (push) and attractive conditions in the destination (pull). (Lee, 1966) Economic instability,

421

political crises, and insecurity typically function as push factors, while opportunities, safety, and cultural familiarity act as pull factors. Although this model is widely used, critics argue it oversimplifies decision-making by overlooking non-economic drivers such as identity, culture, and networks. (De Haas, 2010)

Alternative approaches highlight these dimensions. Transnationalism emphasizes how migrants sustain ties with their countries of origin while integrating into new societies. (Schiller et al., 1992) Similarly, social network theory points to the importance of family, friends, and communities in facilitating migration decisions and adaptation. Together, these perspectives stress that migration is not only a rational calculation but also a socially embedded process. (Massey et al., 1993)

Latin American migration has historically been directed to the United States and Spain, with motivations ranging from economic opportunity to colonial and linguistic ties. Türkiye has traditionally been studied as a transit country or as a host to regional refugees. Yet in recent years it has redefined itself as a global actor through soft power tools: education initiatives, cultural diplomacy, and the global export of Turkish television dramas. These instruments, combined with affordable living and geographic accessibility, make Türkiye a non-traditional but increasingly attractive destination. This paper situates Latin American migration to Türkiye at the intersection of these theoretical debates.

Methodology

This study employs a qualitative research design to explore the motivations, challenges, and perceptions of Latin American migrants in Türkiye. The research focuses on four case countries: Brazil, Colombia, Peru, and Venezuela. They were selected due to their visible but understudied presence in Türkiye. Data collection combined semi-structured interviews with thirty Latin American migrants and discussions with consular staff from the embassies of Colombia, Peru, and Venezuela. Participants were recruited through snowball sampling, reflecting the difficulty of accessing small and dispersed migrant communities. The sample included both men and women, aged 19 to 41, in Türkiye more than a year, with diverse motivations.

Interviews explored pre-migration factors, decision-making processes, adaptation challenges, and evolving perceptions of Türkiye. They were conducted in person where possible, and online when necessary, lasting 40–60 minutes each. Secondary sources including embassy data, policy documents, and academic studies, supplemented primary material, compensating for the absence of official statistics on Latin American migrants in Türkiye.

Findings & Discussion

Push Factors: Leaving Latin America

Across all four case countries, participants emphasized structural crises in their home countries as the primary triggers of migration. While individual motivations varied, three interconnected themes emerged: economic instability, political turmoil, and insecurity.

Economic instability was consistently highlighted. Participants from Venezuela described the collapse of the economy, hyperinflation, and shortages of basic goods as unbearable. For example, one interviewee noted that earning a monthly salary at home could not cover a week of groceries, making life "unsustainable." Colombians and Peruvians pointed to limited job opportunities, underemployment, and income inequality. Even Brazilians, despite coming from the region's largest economy, described corruption and inflation as drivers pushing them abroad.

Political crises also played a significant role. Venezuelans and Colombians mentioned lingering instability while Peruvians highlighted the persistent cycle of political unrest and corruption scandals. These factors created an atmosphere of unpredictability, eroding confidence in the future.

Insecurity and social factors were further push elements. Colombians described threats of violence and the impact of organized crime, while some Brazilian and Venezuelan participants mentioned fears of urban violence. In addition, limited educational opportunities and constrained social mobility convinced many young people to look abroad.

Taken together, these push factors reveal that migration was not a choice made lightly but a response to multidimensional crises. As one participant put it, "Leaving was not just about wanting something better, it was about survival and dignity."

Pull Factors: Why Türkiye?

The decision to choose Türkiye rather than traditional destinations such as the U.S. or Spain reflected a combination of affordability, accessibility, and emerging opportunities.

Affordability and accessibility were mentioned by nearly all participants. Compared to Europe or North America, Türkiye was perceived as less expensive in terms of daily living, travel, and tuition for education. Several participants emphasized that visa procedures were easier and less restrictive, making Türkiye more approachable. For migrants lacking European ancestry or strong family networks abroad, Türkiye offered a feasible alternative

Education emerged as the most common pull factor. Twenty-one out of thirty participants arrived primarily for higher education, often through scholarships or university admission programs. Türkiye's universities were seen as increasingly internationalized, and degrees from Turkish institutions carried value both regionally and globally.

Employment and family formation also mattered. Some participants came for job opportunities in tourism, trade, or language teaching, while others migrated through marriage to Turkish spouses.

Safety and quality of life were additional attractions. Participants contrasted Türkiye's relative stability and social services with the insecurity they left behind. For example, Colombians emphasized that despite bureaucratic hurdles, Türkiye felt "safer than home." Venezuelans similarly described a sense of relief at being able to walk freely in public spaces without fear of shortages or violence.

Overall, Türkiye was seen not as a perfect destination but as an achievable and promising one. It provided an alternative pathway for individuals who were excluded from or disillusioned with traditional migration corridors.

Soft Power as a Pull Factor

While structural pull factors played a key role, the findings show that Türkiye's soft power instruments were decisive in shaping perceptions and decisions.

Scholarships and educational programs were the most influential. The Türkiye Scholarships program was frequently mentioned, offering full funding and fostering goodwill. Several participants explained that hearing about these opportunities through friends or social media directly motivated their move. The presence of exchange programs and initiatives by the Turkish Maarif Foundation further strengthened this effect.

Cultural diplomacy also resonated. Institutions such as the Yunus Emre Institute and TİKA supported cultural events, Turkish language courses, and development projects in Latin America. Participants recalled encountering

Turkish cultural promotion in their home countries and developing a curiosity that later translated into migration interest.

Media and entertainment were particularly striking. Turkish television series, widely popular across Latin America, created a sense of familiarity with Turkish culture. Participants often mentioned dramas like Magnificent Century and Fatmagül, saying these shows shaped positive images of Türkiye and sparked curiosity about everyday life. Embassy officials also confirmed that Turkish series generated a surge of interest, especially among younger audiences. This demonstrates how cultural exports can indirectly function as migration drivers.

Diaspora and historical narratives further reinforced these dynamics. Some participants referenced stories of Ottoman migration to Latin America, particularly the "Los Turcos" communities, which created a sense of historical connection. Although often misunderstood, these legacies contributed to shaping perceptions of Türkiye as accessible.

Linking Findings to Theory

The findings support but also expand classical migration theories. The push–pull model clearly explains much of the movement: Latin Americans were pushed by instability and pulled by opportunity. However, this framework alone is insufficient. Türkiye's attraction cannot be reduced to material benefits; instead, it reflects the influence of soft power and cultural narratives that shaped perceptions long before actual migration occurred.

Transnationalism helps explain how migrants sustained ties to Latin America while building lives in Türkiye. Many participants remained active in online communities, sent remittances, and engaged in transnational networks. Similarly, social network theory was evident: participants often decided to migrate after hearing positive stories from friends or family who had already settled in Türkiye.

Conclusion

This study sheds light on the underexplored phenomenon of Latin American migration to Türkiye, revealing a migration corridor shaped by both structural and symbolic factors. Economic instability, political crises, and insecurity in the origin countries clearly function as push factors, compelling migrants to seek alternatives beyond traditional destinations. Türkiye, in turn, offers affordability, accessibility, educational opportunities, and relative safety, making it an attractive destination for diverse groups from Brazil, Colombia, Peru, and

Venezuela. Crucially, this paper demonstrates that Türkiye's soft power through scholarships, cultural diplomacy, and globally popular media reinforces its appeal, creating a narrative of accessibility and modernity that influences migration decisions alongside material incentives.

The findings expand classical migration theories by illustrating how push–pull dynamics operate in tandem with cultural and social influences. Transnational networks and social ties further facilitate migration, highlighting the socially embedded nature of mobility. By focusing on this migration route, this study challenges assumptions about Latin American migration patterns and positions Türkiye as an emerging global actor in migration flows. Future research could explore long-term integration, community formation, and the evolving impact of soft power, offering a richer understanding of how non-traditional destinations shape contemporary migration landscapes.

References

De Haas, H. (2010). The Internal Dynamics of Migration Processes: A Theoretical inquiry. *Journal of Ethnic and Migration Studies*, *36*(10), 1587–1617. https://doi.org/10.1080/1369183x.2010.489361

Massey, D. S., Arango, J., Hugo, G., Kouaouci, A., Pellegrino, A., & Taylor, J. E. (1993). Theories of International Migration: A Review and Appraisal. *Population and Development Review*, *19*(3), 431. https://doi.org/10.2307/2938462

Schiller, N. G., Basch, L. G., & Blanc-Szanton, C. (1992). *Towards a transnational perspective on migration: race, class, ethnicity, and nationalism reconsidered.* http://ci.nii.ac.jp/ncid/BA18432971

REFUGEE RESEARCH ETHICS: MOVING FROM PARTICIPATION TO MATTERING

Maria Psoinos[1]

Introduction

Pragmatic methodological approaches in social research are epistemologically informed, but also practical, that is, they give voice to the participants and through the research process where they actively participate, they explore the issues under examination so that actual solutions are derived for real-life problems (Flyvbjerg, 2001; Morgan, 2007; Patton, 2014). Participation in this context means doing research 'with' rather than 'on' groups of people.

One example of a methodology belonging to this pragmatic approach is Community-Based Participatory Research (CBPR); it has been identified as having the potential to make substantial contributions to improving the well-being of traditionally disenfranchised populations- such as refugees- while building capacity within these communities (Betancourt et al., 2015).

In recent refugee studies, these pragmatic approaches are increasingly being supported (Filler et al., 2021; Kia-Keating & Huang, 2022). In this paper a narrative review is carried out of refugee studies which have adopted this pragmatic approach. In particular the focus is on reviewing these studies' research ethics and critically looking at the ethical principles adopted, the Institutional Review Board procedures followed and the ethical concerns addressed.

Rationale/ Justification

This is an important and timely topic to be explored firstly because of ongoing challenges in the refugee studies area : the research field is becoming saturated, and refugees and other forcibly displaced people often do not wish to participate in more studies or hesitate about how they will be involved in research,

---

[1] Maria Psoinos, Canterbury Christ Church University, UK/ University of Western Macedonia, Greece

especially during the recruitment phase of a study (Hanza et al., 2016).

In addition, given an increasing demand for social scientists to expand their data collection beyond WEIRD (Western, educated, industrialized, rich and democratic) populations, there is an urgent need for transdisciplinary conversations on the logistical, scientific and ethical considerations inherent to this type of scholarship (Broesch et al. 2020)

Literature Review

When designing and carrying out social research with refugee populations, there are various ethical issues involved. Scholars have extensively discussed refugee research ethics, especially with regards to the particularities of these types of studies, e.g. vulnerabilities of the study population and the asymmetric power relationship between researcher(s) and participant(s) (Deps et al., 2022; Psoinos, 2015); the difficulties of constructing an ethical consent process (Mackenzie et al., 2007); the variation across ethno-cultural groups in migrants' and refugees' motivations to participate in research projects, even if they actively engage members of the community (van der Velde et al. 2009).

Systematic reviews of refugee studies and their ethical considerations have been conducted (Davidson et al., 2023). However, what is missing is a more qualitative review and then an in-depth analysis of ongoing and emerging issues in this area. Very recently, some scholars have explored ethical issues in health-related research with forced migrants based on qualitative data and thematic analysis (Inge et al., 2025) but more similar studies are required.

Methodology

This study set out to explore the ethics procedures in recent refugee studies which adopt the aforementioned pragmatic approaches. This exploration is implemented via a narrative review.

Narrative reviews are typically concerned with questions such as *"What do we know about the causes of a particular social and/or health problem?"* Increasingly however, narrative reviews are also addressing questions of evidence of effectiveness and cost-effectiveness when a program/intervention is developed (Mays et al., 2005).

This study adopts the first traditional approach to a narrative review, which means it is less concerned with assessing the quality of evidence and more interested in mapping the field of research ethics in refugee studies today and making recommendations for future research and practice with this population, in this context.

Searching and identifying material

First, a literature search was conducted on the topic of ethics in refugee studies. The following databases were accessed: ASSIA; Sociological Abstracts; Social Care Online; MEDLINE; PsycINFO; Social Sciences Abstracts; OECD iLibrary. A search was also carried out within journals related to the areas of migration; integration; ethnic & migration studies; diversity & equality.

Searches were limited to articles from January 2015 (when the refugee crisis started to unfold in Europe) to the present date. Based on the inclusion criteria the focus was on sources that: were original studies; adopted systematic or narrative reviews as their methodology; had participants who were refugees or other forcibly displaced people; and included discussions-even brief- of methods and ethics.

The emerging material could be roughly divided in the following two areas: 1) studies from the fields of sociology and human geography that focused on migration/refugee flows and 2) studies from the fields of psychology, social work, and health policy that focused on refugees' psychosocial status & its fluctuations.

Findings and Discussion

In most of the reviewed studies, in the ethics sections, even though the typical issues related to securing consent, ensuring confidentiality and participant anonymity, doing-no-harm and the 'dual imperative' of balancing academic rigour with the relevance of research on policy are addressed, other aspects are missing, such as the need to ensure that refugees derive benefit from the research to which they have contributed (Deps et al., 2022).

This gap can be addressed by drawing on relevant theoretical developments from the field of liberation psychology (Garcia-Ramirez et al., 2010) and pertinent community psychology concepts such as 'mattering' (Prilleltensky, 2020). 'Mattering' is an ideal state of affairs that consists of two complementary psychological experiences: feeling valued and also adding value. Human beings can feel valued by, and add value to, self, others, work, and community (Prilleltensky, 2020)

The importance of 'meaningful participation' has been noted in previous research (Deps et al (2022) and indeed 'mattering' as a theoretical framework has been used in empirical research with refugees (Moe & Ytterhus, 2022). However, what is suggested here is that mattering becomes part of the ethics procedures. In the same manner that informed consent is secured from participants, their understanding of how much they feel valued and how much they feel they give value to others, should also be secured.

The above findings contribute to the emerging field of 'research on research ethics' and as noted by Makhoul et al (2028) may be valuable to 'relief agencies and researchers in their pursuit of ethically sound research in times of crisis'.

Conclusions

The study's findings suggest that it is important not only to include refugee research participants in the design and implementation of the studies for the sake of paying lip service to notions of inclusion (Albtran et al., 2024).

Precisely because in refugee studies which adopt the pragmatic approach the lived experiences of migration and resettlement are explored in a collaborative and interdisciplinary manner (Jacquez et al., 2021) and structural coercion (Fisher, 2013) is strongly criticised, research ethics should set up a context where greater equity is promoted.

Notions such as 'mattering' can significantly contribute to this goal. And for community-based, participatory research methodologies and similar approaches to be implemented truly meaningfully, they have to be present throughout the entire research process (*formulating the research question, getting funding, research design, engaging the community, data collection and analysis, dissemination of findings*).

References

Albtran, A. et al. (2024). Building an ethical research culture: Scholars of refugee background researching refugee-related issues. *Journal of Refugee Studies*, 37(2): 579-588.

Betancourt, T.S., Frounfelker, R., Mishra, T., Hussein, A. & Falzarano, R. (2015) Addressing health disparities in the mental health of refugee children and adolescents through community-based participatory research: a study in 2 communities. *American Journal of Public Health,* 105(Suppl 3):S475–82.

Broesch, T., Crittenden, A.N., Beheim, B.A. et al. (2020). Navigating cross-cultural research: methodological and ethical considerations. *Proceedings: Biological Sciences*, 287(1935):20201245.

Davidson, N., K. Hammarberg, and J. Fisher. 2023. Ethical considerations in research with people from refugee and asylum seeker backgrounds: A systematic review of national and international ethics guidelines. *Journal of Bioethical Inquiry,* 21(2): 261–2.

Deps, P.D., Rezende, I., Andrade, M.A.C., & Collin, S.M. (2022). Ethical issues in research with refugees. *Ethics, Medicine and Public Health*. 24.

Filler, T. et al (2021). A chair at the table: a scoping review of the participation of refugees in community-based participatory research in healthcare. *Globalisation and Health*, 17: 103.

Fisher, J.A. 2013. Expanding the frame of "voluntariness" in informed consent: Structural coercion and the power of social and economic context. *Kennedy Institute of Ethics Journal*, 23(4): 355–379.

Flyvbjerg, B. (2001). *Making social science matter. Why social inquiry fails and how it can succeed again.* Cambridge University Press.

García- Ramírez, M., de la Mata, M., Paloma, V. and Hernández-Plaza, S. (2010). A liberation psychology approach to acculturative integration of migrant populations. *American Journal of Community Psychology*, 47(1-2): 86-97.

Hanza, M.M., Goodson, M., Osman, A. *et al.* (2016). Lessons Learned from Community-Led Recruitment of Immigrants and Refugee Participants for a Randomized, Community-Based Participatory Research Study. *Journal of Immigrant and Minority Health*, 18: 1241–1245.

Inge, E., Elmi, N., Omar, Y. *et al.* (2025). Patient and public involvement with forced migrants: an empirical exploration of ethical issues. *Bioethical Inquiry* https://doi.org/10.1007/s11673-025-10438-3.

Jacquez, F., Dutt, A., Manirambona, E., & Wright, B. (2021). Uniting liberatory and participatory approaches in public psychology with refugees. *American Psychologist, 76*(8): 1280–1292.

Kia-Keating & Huang. (2022). Participatory science as a decolonizing methodology: Leveraging collective knowledge from partnerships with refugee and immigrant communities. *Cultural Diversity and Ethnic Minority Psychology, 28*(3): 299-305.

Mackenzie, C., Christopher McDowell, C., & Eileen Pittaway, E. (2007) Beyond 'Do No Harm': The Challenge of Constructing Ethical Relationships in Refugee Research. *Journal of Refugee Studies*, 20(2): 299–319.

Makhoul, J., Chehab, R.F., Shaito, Z. *et al.* (2018). A scoping review of reporting 'Ethical Research Practices' in research conducted among refugees and war-affected populations in the Arab world. *BMC Medical Ethics* 19: 36.

Mays, N., Pope, C., & Popay, J. (2005) Systematically reviewing qualitative and quantitative evidence to inform management and policy-making in the health field. *Journal of Health Services Research and Policy*, Jul;10 Suppl 1:6-20.

Moe, G. & Ytterhus, B. (2022). Health and meaning through "doings": A qualitative study with young unaccompanied refugees in Norway. *Social Science and Medicine*, 315:115542.

Morgan, D.L. (2007). Paradigms lost and pragmatism regained: Methodological implications of combining qualitative and quantitative methods. *Journal of Mixed Methods Research*, 1: 48-76.

Patton, M.Q. (2014). Strategic themes in qualitative inquiry. In *Qualitative Research and Evaluation methods, Integrating Theory and Practice*, (pp. 37-73). Sage Publications.

Prilleltensky, I. (2020). Mattering at the intersection of psychology, philosophy and politics. *American Journal of Community Psychology*, 65 (1-2): 16-34.

Psoinos, M. (2015). Researching migrants who hold nomadic identities: analysing multi-level dynamic discourses of power. *Equality, Diversity and Inclusion: An International Journal*, 34(4): 293-307.

van der Velde, J., Williamson, D. L., & Ogilvie, L. D. (2009). Participatory action research: Practical strategies for actively engaging and maintaining participation in immigrant and refugee communities. *Qualitative Health Research, 19*(9): 1293–1302.

THE ROLE OF THE HICK-HYMAN LAW ON HUMAN-COMPUTER INTERACTION (HCI) SYSTEMS IN EXTRATERRESTRIAL MIGRATION: CONTEMPORARY PERSPECTIVES AND CHALLENGES

Stefani Stojchevska

Introduction

The concept of *Extraterrestrial Migration* represents an ambitious endeavor toward mankind's advancement beyond the confinements of Planet Earth despite many multidisciplinary challenges, including Human-Computer Interaction (HCI) Systems incorporated in man-made objects. When considering an effective HCI System, as depicted in Figure 1, the astronaut fulfils specific tasks or purposes related to specified activities that are regarded as natural toward the factors dependent.

Figure 1: Schematic Diagram of a Human-Computer Interaction (HCI) System in Manned Spacecrafts

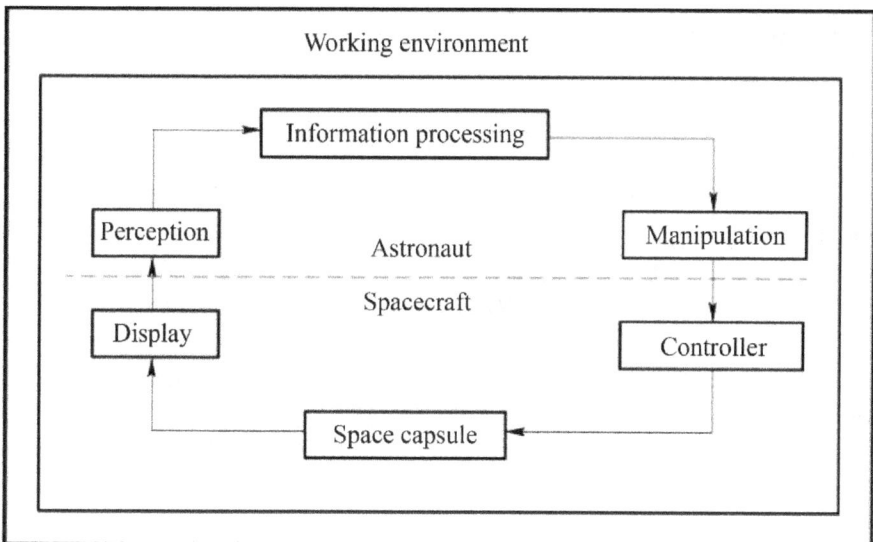

Note. From "Manned Spacecraft Technologies" by Hong Yang, 2020, p.53.

By operating together as part of a complex interconnected mechanism, a series of related measures is often based on four main functions: (1) *information reception*; (2) *information storage*; (3) *information processing and decision-making*; and (4) *information execution*. The frequent disruption of the cognitive consequentiality of astronauts and pilots could cause life-threatening outcomes. Further, according to the National Aeronautics and Space Administration (NASA) Report titled *"Evidence Report: Risk of Inadequate Human-Computer Interaction"*, the risk of inadequate HCI includes eight core contributing factors:

1. Requirements, policies, and design processes;
2. Information resources/support;
3. Allocation of attention;
4. Cognitive overload;
5. Environmentally induced perceptual changes;
6. Misperception/misinterpretation of displayed information;
7. Spatial disorientation;
8. Design of displays and controls (Holden at al., 2013);

On that account, this scientific research paper attempts to improve the practical manifestation of selective contributing factors in relation to inadequate HCI predominantly concerning engineering psychology and human performance during manned spacecraft missions.

Mathematically Modeling the Hick-Hyman Law to Hypothetical Extraterrestrial Migration Missions

The Hick-Hyman Law was formulated in 1952 by psychologists William Edmund Hick and Ray Hyman, who were examining the relationship between the number of stimuli present and an individual's reaction time to any given stimulus. It was found that increasing the number of choices available logarithmically increases decision time (Yablonski, 2020), in addition to the time to make a decision being affected by two factors: (1) *familiarity with the choices* (repeated use); and (2) *the format of the choices* (sounds, words, videos and buttons) (Saffer, 2010). Regarding a hypothetical manned spacecraft mission, situations involve an astronaut having a choice to select a certain response among several possible responses and make the selected response. The further adaptation of the following mathematical manifestations is considered. Namely, the average number of bits for a set of "N" equally likely stimuli is $\log_2 N$. Because uncertainty also varies as a function of the probabilities with which individual stimuli occur, the average amount of information for a set of stimuli that occur with unequal probability will be less than $\log_2 N$ (Proctor & Vu, 2006).

Adaptation of the Astronaut's Alternative of Equal Probability Choices

Given a set of *"n"* stimuli, associated for one-for-one with *"n"* responses, the time to react (RT) to the onset of a stimulus and to make the appropriate response is given by Hick's 1952 Law of Information Processing, which is stated as follows:

$$RT = a + b \, log_2 \, (n+1)$$

(1)

, where:

- *"RT"* is the astronaut's reaction time;
- *"n"* is the number of equally likely stimuli (number of choices);
- *"a"* is an empirically determined constant by fitting a line to measured data which comes from factors that are outside the choice itself, such as environmentally induced perceptual changes (example of *environmental constraints*);
- *"b"* is an empirically determined constant by fitting a line to measured data which comes from factors inherent in the design of choices, including font and spacing of buttons (example of *technological diversification*);
- *"log2"* is a binary research performed;
- *"n+1"* is the astronaut's uncertainty about whether to respond or not or which response to make;

One aspect of equation (1) is that the RT increases by a constant amount each time the number of choices doubles (Albers, 2012). Although uncertainty can be reduced by decreasing set-size, it also can be reduced by cuing a sub-set of stimuli and responses ahead of the stimulus onset or making some stimuli and responses more likely than others. Generally speaking, the Hick-Hyman Law states that it is the *information* extracted from the stimulus to select the response (defined as reduction in uncertainty) that determined the RT (Johnson & Proctor, 2016). The information (H) measured in *"bits"* is a measure of uncertainty. The value of information is directly related to the amount of uncertainty reduced. Thus, the amount of information (H) in a choice reaction situation that the astronaut in the manned spacecraft mission as a decision-maker processes by associating to an event (choice) among a set of *"N"* equally likely events (i.e., each of the *"N"* events occurs with equal probability of $p = 1/N$) is defined as follows:

$$H = log_2 \left(\frac{P_A}{P_B}\right)$$

(2)

, where:

- **"PA"** is the probability at the receiver of the event *after* the information is received;
- **"PB"** is the probability at the receiver of the event *before* the information is received;

In the case when the events are equally likely:

$$H = \log_2(1/p) = \log_2 N \tag{3}$$

The assumption of all choices being equally likely is not applicable to situations commonly occurring in the real world, where possible choices have different probabilities (Bhise, 2016). Hence, the assessment of astronauts' cognitive information capacity in choice reaction within the working process of the HCI System is considered through two factors influencing inadequate HCI in an extraterrestrial environment – *technological diversification* and *environmental constraints* – where the forthcoming relationships among the astronaut, the spacecraft and the environment displays how the HCI interface provides both perceptional and intuitive images for astronauts in order to acquire interface information with the aid of their knowledge, experience, perception and thinking. Such interface manifests the manner in which astronauts use control equipment for information output to complete HCI, while the spacecraft processes the received information and sends back the response information or operation results to the astronaut through the human-computer interface.

Adaptation of the Astronaut's Alternative of Unequal Probability Choices

Given the average amount of information for stimuli that occur with unequal probability would be less than log2N, the Hick-Hyman Law is generalized when considering choices with unequal probabilities *"pi"*, of occurring, to:

$$T = bH \tag{4}$$

The average amount of information (*H*) conveyed by a stimulus for a set of size *"N"* is:

$$H = \sum_i^n p_i \log_2(1/p_i + 1) \tag{5}$$

, where:

- **"H"** is the average amount of information conveyed by a stimulus for a set of size *"N"*;
- **"pi"** is the probability of alternative;

Taking into account the unequal probabilities of the "N" possible choice events, the following may be stated:

$$RT = a + b \sum_{i=1}^{N} p_i \log_2 \left(\frac{1}{p_i} \right)$$

(6)

The combination of equations (4), (5) and (6) is applicable to extraterrestrial migration missions, where the astronaut receiving the average amount of information for stimuli that occur with unequal probability would be conveyed by a stimulus for a set of size "N". This results in stating the RT by addressing previous components, including the binary research performed or the arbitrary constants "a" and "b" by fitting a line to measured data which come from factors that are outside and/or inherent to the choice itself, respectively.

The Mathematical Adaptation of Roth's Correlation between Intelligence Quotient (IQ) Assessment in Information Processing Speed and Astronaut Screening and Evaluation

Erwin Roth, using multiple-choice *RTs* in an experimental paradigm conforming to the Hick-Hyman Law, found that individual differences in the slope of *RT* as a function of bits (i.e., the rate of information processing) are correlated with intelligence quotient (IQ), which serves as the reciprocal of the slope of the function, as follows:

$$\text{Reaction Time} = \text{Movement Time} + \frac{\log_2(n)}{\text{Processing Speed}}$$

(7)

The same components are present in the Hick-Hyman Law equations; with the notion of the time it takes for the astronaut to come to a decision in the extraterrestrial migration mission is said to be proportional to the following equation:

$$\frac{\log_2(n)}{\text{Processing Speed}}$$

(8)

Other things being equal, astronauts with greater speed of information processing acquire more cognitively integrated knowledge and skill per unit of time that they interact with their working environment. Seemingly small individual differences in speed of information processing, amounting to only a few milliseconds per bit of information, when multiplied by months or years of interaction with such environment may partially account for the relatively large differences observed between astronauts regarding developed cognitive skills obtained by IQ assessment (Eysenck, 2012).

Figure 2: Roth's Application of Hick's Law "Bit" is the Unit of log2*N*

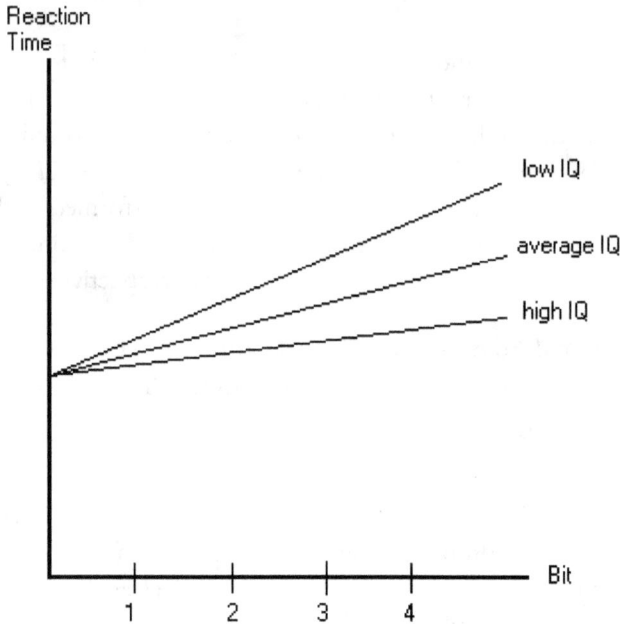

Note. From "Die Geschwindigkeit der Verarbeitung von Information und ihr Zusammenhang mit Intelligenz" by Erwin Roth, 1964, p.616.

Regarding extraterrestrial migration missions, the astronauts' speed of information processing in parallel with interactions within their environment greatly depends on the temporal duration of the mission, besides measures of cognitive and intellectual capacity in the screening and evaluation of astronaut candidates (Bishop, et al., 1996). Test pilots and astronauts are assumed to be a highly unique and talented group of individuals, whose abilities for mastering the stresses and demands of high altitude flying, testing and crisis management, all of which require instantaneous reactions, are highly specialized. Consequently, high intelligence requirements are assumed (Itzkoff, 1994). IQ tests measure intelligence in its most general sense, where scores reflect the astronauts' ability to comprehend the world, accurately perceive relationships, and solve problems. By way of illustration, although early astronauts seemed tongue-tied to some observers, they were actually extremely bright. Their overall IQ scores tended to fall in what psychologists call the superior (IQ of 115 to

129) and very superior (IQ of 130 and above) ranges. On occasion, people of average IQ have been selected, but only 10 percent of the astronaut corps has an average IQ, while 48 percent and 42 percent are classified as superior and very superior, respectively (Harrison, 2002).

Conclusions and Recommendations

Effective HCI systems are crucial for routine operations and unpredicted situations in successful extraterrestrial migration missions, although their development is a challenging task that requires coordinated efforts of multiple fields. While the application of the Hick-Hyman Law to HCI remains controversial due to misunderstandings, the importance of this research may be reflected on technology policy and the space industry.

References

Albers, M.J. (2012). Human-Information Interaction and Technical Communication: Concepts and Frameworks. Hershey, Pennsylvania: Information Science Reference.

Bhise, V.D. (2016). Ergonomics in the Automotive Design Process. Boca Rato, Florida: Taylor & Francis Group.

Bishop, S.L., Faulk, D., & Santy, P.A. (1994). The Use of IQ Assessment in Astronaut Screening and Evaluation. Aviation Space and Environment Medicine, 67(12), 1130-1137.

Eysenck, H.J. (2012). A Model for Intelligence. Berlin, Germany: Springer-Verlag.

Harrison, A.A. (2002). Spacefaring: The Human Dimension. California, United States: Univeristy of California Press.

Holden, K., Ezer, N., & Vos, G. (2013). Evidence Report: Risks of Inadequate Human-Computer Interaction. Houston, Texas: National Aeronautics and Space Administration Lyndon B. Johnson Space Center.

Itzkoff, S.W. (1994). The Decline of Intelligence in America: A Strategy for National Renewal. Westport, Connecticut: Praeger Publishers.

Johnson, A., & Proctor, R.W. (2016). Skill Acquisition and Training: Achieving Expertise in Simple and Complex Tasks. New York, NY: Routledge.

Proctor, R.W., & Vu, K.L. (2006). Stimulus-Response Compatibility Principles: Data, Theory and Application. Boca Rato, Florida: Taylor & Francis Group.

Roth, E. (1964). Die Geschwindigkeit der Verarbeitung von Information und ihr Zusammenhang mit Intelligenz. Zeitschrift für Experimentelle und Angewandte Psychologie, 11(4), 616–622.

Saffer, D. (2010). Designing for Interaction. Second Edition: Creating Innovative Applications and Devices. Berkley, California: New Riders.

Yablonski, J. (2020). Laws of UX: Using Psychology to Design Better Products & Services. Sebastool, California: O'Reilly Media.

Yang, H. (2020). Manned Spacecraft Technologies. Singapore, Singapore: Springer Nature.

PAPERS IN SPANISH

MIGRACIÓN ITALIANA A MÉXICO: UNA PERSPECTIVA HISTÓRICA

Sara D'Anna

Introducción

La historiografía sobre la migración italiana hacia México es escasa y marginal en el campo más amplio de los estudios migratorios internacionales. Esta marginalidad parece estar vinculada a la escala cuantitativamente limitada del fenómeno, una condición que, no obstante, no justifica la poca atención que ha recibido por parte de los académicos, quienes han preferido centrarse en rutas migratorias de mayor envergadura y mejor documentadas. A ello se suman otras limitaciones de la reducida literatura sobre el tema: la brecha entre el país de origen y el país de destino, que ha dado lugar a un análisis fragmentado de las fuentes disponibles y a una subestimación de los datos que surgen en la comparación entre ambas realidades.

El presente estudio, basado en fuentes de naturaleza institucional, tiene como objetivo contribuir a subsanar, en parte, esta laguna promoviendo un diálogo entre los lugares de partida y de llegada y, sobre todo, ofreciendo una perspectiva diferente respecto a la narrativa hasta ahora consolidada.

Las investigaciones existentes, aunque pocas, han descrito la emigración italiana hacia México como un fenómeno procedente del norte, de carácter colonial y centrado en asentamientos permanentes, cuyo legado aún es rastreable en las comunidades descendientes. Sin embargo, el análisis propuesto aquí demuestra que esta no representa la única dimensión del fenómeno migratorio: otras trayectorias y experiencias configuran un panorama más amplio y complejo. En particular, el estudio muestra que también existieron flujos originarios del sur de Italia, caracterizados por un proyecto migratorio temporal e integrados en iniciativas económicas privadas y transnacionales.

La migración de 1900

A partir de la independencia en 1821, los gobiernos mexicanos delinearon políticas de colonización agrícola destinadas a poblar áreas escasamente habitadas, impulsar la agricultura local y contrarrestar posibles amenazas de potencias extranjeras. Las leyes de 1824 y 1854 establecieron los criterios de admisión, dando preferencia a migrantes europeos, considerados más adecuados para el entorno local y compatibles, desde el punto de vista cultural y religioso, con la población local.

Entre 1858 – año en que se obtuvieron los primeros resultados de las políticas migratorias – y 1900 llegaron alrededor de 4.000 italianos, muy por debajo del objetivo de los gobiernos, que esperaban cientos de miles de migrantes europeos, entre ellos italianos.

El flujo de italianos más numeroso se produjo entre 1881 y 1882, con migrantes provenientes de Trentino, Piamonte, Véneto y Lombardía. Estos fueron asentados por el gobierno en seis colonias distribuidas en diversos estados – siendo la más famosa, aun existente, comunidad de Chipilo – donde se dedicaron a la actividad agrícola.

En línea con los proyectos del siglo XIX implementados por el gobierno mexicano para promover la inmigración extranjera como instrumento de desarrollo socioeconómico nacional, el éxodo de 1900 también formó parte de estrategias orientadas al progreso y a la valorización de los recursos nacionales mediante el uso de mano de obra extranjera, aunque con dinámicas diferentes.

La falta de una distribución demográfica equilibrada en México, dejaba amplias extensiones de tierra deshabitada entre los centros poblados, que debían ser aprovechadas no solo mediante el cultivo agrícola, sino también mediante el desarrollo de infraestructuras de utilidad pública y de interés comercial y económico, capaces de conectar las regiones interiores de México con los principales centros urbanos y también con los vecinos Estados Unidos, interesados en invertir capital y fortalecer los lazos comerciales y la influencia económica en la región. El flujo migratorio italiano de 1900 responde a este sistema de desarrollo nacional de líneas ferroviarias. Los documentos archivísticos registran que un contingente de poco más de 500 migrantes partió del puerto de Nápoles hacia México el 5 de abril de 1900, llegando a Veracruz el 27 del mismo mes a bordo del transatlántico *Centro America*[1]. Los migrantes fueron reclutados, a petición del gobierno mexicano y con la aprobación del Ministerio del Interior del Reino de Italia, por una de las agencias de emigración italianas más importantes de la época, la *Società Commerciale Marittima*, que operaba, entre otras ciudades, en Nápoles, Cosenza,

---

[1] Poco después, otros aproximadamente 500 migrantes se habrían embarcado hacia Veracruz a bordo del vapor *San Gottardo*.

Catanzaro y Reggio Calabria. En consecuencia, mientras que en los proyectos anteriores de inmigración promovidos por el gobierno la mayoría de los migrantes procedía del norte de Italia, el flujo de 1900 mostró una "meridionalización" de la migración, compuesta casi en su totalidad por trabajadores del sur de Italia, en lugar de casos aislados. En particular, los migrantes provenían de las regiones de Campania y Calabria, donde se desarrolló una emigración comunitaria desde las localidades de Ercolano (en aquella época, más conocida como Resina) y la cercana Torre del Greco (Nápoles), así como de Limbadi, Gerace y Nicotera. Una elección bastante singular, considerando que las autoridades habían expresado tradicionalmente una clara preferencia por los migrantes del norte debido a su percibida "naturaleza dócil" (Zilli Manica 1981, 74 y 99).

Los trabajadores fueron contratados por una empresa privada estadounidense, la *Veracruz & Pacific Railroad*, representada por el abogado Alfred Bishop Mason y con sede en Orizaba (Estado de Veracruz). Este proyecto ferroviario estaba destinado a conectar Veracruz con Salina Cruz (Oaxaca) en el lado sur del Istmo de Tehuantepec, enlazando así la costa norte del Golfo de México con la costa sur del Pacífico. Según el contrato, el empleo de los migrantes estaba garantizado por dos años, generalmente coincidiendo con el trabajo estacional, precario e irregular típico del sector ferroviario. Sin embargo, no se cumplieron todas las cláusulas contractuales.

Las condiciones de hacinamiento en el campamento de trabajadores, en Tierra Blanca, y las criticas condiciones higiénicos-sanitarias, que podían favorecer casos de fiebre amarilla y su propagación entre los inmigrantes fueron a la base de la huelga. Una situación de la que el gobierno italiano estaba al tanto desde el principio y que suscitó preocupaciones entre sus representantes locales.

El campamento fue visitado por una delegación – compuesta por médicos, el Cónsul Real italiano en México y, por su propia voluntad, por el salesiano italiano Padre Antonio Riccardi – encargada de verificar las condiciones en que se encontraban los trabajadores, considerándolas en última instancia óptimas. La comisión concluyó que las *quejas* y la consiguiente sublevación eran *irracionales* e *infundadas*. Por lo tanto, la empresa estadunidense contratante, que rechazó cualquier responsabilidad respecto a las causas – a pesar de que las condiciones higiénicas y de alojamiento debían estar garantizadas por contrato – y a las consecuencias de la huelga. Según la empresa, cumplió con todas las obligaciones previstas en el contrato y no existía ninguna violación que justificara la obligación de continuar pagando a los trabajadores ni repatriarlos

su   cargo.
Con la protesta de los migrantes, fue necesario la intervención militar, de la cual
resultaron el arresto de algunos de los sublevados y la huida de embajadores y
autoridades locales que, al igual que la empresa, se desentendieron de la situación
incierta.

Abandonados en este limbo de dependencias y relaciones internacionales,
muchos quedaron sin trabajo, vagando por los estados mexicanos.

Conclusiones

El análisis de las fuentes de lo archivos italianos nos ha permitido descubrir una
nueva faceta de la migración a México y proponer una lectura alternativa, capaz
de incluir las condiciones sociales de partida, los desarrollos inmediatos del
fenómeno y, de manera indirecta, las dinámicas socioeconómicas de las
relaciones entre los países implicados – el Reino de Italia, México y USA, cuyo
papel de intermediación resultó crucial.

Además, esta contribución da voz a una historia distinta de las habituales
narraciones de éxito financiero de los italianos en el extranjero, acercándose en
cambio a experiencias marcadas por el fracaso económico – al menos en suelo
mexicano – y por condiciones laborales precarias y carentes de protecciones, un
tema que todavía hoy sigue siendo actual.

La reivindicación de mejor condiciones de trabajo se tradujo, en la retórica
política de la época, en etiquetas de *instigadores, exaltados, malvados agitadores* y
miembros de la categoría de los *inadaptados de mayor especie*, descritos como
implicados en conspiraciones y asociados a las mafias italianas. No obstante,
estos trabajadores fueron capaces de sacudir las conciencias y arrojar luz sobre
temas que poco después habrían involucrado al mundo laboral a nivel global,
aunque con tiempos distintos.

Referencias bibliográficas

Zilli Manica, J. B. (1981). Italianos en México: Documentos para la historia de los colonos italianos
en México. México: Ediciones San José.

ECUADOR VIVE UNA NUEVA OLA DE MIGRACIÓ

Jessica Ordóñez Cuenca[1]

Este documento describe las tres olas migratorias que ha vivido Ecuador en los u ltimos veinticinco an os. El actual e xodo surge desde una coyuntura crí tica de crisis siste mica internacional y esta impulsada por los efectos adversos que dejo la pandemia por el COVID19.

Los primeros indicios de la migracio n internacional en Ecuador se producen en los an os cincuenta, el destino fue Estados Unidos y admitio a hombres con formacio n primaria. A partir de este hecho se conformaron las primeras redes migratorias, que ma s adelante facilitarí an los futuros procesos migratorios. En los u ltimos an os de la de cada de 1990 y a inicio de los an os 2000, se registra una primera ola migratoria de particular importancia, la cual estuvo generada por una grave crisis econo mica y financiera, los destinos migratorios se diversificaron, adema s de Estados Unidos se generalizo la migracio n hacia Espan a y otros paí ses europeos.

Este proceso migratorio afecto tanto a hombres como mujeres con educacio n secundaria y superior. Las remesas han sido y continu an siendo el principal efecto econo mico de la migracio n. Constituyen uno de los principales mecanismos de ingresos de do lares para la economí a dolarizada, junto con las exportaciones de camaro n y de petro leo, que tambie n son de gran importancia. Entre 1993 y 2004, estas pasaron de 201 a 1604 millones (Serrano, 2008, p. 5). Contribuyen a mitigar los efectos sociales de la emigracio n a trave s de las inversiones en vivienda, implementacio n de nuevas empresas, inversio n en educacio n de los hijos de migrantes que quedaron en Ecuador, entre otros.

> Los datos macroecono micos en este periodo evidencian una importante crisis econo mica y social. Segu n Serrano (2008), entre 1998 y 1999 el Producto Interno Bruto de Ecuador (PIB) se redujo en un 30%, lo que aumento la pobreza y el desempleo. Adicionalmente, de acuerdo con Acosta (2005) en este periodo, la pobreza y la desigualdad aumentaron, una muestra de ello es que el "nu mero de pobres crecio de 3,9 a 9,1 millones; en te rminos porcentuales, de 34% al

[1] Jessica Ordóñez Cuenca, Universidad Técnica Particular de Loja. E-mail: jaordonezx@utpl.edu.ec

71%" (p.2), la desigualdad tambie n aumenta, segu n el mismo autor, el 20% ma s pobre paso de recibir el 5% del ingreso nacional en 1990 al 3% en 1999, mientras que el ma s rico aumento su participacio n del 52% al 61% en ese mismo periodo.

La segunda ola migratoria se da en el contexto de la crisis financiera internacional del 2008, la cual afecto la economí a en los paí ses de residencia de nuestros ecuatorianos, principalmente a Espan a. En este contexto como lo menciona Cardoso y Gives (2008), el sector de la construccio n sufrio el mayor estancamiento, lo cual afecto substancialmente a la poblacio n inmigrante residente en Estados Unidos y Espan a motivo por el cual muchos ecuatorianos optaron por volver a migrar "dando como resultado la llamada dia spora ecuatoriana" (p.1); este contexto evidencio el retorno migratorio de muchos migrantes ecuatorianos.

Como se menciono , el retorno migratorio fue motivado por la falta de empleo en el paí s de residencia, el crecimiento y estabilidad econo mica experimentada en Ecuador, y por la polí tica migratoria local que fomentaba el retorno a trave s de la difusio n del Plan de retorno migratorio denominado "Bienvenidos a casa", que fue impulsado en el gobierno del presidente Rafel Correa para promover el emprendimiento y la inversio n de los ahorros de las personas migrantes. Esta migracio n (retorno) afecto ma s a los hombres que a las mujeres, debido a la caí da del sector de la construccio n en los paí ses de residencia anterior.

En el 2016, el paí s fue afectado por un terremoto que produjo devastacio n en algunas provincias del paí s y provoco la caí da del PIB en el 1.2%. En el 2017, se registro una recuperacio n del crecimiento del 2.4%, pero en 2018 regresan los problemas fiscales, lo que resulto en un crecimiento moderado del 1.3%. En el 2019, el PIB del paí s no crecio , por efecto del estancamiento econo mico a nivel internacional y a una marcada desaceleracio n de la demanda interna.

A lo anterior se suman los efectos negativos de la pandemia por el COVID-19, que contrajo el PIB del paí s al -7.8% (CEPAL,2021). Este contexto macroecono mico ha influido en otros agregados nacionales como el desempleo, la pobreza y principalmente en la desigualdad. Segu n el portal de datos del Banco Mundial, la desigualdad disminuyo entre el 2000 y 2017, pero a partir del 2020 tiende a incrementarse, retrocediendo a niveles similares a los de 2010. En la actualidad, el paí s vive una crisis de seguridad y de violencia generalizada que ha influido negativamente en la economí a. Esta situacio n abarca desde la crisis carcelaria hasta el incremento de percepcio n de inseguridad, debido a la existencia de grupos de delincuencia organizada. Estos extorsionan a trave s de las llamadas "vacunas" o chantajes que obligan a las personas a pagar un valor semanal o mensual a cambio de "proteger su vida".

Ante este contexto de inseguridad el Estado ha respondido estableciendo estados de excepcio n; hasta septiembre de 2024 se han instaurado ma s de cinco. Esta media tiene por motivo resguardar la seguridad en el paí s, pero produce efectos perversos en la democracia, ya que incrementa la desconfianza en las instituciones del paí s e incrementa la inestabilidad polí tica. Esta estrategia se ha popularizado entre los u ltimos gobiernos, puesto que se contabilizan 47 estados de excepcio n en los u ltimos 15 an os, es decir, un promedio 3 por an o.

Este escenario de inseguridad se ha convertido en el nuevo factor de expulsio n migratoria, suma ndose a la falta de oportunidades y la intencio n de mejorar las condiciones de vida. Las personas migran tanto hacia ciudades ma s seguras dentro del mismo paí s como a otros paí ses. A diferencia de los anteriores procesos migratorios, este movimiento se caracteriza por ser un e xodo familiar e irregular. Este nuevo e xodo se desarrolla por rutas irregulares y peligrosas como es la Selva del Darie n. Las estadí sticas oficiales exhiben un saldo migratorio negativo y creciente, en el 2022 asciende a 137545 ecuatorianos, no obstante, las cifras reales superan con creces a esta estadí stica.

La situacio n de crisis generalizada a nivel social, econo mica, ambiental es una causa como una consecuencia de la migracio n. Ecuador, ha vivido tres olas migratorias importantes, las cuales, como se establece en la teorí a, las consecuencias econo micas y sociales son significativas. La migracio n actual se intensifico a partir de la crisis por la pandemia por el COVID19, la cual produjo el cierre masivo de empresas, la pe rdida de empleos y un aumento en la pobreza y la desigualdad. Consecuentemente, esta migracio n afecta particularmente a personas pobres que, con el objetivo de mejorar sus oportunidades, optan por retomar un destino migratorio ya conocido: Estados Unidos. Sin embargo, las rutas informales que utilizan son peligrosas, y muchas personas no llegan a su destino.

Bibliografía

CEPAL (2017). Balance Preliminar de las Economí as de Ame rica Latina y el Caribe. En lí nea: https://repositorio.cepal.org/server/api/core/bitstreams/3cec2241-83b0-4475-b57a-c790c8a4fa37/content

CEPAL (2018). Balance Preliminar de las Economí as de Ame rica Latina y el Caribe. En lí nea: https://repositorio.cepal.org/server/api/core/bitstreams/1ec52cf2-976a-481fb82e-a2cfca6eb0d7/content CEPAL (2019). Balance

Caribe. En lí nea: https://repositorio.cepal.org/server/api/core/bitstreams/00d048e5-08cb-4b40- 8c41-18fd99b3a337/content

Cardoso Ruiz, Rene Patricio; Gives Ferna ndez, Luz del Carmen Migracio n ecuatoriana, ge nero y retorno en el siglo XXI CIENCIA ergo-sum, Revista Cientí fica Multidisciplinaria de Prospectiva, vol. 28, nu m. 2, 1, 2021 Universidad Auto noma del Estado de Me xico, Me xico Disponible en: https://www.redalyc.org/articulo.oa?id=10466283006 DOI: https://doi.org/ 10.30878/ces.v28n2a5

Serrano, A. (2008). Perfil migratorio del Ecuador. OIM. Quito. En lí nea: https://publications.iom. int/system/files/pdf/ecuador_profile.pdf.

ANÁLISIS (DE)CONSTRUCTIVISTA DEL DERECHO MIGRATORIO INTERNACIONAL: LAS IDEAS DE LA CONTRADICCIÓN

Juan Carlos Valarezo[1]

Introducción

El siguiente artículo nace del avance de una investigación sobre las paradojas legales en torno a la migración, con el objetivo de construir puentes de entendimiento entre campos académicos como el derecho, particularmente el derecho internacional, y las relaciones internacionales, en donde las ontologías y epistemologías de la migración pueden ser vistas desde diversas perspectivas. Específicamente se busca ver, a través de las premisas teóricas del constructivismo de Alexander Wendt en las Relaciones Internacionales, la evolución del marco normativo del Derecho Migratorio Internacional (DMI).

Conceptualmente, se parte también de la definición de deconstrucción de Jacques Derrida, debido a la relación que el autor plantea entre texto y significado, en un intento por reorganizar el pensamiento, en especial el occidental, ante un variado surtido de contradicciones y desigualdades no lógico-discursivas que se aprecian en la evolución de la normativa internacional de la migración (Derrida, 1997). Es por eso que se da especial atención al lenguaje a nivel histórico, especialmente los conceptos de migrante y migración. A nivel teórico, se toman las ideas de Alexander Wendt, en especial las del poder de las ideas, la constitución mutua entre agentes y estructuras, y el rol constitutivo y regulativo de las normas en el comportamiento estatal (Wendt, 1987, Wendt 1995, Wendt 1999).

Desarrollo

Las ideas son rutas de camino, puntos focales, que crean institucionalización a través de la socialización de y entre las unidades. Estas unidades no sólo poseen distintos grados de recursos de poder, sino también distintos conjuntos de ideas y de intereses. En su argumentación teórica, el constructivismo sostiene que los

---

[1] Juan Carlos Valarezo, Pontificia Universidad Católica del Ecuador.

intereses dan sentido al poder y que éstos descansan en gran medida en las ideas; por lo que las unidades ya no sólo se diferencian a partir de su poder relativo. Esta nueva forma de caracterizar las unidades abre espacios para entender la estructura en términos más amplios. Hay un reconocimiento de que la acción del Estado es posible sólo si existen instrumentos por medio de los cuales la acción puede ser, de hecho, llevada a cabo. Estas ideas dan paso al conocimiento compartido, a través del cual un recurso material (sea este el territorio, frontera, etc.), crea una práctica. Esto es en sí, desde el constructivismo, el proceso de creación de la estructura social.

En el caso del derecho migratorio internacional (DMI), este puede puede ser definido como el conjunto de normas internacionales que gobiernan el movimiento de personas entre Estados, así como el estatus legal de los migrantes en los Estados receptores. También puede ser descrito y conceptualizado literal y metafóricamente como una arquitectura de-constructivista de fragmentación basada en la disonancia y asimetría que cuestiona las tradiciones de armonía, unidad y estabilidad. La migración como tal es un campo transversal cuya gobernanza se caracteriza por una ecléctica serie de normas dispersas en una variedad de campos superpuestos: derechos humanos, derecho comercial, derecho laboral, derecho de refugio, derecho marítimo, etc.

Haciendo un análisis histórico de la doctrina legal del DMI (Chetail, 2016), se puede apreciar la disonancia y asimetría del significado de migración y migrante, yendo de un libre movimiento de personas como norma obligatoria del derecho internacional basada en la sociabilidad natural de los seres humanos (como lo establecía De Vitoria), a una separación entre el derecho a salir y el derecho a permanecer en un país extranjero, con ciertas restricciones (según Grocio), y luego a una concepción patrimonial del Estado donde la propiedad del territorio iguala a su soberanía (derecho de la propiedad), que luego captura a la inmigración y a la emigración como jurisdicción doméstica (desde la visión de Wolff), hasta concebir que la emigración es un derecho fundamental cuando el Estado de origen no puede proveer subsistencia o falla en proteger a sus ciudadanos; sin embargo, cae en la competencia del Estado anfitrión como consecuencia de la soberanía territorial (como lo percibía De Vattel).

Por otro lado, el constructivismo de Wendt cuestiona el carácter unidimensional de la estructura. Así, la estructura debe entenderse no simplemente conformada por la distribución material de los atributos de poder de las unidades, sino también por la distribución de intereses y de ideas de éstas. Al volver multidimensional el análisis de la estructura, el enfoque constructivista nos lleva necesariamente a sostener que la estructura no sólo restringe las acciones de los agentes (como lo sostiene el neorrealismo de Waltz), sino que también las posibilita. Es decir, dado que la estructura no sólo está constituida por la distribución material de los recursos de poder, sino también por la distribución de ideas, la estructura es tanto un medio como un límite para el accionar de los Estados. La estructura del Sistema hace posible las acciones al constituir actores con ciertas identidades e intereses y con capacidades materiales con ciertos significados. La agencia, por su parte, será la interacción que produce y reproduce estructuras de conocimiento compartido a lo largo del tiempo.

Para el caso del DIM, esta asimetría normativa entre emigración e inmigración se ha convertido en la ortodoxia del DMI actual. Por ejemplo, el control migratorio, como práctica, es una invención mucho más reciente (fin del siglo XIX) sentada las bases de ideas de siglos pasados. No es sino hasta 1920, sin embargo, que la Sociedad de Naciones estableció por primera vez un estándar mundial para pasaportes, por ejemplo. Paralelo a esta evolución estructural, Louis Varlez es quien usa por primera vez el término DMI en 1927, antes de que Richard Plender publicara su libro DMI en 1972. Con esto, se puede apreciar el carácter dialógico que hay entre la estructura creada por ideas y la posterior agencia que posibilita prácticas que hasta el día de hoy mantienen un carácter restrictivo y exclusivo para la migración.

Finalmente, en cuanto a la idea de Wendt sobre el rol constitutivo y regulativo de las normas en el comportamiento estatal, se denota que las reglas normativas prescriben y proscriben el comportamiento bajo circunstancias determinadas, mientras que las reglas constitutivas crean o definen nuevas formas de comportamiento. Las reglas constitutivas, también denominadas convenciones, son prácticas estandarizadas y relativamente constantes que constituyen un vocabulario que permite una suerte de comunicación internacional. Las reglas normativas están definidas por demandas públicas, respaldadas por sanciones, que prescriben, proscriben o permiten ciertos comportamientos para determinados actores en circunstancias dadas. La construcción de estas reglas implica dividir a los actores entre aquellos que siguen (o infringen) las reglas y aquellos que velan porque se cumplan; sin embargo, estas reglas aplican para ambos tipos de actores.

Para poder aplicar esta idea al caso de estudio, hay que referirse a las bases y pilares del DMI en las fuentes del derecho internacional, en especial el derecho consuetudinario. Es así que en esta fuente emergen dos pilares desiguales: el derecho de tratados y el "soft law" (derecho no vinculante). En el continuo de la migración (salida, admisión y estadía), la salida se ha divorciado de la admisión, que tiene requisitos sustantivos y procedimentales del derecho consuetudinario. En cuanto al derecho de tratados, según Chetail (2016) los mismos se enfocan en 3 categorías de migrantes: refugiados (Convención de Ginebra de 1951), trabajadores migrantes (Convenciones de trabajadores de 1949, 1975, 1990), y migrantes en contexto de tráfico (Protocolo de 2000), es decir que la lógica entre normas constitutivas y regulativas pone a las primeras como la base de la normativa internacional.

En cuanto al "soft law", pese a no ser una fuente formal, un número considerable de instrumentos no vinculantes han sido adoptados en las últimas décadas para guiar y fomentar la cooperación, creando gobernanza multinivel basada en 5 capas de instituciones y procesos: la Asamblea General de la ONU, el Foro Global de Migración y Desarrollo, el Grupo Global de Migración, organismos internacionales (OIM, ACNUR, OIT), y Estados (Chetail, 2019). Esto crea una proliferación de estándares no vinculantes y procesos consultivos entre actores con agendas diferentes y a veces conflictivas. Al mismo tiempo crea un fenómeno ambivalente: con el "soft law" la migración cae en el campo discreto de la "cooperación internacional" y muestra la renuencia del receptor de comprometerse a una forma obligatoria de gobernanza global.

Conclusiones

Como se puede observar, existe una clara disyuntiva entre la práctica y la normativa del DMI a nivel histórico y conceptual. Por ejemplo, el derecho consuetudinario y el derecho de tratados regula la emigración y estadía de migrantes, mientras que la admisión sigue "en construcción". Desde una lógica constructivista, el poder de las ideas, la constitución mutua entre agentes y estructuras, y el rol constitutivo y regulativo de las normas en el comportamiento estatal, dan luces para una mejor comprensión sobre la creación y contradicción del marco regulatorio en el campo de la migración.

Hay heterogeneidad y transversalidad que trasciende las ramas del derecho internacional, y por ello, a través de la plasticidad del DMI, se debe repensar a la migración como un fenómeno global, que se puede "de-construir" desde varias perspectivas, como el constructivismo en las relaciones internacionales, los estudios jurídicos críticos y el pluralismo legal en el derecho, o desde una perspectiva género y de ópticas del sur, entre otras.

Referencias

Chetail, V. (2016). Sovereignty and Migration in the Doctrine of the Law of Nations: An Intellectual History of Hospitality from Vitoria to Vattel. European Journal of International

Law.

Chetail V. (2019). International Migration Law. Oxford: Oxford University Press.

Derrida, J. (1972). Marges de la philosophie. Collection Critique. Paris: Minuit.

Derrida, J. (1997). Una filosofía deconstructiva. Barcelona: Anthropos.

Wendt, A. (1987). The Agent-Structure Problem in International Relations Theory. International Organization, Vol. 41, No. 3, pp. 335-370.

Wendt, A. (1995). Constructing International Politics. *International Security*, Vol. 20, No 1, pp 71-81.

Wendt, A. (1999). Social Theory of International Politics. Cambridge: University Press.

SITUACIÓN DE LOS Y LAS ADOLESCENTES MIGRANTES NO ACOMPAÑADAS EN CHILE, COLOMBIA, ECUADOR Y PERÚ: UN ANÁLISIS DE LA RESPUESTA ESTATAL DESDE LOS ESTÁNDARES INTERNACIONALES DE DERECHOS HUMANOS

Marcela Huaita, Julissa Chávez y Diana Manrique[1]

Introducción

La crisis política y humanitaria que ha atravesado Venezuela desde el 2015 ha desencadenado una migración masiva especialmente hacia países latinoamericanos. Se calcula que los/as niños, niñas y adolescentes (NNA) representan el 16% de migrantes venezolanos (Palomo et al., 2022). En este contexto, los/as adolescentes migrantes no acompañados (AMNA), han emergido como un grupo especialmente vulnerable y desatendido, dado que, si bien son personas menores de edad, y como tales deben ser sujetos de protección por parte de los Estados, al mismo tiempo se debe respetar y promover su autonomía progresiva, reconociéndoles su condición de sujetos de derecho. Al respecto, resulta importante reconocer que los/as NNA migrantes no acompañados/as[2] no son un grupo homogéneo (Pavez-Soto, 2017), y que podemos encontrar una diversidad de situaciones en la que se encuentran durante su tránsito por la región.

Una investigación centrada en adolescentes venezolano/as que llegan al Perú (GRIDEH, 2021), reveló que en muchos casos los/as adolescentes que emprenden rutas migratorias ya han enfrentado retos en su país de origen: violencia intrafamiliar, abandono escolar, desvinculación familiar, pobreza y deprivación, y que estos elementos configuran fuertes antecedentes para el inicio de su trayectoria migratoria y su capacidad de agencia para enfrentar las

---

[1] Marcela Huaita, GRIDEH member and professor at the Pontifical Catholic University of Peru.
Julissa Chávez, professor at the Pontifical Catholic University of Peru.
Diana Manrique, GRIDEH member at the Pontifical Catholic University of Peru.

[2] Niña, niño o adolescentes no acompañado a quien está separado de ambos padres y de otros parientes mayores de edad, y al momento no está al cuidado de un adulto al que, por ley o costumbre, le incumbe esa responsabilidad. Los/as adolescentes que estén únicamente con sus parejas, incluso si tienen hijos en común, corresponden a este grupo (Comité de los Derechos del Niño, 2005).

dificultades en la ruta.

Los sistemas de protección que acogen a AMNA en Chile, Colombia Ecuador y Perú

Los países andinos referidos tienen en común un marco internacional sólido en materia de derechos humanos (Palomo et al., 2022), tanto en niñez como en personas en movilidad, en virtud de ello, los Estados están obligados a respetar y garantizar sus derechos, en el marco de su interés superior y su capacidad evolutiva. Respecto a sus marcos nacionales, si bien la normativa migratoria prevé la obligación estatal de brindar una protección especial a los/as NNA en general, por el principio de igualdad y no discriminación cuando se está frente a NNA migrantes no acompañados/as se activan sistemas de protección que han sido previstos para la población nacional.

Del análisis realizado sobre esta normativa, se resalta que estos países han priorizado un enfoque de protección y asistencia a los/as NNA en contexto de migración, lo que implica proporcionar albergue, alimentación, atención médica y psicológica, garantizar el acceso a educación y oportunidades de capacitación, así como facilitar la reunificación familiar cuando sea posible, teniendo en cuenta expresamente al establecer sus procedimientos el interés superior del niño. Sin embargo, el fenómeno de la migración venezolana ha puesto en jaque a estos sistemas de protección nacionales, que no han sido pensados para atender las necesidades particulares de adolescentes en situación de movilidad transfronteriza. Por ello, en los últimos años se ha visto la necesidad de desarrollar protocolos ad hoc[3] como en Chile, Ecuador y Perú, lo que constituye una buena práctica. En Colombia se aplica el mismo procedimiento que a los/as adolescentes nacionales, aunque se ha desarrollado una estrategia ad hoc que prioriza la estrategia de reunificación familiar, a través del proyecto "Unidos reunificamos" (Instituto Colombiano de Bienestar Familiar, 2021).

Reconocimiento expreso de la categoría adolescente y grados de autonomía

Aunque sabemos que la Convención por los Derechos del Niño (CDN) no establece una edad divisoria entre niños/as y adolescentes (art. 1), sí reconoce su capacidad evolutiva (art. 5) lo que permite la caracterización de "adolescentes". Por ello, consideramos una buena práctica que en el marco estatal se haga hincapié en la necesidad de un tratamiento acorde a la edad, tal

---

[3] Ver en las referencias

como lo propone Chile, cuando se trata de la entrevista que debe realizar la judicatura para determinar las necesidades de protección del/a AMNA (Pleno de la Corte Suprema de Chile, 2021). Asimismo, Ecuador prevé expresamente que cuando no exista posibilidad de reinserción familiar, acogimiento familiar o adopción, la unidad de atención debe iniciar el proceso de autonomía siempre que él o la adolescente sea mayor de 15 años (Ministerio de Inclusión Económica y Social de Ecuador, 2023). Esta previsión, nos parece importante - en especial en el caso de las/os AMNA, dado que por sus singulares condiciones es altamente probable que no puedan ser reunificados con sus familias.

De acuerdo con las directrices de Naciones Unidas, los/las AMNAS, incluidos aquellos que llegan a un país de un modo irregular, no deberían ser privados de su libertad por el mero hecho de haber incumplido cualquier disposición legal por la que se rijan la entrada y estancia en el territorio (Naciones Unidas, 2010). Sin embargo, también es cierto que los Estados receptores deben proteger sus derechos y que muchas veces, esto requiere que sean institucionalizados/as, dados en adopción, u otras alternativas. Así, en muchos casos el juzgado o la autoridad administrativa disponen la institucionalización de los/as adolescentes como medida preferente, en lugar de aplicarla como último recurso, sin considerar la idoneidad de otras medidas como la previsión de viviendas que les permitan una semi autonomía. En ese sentido, es relevante que Ecuador cuente con la modalidad de "Alojamiento Independiente y Tutelado", especialmente para adolescentes cabeza de hogar (con hijos, con grupos de hermanos, entre otros), y adolescentes en proceso de independencia entre 16 y 17 años (Consejo Nacional para la Igualdad Intergeneracional, 2021).

La normativa peruana (Ministerio del Interior del Perú, 2017) contempla la posibilidad de otorgar una "visa humanitaria" a quienes, siendo extranjeros, se encuentren en territorio nacional sin reunir los requisitos para acceder a la condición de asilado o refugiado, y se encuentren en gran vulnerabilidad o peligro de vida en caso de abandono del territorio peruano o para quien requiere protección en atención a una grave amenaza o acto de violación o afectación de sus derechos fundamentales, siendo ello aplicable para los/as AMNA (Ministerio de la Mujer y Poblaciones Vulnerables de Perú, 2023). Esta calidad migratoria permite realizar actividades lucrativas de manera subordinada, autónoma o por cuenta propia. Si se concuerda con el Código de Niños y Adolescentes de dicho país, se tiene que, en general, la edad mínima para el trabajo son los 14 años, siempre que las labores a realizar no perjudiquen su salud o desarrollo, ni interfieran o limiten su asistencia a los centros educativos y permitan su participación en programas de orientación o formación profesional.

En virtud de esta norma, por el principio de igualdad y no discriminación, los/as AMNA deberían acceder a trabajos que no constituyan un peligro y más bien, lo que debería exigirse es que los Estados tengan la capacidad suficiente para supervisar las condiciones en las que este trabajo se estaría desarrollando. Ello resulta clave porque los/as adolescentes para obtener ingresos evitan estar en contacto con las autoridades, por temor a ser institucionalizados/as. Así, tratándose de un/a AMNA resulta importante reevaluar la posibilidad de permitirles que generen ingresos como parte de la determinación de su interés superior en casos concretos, especialmente, porque muchos buscan trabajar al provenir de familias con necesidades extremas.

Otro nudo problemático identificado es la situación de adolescentes mujeres que migran y que establecen relaciones de pareja con hombres adultos. Si bien la legislación establece principios y garantías para la protección de los/as AMNA, la reunificación familiar con parejas mayores de edad puede enfrentarse a desafíos legales, por el riesgo de abuso o explotación. Por ello, resulta relevante que Colombia prevea algunas modalidades de atención como el apoyo psicosocial dirigido a su desarrollo personal y a su condición particular, así como la intervención de apoyo que es la prestación de servicios ambulatorios con un mínimo de 10 sesiones y que constituyen un proceso de orientación individual y familiar (Instituto Colombiano de Bienestar Familiar, 2016).

Conclusiones

Aunque los países de la región andina han avanzado en la adopción de estándares internacionales en materia de protección de AMNA, persisten importantes vacíos en la implementación de normativas adecuadas para abordar las necesidades específicas de este grupo. Las respuestas estatales en Chile, Colombia, Ecuador y Perú han sido insuficientes ante el aumento de adolescentes en situación de movilidad transfronteriza, lo que ha llevado a la creación de protocolos especializados que, aunque valiosos, requieren fortalecimiento. De ahí la importancia de reconocer la autonomía progresiva de los AMNA en las decisiones migratorias, la protección de su derecho a la reunificación familiar, y el acceso a una calidad migratoria especial que les permita ejercer actividades laborales sin caer en situaciones de explotación. Las buenas prácticas reseñadas ofrecen ejemplos replicables. Sin embargo, es crucial que los sistemas de protección de la región evolucionen para garantizar los derechos de estos adolescentes, considerando su situación de vulnerabilidad y sus capacidades de agencia.

Referencias

Pleno de la Corte Suprema de Chile (2021). *Protocolo para la protección de niños, niñas y adolescentes no acompañados y separados en el contexto de la migración y/o en necesidad de protección internacional.* (AD-1251-2018). https://www.pjud.cl/prensa-y-comunicaciones/docs/download/30475

Consejo Nacional para la Igualdad Intergeneracional. (2021). Informe de Observancia - Movilidad humana de niños, niñas y adolescentes de nacionalidad venezolana en Ecuador. https://www.igualdad.gob.ec/wp-content/uploads/downloads/2021/06/informe_obs_movhumana_nnvenez2.pdf

Comité de los Derechos del Niño. (2005). *Trato de los menores no acompañados y separados de su familia fuera de su país de origen.* Observación general 6. https://tbinternet.ohchr.org/_ layouts/15/ treatybodyexternal/ Download.aspx?symbolno=CRC%2FGC%2F2005%2F6&Lang=en

GRIDEH – Grupo Interdisciplinario de Investigación en Derechos Humanos y Derecho Internacional Humanitario (2021). Proyecto de investigación *"Adolescentes venezolanos/as ¿no acompañados/as?: trayectorias migratorias al desafío de las violencias de género y el acceso a los servicios sociales en Perú"*, financiado por la Dirección de Gestión de la Investigación de la PUCP mediante la subvención DGI-*2021-C-0019 / PI0747.*

Instituto Colombiano de Bienestar Familiar. (2016). *Lineamiento técnico del programa especializado para la atención a adolescentes y mujeres mayores de 18 años, gestantes o en periodo de lactancia, con sus derechos inobservados, amenazados o vulnerados* https://www.icbf.gov.co/sites/default/files/procesos/lm6.p_lineamiento_tecnico_ para_ la_ atencion_de_adolescentes_y_mujeres_mayores_de_18_anos_gestantes_o_en_periodo_de_lactancia_v1.pdf

Instituto Colombiano de Bienestar Familiar. (2021). Estrategia de estabilización, integración y futuro de niños, niñas, adolescentes, jóvenes migrantes y sus familias provenientes de Venezuela. https://www.icbf.gov.co/ sites/default/files/30122021_estrategia_migracion_v2._final_esta_si.pdf

Naciones Unidas. (2010). *Directrices sobre las modalidades alternativas de cuidado de los niños* (Resolución de Asamblea General N° A/RES/64/142). https://www.acnur.org/fileadmin/Documentos/ BDL/2010/8064. pdf? file=fileadmin/Documentos/BDL/2010/8064

Ministerio de Inclusión Económica y Social de Ecuador. (2022). Acuerdo Interministerial No. 0001, de 20 de octubre de 2022, suscrito por el Ministerio de Inclusión Económica y Social, Ministerio de Relaciones Exteriores y Movilidad Humana, y Ministerio del Interior. https://servicios.inclusion.gob.ec/Lotaip_ Mies/ phocadownload/02_feb_2024/numeral_21_politicas-publicas-o-informacion-grupo-especifico/ Acuerdo%20Interministerial%20 Nro.%200001, %20de %2020 %20de%20octubre%20de%202022%20-%20MIES,%20MREMH,%20MDI.pdf

Ministerio de Inclusión Económica y Social de Ecuador. (2023). *Norma técnica para el servicio de acogimiento institucional.* https://www.inclusion.gob.ec/wp-content/uploads/2023/05/Norma-Tecnica-Acogimiento-Institucional_2023.pdf

Ministerio del Interior del Perú. (2017). Decreto Supremo que aprueba el Reglamento del Decreto Legislativo N.° 1350, Decreto Legislativo de Migraciones y aprueban nuevas calidades migratorias (Decreto Supremo N.° 007-2017-IN).

Ministerio de la Mujer y Poblaciones Vulnerables de Perú. (2023). *Protocolo de las unidades de protección especial para la atención de niñas, niños y adolescentes refugiadas/os o migrantes en situación de riesgo de desprotección familiar o desprotección familiar* (Resolución Directoral 076-2023-MIMP-DGNNA). https://www.gob.pe/institucion/mimp/normas-legales/4415795-076-2023-mimp-dgnna

Colombia (2021), Resolución 971 de 2021, Título IV, regula la aplicación del Estatuto Temporal de Protección para Migrantes Venezolanos a los niños, aplicándose el Proceso administrativo de restablecimiento de derechos (PARD) creado por el Código de la infancia y la adolescencia.

Palomo, N.; Machado, A.; Sato, L. (2022). Niñas, niños y adolescentes en movimiento: Dimensión y respuesta pública desde la protección social - Un análisis de la migración venezolana en países de América Latina y el Caribe, Research Report, No. 71, International Policy Centre for Inclusive Growth (IPC-IG), Brasilia. ISSN:2526-0499. https://ipcig.org/sites/default/ files/ pub/ es/RR70_Sumario_Ejecutivo_Ninas_ninos_y_adolescentes_en_movimiento.pdf

Pavez-Soto, I. (2017). La niñez en las migraciones globales: perspectivas teóricas para analizar su participación. *Tla-melaua*, 10(41), 96-113. ISSN 2594-0716. https://www.scielo.org.mx/ scielo. php?pid=S1870-69162017000100096&script=sci_abstract&tlng=es

PAPERS IN TURKISH

AKIŞKAN SINIRLARIN GÜVENLIĞINI SAĞLAMA: TÜRKIYE-İRAN SINIRINDA GÖÇ YÖNETIMINDEKI ZORLUKLAR VE FIRSATLAR

Güven Şeker

Giriş

Türkiye-İran sınırı, yüzyıllık tarihsel etkileşimler ve karmaşık jeopolitik oyunların yoğurduğu, göç yönetiminde kritik bir alanı temsil ettiği düşünülmektedir (Oztig ve Okur, 2022; Ceylan, 2023). Bu çalışma, coğrafi konumu ve bölgesel dinamikleri göz önüne alındığında, konu sınırın kendine özgü zorluklarını ve fırsatlarını keşfetmeyi amaçlamaktadır. Birincil hedefimiz, Türkiye-İran sınırında göçü ve sınır güvenliğini yöneten kurumsal, yasal ve operasyonel çerçeveleri incelemektir. Ayrıca, düzensiz göç, sınır ötesi kaçakçılık ve insan ticareti gibi acil sorunları tanımlamayı ve bölgesel iş birliğini ve politika uygulamasını iyileştirmek için kanıta dayalı öneriler sunmayı hedeflemektedir. Bu araştırma, Türkiye-İran sınırının etkin yönetiminin, ulusal güvenliği, ekonomik kalkınmayı, insan haklarına saygıyı ve bütünleşmiş bölgesel iş birliğini bir bütün olarak ele alan dengeli bir strateji gerektirdiği temel varsayımına dayanmaktadır.

Türkiye-İran sınırının operasyonel uygulama alanı, köklü anlaşmalar ve yasal çerçevelerle şekillenmiştir. Bu temelleri anlamak, çağdaş sınır yönetiminin karmaşıklığını kavramak için hayati öneme sahiptir. İkili ilişkilerin temel taşı, 14 Mart 1937'de Tahran'da imzalanan 1937 Güvenlik Anlaşması' dır (Türkiye Büyük Millet Meclisi, 1937). Bu anlaşma, sınır bölgelerindeki anlaşmazlıkları çözme ve güvenliği sağlama konusunda kapsamlı yönergeler belirlemiştir. Özellikle Madde 5, Birinci Derece Sınır Komiserlikleri (Kaymakamlıklar) arasında iki ayda bir, İkinci Derece Sınır Komiserlikleri (Valilikler) arasında ise yılda iki kez düzenli toplantıları zorunlu kılmaktadır. Bu çok katmanlı yaklaşım, sürtüşmelere rağmen istikrarı sürdürmeyi amaçlayan uzun soluklu bir diplomatik geleneği vurgulamaktadır (Omidi ve Özdağ, 2023; Oztig ve Okur, 2022).

Türkiye'nin iç hukuk mevzuatı da sınır yönetimi stratejilerini belirlemede önemli bir rol oynamaktadır. 3497 Sayılı Kanun, kara sınır güvenliği sorumluluğunu Türk Kara Kuvvetleri Komutanlığı'na verirken, belirli alanları Jandarma Genel Komutanlığı'nın yetki alanına bırakmaktadır (Koca, 2020; Luerdi ve Hakim,

2020). Bu, ulusal güvenlik stratejisinin bir yansımasıdır. Ayrıca, Kara Sınırlarının Korunması ve Güvenliği Hakkında Yönetmelik, askeri birimlerin rollerini, fiziksel güvenlik sistemlerini ve ortak teknik komisyonların işlevlerini detaylandırmaktadır. Bu yasal araçlar, ileri gözetim sistemleri gibi teknolojilerin bütünleşmesi yolu ile kaçakçılığı ve terörü önlemeyi amaçlamaktadır (Koca, 2020; Ollier, 2023).

Türkiye-İran sınırının etkin yönetimi, sivil ve askeri otoritelerin iş birliğini ve ortak güvenlik komitelerini içeren karmaşık bir kurumsal çerçeveye dayanmaktadır.

Sınır yönetiminin merkezinde, sivil yöneticilerin ve askeri birimlerin farklı ancak işbirlikçi rolleri yer almaktadır. Vali ve Kaymakam gibi Sivil Yöneticiler, Sınır Komiserleri olarak görev yapar; uluslararası anlaşmaları uygulamak, kamu düzenini sağlamak ve yasa dışı faaliyetleri önlemekle doğrudan sorumludurlar, (Ekmekcioğlu ve Yıldız, 2023) bu sorumlu yöneticiler adına genellikle polis birimleri iş ve işlemleri takip ederler. Askeri Birimler (Kara Kuvvetleri Komutanlığı ve Jandarma Genel Komutanlığı), fiziki güvenlik ve uygulamayı sağlar. Devriyeler, sınır izleme ve tehditlere müdahale görevlerini yürütürler ve sivil otoritelerle ortak operasyonlarda iş birliği yaparlar. Sınır boyunca inşa edilen duvarlar gibi fiziksel engeller, bu askeri rolün bir kanıtıdır (Ollier, 2025.; Olejárová, 2018).

Kapsamlı sınır yönetimi için her iki ülke de Ortak Güvenlik Komiteleri sistemini kullanmaktadır. Yüksek Güvenlik Komisyonu (1989 anlaşmasıyla kurulan), ulusal güvenlik ve bölgesel istikrar tehditlerini ele alır. Stratejik tartışmalar ve terörle mücadele, organize suç ve düzensiz göçle ilgili politikaların belirlenmesi için üst düzey yetkilileri bir araya getirir (Omidi ve Özdağ, 2023). Daha alt düzeyde ise, Alt Güvenlik Komitesi ve Ortak Teknik Komisyonlar gibi Alt Komiteler bulunur. Bu komiteler, kaçakçılık rotaları ve yasa dışı geçişler gibi yerelleşmiş konulara odaklanır, günlük operasyonel etkinliği sağlarlar. Bu çok katmanlı yapı hem stratejik koordinasyonu hem de yerel düzeyde operasyonel duyarlılığı mümkün kılar.

Türkiye-İran sınırının yönetimi, sosyo-ekonomik farklılıklar, güvenlik tehditleri ve operasyonel sınırlamalardan kaynaklanan önemli zorluklarla karşı karşıyadır. Türkiye ve İran arasındaki ekonomik farklılıklar, düzensiz göç ve kaçakçılığın temel nedenidir. Sınır bölgelerindeki işsizlik ve yoksulluk, yerel halkı kaçakçılığa yöneltir; bu, birçok sınır köyünde bir yaşam biçimi haline gelmiştir (Deniz ve Doğu, 2008). Bu durum, sadece ekonomik değil, aynı zamanda kültürel ve sosyal değişimlere de yol açar. Kaçakçılar genellikle AB sınır kontrolleri düzenine uygun olarak formüle edilmiş uygulamalar ve yolsuzluk gibi sorunlarla karşılaşırlar (Augustova ve Suber, 2023). Bu köklü nedenleri ele almak için sosyo-ekonomik kalkınma girişimleri hayati öneme sahiptir.

Sınırda çeşitli güvenlik tehditleri sürekli dikkat gerektirir. Kaçakçılık, narkotik, yakıt, tekstil ve elektronik gibi yasa dışı malları içerir ve Türkiye'yi uluslararası uyuşturucu ticaretinde kritik bir geçiş noktası yaptığı bilinmektedir (Soykan ve Karasoy, 2022). İnsan kaçakçılığı da önemli bir sorundur, binlerce düzensiz göçmenin istismara uğramasına neden olur (Deniz, 2022). Ayrıca, IŞİD ve PKK/PYD/YPG gibi terör örgütlerinin sınır ötesi hareketleri ciddi risk oluşturur (Luerdi ve Hakim, 2020; Avatkov ve Sbitneva, 2022). Bu gruplar, kaçakçılık rotalarını kullanarak insan kaynağı ve silah transferi yaparlar. Kaçakçılık ve terör arasındaki bağlantı, bütünleşik güvenlik stratejilerini zorunlu kılar (Achilli ve Tinti, 2019; Musayev, 2023). Bunların yanında sadece bir konu bazlı değil, kaçakçılık (insan ve eşya gibi) ve terör (farklı gruplar) gibi farklı konuların tek aktörler tarafından yönetilerek sınırda kar ve menfaat amaçlı olarak yürütülebildiği de görülmektedir.

Yasal ve kurumsal çerçevelere rağmen, pratik operasyonel sınırlamalar optimal sınır yönetimini engellemektedir. Yetersiz kaynaklar (insan gücü, maliyet, eski altyapı) devriye, gözetim ve hızlı müdahale etkinliklerini sınırlar. Yeterince eğitimli personel eksikliği de etkin uygulamayı zorlaştırır. Özellikle asker, polis ve sivil görev alanların sürekli yer değiştirmesi de diğer bir problemli konu olarak da görülmektedir. En kritik sorunlardan biri, sınır yetkilileri arasındaki iletişim boşluklarıdır; bu, olaylara müdahaleyi geciktirir (Deniz ve Doğu, 2008). Dağlık arazi gibi coğrafi zorluklar bu durumları daha da kötüleştirir. Bu sınırlamaları aşmak için yatırım ve bütünleşik bilgi yönetimi gereklidir (Yang vd., 2022; Setiawan vd., 2020).

Yöntem

Bu çalışma, jeopolitik gerginlikler, ekonomik farklılıklar ve kültürel bağların etkilediği Türkiye-İran sınırındaki göç yönetiminin karmaşık yapısını anlamayı amaçlamaktadır. Bu bağlamda göçü ve sınır güvenliğini denetleyen kurumsal, yasal ve operasyonel çerçeveleri ortaya koymaktır. Ayrıca, düzensiz göç, sınır ötesi kaçakçılık ve insan ticareti gibi acil sorunları belirleyerek, bölgesel iş birliğini ve politika uygulamasını iyileştirmek için kanıta dayalı öneriler sunmayı hedeflemektedir. Araştırma, sınır güvenliği, insan hareketliliği ve uluslararası iş birliği hakkında mevcut bilgi birikimine dayanmaktadır. İran ve Türkiye arasındaki 1937 Güvenlik Paktı ve Alt Güvenlik Komitesi gibi karşılıklı güvenlik komitelerinin işleyişi de dahil olmak üzere önemli tarihi anlaşmalara atıfta bulunulmuştur. Ayrıca, devletlerin sınır ötesi dinamiklere nasıl tepki verdiğini daha iyi anlamak için "sınır güvenliği" ve "göç diplomasisi" etrafındaki teorik çerçeveleri birleştirilecektir.

Araştırmamızda, karma yöntemli bir yaklaşım kullanılmıştır. Bu yaklaşım, ikili anlaşmalar, protokoller ve Hudut Komiserliği gelen raporları (2009-2011) gibi resmî belgelerin nitel içerik analizini, yerel yetkililer, güvenlik personeli ve göç uzmanlarının katıldığı yarı yapılandırılmış görüşmelerle birleştirmektedir. Van ve Ağrı illeri gibi önemli sınır bölgelerinde yürütülen gözlemsel araştırmalar, bu bölgelerin yerel gerçeklikleri ve zorlukları hakkındaki anlayışımızı zenginleştirmiştir.

Bulgular ve Tartışma

Türkiye'nin doğusunda yer alan ve İran ile önemli bir sınır kesimini paylaşan Van İli, bu karmaşık bölgedeki sınır yönetiminin pratik uygulamasını ve zorluklarını anlamak için çok önemli bir vaka çalışması niteliğindedir. Coğrafi özellikleri, düzensiz göç için önemli bir giriş noktası olmasıyla birleştiğinde, burayı güvenlik ve insani endişeler için bir odak noktası haline getirmektedir. Türkiye ile İran arasındaki toplam sınır, 314 sınır taşını kapsamakta ve yaklaşık 278 km uzunluğundadır; bunun önemli bir kısmı Van İli içinde yer almaktadır. Özellikle dağlık ve engebeli arazi gibi olumsuz doğal koşullar, her iki ülke için de sınır güvenliğini sağlamada önemli zorluklar yaratmaktadır. Bu zorlu koşullar, kaçakçılık faaliyetlerinin, üçüncü ülkelere yasa dışı geçişlerin ve çeşitli sınır olaylarının artmasına doğrudan katkıda bulunmaktadır.

İdari Yapı ve Yetki Alanları

Van İl'inde sınır güvenliği ve yönetim protokollerinin uygulanması, 1937 Güvenlik Anlaşması'nda belirtilen çok katmanlı yaklaşıma uygun olarak titizlikle yapılandırılmış bir idari çerçeveye bağlıdır. Birincil operasyonel düzeyde, genellikle Kaymakam olan Birinci Derece Sınır Komiserleri bulunmaktadır; bunlar sınırın belirli kesimlerini denetlerler. Bu kesimler, sınır taşı numaraları ile titizlikle belirlenmiştir ve her komiser, kendi belirlenmiş alanındaki acil güvenlik, kamu düzeni ve olaylara müdahaleden sorumludur. Bu sorumluluklar, İranlı mevkidaşlarının sorumluluklarıyla doğrudan örtüşmekte, ikili iş birliğinin yerelleşmiş doğasını vurgulamaktadır (Türkiye Büyük Millet Meclisi, 1937).

Van İli'ndeki bu yetki alanlarının ayrıntılı bir dökümü, operasyonel özelliklere ilişkin kritik bir içgörü sağlamaktadır:

• Çaldıran Kaymakamlığı, İran tarafındaki Kilisekent ve Siyahçeşme Sınır

Komiserlikleri ile iş birliği yapar.

• Özalp Kaymakamlığı, mevkidaşları Siyahçeşme ve Belesor Sınır Komiserlikleri'dir.

• Saray Kaymakamlığı, Belesor ile Kotur Sınır Komiserlikleri ile iş birliği yapar.

• Başkale Kaymakamlığı, İranlı mevkidaşları Kotur, Sinci ve Sero Sınır Komiserlikleri'dir.

Sınırı Derece Sınır Komiseri düzeyinde, Van Valiliği geniş vilayet kesiminden sorumludur. İlgili İranlı Birinci Derece Sınır Komiserlikleri Makü, Hoy, Salmas ve Urumiye'dir. Vali ve Kaymakamların sınır komiseri olarak başlıca görevleri, uluslararası anlaşmaları uygulamak, iyi komşuluk ilişkilerini geliştirmek, ulusal çıkarları korumak ve sınır olaylarını çözmektir. Bu çok katmanlı yaklaşım, karmaşık sınır yönetimine yönelik ayrıntılı idari çabayı vurgular. Ancak, sistemin başarısı, Van bölgesinin engebeli arazisi ve düzensiz göç için bir geçiş noktası olması nedeniyle zorlu olabilen ön saflardaki yöneticiler arasındaki tutarlı iletişim ve güven inşasına bağlıdır (Ekmekcioğlu ve Yıldız, 2023; Deniz, 2022).

Olaylara Müdahale Mekanizmaları ve Operasyonel Gerçekler

Sınır olaylarına müdahale için resmi protokoller, sistematik ve koordineli yanıtları sağlamak üzere tasarlanmıştır. Bu mekanizmalar genellikle ortak soruşturmaları, olayın belgelenmesini ve üzerinde anlaşmaya varılmış takip eylemlerini içerir. 1937 Güvenlik Anlaşması (Madde 5) ile öngörülen düzenli toplantılar, bu tür olayların gözden geçirilmesi ve bilgi alışverişi için platformlar olarak hizmet etmeyi amaçlamaktadır (Türkiye Büyük Millet Meclisi, 1937).

Ancak, bu köklü protokollere rağmen, Van İl'inde ve daha geniş sınır boyunca olaylara müdahale verimliliğini ve etkinliğini önemli ölçüde engelleyen ciddi zorluklar sıklıkla yaşanmaktadır. Yetkililer tarafından tespit edilen tekrarlayan bir sorun, özellikle daha düşük operasyonel düzeylerdeki Türk ve İranlı yetkililer arasında toplantıların yapılmasındaki gecikmelerdir. Bazen olaydan altı ay sonra bile toplantıların yapılabildiği gözlemlenmiştir. Bu gecikmeler, bürokratik atalet ve yetersizlikler, lojistik zorluklar veya siyasi hassasiyetler gibi faktörlerden kaynaklanabilmektedir.

Ayrıca, doğru belgeleme için yetersiz malzeme kaynakları yaygın bir sorundur. Kamera, ulaşım aracı ve nitelikli personel eksikliği, "kaliteli durum tespitlerinin" yapılmasını engellemektedir. Sınırla ilgili konularda çok boyutlu yaklaşabilecek uzman personel eksikliği ve sekreterya personelinin olay yerinde bulunmaması da belgeleme sürecini olumsuz etkilemektedir.

Sınır makamlarının yönetmesi gereken olay türleri, çeşitlilik göstermektedir: Yasa dışı geçiş, kasıtlı veya kasıtsız insan ve hayvan sınır ihlalleri, adam öldürme, yaralama, hırsızlık, kaçakçılık, yangın çıkarma, hava sahası ihlali, sınır işaretlerinin değiştirilmesi, karşı tarafa ateş edilmesi, akarsuların talveg hattının değiştirilmesi, yasa dışı avlanma, mayın sökme, demiryolu tahribatı, yasa dışı kaynak kullanımı, gözetimsiz hayvanlar, resmi temaslar dışında tehdit/tahrik/tahkir, toprak fotoğraflama, özel aydınlatma ile kasıtlı aydınlatma, propaganda faaliyetleri ve diğer anlaşmalarla belirtilen fiiller. Bu kapsamlı liste, sorumlulukların genişliğini ve tehditlerin çeşitliliğini vurgulamaktadır.

Sonuç

Türkiye-İran sınırı, karmaşık jeopolitik ve sosyo-ekonomik baskılarla şekillenmiş, dinamik bir sınırdır. Başarılı yönetimi, ulusal güvenliği, bölgesel ekonomik kalkınmayı ve insan haklarını dengeleyen nüanslı bir yaklaşım gerektirir. Mevcut anlaşmalar ve kurumsal çerçeveler iş birliği için zemin sağlasa da ekonomik farklılıklar, güvenlik tehditleri ve operasyonel sınırlamalar önemli zorluklar yaratmaktadır.

Kurumsal çerçevenin analizi, sivil ve askeri otoriteler arasındaki kritik iş birliğini ve ortak güvenlik komitelerinin rolünü göstermiştir. Van İli vaka çalışması, idari yapıların ve olay müdahale mekanizmalarının, kaynak eksiklikleri ve iletişim engelleri nedeniyle karşılaştığı pratik zorlukları ortaya koymuştur. Kurumsal belgelerden elde edilen bilgiler, toplantılardaki gecikmeler, yetersiz belgeleme ve uzman personel ihtiyacı gibi operasyonel darboğazları vurgulamaktadır.

Bu zorlukları hafifletmek ve sürdürülebilir bir sınır yönetimi modeli geliştirmek için, bu çalışma çok yönlü bir yaklaşım önermektedir: kurumsal kapasitenin güçlendirilmesi (eğitim ve bilgi paylaşımı), ileri teknolojiden yararlanma (gözetim sistemleri ve iletişim altyapısı) ve topluluk katılımının derinleştirilmesi (yasal yollar hakkında farkındalık ve STK iş birliği) gibi yaklaşımlar önerilmektedir. Bu öneriler, insan haklarını ve sosyo-ekonomik kalkınmayı güvenlik gereklilikleriyle dengeleyerek, Türkiye ve İran'ın ortak sınırlarını istikrar ve karşılıklı fayda bölgesine dönüştürebilir. Bu yaklaşım, sadece ulusal çıkarların güvenliğini değil, aynı zamanda bu hayati sınır boyunca yaşayan ve etkileşimde bulunan toplulukların refahını da sağlamaktadır.

References

Achilli, L., & Tinti, A. (2019). Debunking the smuggler-terrorist nexus: Human smuggling and the Islamic State in the Middle East. Studies in Conflict & Terrorism, 45(5), 463–478. https://doi.org/10.1080/1057610X.2019.1678884

Altunbaş, Ç., & MemiSoglu, F. (2024). Securitization of European Union migration policies and its impact on border security: A comparative analysis of Greece and Turkey. Lectio Socialis, 8(1), 35–56. https://doi.org/10.47478/lectio.1412017

Augustova, K., & Suber, D. (2023). The Kurdish kaçakçı on the Iran-Turkey border: Corruption and survival as EU sponsored counter-smuggling effects. Trends in Organized Crime, 26(1), 48–63. https://doi.org/10.1007/s12117-023-09484-3

Avatkov, V. A., & Sbitneva, A. I. (2022). Transformation of Turkey's Anti-Terrorism Policy under the AKP. MGIMO Review of International Relations, 15(3), 143–174. https://doi.org/10.24833/2071-8160-2022-3-84-143-174

Ceylan, T. İ. (2023). Peace at home, a minor intervention abroad? Explaining the Turkish-Iranian border revision of 1932. DIYÂR, 4(2), 262–280. https://doi.org/10.5771/2625-9842-2023-2-262

Das, P. (2021). Border management and threats to internal Security. Electronic Journal of Social Sciences and Strategic Studies, 2(1), 89–110. https://doi.org/10.47362/EJSSS.2021.2106

Deniz, O. (2022). Türkiye İran Sinirinda Düzensiz Göç Ve Göçmenlerin Sinir Geçme Pratikleri. İstanbul Ticaret Üniversitesi Sosyal Bilimler Dergisi, 21(Özel Sayı), 254–273. https://doi.org/10.46928/iticusbe.1148196

Deniz, O., & Doğu, A. F. (2008). Türkiye-İran Sınırı: Sınırın Coğrafi Durumu Ve Sınır Köylerimizin Sosyo-Ekonomik Yapıları / Turkish-Iran Border: Geographical Condition of the Border and Socio-Economic Structure of Our Border Villages. Doğu Coğrafya Dergisi, 13(19), 49–72. https://doi.org/10.17295/DCD.78377

Doyle, T. (2010). Collaborative border management. World Customs Journal, 4(1), 15–22. https://doi.org/10.55596/001c.91376

Ekmekcioğlu, A., & Yıldız, M. (2023). How Street-Level Bureaucrats Perceive and Deal with Irregular Migration From Borders: The Case of Van, Türkiye. Journal of Borderlands Studies. https://doi.org/10.1080/08865655.2023.2202209

Guven, M. (2024). An AI-based surveillance system proposal for the second line of defense against irregular migration, smuggling, and terrorism: Gendarme assessment. Güvenlik Bilimleri Dergisi, 13(1), 63–84. https://doi.org/10.28956/gbd.1454962

Husain, T. (2024). Cross Border Security Challenges for Bangladesh. Society & Sustainability, 6(1), 617. https://doi.org/10.38157/ss.v6i1.617

Kheirkhah, M., Allen, M. B., & Emami, M. (2009). Quaternary syn-collision magmatism from the Iran/Turkey borderlands. Journal of Volcanology and Geothermal Research, 182(1–2), 1–12. https://doi.org/10.1016/J.JVOLGEORES.2009.01.026

Koca, B. (2020). Bordering processes through the use of technology: The Turkish case. Journal of Ethnic and Migration Studies, 48(11), 1909–1926. https://doi.org/10.1080/1369183X.2020.1796272

Laouira, M., Abdelkrim, A., Othman, J., & Kim, H. (2021). An Efficient WSN Based Solution for Border Surveillance. IEEE Transactions on Sustainable Computing, 6(1), 54–65. https://doi.org/10.1109/TSUSC.2019.2904855

Luerdi, L., & Hakim, A. (2020). Turkey's border security policy against non-state actors (2016–2019). The Journal of International Studies, 4(2), 179–200. https://doi.org/10.24198/intermestic.v4n2.5

Miller, D., & Chtouris, S. (2017). Borderland Security and Migration: Balancing Humanitarian

Response with Crisis Preparedness & Emergency Management—The Social and Cultural Challenges to Homeland Security. Journal of Applied Security Research, 12(1), 1–6. https://doi.org/10.1080/19361610.2017.1227620

Musayev, N. H. (2023). Terrorism As A Threat To Border Security. International Journal of Innovative Technologies in Social Science, 3(39). https://doi.org/10.31435/rsglobal_ijitss/30092023/8019

Okyay, A. (2017). Turkey's post-2011 approach to its Syrian border and its implications for domestic politics. International Affairs, 93(4), 829–846. https://doi.org/10.1093/IA/IIX068

Olejárová, B. (2018). The Great Wall of Turkey: From „The Open-Door Policy" to Building Fortress? https://doi.org/10.25167/PPBS55

Ollier, J. (2023). Border Securitization Cycles: Periodizing Turkey's management of its Iranian border (1920–2020). DIYÂR, 4(2), 210–231. https://doi.org/10.5771/2625-9842-2023-2-210

Ollier, J. (2025). Turkey's Walled Borders: A Multiscalar Approach. Journal of Borderlands Studies, 1–18. https://doi.org/10.1080/08865655.2025.2457610

Omidi, A., & Orhon Özdağ, H. (2023). Analyzing the Mutual Geopolitical and Security Complementarity of Iran and Turkey: Border, energy, and water. Journal of Balkan and Near Eastern Studies, 25(5), 923–943. https://doi.org/10.1080/19448953.2023.2167182

Oztig, L. I., & Okur, M. A. (2022). Border Settlement Dynamics and Border Status Quo: A Comparative Analysis of Turkey's Borders. Geopolitics, 28(7), 1892–1919. https://doi.org/10.1080/14650045.2022.2084385

Setiawan, M.R.S., Mendrofa, E.L.a.M., & Pramana, G.M.a.P. (2020). Border Management: Challenges And Issues At the Border In Indonesia. Customs Research and Applications Journal, 2(2), 84–104. https://doi.org/10.31092/craj.v2i2.65

Soykan, M., & Karasoy, H. (2022). The fight against drugs and border security policy in Turkey. Pamukkale Journal of Eurasian Socioeconomic Studies, 9(2), 132–146. https://doi.org/10.34232/pjess.1183006

Sun, Z., Wang, P., Vuran, M. C., Al-Rodhaan, M. A., Al-Dhelaan, A. M., & Akyildiz, I. F. (2011). BorderSense: Border patrol through advanced wireless sensor networks. Ad Hoc Networks, 9(3), 468–477. https://doi.org/10.1016/j.adhoc.2010.09.008

Tholen, B. (2010). The changing border: Developments and risks in border control management of Western countries. International Review of Administrative Sciences, 76(2), 259–278. https://doi.org/10.1177/0020852309365673

Türkiye Büyük Millet Meclisi. (1937). Türkiye Cumhuriyeti ile İran Devleti Şehinşahisi arasındaki antlaşma (Law No. 3215, Enacted: June 7, 1937; Published in Resmî Gazete : June 21, 1937, Issue No. 3636). https://www5.tbmm.gov.tr/tutanaklar/KANUNLAR_KARARLAR/kanuntbmmc017/kanuntbmmc017/kanuntbmmc01703215.pdf . Accessed June 16, 2025.

Yang, J., Kang, J., & Jeon, Y. (2022). A functional integration model of border information management. Crisisonomy, 18(6), 1–19. https://doi.org/10.14251/crisisonomy.2022.18.6.1

ULUSLARARASI ÖĞRENCILER VE UYUM SÜREÇLERI: ANADOLU ÜNIVERSITESI ÖRNEĞI

Filiz Göktuna Yaylacı[1]

Giriş

Son elli yıllık dönemde yükseköğretim giderek daha yüksek düzeyde uluslararası bir nitelik kazanmıştır. Bu süreçte uluslararası öğrenci sayısı 800 binlerden 6 milyona ulaşmıştır. Uluslararasılaşma aynı zamanda yoğun bir rekabet alanı oluşturmaktadır (YÖK, 2017; Altbach, 1991; Yu & Moskal, 2019; IOM, 2024; YÖK, 2017; Zhao, 2021; Topal & Tauscher, 2020; Türel, 2021). Yükseköğretimde uluslararasılaşmanın etkili olduğu bu süreçte uluslararası öğrencilerin refahı, uyumu ve memnuniyeti gibi meseleler daha fazla gündeme gelmektedir (Sin & Tavares, 2019).

Yükseköğretimde uluslararasılaşma artan bir akademik bir ilginin de hedefi olmuştur. Özellikle öğrencilerin yaşamış olduğu sorunlarla ilgili çok sayıda araştırma yapılmıştır. Genel olarak bakıldığında araştırmalar, dil yetersizliği, kültür şoku, sosyal ilişkilerde güçlükler ve ekonomik sorunlara işaret etmektedir (Taylor & Ali, 2017; Göktuna Yaylacı, Yaylacı & Uzun, 2023; Ballo, Mathias ve Weimer, 2019).

Türkiye de son yıllarda uluslararası öğrenciler için cazibe merkezi haline gelen ülkeler arasında yer almaktadır. Türkiye'de artan uluslararası öğrenci varlığı yükseköğretim kurumlarının yanında yerel toplulukları ekonomik, sosyal ve kültürel açılardan etkilemektedir. Bununla birlikte söz konusu alanlarda yapılan akademik çalışmaların sınırlı olduğu söylenebilir (Erişti, Polat & Erdem, 2018; Türel, 2021). Bu bağlamda Türkiye'de yükseköğretimde uluslararasılaşmanın sonuçları, ulusları öğrencilerin yaşadığı sorunlar ve uyum süreçleri hakkında daha fazla çalışma yapılması hem uluslararasılaşmanın sağlıklı gelişimi hem de uluslararası öğrencilerin uyum süreçlerinin zenginleştirilmesi için önem taşımaktadır. Bu doğrultuda bu çalışmanın temel amacı Anadolu Üniversitesi örneğinde uluslararası öğrencilerin uyum süreçleri hakkındaki görüşlerini

---

[1] Filiz Göktuna Yaylacı, Prof. Dr., Anadolu Üniversitesi, Eskişehir, Türkiye, fgoktuna2@yahoo.com, ORCID:0000-0002-7937-8676

değerlendirebilmektir. Anadolu Üniversitesi de oldukça çeşitli bir öğrenci profiline sahiptir. Bugün itibarıyla üniversitede 100'ü aşkın farklı ülkeden gelen 1970 uluslararası öğrenci eğitim görmektedir.

Yöntem

Araştırma, Anadolu Üniversitesi'nde öğrenim gören uluslararası öğrencilerin uyum süreçleri hakkındaki görüşlerini değerlendirebilme amacı doğrultusunda nitel bir araştırma olarak desenlenmiştir.

Araştırma sürecinde veriler araştırmacılar tarafından hazırlanan yarı yapılandırılmış görüşme formu aracılığıyla toplanmıştır. Bu doğrultuda kartopu tekniği ile belirlenen ve ulaşılan katılımcılarla görüşmeler yapılmıştır. Araştırmanın çalışma grubunu Anadolu Üniversitesi'nde öğrenim gören 50 uluslararası öğrenci oluşturmuştur. Çalışma grubundaki öğrencilerin geldikleri ülkeler, cinsiyet ve öğrenim alanları bakımından çeşitliliği yansıtabilmesine özen gösterilmiştir. Bu doğrultuda üniversitenin ilgili birimleri ile iletişim kurularak gerekli düzenlemeler yapılmıştır. Ses kaydı alınarak kaydedilen görüşmeler daha sonra deşifre edilerek metinlere dönüştürülecek ve amaç ve alt amaçlar doğrultusunda çözümlenmiştir. Belirlenen ana tema ve alt temalara dayalı bir şekilde katılımcıların görüşleri uluslararasılaşma ve uluslararası öğrencilerin uyumuna ilişkin alanyazın bağlamında tartışılmıştır.

Araştırmanın çalışma grubunu 23 farklı ülkeden 50 uluslararası öğrenci oluşturmuştur. Katılımcıların köken ülkelerine bakıldığında en fazla katılımcı 9 kişi ile Kazakistan'dan gelmiştir. Kazakistan'ı, Endonezya (7), Rusya-Dağıstan (6), Azerbaycan (4), Mısır (3), Irak, Türkmenistan, Afganistan (2'şer), Bosna-Hersek, Somali, Gambiya, Burundi, Panama, Özbekistan, Malezya, Gine, Tunus, Tacikistan, S. Arabistan, Libya, Nijer ve Ürdün (1'şer) izlemiştir. Katılımcıların 27'si kadın 23'ü erkektir. Katılımcıların yaşları 18 ile 32 arasındadır, Türkiye'de bulunma süreleri ise 6 ay ile 10 yıl arasında değişmektedir. Katılımcılar Türkçeyi bilme düzeylerini ise genellikle orta ve iyi olarak belirtmiştir.

Bulgular ve Tartışma

Bu bölümde araştırmanın Eskişehir'e uyum ve Anadolu Üniversitesi Kampüsünde yaşam ve üniversiteye uyumla ilgili görüşlerine ait bulgulara yer verilmiştir.

Eskişehir'e Uyum

Katılımcıların Eskişehir'e uyum sağlama durumlarına ilişkin görüşleri 7 alt boyutta ifade edildiği söylenebilir; a) Genel Kabul ve Olumlu Deneyimler; b) Zorluklar ve Olumsuz Deneyimler, c) Ulaşım ve Şehir İçi Olanaklar, d) Sağlık Hizmetleri ve Hastane Deneyimleri, e) Göç İdaresi ve Bürokratik İşlemler, f) Sosyal Hayat ve Aktivite Olanakları, g) Ekonomik Durum ve Yaşam Maliyeti

a) Genel Kabul ve Olumlu Deneyimler

Katılımcıların önemli bir kesimi Eskişehir'de yaşamaya alıştığını, şehirden memnun olduklarını ve rahat ettiklerini belirtmiştir. Bu yönde görüş belirten katılımcılar çoğunlukla günlük yaşamda zorluk yaşamadıklarını ve şehri sevdiklerini ifade etmiştir; *Evet alıştım Eskişehir'de belki kendimi evde gibi hissediyorum* (K7) Eskişehir'de yaşamaya alıştığını, şehirden memnun olduğunu ve genel olarak zorluk yaşamadığını ifade eden katılımcıların görüşleri, literatürde uluslararası öğrencilerin sosyal destek ve çevresel faktörler aracılığıyla zamanla olumlu uyum geliştirdiğini gösteren bulgularla örtüşmektedir (Andrade, 2006; Almukdad, 2020).

b) Zorluklar ve Olumsuz Deneyimler

Türkiye'deki üniversitelerde eğitim gören çok sayıda uluslararası öğrenci, zorunlu göç yoluyla ülkeye gelen grupların yaşadığı zorluklarla birebir aynı deneyimleri yaşamamakla birlikte, farklı bir kültürel ortamda bulunmanın doğasında yer alan çeşitli uyum sorunlarıyla karşı karşıya kalmaktadır (Göktuna Yaylacı, Yaylacı ve Uzun, 2023). Bu araştırmanın katılımcılarından bazıları da şehirde yaşamaya alışmakta zorlandıklarını, çeşitli sosyal, kültürel veya dil engelleriyle karşılaştıklarını ifade etmiştir. Göç idaresi ile işlemler, hastane gibi hizmetlerden yararlanma veya sosyal hayatta yaşanan sıkıntılar bu bağlamda dile getirilmiştir. Uluslararası öğrencilerin çeşitli hizmetlerden yararlanırken dil yetersizliği ya da bilgi eksikliği gibi nedenlerle sorunlar yaşadıklarına ilişkin alanyazındaki bulgularla örtüşmektedir (Masai vd., 2021; Smith ve Khawaja, 2011).

c) Ulaşım ve Şehir İçi Olanaklar

Çeşitli araştırmalarda öğrencilerin günlük yaşam pratiklerindeki (ulaşım, kampüs mekânlarını bulma vb.) zorlukların ilk dönemlerde önemli bir stres kaynağı olduğu ve kampüs yaşamına yönelik pratik zorlukların öğrencilerin zaman yönetimi ve ders uyumunu etkilediğine ilişkin bulgular söz konusudur (Brown ve Holloway, 2008; Poyrazli ve Grahame 2007), Bu araştırmanın katılımcıların önemli bir kesimi de Eskişehir'de ulaşımın kolaylığını, toplu taşıma araçları ve maliyetleri hakkındaki olumlu duruma işaret etmiştir. Çoğu katılımcı şehir içi ulaşımın pratik ve uygun fiyatlı olmasından memnundur; *Otobüs ve tramvay çok güzel ve abonman kart öğrenciler için çok güzel çok ucuz. Burada çok iyi. Benim İstanbul arkadaşlar daha pahalı* (K28)

d) Sağlık Hizmetleri ve Hastane Deneyimleri

Uluslararası öğrencilerin sağlık sistemine erişimde yaşanan zorluklar ve olumlu deneyimlerle ilgili farklı bulgular (Masai vd., 2021) söz konusudur. Bu çalışmada da katılımcılar, hastane, eczane ve sağlık sisteminden alınan hizmetlerle ilgili yaşanan olumlu ya da olumsuz deneyimlerini şehre uyum açısından önemine işaret etmiştir. Sağlık hizmetlerine erişimdeki kolaylıklar veya karşılaşılan güçlükler bu bağlamda dile getirilmiştir.

e) Göç İdaresi ve Bürokratik İşlemler

Göç idaresi ve evrak işlemlerinde yaşanan zorluklar, katılımcılarınızın dikkat çektiği önemli bir sorundur. Türkiye'deki göç politikaları üzerine yapılan araştırmalar, uluslararası öğrencilerin oturum ve belge işlemlerinde sistematik bilgilendirme eksiklikleri nedeniyle sıkıntı yaşadığını göstermektedir (Güngör ve Tansel, 2019). Bu araştırmanın bazı katılımcıları tarafından da göç idaresi ile yapılan işlemler, evrak işleri ve bürokratik işlem ve süreçlerde yaşanan sorunlar veya kolaylıklar, çalışanların tutumu da uyum sürecindeki etkileri açısından önemi vurgulanmıştır.

f) Sosyal Hayat ve Aktivite Olanakları

Eskişehir'e uyum sağlama açısından şehirdeki sosyal aktiviteler, kulüpler, arkadaşlık kurma olanakları ve sosyal çevre ile ilgili deneyimler olumlu etkenler olarak dile getirilmiştir. Katılımcıların kulüpler, etkinlikler, Erasmus ve sosyal faaliyetler sayesinde sosyal uyumu kolaylaştırdıklarına ilişkin bulgular alanyazındaki benzer çalışmaların sosyal faaliyetlere katılımın uyumu artırmasıyla ilişkili bulgularla örtüşmektedir (Andrade, 2006; Ward, Bochner ve Furnham; 2001; Brown ve Holloway, 2008).

g) Ekonomik Durum ve Yaşam Maliyeti

Finansal zorluklar uluslararası öğrencilerin önemli stresin kaynaklarından biridir ve ekonomik belirsizlikler öğrencilerin uyum süreçlerini olumsuz etkilemektedir (Smith ve Khawaja, 2011; Özoğlu, Gür & Coşkun, 2015). Bu araştırmanın katılımcıların görüşleri doğrultusunda da Eskişehir'de yaşamın maddi boyutu, kira, ulaşım ve diğer harcamaların şehir yaşamına uyumu etkilediği anlaşılmaktadır. Kimi katılımcılar enflasyon ve yaşam maliyetlerindeki değişimlerin olumsuz etkilerini dile getirmiştir.

Kampüste Yaşam ve Üniversiteye Uyum

Bazı araştırmalar uluslararası öğrencilerin Türkiye'deki deneyimlerine dair olumlu algılar geliştirdiklerini ortaya koymakla birlikte (Erdem ve Polat, 2019), çeşitli sorunların da yaygın biçimde yaşandığını göstermektedir. Bu sorunlar, dil ve eğitim gibi temel konuların yanı sıra, çok boyutlu sosyo-kültürel ve ekonomik zorlukları da kapsamaktadır. Araştırma bulguları, uluslararası öğrencilerin günlük yaşamlarında, barınma ortamlarında, kampüs içi deneyimlerinde, sosyal ilişkilerinde ve akademik süreçlerinde çeşitli güçlükler yaşadıklarını göstermektedir (Gebru ve Yüksel-Kaptanoğlu, 2020). Bu araştırmanın katılımcılarının Anadolu Üniversitesi Kampüsünde yaşamla ilgili soruya verilen cevaplar a) Sorunlar-Olumsuzluklar ve b) Olumlu Yönler-Avantajlar olmak üzere iki boyutta ifade edilebilir.

Sorunlar ve Olumsuzluklar boyutunda ulaşım ve kampüs büyüklüğü, yemekhane ile ilgili sorunlar, sınıf ve fiziksel alanlar, güvenlik ve ortam ile diğer sorunlar yer almıştır. Bazı katılımcılara göre kampüsün çok büyük olması ve kampüs içinde otobüs olmaması önemli bir sorundur. Kampüs büyük olduğu için derslere, spor alanlarına ulaşmak zaman almaktadır. Katılımcılar genel olarak yemekhane hizmetlerinden memnuniyetini dile getirmiştir. Bununla birlikte bazı katılımcılar ise yemekhane fiyatlarının hızlı değişmesini, yemekhane rezervasyonu ve önceden ödemedeki zorlukları dile getirerek yemeklerin iyileştirilmesinin gerekliliğini vurgulamıştır. Bazı katılımcılar sınıflarda klima olmamasını bir sorun olarak dile getirirken bazı katılımcılar sınıflardaki iletişim sorunlarına işaret etmiştir. Yine bazı katılımcılara göre ise derslerin farklı binalarda olması ve bu durumun zorluk yaratması Katılımcıların önemli bir kesimi kampüste çok köpek olmasının korkutucu ve rahatsız edici olduğunu ifade ederek güvenlik açısından olumsuzluğuna işaret etmiştir. Bu sorunların yanında sınav haftalarının sıkışık ve yorucu olması; kampüste sosyal aktivitelerin yetersizliği; idari süreçlerde yavaşlık ve ilgisizlik; kampüs dışı ulaşım ve konum zorlukları; fiyatlar ve ekonomik zorlukları dile getirmiştir.

Olumlu Yönler ve Avantajlar boyutunda kampüsün doğası, sosyal ve akademik olanaklar, güvenlik ve rahatlık bağlamındaki görüşler yer almıştır.

Katılımcıların büyük kesimi, yeşil alanların çokluğu, parklar, Japon Bahçesi'nin varlığı, çok sayıda ağaçlık bölgenin olması ve kampüsün doğal güzelliği ile temiz olmasını olumlu yönler arasında göstermiştir. Benzer şekilde birçok katılımcı, Erasmus ve değişim programlarının çok aktif ve avantajlı olmasını, spor olanaklarının zenginliğini ve gençlik merkezinin etkinliğini, kampüste kafeler, marketler, kütüphanelerin mevcut olmasını; kütüphane ve çalışma odalarının iyi olmasını; etkinliklerin ve kulüplerin çok ve çeşitli olmasını, sosyal aktivitelerin zenginliğini; kampüs içinde caminin olmasını, sağlık hizmetlerinin sunulduğu merkezlerin olmasını kampüsün olumlu yönleri bağlamında önemli avantajlar olarak dile getirmiştir.

Katılımcıların önemli bir kesimi kampüsün güvenlikli bir alan olmasını dolayısıyla buradaki herkesin öğrenci olmasının güven hissi verdiğini ifade etmiştir. Katılımcılara göre kampüs içinde öğrencilerin gündelik yaşamlarında ihtiyaç duyacakları her şeyin bir arada olması rahatlık sağlamaktadır

Yapılan çalışmalar, bu öğrencilerin yalnızlık hissi, sosyal uyumsuzluk, çekingenlik, kültürel şok ve psikolojik sıkıntılar gibi bireysel düzeyde etkileyici sorunlarla karşılaştığını ortaya koymaktadır (Kıroğlu, Kesten ve Elma, 2010). Üniversiteye uyum hakkında bu araştırmanın katılımcılarının görüşleri incelendiğinde öğrencilerin üniversiteye uyum sağlama sürecindeki deneyimlerinin akademik ve sosyal uyum, dil ve kültür zorlukları, zaman yönetimi ve kampüs dinamikleri gibi faktörlere göre şekillendiği görülmektedir. Öğrencilerin önemli bir kesimi üniversiteye ve akademik yaşama tamamen veya büyük ölçüde uyum sağladıklarını, kendilerini rahat hissettiklerini, derslere, kampüse ve sosyal hayata alıştıklarını ifade etmiştir;

"Evet alıştım okula, fakülteye." (K7)

"Evet üç yıl olduğu için alıştım. Öğrendim." (K9)

"Evet, ben sadece akışına uyuyorum ve her gün yeni bir kültür öğreniyorum." (K31)

"Evet adapte oldum. Çok güzel, çok kolay." (K48)

Öğrencilerin bir kısmı genel olarak uyum sağladıklarını belirtirken, dil, ders çalışma, fakülte ortamı gibi bazı alanlarda hâlâ zorluk yaşadıklarını ifade etmiştir;

"Dil öğreniyoruz ama akademik dil zor, hocaları zor anlıyoruz." (K15)

"Alıştım ama Türkçeyi bilmediğim için ders çalışmaya, anlamaya alışmadım." (K36)

"Derslere alışmaya başladım, hocaların sınav sistemine alışmak zor oldu." (K26)

Üniversiteye uyumda en çok zorlanan konu olarak dil bariyerini gösteren öğrenciler, TÖMER'in kolaylığı ile fakültelerdeki dilinin zorluklarını karşılaştırmıştır;

"TÖMER çok kolay, fakültede zor." (K3)

"Türkçem zayıftı, şimdi dil öğreniyorum, akademik dil zor." (K4)

"Ben 3 ayda Türkçeyi öğrendim, dizilerden öğrendim." (K16)

Katılımcıların görüşlerine bakıldığında arkadaş çevresi, kampüs yaşantısı, kulüp ve etkinliklere katılım ile üniversite ortamına sosyal olarak uyum sağlama deneyimlerini olumlu etkilemiştir;

"Arkadaşlarımla birlikte yaşıyoruz, sınıfta 56 kişiyiz, uyum sağladım." (K2)

"Uluslararası öğrenci kulübünün başkanlığını yaptım, sunuculuk yaptım." (K40)

"TÖMER'de arkadaşlarımızla çok iyi ilişkilerimiz var." (K41)

"Tatilde evde sıkılıyorum, üniversiteye gitmeyi özlüyorum." (K27)

Bazı katılımcılara göre zaman yönetimi, iş ve ders yoğunluğu nedeniyle uyum sürecinde yaşanan zorluklar, kampüs içindeki mekanların büyüklüğü ve karmaşıklığı gibi pratik sorunlar uyumu olumsuz etkilemektedir; "Kampüs büyük, Google Maps kullanıyordum ama alıştım." (K1)

Katılımcıların önemli bir kesimi tarafından farklı ülkelerden gelen öğrenciler arasındaki dilsel ve kültürel çeşitliliğin uyumu kolaylaştırıcı etkisi vurgulanmıştır

"Farklı diller biliyorum, bu yüzden uyum zor olmadı." (K34)

"Kazaklar, Tacikler, Koreliler var, iletişim kurmak zor olmadı." (K35)

"Farklı kültürlerden arkadaşlar buldum, hızlı adapte oldum." (K44)

Sonuç

Bu araştırma, Eskişehir'de eğitim gören uluslararası öğrencilerin şehir ve üniversite yaşamına uyum süreçlerinin çok boyutlu bir yapıya sahip olduğunu ortaya koymuştur. Bulgular, öğrencilerin genel kabul, sosyal etkinliklere katılım ve ulaşım kolaylıkları gibi olumlu deneyimlere sahip olduklarını göstermektedir. Bununla birlikte, dil engeli, bürokratik işlemlerde yaşanan güçlükler, sağlık hizmetlerine erişimde karşılaşılan sorunlar ve ekonomik zorluklar gibi çeşitli faktörler öğrencilerin uyum sürecini olumsuz etkileyen unsurlar olarak öne çıkmaktadır. Katılımcıların ifadeleri, literatürde dile getirilen sosyal destek ağlarının, kültürel etkileşimlerin ve üniversite olanaklarının öğrencilerin uyumunu kolaylaştırdığına ilişkin bulgularla büyük ölçüde örtüşmektedir.

Kampüs yaşamına ilişkin değerlendirmeler de uyum sürecinin farklı yönlerini ortaya koymuştur. Katılımcılar, kampüsün doğal güzellikleri, sosyal ve akademik olanakların çeşitliliği, güvenlikli bir alan olması gibi unsurları olumlu olarak nitelendirirken; ulaşım güçlükleri, yemekhane ve dersliklere dair sorunlar, sosyal aktivitelerin yetersizliği ve idari süreçlerde yaşanan aksaklıklar olumsuz deneyimler arasında yer almıştır. Dolayısıyla Eskişehir'deki uluslararası öğrencilerin uyum sürecinin, bireysel, kültürel ve yapısal koşulların etkileşimiyle şekillendiği ve bu sürecin yalnızca öğrencilerin bireysel çabalarıyla değil, aynı zamanda üniversite ve şehir tarafından sunulan destek mekanizmalarıyla da yakından ilişkili olduğu sonucuna ulaşılmaktadır.

Kaynakça

Altbach, P. G. (1991). Impact and adjustment: Foreign students in comparative perspective. Higher Education, 21, 305–323.

Almukdad, M. (2020). Uluslararası öğrencilerin kültür şoku, öz-yeterlik, yaşam doyumu ve uyum stratejileri: Bir karma yöntem araştırması (Doktora tezi). Akdeniz Üniversitesi, Eğitim Bilimleri Enstitüsü.

Anadolu Üniversitesi. (2024). Anadolu hakkında. Erişim adresi: https://www.anadolu.edu.tr/universitemiz/anadolu-hakkinda/hakkinda (Erişim tarihi: 31.08.2025)

Andrade, M. S. (2006). International students in English-speaking universities: Adjustment factors. Journal of Research in International Education, 5(2), 131–154.

Ballo, A., Mathias, C., & Weimer, L. (2019). Applying student development theories: Enhancing international student academic success and integration. Journal of Comparative and International Higher Education, 11(Winter), 18–24.

Brown, L., & Holloway, I. (2008). The adjustment journey of international postgraduate students at an English university: An ethnographic study. Journal of Research in International Education, 7(2), 232–249. https://doi.org/10.1177/1475240908091306

Ercan, M. S. (2012). Uluslararası öğrencilerin uyum sorunlarının incelenmesi ve bu sorunların çözümüne yönelik beklentilerin araştırılması (Uzmanlık tezi). T.C. Başbakanlık Yurtdışı Türkler ve Akraba Topluluklar Başkanlığı.

Erdem, C., & Polat, M. (2019). Türkiye'de uluslararası öğrenci olma deneyimi: Bir metafor analizi. Turkish Studies - Educational Sciences, 14(6), 3089–3109.

Erişti, B., Polat, M., & Erdem, C. (2018). Yükseköğretimde uluslararasılaşma: Uluslararası öğrencilerin bulunduğu sınıflarda ders veren öğretim elemanlarının öğretim sürecinde yaşadıkları sorunlar ve çözüm önerileri. Journal of History Culture and Art Research, 7(2), 352–375.

Gebru, M. S., & Yuksel-Kaptanoglu, I. (2020). Adaptation challenges for international students in Turkey. Open Journal of Social Sciences, 8, 262–278. https://doi.org/10.4236/jss.2020.89021

Göktuna Yaylacı, F., Yaylacı, A. F., & Uzun, K. (2023). To be with the other on campus: Learning for intercultural understanding through participatory photography. In P. Holmes & J. Corbett (Eds.), Critical intercultural pedagogy for difficult times (pp. 87–116). Routledge.

Güngör, N. D., & Tansel, A. (2019). Brain drain from Turkey: Return intentions of Turkish students abroad. International Migration, 57(5), 235–252. https://doi.org/10.1111/imig.12537

International Organization for Migration (IOM). (2024). Migration and migrants: A global overview: International students. Erişim adresi: https://worldmigrationreport.iom.int/what-we-do/world-migration-report-2024-chapter-2/international-students

Kıroğlu, K., Kesten, A., & Elma, C. (2010). Türkiye'de öğrenim gören yabancı uyruklu lisans öğrencilerinin sosyal-kültürel ve ekonomik sorunları. Mersin Üniversitesi Eğitim Fakültesi Dergisi, 6(2), 26–39.

Masai, A. N., Güçiz-Doğan, B., Ouma, P. N., Nyadera, I. N., & Ruto, V. K. (2021). Healthcare services utilization among international students in Ankara, Turkey: A cross-sectional study. BMC Health Services Research, 21(1), 1166. https://doi.org/10.1186/s12913-021-06301-x

Özoğlu, M., Gür, B. S., & Coşkun, İ. (2015). Factors influencing international students' choice to study in Turkey and challenges they experience in Turkey. Research in Comparative and International Education, 10(2), 223–237. https://doi.org/10.1177/1745499915571718

Poyrazli, S., & Grahame, K. M. (2007). Barriers to adjustment: Needs of international students within a semi-urban campus community. Journal of Instructional Psychology, 34(1), 28–45.

Sin, C., & Tavares, O. (2019). Integrating international students: The missing link in Portuguese higher education institutions. Journal of Comparative and International Higher Education, 11(Winter), 59–65.

Smith, R. A., & Khawaja, N. G. (2011). A review of the acculturation experiences of international students. International Journal of Intercultural Relations, 35(6), 699–713. https://doi.org/10.1016/j.ijintrel.2011.08.004

Taylor, G., & Ali, N. (2017). Learning and living overseas: Exploring factors that influence meaningful learning and assimilation: How international students adjust to studying in the UK from a socio-cultural perspective. Education Sciences, 7, 35. https://doi.org/10.3390/educsci7010035

Topal, F., & Tauscher, S. (2020). Uluslararası öğrencilerin akademik ve sosyal yaşamlarında karşılaştıkları sorunlar üzerine inceleme. Akademik İncelemeler Dergisi, 15(1), 309–336.

Türel, M. T. (2021). Uluslararası öğrencilerin sosyokültürel uyumu. Avrasya Beşeri Bilimler Araştırmaları Dergisi, 1(2), 73–89.

Ward, C., Bochner, S., & Furnham, A. (2001). The psychology of culture shock (2nd ed.). Routledge.

Yükseköğretim Kurulu (YÖK). (2017). Yükseköğretimde uluslararasılaşma strateji belgesi 2018-2022. YÖK.

Yu, Y., & Moskal, M. (2019). Missing intercultural engagements in the university experiences of Chinese international students in the UK. Compare: A Journal of Comparative and International Education, 49, 654–671.

Zhao, X. (2021). Understanding international postgraduate students' adjustment in a British university: Motivations for study abroad and subsequent academic, sociocultural and psychological experiences (Doktora tezi). School of Education, Communication, and Language Sciences, Faculty of Humanities and Social Sciences, Newcastle University.

"KADIN BAŞINA GÖÇ": KONYA'DAKI AFGAN GENÇ KADINLARIN KAÇIŞ HIKAYELERI VE ERIL ŞIDDETLE MÜCADELELERI

Filiz Göktuna Yaylacı ve Gamze Kaçar Tunç[1]

Giriş

Bu çalışmada, Afganistan'dan ve İran'dan Türkiye'ye göç eden genç Afgan kadınların yaşam öykülerini feminist bir bakış açısıyla inceleyen anlatı temelli bir araştırmanın erken bulgularına dayanmaktadır. Araştırmada kadınların göç deneyimleri; göç öncesi yaşam koşulları, göç kararı alma süreçleri, sınır geçiş deneyimleri ve Türkiye'ye girişteki ilk temaslar bağlamında çözümlemeye tabi tutulmuştur.

Türkiye, uzun yıllardır Afgan göçünde hem bir geçiş hem de varış ülkesi olarak rol oynamaktadır. Özellikle 2011 sonrası Suriye krizine bağlı olarak izlenen açık kapı politikasının ardından göç rotaları değişmiş, Taliban'ın 2021'de yeniden iktidara gelişiyle birlikte Afganistan'dan Türkiye'ye doğru yönelen göç dalgalarında ve bu göçün toplumsal görünürlüğünde belirgin bir artış yaşanmıştır.

Medyada sıklıkla "genç erkek göçü" olarak temsil edilmesine karşın, Afgan göçünün önemli bir bölümü kadınlardan, özellikle de genç kadınlardan oluşmaktadır. 2022 itibarıyla Türkiye'deki yaklaşık 140.000 kayıtlı Afgan sığınmacı ve şartlı mültecinin %35'ini kadınlar oluşturmaktadır. Mixed Migration Centre (2024) ve UN Women (2023) gibi kuruluşların raporları, 18–30 yaş grubundaki Afgan kadınlar arasında cinsiyete dayalı şiddet, toplumsal baskı, eğitim hakkının gaspı ve kişisel özgürlük arayışları nedeniyle gerçekleşen göçte belirgin bir artış olduğunu göstermektedir.

Toplumsal Cinsiyetli Sınırlar ve Göç

Kadınların sınır geçişleri yalnızca fiziksel bir yer değiştirmeye indirgenemez; bu

---

[1] Filiz Göktuna Yaylacı, Prof. Dr., Anadolu Üniversitesi, Eskişehir, Türkiye, fgoktuna2@yahoo.com, ORCID:0000-0002-7937-8676

Gamze Kaçar Tunç, Dr. Öğretim Ü., Karamanoğlu Mehmetbey Üniversitesi, Karaman, Türkiye ORCID: 0000-0001-6291-8683 süreç, aynı zamanda ataerkil normların, kültürel kodların ve kimlik rejimlerinin aşılmasıyla da yakından ilişkilidir. Anzaldúa'nın (1987) geliştirdiği "sınırda olma hali" (borderlands) ve "mestiza bilinci" kavramları, kadın göçmenlerin hem yerinden edilme hem de kimliksel dönüşüm süreçlerini anlamada önemli bir teorik çerçeve sunar. Bu bağlamda, göç eden kadınların yaşadığı "arada kalma", parçalanma ve yeniden yapılanma deneyimleri, hem fiziksel hem de kültürel sınırları aşmanın çok katmanlı doğasını gözler önüne serer.

Zorunlu göç sürecinde kadınların maruz kaldığı eril şiddet yapısal ve sembolik şiddet biçimleriyle onları derinden etkilediği için çok katmanlı mücadele yöntemleri söz konusu olmaktadır (Borges, 2024; Başkan, 2022). Sınırların yalnızca coğrafi çizgiler olmadığı, aynı zamanda toplumsal cinsiyet temelli ideolojilerle örülü olduğu literatürde sıkça vurgulanmaktadır (Aaron vd., 2010; Yuval-Davis, 1997). Bu ideolojik çerçevede kadınlar, sınır geçişlerinde erkeklerden farklı biçimlerde denetlenmekte, daha yoğun kontrole tabi tutulmakta ve sıklıkla cinsiyete özgü şiddet biçimlerine maruz kalmaktadır. Kadın bedeni çoğu zaman "korunması gereken" kırılgan bir varlık olarak temsil edilirken, bu koruma söylemi aynı zamanda denetimin meşrulaştırıcı aracı hâline de gelmektedir. Bununla bağlantılı olarak, sınırların giderek militarize edilmesi, kadın bedeni üzerindeki denetimi daha da yoğunlaştırmaktadır. Enloe'nun (2000, 2007) ve Tyszler'in (2023) çalışmalarında da vurgulandığı gibi, militarize sınır rejimleri kadınların bedenini hem potansiyel bir tehdit nesnesi hem de sembolik bir güvenlik göstergesi olarak kodlamaktadır. Kaçakçılarla kurulan temaslar, sınır geçiş noktalarında uygulanan güvenlik politikaları ve göçmen toplama merkezlerindeki denetim pratikleri, bu eril militarist yapının somut uzantıları olarak işlev görmektedir.

Tüm bu deneyimlerin farklı kadın grupları tarafından nasıl yaşandığını anlayabilmek için kesişimsel bir bakış açısının gerekliliği ortaya çıkmaktadır. Crenshaw'ın (1989) ortaya koyduğu ve Yuval-Davis (2006) gibi feminist yazarlar tarafından geliştirilen kesişimsellik kuramı, kadınların göç deneyimlerinin yalnızca "kadın olmak" temelli bir kategoriyle açıklanamayacağını, aksine bu deneyimlerin sınıf, etnisite, yaş, medeni durum, annelik gibi birçok kimlik ekseniyle iç içe geçtiğini savunur. Bu çoklu aidiyetler, kimi zaman bireyleri daha korunaklı kılabilirken, kimi durumlarda ise daha derinleşmiş ayrımcılıklara ve dışlanmalara zemin hazırlamaktadır. Dolayısıyla, kadın göçmenlerin sınır geçişleri, çok katmanlı toplumsal süreçlerin ve iktidar ilişkilerinin kesiştiği bir alan olarak düşünülmelidir. Bu alanda hem fiziksel hem de sembolik sınırların yeniden üretildiği; toplumsal cinsiyet, militarizm ve kimlik siyasetinin iç içe geçtiği karmaşık bir deneyim alanı söz konusudur.

Amaç

Göç, birçok kadın için yalnızca mekânsal bir yer değişimi değil; aynı zamanda ataerkil düzene karşı bir hayatta kalma, direnme ve özneleşme stratejisine dönüşmektedir. Kadınlar bu süreçte sadece göçün nesnesi değil, aynı zamanda aktif failleri olarak da karşımıza çıkmaktadır. Bu durum, sınırların artık yalnızca erkekler tarafından aşılmadığını, kadınların da sınır geçişlerinde özneleştiğini ve göçün eril yapısına müdahale ettiğini göstermektedir. Bu doğrultuda bu çalışmada Afgan kadınların göç deneyimleri ve göç sürecinde eril şiddetle baş etme stratejileri konu edilmiştir. Çalışmanın temel amacı Afgan kadınların göç deneyimlerinde eril şiddetle baş etme stratejilerini derinlemesine inceleyebilmektir. Bu doğrultuda kadınları göçe iten temel faktörler, göç kararını alma süreci, Türkiye'ye giriş sürecinde toplumsal cinsiyet açısından yaşananlar değerlendirilmiştir.

Yöntem

Afgan kadınların göç deneyimlerinde eril şiddetle baş etme derinlemesine inceleyebilme amacı doğrultusunda araştırma nitel bir çalışma olarak desenlenmiştir. Araştırmanın verileri anlatı görüşmeleri ve anlatı analizleri yoluyla gerçekleştirilmiştir. Veriler betimsel yaklaşıma analiz edilmiştir. Araştırmanın çalışma grubunu Konya'da yaşayan 15-25 yaş aralığında 20 Afgan kadın oluşturmuştur. Katılımcılarla derinlemesine anlatı görüşmeleri yapılmıştır.

Bulgular

Araştırmanın bulguları, göçe sürükleyen faktörler, göç kararının alınması süreci ve Türkiye'ye girişte kadınların aktif rolleri boyutlarına ifade edilmiştir.

Göçe Sürükleyen Faktörler

Farklı araştırmaların bulgularına göre göçler çoğu zaman savaş, yoksulluk, ailevi baskılar ve toplumsal cinsiyet temelli ayrımcılığın sonucu olarak ortaya çıkmaktadır (Başkan, 2022). Toplumsal cinsiyet temelli şiddet, zorunlu göç literatüründe kadınların hareketlilik deneyimlerini biçimlendiren başlıca faktörlerden biri olarak öne çıkmaktadır. Benzer coğrafyalardan göç eden kadınlara ilişkin araştırmalar, özellikle eril şiddetten kaçışın göç anlatılarında sürekli yinelenen bir tema olduğunu göstermektedir (Buz, 2007; Mehta, 2025; MMC, 2018). Taliban'ın Afganistan'da yeniden iktidarı ele alması, kadınların yalnızca fiziksel güvenliklerini tehdit eden bir unsur değil, aynı zamanda toplumsal cinsiyet kimliklerinden kaynaklı özgürlük arayışlarını da güçlendiren bir faktör olarak ortaya çıkmıştır (MMC, 2024). Bu bağlamda, katılımcı kadınların deneyimlerinde hem yakın erkek akrabaların hem de Taliban'ın temsil ettiği maskülen iktidar pratiklerinin yaşamlarını doğrudan şekillendiren baskılar yarattığı görülmektedir. UN Women ve diğer kurumların (2023) raporunda da vurgulandığı üzere, Afgan kadınların maruz kaldıkları hak ihlalleri geçici olarak algılanmamakta, tersine "belirsiz süreli" bir durum olarak değerlendirilmektedir. Bu algı, kadınlar açısından ülkeden ayrılmayı kısa vadede en işlevsel hayatta kalma ve özgürleşme stratejisi haline getirmektedir. Nitekim bu araştırmada da göç kararlarının temelinde kadınlara yönelik toplumsal cinsiyet temelli baskıların öne çıktığı görülmüştür. Katılımcıların anlatıları, zorla evlendirilme, aile içi şiddet, eğitim hakkının ellerinden alınması, Taliban yönetimi ve aşiret/akrabalık ilişkileri çerçevesinde kadın bedenine yöneltilen tehditlerin göçe sürükleyici faktörler olduğunu açıkça ortaya koymaktadır. Bu noktada katılımcıların bireysel ifadeleri, söz konusu baskıların kadınların göç kararlarını nasıl şekillendirdiğini somut biçimde yansıtmaktadır. Aliye, ailesiyle yaşadığı gerilimi şu sözlerle dile getirmiştir: *"Babam bana 'kadın evden çıkmaz' dedi. Üniversiteyi kazandığım için kavga ettik."* Bu ifade, kadınların eğitim hakkı taleplerinin dahi patriyarkal sınırlarla karşılaştığını göstermektedir. Feride'nin anlatısı ise aile içi baskı ve eşin bağımlılığı gibi çoklu şiddet biçimlerinin göçe nasıl zorladığını gözler önüne sermektedir: *"Amcam annemi zorla eş almak istedi. Zaten kocam da madde bağımlısıydı. Kaçtık."* Benzer biçimde Fatma, kız kardeşini zorla evlendirilmekten korumak için annesiyle birlikte göç kararı aldıklarını şu şekilde aktarmaktadır: *"Kız kardeşim evlendirilecekti. Annem 'aynı hayatı yaşamayacak' dedi. Bu kararı birlikte aldık."* Bu örnekler, toplumsal cinsiyet temelli şiddetin göç kararlarının merkezinde yer aldığını, kadınların ise baskı ve tehdit koşullarında hem kendi hem de aile üyelerinin özgürlüğünü ve güvenliğini korumak için stratejik kararlar alabildiklerini ortaya koymaktadır.

Göç Kararı: Faillik ve Aile İçi Müzakere

Kadınlar, göç kararlarında pasif ve ikincil aktörler değil; ailevi stratejilerin oluşturulmasında, toplumsal rollerin yeniden müzakere edilmesinde ve göç imkanlarının değerlendirilmesinde etkin konumdadır (Aryal, 2024; Boyles, 2015; Oucho, 2011). Bu araştırmanın bulguları da kadınların failliklerine ilişkin önemli ipuçları sunmaktadır. Katılımcıların anlatıları, kadınların çoğu durumda göç kararına doğrudan katıldıklarını, hatta bazı durumlarda bu kararın belirleyicisi olduklarını göstermektedir. Kimi katılımcılar göç kararını eşleriyle ya da anneleriyle birlikte alırken, bazıları ise tek başına karar vermiştir. Bu karar alma süreçlerinde aile içi ikna mekanizmaları, direnç gösterme pratikleri ve stratejik planlama girişimleri dikkat çekici bir biçimde öne çıkmaktadır.

Katılımcı kadınların doğrudan ifadeleri bu durumu somut biçimde gözler önüne sermektedir. Şükran, ailelerinin evlenmelerine karşı çıkmasına rağmen kendi kararlılığını ortaya koyarak *"Ailem evlenmemizi istemedi. Hamileydim. Yine de kaçtık."* sözleriyle hem direncini hem de aldığı riski ifade etmektedir. Farima'nın anlatısı ise göç sürecinde aile içi dayanışmanın önemini göstermektedir: *"Kaçmak için ablamın desteğiyle para topladık. Annemle bir haftalık plan yaptık."* Burada kadınların maddi kaynak yaratma ve stratejik plan yapma becerilerinin süreci nasıl şekillendirdiği açıkça görülmektedir. Benzer biçimde Malika'nın deneyimi, göç kararının annesi tarafından verilmesiyle kadınların aile içi otoriteyi yönlendirebildiğini ortaya koymaktadır: *"Amcamlar İran'da peşimizi bırakmaz diye Türkiye'ye geçmeye annem karar verdi."* Bu bağlamda göç literatüründe kadınların çoğu kez edilgen öznelermiş gibi ele alınmasına karşın, onların aktif failliklerini güçlü biçimde görünür kıldığı söylenebilir. Kadınlar hem bireysel iradeleriyle hem de ailevi dayanışma ve müzakere süreçleri aracılığıyla göç kararının şekillenmesinde belirleyici aktörler olarak ortaya çıkmaktadır.

Türkiye'ye Girişte Kadınların Aktif Rolü

Bulgular, Türkiye'ye giriş sürecinde kadınların yalnızca pasif özne olarak konumlanmadıklarını, aksine yanlarındaki erkek akrabaların kabulü için kurumlarla müzakere yürüterek aktif roller üstlendiklerini göstermektedir. Kadınların erkek kardeş, eş veya çocuklarına ilişkin işlemleri organize etmeleri, yol izinlerini temin etmeleri ve gerekli belgeleri toplamaları, onların bürokratik alanlarda da stratejik bir faillik sergilediklerini ortaya koymaktadır. Bu durum, "kadın olarak korunma" söyleminin ardında aslında bilinçli bir strateji ve yönlendirici bir kapasite bulunduğuna işaret etmektedir. Katılımcıların kişisel anlatıları da bu failliği somut biçimde gözler önüne sermektedir: Aliye, kaçakçılar tarafından alıkonulduklarında sakladığı telefonu kullanarak polisi aramış ve kurtuluşlarını sağlamıştır; *"Kaçakçılar bizi alıkoydu ama ben bir telefonumu saklamıştım onlardan, onunla polisi aradım ve kurtulduk."* Şukufe, kızının ihtiyaçları için talepte bulunarak, resmi belgelerin temini sonrasında göç yolculuğunu sürdürmüştür; *"Kızım için battaniye istedim. Göl kenarındaydık. Sonra belge verdiler. Üç gün sonra yola çıktık."* Feride ise Türkçe bilmemesine rağmen İngilizce aracılığıyla polisle müzakere etmiş ve kardeşini yanına almayı başarmıştır; *"Türkçe bilmiyordum ama İngilizce konuştum, kardeşimi almak için polisle pazarlık ettim."*

Göç literatüründe kadınların deneyimleri sıklıkla "kırılganlık" ve "faillik" ikiliği üzerinden ele alınmaktadır. Bu araştırmada da kadınların bir yandan sınır geçişlerini defalarca denemeleri, ailelerini ve çocuklarını korumaları gibi direniş ve stratejik karar pratikleri dikkat çekmektedir. Ancak diğer yandan, bulgular bu aktif rollerin çoğu kez gölgede kaldığını ve kadınların daha çok kırılganlıklarını ön plana çıkardıklarını göstermektedir. Freedman'ın (2018) ve Latouche'nin

(2023) vurguladığı üzere, kırılganlık söylemi sınır siyaseti bağlamında kadınların kabul edilme ihtimalini artırsa da göç sonrasında onların öznelliklerini ve otonomilerini görünmez kılmaktadır. Militarize sınır geçişlerinde kadınların cesaret ve faillik pratiklerinin göz ardı edilmesi, göç deneyimlerinin yalnızca mağduriyet penceresinden okunmasına yol açmaktadır. Bu nedenle, katılımcıların kendi anlatılarında dahi failliğin çoğu kez fark edilememesi, göç çalışmalarında kırılganlık–faillik ikiliğinin eleştirel bir biçimde yeniden değerlendirilmesi gerektiğini ortaya koymaktadır.

Sonuç

Bu araştırmanın bulguları, toplumsal cinsiyet temelli şiddetin kadınların göç deneyimlerinde belirleyici bir faktör olduğunu ve kadınların göç kararlarını hem baskıcı toplumsal yapılara karşı bir direniş hem de hayatta kalma stratejisi olarak aldıklarını göstermektedir. Katılımcıların anlatıları, zorla evlendirilme, aile içi şiddet, eğitim hakkının gaspı, Taliban yönetimi ve akrabalık/aşiret baskıları gibi unsurların kadınların göç etme gerekçeleri arasında öne çıktığını ortaya koymuştur. Bununla birlikte, göç sürecinin yalnızca kırılganlık üzerinden okunamayacağı, kadınların aktif faillik pratikleriyle de şekillendiği anlaşılmaktadır.

Kadınların göç kararlarına doğrudan katıldıkları, kimi zaman aile içi müzakereler aracılığıyla, kimi zaman ise tek başlarına göç kararını aldıkları bulgusu, göç literatüründe kadınların pasif aktörler olarak konumlandırılmasına yönelik eleştirileri destekler niteliktedir. Katılımcılar, yalnızca bireysel güvenlikleri için değil, aile bireylerini korumak ve süreci organize etmek amacıyla da aktif roller üstlenmişlerdir. Türkiye'ye giriş sırasında erkek akrabaların kabulü için yürütülen bürokratik müzakereler, kadınların göç sürecindeki stratejik yönelimlerinin somut göstergelerinden biridir.

Bununla birlikte, araştırma bulguları kadınların çoğu kez kendi failliklerinin farkında olmadıklarını, anlatılarında kırılganlıklarını daha fazla öne çıkardıklarını göstermektedir. Literatürde de belirtildiği üzere, kırılganlık söylemi sınır politikaları bağlamında kadınların kabul edilme ihtimalini artırsa da göç sonrasında öznelliklerinin ve özerkliklerinin görünmez olmasına yol açabilmektedir. Bu durum, göç süreçlerinin yalnızca mağduriyet üzerinden okunmasının eksik kaldığını ve kadınların faillik pratiklerinin görünür kılınması gerektiğini ortaya koymaktadır.

Sonuç olarak, bu araştırma kadınların göç deneyimlerinin kırılganlık ve faillik ikiliği üzerinden yeniden düşünülmesi gerektiğine işaret etmektedir. Kadınların anlatıları, göç sürecinde hem baskı ve şiddetten kaçan kırılgan özneler hem de stratejik kararlar alarak, direnerek ve müzakere ederek hareket eden failler olduklarını göstermektedir. Bu ikiliğin eleştirel bir biçimde ele alınması, göç literatüründe kadın deneyimlerinin daha bütüncül ve çok boyutlu biçimde anlaşılmasına katkı sağlayacaktır.

Kaynaklar

Aaron, J., Altink, H., & Weedon, C. (Eds.). (2010). *Gendering border studies*. Cardiff: University of Wales Press.

Anzaldúa, G. (1987). *Borderlands/La Frontera: The new mestiza*. San Francisco, CA: Aunt Lute Books.

Aryal, S. (2023). Gender or gendered demand of care? Migration decision-making processes of Nepali care workers. *Gender Issues, 40*(3), 275–295.

Başkan, B. (2022). Zorunlu göç, toplumsal cinsiyet ve mülteci kadınlar. In B. Başkan & M. E. Kula (Eds.), *Uluslararası göç ve mültecilik* (ss. 115–134). Ankara: Siyasal Kitabevi.

Borges, G. M. (2024). Journey of violence: Refugee women's experiences across three stages and places. *Journal of International Migration & Integration, 25*(3), 673–693.

Boyles, J. (2015). Male migration and decision making: Are women finally being included? *Migration and Development, 4*(2), 200–219.

Buz, S. (2007). Göçte kadınlar: Feminist yaklaşım çerçevesinde bir çalışma. *Toplum ve Sosyal Hizmet, 18*(2), 37–50.

Crenshaw, K. (1989). Demarginalizing the intersection of race and sex: A Black feminist critique of antidiscrimination doctrine, feminist theory and antiracist politics. *University of Chicago Legal Forum, 1989*(1), 139–167.

Enloe, C. (2000). *Maneuvers: The international politics of militarizing women's lives*. Berkeley, CA: University of California Press.

Enloe, C. (2007). *Globalization and militarism: Feminists make the link*. Lanham, MD: Rowman & Littlefield.

Freedman, J. (2018). The uses and abuses of "vulnerability" in EU asylum and refugee protection: Protecting women or reducing autonomy? *Papeles del CEIC, 2019*(1), 1–15.

Latouche, A. (2023). Crossing the borders of intimacy: Gender, extimacy and vulnerability assessment in Greece. In J. Freedman, A. Latouche, & A. Miranda (Eds.), *The gender of borders: Embodied narratives of migration, violence and agency* (pp. 33–50). Routledge.

Mehta, R. (2025). Circularity of violence and institutionalisation: Understanding women's (im)mobility across borders. *Journal of Gender-Based Violence, 9*(2), 234–251.

Mixed Migration Centre. (2018, September). *Experiences of female refugees & migrants in origin, transit and destination countries: A comparative study of women on the move from Afghanistan, East and West Africa*. Mixed Migration Centre.

Mixed Migration Centre. (2024, April). *Implications of the Taliban takeover on Afghan women's migration to Türkiye: MMC Asia and the Pacific 4Mi snapshot*. Mixed Migration Centre.

Oucho, L. A. (2011). *Migration decision-making of Kenyan and Nigerian women in London: The influence of culture, family and networks* (Unpublished doctoral thesis). University of Warwick.

Tyszler, E. (2023). Between violence and power to act. In J. Freedman, A. Latouche, A. Miranda, N. Sahraoui, G. Santana de Andrade, & E. Tyszler (Eds.), *The gender of borders: Embodied narratives of migration, violence and agency* (pp. 88–102). Routledge.

UN Women, UNAMA, & IOM. (2023, March). *Afghan women's voices – Summary report of country-wide women's consultations March 2023*. UN Women.

Yuval-Davis, N. (1997). *Gender and nation*. London: Sage.

Yuval-Davis, N. (2006). Intersectionality and feminist politics. *European Journal of Women's Studies, 13*(3), 193–209.

www.ingramcontent.com/pod-product-compliance
Lightning Source LLC
Chambersburg PA
CBHW052110230326
41599CB00055B/5384